OCT 2 1 2016

14th Edition

Michigan History Directory

Historical Societies • Museums • Historic Sites • Archives
Historical Collections • Genealogical Societies • Agencies • Commissions

Edited by
Larry J. Wagenaar
and Nancy Feldbush

Sponsored by

HUIZENGA GROUP

Rollin M. Gerstacker Foundation

An official publication of the

© 2015 The Historical Society of Michigan. All rights reserved.

On the front cover: Photo of the William Upton House in Sterling Heights, which is maintained by the Sterling Heights Historical Commission. Photo courtesy of Colleen Parker.

On the back cover: Photo was taken inside the Dearborn Historical Museum's 1833 Commandant's Quarters, which is maintained by the Dearborn Historical Society. Photo courtesy of John D. Little.

No portion of this book may be reproduced, reprinted, entered into a computer database, or otherwise copied or distributed without the written permission of the Historical Society of Michigan.

Printed in the United States of America.

Preface

I've had the privilege of being a part of this publication since 2002, shortly after becoming Executive Director the previous year. The first *Michigan History Directory* was published by the Historical Society of Michigan (HSM) in 1975. Back then, there were just a handful of resources listed. Now, we collect and track information on more than 1,000 historical societies, museums, historic sites, archives, historical collections, genealogical societies, agencies, and commissions in Michigan.

We take the compilation and maintenance of this comprehensive tool very seriously and regularly invest significant resources to keep it up to date. The process that we follow to assemble the Directory has changed over time, and it will continue to evolve—especially since we hope to launch a new mobile app in 2015 that will include this information commingled with the content of the *Historic Michigan Travel Guide*.

To create the listings, we continually survey our members and other historical entities. We send out e-mails, letters, and forms, asking them to review the material already on hand and to contact HSM about any updates or changes. If an organization did not respond to our efforts, we have added the note "Information may not be current" to the end of its listing. This does not mean that the description is incorrect—it means the information was secured sometime prior to 2014.

Organizations that were HSM members at the time we pulled the data to compile this 14th edition have a picture (if one was provided) within their listing that represents their historical entity. In addition, those members have a QR code included that can be scanned by a smartphone and will connect you to their website or other online presence. Sites and organizations are listed under the cities in their mailing address. For your convenience, we have cross referenced any site that is in a different city than the mailing address. At the back of the Directory, we have included a cross index so that you can search for organizations by name.

Our member organizations are also listed on our website at *www.hsmichigan.org* under the Resources tab with links to their websites. To learn more about HSM membership benefits, look for information on our website, on the back of this page, and on the last page of this book.

The 14th edition of the *Michigan History Directory* could not have come together without the hard work of several HSM staff. They include my co-editor, Director of Communications Nancy Feldbush; Membership Coordinator Jordan Stoddard; Editorial Assistant Amy Wagenaar; Editorial Assistant Jodi Lynn Fry; and proofreader Julie Kampling. Many former HSM staff members were also a part of the foundational information on which this new edition is based.

If you find any inaccuracies in the following listings, please notify HSM at (517) 324-1828 or hsm@hsmichigan.org.

I hope you enjoy this Directory and all it offers as you explore the story of Michigan's past.

Larry J. Wagenaar

JOIN HSM TODAY!

To become a member of the Historical Society of Michigan, complete this form and mail or fax it to:

Historical Society of Michigan
5815 Executive Dr.
Lansing, MI 48911
Fax: (517) 324-4370

You may also join online at www.hsmichigan.org.

_____
Name (please print)

_____
Address

_____
City, State, Zip

_____
Phone

_____
E-mail*

*HSM protects your privacy. Your e-mail will be used for HSM Member communications only.

MEMBERSHIP OPTIONS

☐ Basic (includes the *Chronicle* magazine)	$25
☐ Regular (adds *Michigan Historical Review* journal)	$35
☐ Historical Society*	$35
☐ Museum or Library**	$50

Enhanced membership adds *Michigan History* magazine for $15 more (nearly $5 off the subscription price!)

☐ Enhanced Basic	$40
☐ Enhanced Regular	$50
☐ Enhanced Historical Society*	$50
☐ Enhanced Museum or Library**	$65

*Historical organization with budget less than $25,000/year
**Historical organization with budget more than $25,000/year

PAYMENT

☐ Check payable to the Historical Society of Michigan
☐ Credit card: Visa, Discover, MasterCard, American Express

_____
Card Number

_____   _____
Exp. Date (mm/yy)   Billing Zip Code

_____
CVV Code (V/MC/DC on back, AMEX on front)

_____
Signature

Michigan History Directory

Acme
(Grand Traverse County)

HSM MEMBER

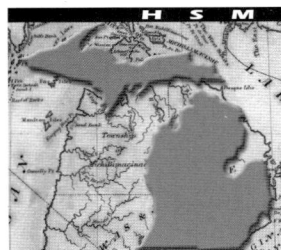

Music House Museum
Mailing Address: P.O. Box 297 • Acme, MI 49610
Contact: Dorothy Clore
E-Mail: info@musichouse.org
Phone: (231) 938-9300
Fax: (231) 938-3650
Physical Location: 7377 US 31 North • Acme, MI 49610
Hours: May-Oct: Mon-Sat 10 a.m.-4 p.m., Sun 12-4 p.m.; Nov, Dec: Sat 10 a.m.-4 p.m.; Dec 26-31: Daily 10 a.m.-4 p.m.
Admission: $11/adult, $4/children (6-15), $25/family. Tour groups (20+) $9/individual.
Visitor Accessibility: Onsite parking available. Wheelchair accessible. Guided tours available.
Website: www.musichouse.org

About: The Music House Museum collects, restores, and preserves automated music machines and instruments from the 1870s to the 1930s. Guided tours explain and demonstrate the unique instruments, which include a Belgian dance organ, nickelodeons, music boxes, pipe organs, and a Wurlitzer Theater Organ. The museum also features a scale model of Traverse City (c.1930).
Annual Events: Silent movie with Wurlitzer Theater Organ accompaniment. Visit website or call for concert/event schedule.

Ada
(Kent County)

HSM MEMBER

Ada Historical Society
Mailing Address: P.O. Box 741 • Ada, MI 49031
Contact: Kristen Wildes, Board Member
E-Mail: adahistoricalsociety@gmail.com
Phone: (616) 676-9346
Site/Location: **Averill Historical Museum of Ada**
Physical Location: 7144 Headley St. • Ada, MI 49301
Hours: Fri-Sat 1-4 p.m. Closed Jan-Feb. Also by appointment.
Admission: Donations accepted.
Visitor Accessibility: On-site parking. Wheelchair accessible. Tour guides available.
Website: www.adahistoricalsociety.org

About: The Averill Historical Museum exhibits the collections of the Ada Historical Society. The museum features a pantry, bedroom, and parlor from an early twentieth-century farmhouse. Additional exhibits feature artifacts from Ada's participation in WWI and WWII, the railroad in Ada, early twentieth-century children's toys, early schools in Ada, Rix Robinson, and Native Americans of the region. Adjacent to the museum is a barn with several exhibits and a historic garden.
Exhibits/Collections: Oral history collection and photo collection. Objects exhibited tell the story of Ada history. Pictures and information about Rix Robinson.
Annual Events: Forest Hills Community Expo; Lecture Series; Music On the Lawn (summer); Visit the Gardens Event; Pioneer Days Summer Camp; Ada Parks River Festival; Tinsel, Treats and Trolley; Tri Rivers Small Museums Tour; 4th of July Parade; August in Ada Children's Festival; Santa Parade; Holiday Wreath Sale Fundraiser. Meetings 2nd Sat monthly, 10:30 a.m.
Publications: "A Snug Little Place: Memories of Ada, Michigan 1821-1930."

Adrian
(Lenawee County)

A

HSM MEMBER

Adrian Dominican Sisters
Mailing Address: 1257 E. Siena Heights Drive • Adrian, MI 49221
Contact: Nadine Foley, Congregation Historian
E-Mail: nfoley@adriandominicans.org
Phone: (517) 266-3580
Fax: (517) 226-3584
Site/Location: **Madden Hall Historical Area**
Hours: Mon-Fri 9 a.m.-5 p.m. Also by appointment.
Admission: Free.
Visitor Accessibility: Parking across the street. Wheelchair accessible. Tour guide available upon request.
Website: www.adriandominicans.org

About: The Adrian Dominican Sisters seek to discover and identify themselves as women called together to share faith and life with one another. The historical display in Madden Hall is organized into three time periods: 1879 to 1933, 1933 to 1962, and 1963 to the present. Each contains narrative panels, photos, documents, and artifacts of its respective period. Also located within Madden Hall is the Historic Holy Rosary Chapel, which was built in 1905-1907.
Exhibits/Collections: Biographies of 1,200 deceased sisters are cataloged for easy reference. Records, letters, documents, papers, photographs. Histories of schools, universities, hospitals, and other missions and ministries.
Publications: "Histories of the Congregation," "Amid the Alien Corn," "Seeds Scattered and Grown," Guides for the Historical Area and Holy Rosary Chapel.

Adrian Historic District Commission
Mailing Address: c/o Adrian City Hall, 135 E. Maumee St. • Adrian, MI 49221
Contact: Clarke Baldwin, Chairperson
E-Mail: cfbaldwin@yahoo.com
Phone: (517) 263-2161
About: The Adrian Historic District Commission reviews applications for renovations, additions, and demolitions of buildings in Adrian's historic district.
Annual Events: Meetings 3rd Tue monthly, 7 p.m. at 204 E. Church St.
*Information may not be current.

HSM MEMBER

Adrian Public Library
Mailing Address: 143 E. Maumee St. • Adrian, MI 49221
Contact: Shirley Ehnis, Library Director
E-Mail: adrianpubliclibrary@ci.adrian.mi.us
Phone: (517) 265-2265
Fax: (517) 265-8847
Hours: Mon, Tue, Thu 10 a.m.-8 p.m.; Wed, Fri 10 a.m.-5:30 p.m.; Sat 10 a.m.-3:30 p.m.
Visitor Accessibility: Wheelchair accessible. Free parking along Maumee Street and behind building in the Toledo Street parking lot.
Website: www.adrian.lib.mi.us

About: The Heritage Room at the Adrian Public Library houses local history and genealogy resources with a focus on Adrian and Lenawee Counties. The room provides access to electronic databases, newspaper archives, Ancestry.com, and Heritage Quest.

Historical Society of Michigan

A

Exhibits/Collections: Local newspapers, microfilm, local history indexes, documents, and governmental proceedings.
Annual Events: Art-A-Licious Cultural Arts Festival.

Lenawee County Family Researchers
Mailing Address: P.O. Box 623 • Adrian, MI 49221
E-Mail: lcfamilyresearchers@gmail.com
Visitor Accessibility: Wheelchair accessible. Self-guided.
Website: http://lcfamilyresearchers.wix.com
About: The Lenawee County Family Researchers exist to foster interest in historical and genealogical information related to Lenawee County, Michigan, by preserving the county's historical and genealogical records and providing support to researchers everywhere seeking that information.
Exhibits/Collections: See website for information.
Annual Events: Meetings 2nd Tue monthly Sep-Jun, 7 p.m. at Vo Tech Center, Adrian. Check website, dates viable to change.

Lenawee County Historical Society

Mailing Address: 110 E. Church St. • Adrian, MI 49221
Contact: Bruce Neal, President
E-Mail: lenaweemuseum@yahoo.com
Phone: (517) 265-6071
Site/Location: **Lenawee County Historical Museum**
Hours: Tue-Fri 10 a.m.-2 p.m., Sat 10 a.m.-4 p.m.
Admission: Free.
Visitor Accessibility: Free on-site parking. Wheelchair accessible. Tour guide available; group tours available by appointment.
Website: http://www.lenaweemuseum.org

About: The Lenawee County Historical Museum collects, maintains, preserves, and displays items of historical nature and significance to Lenawee County. Exhibits in the museum feature the history of Lenawee County and its pioneers, railroads, and industries, plus other items linked to the county's history. The 100-year-old museum building is listed on the National Register of Historical Places and also includes an auditorium and a large archive of genealogical information.
Exhibits/Collections: Emphasis on objects, documents, and photographs related to Lenawee County. Special emphasis on genealogical documents related to the county.
Annual Events: Christmas Tree Open House. Bimonthly meetings and programs held in museum auditorium.
Publications: Newsletter (From the Tower), "Seeds of Time."

Shipman Library
Mailing Address: Adrian College, 110 S. Madison St. • Adrian, MI 49221
Contact: Rebecca McNitt
E-Mail: emaertens@adrian.edu
Hours: By appointment only.
Visitor Accessibility: Street parking. Wheelchair accessible.
Website: www.adrian.edu/library
About: The United Methodist Archives of the Detroit Conference documents the churches in the Detroit Conference of the United Methodist Church. The archives accept personal papers and manuscripts from ministers, church leaders, organizations, and others involved in the history of the conference and its churches.
Exhibits/Collections: Detroit Conference records and publications; district records; local church histories, directories, newsletters, and records; and information concerning clergy and bishops.
Publications: Biannual newsletter (The Historical Messenger).
*Information may not be current.

Alanson
(Emmet County)

Inland Water Route Historical Society
Mailing Address: P.O. Box 433 • Alanson, MI 49706
Contact: Wayne Blomberg
E-Mail: wcblomberg@hotmail.com
Phone: (231) 838-5309
Physical Location: 9088 Marina Dr. • Alanson, MI 49706
Hours: Call for current hours.
Admission: Donations accepted.
Visitor Accessibility: Free on-site and street parking. Wheelchair accessible. Tour guide available.
Website: www.iwrhs.com
About: Organized in 2004, the Inland Water Route Historical Society preserves and presents the history of the Inland Water Route of Northern Michigan, which comprises the waters of Crooked, Burt, and Mullett Lakes and Crooked, Indian, and Cheboygan Rivers.
Exhibits/Collections: Artifacts and photos of route, activities, facilities, and equipment used in Inland Water Route.
Annual Events: 4th of July celebration. Meetings 3rd Tue monthly, 6:30 p.m. at museum.
Publications: Newsletter (On the Waterway).

Alba
(Antrim County)

Alba Historical Society
Mailing Address: P.O. Box 62 • Alba, MI 49611
Contact: Linda Rebec
Phone: (231) 584-2593
Website: http://www.ole.net/~maggie/antrim/alba.htm
About: The Alba Historical Society maintains a museum in an 1881 one-room schoolhouse, which was the first school built in Alba.
Exhibits/Collections: Original register with planning and construction records. Also contains original teachers' contracts. Genealogy department for information on people who resided in area.
*Information may not be current.

Albion
(Calhoun County)

Albion College
Mailing Address: Stockwell Mudd Library, 602 E. Cass St. • Albion, MI 49224
E-Mail: archives@albion.edu
Phone: (517) 629-0382 • *Fax:* (517) 629-0504
Hours: By appointment.
Admission: Free.
Visitor Accessibility: On-site parking.
Website: http://campus.albion.edu/library/
About: The archives are located on the 2nd floor of the Stockwell Mudd Library.
Exhibits/Collections: See website for complete list of collections.

Albion College Archives & Special Collections
Mailing Address: 602 E Cass St. • Albion, MI 49224
Contact: Nicole Garrett, College Archivist
E-Mail: archives@albion.edu
Phone: (517) 629-0487 • *Fax:* (517) 629-0504

Physical Location: 602 E. Cass Street • Albion, MI 49224
Hours: By appointment only.
Website: www.albion.edu/library/specialcollections/
About: The Albion College Archives and Special Collections collects, preserves, and makes available records, manuscripts, artifacts, and ephemera that accurately document the history of Albion College and the West Michigan Conference of the United Methodist Church.
Exhibits/Collections: Albion College archives, rare books, archives of West Michigan Conference of the United Methodist Church.
Annual Events: Marilyn Crandell Schleg Memorial Lecture for visiting archivists, preservationists, curators, or historians.
*Information may not be current.

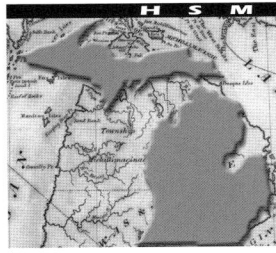

Albion District Library Local History Room
Mailing Address: 501 S. Superior St. • Albion, MI 49224
Contact: Jennifer Wood, Local History Archivist
E-Mail: history@albionlibrary.org
Phone: (517) 629-3993
Fax: (517) 629-5354
Hours: Tue 12-8 p.m., Wed 2-4 p.m., Sat 1-5 p.m.
Admission: Free.
Visitor Accessibility: Free street parking. Wheelchair accessible.
Website: www.albionlibrary.org/local-history

About: The Albion District Library's Local History Room collects, preserves, and makes available to the public books, manuscripts, records, photographs, and other materials that document the history of the Albion area, including its people; organizations; businesses; social, cultural, ethnic, and religious groups; and built environment.
Exhibits/Collections: Local obituary database, family history and subject files, photographs and maps, newspapers on microfilm, Albion residents, publications, Albion yearbooks, manuscript collections.

Albion Historical Society
Mailing Address: 509 S. Superior St. • Albion, MI 49224
Contact: Andy Zblewski, President
E-Mail: info@albionhistoricalsociety.org
Phone: (517) 629-5100
Site/Location: **Gardner House Museum**
Hours: May-Sep: Sat-Sun 2-4 p.m. Also by appointment.
Admission: Donations accepted.
Visitor Accessibility: Free street parking. Partially wheelchair accessible; first floor only. Tour guides available.
Website: www.albionhistoricalsociety.org

About: The society owns and operates the Gardner House Museum, featuring period furniture and three floors. In the basement, visit a neighborhood grocery store and kitchen. On the first floor, see antique furniture, decorations, musical instruments, and pictures; on the second floor, antique beds and clothing in the Victorian bedroom and a Victorian bathroom. The second floor also features clothes worn between 1870-1970 and a World War II exhibit showcasing 400 photos, as well as memorabilia.
Exhibits/Collections: Historical society's research collection in Local History Room, Albion Public Library, 501 South Superior Street, Albion, Michigan 49224. (517) 629-3993.
Annual Events: Twelfth Night Celebration (Jan), Mother's Day Tea (May).

Alden
(Antrim County)

A

Helena Township Historical Society
Mailing Address: P.O. Box 204 • Alden, MI 49612
Contact: Paul Delange, President
E-Mail: ddelange@juno.com
Phone: (231) 331-4274
Site/Location: **Alden Depot Museum**
Physical Location: 10670 Coy • Alden, MI 49612
Hours: Memorial Day-Labor Day: Fri-Sun 1-4 p.m.
Admission: Free.
Visitor Accessibility: On-site public parking. Wheelchair accessible. Free tour guide available.
About: The Helena Township Historical Society maintains a museum in the renovated 1908 Pere Marquette railroad station. The Alden Depot Museum details the township's local history with displays about railroads, lumbering, and tourism. Exhibits focus on the local town, residents, and resorts. Attractions include several large-scale train layouts as well as a 1903 Pere Marquette caboose, flat car, and engine.
Exhibits/Collections: Model train collection. Artifacts of area, lumber, railroad, business, farming, and boating.
Annual Events: Arts and Crafts Show (Aug), Quilt Show (Jul), Cottage Sale (Jun), Train Show (Aug-Labor Day). Meetings 1st Thu monthly, 10 p.m. at Helena Township Community Building.

Algonac
(St. Clair County)

Algonac-Clay Township Historical Society
Mailing Address: 1240 St. Clair River Drive, P.O. Box 228 • Algonac, MI 48001
Contact: Don LaCombe, President
E-Mail: achs@algonac-clay-history.com
Phone: (810) 794-9015
Site/Location: **Algonac Clay Township Museum**
Physical Location: 1117 St. Clair River Dr. • Algonac, MI 48001
Hours: May-Dec: Sat-Sun 1-4 p.m. Summer: Wed 6-8 p.m. Also by appointment.
Admission: Donations accepted.
Visitor Accessibility: Free on-site parking. Wheelchair accessible. Free tour guides available.
Website: www.achistory.com

About: The Algonac-Clay Township Historical Society preserves and promotes the history of the Algonac and Clay Township area, the home of pleasure boating started by Chris Smith who created Chris-Craft, Gar Wood, and his historical racing boats. The society maintains the Algonac Clay Township Museum, which features an exhibit of the area's Native-American Tribes, a military display, a freighter exhibit, Tall Ship memorabilia, and an exhibit that changes yearly.
Exhibits/Collections: Boat-building and boat-racing heritage and memorabilia, including Chris-Craft, Gar Wood, and other local boat builders. More than 10,000 artifacts concerning business, industry, schools, churches, military, local history, and Harsens Island.
Annual Events: Memorial Day Celebration, Log Cabin Day, Quilt/Craft Show, Yearly Picnic, Labor Day Art Show, Victorian Tea, Classic Car Show. Board meeting 2nd Tue, 6 p.m. General meeting 4th Tue, 7 p.m.
Publications: Monthly museum newsletter, Algonac Community Centennial Book, Memorial Afghan Book
Other Sites/Locations: **Maritime Museum** • Location: 1117 St. Clair River Dr., Algonac, MI 48001 • Hours: Not open yet • Admission: TBD

Historical Society of Michigan

A

- Visitor Accessibility: Free on-site parking. Wheelchair accesibe. Tour guides available • The Maritime Museum will have full-size boats of many makers on a rotating basis. Boating artifacts will be featured along with the history of boating.

Log Cabin and Detroit Urban Railway Wait Station and Annex • Location: 4710 Point Tremble Rd., Clay Township • Hours: Open Log Cabin Day • Admission: Donations accepted • Visitor Accessibility: Free on-site parking. Wheelchair accessible. Tour guides available • The Log Cabin shows life as it was in 1850. The DUR Wait Station and section of tracks show where people waited for the train from Detroit to Port Huron. The annex has boats and farming implements.

Allegan
(Allegan County)

Allegan County Historical Society
Mailing Address: 113 Walnut St. • Allegan, MI 49010
Contact: Amanda Strickfaden, President
E-Mail: oldjailmuseum06@yahoo.com
Phone: (269) 673-8292
Site/Location: **Old Jail Museum**
Hours: May-Aug: Fri-Sat 10 a.m.-4 p.m.; Sep-Apr: Sat 10 a.m.-4 p.m. Also by appointment.
Admission: Donations accepted.
Visitor Accessibility: Free street parking. Not wheelchair accessible. Guided tours available; advance notice required for large groups.
Website: www.alleganoldjail.org

About: The Allegan County Historical Society encourages historical study and research. The society also collects and preserves historical material connected with the Allegan County area. In 1963, the Allegan County Historical Society acquired the former jail (b.1906) and converted it into the Old Jail Museum with period rooms and displays. Exhibits contain items from the pioneer days up to 1950 and include artifacts from the War of 1812, Civil War, Spanish American War, World War I, and World War II.
Exhibits/Collections: Large photographic collection and written local histories. Collection on Civil War General Benjamin Pritchard, captor of Jefferson Davis, President of the Confederacy.
Annual Events: Fiber Festival, Allegan County Fair (Sep). Meetings 3rd Thu Apr-Nov at 7 p.m.; see website for location.
Publications: Monthly newsletter.
Other Sites/Locations: **John C. Pahl Historic Village** • Location: 150 Allegan County Fair Grounds, Allegan, MI 49010 • Hours: Vary • Admission: Included in admission to county fair event • Visitor Accessibility: Parking fees apply during Allegan County Fair events. Wheelchair accessible. Tour guides available when village is open; special tours can be arranged with advance notice • The John C. Pahl Historic Village is set during the 1800s to 1900s and includes a gas station, fire barn with a 1929 REO fire truck, woodworker's shed, carriage barn, 1840 home, log cabin, doctor's office, log church, one-room school, blacksmith shop, Native-American building, depot, and C&O caboose.

Allen
(Hillsdale County)

Allen Area Historical Society
Mailing Address: P.O. Box 68 • Allen, MI 49227
Contact: Ken Todd, President
E-Mail: allenareahistoricalsociety@yahoo.com
Phone: (517) 869-2147
Physical Location: 151 West Chicago Road • Allen, MI 49227
Hours: May-Oct: 1st Sat monthly 12-2 p.m.
Admission: Donations accepted.
Visitor Accessibility: On-site parking available. Not wheelchair accessible.
Website: www.allenareahistoricalsociety.org
About: The Allen Area Historical Society focuses on the preservation of the area's history. The society's museum is located in the former office of Dr. Charles Clobridge, Allen's last resident physician.
Exhibits/Collections: Artifacts, written and oral histories of the area, records of sites and buildings.
Annual Events: Community Day (Jul), Meetings 4th Thu monthly at Allen Township Community Building (Apr-Oct).

Allen Park
(Wayne County)

Allen Park Museum & Historical Commission
Mailing Address: Allen Park Historical Museum, 16850 Southfield Rd. • Allen Park, MI 48101
Contact: Sharon Broglin
Phone: (313) 928-1400, ext. 221
Hours: Wed 1:30-4 p.m. Also by appointment.
About: The Allen Park Historical Commission maintains its museum in the 1888 Backhaus Farmhouse. On display are items such as clothing and farm tools, which depict life from 1900s to present. The commission also fundraises to continue restoration and operation.
Exhibits/Collections: Yearbooks, photos, documents from village and city of Allen Park. Church, school, and organization records.
Annual Events: Plant/Garage Sale (spring), Garden Tour (Jul), Arts and Crafts Fair (Aug), Tree Lighting and Fundraiser Dinner (Dec).
Information may not be current.

Allendale
(Ottawa County)

Allendale Historical Society
Mailing Address: Knowlton House Museum, P.O. Box 539 • Allendale, MI 49401
Contact: Betty Groendyk
Phone: (616) 895-9777
Site/Location: **Knowlton House and Retro Museums**
Physical Location: 11080 68th Avenue • Allendale, MI 49401
Hours: 1st Mon monthly 7-9 p.m. or by appointment.
About: The Allendale Historical Society is dedicated to preserving the diverse history of Allendale and the vicinity. The society collects and preserves historical material connected with Allendale as well as historical plat books and town records and houses them at the Knowlton House and Retro Museums both located at 11080 68th Avenue, adjacent to the township park.
Annual Events: Good Ol' Days Festival, workshops, rotating exhibits, cemetery tour known as "Meet the Skeletons in Allendale's Closet."
Information may not be current.

Engine House No. 5
Mailing Address: 6610 Lake Michigan Dr. • Allendale, MI 49401
Contact: Jeff DuPilka
E-Mail: jdupilka@westshorefire.com
Phone: (616) 895-4347 • *Fax:* (616) 895-7158
Hours: By appointment.
Admission: $2/individual donation.
Visitor Accessibility: Adjacent parking lot. Partially wheelchair accessible; main floor only. Tour guides avilable by appointment only.
Website: www.enginehouse5.org
About: Engine House No. 5 was constructed on the corner of Leonard & Monroe Street in Grand Rapids in 1880. Disassembled in 1980 to allow construction of a new firehouse on same site. Transported to

Allendale, Michigan, and reconstructed in 1984 as a fire museum to save artifacts of historical and technological interest.
Exhibits/Collections: Fire trucks and fire-fighting equipment, such as hand pumpers and horse-drawn wagons.

Michigan Council for History Education
Mailing Address: Grand Valley State University, D-1-160 Mackinac Hall • Allendale, MI 49401
Fax: (734) 429-8036
Website: www.michiganhistoryed.org
About: Association of K-12 educators organized to advocate and advance the study and teaching of history in schools throughout the state.
Annual Events: K-12 History Education Conference.
Information may not be current.

Special Collections, Grand Valley State University Libraries
Mailing Address: Library Serials, 1 Campus Dr. • Allendale, MI 49401
Contact: Robert Beasecker, Director
E-Mail: collections@gvsu.edu
Phone: (616) 331-2749 • *Fax:* (616) 331-2720
Hours: Mon-Fri 8 a.m.-4:30 p.m. Appointments preferred; call ahead.
Visitor Accessibility: Free on-site visitor parking with appointment. Wheelchair accessible.
Website: www.gvsu.edu/library/specialcollections/
About: The Special Collections and University Archives at Grand Valley State University Libraries houses rare books, manuscripts, documents, and artwork, which supplement and enhance resources available in the GVSU libraries. GVSU is an institution of higher education (masters-level, regional comprehensive).
Exhibits/Collections: Abraham Lincoln & Civil War collection; history of West Michigan, Michigan, Old Northwest, Midwest; history of books and printing; Bergers Presidential Writings collection; Markel Espionage collection; Modern first editions; substantial collections of writings.
Publications: "Fifty at Fifty: A Catalogue of Incunabula in the University Libraries, Grand Valley State University."

Alma
(Gratiot County)

Alma College Archives
Mailing Address: 614 W. Superior St. • Alma, MI 48801
Contact: Viki Everhart, Acquisitions & Special Collections
E-Mail: bookorder@alma.edu
Phone: (989) 463-7310
Hours: By appointment.
Visitor Accessibility: Free street parking. Partially wheelchair accessible.
Website: http://www.alma.edu/library
About: The purpose of the Alma College Archives is to collect and preserve historical materials of events or people associated with Alma College. These records shall be accessible to those interested by contacting a library staff member, preferably the Special Collections Specialist.
Exhibits/Collections: Alma College institutional records.

Alma Public Library
Mailing Address: 351 N. Court St. • Alma, MI 48801
Contact: Bryan Dinwoody, Director
E-Mail: tleonard@alma.lib.mi.us
Phone: (989) 463-3966
Fax: (989) 466-5901
Hours: Mon and Fri 12-9 p.m., Tue-Thu 9:30 a.m.-9 p.m., Sat 9:30 a.m.-5:30 p.m.
Admission: Free.
Visitor Accessibility: Free on-site parking. Wheelchair accessible. Tours provided with previous notice.
Website: www.alma.lib.mi.us

About: The library exists to provide an educational and entertaining option through the written word and visual presentation. Access to this information is provided by print, media, and electronic formats. The library also maintains a historical repository for the legacy of our community.

Almont
(Lapeer County)

Almont Community Historical Society
Mailing Address: P.O. Box 635 • Almont, MI 48003
Contact: Tom Spencer, President
E-Mail: almonthistorical@yahoo.com
Phone: (248) 628-3976
Physical Location: 149 S. Main St. • Almont, MI 48003
Hours: By appointment.
Admission: Donations accepted.
Visitor Accessibility: Free on-site parking. Wheelchair accessible through front door.
About: The Almont Community Historical Society gathers, displays, and shares Almont historical items at its museum. Exhibits focus on the military, Hurd Lock Company, and the Congregational Church.
Exhibits/Collections: Extensive photo collection of Almont.
Annual Events: Meetings 2nd Mon monthly, 7 p.m. at the museum.

Almont District Library
Mailing Address: P.O. Box 517 • Almont, MI 48003
Contact: Kay Hurd, Director
E-Mail: almontdistrictlibrary@adlmi.org
Phone: (810) 798-3100
Fax: (810) 798-2208
Hours: Mon-Thu 11 a.m.-8 p.m., Fri 11 a.m.-5 p.m., Sat 10 a.m.-2 p.m.
Visitor Accessibility: Wheelchair accessible.
Website: www.adlmi.org

About: The Almont District Library's mission is to provide learning and knowledge to individuals and the community.
Exhibits/Collections: Genealogy and local history.

Alpena
(Alpena County)

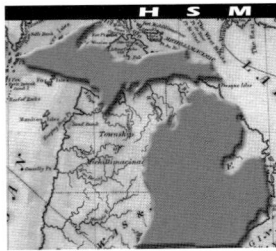

Alpena County Library
Mailing Address: 211 N. First Ave. • Alpena, MI 49707
Phone: (989) 356-6188
Fax: (989) 356-2765
Website: www.alpenalibrary.org
Exhibits/Collections: Alpena History, Great Lakes Maritime History, Genealogy.

Historical Society of Michigan

A

Alpena Historic Preservation Society
Mailing Address: 422 W. Washington Ave. • Alpena, MI 49707
Information may not be current.

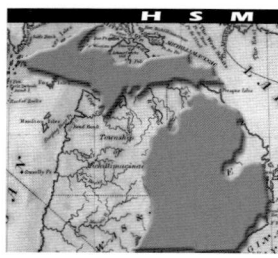

Besser Museum for Northeast Michigan
HSM MEMBER
Mailing Address: 491 Johnson St. • Alpena, MI 49707
Contact: Amanda Dozier, Public Relations Manager
E-Mail: adozier@bessermuseum.org
Phone: (989) 356-2202
Fax: (989) 356-3133
Hours: Mon-Sat 10 a.m.-5 p.m.
Admission: $5/adult, $3/senior, $3/children.
Visitor Accessibility: On-site parking. Wheelchair accessible. Self-guided.
Website: www.bessermuseum.org

About: The Besser Museum for Northeast Michigan is dedicated to inspiring curiosity and cultivating legacy through art, history, and science. Through research, it collects, preserves, and interprets artifacts and information concerning 15 counties in Northeast Michigan. Through programs and exhibits, it promotes understanding and appreciation. The museum hosts four permanent and five rotating exhibits. Exhibits include Native-American artifacts, historic Alpena, natural history, and more.
Exhibits/Collections: 20,000-plus artifacts include the Haltiner Collection of Native-American Artifacts and taxidermy specimens by Jan Van Houssen.
Annual Events: Log Cabin Day (Jun), Fossil Fest and Fall Harvest Day.

Great Lakes Lighthouse Festival Museum.
Please see entry under Macomb: Great Lakes Lighthouse Festival Museum.

Great Lakes Maritime Heritage Center.
HSM MEMBER
Please see entry under Lansing: Michigan Historical Center.

Middle Island Museum on Wheels
Mailing Address: 7406 US 23 North • Alpena, MI 49707
Phone: 989-595-3600
Information may not be current.

Northeast Michigan Genealogical Society
Mailing Address: c/o Besser Museum of Northeast Michigan, 491 Johnson St. • Alpena, MI 49707
Contact: Janet Romas, Secretary
E-Mail: nemgs@charter.net
Website: www.nemgs.com
About: Organized in 1976, the Northeast Michigan Genealogical Society fosters genealogical interest and activities in the counties of Alcona, Alpena, Montmorency, and Presque Isle. The society encourages and preserves family history and genealogical records, encourages area entities to expand and publicize their genealogical holdings, and makes materials of interest available to genealogists and the general public.
Exhibits/Collections: 10-volume death entries from Alpena newspapers, naturalization index of 26th Judicial Court 1878-1978, unpublished manuscript files.
Annual Events: Meets Jan-Nov: 3rd Thu of each month, 7-9 p.m. at Besser Museum.

Publications: "Alpena County Sesquincentennial 1857-2007," "Smugglers of Thunder Bay; Index to 1903 Aplena Plat," "Cemetery: Calvary & Holycross," "Churches: St. Anne, St. Bernard, St. Marys, Immanuel Lutheran," "Pleasant Valley Free Methodist."

Alto
(Kent County)

Bowne Township Historical Commission
HSM MEMBER
Mailing Address: P.O. Box 35 • Alto, MI 49302
Contact: Richard Johnson, President
E-Mail: srjohnson4@charter.net
Phone: (616) 868-6424
Site/Location: Bowne Center School House
Physical Location: 8240 Alden Nash Ave. • Alto, MI 49302
Hours: Jun-Aug 1st Sun monthly 2-4 p.m. Also by appointment.
Admission: Donations accepted.
Visitor Accessibility: Free on-site parking. Partially wheelchair accessible. Self-guided.
Website: http://bownetwp.org

About: The purpose of the Bowne Township Historical Commission is to preserve the agricultural, residential, and commercial history and integrity of our community. To bring together those people interested in the history of our community in order to educate the present generations so that we might forever leave a historical legacy to those who come after. Visitors see artifacts from the mid-1800s thru the 1900s from home to business to military.
Exhibits/Collections: Local memorabilia and family histories.
Annual Events: Spring Into the Past (May), Open House (Dec). Meetings 2nd Mon monthly, 10 a.m. at museum.
Publications: "The Mission of a People Within The Valley of the Little Thornapple," quarterly newsletter.
Other Sites/Locations: Bowne Center School House • Location: S.E. Corner of 84th Avenue and Alden Nash Road, Alto, MI 49302 • Hours: Jun-Sep 1st Sun monthly 2-4p.m. Also by appointment • Admission: Donations accepted • Visitor Accessibility: Free on-site parking. Partially wheelchair accessible. Self-guided. • The Bowne Center School House is filled with old desks, books, and other school artifacts and historical information.

Farmall Acres Farm Museum
Mailing Address: 5253 Morse Lake Ave SE • Alto, MI 49302
Contact: Harold Metternick Jr.
E-Mail: ihgrandpat340@yahoo.com
Phone: (616) 868-6639
Physical Location: 170 McCormick St. • Clarksville, MI 48815
Hours: Jan-Aug: 2nd and 4th Sun monthly 1-5 p.m. Also by appointment.
Admission: $5/individual donation. Children 13 and under free.
Visitor Accessibility: Free on-site parking. Wheelchair accessible. Tour guide available.
About: 12,000 square feet of restored old farm equipment from 1900-1950 and tractors from 1938-1956, show boxes full of Mc Cormick, McCormick-Deering, and IH collections and much more. Museum contents collected from 11 states and Canada.
Exhibits/Collections: Private collection of McCormick, McCormick-Deering, IH items collected over the past 20-plus years.
Annual Events: Clarksville Steam Engine Show (Aug), Clarksville Ox Roast (Aug).

Michigan History Directory

Amasa
(Iron County)

Amasa Historical Society
Mailing Address: Amasa Historical Museum, P.O. Box 111 • Amasa, MI 49903
Contact: Helen Hord, Secretary
E-Mail: mullinaxk@sbcglobal.net
Phone: (906) 822-7210
Site/Location: **Amasa Historical Museum**
Physical Location: 208 W. Pine St. • Amasa, MI 49903
Hours: Open by appointment.
Admission: Donations accepted.
Visitor Accessibility: Street parking. Not wheelchair accessible. Docent available at no cost.
Website: www.amasahistoricalsociety.org
About: The Amasa Historical Society preserves local history and maintains a museum in the 1894 Township Hall. Displays feature logging, mining, and old streets of Amasa.
Exhibits/Collections: Amasa school memorabilia, township artifacts, Amasa folklore, logging and mining artifacts, photographs, and business records.
Annual Events: Heritage Day (Memorial Day). Meetings 2nd Wed monthly.
Publications: Annual newsletter (Apr).

Ann Arbor
(Washtenaw County)

African American Cultural & Historical Museum
Mailing Address: P.O. Box 130724 • Ann Arbor, MI 48113
Contact: Joyce M. Hunter, President
E-Mail: aachmuseum@gmail.com
Phone: (734) 761-1717
Physical Location: 3261 Lohr Road • Ann Arbor, MI 48108-9515
Website: www.aachmuseum.org

About: The African American Cultural and Historical Museum researches, collects, preserves, and exhibits cultural and historical materials about the life and work of African Americans in Washtenaw County. In 2005, the museum moved administrative offices to the David R. Byrd Center, an 1830s farmhouse restored by the late African-American architect David R. Byrd. (Byrd also built the chapel that is on the adjacent property.) The museum is currently working to secure 1528 Pontiac Trail as its permanent home.

Ann Arbor Hands-On Museum
Mailing Address: 220 E. Ann St. • Ann Arbor, MI 48104
Contact: Mel Drumm, Executive Director
Phone: (734) 995-5439
Hours: Mon, Wed, Fri, Sat 10 a.m.-5 p.m., Tue 9 a.m.-5 p.m. Thu 10 a.m.-8 p.m., Sun 12-5 p.m.
Admission: $11/individual.
Website: www.aahom.org
About: The Ann Arbor Hands-On Museum has been a cornerstone of informal science education in Ann Arbor for more than 30 years. Located in a 125-year-old firehouse, the museum inspires people to discover the wonder of science, math, and technology. The Lyons Country Store exhibit is an interactive replica of a 1920s country store, where visitors can listen to historic radio broadcasts and examine a collection of items sold in rural country stores.
Annual Events: See website for listing of events.

Ann Arbor Historic District Commission
Mailing Address: 301 E. Huron St., P.O. Box 8647 • Ann Arbor, MI 48107
Contact: Jill Thacher, City Planner/Hist Pres Coordinator
E-Mail: HDC@a2gov.org
Phone: (734) 994-6265 x42608 • *Fax:* (734) 994-8312
Hours: Mon-Fri 8 a.m-5 p.m.
Website: www.a2gov.org
Annual Events: Meetings 2nd Thu monthly, 7 p.m. at Ann Arbor City Hall.

Ann Arbor Train and Trolley Watchers
Mailing Address: 306 N. Division • Ann Arbor, MI 48103
Contact: Gary Sample
E-Mail: swkindschy@sbcglobal.net
Phone: (734) 996-8345
About: The Ann Arbor Train and Trolley Watchers is an informal but dedicated group of rail fans who meet to enjoy friendship, exchange news of interest, and share slide shows and videos about railroad and transportation subjects.
Annual Events: Meetings 3rd Fri Sep-Nov and Jan-May, 7:30 p.m. at St. Andrew's Episcopal Church.

Bentley Historical Library
Mailing Address: University of Michigan, 1150 Beal Ave. • Ann Arbor, MI 48109
Contact: Karen L. Jania, Head, Reference & Access Services
E-Mail: kljania@umich.edu
Phone: (734) 764-3482
Fax: (734) 936-1333
Hours: Mon-Fri 9 a.m.-5 p.m.
Admission: Free.
Visitor Accessibility: Free on-site parking. Wheelchair accessible.
Website: http://bentley.umich.edu/

About: The Bentley Historical Library was established in 1935 by the University of Michigan Regents to carry out two functions: to serve as the official archives of the University and to document the history of the state of Michigan and the activities of its people, organizations, and voluntary associations. Includes more than 50,000 linear feet of archives and manuscripts, 90,000 printed volumes, 1.5 million photographs and other visual materials, 10,000 maps, and 60 terabytes of digital content.
Exhibits/Collections: Michigan Historical Collections, University of Michigan archives, historical manuscripts, archival materials, printed works, visual images, and audio holdings relating to the history of the state of Michigan, its organizations, and people.
Other Sites/Locations: **Detroit Observatory** • Location: 1398 E. Ann, Ann Arbor, MI 48109 • Admission: By donation • Visitor Accessibility: Street parking is available for a fee. Not wheelchair accessible. Tour guide available. • Managed by the Bentley Historical Library, the Detroit Observatory is open to the public once a month from Sep-Dec and Mar-Jun. For more information, visit http://bentley.umich.edu/observatory/activities.php.

Cobblestone Farm Association
Mailing Address: 2781 Packard Rd. • Ann Arbor, MI 48108
Contact: George Taylor, President
E-Mail: cobblestonefarm@proo.de.net

Historical Society of Michigan

A

Phone: (734) 794-7120
Hours: Thu 11 a.m.-2 p.m. or by appointment.
Admission: $2/adult, $1.50/seniors and youth (4-17), $5/families, children 3 and under are free.
Visitor Accessibility: Free on-site parking. Partially wheelchair accessible. Free volunteer docents available.
Website: www.cobblestonefarm.org
About: The Cobblestone Farm is administered through the Department of Parks and Recreation in partnership with the Cobblestone Farm Association. The association preserves and interprets the history of the mid-19th-century cobblestone farmhouse and the families who called it home. Attractions include a restored and furnished 1844 cobblestone home, 4.5 acres of original farm, reproduction barnyard with live animals, and an 1837 log cabin.
Annual Events: Cobblestone Farm Market Tue 4-7p.m. Winter Happening (Feb), Spring Cleaning (Apr), Mid-19th-Century July 4th Celebration, Fall Harvest Event (Sep).
Publications: Newsletter (Field Notes).

Genealogical Society of Washtenaw County
Mailing Address: P.O. Box 7155 • Ann Arbor, MI 48107
Contact: Marcia McCrary,
E-Mail: president@washtenawgenealogy.org
Phone: (734) 483-2799
Hours: Call or see website.
Visitor Accessibility: Free parking. Wheelchair accessible.
Website: www.washtenawgenealogy.org
About: The Genealogical Society of Washtenaw County, organized in 1974 to assist in genealogical studies, encourages the collection and preservation of family and public records and promotes the exchange of genealogical information.
Annual Events: Meetings 4th Sun of the month Sep-May (Nov-Dec combined 1st Sun Dec) at Educational Center Auditorium in St. Joseph Hospital, 5305 Elliot Dr. in Ypsilanti.

Gerald R. Ford Presidential Library
Mailing Address: National Archives Records Administration, 1000 Beal Ave. • Ann Arbor, MI 48109
Contact: Elaine Didier
E-Mail: ford.library@nara.gov
Phone: (734) 205-0555
Fax: 734-205-0571
Hours: Mon-Fri 8:45 a.m.-4:45 p.m. Closed Federal holidays.
Admission: Free.
Visitor Accessibility: Free on-site parking. Wheelchair accessible.
Website: www.fordlibrarymuseum.gov

About: The Gerald R. Ford Presidential Library, part of the National Archives Records Administration, preserves the written record and physical history of presidents while providing special programs and exhibits that serve the community. Located on the campus of the University of Michigan, the library offers research materials as well as educational programs.
Exhibits/Collections: 25 million pages of letters, memos, meeting notes, plans, and reports; oral histories; audiovisual materials from the congressional; vice presidential and presidential papers of Gerald Ford and his White House staff; and personal papers.

Kempf House Museum
Mailing Address: 312 S. Division St. • Ann Arbor, MI 48104
Contact: Ann Dilcher
E-Mail: kempfhousemuseum@gmail.com
Phone: (734) 994-4898
Hours: Spring and fall: Sun 1-4 p.m. Also by appointment.
Admission: Donations accepted.
Visitor Accessibility: Street parking. Wheelchair accesible. Tour guide available.
Website: www.kempfhousemuseum.org

About: The 1853 Greek Revival Kempf House interprets Ann Arbor history and Victorian lifestyles from 1850 to 1910.
Exhibits/Collections: Late-18th- and early-19th-century furnishings.
Annual Events: German Holiday Open House, Valentine Teas, spring and fall noon lectures. Board meeting 2nd Mon monthly at 7 p.m.
Information may not be current.

Margaret Dow Towsley Sports Museum
Mailing Address: Schembechler Hall, 1000 S. State • Ann Arbor, MI 48104
Phone: (734) 747-2583
About: The Margaret Dow Towsley Sports Museum captures the tradition and spirit of more than 100 years of athletic competition at the University of Michigan. Exhibits share the story of Michigan athletes as part of the Rose Bowl, Big Ten Championship competitions, and U.S. Olympic teams. See the Little Brown Jug, the trophy for the winner of the Michigan-Minnesota Football game.
Information may not be current.

Michigan Theater Foundation
Mailing Address: 603 E. Liberty St. • Ann Arbor, MI 48104
Contact: Barbara Twist, Executive Assistant
E-Mail: info@michtheater.org
Phone: (734) 668-8397
Fax: (734) 668-7136
Hours: Mon-Sat 3-10 p.m.; Sun 3-9 p.m.
Admission: $7-$10/individual for films.
Visitor Accessibility: Street parking for a fee; multiple parking structures in area (Maynard and Liberty Square structures are closest). Wheelchair accessible. Tour guide available; by appointment.
Website: www.michigantheater.org

About: The Michigan Theater Foundation operates, preserves, and maintains the historic Michigan Theater for the benefit of the community and the arts. In addition to hosting various live events and performing art programs, the foundation exhibits fine film 365 days a year. The Ford Gallery exhibits and highlights the founding of Ann Arbor, the building of the Michigan Theater, the restoration of the theater.
Annual Events: Cinetopia International Film Festival.

Old West Side Association
Mailing Address: P.O. Box 2114 • Ann Arbor, MI 48106
Contact: Christine Brummer, President

Michigan History Directory

A

E-Mail: brummer@umich.edu
Phone: (248) 593-8856
Website: www.oldwestside.org
About: The Old West Side Association formed in 1967 to promote neighborhood conservation of the Old West Side, a historic neighborhood with architecture, streetscape, history, and environment characteristic of 19th-century Midwestern America.
Annual Events: Fall Homes Tour, Old West Side Week, and Children's Festival at Wurster Park.
Publications: The Old West Side News.

Pittsfield Township Historical Society
Mailing Address: P.O. Box 6013 • Ann Arbor, MI 48106
Contact: Emily Hopp Salvette, President
E-Mail: pittsfieldhistory@yahoo.com
Phone: (734) 668-2607
Site/Location: **Sutherland-Wilson Farm Museum**
Physical Location: 797 Textile Road • Ann Arbor, MI 48108
Hours: By appointment.
Admission: Free.
Visitor Accessibility: Free on-site parking. Wheelchair accessible. Tour guide available by appointment.
Website: www.pittsfieldhistory.org

About: The Pittsfield Township Historical Society promotes, stimulates, and supports interest in all aspects of the history of America, Michigan, Washtenaw County, and especially Pittsfield Township. The Sutherland-Wilson Farm Museum is located in an 1830s Greek Revival home and features furniture from the 1830s to 1900s. Outbuildings consist of a barn, carriage house, ice house, wood shed, and pump house.
Exhibits/Collections: Plat maps, newspaper clippings, and historical information about the township. The archives are open by appointment only.
Annual Events: Harvest Festival (Sep). Quarterly meetings held at 6:30 p.m. at Pittsfield Community Center, 701 Ellsworth, Ann Arbor.
Publications: Quarterly newsletter.

Sindecuse Museum of Dentistry
Mailing Address: 1011 N. University, G565 School of Dentistry • Ann Arbor, MI 48109-1078
Contact: Shannon O'Dell, Curator & Director
E-Mail: dentalmuseum@umich.edu
Phone: (734) 763-0767 • *Fax:* (734) 615-1429
Physical Location: Ground floor of Kellogg Foundation Inst., building (corner of N. Univeristy & Fletcher) • Ann Arbor, MI 48109-1078
Hours: Mon-Fri 8 a.m.-6 p.m. Closed university holidays.
Admission: Free.
Visitor Accessibility: Parking available for a fee. Refer to website for detailed directions. Wheelchair accessible. To schedule a group tour, e-mail at least 30 days in advance.
Website: www.dent.umich.edu/sindecuse
About: The Sindecuse Museum of Dentistry encourages learning about the history of dentistry through museum exhibition, related programs, research, and preservation of its collections. More than 18,000 objects have been collected and cataloged and approximately 15 percent are on display in permanent and temporary exhibitions. There are 13 museum exhibit cases, most located on the ground level of the Kellogg Building of the School of Dentistry. These feature the history of dentistry, with emphasis on the United States and Michigan.
Exhibits/Collections: More than 18,000 objects focused on the history of American dentistry from the 18th century to present with particular interest on dental practice and technology in Michigan.
Annual Events: School of Dentistry Hall of Honor Induction Ceremony (Homecoming Weekend).

Stearns Musical Collection
Mailing Address: E.V. Moore Building, 1100 Baits Dr. • Ann Arbor, MI 48105
Phone: (734) 763-4389
Site/Location: **University of Michigan School of Music**
Visitor Accessibility: Housed in the School of Music on the UM North Campus.
About: The Stearns Musical Collection has more than 2,000 musical instruments that have been acquired since Frederick Stearns donated the original collection in 1899, making this one of the largest, most distinctive collections around the world.
*Information may not be current.

University of Michigan: Exhibit Museum of Natural History
Mailing Address: 1109 Geddes Ave. • Ann Arbor, MI 48109
Phone: (734) 764-0478 • *Fax:* (734) 647-2767
Hours: Mon-Sat 9 a.m.-5 p.m.; Sun 12-5 p.m.
Admission: $6/individual suggested donation.
Visitor Accessibility: Parking available for a fee ($1.10/hr, $.50/half hr). Wheelchair accessible.
Website: www.lsa.umich.edu/exhibitmuseum
About: The Exhibit Museum of Natural History at the University of Michigan explores prehistoric life, Michigan wildlife and ecology, anthropology, geology, and archaeology. Attractions include a planetarium.
Annual Events: See website.
*Information may not be current.

University of Michigan: pecial Collections Library
Mailing Address: 7th Floor, Hatcher Graduate Library, 913 S. University Ave. • Ann Arbor, MI 48109-1205
Contact: Martha O'Hara Conway, Director
Phone: (734) 764-9377 • *Fax:* (734) 764-9368
Hours: Mon-Fri 10 a.m.-5 p.m., Sat 10 a.m.-12 p.m.
Admission: Free.
Visitor Accessibility: Several on-site parking options for a fee. Wheelchair accessible. Free tour guides; appointment only.
Website: http://www.lib.umich.edu/special-collections-library
About: In keeping with the University Library's mission to collect, describe, preserve, and make available the record of human knowledge, the Special Collections Library acquires, cares for, interprets, and promotes the use of important collections of unique, rare, primary source, and other material in all formats and in a variety of subject areas.
Exhibits/Collections: Include papers of distinguished authors, poets, and filmmakers; American culinary history; anarchism, radicalism, and social protest; children's literature; the early histories of astronomy, mathematics, and medicine; and transportation history.

Washtenaw County Historic District Commission
Mailing Address: 110 N. Fourth Ave., P.O. Box 8645 • Ann Arbor, MI 48107-8645
Contact: Melissa Milton-Pung, Project Manager
E-Mail: miltonpungm@ewashtenaw.org
Phone: (734) 222-6878 • *Fax:* (734) 222-6531

A

Visitor Accessibility: On-site parking. Wheelchair accessible.
Website: http://preservation.ewashtenaw.org
About: The Washtenaw County Historic District Commission consists of nine members who are appointed by the county's Board of Commissioners and protect historic buildings, sites, objects, and landscapes of Washtenaw County.
Annual Events: Meetings 1st Thu (Feb, May, Sep, Nov) at WCL Learning Resource Center, 4135 Washtenaw Ave. in Ann Arbor.
Publications: "Four Heritage Driving Tours: Greek Revival Architecture, Historic Barns, German Heritage, and Esek Pray Trail."

Washtenaw County Historical Society
Mailing Address: P.O. Box 3336 • Ann Arbor, MI 48106
Contact: Leslie L. Loomans, President
E-Mail: wchs-500@ameritech.net
Phone: (734) 662-9092
Site/Location: **Museum on Main Street**
Physical Location: 500 N. Main St. • Ann Arbor, MI 48106
Hours: Sat-Sun 12-4 p.m.
Admission: Donations accepted.
Visitor Accessibility: Free on-site parking. Wheelchair accessible. Tour guide available.
Website: www.washtenawhistory.org

About: The Washtenaw County Historical Society educates and inspires the community to engage in the preservation and presentation of area history by exhibit, assembly, and publication. The Museum on Main Street is located at the corner of East Kingsley and Beakes streets.
Exhibits/Collections: More than 5,000 artifacts. Archival materials, including ledgers and writings of a few local businesses and personal papers of some families, are filed at Bentley Historical Library under "WCHS Collection."
Annual Events: Meetings 3rd Sun Feb-Apr and Sep-Nov, 2 p.m.
Publications: Newsletter (Washtenaw Impressions).
Other Sites/Locations: **The Argus Museum** • Location: 525 West William • Hours: 9 a.m.-5 p.m. Mon-Fri (closed holidays).

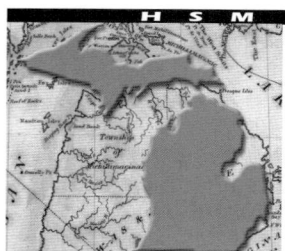

William L. Clements Library
Mailing Address: University of Michigan, 909 S. University Ave. • Ann Arbor, MI 48109
Contact: J. Kevin Graffagnino, Director
Phone: (734) 764-2347
Fax: (734) 647-0716
Hours: 9 a.m.-4:45 p.m.
Website: www.clements.umich.edu

About: The William L. Clements Library is a major academic research library that collects and preserves primary source materials and creates an environment that supports and encourages scholarly investigation of our nation's past. Public functions are restricted to front hall's changing exhibits, which focus on different aspects of collections that would interest both an expert bibliophile and the casual reader.
Exhibits/Collections: African-American history, the American Revolution, cookery, crime, education, fairs and expositions, intellectual life in America (1750-1900), military history, Native-American history, reform movements, religious history, theatre, social impact of war, women's history.
Other Sites/Locations: **Temporary Relocation** Location: 1580 Ellsworth Road, Ann Arbor, MI 48108 • Hours: Labor Day to Memorial Day: Mon-Fri 9am-4:45pm; Memorial Day to Labor Day: Mon-Thu 9am-5:45pm, Fri 9-11:45 am. • Visitor Accessibility: Metered street parking. Wheelchair accessible. Self-guided. • Prior to visiting the William L. Clements Library during its renovation project (through September 2015), visitors are advised to call beforehand. For updates regarding the site's renovation project, visit www.clements.umich.edu/renovation.php.

Arcadia
(Manistee County)

Arcadia Area Historical Society
Mailing Address: Arcadia Area Historical Museum, P.O. Box 67 • Arcadia, MI 49613
Contact: Joyce Howard, President
Phone: (231) 889-4360
Site/Location: **Arcadia Area Historical Museum**
Physical Location: 3340 Lake St. • Arcadia, MI 49613
Hours: Thu-Sat 1-4 p.m. and Sun 1-3 p.m. Also by appointment; call (231) 889-3389.
Admission: Free.
Visitor Accessibility: Free on-site parking. Wheelchair accessible. Tour guide available.
Website: www.arcadiami.com

About: The Arcadia Area Historical Society collects, preserves, and exhibits materials, artifacts, and data of historical significance to the Arcadia area. The society publishes information regarding these items and makes them available for public inspection, instruction, and use (subject to society regulations and policy). The society is working on a scrapbook pertaining to all veterans from the Arcadia area. The society also manages the Arcadia Area Historical Museum in an 1884 Victorian house built by early settler Howard Gilbert.
Exhibits/Collections: Artifacts pertain to lumbering in Arcadia, old toys and games, children's books, and past businesses.
Annual Events: Meetings 4th Mon monthly, 7 p.m. at museum.
Publications: "A Walk Along Old Lake Street," "The Arcadia Furniture Factory," "Shipping in Arcadia," "Arcadia Railroad," "Lumbering in the Arcadia Area."

Armada
(Macomb County)

Armada Area Historical Society
Mailing Address: 23350 Torrey, P.O. Box 333 • Armada, MI 48005
Contact: Dorothy Heldt, Treasurer
Phone: (586) 784-9074
Physical Location: Armada Free Public Library, 73930 Church Street • Armada, MI 48005
Admission: Single membership $10/individual yearly membership, $18/family yearly membership.
Visitor Accessibility: Free on-site parking. Wheelchair accessible.
About: The Armada Area Historical Society helps individuals trace history of family members, collects area artifacts, and works with the Armada Fair Board to restore Grange Hall at the Fairgrounds.
Exhibits/Collections: Local artifacts, genealogy information from tax records, death records, newspapers, and similar sources.
Annual Events: Meetings 1st Wed monthly, 6:30 p.m. at Armada Library.
Information may not be current.

Athens
(Calhoun County)

Athens Area Historical Society
Mailing Address: Athens Area Museum, P.O. Box 22 • Athens, MI 49011
Contact: Judi Henckel, President

Michigan History Directory

E-Mail: athens.mi.historicalsociety@gmail.com
Phone: (269) 986-2689
Site/Location: **Athens Area Museum**
Physical Location: Athens Area Museum, 101 South Capital Ave. • Athens, MI 49011
Hours: Call for current hours.
Website: athens-mi-historicalsociety.org
About: The Athens Area Historical Society offers programs and supports the Athens Area Museum.
Exhibits/Collections: Artifacts, pictures, and records that reflect culture and history of Athens area.
Annual Events: Living History Tours (May), Athens Homecoming (Jul), Tombstone Tour (Sep) Meetings 3rd Thu quarterly, 7 p.m. at museum.

Au Gres
(Arenac County)

Arenac County Historical Society
Mailing Address: P.O. Box 272 • Au Gres, MI 48703
Contact: Annabell Goodman
E-Mail: achs@centurytel.net
Phone: (989) 876-7029
Site/Location: **Arenac County Historical Museum**
Physical Location: 304 E. Michigan Ave. • Au Gres, MI 48703
Hours: Memorial Day to Labor Day: Sat-Sun 1-4 p.m. Also by appointment.
Admission: Free.
Visitor Accessibility: On-site parking. Tour guide available.
Website: http://www.rootsweb.com/~miachs/
About: The Arenac County Historical Society was organized in 1970 to preserve history. The society maintains a museum in the former Au Gres Methodist Church, which was built in 1883. Exhibits include schoolroom, home settings, barber and apothecary shops, country store, and fishing exhibit. The society is also working to preserve Omer's "Ye Old Courthouse," a former courthouse and Masonic Hall.
Exhibits/Collections: Tax asessment books. Cemetery, church, genealogy, military, school, and census records.
Annual Events: Christmas Walk.
Publications: Quarterly newsletter.
*Information may not be current.

Auburn Hills
(Oakland County)

Walter P. Chrysler Museum
Mailing Address: One Chrysler Dr. • Auburn Hills, MI 48326
Contact: Jim Worton, Executive Director & COO
Phone: (248) 944-0001 • *Fax:* (248) 944-0460
Hours: Tue-Sat 10 a.m.-5 p.m., Sun 12-5 p.m.
Admission: $8/adult, $7/senior, $4/children (6-12), children 5 and under free.
Visitor Accessibility: Free on-site parking. Wheelchair accessible. Tour guides available on request for groups of 15 or more.
Website: www.wpchryslermuseum.org
About: The Walter P. Chrysler Museum interprets the heritage of Chrysler by generating innovative educational experiences that link guests to past, present, and future vehicles. The museum aims at becoming self-sustaining. Attractions include more than 65 vehicles from 1902 to the 1980s, newsreel-type kiosks, hands-on engineering displays, and three short movies.
Annual Events: Summer Cruise Nights (Jun-Aug), Trunk or Treat (Oct), Cars, Trees & Traditions (Nov-Dec).
Publications: "Forward Magazine."
*Information may not be current.

Bad Axe
(Huron County)

Bad Axe Historical Society
Mailing Address: P.O. Box 22, 303 N. Port Crescent • Bad Axe, MI 48413
Contact: Ken Guza, President
E-Mail: badaxehistorical@yahoo.com
Phone: (989) 550-2733
Site/Location: **Bad Axe Museum of Local History**
Hours: Memorial Day to Labor Day: Sun 2-4pm.
Admission: Donations accepted.
Visitor Accessibility: Free street parking. Not wheelchair accessible. Tour guide available.
Website: www.thehchs.org

About: The Bad Axe Museum of Local History features period clothing, advertising, photographs, documents, timeline events, antiques, and education—everything "Bad Axe."
Annual Events: Michigan Log Cabin Day (Jun), Countywide Museum Weekend (Sep).
Other Sites/Locations: **Pioneer Log Cabin Village** • Location: 205 S. Hanselman St., Bad Axe, MI 48413 • Hours: Memorial Day-Labor Day: Sun 2-4 p.m. • Visitor Accessibility: Free street parking. Partially wheelchair accessible; grounds only. Tour guide available. • The Pioneer Log Cabin Village is the largest collection of authentically restored pioneer log buildings in Michigan. The six individual museums include a pioneer home, general store, one-room school, chapel, barn, and blacksmith shop. They were originally built between 1875 and 1900 and moved to this site from elsewhere around Huron County in the 1980s.
*Information may not be current.

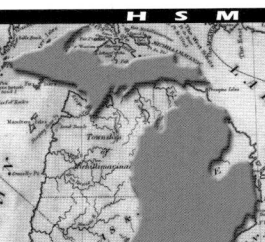

Huron County Historical Society
Mailing Address: P.O. Box 62 • Bad Axe, MI 48413
Contact: David McDonald
E-Mail: huroncountyhistoricalsociety@yahoo.com
Phone: (989) 712-0050
Visitor Accessibility: Contact museum or see website for information about tour guides.
Website: http://www.thehchs.org

About: The Huron County Historical Society consists of 14 historical society chapters located in Huron County. The society preserves, records, and publishes the area's history. See website for information pertaining to the society's member organizations.
Annual Events: Meetings in May, Jul, Oct, and Dec.
Publications: "Celebrating 150 Years, Huron County, Michigan," "Images of America, Huron County, Michigan."
Other Sites/Locations: See website for information pertaining to museums belonging to member societies.

Baldwin
(Lake County)

Lake County Historical Society
Mailing Address: P.O. Box 774 • Baldwin, MI 49304
Contact: Bruce Micinski, President
E-Mail: lakecountyhistory@hotmail.com
Phone: (231) 898-2194
Physical Location: 911 Michigan Ave. • Baldwin, MI 49304

Hours: Fri 1-4 p.m.
Admission: $5/individual society dues.
Visitor Accessibility: Free street parking. Wheelchair accessible. Docent available.
About: Lake County Historical Society was established in 1983.
Exhibits/Collections: Court records of Lake County from 1871 to 1960s, school records, photographs. Attractions include Shrine of the Pines, Martin Johnson Heritage Museum, Idlewild National Historic Sites, Lake County 1927 Courthouse.
Annual Events: Lake County History Days (Jul). Meetings 2nd Wed monthly Mar-Oct, 6 p.m. at Lake County Historical Research Center.
Publications: "Lake County Historical Writings Books I and II," "Lake County 1871-1960 Pictorial History."
Other Sites/Locations: Baldwin Business Center • Location: 830 Michigan Avenue, Baldwin MI 49304 • Hours: Fri 1-4 p.m. • Admission: $5/individual society dues.

Shrine of the Pines
Mailing Address: P.O. Box 548 • Baldwin, MI 49304
Contact: Treasurer
Phone: (231) 745-7892
Physical Location: 8962 S. M37 • Baldwin, MI 49304
Hours: Mid-May to mid-Oct: Mon-Sat 10 a.m.-6 p.m., Sun 1:30-6 p.m. Last daily tour at 5:30 p.m.
Admission: $5/adult, $4/senior, $2.50/children (6-17), $12.50/family, children under 6 free.
Website: www.facebook.com/shrineofthepines

About: The Shrine of the Pines is a museum in a hunting lodge, which displays furniture made from pine stumps by Raymond W. Overholzer, who fashioned beds, chairs, chandeliers, and a dining room table made from a 700-pound stump, without using metal fasteners. He finished the projects using broken glass, handmade sandpaper, and raw deer hide.
Exhibits/Collections: Rustic handmade furniture.

Bancroft
(Shiawassee County)

Historical Society of Bancroft
Mailing Address: P.O. Box 5 • Bancroft, MI 48414
Contact: Rebecca Sedlock, President
Phone: (989) 634-5184• **Fax:** (989) 634-5689
*Information may not be current.

Bangor
(Van Buren County)

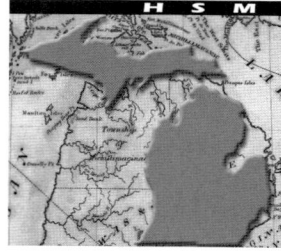

Bangor Historical Society
Mailing Address: P.O. Box 25 • Bangor, MI 49013
Contact: Bob Emmert, Historian
E-Mail: bob@bangormihistory.com
Phone: (269) 427-5206
Website: www.bangormihistory.com

About: The Bangor Historical Society was formed in 2006 for the purpose of collecting, preserving, and interpreting the history and cultural development of the greater Bangor, Michigan, area. The society continues to work toward the goal of building and maintaining a Bangor museum. The museum would serve as a repository for archival materials, be a conduit for research of local history and genealogy, and provide educational material and information about the past.
Annual Events: Annual Yard Sale, Old Time Baseball Game (Sep), Christmas Cookie Walk (Dec). Meetings 2nd Thu Feb, Apr, Jun, Aug, and Oct, 7 p.m. at Simpson United Methodist Church.
Publications: Semi-annual newsletter. "Bangor: Our History in Photographs."

Michigan Flywheelers Museum
Mailing Address: 64958 M-43 Hwy. • Bangor, MI 49013
Contact: Patrick Ingalls, President
E-Mail: michiganflywheelers@yahoo.com
Phone: (269) 639-2010
Physical Location: 06285 68th St. • South Haven, MI 49090
Hours: Memorial Day to Labor Day: Wed, Sat-Sun 10 a.m.-3 p.m.
Admission: Donations accepted. Admission charged during special events.
Visitor Accessibility: Free on-site parking. Wheelchair accessible. Free tour guide available during operational hours or by special request.
Website: www.michiganflywheelers.org

About: The Michigan Flywheelers Museum is an organization of volunteers dedicated to the preservation and education of American farming history and its equipment. The museum offers visitors a look at the lives of our early rural settlers. Guests can visit Old Towne, which is filled with 1920s-era businesses and trades. Displays include the Old Tyme Jail, Peaceful Knoll Church, Abbert & Sons Farm Machinery Repair, Over the Hill Forge and the Farm History Building.
Exhibits/Collections: Antique farm machinery, flywheel tractors, and flywheel engines. Also various collections, such as milk bottles and hand tools, that relate to farming.
Annual Events: Farm History Day (May), Swap Meet/Flea Market (Jun), Blacksmith Hammer-IN (June), Antique Engine & Tractor Show (Sept). Meetings 2nd Sun monthly.
Publications: Monthly newsletter for members.

Baraga
(Baraga County)

Baraga County Historical Society
Mailing Address: P.O. Box 567, 803 U.S. Hwy 41 • Baraga, MI 49908
Contact: Nancy Mannikko, Archivist
E-Mail: baragacountyhistory@gmail.com
Phone: (906) 353-8444
Fax: (906) 353-8444
Site/Location: Baraga County Historical Museum
Physical Location: 803 U.S. Hwy 41 • Baraga, MI 49908
Hours: Memorial Day-Labor Day: Thu-Sat 11 a.m.-3 p.m. Off-season hours by appointment only.
Admission: $2/adult, $1/youth, children 12 and under free
Visitor Accessibility: Free on-site parking. Wheelchair accessible. Tour guide available.
Website: www.baragacountyhistoricalmuseum.com/

About: The Baraga County Historical Museum collects, preserves, and displays artifacts and documents related to Baraga County's past. Exhibits include logging and lumbering artifacts, an exhibit on the life of Captain James Bendry and the Village of Baraga, material about Bishop Frederic Baraga and his missionary work in upper

Michigan, displays on everyday life in the late-19th and early-20th century, and an exhibit on Finnish immigrants and their influence on Baraga County. Outdoor exhibits include a Pettibone Cary-Lift.
Exhibits/Collections: Archives range from the history of the lumber industry in Michigan to individual family genealogy. Records of birth, death, and marriage since 1875. Collections include all of Baraga County.
Annual Events: Meetings Oct-Apr 3rd Wed monthly, 9:30 a.m. at Java by the Bay in L'Anse. Meetings May-Sep 3rd Wed monthly, 6 p.m. at museum.

Bishop Baraga Shrine
Mailing Address: P.O. Box 665 • Baraga, MI 49908
Contact: Nancy Hammerberg, President
Phone: (906) 353-7779
Site/Location: **Shrine of the Snowshoe Priest**
Physical Location: Shrine of the Snowshoe Priest, Lambert Road • L'Anse, MI 49946
Hours: Open year-round, 24 hours a day. Access restricted by snow in winter.
Admission: Donations accepted.
Visitor Accessibility: On-site parking. Wheelchair accessible. Self-guided.
About: Located one mile west of L'Anse next to US-41. Rising six stories above the Red Rocks Bluff near L'Anse, this historic shrine commands a breathtaking view of Michigan's Keweenaw Bay. Holding a cross 7 feet high and snowshoes 26 feet long, this hand-wrought brass sculpture of Bishop Baraga is 35 feet tall and weighs 4 tons. It floats on a cloud of stainless steel supported by five laminated wooden beams, which represent Bishop Baraga's five major missions.
Publications: "The Snowshoe Priest," pamphlets on site contain information and membership information.

Battle Creek
(Calhoun County)

Battle Creek Historic District Commission
Mailing Address: 77 Michigan Ave. E., Suite 204 • Battle Creek, MI 49016
Contact: Glenn Perian
Phone: (269) 966-3200 • *Fax:* (269) 966-3529
About: The Battle Creek Historic District Commission regulates and reviews applications for construction and changes within historic districts.
Annual Events: Meetings 2nd Mon monthly, 4 p.m. at Chamber of Commerce Board Room.
Information may not be current.

Heritage Battle Creek
Mailing Address: 165 N. Washington • Battle Creek, MI 49017
Contact: Mary Butler
Phone: 269-965-2613 • *Fax:* 269-660-9072
Site/Location: **Kimball House Museum**
Physical Location: 196 Capital Ave. NE • Battle Creek, MI 49017
Hours: Office: Mon-Fri 9 a.m.-5 p.m.
Admission: Free.
Visitor Accessibility: Free parking. Partially wheelchair accessible. Self-guided, guided tours of Kimball House available Sun or by appointment.
Website: www.heritagebattlecreek.org
About: Established in 1916 to promote the history of Southwestern Michigan and the Sojourner Truth Institute, which seeks to expand the historical and biographical knowledge of Truth's work. Heritage Battle Creek maintains collections and operates the Kimball House Museum. It also provides two heritage tours: "Freedom Saga" tells the story of Sojourner Truth and the Underground Railroad in Southwest Michigan and "Road to Wellness" traces the Seventh-day Adventist origins of health reform and the development of the cereal industry.

Exhibits/Collections: Documents and artifacts related to Sojourner Truth, cereal industry, Battle Creek Sanitarium, and Battle Creek's unique heritage.
Annual Events: Strawberry Festival and Ice Cream Social (Jun), Child's Christmas Past Victorian Christmas (Dec).
Publications: Journal (Heritage Battle Creek).
Information may not be current.

Historic Adventist Village
Mailing Address: P.O. Box 1414 • Battle Creek, MI 49016
Contact: Don Scherencel, Director
E-Mail: adventistvillage@tds.net
Phone: (269) 965-3000 • *Fax:* (269) 968-9700
Physical Location: 404 W. Van Buren St. • Battle Creek, MI 49037
Hours: Sun-Fri 10 a.m.-4 p.m., Sat 2-4 p.m.
Admission: Donations accepted.
Visitor Accessibility: Free on-site parking. Partially wheelchair accessible. Free tour guide available; call ahead.
Website: www.adventistheritage.org
About: The Historic Adventist Village aims to teach visitors about the history of Battle Creek from 1852 to 1902. The village comprises an 1870s one-room schoolhouse; an 1850s log cabin; a church built in Parkville, Michigan, in 1860; the home of Harriet Henderson Tucker, a former slave who fled north on the underground railroad; and the home of James and Ellen White, two of the early members of the Seventh-day Adventist Church. Another attraction is the Dr. John Kellogg Discovery Center.
Annual Events: Christmas Stroll (Dec).
Publications: Adventist Heritage Ministry quarterly bulletin.

Historic Bridge Park
Please see entry under Marshall: Calhoun County Road Commission.

Historical Society of Battle Creek
Mailing Address: 171 Michigan Ave. W • Battle Creek, MI 49017
Phone: 269-965-2613 • *Fax:* 269-966-2495
Website: www.historicalsocietybc.org
Information may not be current.

Kingman Museum
Mailing Address: 175 Limit St. • Battle Creek, MI 49037
Contact: Donna Roberts, Executive Director
E-Mail: droberts@kingmanmuseum.org
Phone: (269) 965-5117
Hours: Sat 12-4 p.m. Tue, Thu 3-5 p.m.
Admission: $7/adult, $6/seniors and veterans, $5/student, $20/family.
Visitor Accessibility: Free on-site parking. Wheelchair accessible. Groups welcome Mon-Thu by reservation.
Website: www.kingmanmuseum.org
About: The Kingman Museum is a natural history museum featuring three levels of exhibits and a planetarium. Exhibits include everything from geology and dinosaurs to ancient pottery, biology, and taxidermy. Our mission is to provide learning and opportunities in natural history, the universe, and world cultures.
Exhibits/Collections: Animal-mounted specimens, geology, archaeology, anthropology, and paleontology.
Annual Events: Festivus Free-day (Feb), Annual Golf Outing (spring), Drawdown in the Garden (summer), Leilapalooza (summer), Museum Free Day (Sep), Spooky Science Saturday (Oct).

Historical Society of Michigan

MI Alliance for the Conservation of Cultural Heritage
Mailing Address: c/o Kingman Museum, 175 Limit St. • Battle Creek, MI 49037
Contact: Katie Nelson, President
E-Mail: knelson@kingmanmuseum.org
Phone: (269) 965-5117
Website: www.macch.org
About: The Michigan Alliance for the Conservation of Cultural Heritage is a statewide 501(c)(3) organization composed of libraries, archives, museums, historical societies, and preservation networks. The purpose is to promote the protection and preservation of Michigan's cultural and humanities resources for the enjoyment, education, and benefit of present and future generations.
Exhibits/Collections: Archival materials, records, objects, artifacts of everyday life, historic sites, buildings, and landscapes held privately or publicly or collected by libraries, archives, and museums.
*Information may not be current.

Sojourner Truth Institute
Mailing Address: 165 N. Washington • Battle Creek, MI 49017
Phone: (269) 964-2613 • *Fax:* (269) 966-2495
Website: www.sojournertruth.org
*Information may not be current.

Bay City
(Bay County)

Bay City Architectural Review Committee
Mailing Address: 301 Washington Ave. • Bay City, MI 48708
Contact: Stuart Barbier
E-Mail: sibarbie@delta.edu
Hours: 2nd-3rd Wed monthly.
About: Bay City Architectural Review Committee is the ruling body over issues relating to development within the Midland Street and Center Avenue historic districts. The committee also focuses on increasing public awareness of Bay City's heritage and identifies historic and cultural resources for the purpose of preserving the best examples of Bay City's past. The 1896 City Hall clock tower is accessible to public.
*Information may not be current.

Bay County Historical Society
Mailing Address: 321 Washington Ave. • Bay City, MI 48708
Contact: Ron Bloomfield, Director of Operations/Chief Historian
E-Mail: info@bchsmuseum.org
Phone: (989) 893-5733
Fax: (989) 893-5741
Site/Location: **Historical Museum of Bay County**
Physical Location: 321 Washington Avenue • Bay City, MI 48708
Hours: Mon-Fri 10 a.m.-5 p.m.; Sat 12-4 p.m.
Admission: Donations accepted.
Visitor Accessibility: Free parking. Wheelchair accessible. Tour guide available by appointment.
Website: www.bchsmuseum.org

About: Active since 1919, this museum is located in a former armory and features exhibit galleries that detail the distinctive heritage of Bay County, including major sections on Native Americans, the fur trade, lumbering, military history, and local businesses and industries. The society also maintains the Kantzler Maritime Gallery, which details the story of Bay City's rich maritime history and several changing exhibit galleries. The Robert and Ann Hachtel Theatre features several feature-length documentaries.
Exhibits/Collections: More than 225,000 objects and archives relevant to the history of the Bay County area, including Great Lakes shipping, lumbering, sugar beet industry, and area land and early governmental records.
Annual Events: River of Time (Sep), Tour of Homes (Oct).
Publications: Newsletter (The Museum Record).
Other Sites/Locations: **Trombley/Centre House** • Location: 901 John F. Kennedy Drive, Bay City, MI 48706 • Trombley/Centre House is the oldest frame house still standing in Bay County (c. 1840) and operated by the society as an off-site location for some programs. The historic herb garden is managed by Olde Thyme Herb Society (a BCHS affiliate), and the house is open for first-floor viewing during special events, including River of Time and holiday open houses. Interpretive signs and virtual tour coming soon.
*Information may not be current.

Detroit & Mackinaw Railway Historical Society
Mailing Address: 305 S. McClellan St. • Bay City, MI 48708
*Information may not be current.

Saginaw River Marine Historical Society
Mailing Address: P.O. Box 2051 • Bay City, MI 48707
Contact: Don Comtois
E-Mail: wolfgangrosa@gmail.com
Phone: (989) 686-1895
About: The Saginaw River Marine Historical Society preserves the history of the Saginaw River and its connecting waterways.
Exhibits/Collections: Oldest known boat built by Defoe Boat & Motor (1913). Other items and literature related to Saginaw River.
Annual Events: Family Picnic (May), Memorial service for Tri-Cities-area sailors lost in storms and accidents (Nov). Meetings 3rd Sat Jan-May and Sep-Nov, 7 p.m. at Trinity Episcopal Church (Corner of Center & Grant, Bay City).
Publications: Newsletter (Modoc Whistle).

Beaver Island
(Charlevoix County)

Beaver Island Historical Society
Mailing Address: 26275 Main St., P.O. Box 263 • Beaver Island, MI 49782
Contact: William Cashman
E-Mail: history@beaverisland.net
Phone: (231) 448-2254 • *Fax:* (231) 448-2106
Hours: Jun-Labor Day: Mon-Sat 11 a.m.-5 p.m. and Sun 12-3 p.m.
Admission: Donations accepted.
Visitor Accessibility: Free parking. Tour guides available.
Website: www.beaverisland.net/History
About: The Beaver Island Historical Society maintains the Old Mormon Print Shop Museum, which was the printing operation for James Strang's Kingdom of St. James, 1850-1856. The shop now serves as a general history museum for Beaver Island. The Beaver Island Maritime Museum was a net house built in 1906 and restored in 1980 to display fishing and shipping history of the island. Protar Home, the log cabin of Feodor Protar, is undergoing restoration.
Exhibits/Collections: Materials related to Beaver Island. Oral history collections include 245 tapes.
Annual Events: Museum Week (Jul).
Publications: Newsletter three issues per year. Five volumes of "The Journal of Beaver Island History."
*Information may not be current.

Belding
(Ionia County)

HSM MEMBER

Belding Museum
Mailing Address: P.O. Box 45 • Belding, MI 48809
Contact: Joan Miller-Moran, Director
E-Mail: beldingmuseum@gmail.com
Phone: (616) 794-1900, ext. 425
Site/Location: **Belding Museum at the Historic Belrockton**
Physical Location: 108 Hanover St. • Belding, MI 48809
Hours: 1st Sun monthly 1-4 p.m.
Admission: Free.
Visitor Accessibility: Free on-site and street parking. Wheelchair accessible. Self-guided.
Website: http://www.ci.belding.mi.us/museum_history.php

About: The historic Belrockton Dormitory was built in 1906 by the Belding Brothers Manufacturing Company to house single women employed at the silk mills when Belding was know as the "Silk Capital of the World." The museum occupies three floors. The Belrockton, which houses the Belding Museum, is the last remaining dormitory of the original three in Belding.
Exhibits/Collections: Focus on silk mill industry era (1880-1935) and the history of Belding and the surrounding area.
Annual Events: Tri-Rivers "Spring Into the Past" Weekend (May), Labor Day Weekend Open House, "Silk City Quilters" Quilt Show (Nov).
Other Sites/Locations: **Belding Exploration Lab Children's Museum (BEL)** • Location: 108 Hanover St., Belding, MI 48809 • Hours: See website • Admission: Free • Visitor Accessibility: Wheelchair accessible. Self-guided. • The BEL offers children the opportunity to learn through creative play and interaction with others and the exhibits within the eight themed rooms. Exhibits include "Adventure on the Flat," where children can sit in a rowboat that was manufactured in Belding and "fish" for species native to Michigan. Other native birds and animals are showcased in the exhibit.

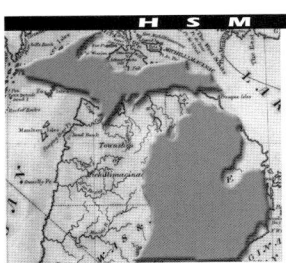

HSM MEMBER

Grattan Township Historical Society
Mailing Address: 12040 Old Belding Rd. Belding, MI 48809
Contact: Diana Force
E-Mail: forcecricket@gmail.com
Phone: (616) 826-1872
Hours: May-Oct: Sun 2-4 p.m.
Website: http://www.grattantownship.org/historicalsociety.html

About: The Grattan Township Historical Society maintains a museum in the 1853 Methodist Episcopal Church, which was used as Grattan Township Hall until 1971.
Exhibits/Collections: Historical artifacts related to Kent County's Grattan Township and its residents. Genealogical records and depository for township records.
Annual Events: Bridge Walk (Memorial Day), Ice Cream Social (Aug). Meetings 1st Tue Feb, Apr, Jun, Aug, Oct, and Dec, 7 p.m. at Grattan Township Hall.
Publications: Newsletter (Grattan Glimpses).
*Information may not be current.

Bellaire
(Antrim County)

HSM MEMBER

Bellaire Area Historical Society
Mailing Address: PO Box 246 • Bellaire, MI 49615
Contact: Don Seman, President
E-Mail: bellairemuseum1@gmail.com
Phone: (231) 533-8631
Site/Location: **Bellaire Historical Museum**
Physical Location: 202 N. Bridge St. • Bellaire, MI 49615
Hours: Tue-Sat 11 a.m.-3 p.m.
Admission: Free.
Visitor Accessibility: Free street parking. Wheelchair accessible. Tour guide available.
About: The Bellaire Area Historical Society informs and educates the residents of and visitors to Bellaire of its history. The Bellaire Historical Museum features Civil War uniforms and weapons, pioneer cabin, history of Bellaire High School, and story of largest woodware factory in the world.
Exhibits/Collections: Newspapers (1885 to present), "Woodenware" products (produced 1879-1905), school pictures, one-room schools, cemetery records, obituaries, "Fisherman's Resort" on Lake Bellaire, Antrim County Atlases (1897 and 1910), Civil War weapons and uniforms.
Annual Events: Annual Home Tour, Memorial Day Walk, Annual Fall Meeting.
Publications: "The Story of Bellaire."
*Information may not be current.

Belleville
(Wayne County)

HSM MEMBER

Belleville Area Museum & Archives
Mailing Address: 405 Main St. • Belleville, MI 48111
Contact: Katie Dallos, Director
E-Mail: kdallos@provide.net
Phone: (734) 697-1944
Fax: (734) 697-1944
Site/Location: **Belleville Area Museum**
Physical Location: 405 Main Street • Belleville, MI 48111
Hours: Fall/winter: Tue 3-7 p.m., Wed-Sat 12-4 p.m. Spring/summer: Tue 3-7 p.m., Mon and Wed-Fri 12-4 p.m.
Admission: $2/adult, $1/child (5-17).
Visitor Accessibility: Street parking. Wheelchair accessible. Self-guided; group bookings call ahead.
Website: www.vanburen-mi.org

About: The Belleville Area Historical Society preserves, promotes, and protects the history of the townships of VanBuren and Sumpter and the city of Belleville. The society maintains a museum in the 1875 Van Buren Township Hall. Exhibits highlight local history of Belleville as well as Van Buren and Sumpter townships.
Exhibits/Collections: Local history, genealogy. Five-foot by five-foot 1860 map of Wayne County.
Annual Events: Third Thu Lectures, Quilt Exhibit, Harvest Fest, Cemetery History Tour, Festival of Holiday Trees, Winterfest, Children's Ornament Workshop.
Publications: Annual historical society calendar.

❊ Historical Society of Michigan

B

HSM MEMBER
Yankee Air Museum
Mailing Address: 47884 D St. • Belleville, MI 48111
Contact: Kevin Walsh, Executive Director
E-Mail: supportyankee@yankeeairmuseum.org
Phone: (734) 483-4030
Fax: (734) 483-5076
Physical Location: 47884 D St. • Belleville, MI 48111
Hours: Tue-Sat 10 a.m.-4 p.m.
Admission: $8/adult, $5/students and children (3 and up), $5/seniors and military. Free for members.
Visitor Accessibility: Free on-site parking. Wheelchair accessible. Tour guide available with advance reservation; call (734) 483-4030.
Website: www.yankeeairmuseum.org

About: The Yankee Air Museum provides unique historical and educational experiences through aviation, military, and home front history based on the museum's collection of objects, archives, and aircraft. The museum challenges, educates, and inspires visitors to embrace aviation's past as a vehicle to the future. Exhibits center on the Willow Run Bomber Plants, along with more recent conflicts such as the Vietnam War. Take a ride in a historic WWII-era bomber: the B-17 "Yankee Lady" or the B-25 "Yankee Warrior!"
Exhibits/Collections: Flyable and static aircraft, military vehicles. Related artifacts and archival materials. Education exhibit "The Exploration Station."
Annual Events: Memorial Day Celebration (May), Thunder Over Michigan Air Show (Aug), Yankee Gala (Veteran's Day Weekend). Meetings 1st Wed monthly.
Publications: Monthly newsletter.

Bellevue
(Eaton County)

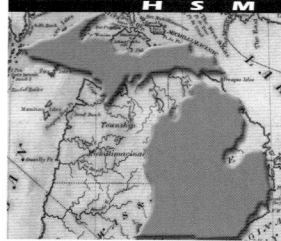

HSM MEMBER
Bellevue Area Historical Society
Mailing Address: 212 N. Main St. • Bellevue, MI 49021
Contact: John Dexter, President
E-Mail: gaddngranny@yahoo.com
Phone: (269) 763-9136
Site/Location: **Bellevue Area Historical Museum**
Hours: Wed 2-4 p.m. Also by appointment.
Admission: Donations accepted.
Visitor Accessibility: Free street parking. Wheelchair accessible. Self-guided.
Website: www.rootsweb.com/~mibhs/

About: The Bellevue Area Historical Society preserves local history. In addition to maintaining a museum, the society is also currently restoring a one-room school in Bellevue. The Bellevue Area Historical Museum houses local history and artifacts.
Exhibits/Collections: Genealogy and school records. Local artifacts of military, agriculture, home, and industry. Period dresses, uniforms, newspaper clippings, and scrapbooks. Microfilm of the Bellevue Gazette.
Annual Events: Meetings 1st Thu monthly (except Jul).
Publications: "History of Bellevue," "Bellevue Area Pictorial Review."

Benton Harbor
(Berrien County)

Berrien County Genealogical Society
Mailing Address: P.O. Box 8808 • Benton Harbor, MI 49023
E-Mail: info@bcgensoc.com
Physical Location: The Church of Jesus Christ of Latter-day Saints, 3711 Niles Rd. • St. Joseph, MI 49085
Visitor Accessibility: Wheelchair accessible.
Website: www.bcgensoc.com
Exhibits/Collections: Records available at Berrien Springs Library.
Annual Events: Meetings 3rd Wed monthly at LDS Family History Center; see website for details.
Publications: Newsletter (Pathfinder), and Berrien County cemetery records.
Information may not be current.

HSM MEMBER
Mary's City of David
Mailing Address: P.O. Box 187 • Benton Harbor, MI 49023
Contact: R. James Taylor, Trustee
E-Mail: rjtaylor@maryscityofdavid.org
Phone: (269) 925-1601
Fax: (269) 925-2707
Physical Location: 1158 E. Britain Ave. • Benton Harbor, MI 49023
Hours: Sat-Sun 1-5 p.m.
Admission: $1/individual for museum admission, $4/individual for guided tour at 1:30 p.m.
Visitor Accessibility: Free on-site parking. Wheelchair accessible. Tour guide available Sundays; call ahead for Saturday availability.
Website: www.maryscityofdavid.org

About: Mary's City of David is a Christian community founded upon the Apostolic communal order of the early Jewish at Jerusalem up to 70 A.D. The religious roots of the movement date back to the Philadelphian Society (1652) in England and is referred to as Christian-Israel. The organization spans 110 years in Michigan and is America's third-oldest practicing Christian community. Today, Mary's City of David, listed on the National Register of Historic Places in 2009, offers a museum and tours.
Exhibits/Collections: Collections are the second-largest holdings of the "Christian-Israelite" movement in the world. Rare manuscripts, hundreds of photographs, paper records, ephemera, complete collections of publications from 1681 to the present.
Annual Events: Baseball game with Blossomtime Festival, "Special Intimate Tours" Fundraiser, 4th of July Base Ball Match, Fables and Mythology About the House of David, Welcome Back to 1934 Vegetarian Lunch.
Publications: "Mary's City of David, A Pictorial History of the Israelite House of David as Reorganized By Mary Purnell," "1996 Vegetarian Cookbook," "Who Is She That Looketh Forth as the Morning," "Portraits: The Face of a Century in Faith."

Morton House Museum
Mailing Address: 501 Territorial Rd. • Benton Harbor, MI 49002
E-Mail: tawana53@aol.com
Hours: Apr-Sep: Mon-Wed 1-4 p.m.; Sun 12-4 p.m.
Admission: $5/adult, $3/senior, $3/children (6-15).
Website: www.mortonmuseum.com
About: The Morton House Museum, built in 1849, is the oldest standing home in Benton Harbor. It was the residence of the first European settlers and remained in the family until it was turned into a museum.
Exhibits/Collections: Clothing, furniture, and artifacts dating from early 1800s through the 1940s.
Annual Events: Cemetery Tour (Sep), Holiday Open House (Nov).
Information may not be current.

Benzonia
(Benzie County)

Benzie Area Historical Society
Mailing Address: 6941 Traverse Ave., P.O. Box 185 • Benzonia, MI 49616
Contact: Louis Yock, Director
E-Mail: bmuseum@att.net
Phone: (231) 882-5539
Fax: (231) 882-4435
Hours: May-Nov: Mon-Sat 11 a.m.-5 p.m.
Admission: Free.
Visitor Accessibility: Free parking. Wheelchair accessible. Self-guided.
Website: www.benziemuseum.org
About: The Benzie Area Historical Society maintains a museum in an 1887 church. Exhibits feature dolls and toys, AA car ferries, early resorts, historian Bruce Catton, railroads, logging, and the Civil War. The society also maintains the One-Room Drake School Museum, located in Honor.
Exhibits/Collections: Photos and documents from early Benzie County history.
Publications: "Benzie Heritage."
Information may not be current.

Bergland
(Ontonagon County)

Bergland/Matchwood Historical Society
Mailing Address: P.O. Box 403 • Bergland, MI 49910
Contact: Brad Livingston, President
E-Mail: berglandmuseum@yahoo.com
Phone: (906) 390-0012
Physical Location: 691 W. M-28 • Bergland, MI 49910
Hours: Wed-Sat 12-4 p.m.
Admission: None
Visitor Accessibility: Free off-site parking (museum). Not wheelchair accessible. Free tour guide available.
Website: www.berglandmuseum.com
About: The Bergland/Matchwood Historical Society preserves local history and artifacts. The society's museum includes a 1920s kitchen and dining room, school room, military exhibit with photos of local veterans, and farm and mining displays.
Exhibits/Collections: Photos and articles of local interest. Photos of schools, images of veterans, pre-century items. Norwich Trail artifacts (from Bergland to the Norwich Bluffs), including saw camps and copper mine artifacts.
Annual Events: Christmas Gathering (Dec). Meetings 2nd Wed monthly, 4:30 p.m. at Bergland Service Center.
Information may not be current.

Friends of Bergland Cultural Heritage Center
Mailing Address: P.O. Box 44 • Bergland, MI 49910
Contact: Phillip Ellsworth
Phone: (906) 236-0312
Physical Location: 691 W. M-28 • Bergland, MI 49910
Hours: Jun-Oct: Mon, Wed, Fri 11 a.m.
Annual Events: Meetings 1st Tue monthly, 1 p.m.
Information may not be current.

Berkley
(Oakland County)

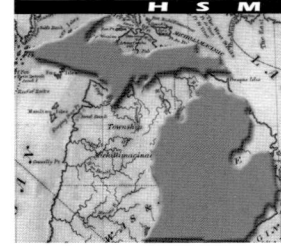

Berkley Historical Committee
Mailing Address: 3338 Coolidge Highway • Berkley, MI 48072
Contact: Sue Richardson, Chair
E-Mail: museum@berkleymich.net
Phone: (248) 658-3335
Fax: (248) 658-3301
Site/Location: Berkley Historical Museum
Hours: Sun 2-4 p.m. Also by appointment.
Admission: Free.
Visitor Accessibility: Free on-site and street parking. Partially wheelchair accessible; slight rise at the front door. Tour guide available.
Website: http://www.berkleymich.org/community_museum.shtm

About: The Berkley Historical Museum is housed in the 1928 historic Village Hall and Fire Station. Major collections include an impressive collection of historic fire and police artifacts. The museum has a large collection of furniture and appliances that were common to Berkley's residents during the 1920s and 1930s. Among major items in the museum are a school bell from Berkley's first school, seats from the Berkley Theater, and a Benjamin Grain Cradle manufactured in the 1830s in Berkley.
Exhibits/Collections: Aerial views of Berkley (1940), photos, village tax receipts, newspapers, scrapbooks, family histories, school memorabilia.
Annual Events: Berkley Days Festival (May), Berkley's Art Bash (Jun), Cruisefest Parade (Aug), Holiday Light Parade (Dec).
Publications: "Images of America: Berkley."

Berrien Springs
(Berrien County)

Berrien County Historical Association
Mailing Address: P.O. Box 261 • Berrien Springs, MI 49103
Contact: Kathy A. Cyr, Executive Director
E-Mail: kcyr@berrienhistory.org
Phone: (269) 471-1202
Fax: (269) 471-7412
Site/Location: History Center at Courthouse Square
Physical Location: 313 N. Cass St. • Berrien Springs, MI 49103
Hours: Sept-May: Mon-Fri 10 a.m.-5 p.m., Jun-Aug: Mon-Sat 10 a.m.-5 p.m.
Admission: Free.
Visitor Accessibility: Free on-site parking. Partially wheelchair accessible. Self-guided.
Website: www.berrienhistory.org

About: The Berrien County Historical Association operates the History Center at Courthouse on the Square, which includes the oldest complex of county government buildings in the Midwest: 1839 courthouse, 1830 log house, 1870 sheriff's residence, and 1860/1873 office building. The museum features permanent and special exhibits highlighting regional history. The association also publishes books and offers on- and off-site programs relevant to the history of the area.
Exhibits/Collections: Corporate records, photographs, films, videos,

Historical Society of Michigan

and artifacts. Records repository of Berrien County records including: marriage records (1831-1929), death records (1867-1929), and probate court files.

Annual Events: Motor Coach Tour, Pioneer Day, Summer Program Series, Annual Meeting with program, Holiday Open House.

Publications: "Greetings from Berrien Springs," "Greetings from Buchanan," "Greetings from St. Joseph," "Greetings from Benton Harbor," "Locomotives Along the Lakeshore," "Historical Sketches of Berrien County," "Clark Equipment County's Aluminum Railcar," "Greetings From Three Oaks."

Horn Archaeological Museum

Mailing Address: 9047 US 21 • Berrien Springs, MI 49104
Contact: Connie Gane, Curator
E-Mail: hornmuseum@andrews.edu
Phone: 269-471-3273 • *Fax:* 269-471-3619
Hours: Sat 3-5 p.m., Mon-Fri by appointment. Closed during university holidays.
Admission: $3/adult, $1/children suggested donation.
Visitor Accessibility: Free on-site parking. Wheelchair accessible. Free tour guides available by appointment.
Website: www.andrews.edu/archaeology
About: The Horn Archaeological Museum houses more than 8,500 artifacts and objects related to ancient and biblical times. Exhibits include a mummified Egyptian Ibis, life-size replica of King Tutankhamen's golden throne, and masonry bricks from Babylon and Ur.
Exhibits/Collections: Hartford Cuneiform Tablet Collection consisting of about 3,000 ancient clay tablets ranging from the Sumerian period to Neo-Babylonian times.
Publications: Newsletter (Near East Archaeological Society Bulletin).

*Information may not be current.

Big Rapids
(Mecosta County)

Big Rapids Historic Preservation Commission

Mailing Address: 220 South Stewart • Big Rapids, MI 49307
Contact: Bryan Ridenour, President
E-Mail: bsridenour@charter.net
Phone: (231) 796-9507
Site/Location: **Old Jail**
Hours: May-Sep Sat 2-4 p.m. Also by appointment.
Website: http://www.ci.big-rapids.mi.us/Bergelin_House.aspx

About: The Big Rapids Historic Preservation Commission maintains the 1873 Queen Anne Old Jail. The commission also maintains the 1873 Italianate home of the Robert Bergelin family, which is being restored to display furniture manufactured in Big Rapids. Tours focus on furniture manufacturing and penal systems at the end of the 19th century.
Exhibits/Collections: Furniture and memorabilia of Big Rapids and Ferris State University. Some jail inmate records.
Annual Events: Yard sales (Aug), Big Rapids Heritage Days. Meetings 2nd Mon monthly, 6:30 p.m.
Other Sites/Locations: **Bergelin House Museum** • Location: 218 Winter, Big Rapids, MI 49307.

*Information may not be current.

Physical Location: 1010 Campus
Hours: Mon-F
Admission: Free. display themes.
Visitor Accessibility: Wheelchair accesible. Tour guide available. Group tours for 10 people or more available by appointment. (Group tours containing children younger than 12 will not be scheduled.)
Website: www.ferris.edu/jimcrow

About: Founded and curated by Dr. David Pilgrim of Ferris State University, the Jim Crow Museum uses objects of intolerance to teach tolerance and promote social justice. It collects, exhibits, and preserves objects and collections related to racial segregation, anti-black caricatures, civil rights, and African-American achievement.
Exhibits/Collections: More than 9,000 pieces of racist artifacts.
Annual Events: See website for list of annual events.

Mecosta County Genealogical Society

Mailing Address: P.O. Box 1068 • Big Rapids, MI 49307
Contact: Maureen Nelson, President
E-Mail: doyle@tucker-usa.com
Physical Location: 424 North Fourth Avenue • Big Rapids, MI 49307
Hours: May 1- Oct 1: 2nd Sat of each month 10 a.m.-2 p.m.; Wed from 5-7 p.m.
Admission: Free and available to the public.
Visitor Accessibility: Free parking on-site. Building is not wheelchair accessible.
Website: www.commoncorners.com/mcgs

About: The Mecosta County Genealogical Society houses 500 binders of historical information about families, townships, businesses, schools, churches, plat maps, and city directories.
Exhibits/Collections: Newspaper clippings from the 1960s to 1990s, with many other prior years also. Obituary file has more than 18,500 obits. Large collection of family genealogies and Pioneer Certificate applications with genealogies.
Annual Events: Veteran's Tribute (Nov), Home for the Holidays (Dec), Pioneer Certificate presentations (ongoing).
Publications: Newsletter

Mecosta County Historical Society

Mailing Address: 129 S. Stewart Ave., PO Box 613 • Big Rapids, MI 49307
E-Mail: verona705@chartermi.net
Phone: (231) 592-5091
Hours: May-Sep: Sat 2-4 p.m. Also by appointment.
Admission: Free.
Visitor Accessibility: Street parking. Not wheelchair accessible. Free tour guide available.

About: Organized in 1894, the Mecosta County Historical Society opened its present museum in 1966 in the former home of lumberman Fitch Phelps. Exhibits include historical displays about the Mecosta County area and lumber industry.
Exhibits/Collections: Local artifacts including 1874 Wooten Desk.
Annual Events: Victorian Tea.
*Information may not be current.

Birmingham
(Oakland County)

Algonquin Club of Detroit & Windsor
Mailing Address: 556 W. Maple • Birmingham, MI 48009
Contact: James Conway, President
E-Mail: AlgonquinClubDW@gmail.com
Phone: (248) 339-0114 • *Fax:* (248) 543-3956
Website: www.AlgonquinClub.info
About: Members of the Algonquin Club of Detroit and Windsor have a broad interest in the history of the Detroit River region, both United States and Canadian shores. We meet in both the United States and Canada.

Birmingham Historic District Commission
Mailing Address: 151 Martin St., P.O. Box 3001 • Birmingham, MI 48012
Contact: Janet Lekas
*Information may not be current.

Birmingham Historical Museum & Park
Mailing Address: 556 W. Maple • Birmingham, MI 48009
Contact: Leslie Pielack, Museum Director
E-Mail: museum@bhamgov.org
Phone: (248) 530-1928
Hours: Wed-Sat 1-4 p.m. Also by appointment. 2nd Thu of the month, open 1-8 p.m.
Admission: $5/adult, $3/members, $3/seniors, $3/students, children under 5 free. Admission fees may be higher during special exhibitions.
Visitor Accessibility: Two hours free parking at Chester Street structure, located across Maple Road from museum. Wheelchair accessible. Guided tours available.
Website: www.bhamgov.org/museum

About: The Birmingham Historical Museum & Park focuses on Birmingham/Bloomfield Township-area history. The four-acre park features two historic buildings: the 1822 John West Hunter House and 1928 Allen House. The Hunter House is the oldest house in Birmingham and is interpreted as a pioneer-era, 19th-century dwelling with period furnishings. The Allen House features changing exhibits that focus on local history and has permanent exhibits of the 1920s, including a Flint Faience Storybook Tile fireplace from a local elementary school.
Exhibits/Collections: Photographs, news clippings, yearbooks, oral history, maps, and other documents relating to local history. Michigan pioneering artifacts (1820-1880). Period garment collection (1840-1960). Special collection of photos and issues of CREEM magazine.
Annual Events: Greenwood Cemetery Tour, Holiday Model Train Exhibit. Call or visit website for more events.
Publications: "Heritage" Newsletter of the Friends of the Birmingham Historical Museum & Park.

Michigan Photographic Historical Society
Mailing Address: P.O. Box 2278 • Birmingham, MI 48102
Contact: Cynthia Motzenbecker, President
E-Mail: motz48073@yahoo.com
Phone: 248-549-6026
Hours: Call or visit website for current hours.
Website: www.miphs.org
About: The Michigan Photographic Historical Society was founded in 1972 to advance the understanding and appreciation of the history of photography. The society provides a venue for people with an interest in collecting and preserving photographic literature, equipment, and images produced with various processes and techniques. The society is interested in the history of photographers and photographic equipment manufacturers, especially those related to Michigan.
Annual Events: Photographic show and dinner meeting.
Publications: Photogram newsletter.

Oakland County Genealogical Society
Mailing Address: P.O. Box 1094 • Birmingham, MI 48012
Contact: Irvin Rabideau, President
E-Mail: list@ocgsmi.org
Phone: (248) 858-0012
Hours: Archive: Mon, Wed, Fri, 8:30 a.m.-5 p.m.; Tue, Thu 8:30 a.m.-8:30 p.m.; Sat 9 a.m.-4 p.m. Hours are subject to change, call ahead for confirmation.
Admission: Free.
Website: http://ocgsmi.org
About: The Oakland County Genealogical Society promotes and encourages an interest in genealogy and related fields. The society locates, publishes, and safeguards public and private genealogical records.
Exhibits/Collections: Collection lcated at the Oakland County Resarch Library, 1200 N. Telegraph Rd., Pontiac. Visit www.oakgov.com/reslib for more info.
Annual Events: Meetings 7 p.m. 1st Tue monthly, Oct-Jun (except Jan), at the St. Andrews Society.
Publications: Quarterly newsletter (Acorns to Oaks), see website for complete list of publications.

Blissfield
(Lenawee County)

Blissfield Area Historical Society
Mailing Address: 105 N. Lane Street • Blissfield, MI 49228
Contact: Paula Saxton
Phone: (517) 486-4816
Hours: Mon-Fri 11 a.m.-5 p.m., also Sat-Sun in summer. Call ahead for current hours.
About: The Blissfield Area Historical Society maintains a museum in the restored Michigan Southern Depot and operates programs for schoolchildren. The society also restored and maintains the one-room Victorsville School at Blissfield High School.
*Information may not be current.

Bloomfield Hills
(Oakland County)

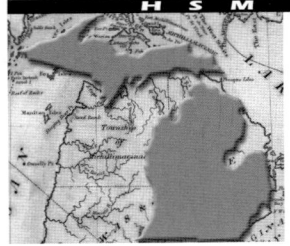

Bloomfield Township Public Library
Mailing Address: 1099 Lone Pine Road • Bloomfield Hills, MI 48302
Contact: Ann Williams, Head of Adult Services
Phone: (248) 642-5800

Historical Society of Michigan

Hours: Mon-Thu 9:30 a.m.-9 p.m.; Fri 9:30 a.m.-6:30 p.m.; Sat 9:30 a.m.-5:30 p.m.
Admission: Free.
Visitor Accessibility: Free on-site parking. Wheelchair accessible. Self-guided.
Website: http://www.btpl.org

About: The Bloomfield Township Public Library serves the members of our community. We have a small local history collection. We collect information about Bloomfield Township. We have a collection of yearbooks from the schools in our area and try to collect information on the Detroit automobile industry.

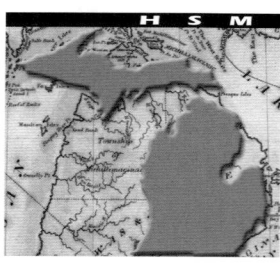

Cranbrook Archives
Mailing Address: P.O. Box 801 • Bloomfield Hills, MI 48303
Contact: Leslie Edwards, Acting Director
Phone: (248) 645-3583
Fax: (248) 645-3029
Hours: Mon-Fri 8:30 a.m.-4:30 p.m.; closed major holidays.
Visitor Accessibility: Free on-site parking. Wheelchair accessible.
Website: www.cranbrook.edu/archives

About: The Cranbrook Archives serves as the research center for study of Cranbrook's heritage in fields of education, science, art, architecture, and design. The archive manages the care and conservation of Cranbrook's cultural properties. It also fosters greater public awareness of Cranbrook's history and cultural heritage.
Exhibits/Collections: Records relating to Cranbrook Foundation, Cranbrook Educational Community, Cranbrook Academy of Art and Art Museum, Cranbrook Institute of Science. Collections of architectural records and audio-visual materials pertaining to Cranbrook.
Information may not be current.

Cranbrook Art Museum
Mailing Address: P.O. Box 801 • Bloomfield Hills, MI 48303
Contact: Gregory Wittkopp, Director
Phone: (248) 645-3323 • **Fax:** (248) 645-3324
Site/Location: Saarinen House
Physical Location: 39221 Woodward Ave. • Bloomfield Hills, MI 48304
Hours: Call for current hours.
Admission: Call for current fees.
Visitor Accessibility: Free on-site parking. Wheelchair accessible. Free tour guide available.
Website: www.cranbrook.edu
About: Cranbrook Art Museum contains approximately 6,000 objects. The Saarinen House is the 1930s restored home and studio of Finnish-American designer Eliel Saarinen.
Exhibits/Collections: Art, architecture, design, decorative arts, crafts, and applied arts from the Arts and Crafts Movement to the present.
Information may not be current.

Leonard N. Simons Jewish Community Archives
Mailing Address: 6735 Telegraph Rd. • Bloomfield Hills, MI 48303
Contact: Robbie Terman, Director of Archives
E-Mail: terman@jfmd.org
Phone: (248) 203-1491 • **Fax:** (248) 645-7879
Hours: Mon-Tue and Thu-Fri by appointment.
Visitor Accessibility: Free on-site parking. Wheelchair accessible. Self-guided.
Website: http://archives.jewishdetroit.org
About: The mission of the Leonard N. Simons Jewish Community Archives is to collect, preserve, and make available for research the records of the Jewish Federation, United Jewish Foundation, Federation's member agencies, local community organizations, and the personal and family papers of Detroit's Jewish citizens.
Exhibits/Collections: Metro-Detroit Jewish organizations, including artifacts, records, memorabilia, photographs. Housed at Walter P. Reuther Library of Labor and Urban Affairs in Detroit and Max M. Fischer Federation Building in Bloomfield Hills.
Publications: Our Story annual publication.

Program Source International
Mailing Address: P.O. Box 444 • Bloomfield Hills, MI 48303
Contact: Al Eicher
E-Mail: info@program-source.com
Phone: (248) 333-2010
Physical Location: 2494 Loch Creek Way • Bloomfield Hills, MI 48303
Hours: 8 a.m.-5 p.m.
Website: www.program-source.com
About: Program Source International presents lectures and creates videos on Michigan communities and events in history. The organization maintains electronic resources for study and presentations related to Michigan history. The organization also maintains a registry of more than 200 individuals who came to Michigan on Orphan Trains from 1854 to 1927. The list includes names, dates, orphanages, and placements.
Exhibits/Collections: Information and photos (15,000 images) about Michigan history, including Civil War, Orphan Trains, lumbering, agriculture, fishing, aviation, Mark Twain in Michigan, Indians, and town histories.

Rabbi Leo M. Franklin Archives
Mailing Address: 7400 Telegraph Road • Bloomfield Hills, MI 48301
Contact: Jan Durecki, Director
E-Mail: franklinarchives@tbeonline.org
Phone: (248) 865-0628
Hours: Mon-Thu 10 a.m.-5 p.m.
Admission: Free.
Visitor Accessibility: On-site parking. Wheelchair accessible. Free docent service available by archivist; schedule in advance.
Website: www.tbeonline.org
About: The Rabbi Leo M. Franklin Archives at Temple Beth El collects, preserves, and makes available to researchers the records of Temple Beth El and the surrounding Jewish community. The Archives has among its collections documents that date to the temple's founding in Detroit in 1850.
Exhibits/Collections: Temple records, Jewish social history, genealogy. The Rabbi Leo M. Franklin Archives is also the custodial repository for the Jewish War Veterans of Michigan and Greater Detroit Chapter of Hadassah.
Annual Events: Mary Einstein Shapero Memorial Lecture Series, Jewish History Detectives Lecture Series.

Bloomfield Township
(Oakland County)

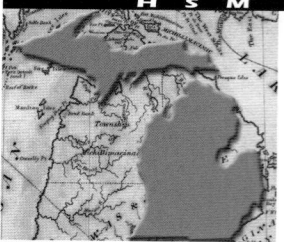

Bloomfield Historical Society
Mailing Address: c/o Bloomfield Township Public Library, 1099 Lone Pine Road • Bloomfield Township, MI 48302
Contact: Pamela Carmichael, President
E-Mail: info@bloomfieldhistoricalsociety.org
Website: www.bloomfieldhistoricalsociety.org

About: The Bloomfield Historical Society seeks to uncover the history of one of Oakland County's original townships, explore the history of the area's original settlers and those who came after, and place local history in context with regional and national history. The society is also actively involved in the restoration of the historic 1859 Wing Lake Schoolhouse, the Benjamin-Barton farmhouse, and the Craig Log Cabin.
Annual Events: Local History/Local Resources Series, Annual Meeting (Apr).
Publications: Biannual newsletter (Legacy).

Bloomingdale
(Van Buren County)

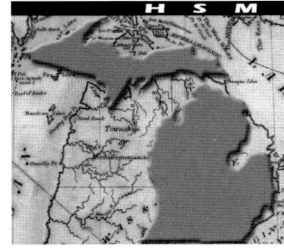

Bloomingdale Area Historical Association, Inc.
Mailing Address: P.O. Box 12 • Bloomingdale, MI 49026
Contact: Pat Bly
Phone: (269) 521-7880
Physical Location: Bloomingdale Depot Museum, 110 N. Van Buren St. • Bloomingdale, MI 49026
Hours: Memorial Day-Oct: Sat 10 a.m.-4 p.m., Sun 1:30-4:30 p.m. Also by appointment.
Admission: Donations accepted.
Visitor Accessibility: On-site parking. Wheelchair accessible. Tour guides available.
Website: www.bloomingdaleareahistoricalassoc.org

About: The Bloomingdale Area Historical Association collects and preserves an accurate record of local history in pictures, written word, and artifacts of the past. The association also maintains the village museum on Kal Haven Trail in Bloomingdale as well as a caboose filled with train memorabilia (which includes a duplicate of a toy train presented to President Reagan by a local company).
Exhibits/Collections: Photos, newspaper clippings dating back to the early 1900s. Medical artifacts dating back to the Civil War. Old iron toys, an oil derrick and pump jack circa late 1930s.
Annual Events: Memorial Day Celebration, Oktoberfest, Parade of Lights, Old Fashioned Christmas in the Park. Meetings 1st Thu Apr-Jan, 7 p.m. in museum history room.
Information may not be current.

Boyne City
(Charlevoix County)

Boyne City Historical Museum
Mailing Address: 319 N. Lake St. • Boyne City, MI 49712
Contact: Michele Hewitt
E-Mail: shelly@boynecity.com
Phone: (231) 582-6597 • ***Fax:*** (231) 582-6506
Physical Location: 317 N. Lake St. • Boyne City, MI 46812
Hours: Mon-Fri 8 a.m.-5 p.m.
Admission: Free.
Visitor Accessibility: Free on-site parking. Wheelchair accessible. Self-guided.
Website: www.boynecity.com
About: The Boyne City Historical Museum features displays on railroading, lumbering, clothing, and military artifacts.
Exhibits/Collections: Railroad artifacts, lumber artifacts, pictures, and farm equipment.

Charlevoix County Genealogical Society
Mailing Address: P.O. Box 7 • Boyne City, MI 49712
Contact: Patrick McCleary, President
E-Mail: ccgseditor@hotmail.com
Phone: (231) 582-3440
Physical Location: Boyne District Library, 201 East Main St. • Boyne City, MI 49712
Hours: Library hours: Sun 12-5 p.m., Mon-Thu 9 a.m.-8 p.m., Fri-Sat 9 a.m.-5 p.m.
Visitor Accessibility: Free on-site parking. Wheelchair accessible.
Website: http://www.cchps.info/
About: The Charlevoix County Genealogical Society promotes and encourages an interest in genealogy. The society instructs members and guests about family history research, assists the Boyne District Library in expanding local history and genealogical holdings, and gathers and preserves genealogical and historical information.
Exhibits/Collections: Genealogical and family history materials focusing on Charlevoix County are available at the Boyne District Library. Collection of local history books. Early local newspapers on microfilm.
Annual Events: Research and Resources Open House (Oct). Meetings 1st Sat (Jan-Apr) at 1 p.m. and 1st Thu (Jun, Aug, Sep, Nov) at 7 p.m.
Publications: Quarterly newsletter (Backtracking Pa's Roots).

Charlevoix County History Preservation Society
Mailing Address: 946 N. Advance Rd. • Boyne City, MI 49712
Contact: Georganna Monk, President
E-Mail: charlevoixchps@yahoo.com
Phone: (231) 582-5326
Hours: Only open to the public by request.
Website: www.cchps.info

About: The Charlevoix County History Preservation Society promotes the understanding and appreciation of the heritage of the people of Charlevoix County and its townships. The society searches out, collects, preserves, and interprets artifacts of historical and cultural significance.
Exhibits/Collections: Books, periodicals, newspapers, family information, public and private records, media presentations, photographs.
Annual Events: Meetings 4th Mon monthly (Mar-Nov).
Publications: Quarterly newsletter.
Information may not be current.

Horton Bay Historical Society
Mailing Address: 5081 Lake St. • Boyne City, MI 49712
Information may not be current.

Breckenridge
(Gratiot County)

Breckenridge-Wheeler Area Historical Society
Mailing Address: P.O. Box 52 • Breckenridge, MI 48615
Contact: Patricia Gillis,
E-Mail: breckenridgewheeler@frontier.com
Phone: (989) 842-1241
Fax: (989) 842-1241

Site/Location: **Plank Road Museum**
Physical Location: 404 E. Saginaw St. • Breckenridge, MI 48615

✤ Historical Society of Michigan

B

Hours: Mon 9 a.m.-12 p.m. Appointments also available.
Admission: Donations accepted.
Visitor Accessibility: Free on-site and street parking. Wheelchair accessible. Tour guide available.
Website: https://www.facebook.com/pages/Breckenridge-Wheeler-Area-Historical-Society-Inc/288330311177232

About: The Breckenridge-Wheeler Area Historical Society preserves area history. The Plank Road Museum is located in an 1890 Baptist Church and its exhibits change on an annual basis.
Exhibits/Collections: Research library with news accounts and oral histories. Artifacts from farming and businesses. War memorabilia from Civil War, WWI, and WWII.
Annual Events: Grand Opening and Plant Sale (May), Cemetery Walk (Sep). Meetings 3rd Wed monthly at 7 p.m.
Publications: "Bygone Era," "The Making of the Drake House."
Other Sites/Locations: **Drake Memorial House Museum** • Location: 328 E. Saginaw St., Breckenridge, MI 48615 • Hours: Mon 9 a.m.-12 p.m. • Admission: Donations accepted • Visitor Accessibility: Free on-site and street parking. Partially wheelchair accessible, main floor doctor's room and gardens wheelchair accessible. Tour guide available. • Drake Memorial House is set in the 1920s era, with a doctor's office featuring physicians instruments that were used from 1920 to 1950. There is also a carriage house on-site.

Brethren
(Manistee County)

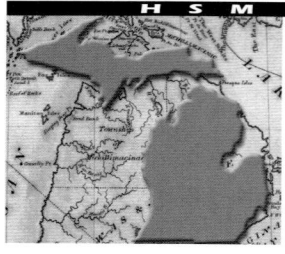

Brethren Heritage Association
Mailing Address: 17955 Coates Hwy. • Brethren, MI 49619
Contact: Janet Stroup, Secretary
E-Mail: janetdonstroup@gmail.com
Phone: (231) 477-5526
Site/Location: **Brethren Heritage Museum**
Physical Location: 14300 Cart Ave. • Brethren, MI 49619
Hours: Jun-Sep: Sun 1 p.m.-4 p.m. Also by appointment.
Admission: Donations accepted.
Visitor Accessibility: Free on-site parking. Wheelchair accessible. Tour guides available by appointment.
About: The purpose of Brethren Heritage Museum is to capture the history of the early 1900s formation of Brethren and its lumbering era. Four buildings on the site include a reconstructed authentic cabin from the 1940's, a reconstructed store from the 30's, and a tool shed containing many artifacts from the lumbering era.
Exhibits/Collections: Artifacts from 1900s. Primarily homesteading, area churches, logging, and farming. Early family records. Materials and pictures from area C.C.C. Camp and building the "High Bridge."
Annual Events: Brethern Days Heritage Lane (Labor Day), Family Fun Fest (Oct). Meetings 1st Monday monthly, 7p.m. at museum.
Publications: Triannual newsletter.

Bridgeport
(Saginaw County)

Historical Society of Bridgeport
Mailing Address: 6190 Dixie Hwy., P.O. Box 591 • Bridgeport, MI 48722
Contact: Diane McCartney, President
E-Mail: damccartney2@yahoo.com
Phone: 989-777-5230
Site/Location: **Bridgeport Historic Village & Museum**
Physical Location: 6190 Dixie Highway • Bridgeport, MI 48722
Hours: Tue-Sat 1-5 p.m.
Admission: Free.
Visitor Accessibility: Free on-site parking. Wheelchair accessible. Tour guide available; larger groups cost $2/person and should schedule in advance.
Website: www.bridgeporthistorical.org

About: The Historical Society of Bridgeport has seven buildings, including an 1896 brick town hall, an 1862 one-room schoolhouse, an 1855 Greek revival house, a replica 1941 fire hall and truck, an 1888 black barn for storage, and a replica little white church from the late 1860s. All buildings contain historical artifacts of the Bridgeport area, from 1835 to the present.
Exhibits/Collections: Native-American artifacts, household furnishings, farm equipment, corn planters, and tools. Bridgeport property tax records 1880-1990; local newspapers and census on microfilm. Genealogy materials, war artifacts, and early school artifacts.
Annual Events: Bridgefest (Jun), Flea and Farm Market (Jun-Sep), Concerts in the Park (Jul-Aug), Pioneer Christmas (Dec).
Publications: Newsletter.

Brighton
(Livingston County)

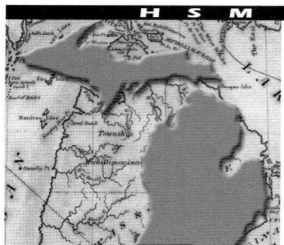

Brighton Area Historical Society
Mailing Address: P.O. Box 481 • Brighton, MI 48116
Contact: James Vichich
E-Mail: info@brightonareahistorical.com
Phone: (810) 250-7276
Site/Location: **1885 Lyon One-Room Schoolhouse Museum**
Physical Location: 14455 Buno Rd. • Brighton, MI 48114
Hours: Thu 9 a.m.-12 p.m.; 3rd Sun monthly 1-4 p.m.
Admission: Free.
Visitor Accessibility: On-site parking. Wheelchair accessible. Prior arrangements required for tour guide.
Website: www.brightonareahistorical.com

About: The Brighton Area Historical Society preserves, advances, and disseminates knowledge of the history of the Brighton area. The society operates two historical buildings. Extensive restoration projects are being performed at Brighton's earliest cemetery, the 1837 Old Village Cemetery. The 1885 Lyon School is a fully restored one-room schoolhouse set in 1900. A small museum highlights local memorabilia, including early veterinarian tools and early photos of Brighton.
Exhibits/Collections: Paper ephemera, pictures, city address listings from the early 1900s, family histories, cemetery records.
Annual Events: Old Village Cemetery Restoration Kick-Off Day (May), Lyon Schoolhouse Pumpkin Decorating for Children (Oct), Lyon Schoolhouse Annual Membership Meetings and Elections (Nov), and Lyon Schoolhouse Christmas with Santa and Mrs. Claus (Dec).
Publications: Monthly newsletter (Trail Tales).
Other Sites/Locations: **City of Brighton Arts Culture and History (COBACH) Center** • Location: 202 W. Main St. Brighton, MI 48114 • Phone: (810) 229-2784 • Hours: Sun-Fri 5 p.m.-8 p.m., Sat 9 a.m.-12p.m. • Admission: Free • Visitor Accessibility: Free street and off-street parking. Wheelchair accessible. Staff volunteers on-site. • Located in a former 1879 firehouse, the COBACH Center is operated by three local non-profits, including the Brighton Area Historical Society. The historical society changes its displays in the center every six to eight weeks.

Michigan History Directory

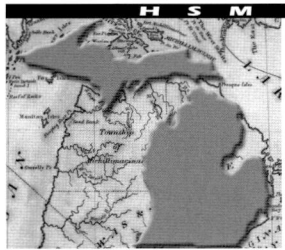

HSM MEMBER
Brighton District Library
Mailing Address: 100 Library Dr. • Brighton, MI 48116
Contact: Mark Mullinax, Genealogy and Local History Librarian
E-Mail: britref@brightonlibrary.info
Phone: (810) 229-6571
Fax: (810) 229-3161
Site/Location: **Brighton Room Collection of Genealogy and Local History**
Hours: Mon-Wed 10 a.m.-9 p.m.; Fri-Sat 10 a.m.-5 p.m.; Sun 1-5 p.m. (closed Sun Jun-Aug)
Admission: Free.
Visitor Accessibility: Free on-site parking. Wheelchair accessible. Self-guided.
Website: http://brightonlibrary.info

About: The Brighton Room Collection of Genealogy and Local History at Brighton District Library provides a full range of services and materials for genealogists, historians, teachers, and other interested hobbyists and scholars. It is one of the largest collections of family and local history information in Livingston County. Knowledgeable librarians and genealogists are available to assist researchers.
Exhibits/Collections: 3,000-plus printed items (family histories, indexes to records, cemetery transcriptions, obituaries, maps, family history magazines, scrapbooks, how-to books, photographs) as well as microfilmed local newspaper, federal census, and Livingston County records.
Annual Events: Genealogy After Hours (fall), special genealogy presentations throughout the year.

Brimley
(Chippewa County)

HSM MEMBER
Bay Mills-Brimley Historical Research Society
Mailing Address: P.O. Box 273 • Brimley, MI 49715
Contact: Janet Russell, President
E-Mail: euprussell@yahoo.com
Phone: (906) 248-3487
Site/Location: **Wheels of History Museum**
Physical Location: 6799 S. M-221 • Brimley, MI 49715
Hours: May 15-Jun 20: 10 a.m.-4 p.m.; June 20-Labor Day: Wed-Sun 10 a.m.-4 p.m.; Labor Day-Oct 15: Sat-Sun 10 a.m.-4 p.m.
Admission: Donations accepted.
Visitor Accessibility: Free street parking. Partially wheelchair accessible. Tour guide available.
Website: www.baymillsbrimleyhistory.org

About: The Bay Mills Brimley Historical Research Society was established April 4, 1981. We preserve the history of the Bay Mills Brimley area. Included are a railroad car and caboose to use as a museum and gift shop, and a replica depot.
Exhibits/Collections: First telephone switchboard in area, logging items, photos of schools, doctor's bag and more.
Annual Events: Fourth of July Celebration, Sault History Fest (Aug), Sault Arts Festival (Aug), Ice Cream Social (Sep), Harvest Dinner Fundraiser (Sep), Quilt Raffle (Oct).
Publications: "Wheels of History Brochure," "Short History of Brimley."
Other Sites/Locations: **Point Iroquois Light Station** • Location: 12942 W. Lakeshore Dr., Brimley, MI 49715 (Six miles west of Brimley) • Hours: May 15-Oct 15: Daily 9 a.m.-5 p.m. • Admission: Donations accepted • Visitor Accessibility: Partially wheelchair accessible. Self-guided; tower is open for climbing. • Built in 1855, the Point Iroquois Light Station was last occupied in the 1950s and was placed on the National Register of Historic Places in 1975. It houses a museum featuring a 1950s living room and kitchen, local artifacts and historical pictures, clothing worn by light keepers, a list of all the past lighthouse keepers, keepers' logs of weather and ships, and a Fresnel Lens.

Brooklyn
(Jackson County)

HSM MEMBER
Walker Tavern Historic Complex.
Please see entry under Lansing: Michigan Historical Center.

Brownstown
(Wayne County)

Brownstown Township Historical Commission
Mailing Address: c/o Charter Township of Brownstown, 21313 Telegraph • Brownstown, MI 48133
Phone: (734) 675-0071
Website: www.brownstown-mi.org/agenda/Historical.html
About: Established in 1992, the Brownstown Township Historical Commission is charged with preserving artifacts, buildings, and other items related to the community's history. The commission is currently working to preserve the 100-year-old Brownstown Acres Farmhouse, located at Telegraph and King Roads, and is developing the site of the 1836 St. Mary's Church at West Jefferson and Lee.
*Information may not be current.

Bruce
(Macomb County)

HSM MEMBER
Historic Memorials Society in Detroit
Mailing Address: 69308 Pine River Dr. • Bruce, MI 48065
Contact: Judy Anders, President
E-Mail: judy_anders@msn.com
Phone: (586) 336-2150
About: The Historic Memorials Society in Detroit was originally founded in 1891 as the Mount Vernon Society of Detroit, a local unit of the Mount Vernon Ladies Association of the Union (the oldest women's charity organization in the United States). In 1922, the organization was renamed the Historic Memorials Society in Detroit and began its current mission of focusing on the preservation of civic memorials around the country and particularly the Detroit area.

Buchanan
(Berrien County)

Buchanan Preservation Society
Mailing Address: 16014 W. Clear Lake Rd. • Buchanan, MI 49107
Contact: Fred Rogers, Treasurer
Phone: (616) 695-5255
Physical Location: Pears Flour & Grist Mill, 121 S. Oak St. • Buchanan, MI 49107
Hours: Memorial Day-Labor Day: Sat 1-5 p.m.
Admission: Donations accepted.
Visitor Accessibility: On-site parking. Partially wheelchair accessible. Guided tours available.
Website: http://www.buchanan.mi.us/pointsofinterest.htm
About: The city-owned Pears Flour & Grist Mill, an 1857 mill and working

museum, was saved from demolition and was restored. It is maintained and operated by the Buchanan Preservation Society. The site features a waterwheel with associated line shafts and pulleys, an operable set of millstones, hand-powered antique machines, and local history displays.
Annual Events: Fruitbelt Woodcarvers, Vintage John Deere Tractors, Historic Manufacturing Techniques, Wool Yarn Spinner (in conjunction with Buchanan Fest).
Information may not be current.

Buckley
(Wexford County)

Northwest Michigan Engine & Thresher Club
Mailing Address: 7428 W. County Line • Buckley, MI 49620
Contact: Jim Luper
Phone: (231) 269-3053
Site/Location: **Buckley Old Engine Club**
Physical Location: N. 13 Road • Buckley, MI 49620
Admission: $25/individual weekend pass, $10/individual, children under 16 free.
Visitor Accessibility: Free on-site parking. Free shuttles. Free handicap shuttle and grounds transportation.
Website: www.buckleyoldengineshow.org
About: Come to see the past in motion with free steam train rides, hands-on demonstrations, and a historic sawmill. Old-time necessities and arts and crafts for sale. On-site prairie tractor plowing ensures fun for any age group.
Exhibits/Collections: Antique tractors, steam engines, gas and oil engines, cars, trucks and farming equipment.
Annual Events: Spring Swap Meet (May), Buckley Old Engine Show (Aug).

Burt
(Saginaw County)

Taymouth Township Historical Association
Mailing Address: P.O. Box 158 • Burt, MI 48417
Contact: Larry Preuter, President
E-Mail: ttha@dishmail.net
Phone: (989) 751-7651 • *Fax:* (989) 624-5466
Physical Location: History Room, Taymouth Township Library, 2361 E. Burt Rd. • Burt, MI 48417
Hours: Mon 10 a.m.-9 p.m.; Tue 9 a.m.-5 p.m.; Thu 10 a.m.-9 p.m.; Fri 9 a.m.-5 p.m.
Admission: Free.
Visitor Accessibility: On-site parking. Wheelchair accessible. Tours by request.
About: Collection of local historical resources at library. Additional resources at township-owned Burt Opera House (1891) and St. Paul's Church (1873).
Annual Events: Memorial Day service at St. Paul's Church Cemetery, Christmas program (Dec). Meeting: 3rd Thu of each month, 7 p.m. at library.
Information may not be current.

Byron Center
(Kent County)

Byron Center Historical Society
Mailing Address: P.O. Box 20 • Byron Center, MI 49315
Contact: Elaine Snyder, President
E-Mail: byronmuseum@sbcglobal.net
Phone: (616) 878-0888
Site/Location: **Byron Area Historical Museum**
Physical Location: Byron Area Historical Museum, 2506 Prescott St. SW • Byron Center, MI 49315
Hours: Tue 9 a.m.- 2 p.m. Also by appointment.
Admission: Free.
Visitor Accessibility: Free on-site parking. Wheelchair accessible. Tour guide available by appointment.
Website: http://www.commoncorners.com/kent/kent_byron_bchs.htm

About: The Byron Center Historical Society preserves and makes available the artifacts and photographs that bring Byron Township's history alive. Located in the historic 1876 Town Hall, a two-story white brick building in the center of Byron Township, the museum features multiple exhibits.
Exhibits/Collections: Genealogy room: mostly data on Byron Township families. Rural Inventory 1939 of the WPA; more than 1,000 photos; church, school, club and old home files. Township records archives. 4,000 artifacts.
Annual Events: Byron Days (Jul). Meetings 1st Mon monthly, 7 p.m. at museum.
Publications: Newsletter (Timekeeper).
Information may not be current.

Cadillac
(Wexford County)

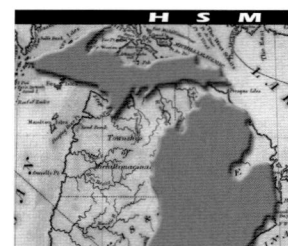
Wexford County Historical Society
Mailing Address: 127 Beech Street, P.O. Box 124 • Cadillac, MI 49601
Contact: Cliff Sjogren, Past President
E-Mail: info@wexfordcountyhistory.org
Phone: (231) 775-1717
Site/Location: **Wexford County Historical Society Museum**
Physical Location: 127 Beech St. • Cadillac, MI 49601
Hours: Call or see website.
Admission: $3/adult, $5/family, children under 16 free.
Visitor Accessibility: Street parking. Not wheelchair accessible. Free tour guides available.
Website: www.wexfordcountyhistory.org

About: The Wexford County Historical Society preserves and presents the history and culture of Wexford County and promotes public awareness of county history; sponsors artistic and cultural activities; and manages the former Carnegie Library as a public museum, library, and meeting place.
Exhibits/Collections: Exhibits include military, tools of trade, medical office, fire station artifacts, Native Americans, lumbering, farming, home appliances, one-room schoolhouse, and manufacturing. Exhibits of a turn-of-the-century home, general store exhibit, etc.
Annual Events: Art Walk (May), Season Opening (May), Art Fair (Jul), Gala (Sep), Cemetery Run (Sep), Train Event (Oct), Ghost Event (Oct), Evening for Educators (Nov), Christmas Event (Dec), New Years Eve Speakeasy (Dec).

Wexford Genealogy Organization
Mailing Address: 601 Chestnut Suite B • Cadillac, MI 49601
Contact: Judy Liptak, President
E-Mail: wegoin@gmail.com
Physical Location: Cadillac Senior Center, 601 Chestnut • Cadillac, MI 49601
Hours: Thu 12-3 p.m. Subject to change.
Visitor Accessibility: Public parking.

Michigan History Directory

Website: www.wexfordgenealogy.org
About: The Wexford Genealogy Organization indexes and copies official records, transcribes and photographs cemetery stones in Wexford County cemeteries, and collects scrapbooks and other unofficial records such as funeral cards and family trees. The organization also hosts seminars and classes pertaining to genealogy.
Exhibits/Collections: Collection focuses on Wexford County with some Missaukee and Osceola records. Resources include obituary collection, newspaper clippings, probate records, burial permits, cemetery records, plat books, family books, death records through 1929.
Annual Events: Spring and fall workshops. Meets 2nd Tue monthly (except Dec), 1 p.m. in resource room. Check website for location changes.

Caledonia
(Kent County)

Caledonia Historical Commission
Mailing Address: 8196 Broadmoor Ave. SE • Caledonia, MI 49316
Contact: Kris Apol, Chairperson
E-Mail: lindawally@charter.net
Phone: (616) 891-0070 • *Fax:* (616) 891-0430
Site/Location: **Barber School**
Hours: Barber School open by appointment.
Website: http://www.caledoniatownship.org/
About: The Caledonia Historical Commission is a township-appointed body, which seeks to preserve the heritage of Caledonia Township. It also maintains the 19th-century Barber School as a museum and repository.
Annual Events: Second-graders field day (Jun), antique appraisal (Jun), Scarecrow Workshop (Oct). Meetings 3rd Mon 7 p.m. at Township Hall (Dec-Mar) or Barber School (May-Aug).
*Information may not be current.

Caledonia Historical Society
Mailing Address: 6260 92nd St. SE • Caledonia, MI 49316
Contact: Kenneth Gackler, Archivist
E-Mail: gackler@iserv.net
Phone: (616) 260-0052
Site/Location: **Caledonia Historical Museum**
Physical Location: 8196 Broadmoor Ave SE • Caledonia, MI 49316
Hours: By appointment.
Admission: Free.
Visitor Accessibility: On-site parking. Wheelchair accessible. Tour guides available by appointment.
About: The Caledonia Historical Society collects the local history, records, and photos of the Caledonia area. Its archives are stored in the Caledonia History Room Archives, located in the Caledonia Township Branch Library (6260 92nd St. SE, Caledonia).
Exhibits/Collections: Local-area history, 1,500 photos, microfilm of early newspapers, early county histories, genealogy database of family names, etc.
Annual Events: Meetings 2nd Wed monthly, 6 p.m. at library.
*Information may not be current.

Calumet
(Houghton County)

Calumet Theatre
Mailing Address: P.O. Box 167 • Calumet, MI 49913
Contact: Laura Miller, Executive Director
E-Mail: laura@calumettheatre.com
Phone: (906) 337-2610 • *Fax:* (906) 337-3763
Physical Location: 340 Sixth St. • Calumet, MI 49913
Hours: Summer Mon-Fri 11 a.m.-5 p.m., winter Wed-Fri 12-5 p.m.
Admission: $4-6/tour. Performance prices vary.
Visitor Accessibility: Wheelchair accessible.
Website: www.calumettheatre.com
About: The restored Calumet Theatre opened as a community opera house in 1900. Today, it is a Heritage Site of the Keweenaw National Historical Park and continues to serve as an entertainment venue.
Exhibits/Collections: Records, articles, and photos related to theatre activities.
Annual Events: Anniversary gathering (Jun).
Publications: Quarterly newsletter.

Coppertown USA Mining Museum
Mailing Address: 1197 Calumet Ave. • Calumet, MI 49913
Contact: Richard Dana
Phone: (906) 337-4354
Fax: (906) 337-3806
Physical Location: 25815 Red Jacket Road • Calumet, MI 49913
Hours: Jun-Oct: Mon-Sat 11 a.m.-5 p.m.
Admission: $4/adult, $2/children (6/15), $3/Golden Age Pass.
Visitor Accessibility: Free parking. Wheelchair accessible. Self-guided.
Website: www.uppermichigan.com/coppertown

About: The Coppertown USA Mining Museum features 100 displays in the former Calumet and Hecla Pattern Shop. These displays introduce the story of the copper country and America's first real mining boom. A copper knife, for instance, dates back hundreds of years to the Copper Culture Indians. Other attractions include a 13-minute video about Keweenaw copper, simulated mine shaft, railroad memorabilia, shoe shop, and old school exhibits.
Exhibits/Collections: Mining history artifacts and local community historical artifacts.
Annual Events: Open House on Heritage Days (Aug).
*Information may not be current.

Houghton-Keweenaw Genealogical Society
Mailing Address: P.O. Box 323 • Calumet, MI 49913
Contact: Avis West, Presdient
E-Mail: avislouise@sbcglobal.net
Phone: (906) 369-4083
Website: http://www.hkcgs.org/
About: The Houghton-Keweenaw County Genealogical Society organized in 1999 to support ancestral research in the local area and to encourage and broaden the understanding and appreciation of genealogical research.
Exhibits/Collections: In Portage Lake District Library, 58 Huron St., Houghton, MI, Indexing Daily Mining Gazette.
Annual Events: Meetings 2nd Tue Jan-Jun and Sep-Nov, 7 p.m. at Portage District Library.
Publications: Newsletter (Tree Climber).

Keweenaw Kernewek
Mailing Address: Cornish Connection of the Copper Country, P.O. Box 263 • Calumet, MI 49913

Historical Society of Michigan

Contact: Jay Rowe
E-Mail: jdrjer@hotmail.com
Website: http://keweenawkernewek.org
About: The Keweenaw Kernewek seeks to preserve the history of the miners and others of Cornish ancestry who came to the Upper Peninsula.
Annual Events: Meetings 2nd Mon monthly, 6 p.m. at Miscowaubik Club, Calumet.
Publications: Biannual newsletter (The Keweenaw Kernewek).
Information may not be current.

Keweenaw National Historical Park
Mailing Address: 25970 Red Jacket Road • Calumet, MI 49913
Phone: (906) 337-3168
Fax: (906) 337-3169
Site/Location: **Calumet Visitor Center**
Physical Location: 98 Fifth St. • Calumet, MI 49913
Hours: Call for current hours.
Admission: Free.
Visitor Accessibility: Free on-site and street parking. Wheelchair accessible. Self-guided.
Website: www.nps.gov/kewe

About: Keweenaw National Historical Park preserves, protects, and interprets the natural and cultural resources relating to the copper mining industry. The Calumet Visitors Center is located at the entrance to Historic Downtown Calumet in the Union Building, a former lodge hall. Visitors are able to experience extensive interactive exhibits on what life was like for people in the mining community from its establishment through the boom times to the closure of the Calumet & Hecla Mining Company in 1968.
Annual Events: Fourth Thursday in History (Apr-Oct).
Publications: Brochure, annual park newspaper, the Keweenaw Guide, and an architectural booklet.

Norwegian Lutheran Church Historical Society
Mailing Address: 608 Elm St. • Calumet, MI 49913
Contact: Susan Rokicki, Trustee
Phone: (906) 337-3731
Site/Location: **Norwegian Lutheran Church**
Physical Location: 338 Seventh Street • Calumet, MI 49913
Hours: June-Oct: Daily 9 a.m.-5 p.m.
Admission: By donation.
Visitor Accessibility: Free street parking. Not wheelchair accessibile. Self-guided.
Website: www.nlc-calumet.org

About: The Norwegian Lutheran Church Historical Society was founded in 2000 to restore and maintain the historic Norwegian Lutheran Church building, which was originally constructed in 1898. The former church contains original alter, pews, organ, chandelier, and tin ceiling. Storyboards in the entry share the church's history, a list of its ministers, and photos of the people who were instrumental in the building and maintaining of the church and attached parsonage.
Exhibits/Collections: Norwegian Lutheran Church and local (Copper Country) historical records.

Annual Events: Open for guided tours during Calumet Heritage Days (Aug). Quarterly meetings (Call for date, time, and place).
Publications: The Norwegian Lutheran Church Historical Society Newsletter.

Upper Peninsula Fire Fighters Memorial Museum
Mailing Address: P.O. Box 503 • Calumet, MI 49913
Contact: Paul Bracco
Phone: (906) 337-4579
Physical Location: 327 Sixth St. • Calumet, MI 49913
Hours: Jun-Labor Day: Mon-Sat 1-4:30 p.m.
Admission: $2/adult, $5/family.
About: Completed in 1900, the Red Jacket Fire Station is now home to the Upper Peninsula Firefighters Memorial Museum. The museum preserves and features exhibits related to the area's firefighting history.
Exhibits/Collections: Fire fighting equipment, including horse-drawn fire wagon and sleigh, hand-pulled carts, fire trucks from 1919 to 1951, tools, uniforms, and personal gear. Photograph collection.
Information may not be current.

Cannonsburg
(Kent County)

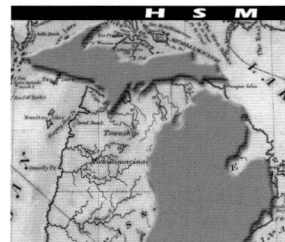

Cannon Township Historical Society
Mailing Address: P.O. Box 24 • Cannonsburg, MI 49317
Contact: Margaret Janose, Director
Phone: (616) 874-6865
Site/Location: **Cannon Township Historical Museum**
Physical Location: 8045 Cannonsburg Road • Cannonsburg, MI 49317
Hours: May-Sep Sun 2-4 p.m. Also by appointment.
Admission: Free.
Visitor Accessibility: Free nearby parking. Wheelchair accessible. Self-guided.
About: The Cannon Township Historical Society preserves township history in the former township hall.
Exhibits/Collections: Cannon township artifacts, including school and family photographs. Machinery, furniture, and household goods. Local genealogy collection.
Publications: Bimonthly newsletter.

Canton
(Wayne County)

Canton Historic District Commission
Mailing Address: 7120 Woonsocket • Canton, MI 48187
Contact: Katherir Martin
E-Mail: bkmartin@wowway.com
Information may not be current

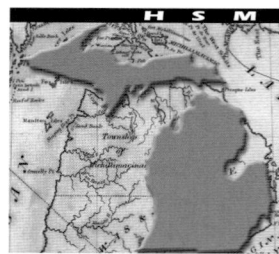

Canton Historical Society
Mailing Address: P.O. Box 87362 • Canton, MI 48187
Contact: Bill Tesen, President
E-Mail: cantonhist@comcast.net
Phone: (734) 495-0274
Site/Location: **Bartlett/Travis House at Preservation Park**

Michigan History Directory

Physical Location: 500 N. Ridge Road • Canton, MI 48187
Hours: Mid-May to Mid-Oct: Sun 9 a.m.-1 p.m. Also by appointment.
Admission: Free.
Visitor Accessibility: Free on-site parking. Partially wheelchair accessible. Call ahead for tour guide availability.
Website: www.cantonhistoricalsociety.org

***About:*** The Canton Historical Society collects, preserves, and makes available objects and records of the history of the township of Canton. The society's main museum, a one-room schoolhouse, is currently closed for restoration, to be reopened late 2014. The agricultural museum consists of old farm equipment, a 1920s kitchen, small hand tools, a 1935 F-20 tractor, fanning mills, corn shellers, plows, etc. The Bartlett/Travis House at Preservation Park is a Victorian-style house built in the 1860s and "Victorianized" about 1900.
Exhibits/Collections: Canton-related artifacts and documents. Military records of Canton soldiers. Archives are temporarily located at the Canton Human Service Building, located at 50430 School House Road. Archives available by scheduled appointment.
Annual Events: Beer, Brats, Bands at the Barn.
Publications: Bi-monthly newsletter, several books on local history.

Canton Township Historic District Commission
Mailing Address: 1150 Canton Center Rd., • Canton, MI 48187
Contact: Gregg King, Staff Liason
E-Mail: gking@canton-mi.org
Phone: (734) 394-5100
Fax: (734) 394-5319
Hours: Mon-Fri 8:30 a.m.-5 p.m.
Website: www.canton-mi.org
About: The Canton Township Historic District Commission preserves historically significant areas of the township which are designated by the board of trustees as historic districts.
Annual Events: Meetings 1st Wed monthly, 7 p.m. at 50440 Cherry Hill Rd. in Canton.

Capac
(St. Clair County)

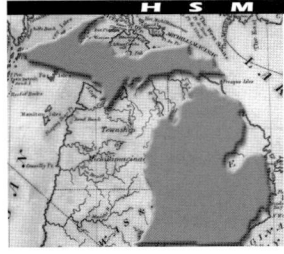### Capac Community Historical Society
Mailing Address: 401 E. Kempf Court • Capac, MI 48014
Contact: John Grzyb, President
E-Mail: capacmuseum@hotmail.com
Phone: (810) 395-2859
Site/Location: **Capac Community Historical Museum**

Physical Location: 401 E. Kempf Court • Capac, MI 48014
Hours: Mon-Fri 12-3 p.m., Sun 1-4 p.m. Appointments available.
Admission: Donations accepted.
Visitor Accessibility: Free on-site parking. Wheelchair accessible. Tour guide available.
Website: http://capachistoricalsocietymuseum.wordpress.com

***About:*** The Capac Community Historical Society preserves the history of the Capac community and Thumb area. The society maintains a museum in the restored Grand Trunk Western Depot, which features exhibits relating to Capac and the Thumb. On display is the Kempf Model City (a mechanical city, 40 feet long and four feet wide). Also on-site is a Grand Truck Western Caboose, which includes several railroad artifacts, and the Kempf Historical Museum, which features artifacts, postcards, and a historical research library.

Exhibits/Collections: Railroad and farm items. More than 200 histories of towns, schools, churches, townships, school classes, businesses, clubs, etc. Atlases, pictures and postcards.
Annual Events: St. Patty Dinner (Mar), Garage Sale (May), Quilt Show (Jul), Bicycle Rally (Aug), Fall Fundraising Dinner (Oct), Craft Show (Dec), Dan Bell Memorial Dinner (Dec).
Publications: "Capac Then and Now 1857-1957," "125 Years of the Capac Community, 1857-1982," "A Pictorial History of Capac, Michigan, 1840s-1970s," "A History of Memphis, Michigan."

Caro
(Tuscola County)

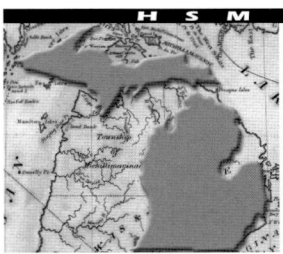### Watrousville-Caro Area Historical Society
Mailing Address: P.O. Box 15 • Caro, MI 48723
Contact: Esther Gorashko, Secretary
E-Mail: dave@watrousville.com
Phone: (989) 823-2360
Site/Location: **Watrousville Museum**

Physical Location: 4607 W. Caro Road (M-81) • Vassar, MI 48768
Hours: Jun-Sep: Thu 1-4 p.m. Also by appointment.
Admission: Free.
Visitor Accessibility: Free on-site parking. Not wheelchair accessible. Tour guide available.
Website: www.watrousville.com

***About:*** The Watrousville-Caro Area Historical Society preserves local history so that it may be passed on to future generations. The Watrousville Museum is located in the former Watrous General Store, which is now a registered Michigan Historic Site.
Annual Events: Veterans Memorial Ceremony (Jun), Founder's Day Dinner (Sep). Meetings 2nd Tue monthly.
Publications: Biannual newsletter (Old News).
Other Sites/Locations: **Leonard-McGlone House** • Location: 4592 W. Caro Rd. (M-81), Vassar, MI 48768 • The Leonard-McGlone House is currently under renovation and is not yet open to the public. It is one of the first homes built in the community.
Information may not be current.

Caseville
(Huron County)

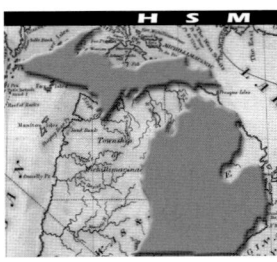### Historical Society of Caseville
Mailing Address: P.O. Box 1973 • Caseville, MI 48725
Contact: Harold Hoelzle, President
E-Mail: chscm@comcast.net
Phone: (989) 856-9090
Site/Location: **Maccabees Hall Museum**

Physical Location: 6733 Prospect St. • Caseville, MI 48725
Hours: Wed-Sat 12-4:30 p.m.
Admission: Free.
Visitor Accessibility: Free on-site parking. Wheelchair accessible. Tour guide available.
Website: www.thehchs.org/caseville

***About:*** The Historical Society of Caseville brings together those interested in learning about the history of the Caseville community. The society discovers, collects, preserves, and displays materials that illustrate the life, conditions, events, and activities of the past. The society maintains a museum in the 1890s Maccabees Hall.

Displays include fishing, farming, lumbering, school, and household exhibits.
Exhibits/Collections: Fishing, farming, lumbering, military, school, and household items, as well as newspapers and yearbooks.
Annual Events: Afternoon Tea (May), Ice Cream Social (May), Cheeseburger Museum and What Is It Contest (Aug) Countywide Free Museum Weekend (Sep). Meetings 3rd Thu monthly, 10 a.m. at museum.
Publications: "Caseville Centennial History, 1898-1998," "Celebrating 150 Years: Huron County History 1859-2009."

Caspian
(Iron County)

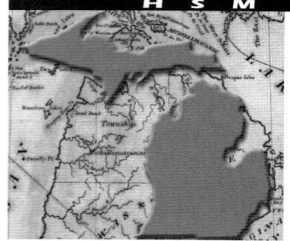

Iron County Historical Society & Museum
Mailing Address: P.O. Box 272 • Caspian, MI 49915
Contact: Bernadette Coates Passamani, Director
E-Mail: info@ironcountyhistoricalmuseum.org
Phone: (906) 265-5399
Site/Location: **Iron County Historical Museum**
Physical Location: 100 Brady Ave. • Caspian, MI 49915
Hours: Jun-Sept: Mon-Sat 10 a.m.-4 p.m., Sun 1-4 p.m.
Admission: $8/adult, $7/senior, $3/youth (5-18), children 5 and under free.
Visitor Accessibility: Free on-site parking. Partially wheelchair accessible. Self-guided.
Website: www.ironcountyhistoricalmuseum.org

About: The Iron County Historical Society preserves and shares Iron County's heritage. Founded in 1962, the Caspian Mine includes a head frame and an engine house that have been converted into a museum. The site includes a log cabin home, lumber camp, mine site, Victorian area with the Carrie Jacobs-Bond Home, cultural center, and two galleries: the LeBlanc Wildlife Art Gallery and the Giovanelli Home and Gallery. The museum's 100-plus displays include mining, lumbering, shops, and the Mining Memorial Room.
Exhibits/Collections: About 200 archival boxes, more than 1,200 photos, more than 8,000 maps, a contemporary file of photos and articles, and 20 file drawers by topics on local history.
Annual Events: Scandinavian/Log Cabin Day, Wine and Cheese Fundraiser, Children's Workshops, LeBlanc Dinner, Italian Heritage Day, and Christmas Tree Galleria. Meetings 4th Mon monthly.
Publications: "Barns, Farms, and Yarns," "Black Rock and Roses," "Caspian: A Caring City 1918-1993," "Frames for the Future," "Forty Years of Sports 1928-1968," "History of Iron County (1870-1954)," "Iron County Historical Sites and Landmarks," "Jewel of Iron County," "Men, Mines, and Memories," "Pine to Popple—People and Places," "Rural School Recollections."

Cass City
(Tuscola County)

Cass City Area Historical and Genealogy Society
Mailing Address: c/o Rawson Memorial Library, 6495 Pine St. • Cass City, MI 48726
Contact: Katie Jackson, President
E-Mail: jacksonk@speednetllc.com
Phone: (989) 872-2856
Hours: Mon-Sat 9 a.m.-5 p.m.
Website: www.rawson.lib.mi.us
About: The Cass City Area Historical and Genealogy Society brings together those interested in local history, promotes knowledge and appreciation of history in the Cass City area, and procures articles worthy of preservation.
Exhibits/Collections: Cass City newspapers from 1881 to present. Oral histories available at Rawson Library. Reproductions of photos of Cass City High School graduates, late 1800s to present. Elkland Township cemetery records.
Annual Events: Genealogy Group meets at Rawson Memorial Library 3rd Thu alternating monthly starting Feb. Historical Society meets 3rd Mon alternating monthly at Rawson Memorial library starting Jan.
Publications: Bi-monthly newsletter. "The Way It Was," "The History of the Cass City Area and Elkland Township 1854-1962." Videos about the old Cass City High School 1927-1999.
Information may not be current.

Sanilac Petroglyphs Historic Site and State Park.
Please see entry under Lansing: Michigan Historical Center.

Cassopolis
(Cass County)

Cass County Historical Commission
Mailing Address: 24785 Cass St. • Cassopolis, MI 49031
Contact: Judith Simpson, Secretary
E-Mail: wuepperj@gmail.com
Phone: (269) 445-4456
Physical Location: 120 N. Broadway, Suite 209 • Cassopolis, MI 49031
Hours: 8 a.m.-5 p.m.
Admission: Free.
Visitor Accessibility: Private parking. Wheelchair accessible.
Website: http://www.casscountymi.org/HistoricalCommission.aspx
About: Created in 1973, the Cass County Historical Commission oversees the Red Brick Schoolhouse Museum and historic Newton House.
Annual Events: Meetings 2nd Thu monthly at Cass County District Library.
Publications: Historic map of Cass County and a booklet of six driving tours. Reprints of histories and atlases.
Other Sites/Locations: **Red Brick Schoolhouse Museum** • Location: 63600 Brick Church Street, Cassopolis, MI 49031 • Hours: By appointment • Visitor Accessibility: On-site parking. • Step back in time to experience education in a one-room, rural school with old books, furniture, and maps.

Newton House • Location: 20689 Marcellus Highway, Decatur, MI 49045 • Hours: May-Oct: 1st Sun monthly 1-4:30 p.m. Also by appointment. • This furnished, restored, mid-19th-century Quaker home is owned by MSU and maintained by the Cass County Historical Commission.

Information may not be current.

Cass County Pioneer Log Cabin Museum
Mailing Address: P.O. Box 72 • Cassopolis, MI 49031
Contact: Marcia Gaskin
E-Mail: mpioneer1@aol.com
Phone: (269) 445-8511
Physical Location: 310 South Broadway • Cassopolis, MI 49031
Hours: Memorial Day-Labor Day Fri-Sun 12-4:30 p.m.
Admission: Donations accepted.
Visitor Accessibility: Free on-site parking. Partially wheelchair accessible; first floor only. Tour guide available during scheduled hours; call (269) 445-8511 for additional appointment times.
Website: www.facebook.com/pioneerlogcabinmuseum
About: The Pioneer Log Cabin Museum was built in 1923 with logs

Michigan History Directory

donated by area farmers. Each log is numbered and identified by species and donor. The museum features many items from the early pioneer days.
Exhibits/Collections: Lewis Cass's rocking chair, quilts, old collection of stuffed birds, pioneer tools, cooking utensils, and clothing.
Annual Events: Log Cabin Days (Jun), Christmas Open House (Dec).

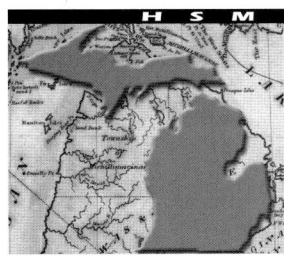

Edward Lowe Foundation
Mailing Address: 58220 Decatur Road • Cassopolis, MI 49031
Contact: Heidi Connor, Collections Manager
E-Mail: heidi@lowe.org
Phone: (269) 445-4200
Fax: (269) 445-4268
Site/Location: **Edward Lowe Information and Legacy Center**
Hours: Mon-Fri 8 a.m.-5 p.m.
Admission: Free.
Visitor Accessibility: Free on-site parking. Wheelchair accessible. Self-guided. Tours held Wed (Apr-Oct) at 2 p.m.; call for reservations.
Website: www.edwardlowe.org

About: The Edward Lowe Foundation was founded by Edward Lowe, who invented kitty litter in 1947. The foundation conducts research, education, and recognition programs for entrepreneurs. The information center features an exhibit of Lowe's business ventures and the foundation and includes videos, print materials, a live web feed, photos, and artifacts dating back to the 1940s.
Exhibits/Collections: Historical Collections Department maintains archival collection of materials about Edward and Darlene Lowe and their foundation.

Cedar Springs
(Kent County)

Cedar Springs Historical Society
Mailing Address: P.O. Box 296 • Cedar Springs, MI 49319
Contact: Sharon Jett, Director
E-Mail: csmuseum@wingsisp.com
Phone: (616) 696-3335
Site/Location: **Cedar Springs Museum**
Physical Location: 60 Cedar St. • Cedar Springs, MI 49319
Hours: Wed 10 a.m.-5 p.m. Also by appointment.
Admission: Free.
Visitor Accessibility: Wheelchair accessible. Self-guided.
Website: www.cedarspringsmuseum.org
About: The Cedar Springs Museum features an old general store, Native-American history, lumbering, farming, and railroad displays. The Payne School was moved to Morley Park in 1971 and has since been restored as a one-room school. There is also a stump-puller that was used to remove stumps in the area so the land could be farmed.
Exhibits/Collections: Artifacts of local interest. Genealogical library includes census data, family histories, newspapers, yearbooks, military records, and local history publications.
Annual Events: Car Show (Jul), Cemetery Walk (May), Antique Tractor Show (Oct). Meetings 3rd Wed monthly, 3:30 p.m. at museum.
Publications: Bimonthly newsletter (Golden Times).
*Information may not be current.

Cedarville
(Mackinac County)

Les Cheneaux Historical Association
Mailing Address: P.O. Box 301 • Cedarville, MI 49719
Contact: Mary Hill, Curator
E-Mail: lcha@lchistorical.org
Phone: (906) 484-2821
Site/Location: **Les Cheneaux Historical Museum**
Physical Location: 105 S. Meridian Rd. • Cedarville, MI 49719
Hours: Mon-Sat 10 a.m.-5 p.m.
Admission: Donations accepted.
Visitor Accessibility: Free on-site and street parking. Wheelchair accessible. Tour guide available.
Website: http://www.lchistorical.org/index.html

About: The Historical Museum is in the middle of Cedarville and withing walking distance of the harbor. There is a new and bright addition connected to a beautiful old and refurbished log cabin. We aspire to tell the unique story of the Les Cheneaux area through museum tours, artist of the week series, a speaker's series, and evenings of music on the grounds.
Exhibits/Collections: Local history, lumber camp model, wooden boat models, full-size boats, videos of social and geological history. Copies of turn-of-the-century photos. Replica of Mackinaw Boat. Nautical artifacts. Research files from 1984 centennial publication.
Annual Events: Antique Wooden Boat Show and Festival of Arts (Aug), Music at the Maritime, Artist Series, Speaker's Series.
Other Sites/Locations: **Les Cheneaux Maritime Museum** • Location: 602 E. M-134, Cedarville, MI 49719 • Hours: Memorial Day Weekend-Sep: Mon-Sat 10 a.m.-5 p.m. • Admission: Donations accepted • Visitor Accessibility: Free parking. Partially wheelchair accessible. Self-guided. • Les Cheneaux Maritime Museum is located in the O.M. Reif Boathouse (circa 1920s). Displays include vintage boats, marine artifacts, antique outboard motors, and historic photos. The association also provides boat-building workshops.

Central Lake
(Antrim County)

Central Lake Area Historical Society
Mailing Address: P.O. Box 404 • Central Lake, MI 49622
Contact: Mary Lou DeTar, President
Site/Location: **Knowels Historical Museum**
Physical Location: 2238 S. Main, Highway M-88 • Central Lake, MI 49032
Hours: Wed-Fri 1-4 p.m. Also by appointment.
Admission: Free.
Visitor Accessibility: Street parking. Not wheelchair accessible.
About: The Central Lake Area Historical Society documents and preserves area history for future generations by collecting and presenting local historic items. The society maintains the Knowels Historical Museum in a restored home that is furnished with local period furniture.
Exhibits/Collections: Donated furnishings for 19th-century renovated frame, some items going back for generations. 100-year collection of local newspaper, "The Central Lake Torch." Many histories, tapes, pictures, books, genealogy research materials.
Annual Events: Meetings 4th Tue 7 p.m.
*Information may not be current.

※ Historical Society of Michigan

Centreville
(St. Joseph County)

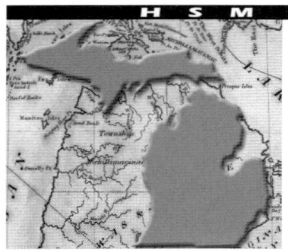

St. Joseph County Historical Society
Mailing Address: P.O. Box 492 • Centreville, MI 49032
Contact: Martha Starmann, President
E-Mail: mstarmann@yahoo.com
Phone: (269) 483-7122
Site/Location: **Centreville Museum & History Library**
Physical Location: 113 E. Main St. • Centreville, MI 49032
Hours: By appointment.
Admission: Donations accepted.
Visitor Accessibility: Free on-site and street parking. Wheelchair accessible. Tour guide available by appointment.
Website: http://hstarmann.wix.com/sjchs

About: The St. Joseph County Historical Society instills an interest in history through its historic sites, publication of history books and maps, and monthly programs. The Centreville Museum & History Library is located in the former Klesner Hotel, which was built about 1860 and is now listed on the State Register of Historic Sites. The building is currently being restored by the society and serves as the organization's main headquarters and library.
Exhibits/Collections: Handmade pioneer clothes, toys, tools, and war items. The history library at the Klesner Hotel has many county deeds, maps, postcards, books, ledgers, photographs, and a one-room school exhibit with photographs and records listed by townships.
Annual Events: Covered Bridge Days (Jun), White Pigeon Days (Jul). Meetings 3rd Sun Feb-Nov; lunch is at 1 p.m. and program is at 2 p.m.
Publications: "St. Joseph Co. History 1827-1877," "St. Joseph Co. 1858 Platt Map," "White Pigeon History," White Pigeon and Mottville Township Plat albums.
Other Sites/Locations: **U.S. Land Office Museum** • Location: 113 W. Chicago Road, US 12 Historic Trail, White Pigeon, MI 49099 • Hours: By apppointment • Admission: Donations accepted • Visitor Accessibility: Free on-site and street parking. • The White Pigeon U.S. Land Office is an 1830s structure restored by the St. Joseph County Historical Society in 1986. It is on the State and National Register of Historic Sites. Eight hand-hewn posts support log rafters, and log joints support the original floor of the building. The land office houses most of the society's collection, which includes 150-year-old primitive tools, toys, instruments, clothing, stuffed birds, and American Indian items.
Wahbememe Memorial Park • Location: Corner of U.S. 12 and U.S. 131, White Pigeon, MI 49099 • Hours: Dusk to dawn • Admission: Free • Visitor Accessibility: Free on-site parking. Wheelchair accessible. Self-guided • This State and National Registered Site is the mound grave of Potawatomi Chief Wahbememe, a signer of the 1795 Treaty of Greenville. According to legend, Wahbememe ran from Detroit to White Pigeon after he heard of a plot to attack the settlement, then collapsed from exhaustion and died. In 1909, a White Pigeon women's group placed a large stone boulder monument at the site. In 2012, the site also became home to a Fallen Solider Memorial.

Ceresco
(Calhoun County)

Union City Genealogical Society
Mailing Address: 11052 B. Dr. N • Ceresco, MI 49033
Contact: Brad Waite, Treasurer
Phone: (269) 979-0207
Physical Location: 195 N. Broadway • Union City, MI 49094
Hours: Tue-Wed 9:30 a.m.-5 p.m., Fri 9:30 a.m.-4:30 p.m., Sat 9 a.m.-12 p.m.
Admission: Free to the public.
About: The Union City Genealogical Society was established 1976.
Exhibits/Collections: Union City-area genealogical information, cemetery books, family histories, and vital statistics.

Champion
(Marquette County)

Champion-Beacon-Humboldt Historical Society
Mailing Address: P.O. Box 126 • Champion, MI 49814
Contact: Dave Mikkola
Phone: (906) 288-3728
Website: www.championmichigan.org
About: Organized in 2006, the Champion-Beacon-Humboldt Historical Society gathers materials for a pictorial history of Champion's first century.
Exhibits/Collections: Area photos, historical documents, mining records, and genealogical information.
Information may not be current.

Charlevoix
(Charlevoix County)

Castle Farms
Mailing Address: 5052 M-66 • Charlevoix, MI 49720
Contact: Anora O'Connor, General Manager
E-Mail: info@castlefarms.com
Phone: (231) 237-0884
Fax: (231) 237-0994

Hours: May 1-Oct 31: Daily 9:30 a.m.-4 p.m. Hours subject to change, call or see website.
Admission: $10/adult, $9/senior, Children (2-12) $6/children (2-12).
Visitor Accessibility: Free on-site parking. Wheelchair accessible. Self-guided.
Website: www.castlefarms.com

About: Built in 1918, Castle Farms was originally designed as a working model dairy farm to showcase farm equipment available in the Sears catalog. Visitors are able to tour the magnificent stone buildings, stroll through the gardens, and view the many collections on display, including castles, antique toys and royal family memorabilia from around the world. The Castle's Model Garden Railroad, with more than 65 G-scale trains and 2,000 feet of track, is one of the largest in Michigan.
Exhibits/Collections: Display of WWI memorabilia, items available in the 1918 Sears catalog, royal family memorabilia, toys, antique cake toppers, and castle collections.
Annual Events: Fiber Arts and Craft Show (Jul), Harvest Festival.

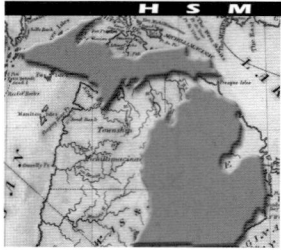

Charlevoix Historical Society
Mailing Address: P.O. Box 525 • Charlevoix, MI 49720
Contact: David L. Miles, Museum Co-Director
E-Mail: info@chxhistory.com
Phone: (231) 547-0373
Fax: (231) 547-4033
Site/Location: **Harsha House Museum**
Physical Location: 103 State St. • Charlevoix, MI 49720
Hours: Call for current hours.
Admission: $1/individual suggested donation.

Michigan History Directory

Visitor Accessibility: Free street and lot parking. Wheelchair accessible. Tour guide available.
Website: www.chxhistory.com

About: The Charlevoix Historical Society is dedicated to the acquisition, preservation, and protection of the Charlevoix-area history. The Harsha House Museum includes three restored 1891 Victorian parlors with vintage furnishings and original works of art by Charlevoix artists. It has kitchen and household objects on display. Other attractions include a large one-horse open sleight, rotating exhibits, a working player piano, pedal pump reed organ, a working wind-up Victrola, and a 3 1/2 order Fresnel Lens from the Gray's Reef lighthouse.
Exhibits/Collections: Artifacts and documents pertaining to the history of Charlevoix. Approximately 20,000 photo images. Oral history tapes, family history binders, city tax records 1900-1980, original 1901 Charlevoix County plat books.
Annual Events: Venetian Festival Weekend Fireworks Potluck (Jul), Ice Cream Social and Volunteer Recognition Night (Sep), Annual Harvest Potluck (Oct), All-You-Can-Eat Fundraising Spaghetti Dinner (Nov), Annual Christmas Dinner (Dec)
Publications: "Historic Charlevoix," "A Guide to Walking and Driving Tours of the Charlevoix Area's Most Historic Sites," "Bob Miles Charlevoix," "Charlevoix Pier Lights," "Charlevoix Hotels," "Charlevoix Railroads," "Charlevoix Bridges."
Other Sites/Locations: **The Depot** • Location: 307 Chicago Ave., Charlevoix, MI 49720 • Hours: Not open on a regular basis • Admission: Donations accepted • Visitor Accessibility: Free on-site and street parking. Wheelchair accessible. Self-guided • Built by the Chicago & West Michigan Railway in 1892, the Depot is used for meetings, events, and occasional exhibits. The Depot is listed on the National Historic register and the interior may be viewed upon request. On the exterior, the Charlevoix Area Garden Club has developed an award-winning Heritage Garden using historic cuttings and design methods. This exterior area is open to the public at all times.
Charlevoix South Pier Lighthouse • Location: Lake Michigan Municipal Beach, Charlevoix, MI 49720 • Hours: Interior not open to the public. Exterior may be visited at anytime • Admission: Free • The Charlevoix Historical Society is responsible for the preservation, restoration, and maintenance of the Charlevoix South Pier Lighthouse (the Federal government owns the pier, the city of Charlevoix owns the light, and the Coast Guard maintains the light as an aid to navigation). The lower portion was built in 1948. The black lens housing at top is from the original Charlevoix light that was built in 1885.

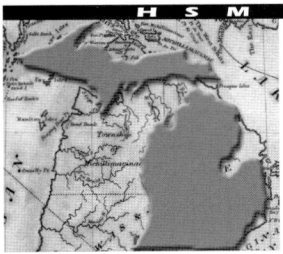
HSM MEMBER
Norwood Area Historical Society
Mailing Address: P.O. Box 595 • Charlevoix, MI 49720
Contact: Yasmin Richmond, President
E-Mail: secretary@norwoodhistory.org
Phone: (231) 547-6220
Physical Location: Norwood Village, 742 Fourth St. • Charlevoix, MI 49720
Website: www.norwoodhistory.org

About: The Norwood Area Historical Society is dedicated to the preservation and dissemination of historical knowledge from the Norwood area of Charlevoix and Antrim counties.
Exhibits/Collections: Collections include documents and photos relating to 19th-century settlement and lumbering, local schools, and famous personages. Also includes some oral history transcripts and tapes.
Annual Events: Meetings 3rd Wed spring-fall.
Publications: "Norwood: A Legacy of North Woods Living."

Charlotte
(Eaton County)

HSM MEMBER
Courthouse Square Association
Mailing Address: P.O. Box 411 • Charlotte, MI 48813
Contact: Julie Kimmer
E-Mail: csamuseum@yahoo.com
Phone: (517) 543-6999
Site/Location: **Courthouse Square Association Museum**
Physical Location: 100 W. Lawrence Ave. • Charlotte, MI 48813
Hours: Mon-Thu 9 a.m.-4 p.m.
Admission: $1/individual.
Visitor Accessibility: Free on-site parking. Partially wheelchair accessible; second and third floors require assistance. Tour guide available; for large groups, call ahead at (517) 543-6999. School tours from within Eaton County are free.
Website: www.csamuseum.net

About: The Courthouse Square Association promotes the preservation and education of history in Eaton County. It maintains three different buildings, including the restored 1885 Courthouse, which features 10 exhibit rooms ranging from the restored courtroom to military exhibits.
Annual Events: Celebrate Charlotte, Frontier Days, Christmas Cuisine. Meetings 1st Tue monthly, 5:30 p.m. at 1885 Courthouse.
Publications: "Charlotte the Beautiful 1907," "Historic Postcards of Eaton County," "Old Charlotte Village," "The Fight to Save the Courthouse," "Elly Peterson 'Mother of the Moderates,'" "The Ledger."
Other Sites/Locations: **1845 Courthouse** • Location: 1305 S. Cochran Ave., Charlotte, MI 48813 • Hours: By appointment • Admission: Varies • Visitor Accessibility: Free on-site parking. Wheelchair accessible. Self-guided. • The 1845 Courthouse is restored to its original time period.
1873 Sheriff's Residence • Location: 100 W. Lawrence, Charlotte, MI 48813 • Hours: Mon-Thu 8:30 a.m.-3:30 p.m. • Admission: Free • Visitor Accessibility: Free on-site parking. Wheelchair accessible. Self-guided. • Exterior restored only; currently home to the Charlotte Chamber of Commerce.

Eaton County Genealogical Society
Mailing Address: P.O. Box 337 • Charlotte, MI 48813
Contact: Sheila Mott, Secretary
E-Mail: ecgsoc@juno.com
Phone: (517) 543-8792
Physical Location: c/o 1885 Historical Courthouse, 100 W. Lawrence • Charlotte, MI 48813
Hours: Mon-Thu 10 a.m.-2 p.m.
Admission: Free.
Visitor Accessibility: Steet and lot parking. Partially wheelchair accessible; first floor only. Self-guided.
Website: www.miegs.org
About: Genealogy library is on ground floor of historic 1885 Courthouse.
Exhibits/Collections: Telephone books, city and rural directories, newspapers, census records, military records, county tax and property records, local and family histories.
Annual Events: Meetings 3rd Wed Feb-Oct and 2nd Wed Nov, 7 p.m. at 1885 Courthouse.
Publications: Newsletter (Eaton County Quest).

*Information may not be current.

❀ Historical Society of Michigan

Eaton County Historical Commission
Mailing Address: P.O. Box 411 • Charlotte, MI 48813
Contact: Julie Kimmer
E-Mail: csamuseum@yahoo.com
Phone: (517) 543-6999
Physical Location: 100 W. Lawrence Ave. • Charlotte, MI 48813
Hours: Call or visit website for current hours.
Website: www.eatoncountyhistory.org
About: The Eaton County Historical Commission fosters public awareness of the county's historical heritage. The commission also encourages organizations and individuals to restore and preserve historic sites, structures, and artifacts.
Annual Events: Meetings 1st Tue alternating months, see website for info.

Chase
(Lake County)

Chase Library Historical Society
Mailing Address: 8400 E. North St., P.O. Box 24 • Chase, MI 49623
Contact: Roxanne Ware, Director
E-Mail: chaselibrary@yahoo.com
Phone: (231) 832-9511 • *Fax:* (231) 832-9511
Site/Location: **Chase Township Public Library**
Physical Location: 8400 E. North St. • Chase, MI 49623
Hours: Mon, Wed-Thu 10 a.m.-6 p.m.; Tue 9 a.m.-5 p.m. Also open Sat 9 a.m.-12 p.m. during the school year.
Admission: Free.
Visitor Accessibility: Wheelhair accessible.
About: The Chase Library Historical Society records and researches local history and families, with a focus on Chase, Pinora, Cherry Valley, and Yates Townships.
Annual Events: Meetings 3rd Tue monthly at 2 p.m.
*Information may not be current.

Chassell
(Houghton County)

Chassell Historical Organization
Mailing Address: P.O. Box 331 • Chassell, MI 49916
Contact: Corinne Hauring, President
Phone: (906) 523-1155
Site/Location: **Chassell Heritage Center**
Physical Location: 42373 Hancock Street • Chassell, MI 49916
Hours: Jul-Aug: Tue 1-4 p.m., Thu 4-9 p.m., Sat 1-4 p.m.
Admission: Donations accepted.
Visitor Accessibility: Free on-site parking. Not wheelchair accessible. Volunteer tour guides available during open hours or by special request.
Website: http://www.einerlei.com/community/CHO.html

About: The Chassell Historical Organization maintains the township museum in a former elementary school. Exhibits include local strawberry farming, the Old School, vintage clothing, a township timeline, three consecutive boys' basketball state championships (1956-58), and Chassell Lions Club. Home of the Friends of Fashion Vintage Clothing Collection. Heritage Site of Keweenaw National Historical Park. Exhibits of Finnish and French-Canadian immigrants and settlers.
Exhibits/Collections: Photograph collection and written local histories. Chassell Township records archived at Michigan Technological University.

Annual Events: Special Summer Evening Programs, Annual Meeting (Jul), Strawberry Festival Open House (Jul), Old Fashioned Christmas Open House (Dec). Board meetings 3rd Mon of Jan, Mar, May, Jul, Sep, and Nov.
Publications: Biannual newsletter.

Cheboygan
(Cheboygan County)

Aloha Historical Society
Mailing Address: PO Box 5071, 4774 1st St. • Cheboygan, MI 49721
Contact: Lois Ballard
Phone: (231) 625-2511
About: Located at Aloha Township Hall.
*Information may not be current.

Cheboygan Area Public Library
Mailing Address: 100 S. Bailey St. • Cheboygan, MI 49721
Contact: Mark Bronson, Director
E-Mail: contactus@cheboyganlibrary.org
Phone: (231) 627-2381
Hours: Mon-Thu 10 a.m.-8 p.m.; Fri 10 a.m.-5 p.m.; Sat 10 a.m.-3 p.m.
Admission: Free.
Visitor Accessibility: Free on-site parking. Wheelchair accessible. Self-guided.
Website: http://www.cheboyganlibrary.org
About: A public district library with a local genealogy room.

Cheboygan County Genealogical Society
Mailing Address: P.O. Box 51 • Cheboygan, MI 49721
Contact: Marie Gouine, President
E-Mail: momgouine@gmail.com
Phone: (231) 627-2691
Website: www.rootsweb.com/~miccgs/ccgsmain.html
About: The Cheboygan County Genealogical Society collects and preserves genealogical records for generations to come.
Exhibits/Collections: Books highlighting local genealogy stored at Cheboygan Area Public Library.
Annual Events: Regular meetings 2nd Wed monthly at Cheboygan Area Public Library.
Publications: Book featuring all county cemeteries.

Cheboygan Historic Resources Commission
Mailing Address: c/o City Hall, P.O. Box 39 • Cheboygan, MI 49721
Contact: Dale A Stuart
E-Mail: dstuart@cheboygan.org
Phone: (231) 627-9931 • *Fax:* (231) 627-6351
Physical Location: City Hall, 403 N. Huron • Cheboygan, MI 49721
Hours: Mon-Fri 8 a.m.-4 p.m.
Visitor Accessibility: Free on-site parking. Wheelchair accessible.
Website: www.cheboygan.org
About: Some information on city of Cheboygan historic resource designations available at the city hall offices. The Cheboygan Historic Resources Commission may be a resource to the DDA regarding the administration of the Building Facade Rehabilitation Program.

Cheboygan River Front Range Light.
Please see entry under Mackinaw City: Great Lakes Lighthouse Keepers Association.

Michigan History Directory

History Center of Cheboygan County
Mailing Address: P.O. Box 5005 • Cheboygan, MI 49721
Contact: Lewis D. Crusoe, President
E-Mail: museum@cheboyganhistorycenter.org
Phone: (231) 627-9597
Fax: (231) 268-3555
Site/Location: **Cheboygan County Historical Museum**
Physical Location: 427 Court Street • Cheboygan, MI 49721
Hours: Jun-Oct: Tue-Sat 1-4 p.m.
Admission: $5/adult.
Visitor Accessibility: Free on-site parking. Partially wheelchair accessible; main exhibit hall is barrier free, but other buildings require stairway access. Tour guide available.
Website: www.cheboyganhistorycenter.org
About: The History Center engages, educates, and entertains residents and visitors in the experience of the area's rich cultural common wealth by collecting, preserving, and presenting the rich history of Cheboygan County. Exhibits portray the various historic eras of the county through the use of artifacts and period settings. Visitors will discover Cheboygan County's place in the history of Northern Michigan and the larger Straits of Mackinac region.
Exhibits/Collections: Exhibits include lumbering, fishing, military, and domestic themes. The 1880s sheriff's residence and newly restored 1912 jail addition portray daily life at the turn of the 19th century.
Annual Events: Winter Lecture Series (Feb-Mar), School Tours (May), Children's Museum Day Camp (Jun), Antique Appraisal Clinic (Jul), Genealogy classes (fall).
Publications: Newsletter (The Chronicles). "When Main Street was a Path Among the Stumps."

Michigan Museums Association
Mailing Address: P.O. Box 5246 • Cheboygan, MI 49721
Contact: Lisa Craig Brisson, Executive Director
E-Mail: lcbrisson@michiganmuseums.org
Phone: (313) 334-7643 • *Fax:* (313) 908-5408
Website: http://michiganmuseums.org
About: With an emphasis on face-to-face collaboration, the Michigan Museums Association (MMA) shares expertise and resources to promote standards and practices that make the Michigan museum community thrive. MMA has been supporting the work of Michigan museums for nearly 60 years. Every type of museum is represented and welcomed, including art, history, science, military, maritime, and youth, as well as aquariums, zoos, botanical gardens, arboretums, historic sites, and science and technology centers.
Annual Events: Workshops, Networking Events, Conference.

Chelsea
(Washtenaw County)

Chelsea Area Historic District Commission
Mailing Address: Village of Chelsea, 305 S. Main St. • Chelsea, MI 48118
Contact: John Frank
E-Mail: jackiefrank@msn.com
Phone: (734) 475-7396 • *Fax:* (734) 475-8722
*Information may not be current.

Chelsea Area Historical Society
Mailing Address: P.O. Box 477 • Chelsea, MI 48118
Contact: Janet Ogle-Mater, President
E-Mail: info@chelseahistory.org
Phone: (734) 476-2010
Website: www.chelseahistory.org
About: The Chelsea Area Historical Society gathers and preserves Chelsea-area history for future generations. The society collects, manages, displays, and maintains area artifacts, archival information, photographs, genealogy records, and oral histories of local citizens.
Exhibits/Collections: Artifacts, memorabilia, photos, and archival collections from the history of Chelsea.
Annual Events: Public programs 2nd Mon monthly, 7 p.m. at the Chelsea Railroad Depot.

Chesaning
(Saginaw County)

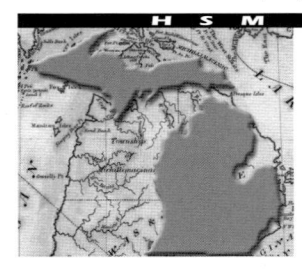

Chesaning Area Historical Society
Mailing Address: P.O. Box 52 • Chesaning, MI 48616
Contact: Greta Temple, President
E-Mail: cahs@centurytel.net
Phone: (989) 845-3155
Site/Location: **Chesaning Historical Museum**
Physical Location: 602 W. Broad St. • Chesaning, MI 48047
Hours: Mon-Wed 10 a.m.-noon. May-Dec: 1st Sat monthly 1-4 p.m. Also by appointment. The museum is temporarily closed with an expected re-opening date in May 2015. Call for details.
Admission: Free.
Visitor Accessibility: Street parking. Wheelchair accessible. Tour guide available.
Website: www.cahs.chesaning.com
About: The Chesaning Area Historical Society preserves the history of the Chesaning area. Displays and permanent exhibits at the Chesaning Historical Museum focus on the area's history from Native-American habitations to present-day local businesses, industries, schools, etc.
Exhibits/Collections: Artifacts of local signficance, clipping files, etc.
Annual Events: Christmas Candlelight Walk, Showboat Music Festival. Meetings 2nd Mon monthly (Apr-Dec) at 6:30 p.m. Board meets 4th Wed monthly at 9 a.m. (time subject to change). All meetings are open to the public.
Publications: Monthly newsletter.

River Rapids Public Library
Mailing Address: Local History/Genealogy Collection, 227 E. Broad St. • Chesaning, MI 48616
Contact: Erin Schmandt, Library Director
E-Mail: d.schell@vlc.lib.mi.us
Phone: (989) 845-3211 • *Fax:* (989) 845-2166
Hours: Mon 10 a.m.-6 p.m., Tue 10 a.m.-8 p.m., Thu 10 a.m.-8 p.m., Sat 12-4 p.m.
Visitor Accessibility: Public parking lot. Wheelchair accessible.
Website: www.chesaninglibrary.org
About: Public library with a local history/genealogy collection.
Exhibits/Collections: Local family history information sheets, a local

Chesterfield
(Macomb County)

Anchor Bay Genealogy Society
Mailing Address: c/o Chesterfield Library, 50560 Patricia Ave. • Chesterfield, MI 48051
Contact: Sue Archambault
Phone: (586) 598-4900
Annual Events: Meets at the Chesterfield Township Public Library.
Information may not be current.

Chesterfield Historical Society
Mailing Address: 47275 Sugarbush Road • Chesterfield, MI 48047
Contact: Eileen Rivard, President
E-Mail: royfrivard@yahoo.com
Phone: (586) 749-3713
Site/Location: Chesterfield Historical Village
Hours: Open for regularly scheduled events and by appointment.
Admission: General admission: Free. Special events: Suggested donations: Adult $1, Family $2.
Visitor Accessibility: Free on-site and street parking. Wheelchair accessible.
Website: www.chesterfieldhistoricalsociety.org
About: The Chesterfield Historical Society collects, safeguards, stores, and displays the history of Chesterfield. The Chesterfield Historical Village includes four buildings: a one-room schoolhouse with outhouse, a log cabin with a springhouse and spiral outhouse, a cobbler shop, and a working blacksmith shop.
Exhibits/Collections: Maintains the Trinity Collection (dedicated to the history of Chesterfield Township), which is stored in the Chesterfield Township Public Library.
Annual Events: Living History Encampment (Jun), Operation Cobra Re-enactment (Jul), Civil War Re-enactment (Aug), Heritage Days (Sep), Fundraising Dinners (May and Oct). Meetings 1st Tue Apr-Dec, 7 p.m. at Chesterfield Senior Center.
Publications: "Chesterfield Township, Michigan."
Information may not be current.

Clare
(Clare County)

Clare County Historical Society
Mailing Address: 3062 E. Colonville • Clare, MI 48617
Contact: Marty Johnson, Communications Director
E-Mail: museum@clarecountyhistory.org
Phone: (734) 755-2638
Site/Location: Clare County Museum Complex
Physical Location: 7050 S. Eberhart Ave. • Clare, MI 48617
Hours: May to mid-Oct: Sat 1 p.m.-4 p.m. Also by appointment.
Admission: Donations accepted.
Visitor Accessibility: Free on-site and street parking. Wheelchair accessible. Tour guide available during open hours and by appointment.
Website: www.clarecountyhistory.org
About: The society (founded 1970) preserves and advances the history of Clare County and the surrounding area. It oversees the museum complex located at the corner of Dover and Eberhart roads north of Clare, Michigan. The museum complex includes the following three buildings: The Clare County Museum, the Dover School House, and the Ott Log Cabin. The museum houses history exhibits, the schoolhouse is a reconstructed 20th-century school room, and the log cabin is a reconstruction from the Ott family.
Exhibits/Collections: Documents and photos pertaining to Clare County's logging, railroad, agricultural, and energy industries. Archives of author/historian Forrest Meek; artifacts of John "Spikehorn" Meyers; early Clare County court records and military displays.
Annual Events: Old Fashion Day (Sep). Meeting 1st Tue May-Oct, 7p.m. on museum grounds.
Publications: Quarterly newsletter (Catchmark).

White Pine Historical Society
Mailing Address: 2865 E. Rock Rd. • Clare, MI 48617
Contact: Forrest Meek,
Phone: (989) 386-7178
About: Research and publish Michigan history.
Exhibits/Collections: Approximately 1,000 items covering logging era, logging railroads, Clare County. Listings of men and mills by county.
Information may not be current.

Clarkston
(Oakland County)

Clarkston Community Historical Society
Mailing Address: 6495 Clarkston Road • Clarkston, MI 48346
Contact: Toni Smith, Director
E-Mail: info@clarkstonhistorical.org
Phone: (248) 922-0270
Fax: (248) 922-0270
Site/Location: Clarkston Heritage Museum
Hours: Mon-Wed 10 a.m.-9 p.m., Thu-Sat 10 a.m.-6 p.m.
Admission: Free.
Visitor Accessibility: Free on-site parking. Wheelchair accessible. Self-guided.
Website: www.clarkstonhistorical.org
About: The society is dedicated to the preservation of local history through family programs, lectures, publications, and the Clarkston Heritage Museum. Located in the library, the museum offers displays that focus on Clarkston history. The museum has featured exhibits detailing every aspect of early life in Clarkston. Exhibits change approximately twice a year and have covered everything from village businesses and local farms to summer tourists and the area's long-standing tradition of 4th of July parades.
Exhibits/Collections: Collects items relating to local history, including artifacts, photographs, and documents.
Annual Events: Art in the Village (Sep). Board of Director meetings 4th Tue monthly.
Publications: "The Heritage," "Our Children's Heritage," "The Way We Remember." Annual newsletter.

Clarkston Historic District Commission
Mailing Address: Village of Clarkston, 375 Depot • Clarkston, MI 48346

Contact: Dennis Ritter, City Manager
Phone: (248) 625-1559
Website: www.villageofclarkston.org
About: The Clarkston Historic District Commission reviews applications to determine if proposed changes are appropriate for structures within historic districts. The commission also acts as a preservation resource for residents.
*Information may not be current.

Clawson
(Oakland County)

Clawson Historical Museum
Mailing Address: c/o City Hall, 425 N. Main St. • Clawson, MI 48017
Contact: Melodie Nichols, Curator
E-Mail: historicalmuseum@cityofclawson.com
Phone: (248) 588-9169
Physical Location: 41 Fisher Court • Clawson, MI 48017
Hours: Sun and Wed 1-4 p.m.
Admission: Free
Visitor Accessibility: Free parking. Not wheelchair accessible.
Website: www.clawsonhistoricalsociety.org
About: The Clawson Historical Museum preserves and promotes the history of Clawson and the surrounding areas. The museum building is a three-story house built by Oswald and Deborah Fischer in the 1920s. It features 11 rooms furnished to reflect that era.
Exhibits/Collections: High school and city yearbooks, genealogical materials, newspaper clippings, and more than 3,000 photographs. Collection also includes furniture, decorative arts, textiles, clothing, tools, and ephemera from the 1920s.
Annual Events: Holiday Open House (Dec). See website for current special events.
Publications: "Two Square Miles," "The Heroes of a Small Town, v. I and II," "Pummychug: the Foundation of the Village of Clawson," "Clawson—The Way It Was," "Images of America: Clawson." Quarterly newsletter.
*Information may not be current.

Climax
(Kalamazoo County)

Prairie Historical Society
Mailing Address: P.O. Box 82 • Climax, MI 49034
Contact: Patrick Harvey, President
Phone: (269) 746-4796 • *Fax:* (269) 746-4125
Hours: Thu 10 a.m.-12 p.m. Other hours by appointment.
About: The Prairie Historical Society maintains its archives in the Lawrence Memorial Public Library.
Exhibits/Collections: Genealogical and property records, business files for the Climax/Scotts area.
Publications: Bimonthly newsletter.

Clinton
(Lenawee County)

Historical Society of Clinton
Mailing Address: P.O. Box 647 • Clinton, MI 49236
Contact: Sharon Scott, Archivist
E-Mail: clinton.historical.society@gmail.com
Phone: (517) 456-7198
Physical Location: Archives, 100 Brown St. • Clinton, MI 49236
Hours: Fri 3-5 p.m. Also by appointment.
Visitor Accessibility: Free street parking. Wheelchair accessible. Self-guided.
Website: www.clinthis.org
About: The Historical Society of Clinton coordinates work of local historians and others interested in collecting and preserving records. The society encourages projects and celebrations in cooperation with other historical societies.
Exhibits/Collections: Collections include maps, documents, newspaper microfilm, photographs, obituary, and subject files and special collections. To make an appointment to use the archives, call ahead.
Annual Events: US 12 Heritage Highway Garage Sale (Aug), Historical Building Marker Program (Oct).
Publications: Biannual newsletter. "Wirt C. Rowland Exhibition," "The Early History of Clintonites: Small Town Stories," "Clinton Community Cookbook," "175th Anniversary Our Home Town."

Southern Michigan Railroad Society
Mailing Address: P.O. Box A • Clinton, MI 49236
Phone: (517) 456-7677 • *Fax:* (517) 456-7677
Physical Location: 320 S. Division St. • Clinton, MI 49236
Hours: Museum open during scheduled train excursions or by appointment.
Admission: Train fares vary; museum admission is free.
Visitor Accessibility: Free on-site and street parking. Not wheelchair accessible. Self-guided.
Website: www.southernmichiganrailroad.com
About: The Southern Michigan Railroad Society is dedicated to building an operating railroad museum using one of the first railroad branch lines in Michigan—a rail corridor that connected the Michigan Southern line with the Michigan Central line in Jackson—and preserving its historical railroad era (1838-1982). The society aims to promote the awareness of railroading to the general public through educational and social activities. The society also maintains the SMRS Tecumseh South and North Rail Yards.
Exhibits/Collections: Vintage railcars, locomotives, tools, equipment. 1878 Sutton Depot. Railroad artifacts, memorabilia. Strap iron and spikes from first Michigan railroad. Magazines, books, videos, maps, pictures, Sanbord Fire Maps of Clinton and Tecumseh.
Annual Events: Train Excursions (Sum), Trains, Trucks & More! (Jun), Clinton Fall Festival and Tecumseh Appleumpkin Festival Train Rides, and Annual Fall Color Train Rides (Oct). Board of directors meeting 2nd Sat monthly.
Publications: Newsletter (Railway Express).

Clinton Township
(Macomb County)

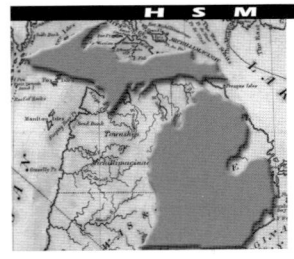

Albert L. Lorenzo Cultural Center
Mailing Address: 44575 Garfield Road • Clinton Township, MI 48038
Contact: Christine Guarino, Director of Cultural Affairs & Commuity
E-Mail: culturalcenter@macomb.edu
Phone: (586) 445-7348
Fax: (586) 286-2079
Hours: Wed-Sat 10 a.m.-4 p.m., Sun 1-4 p.m.
Admission: Free.
Visitor Accessibility: Free on-site parking. Wheelchair accessible. Tour guides available; contact the center at least two weeks in advance to schedule a guided tour.
Website: www.lorenzoculturalcenter.com

About: Albert L. Lorenzo Cultural Center is a unique cultural venue located on the center campus of Macomb Community College. The center provides multi-dimensional cultural experiences in the areas of history, science, literature, current events, visual and performing arts, popular culture, and heritages. Each year, the Lorenzo Cultural Center presents a themed anchor program and numerous presentations that explore the influences that shape the community's heritage; examine topics from a variety of perspectives; and create interactive opportunities for learning and celebration.
Annual Events: See website.
Publications: Video productions include "A Tribute to WWII Veterans," "A Tribute to Vietnam Veterans," and "Remembering the Henry Ford Trade School."

Clinton and Kalamazoo Canal Society
Mailing Address: 42662 Elizabeth Pl. • Clinton Township, MI 48038
Contact: Donald Green,
E-Mail: dwgreen@ameritech.net
Phone: (586) 263-0168 • *Fax:* (586) 263-6937
Hours: By appointment only.
Admission: Free.
About: In addition to maintaining the old canal route, the Clinton & Kalamazoo Canal Society hosts speakers and canal tours.
Annual Events: Festival of the Senses (Sep).
Information may not be current.

Clinton Township Historical Commission
Mailing Address: Attn: James Hungerford, 40700 Romeo Plank Rd. • Clinton Township, MI 48038
Contact: James Hungerford, Chairman
E-Mail: jphungerford@gmail.com
Phone: (586) 263-9173 • *Fax:* (586) 263-6932
Hours: Call or check website for hours.
Admission: Free.
Visitor Accessibility: Free parking. Wheelchair accessible. Tour guide available.
Website: http://ctwphc.org/
About: The Clinton Township Historical Commission is responsible for the general administration of the township's historical properties, including buildings in the Clinton Township Historical Village. The commission also offers interpretive programs with the Greater Clinton Township Historical Society.
Information may not be current.

Greater Clinton Township Historical Society
Mailing Address: 40700 Romeo Plank Rd. • Clinton Township, MI 48038
Contact: Jeri Hungerford, President
Phone: (586) 283-7025
Site/Location: **Clinton Township Historical Village Museum**
Hours: Open during special events and by appointment.
Website: http://www.clintontwphistory.org/
About: The Greater Clinton Township Historical Society studies, preserves, and promotes the history of Clinton Township. The society staffs and maintains the Clinton Township Historical Village Museum, which includes a furnished 1830s Williams Log Cabin and 1880s Moravian Meeting Hall.
Annual Events: Bi-monthly historical presentations. Schedule posted on website.
Publications: Quarterly Newsletter.
Information may not be current.

Clio
(Genesee County)

Clio Area Historical Association
Mailing Address: P.O. Box 295 Clio, MI 48420
Contact: Donna Clevenger
Phone: (989) 871-2213
Site/Location: **Clio Area Historical Depot Museum**
Physical Location: 300 W. Vienna Rd • Clio, MI 48420
Hours: May-Sep: Thu, Sun 1-3 p.m., also by appointment.
Admission: Donations accepted.
Visitor Accessibility: Free parking. Wheelchair accessible. Tour guides available.
About: The Clio Area Historical Association preserves the history of Clio, Vienna, and Thetford Townships. The association's museum is located in the former Flint & Pere Marquette railroad depot. Displays and exhibits feature Clio-area railroad, farming, household artifacts, class pictures of Clio High School, graduating classes 1900-1950s, Native-American display, local businesses, early farm kitchen, and country store.
Exhibits/Collections: Railroad and farm equipment. Genealogical center at the old Thetford Township Hall. Materials and maps from Thetford and Vienna Townships and city of Clio. Clio Messenger newspaper 1914-1980.
Information may not be current.

Clyde
(St. Clair County)

Clyde Historical Society
Mailing Address: 7293 Beard Rd. • Clyde, MI 48049
Contact: Janet Kruger, President
E-Mail: clydehistory@comcast.net
Phone: (810) 324-2572
Site/Location: **Old Clyde Township Hall**
Physical Location: 5080 Wild Cat Road • Clyde, MI 48049
Visitor Accessibility: On-site parking. Wheelchair accessible.
Website: http://home.comcast.net/~jlbearss/CHS/index.html
About: Founded in 2003, the Clyde Historical Society brings together people interested in the history of the area and local genealogy. The society collects, protects, and preserves items of historical significance. The Old Clyde Township Hall (1879) was donated to the society in 2005 and relocated to Bill Bearss Park in Clyde Township. It is used for dances and for storing the society's small collection of toy tractors and artifacts.
Exhibits/Collections: Toy tractors and assorted items from the area.
Annual Events: Annual Ox Roast (Aug), Car Show (Aug). Meetings 3rd Thu Mar-Nov, 7 p.m. in the Old Township Hall.

Coldwater
(Branch County)

Branch County Genealogical Society
Mailing Address: P.O. Box 443 • Coldwater, MI 49036
Contact: David McDonald, Treasurer
E-Mail: bchistorybook@aol.com
Phone: (517) 278-2789
Physical Location: Holbrook Heritage Room, Branch District Library, 10 E. Chicago Street • Coldwater, MI 49036
Hours: Call for current hours.
Visitor Accessibility: On-site public parking.
About: The Branch County Genealogical Society researches and preserves family and local genealogy/history.
Annual Events: Meetings 2nd Tue monthly, 5:30 p.m. at Grahl Conference Room, Burnside Center, Grahl Drive, Coldwater, MI 49036.
Publications: Published a number of reference books on research topics specific to Branch County.

Michigan History Directory

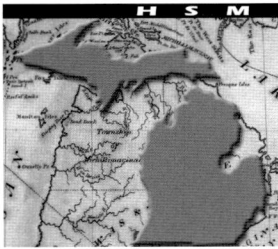

Branch County Historical Society
Mailing Address: 27 S. Jefferson St. • Coldwater, MI 49036
Contact: David McDonald, President
E-Mail: bchistorybook@aol.com
Phone: (517) 278-2871
Site/Location: **Wing House Museum**
Hours: 3rd Sat monthly 12-4 p.m. Also by appointment.
Admission: $3/individual donation.
Visitor Accessibility: Free street parking. Not wheelchair accessible. Tour guide available.
Website: www.branchcountyhistoricalsociety.org

About: Constructed in 1875, the Wing House is an example of Second Empire architecture with a convex mansard roof. It was sold to the Wing family in 1882 and has been restored to reflect the presence of both the Chandler and Wing families through their periods of ownership up to 1974. Most of the furnishings on display in the museum belonged to the two families and include items dating back to the mid-1800s.
Exhibits/Collections: Chandler family furniture dating to the 1850s, a large music box that plays 2.5-foot metal play discs, numerous collectibles from the families and Branch area.
Annual Events: Biannual Branch County Victorian Home Tour, Annual Christmas Wassail (Dec). Meeting 1st Mon monthly, 5:30 p.m.
Publications: "Branch County History, Vol. 1-2," "Harriet Quimby, 1st Lady of the Air," "Sans Soucci Beach."
Other Sites/Locations: **One-Room School House** • Location: Branch County Fairgrounds, 262 S. Sprague St., Coldwater, MI 49036 • Hours: During Branch County Fair Week. Also by appointment. • Admission: Donations accepted • Visitor Accessibility: Free street parking. Not wheelchair accessible. Tour guide available • Originally located in Quincy, the One-Room School House (b. 1846) was moved to the county fairgrounds for display. The building has been restored to represent the classroom accommodations that children experienced in the mid-1800s. It is open with reenactment teachers each year during the Branch County Fair in early August or by appointment.
Batavia Grange • Location: Snow Prairie Road, Coldwater, MI 49036 • This site is not open to the public.

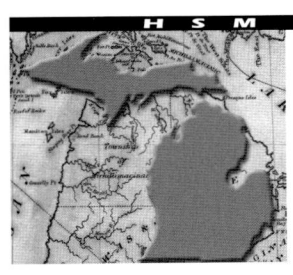

Branch District Library
Mailing Address: 10 E. Chicago St. • Coldwater, MI 49036
Contact: Evette Atkin, Director
E-Mail: hhr@branchdistrictlibrary.org
Phone: (517) 278-2341
Fax: (517) 279-7931
Hours: Mon, Thu 10 a.m.-7 p.m., Tue, Wed, Fri 10 a.m.-5 p.m., Sat 11 a.m.-3 p.m.
Visitor Accessibility: Free on-site parking.
Website: www.branchdistrictlibrary.org
Exhibits/Collections: Holbrook Heritage Room and Genealogy.

Little River Railroad
Mailing Address: 29 W. Park Ave. • Coldwater, MI 49036
Contact: Terry Bloom,
E-Mail: customerservice@littleriverrailroad.com
Phone: (574) 215-0751
Hours: Call or check website for train schedule.
Admission: $20/adult, $13/children (3-11), $65/family. Fares may change for special events. Call to charter the whole train.
Visitor Accessibility: Very old RR equipment with limited handicap capability. Call ahead to determine ability to accomodate.
Website: www.littleriverrailroad.com
About: The Little River Railroad provides steam train rides, which depart from the 1883 Lakeshore & Michigan Southern depot in Coldwater. The railroad maintains the 4-6-2 Pacific-type locomotive, which at 58 tons, is the smallest of its class ever built for standard gauge. Custom built in 1911 for the original Little River Railroad in Townsend, Tennessee, the train served as a logging engine until 1940. It was restored in 1975.

Coloma
(Berrien County)

Coloma Public Library
Mailing Address: P.O. Box 430 • Coloma, MI 49038
Contact: Charles Dickinson, Director
E-Mail: faith@colomapubliclibrary.net
Phone: (269) 468-3431
Fax: (269) 468-8077
Physical Location: 151 W. Center St. • Coloma, MI 49038
Hours: Mon, Fri 10 a.m.-5:30 p.m.; Tue, Wed, Thu 10 a.m.-8 p.m.; Sat 10 a.m.-2 p.m.
Admission: Free.
Visitor Accessibility: Free on-site parking. Wheelchair accessible. Self-guided.
Website: http://www.colomapubliclibrary.net

North Berrien Historical Society and Museum
Mailing Address: P.O. Box 207 • Coloma, MI 49038
Contact: Tracy Gierada, Executive Director
E-Mail: info@northberrienhistory.org
Phone: (269) 468-3330
Fax: (269) 468-4083
Physical Location: 300 Coloma Ave. • Coloma, MI 49038
Hours: May-Sep: Tue-Sat 10 a.m.-4 p.m.; Oct-Apr: Tue-Fri 10 a.m.-4 p.m. Also by appointment.
Admission: Free.
Visitor Accessibility: Free on-site parking. Wheelchair accessible. Self-guided.
Website: www.northberrienhistory.org

About: The North Berrien Historical Society preserves and distributes information regarding the history of North Berrien County. The museum focuses on the local history of northern Berrien. Exhibits cover 10,000 years of human history, from archaeology to modern technology. The main gallery features Native Americans, lake resorts, rural schools, Lake Michigan shipwrecks, daily life, and businesses. The Nichols-Beverly Barn presents lumbering and agricultural history. The Carter House (c.1860) tells the story of the museum property and holds events throughout the year.

✽ Historical Society of Michigan

Exhibits/Collections: More than 8,100 objects, photographs, archival and library holdings significant to the history of northern Berrien County.
Annual Events: Victorian Valentine's Party (Feb), Coastline Children's Film Festival (Mar), Spring Break Activity Day (Mar/Apr), Volunteer Appreciation Dinner (May), Summer Time Travelers (Jun, Jul, Aug), North Berrien Photo Contest & Exhibit (Jun-Oct), Annual Meeting (Oct), Halloween Cemetery Tours (Oct), Holiday Open House (Nov/ Dec).
Publications: Quarterly Newsletter (Glimpses of the Past).

Colon
(St. Joseph County)

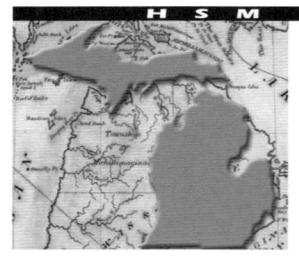

Community Historical Society of Colon
Mailing Address: P.O. Box 136 • Colon, MI 49040
Contact: Joe Ganger, President
Phone: (269) 432-3804
Site/Location: **Community Historical Museum of Colon**
Physical Location: 219 N. Blackstone Ave. • Colon, MI 49040
Hours: Jun-Aug: Tue and Thu 2-4:30 p.m. Also by appointment.
Admission: Donations accepted.
Visitor Accessibility: Parking available in the Methodist Church parking lot. Wheelchair accessible. Tour guide available.
Website: www.colonmi.com/historical.html
About: The Community Historical Society of Colon preserves local history and makes local artifacts available to the community. The society also maintains the Colon Community Historical Museum, which features area artifacts pertaining to medicine, school, Native Americans, pioneers, a general store, toys, military, etc. As Colon is the "Magic Capital of the World," the museum also features a magic collection and a print shop. Also on site is the Farrard/Hockzema Annex, which features multiple interests.
Annual Events: Meetings usually 1st Mon May-Sep.

Columbiaville
(Lapeer County)

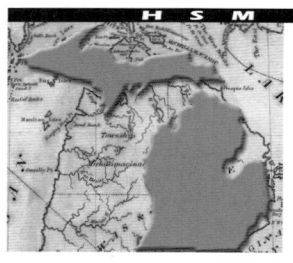

Historic Fort Wayne Coalition
Mailing Address: 3660 Columbiaville Rd. • Columbiaville, MI 48421
Contact: Tom Berlucchi
E-Mail: info@historicfortwaynecoalition.com
Phone: (810) 793-6739
Site/Location: **Historic Fort Wayne**
Physical Location: 6325 Jefferson • Detroit, MI 48209
Hours: May-Oct Sat-Sun 10 a.m.-4 p.m.
Admission: Free to the public.
Visitor Accessibility: On-site parking for a fee ($5).
Website: www.historicfortwaynecoalition.com
About: The Historic Fort Wayne Coalition is dedicated to preserving the history of the Michigan men and women who served their country from 1845-1973 and either sent material to or personally passed through Historic Fort Wayne during U.S. military service. The coalition presents events as well as helps preserve and restore the fort's structures and facilities.
Annual Events: Collectable Show and Flea Market (Apr, Oct), World War II (May), Military Time Line (May), Colonial Days (Jun), Medieval Days (Jul), Civil War Days (Sep), 1812 Living History (Sep), Civil War Christmas (Dec).

Other Sites/Locations: **Tuskegee Airmen National Museum** • Location: 6325 W. Jefferson Ave., Detroit, MI 48209 • Open only by appointment. Call 313-833-8849.

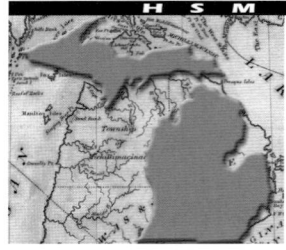

Historical Society of Columbiaville
Mailing Address: P.O. Box 165 • Columbiaville, MI 48421
Contact: Floyd Klauka, President
E-Mail: cville.historical.society.2@gmail.com
Phone: (810) 793-2932
Site/Location: **Columbiaville Historical Society Museum**
Physical Location: 4718 First St. • Columbiaville, MI 48619
Hours: May-Oct: 1st and 3rd Fri monthly 1-4 p.m. Also by appointment.
Admission: Donations accepted.
Visitor Accessibility: Free on-site parking. Wheelchair accessible. Tour guide available.
Website: www.columbiavillehistoricalsociety.blogspot.com
About: The Columbiaville Historical Society was founded immediately following the bicentennial celebration in 1976. The society preserves the story of the community of Columbiaville, Michigan, and the people who made it what it is today. It aims to thoroughly research, collect, preserve, and display in its museum historic evidence related to the village and its extensive, rich history. Attractions at the Columbiaville Historical Society Museum include Native-American arrowheads, mounted birds, quilts, furniture, books, photographs, and antique household and farm implements.
Annual Events: Appraisal Fair. Meetings 3rd Mon Apr-Oct, 7:15 p.m. at museum.

Comins
(Oscoda County)

Comins Restoration Association
Mailing Address: P.O. Box 141 • Comins, MI 48619
Phone: (989) 848-5362
Information may not be current.

Michigan Magazine Museum
Mailing Address: 3309 N. Abbe Rd. • Comins, MI 48619
Phone: 989-848-2246
Hours: Memorial Day-Labor Day: Thu-Sat 10 a.m.-5 p.m., Sun 12-5 p.m.
Website: www.michiganmagazine.com
About: The Michigan Magazine Museum houses articles referred to on the Michigan Magazine TV show, which was broadcast on the Public Broadcasting System (PBS) throughout Michigan.
Information may not be current.

Comstock
(Kalamazoo County)

Kalamazoo Valley Genealogical Society
Mailing Address: P.O. Box 405 • Comstock, MI 49041
Contact: Curt Ingersoll, President
E-Mail: mikvgs@yahoo.com
Phone: (269) 626-8285
Website: www.mikvgs.org
About: The Kalamazoo Valley Genealogical Society preserves family and vital records in the Kalamazoo area. The society also assists members

interested in their family histories.
Exhibits/Collections: Collections held at Western Michigan University Archives and Regional History Center.
Annual Events: Meetings 3rd Mon at Portage District Library, 300 Library Lane (Jan-Jun, Sep-Nov). March meetings held at Western Michigan University Archives, East Hall.
Publications: Newsletter (Kalamazoo Valley Heritage).
Information may not be current.

Comstock Park
(Kent County)

HSM MEMBER

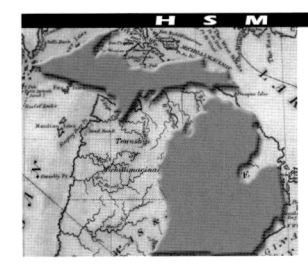

Alpine Township Historical Commission
Mailing Address: 5255 Alpine Ave. NW, • Comstock Park, MI 49321
Contact: Ruth Post, President
E-Mail: b.alt@alpinetwp.org
Phone: (616) 784-1262
Site/Location: Alpine Township Historical Museum
Physical Location: 2408 Seven Mile Rd. NW • Comstock Park, MI 49321
Hours: By appointment.
Admission: Free.
Visitor Accessibility: Public parking. Wheelchair accessible. Free tour guides available.
Website: www.alpinetwp.org
About: Appointed by the township board, the Alpine Township Historical Commission collects, maintains, and preserves the antiquities of Alpine Township. The commission hosts monthly programs featuring speakers on a variety of historical subjects. It also maintains a museum in an 1860 township hall, which was restored in 1987 and is now listed in the State Register of Historic Places.
Exhibits/Collections: Photo galleries of early settlers, 12 one-room schools, and more than 300 township veterans. Furniture and artifacts of pioneer families. Extensive file of township family histories and obituaries.
Annual Events: Meetings 3rd Sun monthly Sep-May, 2 p.m. at Township Community Center, 2015 Seven Mile Rd. NW, Comstock Park.

HSM MEMBER

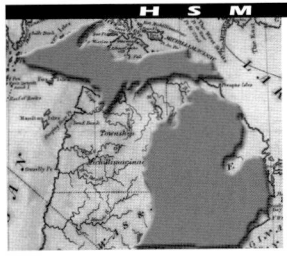

Plainfield Township Historical Commission
Mailing Address: P.O. Box 74 • Comstock Park, MI 49321
Contact: Suzanne Carpenter, President
E-Mail: suzannec@iserv.net
Phone: (616) 784-7264
Site/Location: Hyser Rivers Museum
Physical Location: 6440 W. River Dr. • Belmont, MI 49306
Hours: Apr-Dec: 1st Sun monthly 2-4:30 p.m. Also by appointment.
Admission: Free.
Visitor Accessibility: Free on-site parking. Partially wheelchair accessible; first floor only. Tour guide available.
Website: http://www.plainfieldtwpmi.com/historical_commission.html
About: The Plainfield Charter Township Historical Preservation Committee collects and documents Plainfield Township's history and the histories of its families. The Committee also seeks to educate its residents about the township's connection to the Grand and Rogue Rivers. The Hyser museum is located in the 1852 Greek Revival home of Dr. William Hyser, a pioneer surgeon and Civil War captain. It displays family living quarters and township artifacts and is one of the last remaining structures of the original Plainfield Village.
Exhibits/Collections: Photographic collection of many of the township's early residents. Everyday objects from the typical 1900s home. Dr. Hyser's medical equipment, canteen, and the chess set he carried in the Civil War.
Annual Events: "Spring into the Past" (May), Historic Reenactment Weekend (Sep).
Publications: Township history book.

Concord
(Jackson County)

Heritage Association of Concord
Mailing Address: P.O. Box 381 • Concord, MI 49237
Contact: Gail Snow
E-Mail: gpsnow@frontiernet.net
Phone: (517) 524-6675
Physical Location: 409 Hanover Street • Concord, MI 49237
Hours: Open for monthly meetings, also by appointment.
About: Organized in 1972, the Heritage Association of Concord purchased and restored the 1919 farmhouse built by Homer Cheesbro Simons. The building is furnished with local furniture from its original era.
Annual Events: Concord Heritage Days Open House (Jul), Home Tours (Dec). Meetings 4th Wed monthly.
Information may not be current.

HSM MEMBER

Mann House.
Please see entry under Lansing: Michigan Historical Center.

Constantine
(St. Joseph County)

Governor John S. Barry Historical Society
Mailing Address: 280 N. Washington St. • Constantine, MI 49042
Contact: Dr. Marvin Vercler, President
Phone: (269) 506-1575
Site/Location: Barry Museum
Hours: By appointment.
About: The Governor John S. Barry Historical Society was established in 1944 to collect and preserve antiques, provide historical information, and maintain the Governor John S. Barry Museum, the former home of Michigan's third elected governor.
Annual Events: Meetings 3rd Tue (Apr-Oct at Barry House, Nov-May at Michigan Room, Constantine Township Library).
Information may not be current.

Coopersville
(Ottawa County)

Coopersville & Marne Railway
Mailing Address: 311 E. Danforth St., P.O. Box 55 • Coopersville, MI 49404
Contact: Jerry J. Ricard, General Manager
E-Mail: jerryricard@comcast.net
Phone: (616) 997-7000 • **Fax:** (616) 994-8296
Site/Location: Coopersville & Marne Railway Railroad Station
Physical Location: 306 Main St. • Coopersville, MI 49404
Hours: See website or call ahead for excursion days. Station opens at 9:30 a.m. on train days.
Admission: $11.50/adult, $10.50/senior, $9.50/children (2-12).
Visitor Accessibility: Free on-site and street parking. Not wheelchair accessible.
Website: www.mitrain.net
About: The Coopersville & Marne Railway Company is dedicated to the preservation of historic railroad equipment, buildings, and artifacts.

❋ Historical Society of Michigan

The organization provides narrated excursions and operates on 14 miles of railroad track between Coopersville and Grand Rapids. Remodeled in 2013, the 120-year-old train station has historical railroad-related artifacts on display.

Exhibits/Collections: Locomotives, railroad cars, national commuter car from Montreal, caboose, speeder cars, industrial Brownhoist Crane, signal tower, RR station, RR heaveyweight.

Annual Events: Bunny Train (Spring), Veteran's Troop Train (Memorial Day), Conductor-narrated Excursions (Jun-Oct), The Great Train Robbery (Jul), Summerfeat (Aug), The Famous Pumpkin Trains (Sep-Oct), Santa Train (Nov-Dec), Locomotive Cab Rides.

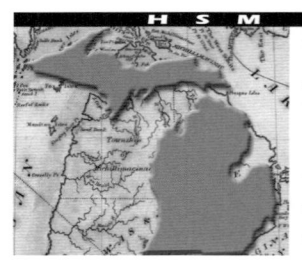

Coopersville Area Historical Society

Mailing Address: 363 Main St. • Coopersville, MI 49404
Contact: James & Lillian Budzynski,
E-Mail: historicalsoc@allcom.net
Phone: (616) 997-7240
Site/Location: **Coopersville Area Historical Society Museum**

Hours: Tue 3-7 p.m.; Wed 10 a.m.-1 p.m.; Fri 1-4 p.m.; Sat 10 a.m.-4 p.m. Also by appointment.
Admission: Donations accepted.
Visitor Accessibility: Free on-site and street parking. Wheelchair accessible. Call ahead for tour guide availability.
Website: www.coopersvillemuseum.com

About: The Coopersville Area Historical Society Museum building is a Michigan Historic Site and on the National Register of Historic Places for its significance as an interurban railway depot and station. Featured are steam and interurban railroad items, an extensive drugstore exhibit, and many local history and household displays. In a connecting building lies a sawmill, along with a schoolroom and other items. Del Shannon memorabilia and Merlin (the interurban car) are popular attractions.

Exhibits/Collections: Del Shannon collection: gold records, photographs. Area history exhibits, railroad and interurban train exhibits, full-size sawmill display, G-gauge model railroad, 1880s drugstore items, and military items.

Annual Events: Del Shannon Days (Aug), Trick or Treat Trail (Oct), Museum by Moonlight (Dec). Monthly meetings with programs; call for time, location, and topics.

Publications: Monthly newsletter.

Coopersville Farm Museum & Event Center

Mailing Address: P.O. Box 64 • Coopersville, MI 49404
Contact: LeeAnn Creager, Museum Director
E-Mail: info@coopersvillefarmmuseum.org
Phone: (616) 997-8555 • *Fax:* (616) 997-9215
Physical Location: 375 Main St. • Coopersville, MI 49404
Hours: Jul-Oct: Tue-Sat 10 a.m.-4 p.m.; Nov-Jun: Tue, Thurs, Sat 10 a.m.-2 p.m.
Admission: $4/adult, $2/youth, children 3 and under free.
Visitor Accessibility: Free on-site parking. Wheelchair accessible.
Website: www.coopersvillefarmmuseum.org

About: The Coopersville Farm Museum & Event Center honors farming, agriculture, and rural life through art, exhibits, and events. The museum also features interactive exhibits and a children's museum.

Exhibits/Collections: Farm equipment of founder Ed Hanenburg; feed sack collection of Corky Pals; assortment of antique farm tools, corn huskers, barbed wire; reconstructed 100-year-old barn. Various tractors, quilts, railroad layout, photos, art.

Annual Events: Monday Night Bingo, Line Dancing, Petting Zoo (Apr), Tractor Show (Aug), Quilts and Their Stories (Aug, Sep). Jam Nights held 1st and 3rd Tue monthly.

Information may not be current.

Copemish
(Manistee County)

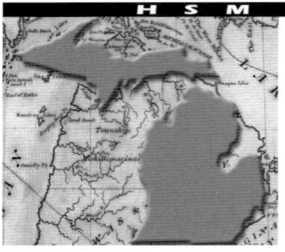

Marilla Historical Society

Mailing Address: 20645 Hulls Road • Copemish, MI 49625
Contact: Jan Thomas, Director
E-Mail: boja@kaltelnet.net
Phone: (231) 362-3430
Site/Location: **Marilla Museum & Pioneer Place**

Physical Location: 9991 Marilla Road • Copemish, MI 49625
Hours: May-Oct: Last Sat monthly 1-5 p.m. Also by special appointment. Subject to change, call before visit.
Admission: $3/adult, $1.50/children (7-17).
Visitor Accessibility: Free on-site parking. Partially wheelchair accessible. Tour guide available.
Website: www.marillahistory.org

About: The Marilla Historical Society promotes the understanding of how communities form and change through interpretive displays and special educational programming and events. The grounds of the Marilla Museum and Pioneer Place include an 1870 fully furnished two-story log "Pioneer House," Nels Johnson Cabin, fully furnished 1900 "Pioneer Barn," and 1920 Standard School.

Exhibits/Collections: Letters, art work, household artifacts, farm machinery and tools, original post office, general store, many school items, maps, books, a large 1920 model of Marilla, and many historic photos.

Annual Events: See website for events. Meetings 3rd Tue monthly, 1 p.m. at Marilla Township Hall.

Publications: "Wildflowers of Orchard Hill Farm Marilla, Michigan," "For the Glory of God and Our Neighbors Good: a Community Identity."

Copper Harbor
(Keweenaw County)

Fort Wilkins Historic Complex and Copper Harbor Lighthouse.
Please see entry under Lansing: Michigan Historical Center.

Delaware Copper Mine Tours.
Please see entry under Mohawk: Delaware Copper Mine Tours.

Covington
(Baraga County)

Covington Township Historical Society

Mailing Address: P.O. Box 54 • Covington, MI 49919
Contact: Mary Tarvainen
E-Mail: marypt@jamadots.com
Phone: (906) 355-2413
Site/Location: **Covington Township Historical Museum**

Physical Location: Elm Street • Covington, MI 49919
Hours: Fri-Sat 11 a.m.-3 p.m.
Admission: Donations accpeted.
Visitor Accessibility: Free street parking. Self-guided.
Website: http://www.ohwy.com/mi/c/covthsts.htm

About: Formed in 1997, the Covington Historical Society preserves local heritage for future generations. The society maintains a museum in the former township hall. Exhibits include the first fire truck, horsedrawn cutter, military display, and jail cell used to house only one prisoner.

Exhibits/Collections: Township board minutes, birth records, obituaries and cemetery plots, justice of the peace court records, some military records, video and audio biographies. 1,500 artifacts, historic photos, Finnish-language books and papers.
Annual Events: Fall Festival. Meetings 3rd Thu May-Sep at museum.
*Information may not be current.

Crystal
(Montcalm County)

Crystal Township Historical Society
Mailing Address: P.O. Box 169 • Crystal, MI 48818
Contact: David Wight
E-Mail: CTHS@CrystalHistory.com
Website: http://www.rootsweb.ancestry.com/~micryshs/CrystalTownshipHistoricalSociety.html

Crystal Falls
(Iron County)

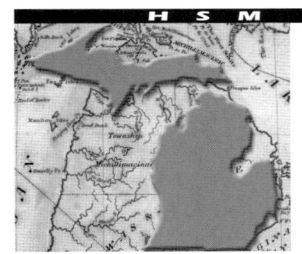

Crystal Falls Museum Society
Mailing Address: P.O. Box 65 • Crystal Falls, MI 49920
Contact: Al Pieper, Treasurer
E-Mail: alfred.pieper@gmail.com
Phone: (906) 875-4341
Site/Location: **Harbour House Museum**
Physical Location: 17 N. 4th St. • Crystal Falls, MI 49920
Hours: Jun-Aug: Thu-Sat 10 a.m.-2 p.m.
Admission: $2/individual, $5/family.
Visitor Accessibility: Free street parking. Partially wheelchair accessible; first floor only. Tour guide available.
Website: www.harbourhousemuseum.org
About: Built in 1900 by master mason and bricklayer Fred Floodstrand, the Harbour House Museum was constructed with cement blocks and designed in the "steamboat" style of architecture with wraparound twin porches. The first floor has been restored to a turn-of-the-century setting, including a kitchen, dining room, parlor, and library.
Exhibits/Collections: Crystal Falls Diamond Drill newspaper (1887-2006), books and pamphlets about the area, etc. Genealogical research done by request; donations are accepted.
Annual Events: Bass Fest (Jul), Reception Open House (Jul), Teddy Bear Picnic (Jul), Crystal Summer Fest (Jul), Fungus Fest (Aug), Mushroom Cook Off (Aug), Victorian Tea (Aug), Annual Meeting (Oct).

Curtis
(Mackinac County)

Curtis Historical Society
Mailing Address: P.O. Box 313 • Curtis, MI 49820
Contact: Lucille Kenyon, President
E-Mail: genilady@hughes.net
Phone: (906) 586-3382
Site/Location: **Curtis Historical Society Museum**
Physical Location: N9224 Portage Ave. • Curtis, MI 49820
Hours: Mon-Fri 1-4 p.m.
Admission: Donations accepted.
Visitor Accessibility: On-site parking. Wheelchair accessible. Self-guided; volunteer available for questions.
About: The Curtis Historical Society Museum houses artifacts from early logging and settlers. Exhibits include displays on school, military, and Native Americans.
Exhibits/Collections: Scrapbooks, pictures, logging items, war memorabilia, school desk, and vertical and obituary files.
Publications: Annual newsletter. Booklets for sale at museum.

D

Davisburg
(St. Clair County)

Springfield Township Historical Society
Mailing Address: P.O. Box 203 • Davisburg, MI 48350
Contact: Kerry Monzo, Prezident
Phone: (248) 634-4453
Physical Location: Andersonville Rd. • Davisburg, MI 48350
About: The Springfield Township Historical Society preserves the heritage of Springfield Township, the James Harvey Davis House, and the Schultz Harness Shop.
Exhibits/Collections: Original furnishings in James H. Davis home from late 1800s. Early records of Springfield Township.
Annual Events: Davisburg Days.
*Information may not be current.

Davison
(Genesee County)

Davison Area Historical Society
Mailing Address: 263 E. Fourth St. • Davison, MI 48423
Contact: Debbie Koski, President
E-Mail: info@davisonmuseum.org
Phone: (810) 658-2286
Site/Location: **Davison Area Historical Museum**
Hours: Thu 10 a.m.-2 p.m.
Admission: Donations accepted.
Visitor Accessibility: Free on-site parking. Partially wheelchair accessible. Tour guides available.
Website: www.davisonmuseum.org
About: The Davison Area Historical Society preserves and educates people about the history of the Davison-Richfield area through old photos and artifacts. The Davison Area Historical Museum features everyday artifacts from the mid-1800s to 1940. Exhibits include display of a 1900 kitchen, toys from that time period, a dry goods store, millinery shop, Davison's first "post office," military uniforms and artifacts from area veterans, a scale of Davison Village as it was about 1903, and school artifacts.
Exhibits/Collections: Military uniforms, medals, and equipment of Davison veterans. Collecting information, artifacts, and photos relating to history, culture, and people of Davison from 1830s to the 1950s.
Annual Events: School Days of Yore (Mar-Apr), Festival of Flags (Jul), Pumpkinfest (fall). Membership meeting 2nd Tue monthly, 7 p.m. at the museum.
Publications: Quarterly newsletter. "Davison, Then and Now," "Davison—Richfield in the Civil War," "Davison in the Day of the Horse."
Other Sites/Locations: **Woolley Veterinarian Building** • Location: Next the Davison Area Historical Museum • Hours:

Thu 10 a.m.-2 p.m. • Admission: Donations accepted • Visitor Accessibility: Free on-site parking. Partially wheelchair accessible. Visitors may access building only when accompanied by a docent. • This local veterinary building has all its original medicines, equipment, and other artifacts. The building was built in 1893 and had several uses before becoming a vet's office in 1905.

Kitchen School • Location: Southwest corner of M-15 (State Road) and Bristol Road • Hours: By appointment • Admission: Free • Visitor Accessibility: Free on-site parking. Partially wheelchair accessible; building is accessible but grounds are unpaved. Tour guides available. • This 150-year-old building is a one-room school as it would have appeared in 1940. It includes an outhouse, wood stove, and a child-powered merry-go-round.

Information may not be current.

Dearborn
(Wayne County)

Arab American National Museum
Mailing Address: 13624 Michigan Ave. • Dearborn, MI 48126
Contact: Kim Silarski, Communications
E-Mail: ksilarski@accesscommunity.org
Phone: (313) 582-2266
Fax: (313) 582-1086
Hours: Wed-Sat 10 a.m.-6 p.m., Sun 12-5 p.m.
Admission: $8/adult, $4/senior $4/student, children 6 and under free.
Visitor Accessibility: Free on-site parking. Wheelchair accessible. Call ahead for group tours (min. 8 individuals); $5/student, $5/senior, $10/adult.
Website: www.arabamericanmuseum.org
About: The Arab American National Museum is the first and only museum in the world devoted to the history, culture, and contributions of Arab Americans. Interactive exhibits discuss Arab immigration to the United States, Arab American lifestyles and traditions, and famous Arab Americans. Two rotating galleries feature traditional and contemporary art, history, and culture.
Exhibits/Collections: Library and Resource Center (multiple collections). Permanent collection of art and artifacts. Education collection includes loanable artifacts.
Annual Events: Arab Film Festival, Global Fridays world music concert series, and Concert of Colors free summer music festival (Jul).
Publications: "Telling Our Story: The Arab American National Museum."

Automotive Hall of Fame
Mailing Address: 21400 Oakwood Blvd. • Dearborn, MI 48124
Contact: William Chapin
E-Mail: AHOF@thedrivingspirit.org
Phone: (313) 240-4000 • *Fax:* (313) 240-8641
Hours: Wed-Sun 9 a.m.-5 p.m., closed holidays.
Admission: $8/adult, $6/senior, $6/student, $4/children (5-18), tour groups of 15 or more $4/individual, school groups $2/child.
Visitor Accessibility: On-site parking. Wheelchair accessible. Free tour guide available.
Website: www.automotivehalloffame.org
About: The Automotive Hall of Fame is dedicated to recognizing outstanding achievement in automotive-related industries, preserving automotive heritage, and educating future generations of industry participants. Automotive history is presented through visual and interactive exhibits, automobiles, and authentic artifacts.
Exhibits/Collections: Various personal artifacts of inductees and their families. Books relating to inductees and automotive industry.
Annual Events: See website.

Information may not be current.

Dearborn Genealogical Society
Mailing Address: P.O. Box 1112 • Dearborn, MI 48121
Contact: Tom Barrett, President
Website: www.rootsweb.com/~midgs/
About: The Dearborn Genealogical Society promotes an interest in genealogy, history, and biography. The society locates, protects, and publishes public and private genealogical records.
Exhibits/Collections: Five-generation ancestor charts. Non-circulating genealogical materials available in Yulon Smith Collection, Henry Ford Centennial Library in Dearborn, MI.
Annual Events: Meetings 4th Thu Jan-Apr, Sep, and Oct, 2nd Thu Dec, 7 p.m. at Cherry Hill Baptist Church, Dearborn Heights.
Publications: Newsletter, Cemetery and vital records.

Information may not be current.

Dearborn Historical Society & Museum
Mailing Address: 915 S. Brady • Dearborn, MI 48124
Contact: Jake Tate, Acting Chief Curator
E-Mail: jtate@ci.dearborn.mi.us
Phone: (313) 565-3000
Fax: (313) 565-4848
Site/Location: McFadden-Ross House
Hours: Tue-Fri 9 a.m.-4 p.m.
Admission: Donations accepted.
Visitor Accessibility: Free on-site and street parking. Not wheelchair accessible. Tour guides available by appointment.
Website: http://thedhm.com/
About: The Dearborn Historical Society preserves and promotes the history of Dearborn. Its museum consists of thee historic structures and a records archive. It has two campuses within two blocks of each other. The museum provides tour brochures and audio of the greater Dearborn area.
Exhibits/Collections: Genealogy records specific to Dearborn-area families. 1820-1920 census records. Yearbooks from area schools. Polk directories from 1928-present. Local newspaper collection from 1905. Local history artifacts, costumes, textiles, decorative arts, agriculture.
Annual Events: Monthly Lecture Series, Victorian Tea, History Hill, and Pioneer School Program.
Publications: The Award-winning Dearborn Historian, Bark Cover House.
Other Sites/Locations: **1831 Richard Gardner House** • Hours: By appointment • Admission: Donations accepted • Visitor Accessibility: Free on-site and street parking. Not wheelchair accessible. Free tour guides available by appointment. • Built in 1831, this building is the oldest home in Dearborn. Richard and Elizabeth Gardner lived in this home with their children. Originally preserved by Henry Ford, the home was moved to the Dearborn Historical Museum in 1996.

1833 Commandant's Quarters • Location: 21950 Michigan Avenue, Dearborn, MI 48124 • Hours: By appointment • Admission: By donation • Visitor Accessibility: On-site parking available for a fee. Some free street parking. Not wheelchair accessible. Free tour guides available by appointment. • Part of the Detroit Arsenal, this structure served as home to 19 different commandants and their families from 1833 to 1875. The current portion of the arsenal wall and entrance gate are replicas. Today, the building is listed on the National Register of Historic Places and features rooms decorated in the style of the era from 1833-1875.

Michigan History Directory

Great Lakes Maritime Institute
Mailing Address: P.O. Box 1990 • Dearborn, MI 48121
Contact: Kathy McGraw, Secretary-Treasurer
E-Mail: mcgrawka@sbcglobal.net
Phone: (313) 441-1155 • *Fax:* (313) 441-1155
Website: www.glmi.org
About: The Great Lakes Maritime Institute promotes maritime history by encouraging the dissemination, production, and viewing of artifact displays, artwork, models, video recording, and written materials. The Institute was organized in 1952 as a Michigan nonprofit corporation. Donations to GLMI have been ruled deductible by the Internal Revenue Service. No member is paid for services.
Exhibits/Collections: Upon request.
Annual Events: Dinner Program (Oct).
Publications: Periodic e-blasts.

Henry Ford Estate—Fair Lane
Mailing Address: University Of Michigan-Dearborn, 4901 Evergreen Rd. • Dearborn, MI 48128
Contact: Gary Rogers, Director
E-Mail: grodgers@umd.umich.edu
Phone: 313-593-5590 • *Fax:* 313-593-5243
Hours: Tours: Year-round: Sun 1-4:30 p.m.; Jan-Mar: Tue-Fri 1:30 p.m.; Apr-Dec: Tue-Sat 10 a.m., 11 a.m., 1 p.m., 2 p.m., 3 p.m. Pool Restaurant Tue-Fri 11 a.m.-2 p.m.
Admission: $10/adult, $9/senior $9/student, $6/children (0-12), children 4 and under free.
Visitor Accessibility: On-site parking. Limited wheelchair accessibility. Guided tours of the residence, power house, and gardens available (call for times, rates, special packages, and group discounts).
Website: www.henryfordestate.org
About: Set on 72 acres of landscaped grounds, the Henry Ford Estate—Fair Lane was the family home of automotive pioneer Henry Ford. The 56-room mansion includes two giant generators placed by Henry Ford and Thomas Edison that still generate electricity today. Designated a National Historic Landmark in 1966.
Annual Events: See website.
*Information may not be current.

Henry Ford Heritage Association
Mailing Address: P.O. Box 2313 • Dearborn, MI 48123
Contact: Mark Campbell, Treasurer
E-Mail: hfha@hfha.org
Phone: (888) 687-4342
Fax: (888) 687-4342
Website: www.hfha.org
About: The Henry Ford Heritage Association works in partnership with other Ford-related museums and groups, including the Benson Ford Research Center, Edison & Ford Winter Estates, Edsel & Eleanor Ford House, Henry Ford Fair Lane Estate, the Model A Ford Foundation, Ford Piquette Avenue Plant Museum, and the Early Ford V8 Museum, to foster interest in the life and accomplishments of Henry Ford and to preserve and interpret the landmarks associated with his life and family.
Exhibits/Collections: The Henry Ford Quiz Show takes place at the Motor Muster and Old Car Festival at Greenfield Village, where the public can test their knowledge on Henry Ford's legacy in a fun and interactive way.
Annual Events: Henry Ford's birthday is celebrated each year on July 30 with a dinner held at a venue important to the Ford story.

Publications: The Ford Legend newsletter is published three times each year. The Legend includes informational updates from all partners and several historical articles about Henry Ford, his family, and his company.

Michigan Railroad Club, Inc.
Mailing Address: P.O. Box 586 • Dearborn, MI 48121
Contact: Anthony Rzucidlo, President
Website: www.michiganrailroadclub.org
About: Founded in 1937, the Michigan Railroad Club, Inc., is Michigan's oldest railroad enthusiast group.
Annual Events: Meetings 1st Wed monthly, 7 p.m. at Henry Ford Centennial Library, 16301 Michigan Ave, Dearborn.
*Information may not be current.

Michigan Regimental Civil War Roundtable
Mailing Address: 1632 N. Silvery Ln. • Dearborn, MI 48128
Contact: Jim Burroughs, Program Director
E-Mail: jwburrough@aol.com
Phone: (313) 277-0355
Physical Location: Farmington Public Library, 23500 Liberty St. • Farmington, MI 48335
Hours: Last Mon of month 6:30-8:45 p.m. No meeting in Oct, Dec.
Admission: $20/yearly membership fee.
Visitor Accessibility: Free on-site parking.
Website: www.farmlib.org/mrrt
About: The Michigan Regimental Round Table has been meeting for 57 years to promote the study of the American Civil War. The roundtable also helped to preserve the 6th Regiment Michigan Heavy Artillery battle flag for state collection.
Annual Events: Fieldtrip (Oct). Meetings last Mon of each month (except Oct and Dec) at Farmington Public Library.

The Henry Ford
Mailing Address: 20900 Oakwood Blvd. • Dearborn, MI 48124
Contact: Nardina Mein, Manager, Archives & Library
E-Mail: research.center@thehenryford.org
Phone: (800) 835-5237
Site/Location: Henry Ford Museum
Hours: Daily 9:30 a.m.-5 p.m. Hours vary by venue, check website for current hours.
Admission: $18/adult, $16/senior (62+), $13.50/children (5-12), children 4 and under free. Members are free.
Visitor Accessibility: On-site parking; $5/vehicle except for members. Wheelchair accessible.
Website: www.thehenryford.org
About: The Henry Ford provides unique educational experiences based on authentic objects, stories, and lives from America's traditions of ingenuity, resourcefulness, and innovation. Its purpose is to inspire people to learn from these traditions to help shape a better future. The Henry Ford consists of the Henry Ford Museum, Greenfield Village, Ford Rouge Factory Tour, IMAX Theatre, and Benson Ford Research Center. It also hosts a tour of the Ford Rouge Factory.
Exhibits/Collections: Transportation, technology, agriculture, industry, domestic life, public life, design, and decorative arts. Archival collection includes the Ford Motor Company archives. Materials at the Archives and Library are available to the public.
Annual Events: Civil War Remembrance, Ragtime Street Fair, Salute

to America (Independence Day Celebration), Historic Baseball Games, Motor Muster, Old Car Festival, Hallowe'en in Greenfield Village, Holiday Nights in Greenfield Village, Summer Discovery Camps.
Publications: The Henry Ford magazine.
Other Sites/Locations: **Greenfield Village** • Hours: Mid-Apr to Nov: Daily 9:30 a.m.-5 p.m.; check website for additional hours • Admission: $24/adult, $22/senior, $17.50/children (5-12), Children 4 and under and members free • Visitor Accessibility: On-site parking; $5/vehicle except for members. Partially wheelchair accessible. • Greenfield Village includes 83 authentic historic structures, including Noah Webster's home, where he wrote the first American dictionary; Thomas Edison's Menlo Park laboratory; and the courthouse where Abraham Lincoln practiced law. Visitors can ride in a genuine Model T, "pull" glass with world-class artisans, watch 1867 baseball, or ride a train with a 19th-century steam engine.

Dearborn Heights
(Wayne County)

Wallaceville School House
Mailing Address: c/o Department of Parks and Recreation, 1801 N. Beech Daly Rd. • Dearborn Heights, MI 48127
Contact: Richard Ensign,
Phone: (313) 791-3600
Physical Location: Off Ann Arbor Trail, Behind St. Sabina School, 8147 Arnold • Dearborn Heights, MI 48127
Hours: Open by appointment.
About: The Wallaceville Schoolhouse is a city-owned 1876 brick schoolhouse. It is located behind the St. Sabina School off of Ann Arbor Trail, but it is not part of the St. Sabina School. A committee of volunteer teachers offers all-day student field trips, provides demonstrations, and raises funds to support school and programs.
Exhibits/Collections: Historical records of Wallaceville School are retained among Dearborn Heights Historical Archives.
*Information may not be current.

Decatur
(Van Buren County)

Newton House.
Please see entry under Cassopolis: Cass County Historical Commission.

Van Buren Regional Genealogical Society
Mailing Address: P.O. Box 143 • Decatur, MI 49045
Contact: Toni Benson
E-Mail: vbrgs@yahoo.com
Phone: (269) 423-4771 • *Fax:* (269) 423-8373
Physical Location: 200 N. Phelps St. • Decatur, MI 49045
Hours: Mon-Thu 9 a.m.-8 p.m., Fri 9 a.m.-5 p.m., Sat 9 a.m.-3 p.m.
Visitor Accessibility: On-site parking. Wheelchair accessible.
Website: www.vbrgs.org
About: The Van Buren Regional Genealogical Society promotes preservation and research for genealogy and local history, with a focus on Allegan, Berrien, Cass, Kalamazoo, St. Joseph, and Van Buren Counties. The society's collection is housed with the Van Buren District Library Local History Collection.
Exhibits/Collections: SW Michigan Pioneer Certificate Project; SW Michigan Military Registry; SW Michigan yearbooks, city and telephone directories, plat books, vital records, family histories, and court records. Photos and manuscript items.
Annual Events: Meetings 4th Mon monthly (except Dec-Jan).
Publications: Quarterly newsletter (Van Buren Echoes), "Van Burden County, Michigan: A Pictorial History." Visit website for online bookstore.

Delton
(Barry County)

Bernard Historical Society & Museum
Mailing Address: P.O. Box 307 • Delton, MI 49046
Contact: Michelle Rastoskey, President
Phone: (269) 623-3565
Physical Location: 7135 West Delton • Delton, MI 49046
Hours: Jun, Sep: Sun 1-5 p.m.; Jul-Aug: Sat-Sun 1-5 p.m. Also by appointment.
Admission: Donations accepted.
Visitor Accessibility: On-site parking. Wheelchair accessible.
Website: http://www.bernardmuseum.org/
About: The Bernard Historical Society was organized in 1962 based on the historical collection owned by Dr. Prosper Bernard. Today, the society collects and preserves the history of Barry, Hope, Orangeville and Prairieville Townships. The society also maintains a former hospital, 1873 Brown School, implement building, general store, seamstress building, and blacksmith shop.
Exhibits/Collections: More than 25,000 artifacts that include buildings, dugout canoe, farm and household items, and a telephone collection.
Annual Events: Meetings 2nd Tue 7 p.m. (Mar-Jun, Sep-Dec).
*Information may not be current.

DeTour Village
(Chippewa County)

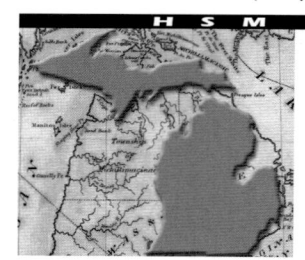

DeTour Passage Historical Museum
HSM MEMBER
Mailing Address: P.O. Box 111 • DeTour Village, MI 49725
Contact: Ruth Ann Hudak
Phone: (906) 297-3231
Physical Location: 104 Elizabeth Street • DeTour, MI 49725
Hours: Daily 1-5 p.m.
Admission: Free.
Visitor Accessibility: Street parking. Wheelchair accessible.
About: The DeTour Passage Historical Museum formed to take possession of the DeTour Light, located at the end of the DeTour Reef, a mile from shore at its nearest point. Today, the museum features displays relating to early marine operations, social and governmental activities, pioneer families, Native-American history, and life in the early years of the DeTour area.
Exhibits/Collections: Displays relating to early marine operations, social and governmental activities, pioneer families.
Annual Events: Community Appreciation Days, Happy Apple Day.
*Information may not be current.

Detroit
(Wayne County)

Archdiocese of Detroit Archives
Mailing Address: 1234 Washington Blvd. • Detroit, MI 48226
Contact: Heidi Christein, Archivist
E-Mail: archives@aod.org
Phone: (313) 237-5846
Hours: 9 a.m.-4 p.m. By appointment only.
Admission: Free.
Visitor Accessibility: Free on-site parking available. Wheelchair accessible. Tour guide available upon request.
Website: www.aod.org

About: The Archdiocese of Detroit Archives serves as the archives of the Roman Catholic Archdiocese of Detroit.

Exhibits/Collections: Manuscripts, photographs, and audiovisual materials. Sacramental records, parish history records, records of closed Catholic schools, the bishops and departments of the six countywide Archdiocese of Detroit, and limited Catholic organizations records.

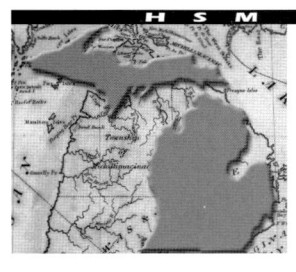

Charles H. Wright Museum of African American History
Mailing Address: 315 E. Warren Ave. • Detroit, MI 48201
Contact: Ted Canaday, Marketing/Communications Director
E-Mail: ted@chwmuseum.org
Phone: (313) 494-5800
Fax: (313) 494-5855
Hours: Tue-Sat 9 a.m.-5 p.m.; Sun 1-5 p.m.
Admission: $8/adult (13-61), $5/senior (62+), $5/youth (3-12), Members and children under 3 free.
Visitor Accessibility: On-site and street parking. Wheelchair accessible. Guided tours available.
Website: www.thewright.org
About: Founded in 1965, the Charles H. Wright Museum of African American History is the world's largest institution dedicated to the African-American experience. The museum provides learning opportunities, exhibitions, programs, and events based on collections and research that explore the diverse history and culture of African Americans and their African origins.
Exhibits/Collections: The Library and Research Center houses more than 35,000 artifacts and is home to the Blanche Coggin Underground Railroad Collection, Harriet Tubman Museum Collection, Coleman A. Young Collection, and Sheffield Collection.
Annual Events: Martin Luther King, Jr. Day (Jan), Black History Month (Feb), Women's History Month (Mar), Poetry and Spoken Word Month (Apr), Ford Freedom Awards (May), Malcolm X Day (May), Black Music Month (Jun), Concert of Colors (Jul), African World Festival (Aug), The Wright Gala (Sep), Noel Night (Dec), Kwanzaa (Dec). Association for the Study of African American Life & History (ASALH) organizing branch of Detroit meets 3rd Wed monthly 6 p.m. at the museum.
Publications: Quarterly membership/visitor newsletter (The Wright Times).
Information may not be current.

Detroit Historic Designation Advisory Board
Mailing Address: 204 Coleman A. Young Municipal Center, 2 Woodward Ave. • Detroit, MI 48226
Contact: Patricia Cagle
Phone: (313) 224-3487 • *Fax:* (313) 224-6110
About: Advises City Council on matters relating to historic preservation and proposals for the designation of local historic districts. Provides citizens with assistance in preservation questions and problems, and serves as a resource to community in matters pertaining to historic buildings.
Information may not be current.

Detroit Historic District Commission
Mailing Address: 65 Cadillac Square, Suite 1300 • Detroit, MI 48226
Contact: Susan McBride
E-Mail: smcbride@detroitmi.gov
Phone: (313) 224-6536 • *Fax:* (313) 224-1310
Hours: Mon-Fri 9 a.m.-5 p.m.
Admission: Free.
Visitor Accessibility: Private parking lots ($20/day), steet parking (meters starts at $0.25/15 minutes). Wheelchair accessible.
Website: www.detroitmi.gov/historic
About: The Detroit Historic Designation Advisory Board advises the city council on matters relating to historic preservation and proposals for the designation of local historic districts. The board also provides citizens with assistance in preservation questions and problems, and serves as a resource to community in matters pertaining to historic buildings.
Exhibits/Collections: Files pertaining to every address that is locally designated historic. This includes the date each district is designated and a baseline photo/slide of the property.
Annual Events: Meetings: 2nd Wed monthly at 5:30 p.m. in the auditorium (13th floor) of the Coleman A. Young Municipal Center.
Information may not be current.

Detroit Historical Society
Mailing Address: 5401 Woodward Ave. • Detroit, MI 48202
Contact: Bob Sadler, Director of Marketing & Sales
E-Mail: bobsadler@detroithistorical.org
Phone: (313) 833-7935
Fax: (313) 833-5342
Site/Location: **Detroit Historical Museum**
Hours: Call for current hours.
Admission: Free.
Visitor Accessibility: Self-guided.
Website: www.detroithistorical.org
About: Established in 1921, the Detroit Historical Society's mission is to educate and inspire our community and visitors by preserving and portraying our region's shared history through dynamic exhibits and experiences. The society is responsible for the overall management and operations of the Detroit Historical Museum, the Dossin Great Lakes Museum, and a collection of more than 250,000 artifacts.
Exhibits/Collections: More than 250,000 artifacts representing social history of metropolitan Detroit over the past 300 years: costumes, decorative arts, toys, Native-American artifacts, industrial and automotive history, maritime history, sports memorabilia, and domestic life.
Annual Events: African American History Day (Feb), Treats in the Streets (Oct), Noel Night (Dec).
Other Sites/Locations: **Dossin Great Lakes Museum** • Location: 100 Strand Dr., Belle Isle, Detroit, MI 48207 • Hours: Sat-Sun 11 a.m.-4 p.m. • Admission: Free • Visitor Accessibility: Free on-site and street parking. Wheelchair accessible. Self-guided. • Permanent exhibits include Built by the River, the Miss Pepsi vintage 1950s championship hydroplane, the Gothic Room from the City of Detroit III, a bow anchor from the S.S. Edmund Fitzgerald, the pilothouse from the S.S. William Clay Ford, and one of the largest known collections of scale model ships in the world.

Detroit Public Library
Mailing Address: Detroit Public Library, 5201 Woodward Ave. • Detroit, MI 48202
Contact: Mark Bowden, Coordinator of Special Collections
E-Mail: bhc@detroitpubliclibrary.org
Phone: (313) 481-1401
Fax: (313) 481-1475
Site/Location: **Burton Historical Collection**
Hours: Tue-Wed 12 p.m.-8 p.m., Thu-Sat 10 a.m.-6 p.m.
Admission: Free.
Visitor Accessibility: Metered street parking. Wheelchair accessible.

❊ Historical Society of Michigan

Website: www.detroitpubliclibrary.org

About: The Burton Historical Collection began as the private collection of Detroit attorney Clarence M. Burton. The collection built upon its foundation of Detroit history to also include the history of the Old Northwest, New France, and Canada. The collection is located on the first floor of the Detroit Public Library.

Exhibits/Collections: Books, pamphlets, bound newspapers, atlases, maps, pictures, photographs, and ephemeral. Personal papers; records of organizations, businesses, and churches; and the governmental archives of Detroit and Wayne County. Genealogical materials.

Annual Events: Family History Festival (Sep).

Detroit Society for Genealogical Research, Inc.

Mailing Address: c/o Burton Historical Collection, DP Library, 5201 Woodward Ave. • Detroit, MI 48202
Contact: Richard Doherty, President
Phone: (313) 481-1395 • *Fax:* (313) 481-1475
Website: http://www.dsgr.org
About: The Detroit Society for Genealogical Research was organized in 1936.
Annual Events: Meetings 2nd Sat of month Sep-Jun at Detroit Public Library. Times vary, visit website for details.
Publications: Quarterly genealogy magazine.

El Museo del Norte

Mailing Address: 412 W Grand Blvd • Detroit, MI 48216
E-Mail: elmuseodelnorte@gmail.com
Website: http://www.elmuseodelnorte.org/
Information may not be current.

Ford Piquette Avenue Plant

Mailing Address: P.O. Box 2127 • Detroit, MI 48202
Contact: Nancy Darga, Executive Director
E-Mail: nancy.darga@tplex.org
Phone: (313) 872-8759
Physical Location: 461 Piquette Avenue • Detroit, MI 48202
Hours: Apr-Oct: Wed-Fri 10 a.m.-4 p.m., Sat 9 a.m.-4 p.m., Sun 12 p.m.-4 p.m.
Admission: $10/adult, $8/senior, $5/student (w/ID).
Visitor Accessibility: Free parking. Wheelchair accessible. Guides available.
Website: www.tplex.org
About: Ford Piquette Avenue Plant is dedicated to preservation of the 1904 Piquette Avenue Plant, the first factory owned/built by Ford Motor Company (1904-1910) and the birthplace of the Model T Ford. The 67,000-square-foot, three-story plant is located in the Milwaukee Junction Industrial District, the birthplace of Detroit's auto industry. This National Historic Landmark is listed on the U.S. Department of Interior Registered Historic Places and State Register of Historic Sites.
Exhibits/Collections: Changing exhibits and vintage vehicles tell the story of Ford Motor Company during Piquette Era.
Annual Events: City Fest (Jul).

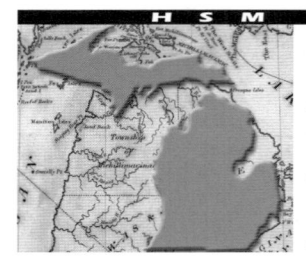

Fred Hart Williams Genealogical Society

Mailing Address: Detroit Public Library—Burton Historical Collection, 5201 Woodward Ave. • Detroit, MI 48202
Contact: Leslie Williams, President
E-Mail: fhwgsmail@yahoo.com
Website: www.fhwgs.org
About: The Fred Hart Williams Genealogical Society was organized in 1979 to increase interest in African-American family history and genealogical research. The society sponsors educational programs and research workshops and takes field trips to examine historical sites and collections of family history records. The society also collects, preserves, and makes available manuscripts, documents, genealogical records and historical materials.
Information may not be current.

Hellenic Museum of Michigan

Mailing Address: 67 E. Kirby • Detroit, MI 48202
Contact: Sam Constantine, President
E-Mail: hellenicmi@gmail.com
Phone: (313) 871-4100
Hours: Sat 12-4 p.m.
Visitor Accessibility: Metered street parking. Partially wheelchair accessible; first floor only. Self-guided.
Website: http://www.hellenicmi.org/
About: The Hellenic Museum of Michigan strives to share the struggles, triumphs, and contributions of the vibrant Greek immigrant community not only in Detroit but across the state of Michigan as well. Our mission is to share the richness of Hellenic heritage and conserve the contributions of Hellenic culture in shaping our world today and in the future.
Exhibits/Collections: Musical instruments, paintings, photogrpahs, period clothing, pottery, and artwork relating to Greek-American life.
Annual Events: Kefi Dinner (Thu Jun-Aug), Noel Night (Dec).

Historic Boston-Edison Association

Mailing Address: P.O. Box 02100 • Detroit, MI 48202
Contact: Pamela Miller Malone,
E-Mail: bostonedison@gmail.com
Phone: (313) 883-4360
Website: www.historicbostonedison.com
About: Formed in 1921, the Historic Boston-Edison Association is one of the oldest continuously operating neighborhood associations in Michigan. The association is dedicated to preserving the historical and architectural integrity of more than 900 homes in the Boston-Edison Historic District. It educates residents and the public about the district and the importance of historic preservation. Information about driving and walking tours is available on website.
Annual Events: Annual dinner meeting (May), Attic Sale (Aug), Holiday Homes Tour (Dec). Meetings at Sacred Heart Seminary, Chicago & Linwood, Detroit (Mar, Oct).
Information may not be current.

Michigan History Directory

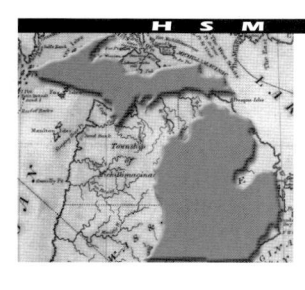

Historic Elmwood Cemetery
Mailing Address: 1200 Elmwood Ave. • Detroit, MI 48207
Contact: Joan Capuano, Executive Director
Phone: (313) 567-3453
Fax: (313) 567-8861
Hours: Winter: 8 a.m.-4 p.m. summer: 7 a.m.-7 p.m.
Admission: Free.
Visitor Accessibility: On-site parking. Wheelchair accessible. Tours available May-Nov.
Website: www.elmwoodhistoriccemetery.org
About: The Elmwood Historic Cemetery is the oldest non-denominational cemetery in the state. The site features an extensive arboretum, as well as many monuments for prominent Detroiters dating back to the 1800s.
Annual Events: Ceremonies on Veterans Day, Arbor Day, Memorial Day. African American Heritage Tours (Feb).

Historic Fort Wayne.
Please see entry under Columbiaville: Historic Fort Wayne Coalition.

Historical Society for the U.S. District Court
Mailing Address: Theodore Levin U.S. Courthouse, 231 W. Lafayette • Detroit, MI 48226
Contact: Judith Christie, Executive Director
E-Mail: jkchristie@hotmail.com
Phone: 313-234-5049
Site/Location: Theodore Levin U.S. Courthouse
Hours: Mon-Fri 8:30 a.m.-5 p.m.
Admission: Free.
Visitor Accessibility: Metered street parking. Wheelchair accessible. Self-guided.
About: The society was formed in 1992 to preserve the history of the United States District Court for the Eastern District of Michigan. The program includes assisting federal district judges in preserving their records and personal papers and sponsorship of publications and exhibitions relating to the history of the court. The society operates a museum space in the Theodore Levin U.S. Courthouse. Exhibits feature important cases and historic photographs and artifacts.
Exhibits/Collections: Oral histories of federal judges available for research by request from responsible researchers. Contact for further information.
Annual Events: Annual Meeting (Nov), Quarterly Board of Trustees Meeting.
Publications: The Court Legacy newsletter. "The United States District Court for the Eastern District of Michigan: People, Law and Politics."

Indian Village Historical Collections
Mailing Address: P.O. Box 14340 • Detroit, MI 48214
Contact: Dot Martin
E-Mail: damartin48214@att.net
Phone: (586) 482-7150
Hours: By appointment.
Admission: Free.
Visitor Accessibility: Free on-site parking. Not wheelchair accessible. Tour guides available; call ahead for an appointment.
Website: http://www.historicindianvillage.org/
About: The Indian Village Historical Collections researches and records the history of the homes and residents of Detroit's Indian Village, which includes 351 homes built from 1895 to 1966. It is listed on the National Register of Historic Places and on the Michigan State Register of Historic Sites and is designated a Historic District by the City of Detroit.
Annual Events: Home and Garden Tour (Jun).
Publications: Neighborhood newsletter (Smoke Signals).

Irish Genealogical Society of Michigan
Mailing Address: 2068 Michigan Ave. • Detroit, MI 48216
Contact: Dave Keem, President
E-Mail: president@miigsm.org
Phone: (734) 287-3143
Visitor Accessibility: Free on-site parking. Wheelchair accessible. Self-guided.
Website: http://miigsm.org
About: The Irish Genealogical Society of Michigan focuses on genealogical research in all 32 counties of the Emerald Isle.

Lawrence Fisher Mansion
Mailing Address: 383 Lenox St. • Detroit, MI 48215
Phone: (313) 331-6740
Hours: Tours: Sat-Sun 10 a.m.-9 p.m.
Admission: $5/individual.
About: Designed in 1927 by theatre architect C. Howard Crane for auto tycoon Lawrence Fisher, the Lawrence Fisher Mansion now serves as the Bhaktivedanta Cultural Center of the Hare Krishna group.

Michigan Archival Association
Mailing Address: Walter P. Reuther Library, 5401 Cass Ave. • Detroit, MI 48202
Contact: Kristen Chinery, President
E-Mail: ac9538@wayne.edu
Phone: (313) 577-8377
Website: http://miarchivists.wordpress.com/
About: The Michigan Archival Association is a membership organization devoted to promoting archival activities and interests in the state. The association offers professional and educational opportunities within Michigan and cooperates with regional and national archival organizations in matters of mutual interest.
Annual Events: Annual meeting (Jun).
Publications: Newsletter (Open Entry).

Michigan Labor History Society
Mailing Address: c/o Walter P. Reuther Library, 5401 Cass Ave. • Detroit, MI 48202
Contact: Alberta Asmar, Secretary
E-Mail: ad3196@wayne.edu
Phone: (313) 577-4003 • *Fax:* (313) 577-4300
Hours: Call or see website for current hours.
Visitor Accessibility: Wheelchair accessible. Tour guides available by appointment.
Website: http://mlhs.wayne.edu
About: Fosters interest, understanding, and research regarding the contributions made by working men and women of Michigan. Disseminates labor history information to encourage public interest. Supports the endeavors of professional archival institutions in Michigan.
Annual Events: Annual Membership Meeting, Annual Labor Day Mobilization Lunch (Aug). Officers and Programs Committee Meetings: Locations and times vary.
Publications: Newsletter (Looking Back-Moving Forward).

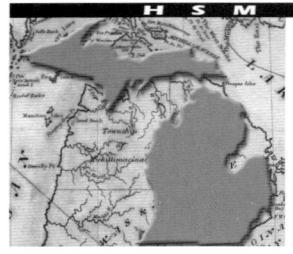

Historical Society of Michigan

MotorCities National Heritage Area
Mailing Address: 200 Renaissance Circle, Suite 3148 • Detroit, MI 48243
Contact: Lisa Ambriez, Outreach Coordinator
E-Mail: lambriez@motorcities.org
Phone: (313) 259-3425, ext. 302
Fax: (313) 259-5254
Hours: Mon-Fri 8 a.m.-5 p.m.
Visitor Accessibility: Off-site parking. Wheechair accessible.
Website: www.motorcities.org
About: The MotorCities National Heritage Area encourages economic revitalization through preservation, tourism, and the development of educational and interpretive programs that tell the story of the American automobile industry and labor in the region.
Annual Events: Autopalooza (May-Sep), Annual Meeting (Apr). Board meets bi-monthly; Stewardship Council public meetings are held quarterly.
Publications: MotorCities (Story of the Week).
Information may not be current.

Motown Historical Museum
Mailing Address: 2648 W. Grand Blvd. • Detroit, MI 48208
Contact: Allen Rawls, CEO
E-Mail: arawls@motownmuseum.org
Phone: (313) 875-2264
Fax: (313) 875-2267
Hours: Tue-Sat 10 a.m.-6 p.m.
Admission: Call for current prices.
Visitor Accessibility: Free street parking. Wheelchair accessible. Tours included in price of admission.
Website: www.motownmuseum.org
About: The Motown Museum, which was founded by Esther Gordy Edwards in 1985, is one of Southeast Michigan's most popular tourist destinations. Visitors come from across America and throughout the world to stand in Studio A, where their favorite artists and groups recorded much-loved music and to view the restored upper flat where Berry Gordy lived with his young family during the company's earliest days.
Exhibits/Collections: Home to an extensive array of Motown artifacts, photographs and other memorabilia. The Museum features the original Hitsville U.S.A. building, a permanent gallery, a special gallery that changes annually, and Studio.
Annual Events: Esther Gordy Edwards Community Day (Apr), Motown EDU: Learning In the Key of Life, Motown MIC: Spoken Word Competition, Studio DNA.

National Automotive History Collection
Mailing Address: Skillman Branch Detroit Public Library, 121 Gratiot Ave. • Detroit, MI 48226
Phone: (313) 628-2851 • *Fax:* (313) 628-2785
Hours: Memorial Day-Labor Day: Mon-Fri 10 a.m.-6 p.m. Labor Day-Memorial Day: Mon-Thu, Sat 10 a.m.-6 p.m.
Admission: Researchers living outside of Detroit must have $10/individual day pass or $100/inidividual annual library card.
Website: www.detroitpubliclibrary.org
About: The National Automotive History Collection at the Detroit Public Library is regarded as the nation's premier automotive archive. The collection documents the history and development of the automobile in the United States and abroad.
Exhibits/Collections: Books, periodicals, automotive art, photographs, factory service manuals, sales brochures, advertisements, owners manuals, historical documents and manuscript collections, including papers of William and Semon Knudsen, Charles Brady King, and Henry Leland.
Annual Events: Holiday for selection of "Collectible Car of the Future."
Publications: Periodic Friends of the NAHC publication, Wheels: Journal of the National Automotive History Collection.

Pewabic Pottery
Mailing Address: 10125 E. Jefferson Ave. • Detroit, MI 48214
Contact: Terese Ireland, Executive Director
E-Mail: pewabic1@pewabic.org
Phone: (313) 822-0954 • *Fax:* (313) 822-3477
Hours: Mon-Sat 10 a.m.-6 p.m., Sun 12-4 p.m.
Admission: Free.
Visitor Accessibility: On-site parking. Tour guide available upon request ($5/person, 20 person miniumum).
Website: www.pewabic.org
About: Founded in 1903 during the Arts and Crafts Movement, Pewabic Pottery is nationally renowned for its tile and pottery in unique glazes. Today, it is a nonprofit design museum, store, and education center that provides classes and workshops for all skill levels.
Exhibits/Collections: Collection dedicated to works by and about founder Mary Chase Stratton and Pewabic Pottery. Archival collection of her business records, architectural renderings, articles, notes, and books.
Annual Events: Garden Party (Jun), Earthy Treasures (winter)
Information may not be current.

Polish Genealogical Society of Michigan
Mailing Address: Burton-Detroit Public Library, 5201 Woodward Ave. • Detroit, MI 48202
Contact: Valerie Koselka
E-Mail: nfo@pgsm.org
Website: www.pgsm.org
About: The Polish Genealogical Society of Michigan promotes and encourages research in Polish genealogy, as well as the preservation of historical materials which aid in the documentations of family histories. PGSM is dedicated to educating its members and the public on Polish Genealogy, genealogical research methods and techniques, and the Polish culture.
Annual Events: October Seminar. Meetings: 3rd Sat monthly (except Jan, Feb, July, Aug, Dec). Locations vary. Annual Seminar at the American Polish Cultural Center in Troy. Includes renowned Polish speakers and a Polish lunch.
Publications: The Polish Eaglet, a triennial membership publication. "News from the Nest," published in between mailings of The Eaglet.

Preservation Detroit
Mailing Address: 4735 Cass Ave. • Detroit, MI 48202
Contact: Claire Nowak-Boyd, Executive Director
E-Mail: info@preservationdetroit.org
Phone: (313) 577-3559
Hours: Mon, Tue, Thu 12-5 p.m.
Visitor Accessibility: On-site parking, street parking for a fee. Walking tours available May-Sep; visit website for details.
Website: www.preservationdetroit.org
About: Since 1975, Preservation Detroit is dedicated to promoting, preserving, and protecting Detroit's architectural and cultural heritage through education and advocacy. We also have regular tours, lectures, and special events.
Annual Events: Theatre Tour, Membership Event, Awards Event, Bootlegging Boat Tour, Historic Cemetery Tours (Oct), Detroit Heritage Walking Tours (weekly).

Michigan History Directory

Tuskegee Airmen National Museum.
Please see entry under Columbiaville: Historic Fort Wayne Coalition.

Ukrainian American Archives & Museum
Mailing Address: 11756 Charest St. • Detroit, MI 48212
Contact: Chrystyna Nykorak, Executive Director
E-Mail: ukrainianmuseum@sbcglobal.net
Phone: (313) 366-9764
Hours: Tue-Fri 9 a.m.-5 p.m. Also by appointment.
Admission: $3/individual.
Visitor Accessibility: Free street parking. Not wheelchair accessible. Tour guide available by donation.
Website: www.ukrainianmuseumdetroit.org
About: The Ukrainian American Archives & Museum opened in 1958 to educate and inform the general public about the culture, art, and history of Ukrainians; their immigration to the United States; and their contributions to America. Exhibits include paintings, famous personalities, costumes, lectures, artist exhibits, sculptures, and pottery. The organization also sponsors public programs to preserve the heritage of Ukrainian Americans.
Exhibits/Collections: Artifacts include folk and ethnic costumes, headdresses, woodcarvings, ceramics, paintings, Easter eggs, musical instruments, historic photos, coins, stamps, and medals. Immigration history, oral histories, films, videos, and books.
Annual Events: Board meets bimonthly at museum or Ukrainian Cultural Center in Warren.
Publications: Quarterly member newsletter (Info).

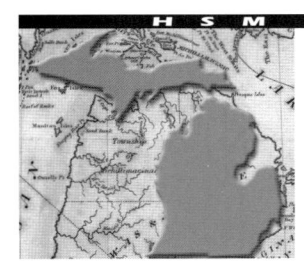

University of Detroit Mercy Library
Mailing Address: Acquisitions & Receiving, 4001 W. McNichols Rd. • Detroit, MI 48221
Contact: Patricia Higo, Archive and Special Collections Libraria
E-Mail: edesk@udmercy.edu
Phone: (313) 578-0435
Fax: (313) 993-1780
Hours: Mon-Fri 8 a.m.-5 p.m. Marine Historical Collection open by appointment only.
Visitor Accessibility: Free on-site parking. Wheelchair accessible. Tour guide available.
Website: http://research.udmercy.edu/
About: The Fr. Edward J. Dowling, S.J., Marine Historical Collection, which was donated to the University of Detroit Mercy in 1993, is considered one of the most complete private collections of information on the subject of Great Lakes marine history. The collection consists of close to 58,000 photographs, plastic and glass negatives, postcards, color plates, sketches, and paintings, as well as detailed information on nearly every commercial ship that sailed the Great Lakes since 1850.
Exhibits/Collections: Extensive collection. For complete list, see website.

DeWitt
(Clinton County)

Clinton County Historical Commission
Mailing Address: 310 W. Washington St. • DeWitt, MI 48820
Contact: Ken Coin, Chairman
Phone: (517) 669-0960
*Information may not be current.

Dexter
(Washtenaw County)

Dexter Area Historical Society
Mailing Address: 3443 Inverness St. • Dexter, MI 48130
Contact: Bene Fusilier, President
E-Mail: dexmuseum@aol.com
Phone: (734) 426-2519
Site/Location: Dexter Area Museum
Hours: May-Nov: Fri-Sat 1 p.m.-3 p.m.
Admission: Free.
Visitor Accessibility: Free on-site parking. Not wheelchair accessible. Self-guided.
Website: www.dextermuseum.org
About: Founded in 1971, the Dexter Area Historical Society acquired the old St. Andrews Church (b. 1883) and had it moved to its present location, where it now serves as the society's museum. Displays include furniture, clothing, toys, medical equipment, a dentist office, military artifacts from Civil War to WWII, a carriage, farm implements, school materials, and a model railroad layout replicating the Village of Dexter.
Exhibits/Collections: Doll collection, artifacts of Dexter's founder, Judge Samuel W. Dexter. Genealogical and local history library has photos; business, organization, and building records; maps; and cemetery records. Local land records and church records.
Annual Events: Dexter Artisan Fair (Mar), Civil War Days at Gordon Hall (Jun), Christmas at the Mansion (Dec), and Holiday Bazaar at the Museum (Dec). Board meetings 1st Thu Oct-May (except Jan), 7:30 p.m. in museum. Also 1st Thu Jun-Sep, 7:30 p.m. at Gordon Hall.
Publications: Quarterly newsletter. "Samuel William Dexter," "Voice of the Past: The Saga of Gordon Hall."
Other Sites/Locations: **Gordon Hall** • Location: 8347 Island Lake Road, Dexter, MI 48130 • Visitor Accessibility: Free on-site parking. Partially wheelchair accessible, first floor only. Tour guide available during Dexter Days in Aug for $5/individual. Group tours also available by appointment for a donation. • Built in 1843 for Judge Samuel Dexter, Gordon Hall was once known as one of the most beautiful Greek Revival buildings in Michigan. It was donated to the University of Michigan in 1950 to be used as an apartment building. In 2005, the society acquired the building and now provides tours discussing its history.

Dorr
(Allegan County)

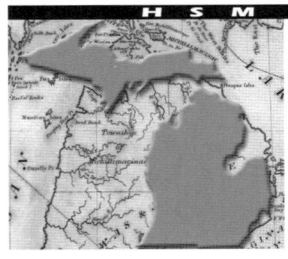

Then & Now Genealogical Library of Allegan County
Mailing Address: P.O. Box 389 • Dorr, MI 49323
Contact: Linda Stoepker
E-Mail: thenandnow1807@yahoo.com
Phone: (616) 681-0333
Physical Location: 1807 142nd Ave. • Dorr, MI 49323
Hours: Wed 1-5 p.m.; Sat 10 a.m.-3 p.m.
Admission: Free.
Visitor Accessibility: On-site parking. Wheelchair accessible.
Website: www.rootsweb.ancestry.com/~mitanhgs/
About: The Then & Now Genealogical Library of Allegan County collects, preserves, and displays the history of Allegan in records, obits, and articles for historical and genealogical research.
Exhibits/Collections: Family histories, obituaries, farm histories, photographs, township and county histories,

atlases, directories, local business information, church, cemetery and tax records, and military records.
Annual Events: Meetings 2nd Tue monthly, 7 p.m. at library.
Publications: Quarterly newsletter (History of Moline), 1864 plat map of Allegan County, photo calendar.

Douglas
(Allegan County)

Saugatuck-Douglas Historical Society
Mailing Address: P.O. Box 617 • Douglas, MI 49406
Contact: Fred Schmidt
E-Mail: fnschmidt@wmol.com
Phone: (269) 857-5751
Site/Location: History Center (The Old Schoolhouse)
Physical Location: 130 Center Street • Douglas, MI 49406
Hours: Call or visit website for current hours.
Admission: Donations accepted.
Visitor Accessibility: Lot and street parking. Wheelchair accessible. E-mail for tour information.
Website: www.sdhistoricalsociety.org
About: The Saugatuck-Douglas Historical Society discovers, procures, and preserves items relating to the civil, religious, social, cultural, and natural history of Saugatuck, Douglas, and the surrounding area. The 1866 Old School House (the Douglas Union School) is the oldest multi-classroom school building in Michigan. Today, it is used as a "History Center," and its attractions include a lifeboat exhibit, back-in-time garden, history room, archives, and more.
Exhibits/Collections: More than 10,000 photographs and paper materials. Website includes extensive collection of materials on local history.
Annual Events: Annual Exhibition at Pump House Museum (Memorial Day-Oct), Heritage Festival (Sep), Tuesday Talks (Jul-Aug). Meetings 2nd Wed Feb-Nov at 7 p.m.
Publications: Published 10 books pertaining to local history.
Other Sites/Locations: The Pumphouse Museum • Location: 735 Park Street, Saugatuck • Hours: Memorial Day-Aug: Sun-Sat 12-4 p.m.; Sep-Oct: Sat-Sun • Admission: Donations accepted • Visitor Accessibility: Free on-site parking. • The museum's building was originally built as the city of Saugatuck's first water-pumping station, completed in 1904. The main gallery features changing exhibits that cover everything from shipwrecks and dancing to artists and gangsters.

Dowagiac
(Cass County)

Dowagiac Area History Museum
Mailing Address: P.O. Box 430 • Dowagiac, MI 49047
Contact: Steve Arseneau, Director
E-Mail: museum@dowagiac.org
Phone: (269) 783-2560
Physical Location: 201 E. Division St. • Dowagiac, MI 49047
Hours: Tue-Fri 10 a.m.-5 p.m., Sat 11 a.m.-3 p.m.
Admission: Free.
Visitor Accessibility: Free on-site and street parking. Wheelchair accessible. Self-guided.
Website: www.dowagiacmuseum.info

About: The Dowagiac Area History Museum educates visitors about the history of the Cass County-Sister Lakes area. The museum provides exhibits, school tours, and public programming. The facility is 4,000 square feet of exhibit space on two floors, with exhibits including "Industrial Dowagiac," a model train set of 1920 Dowagiac, the Round Oak Stove Company, Heddon Bait Company, Underground Railroad, Potawatomi Indians, and early settlement. "Small Town, Big World" examines locals who impacted the world.
Exhibits/Collections: Dowagiac and Cass County photos, records and artifacts; Round Oak Stove Company; Heddon Bait Company; test pilot Captain Iven Kincheloe; journalist Webb Miller.
Publications: "Indentification and Dating of Round Oak Heating Stoves."

Heddon Museum
Mailing Address: 204 W. Telegraph St. • Dowagiac, MI 49047
Contact: Joan Lyons, Co-Curator
E-Mail: heddonmuseum@lyonsindustries.com
Phone: (269) 782-4068
Physical Location: 414 West St. • Dowagiac, MI 49047
Hours: Tue 6:30-8:30 p.m., last Sun monthly 1:30-4 p.m. Also by appointment.
Admission: Donations accepted.
Visitor Accessibility: Free on-site and street parking. Wheelchair accessible. Tour guides available; donations accepted from large groups.
Website: www.heddonmuseum.org
About: Located in the old Heddon factory, the Heddon Museum is dedicated to preserving the history of the James Heddon family's many contributions to the fishing tackle industry, the city of Dowagiac, and the world. On display are more than 1,000 Heddon lures, 140 reels, and 150 Heddon rods, including an original James Heddon frog, one of the most sought after of all collector lures. Other highlights include the Heddon truck, a Heddon boat, and a second room showing some classic cars and car-related memorabilia.
Exhibits/Collections: Photographs of former employees and research library available.

Historic Association of Dowagiac
Mailing Address: 307 Center Street • Dowagiac, MI 49047
*Information may not be current.

Drummond Island
(Chippewa County)

DeTour Reef Light Preservation Society
Mailing Address: P.O. Box 307 • Drummond Island, MI 49726
Contact: Ann Method Green, President
E-Mail: drlps@drlps.com
Phone: (906) 493-6303
Site/Location: DeTour Reef Light
Hours: Summer: By appointment.
Admission: $95/tour ($75 to DRLPS members). Children accompanied by parent or guardian receive 50 percent discount.
Visitor Accessibility: Free on-site parking. Not wheelchair accessible. Guided tours.

Michigan History Directory

Website: www.drlps.com

About: The DeTour Reef Light, completed in 1931, is a significant monument to Michigan's maritime history in the areas of maritime history, transportation, and architecture. It has been listed on the National Register of Historic Places since 2004. It exemplifies the distinctive architectural characteristics of an early-20th-century Great Lakes crib foundation lighthouse. Located where the St. Marys River joins Lake Huron at the south end of DeTour Passage, the lighthouse has been an important aid to navigation throughout its.

Exhibits/Collections: Oral history interviews of five previous lighthouse keepers available at libraries in DeTour Village and Drummond Island. Copies of original lighthouse logbooks at the DeTour Village Public Library.

Annual Events: Weekend Light Keeper Prgroam (Jun-Aug), Father's Day Cruise on the St. Marys River, Evening Under the Stars.

Publications: "DeTour Reef Light: History, Restoration, and Preservation of an Offshore Michigan Lighthouse."

Drummond Island Historical Museum
Mailing Address: PO Box 293 • Drummond Island, MI 49726
Phone: (906) 493-5746
Hours: Jun-Oct: Daily 1-5 p.m.
Website: http://www.drummondislandchamber.com/index.php?page=Historic

About: "Hands-On Museum" of history of early settlers, plus Native-American and Finnish artifacts. Fort Drummond display of the British era, marine and sportsman's exhibits, and a display of the early lumbering era. The museum is constructed of hand-hewn Drummond Island logs.

Annual Events: Meetings 2nd Mon monthly at Drummond Island Museum.

*Information may not be current.

Dryden
(Lapeer County)

HSM MEMBER

Dryden Historical Society
Mailing Address: P.O. Box 93 • Dryden, MI 48428
Contact: Jan Chisnell
E-Mail: drydenhistoricalsociety@gmail.com
Phone: (810) 796-3611
Site/Location: **Dryden Historical Depot**
Physical Location: 5488 Main St. • Dryden, MI 48428
Hours: Mon 5:30-7 p.m. Also by appointment. Closed Jan-Apr.
Admission: Donations accepted.
Website: www.drydenhistoricalsociety.webs.com

About: The Dryden Historical Society preserves the history and artifacts of Dryden and its surrounding community. Built in 1883, the Dryden Historical Depot moved to its current location in 1970 and is now used as a museum by the Dryden Historical Society.

Exhibits/Collections: Large collection of historical photos, graduation information from Dryden High School 1881-2013, depot museum, and General Squier's personal effects display.

Annual Events: Plant Sale (May), Christmas Cookie Sale (Dec), Quilt Raffle.

Publications: Annual newsletter.

Dundee
(Monroe County)

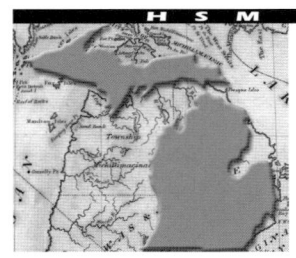

HSM MEMBER

Historical Preservation Society of Dundee
Mailing Address: 242 Toledo St. • Dundee, MI 48131
Contact: Shirley Massingill, Administrative Director
E-Mail: museum@dundeeoldmill.com
Phone: (734) 529-8596
Site/Location: **Old Mill Museum**
Hours: Fri-Mon 12-4 p.m.
Admission: Donations accepted.
Visitor Accessibility: Free on-site parking. Wheelchair accessible. Tour guide available; call ahead to schedule a group tour.
Website: www.dundeeoldmill.com

D

About: The Historical Preservation Society of Dundee preserves and shares the history of Dundee and surrounding areas using exhibits chronicling local history at the Old Mill Museum. Exhibits consider the Ford Village Industries, farm and small-town life in the 19th and 20th centuries, and Native-American life on the Macon Reserve. The museum hosts paranormal tours by reservation on Friday and Saturday nights. The Old Mill Museum displays historical papers/artifacts from the Dundee area, with a primary focus on 1900-1950.

Exhibits/Collections: Early-20th-century household items; Native-American tools, reproductions, and beadwork; photographs; yearbooks; scrapbooks; and obituaries.

Annual Events: '80s Dance Party (Jan), Easter Bunny Brunch (Feb), Women's Expo, Jazz at the Mill (May), Mayfly Music Festival (Jun), Children's Halloween Party, Chocolate Bingo (Oct), Lunch and Crafts with Mrs. Claus (Nov), Paranormal Book Signing and Tours (Jun-Aug), Paranormal Convention (Nov). Board meetings 1st Mon monthly, 6:30 p.m. at the museum.

Publications: "Images of America: Dundee."

Durand
(Shiawassee County)

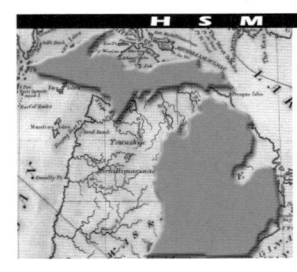

HSM MEMBER

Durand Union Station, Inc.
Mailing Address: P.O. Box 106 • Durand, MI 48429
Contact: Mary Warner-Stone
E-Mail: dusi@durandstation.org
Phone: (989) 288-3561
Fax: (989) 288-3494
Site/Location: **Michigan Railroad History Museum**
Physical Location: 200 Railroad St. • Durand, MI 48429
Hours: Tue-Thu, Sun 1-5 p.m.; Fri-Sat 10 a.m.-5 p.m.
Admission: Free.
Visitor Accessibility: On-site parking. Wheelchair accessible. Tour guides available, group tours by appointment.
Website: www.durandstation.org

About: The Michigan Railroad History Museum supports the rehabilitation, development, and maintenance of the Durand Union Station. The museum collects, preserves, and interprets artifacts, records, and documents related to history of railroads and railroading in Michigan. It engages in activities that encourage interest in railroad industry and is a source of information on railroad groups and structures throughout Michigan.

Exhibits/Collections: Variety of print, graphic, and railroading resources.
Annual Events: Railroad Days (May), Christmas Event (Dec).
Publications: Monthly newsletter (The Conductor).

*Information may not be current.

❋ 55 ❋

Historical Society of Michigan

Eagle Harbor
(Keweenaw County)

Keweenaw County Historical Society
Mailing Address: 670 Lighthouse Rd. • Eagle Harbor, MI 49950
Contact: Virginia Jamison, President
E-Mail: vjamison@pasty.com
Phone: (906) 289-4990
Fax: (906) 289-4911
Site/Location: Eagle Harbor Lighthouse Complex
Hours: Jul-Aug: Mon-Sat 10 a.m.-5 p.m. Jun, Sep-Oct: Sun 12-5 p.m.
Admission: $4/adult.
Website: www.keweenawhistory.org
About: Organized in 1981, the Keweenaw County Historical Society maintains the Eagle Harbor Lighthouse Complex, which includes an 1871 light station and museums pertaining to maritime, mining, life-saving, and commercial fishing history. Heritage Site of Keweenaw National Historical Park.
Publications: Quarterly newsletter (The Superior Signal).
Other Sites/Locations: **Rathbone School** • Location: 200 Center Street • Hours: Jun-Oct • Admission: Donations accepted • Exhibits in restored 1853 Eagle Harbor School commemorate birthplace of Knights of Pythias, fraternal order founded by Justus H. Rathbone in the 1860s.
Central Mine Village • Location: US-41 at Central Road • Hours: Visitor Center open in summer • Admission: by donation • Mine opened in 1854, closed 1898. Society acquired former company town in 1996. Annual reunion of Central families' descendents; reunion in 1868 Methodist Church last Sun of Jul.
Bammert Blacksmith Shop and Phoenix Church • Location: MI-26 and US-41, Phoenix • Hours: May-Oct • Restored shop of Amos Bammert located in Phoenix. Church of the Assumption at junction US-41 & M-26. Restored.

East Jordan
(Charlevoix County)

Banks Township Historical Society
Mailing Address: 3944 Homestead Ln. • East Jordan, MI 49727
Contact: Walter Murphy, President
Physical Location: 6520 Center St. • Ellsworth, MI 49729
Visitor Accessibility: On-site parking. Not wheelchair accessible. Free tour guide available.
About: The Banks Township Historical Society preserves local history and heritage, encourages educational activities and culture, and provides scholarships for students at Ellsworth High School each year.
Exhibits/Collections: Antique items, photos, family trees, old newspapers, calendars, books, clothing, etc.
Annual Events: Meetings 4th Tue Apr-Oct, 7 p.m. at the Banks Township Historical Society.
Publications: "Humanities Class Book," "Elmer Road's Memoirs," "Pioneer Notes."

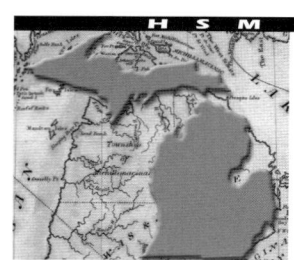

East Jordan Portside Art & Historical Society
Mailing Address: P.O. Box 1355 • East Jordan, MI 49727
Contact: Kim Prebble, Treasurer
E-Mail: kprebble@ejps.org
Phone: (231) 536-3282
Site/Location: East Jordan Portside Art & Historical Society Museum
Physical Location: 01656 S M66 Hwy • East Jordan, MI 49727
Hours: Jun-Sep: Sat-Sun 1:30-4:30 p.m.
Admission: Donations accepted.
Visitor Accessibility: Free on-site parking. Wheelchair accessible. Tour guide available.
Website: www.portsideartsfair.org
About: The East Jordan Portside Art & Historical Society collects the history of East Jordan and makes it available to the public through the museum and information shared with the Jordan Valley District Library. The society's museum is located in Elm Pointe Park, a Michigan historic site located on Lake Charlevoix. First historical museum in Charlevoix County. Established in 1976 to preserve the history of the local area. Collections include lumbering era, train, agriculture, home life, doctor, military, and industry.
Exhibits/Collections: Train, lumber, home life, agriculture, military, industry, and medical and veterinary instruments.
Annual Events: Portside Arts Fair (Aug).
Publications: "East Jordan Pictorial History," "Local Industrialist William Pitt Porter."
Other Sites/Locations: **East Jordan City Hall** • Location: 201 Main Street • East Jordan, MI 49727 • Hours: Mon-Fri 8:30 a.m.-4:30 p.m. • Admission: Donations accepted • Visitor Accessibility: Free street parking. Not wheelchair accessible. Self-guided. • Collections include ladies furnishings, train memorabilia, woodworking tools, newspaper typeset, and revolving exhibits.

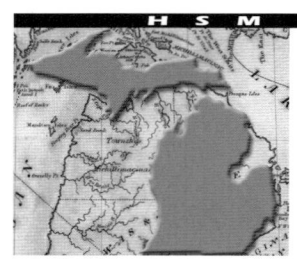

Jordan Valley District Library
Mailing Address: P.O. Box 877, One Library Ln. • East Jordan, MI 49727
Contact: Dawn LaVanway, Library Director
E-Mail: dir@jvdl.info
Phone: (231) 536-7131
Fax: (231) 536-3646
Hours: Mon Tue Thu Fri 9 a.m.-5 p.m., Wed 9 a.m.-7 p.m., Sat 9 a.m.-1 p.m., Sun 1-5 p.m.
Visitor Accessibility: Free on-site parking, Wheelchair accessible. Self guided.
Website: http://jvdl.info
About: Curious to explore and discover!
Exhibits/Collections: Art displays, local newspapers (digital), genealogy.

East Lansing
(Ingham County)

East Lansing Historic District Commission
Mailing Address: East Lansing City Hall, 410 Abbot Rd. • East Lansing, MI 48823
Contact: Timothy Schmitt, AICP—Historic Preservation Officer
Phone: (517) 319-6828 • *Fax:* (517) 337-1607
Hours: Mon-Fri 8 a.m.-5 p.m.
Website: www.cityofeastlansing.com
About: The East Lansing Historic District Commission administers the Historic Preservation Code, which was adopted in July 1989. East Lansing has more than 800 properties in historic districts.
Exhibits/Collections: East Lansing Study Committee, Final Report of March 1988, with photos of all houses in East Lansing at that time. Final Report: Historical/Architectural Survey 1986-1987.

Information may not be current.

East Lansing Historical Society
Mailing Address: P.O. Box 6146 • East Lansing, MI 48826
Contact: Pat McCarthy
E-Mail: thomps3469@hotmail.com
Phone: (517) 337-1731 • *Fax:* (517) 337-1607
About: The East Lansing Historical Society is a membership program that partners with the city for historical occasions and is recognized as the city's official historical society. The society has also produced DVD recordings of local WWII veterans.
Exhibits/Collections: Photographs and archival materials in storage at Hannah Community Center.
Annual Events: Meetings 1st Sun monthly 12 p.m. at Hannah Community Center.
Publications: Newsletter (Lamplighter).
*Information may not be current.

G. Robert Vincent Voice Library of the MSU Libraries
Mailing Address: Michigan State University Main Library, 100 Library • East Lansing, MI 48824
Contact: John D. Shaw, Supervisor
E-Mail: shawj@msu.edu
Phone: (517) 884-6470 • *Fax:* (517) 432-3693
Hours: Mon-Fri 8 a.m.-5 p.m.
Admission: Free; charges may apply for Inter-Library loan.
Visitor Accessibility: On-site parking for a fee. Wheelchair accessible. Library staff available as guides; call ahead if possible.
Website: vvl.lib.msu.edu
About: The G. Vincent Voice Library is a unit of the Michigan State University Libraries. Bibliographic record available in MSU Libraries' OPAC.
Exhibits/Collections: Collection of primary source sound material, found in more than 40,000 hours of sound recordings and includes the voices of 100,000 different individuals dating back to 1888.

Michigan Political History Society
Mailing Address: P.O. Box 4684 • East Lansing, MI 48826
Contact: Linda Cleary
E-Mail: linda.cleary@sbcglobal.net
Phone: (517) 336-5742 • *Fax:* (517) 337-2490
Website: www.miphs.com
About: Videotapes of significant figures in Michigan political history.
*Information may not be current.

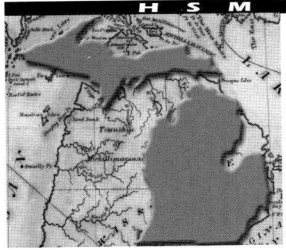

Michigan State University Archives & Historical Collection
Mailing Address: 101 Conrad Hall • East Lansing, MI 48824-1327
Contact: Portia Vescio, Assistant Director
E-Mail: archives@msu.edu
Phone: (517) 355-2330
Fax: (517) 353-9319
Hours: Mon-Tue, Thu-Fri 9 a.m.-5 p.m., Wed 10 a.m.-5 p.m. Closed university holidays.
Visitor Accessibility: On-site parking for a fee. Wheelchair accessible. Self-guided.
Website: www.archives.msu.edu
About: The Michigan State University Archives & Historical Collection preserves and provides access to the university's historical records. Our mission is to collect the official records of the institution and preserve the legacy of the nation's pioneer land-grant university. The archives also has an active interest in records pertaining to the state of Michigan and the Great Lakes region, with emphasis on materials that complement existing collections or have a relation to the university.
Exhibits/Collections: Changing exhibits. See website for current exhibits and archive collections.
Publications: Newsletter (The Insight), blog.

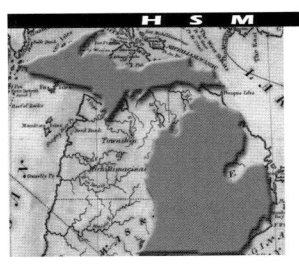

Michigan State University Museum
Mailing Address: 409 W. Circle Dr. • East Lansing, MI 48824
Contact: Gary Morgan, Director
E-Mail: schmi140@msu.edu
Phone: (517) 884-6894
Fax: (517) 432-2846
Hours: Mon-Fri 9 a.m.-5 p.m.; Sat 10 a.m.-5 p.m.; Sun 1-5 p.m. Closed university holidays.
Admission: $5/individual suggested donation.
Visitor Accessibility: Street parking for a fee. Wheelchair accessible.
Website: http://museum.msu.edu/
About: Organized in 1857, the Michigan State University Museum is a resource for natural and cultural history, particularly of the Great Lakes region. The museum features country store and print shop exhibits and a Michigan fur trade display.
Exhibits/Collections: One million objects include Michigan folk life, rural history, and Great Lakes archeology and ethnography. Michigan Traditional Art Program Research Collection is repository of materials documenting traditional culture of Michigan.
Annual Events: Chocolate Party Benefit (Feb), Darwin Discovery Day Natural History Program (Feb), Great Lakes Folk Festival (Aug), Dinosaur Dash (Oct).
*Information may not be current.

East Tawas
(Iosco County)

Iosco County Historical Society & Museum
Mailing Address: 405 W. Bay St. • East Tawas, MI 48730
Contact: Marguerite Schmidt, Executive Director
E-Mail: iosco.history@gmail.com
Phone: (989) 362-8911 • *Fax:* (989) 362-8911
Hours: June-Labor Day Tue-Sat 10 a.m.-4 p.m. Check website for times.
Admission: Donations accepted.
Visitor Accessibility: Public parking lot adjacent to museum. Wheelchair accessible. Free tour guide.
Website: www.ioscomuseum.org
About: The Iosco County Historical Society formed in 1967 to preserve local history for current and future generations. In 1978, the society opened its museum as a depository of historic artifacts reflecting Iosco County's history and growth. Historical displays and exhibits change regularly and include class pictures; a Victorian parlor; an early kitchen; medical displays; ship models; and the military during WWI, WWII, and the Spanish American and Civil Wars.
Annual Events: Garden Tour (Jul), Folk Art Festival (Sep), Adult Halloween Tales (Oct), and Holiday House Tour & Tea (Dec). Meetings 3rd Thu monthly, 4 p.m. at museum.
*Information may not be current.

Tawas Point Lighthouse.
Please see entry under Lansing: Michigan Historical Center.

Eastpointe
(Macomb County)

East Detroit Historical Society
Mailing Address: P.O. Box 110 • Eastpointe, MI 48021
Phone: (586) 775-1414
Site/Location: **Halfway Schoolhouse**
Physical Location: 15500 Nine Mile Road • Eastpointe, MI 48021
Hours: Open for special events and by request.
Admission: Free
Visitor Accessibility: On-site parking. Wheelchair accessible
Website: www.erin-halfwaydays.org
About: The East Detroit Historical Society maintains a museum in the 1872 Halfway Schoolhouse.
Exhibits/Collections: Pictures and biographies related to early Halfway, later East Detroit, now Eastpointe.
Annual Events: Erin Halfway Days featuring Civil War reenactors and American Indian encampment.
Information may not be current.

Michigan Military Technical & Historical Society
Mailing Address: P.O. Box 137 • Eastpointe, MI 48021
Contact: Chris Causley, President
E-Mail: mimths@mimths.org
Phone: (586) 872-2581
Physical Location: 16600 Stephens Rd. • Eastpointe, MI 48021
Hours: Sat 10 a.m.-5 p.m., Sun 12-5 p.m.
Admission: $5/individual, $7 family, $3 senior/military/student, children under 16 free.
Visitor Accessibility: Free on-site parking. Wheelchair accessible. Tour guide available; call ahead for groups of 10 or more.
Website: www.mimths.org
About: The Michigan Military Technical & Historical Society is dedicated to portraying and preserving the story of the role played by Michigan's civilian and military personnel in 20th-century conflict and showcasing the products of Michigan's "Arsenal of Democracy." The society's museum features exhibits on Michigan-related military production, units, and veterans dating back to the 1900s.
Exhibits/Collections: Military items connected to Michigan from 1900 to today.

Eastport
(Antrim County)

Wilkinson Homestead & Historical Society
Mailing Address: 5940 N. M-88, P.O. Box 102 • Eastport, MI 49627
Contact: Richard Hendershott, President
Phone: (231) 599-2985
Hours: Jul-Sep Sun 12 p.m.-3 p.m.. Other times by appointment.
Admission: Donations accepted.
Visitor Accessibility: Partially wheelchair accessible; main floor only. Tour guide available.
Website: http://torchlakeviews.wordpress.com/about/wilkinson-homestea
About: The Wilkinson Homestead and Historical Society was founded in 2000 to renovate an 1880s home that was vacant for 45 years. The society hosts a lecture series held at the Torch Lake Township Hall.
Publications: Newsletter (Society Pages).

Eaton Rapids
(Eaton County)

Eaton Rapids Area Historical Society
Mailing Address: 635 State St. • Eaton Rapids, MI 48827
Contact: Deb Malewski, Trustee
E-Mail: info@eatonrapidshistory.com
Phone: (517) 256-9460
Site/Location: **The Miller Farm**
Hours: Wed 10 a.m.-5 p.m.
Visitor Accessibility: Free on-site parking. Partially wheelchair accessible. Tour guide available by reservation.
Website: www.eatonrapidshistory.com
About: The Eaton Rapids Area Historical Society collects, preserves, and educates the public about the rich history of Eaton Rapids. The Miller Farm is where Miller Dairy operated and the Miller family lived and helped make Eaton Rapids into the "Ice Cream Capital of the World" for many years. The Miller Barn #1 is one of the largest barns in Michigan and showcases a full hay loft and historical displays.
Exhibits/Collections: Other buildings include the 1870 Wright Schoolhouse, a working blacksmith shop (open only during events), the Plains Road Bible Church, the Jean Kline Block, and a Horner Woolen Display.
Annual Events: Dam Festival, Fall Farm Festival, Christmas on the Farm, Historical Cemetery Tour, Mrs. Miller's Pantry. Board meetings 3rd Thu monthly, 7 p.m. at the Miller Farm's Ice Cream Factory.
Publications: "The Pictorial Guide to Eaton Rapids."

GAR Memorial Hall and Museum
Mailing Address: 224 S. Main St. • Eaton Rapids, MI 48827
Contact: Keith Harrison, President
E-Mail: garmichigan@gmail.com
Phone: (517) 694-9394
Hours: Call or see website.
Admission: Free.
Visitor Accessibility: Street parking. Partially wheelchair accessible. Tour guide available upon request.
Website: www.garmuseum.com
About: It is the mission of the GAR Memorial Hall and Museum to collect, preserve, and display artifacts relating to the Grand Army of the Republic and the United Confederate Veterans and their related organizations in order to educate and inform the public about the people and the history of the post-Civil War time period.
Exhibits/Collections: Artifacts of the Grand Army of the Republic, including uniforms, ribbons, flags, banners, photos, and documents. The scope is not limited to the local area; emphasis is on the entire GAR organization.
Annual Events: GAR Historic Walking Tour (May), Urban Air (Oct).

Edmore
(Montcalm County)

Old Fence Rider Historical Center
Mailing Address: P.O. Box 451 • Edmore, MI 48829
Contact: Lon Leonard, President
Phone: (989) 506-9562
Physical Location: 222 S Shedon • Edmore, MI 48829
Hours: Sat 10 a.m.-2 p.m.

Admission: $2/individual donation requested.
Visitor Accessibility: Free on-site parking. Wheelchair accessible. Tour guide available; call for appointment.
Website: http://www.montcalm.org/culture0015.asp
About: The Old Fence Rider Historical Center contains displays on early America, pioneers, the logging industry, the Civil War, and the major wars of the 20th century. Also included are life-size displays and recreations of old-fashioned drugstores, a 1950s diner, and a gas station. Local history is also displayed.
Annual Events: Edmore Potato Festival (Aug), Edmore Hometown Christmas (Dec). Meetings 1st Sat monthly at museum.

Edwardsburg
(Cass County)

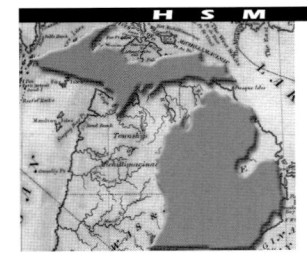

Edwardsburg Area Historical Museum
Mailing Address: P.O. Box 694 • Edwardsburg, MI 49112
Contact: Jo-Ann Boepple
E-Mail: JoBoepple@aol.com
Physical Location: 26818 Main St. • Edwardsburg, MI 49112
Hours: May-Dec: Tue-Sat 1-4 p.m. Sat 11 a.m.-2 p.m.
Admission: $2/individual donation.
Visitor Accessibility: Free street parking. Wheelchair accessible. Tour guides available.
Website: https://www.facebook.com/pages/Edwardsburg-Area-Historical-Museum/106608379400372
About: The Edwardsburg Historical Collection is dedicated to the preservation of the past from the 1800s to the future.
Exhibits/Collections: Historical photographs and documents from businesses, organizations, railroads, farms, lakes, churches, and schools. A collection of household goods depict life of early settlers.
Annual Events: Annual Plant Sale (May), meetings Wed weekly, 10 a.m. at museum.
Publications: "Edwardsburg: The First 150 Years."

Elk Rapids
(Antrim County)

Elk Rapids Area Historical Society
Mailing Address: P.O. Box 2 • Elk Rapids, MI 49629
Contact: Dan LeBlond, President
E-Mail: president@elkrapidshistory.org
Phone: (231) 264-5692
Site/Location: Elk Rapids Area Historical Musuem
Physical Location: 301 Traverse St. • Elk Rapids, MI 48629
Hours: May-Sep: Fri-Sun 1 p.m.-4 p.m. Closed holidays.
Admission: Donations accepted.
Visitor Accessibility: Free street parking. Partially wheelchair accessible. Tour guide available; for group tours during open hours, call (231) 264-5692; for group tours after open hours, call (231) 264-8984.
Website: www.elkrapidshistory.org
About: Exhibits and displays at the Elk Rapids Area Historical Museum focus on the Village of Elk Rapids' role in the "Chain of Lakes Region" during the 19th and 20th centuries as an important lumbering, cement, and pig iron smelting center.
Exhibits/Collections: Artifacts from the pig iron and lumber industries. Vintage clothing, antique tools, and office furniture and machines. Genealogical, business, school, organization, and family records. Regional photo collection of 3,000 images.
Annual Events: Monthly programs Apr-Oct; see website for info.
Publications: Newsletter (Museum Matters), "Water Under the Bridge: Poems from the Elk Rapids Elders Project," "Bay Breezes: Local History Unfolding: The Grand Traverse Country Through the Pen of a Small Town Editor (Vol. 1-3)," "Bay Breezes: The Grand Traverse Country Abundance for All."

Elkton
(Huron County)

Elkton Area Historical Society
Mailing Address: P.O. Box 342 • Elkton, MI 48371
Contact: Randy Haley
E-Mail: rhaley184@comcast.net
Phone: (989) 375-1933 • **Fax:** (989) 375-4361
Site/Location: Mayhew Log Cabin & Blacksmith Barn
Physical Location: Ackerman Memorial Park • Elkton, MI 48731
Hours: Log Cabin Day (last Sun of Jun) 1-5pm; Labor Day Weekend Fri 1-8 p.m., Sat 1-9 p.m., Sun 1-5 p.m.; Huron County Museum Days 9 a.m.-5 p.m.
Admission: Donations accepted.
Visitor Accessibility: Free street parking. Partially wheelchair accessible, limited to first-floor displays. Free tour guides available.
Website: www.thehchs.org/elkton
About: The Elkton Area Historical Society brings together and makes available the collection and display of material that helps establish or illustrate the area's history. The society maintains the 1865 Mayhew Log Cabin and Blacksmith Barn. Attractions include a 1916-80 HP Case stationary-type steam engine, farm-related artifacts, displays of memorabilia, and items of local interest.
Exhibits/Collections: Various household, farm, merchant items. Public memorabilia, including books, photographs, bottles, school yearbooks, and trophies. Kitchen items, barber chair, old newspapers of special events, and Log Cabin Society of Michigan publications.
Annual Events: Log Cabin Day (Jun), Autumn Fest (Sep), Huron County Museum Days (Sep).

Ellsworth
(Keweenaw County)

Ellsworth/Banks Township Historical Association
Mailing Address: 6387 Ellsworth Rd. • Ellsworth, MI 49729
Information may not be current.

Elsie
(Clinton County)

Elsie Historical Society
Mailing Address: P.O. Box 125 • Elsie, MI 48831
Contact: Nancy Conklin, President
Physical Location: 145 W. Main St. • Elsie, MI 48831
Hours: Wed 2-5 p.m. Also by appointment.
Admission: Donations accepted.
Visitor Accessibility: Street parking. Wheelchair accessible.
Website: www.elsie.org/Historical%20Society.html
About: Connected to the Elsie Public Library and Duplain Township Hall, the Elsie Library Historical Society maintains and assembles historical information concerning Elsie, including its residents and the surrounding area.
Exhibits/Collections: Library of indexed scrapbooks, copies of death certificates in Elsie area, books of surrounding cemeteries.
Annual Events: Meetings 3rd Wed monthly at 5 p.m.
Publications: "Elsie 1857-2007."

Empire
(Leelanau County)

Empire Area Heritage Group
Mailing Address: P.O. Box 192 • Empire, MI 49630
Contact: David Taghon, President
E-Mail: empiremuseum@centurytel.net
Phone: (231) 326-5568
Site/Location: Empire Area Museum Complex
Physical Location: 11544 S. LaCore St. • Empire, MI 49630
Hours: Memorial Day until Jul 1: Sat-Sun 1-4 p.m. Jul -Aug: Mon-Sun (closed Wed) 1-4 p.m. Labor Day-Oct: Sat-Sun 1-4 p.m.
Admission: $2/person suggested donation.
Visitor Accessibility: Free on-site parking. Wheelchair accessible. Self-guided.
Website: empiremimuseum.org
About: The Empire Area Heritage Group preserves and displays Empire's past through the Empire Area Museum Complex, which is made up of four buildings. The main building houses Roen Saloon, a theater room, a pioneer parlor, a blacksmith shop, a woodworking shop, and Empire's 1924 gas station. The Billy Beeman Barn contains farming items. The third building is a turn-of-the-century one-room school combined with a church. The relocated vintage Hose House (firehouse) features a display of early "hand pulled" firefighting equipment.
Exhibits/Collections: Genealogical records, written documents, and thousands of photographs pertaining to the area's history.
Annual Events: Heritage Day (Oct). Meetings last Thu monthly (except mid-winter months), 1 p.m. at museum complex.
Publications: "Empire Cook," "Remembering Empire Through Pictures," "Some Other Day," "The Boizard Letters."

Friends of Sleeping Bear Dunes
Mailing Address: P.O. Box 545 • Empire, MI 49630
Contact: Kerry Kelly, Chairman
E-Mail: info@friendsofsleepingbear.org
Phone: (231) 326-5011
Physical Location: 9922 Front St. • Empire, MI 49630
Hours: Call or see website.
Visitor Accessibility: Most sites at the National Lakeshore are wheelchair accessible. Public parking free with entrance pass. Rangers and volunteers available Jun-Aug.
Website: www.friendsofsleepingbear.org
About: Friends of Sleeping Bear Dunes protect resources and heighten visitor experiences in partnership with Sleeping Bear Dunes National Lakeshore. The all-volunteer nonprofit organization with more than 150 volunteers is involved in a wide variety of projects each year.

Manitou Islands Memorial Society
Mailing Address: P.O. Box 177 • Empire, MI 49630
Contact: Paul Rocheleau, President
E-Mail: info@manitouislandsmemorialsociety.org
Phone: (720) 808-4719
Site/Location: North and South Manitou Islands
Admission: Fees are set by the National Park Service.
Visitor Accessibility: On-site parking for a fee. Not wheelchair accessible. Tour guide available.
Website: http://www.manitouislandsmemorialsociety.org
Annual Events: Annual Potluck (Jul).

Preserve Historic Sleeping Bear
Mailing Address: P.O. Box 453 • Empire, MI 49630
Contact: Susan Pocklington, Director
E-Mail: phsb@leelanau.com
Phone: (231) 334-6103
Site/Location: Charles and Hattie Olsen Farm
Physical Location: 3164 W. Harbor Hwy. • Maple City, MI 49664
Hours: To be determined.
Admission: A National Park Pass is required for admission.
Visitor Accessibility: Free on-site parking. Wheelchair accessible. Tour guide available.
Website: www.phsb.org
About: Preserve Historic Sleeping Bear partners with Sleeping Bear Dunes National Lakeshore to preserve and interpret its rich heritage of 366 historic buildings and landscapes. The organization facilitates volunteer preservation projects, tours of historic properties in the National Lakeshore, and related programs.
Exhibits/Collections: Oral histories and information about families who lived in what is now Sleeping Bear Dunes National Lakeshore.
Annual Events: Port Oneida 5K Barn to Barn Trail Run Fundraiser, Port Oneida Cultural Fair and Picnic Dinner (Aug).
Publications: "Port Oneida Field Guide."

Sleeping Bear Dunes National Lakeshore
Mailing Address: 9922 Front St. • Empire, MI 49630
Contact: Lisa Myers
Phone: (231) 326-5134 • **Fax:** (231) 326-5382
Hours: Call or see website.
Admission: Park Entrance Pass $10/week per vehicle, Annual $20/park entrance pass for vehicles, $5/individual with no car. Also admittance by National Park Pass.
Visitor Accessibility: Most sites at the National Lakeshore are wheelchair accessible. Public parking free with entrance pass. Rangers and volunteers available Jun-Aug.
Website: www.nps.gov/slbe
About: Along with the Friends of Sleeping Bear Dunes, preserve, restore, and interpret the natural, cultural, historical, and recreational resources of Sleeping Bear Dunes National Lakeshore. Attractions include Glen Haven Historic Village with a working blacksmith shop, general store, and cannery boat museum; Maritime Museum (circa 1901) with Coast Guard station and boathouse; and Port Oneida Rural Historic District historic farms.
Annual Events: Port Oneida Rural Arts & Culture Fair.
Publications: Annual Visitors Guide.
Other Sites/Locations: Glen Haven Historic Village • Location: M-209, 2 miles west of Glen Arbor • Hours: Memorial Day-Labor Day: 11 a.m.-5 p.m. • Company-owned steamboat stop 1865-1931 and museums. Inquire about ranger programs. Blacksmith shop demonstrations in restored 1920s shop.
Cannery Boat Museum • Hours: Late-May-Labor Day: 11 a.m.-5 p.m. • Former cherry and apple cannery houses Great Lakes boats and equipment.
Glen Haven General Store • Hours: Open: May-Jun: Fri, Sat-Sun 12-5 p.m.; Jul-Labor Day: Daily 12-5 p.m. • An 1867 company store with typical general store merchandise and park bookstore.
Maritime Museum • Hours: May-Sep: Daily 12-5 p.m. Oct 1-mid-Oct: Weekends 12-5 p.m. • Crew quarters and boathouse of Sleeping Bear Point Life Saving Station. Steamer wheelhouse, surfmen's quarters, rescue boat, and equipment. Collections include Great Lakes maritime items, U.S. Life-Saving Service, U.S. Lighthouse Service.

*Information may not be current.

Engadine
(Mackinac County)

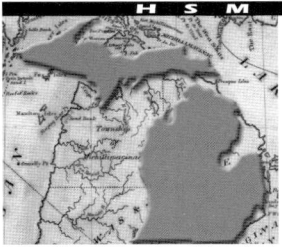

Engadine Historical Society
Mailing Address: P.O. Box 114 • Engadine, MI 49827
Contact: Edward Schmitt, President
E-Mail: edchar1@earthlink.net
Phone: (906) 477-6908
Site/Location: **Engadine Historical Museum**
Physical Location: W14075 Melville St. • Engadine, MI 49827
Hours: Tue and Sat 10 a.m.-2 p.m.
Admission: Free.
Visitor Accessibility: Free street parking. Wheelchair accessible. Tour guide available.
About: The Engadine Historical Museum reflects life in the late 1800s and early 1900s. Displays focus on lumbering and agricultural eras and include furnishings; a one-room schoolhouse replica; and displays of military artifacts, pictures, and artifacts from the Cooperidge Mill and old Mackinac County Bank. There is also a restored log house (b. 1895) on the property.
Exhibits/Collections: Log house, display of barns in the area, and old washing machines. Original Register of Deeds books from the 1900s. Family records.
Annual Events: Heritage Day (Jul). Meetings 2nd Thu Mar-Sep.
Publications: Biannual newsletter.

Luce-Mackinac Genealogical Society
Mailing Address: P.O. Box 113 • Engadine, MI 49827
Contact: Georgianna Kuebler
Phone: (906) 477-6790
Website: http://luce.migenweb.net/
About: The Luce-Mackinac Genealogical Society promotes genealogy and works to preserve local records and historical information.
Annual Events: Meetings 1st Thu 1:30 p.m., location shifts among Engadine, Newberry, and Curtis Libraries.
Publications: Newsletter and numerous compilations of local records.

Escanaba
(Delta County)

Delta County Genealogical Society
Mailing Address: P.O. Box 442 • Escanaba, MI 49829
Contact: Richard Rieffers, President
Phone: (906) 786-1893
Physical Location: Escanaba Public Library, 400 Ludington St. • Escanaba, MI 49829
Website: www.dcmigs.org
About: Collection housed in Escanaba Public Library. Records of all Delta County cemeteries; indexes to birth, death, marriage, probate, and divorce records. Delta County Civil War and pioneer records.
Annual Events: Meetings 2nd Wed Mar-May and Sep-Nov, 7 p.m. at Escanaba Civic Center.
*Information may not be current.

Delta County Historical Society & Museum
Mailing Address: 16 Beaumier Way • Escanaba, MI 49829
Contact: Charles Lindquist, President
E-Mail: deltacountyhistsoc@sbcglobal.net
Phone: (906) 789-6790
Hours: Museum and lighthouse: Memorial Day-Labor Day Daily 11 a.m.-4 p.m. Archives: Jun- Aug: Mon-Fri 1-4 p.m., Sep-May: Mon 1-4 p.m.
Admission: $3/adult, $1/child, $5/family, $50-75/bus tours.
Visitor Accessibility: Free parking. Partially wheelchair accessible. Self-guided.
Website: www.deltahistorical.org
About: The society organized in 1948 to collect and preserve materials related to Delta County. In 1956, the society opened its museum in a former radio station, where exhibits highlight local history. A new building now contains the museum and the archives. The society also maintains Sand Point Lighthouse. Lighthouse home, tower, and boathouse open to visitors.
Exhibits/Collections: Marine Lighthouse Services, U.S. Coast Guard, lumbering, Elliott Letters, Brotherton Journals, C&NW Railroad, county newspapers 1873-1954, glass negatives.
Annual Events: Annual Open House (Dec).
Publications: Newsletter (Delta Historian).

Essexville
(Bay County)

7th Michigan Cavalry Civil War Roundtable
Mailing Address: 1605 Carla Dr. • Essexville, MI 48732
Contact: Edith Wacksman
E-Mail: dswacks@hotmail.com
Phone: (989) 892-1136
Admission: $20/family per year or $5/family per program.
Visitor Accessibility: Free on-site parking.
About: The 7th Michigan Cavalry Civil War Roundtable meets to learn about the American Civil War. Speakers come from throughout the state.
Annual Events: Annual Meeting (Apr). Meetings 2nd Wed Oct-Apr, 7 p.m. at the Wirt Library or Stein Haus Restaurant in Bay City.

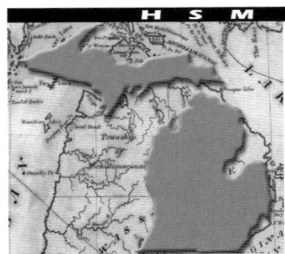

Heritage House Farm Museum
Mailing Address: P.O. Box 103 • Essexville, MI 48732
Contact: Lois Englehardt, President
E-Mail: lenglehardt7025@charter.net
Phone: (989) 686-7025
Physical Location: 305 Pine St. • Essexville, MI 48732
Hours: Summer: Sun 2-4 p.m. Also by appointment.
Admission: Donations accepted.
Visitor Accessibility: Not wheelchair accessible. Nearby parking available. Tours by appointment only.
Website: www.theheritagemcc.org
About: The Heritage House Farm Museum is a fully furnished nine-room home from early 1890s. The home was built by John Garber, whose family members were the building's only residents. Today, the home features furniture that belonged to both the Garber family and the community. Also on-site are a German-style shed, corn crib, and herb garden.
Annual Events: Meetings 2nd Mon monthly, 1 p.m. at museum.
Publications: Annual newsletter.

Evart
(Osceola County)

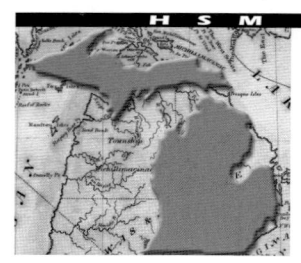

Evart Public Library Museum
Mailing Address: P.O. Box 576 • Evart, MI 49631
Contact: Aloha Hodges, Curator
E-Mail: evartlibrary@yahoo.com
Phone: (231) 734-5542
Fax: (231) 734-5542
Physical Location: 105 N. Main St. • Evart, MI 49631
Hours: Mon 9 a.m.-6 p.m., Tue-Fri 9 a.m.-4 p.m.
Admission: Free.
Visitor Accessibility: Street and lot parking. Wheelchair accessible. Tour guide available part-time.
About: The Evart Public Library Museum collects artifacts, records, and archival materials that document and/or illustrate local history. Rotating exhibits and freestanding items relate to the history of the Evart area and the interests of its citizens.
Annual Events: Annual Open House and Victorian Tea (Sep).

Farmington
(Oakland County)

Farmington Genealogical Society
Mailing Address: 28870 Summerwood Rd. • Farmington, MI 48335
Contact: Byron Bailey, President
Phone: (248) 553-0300
Physical Location: 23500 Liberty St. • Farmington, MI 48335
Website: www.rootsweb.ancestry.com/~mifarmgs
About: Founded in 1973, the Farmington Genealogical Society encourages, instructs, and assists members and other interested persons in researching and compiling their family histories.
Annual Events: Meetings 3rd Tue monthly (Sep-Nov, Jan-May) at Farmington Community Library Downtown Branch. Genealogy basics pre-meeting at 5:45 p.m., main meeting at 7 p.m. featuring speakers on various genealogical topics.
Publications: Monthly newsletter (Footprints to the Past), books with local information, see website.
Information may not be current.

Farmington Historical Commission
Mailing Address: 23600 Liberty St. • Farmington, MI 48335
Contact: Susan Wendel, Deputy Clerk
E-Mail: swendel@ci.farmington.mi.us
Phone: (248) 474-5500
Fax: (248) 473-7261
Site/Location: **Governor Warner Mansion**
Physical Location: 33805 Grand River Ave. • Farmington, MI 48335
Hours: Wed 1-5 p.m.; 1st Sun monthly 1-5 p.m.
Admission: $3/adult, $1/youth (7-12).
Visitor Accessibility: Free on-site and street parking. Not wheelchair accessible. Group tours by appointment.
Website: http://www.ci.farmington.mi.us/government/boards/historicalcommission.asp
About: Collects and preserves the artifacts of Farmington and the Warner family from 1867-1911. The Governor Warner Mansion is a Victorian home, where visitors learn about Governor Warner and his family. The Carriage House houses a classroom, 19th-century tools, and an early 20th-century printing press and loom.
Exhibits/Collections: Victorian clothing, home furnishings, 19th-century kitchen. Display of the governor's three terms, 1905-1911; family and city of Farmington photos; children's belongings; 1,000 eye-pressed glassware; 19th-century gardening tools.
Annual Events: Open House (Apr), Fashion Show and Luncheon Fundraiser (May), Founders Festival Events and Parade (Jul), Summer Porch Parties (May-Aug), Ghost Walk (Oct), Open House (Dec).
Information may not be current.

Farmington Historical Society
Mailing Address: P.O. Box 551 • Farmington, MI 48332
Contact: Brian Golden, President
E-Mail: bgolden@pastways.info
Phone: (248) 701-8112
Fax: (248) 987-6899
Physical Location: Heritage & History Center, 24725 Farmington Rd. • Farmington Hills, MI 48335
Hours: Tue, Thu, Sat 10 a.m.-2 p.m.
Admission: Donations accepted.
Website: www.farmingtonhistoricalsociety.org
About: Founded in 1962, the Farmington Historical Society strives to preserve and share the history and heritage of the Farmington and Farmington Hills areas. It supports two local museums, the Governor Warner Mansion and the Heritage & History Center in Farmington Hills.
Annual Events: Annual Banquet (May), Founder's Festival (Jul).

Farmington Hills
(Oakland County)

Abraham Lincoln Civil War Roundtable of Michigan
Mailing Address: 23959 Brookplace Ct. • Farmington Hills, MI 48336
Contact: Liz Stringer
E-Mail: stringerl@aol.com
Phone: (248) 473-4118 • *Fax:* (248) 548-2403
Website: www.alcwrt.org
About: This Civil War Round Table meets nine times a year hosting speakers on various topics related to the Civil War and promotes preservation activities.
Annual Events: Field trips, meetings 3rd Thu Feb-Jun and Sep-Nov, 8 p.m. at Plymouth Township Offices.
Publications: Newsletter.
Information may not be current.

Cadillac LaSalle Club Museum & Research Center
Mailing Address: 35105 W. Thirteen Mile Rd. • Farmington Hills, MI 48331
Contact: Paul Ayres, President
E-Mail: payres@flash.net
Phone: (313) 553-2053 • *Fax:* (313) 553-2053
Site/Location: **Gilmore Car Museum**
Physical Location: 6865 Hickory Rd. • Hickory Corners, MI 49060
Hours: 9 a.m.-5 p.m.
Admission: $10/individual.
Visitor Accessibility: Free on-site parking. Wheelchair accessible. Free tour guide available.
Website: www.cadillaclasallemuseum.org
About: Collects, preserves, and displays automobiles, literature, and artifacts associated with Cadillac and LaSalle automobiles and their manufacture and sale. Attractions include automobile and artifact

displays in the Cadillac Gallery at the Gilmore Car Museum Carriage House Building. A new museum building is also under construction at the Gilmore.
Exhibits/Collections: Cadillac and La Salle automobiles, literature, and artifacts.
Annual Events: Cadillac Weekend at Gilmore Car Museum (Sep), Labor Day Weekend Anniversary.
Publications: Annual Cadillac and La Salle photo calendar.

Farmington Community Library
Mailing Address: 32737 W. Twelve Mile Rd. • Farmington Hills, MI 48334
Contact: Judy Donlin, Librarian
E-Mail: heritage.vols@farmlib.org
Phone: (248) 553-0300
Fax: (248) 553-3228
Hours: Mon-Thu 9 a.m.-9 p.m.; Fri-Sat 10 a.m.-6 p.m.; Sun 1-5 p.m.
Admission: Free.
Visitor Accessibility: Free on-site parking. Wheelchair accessible. Self-guided.
Website: www.farmlib.org
About: The Farmington Community Library is a major public library in metropolitan Detroit that has a local history room, which is staffed by volunteers on a part-time basis. Many items of the collection have been digitized, including the Farmington Enterprise/Observer as well as monographs, telephone directories, and more.

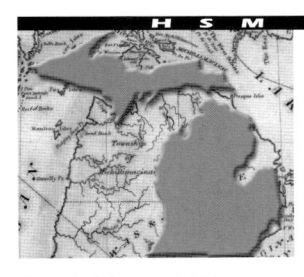

Farmington Hills Historic District Commission
Mailing Address: City Hall Planning Department, 31555 W. Eleven Mile Road • Farmington Hills, MI 48336
Contact: Mark Stec, HDC Staff Liaison
E-Mail: mstec@fhgov.com
Phone: (248) 871-2544
Fax: (248) 871-2451
Website: http://fhgov.com/Community/HistoricDistrict.asp
About: The Farmington Hills Historic District Commission safeguards heritage by preserving districts in the city that reflect cultural, social, economic, political, or architectural history. The commission also provides for maintenance of municipally owned structures.
Annual Events: Meetings 2nd Wed monthly at 7:30 p.m. in the community room of City Hall. All meetings are open to the public.

Finnish American Historical Society
Mailing Address: 35200 W. Eight Mile • Farmington Hills, MI 48335
Contact: Mia Lamminen, President
E-Mail: fcacenter@sbcglobal.net
Phone: (248) 478-6939 • *Fax:* (248) 478-5671
Hours: Mon, Wed, Fri. See website for current hours.
Admission: None.
Visitor Accessibility: Free on-site parking. Wheelchair accessible.
Website: www.finnishcenter.org
About: The Finnish American Historical Society preserves and promotes the history, culture, knowledge, and activities of Finland and Finnish Americans. The society sponsors the Finlandia Foundation National's Performer and Lecturer of the Year as well as Finnish American Theater programs. It also presents historical works by Finnish-American authors and poets from Michigan and hosts programs about Finnish-American communities in Michigan.

Annual Events: Celebration of Finland's Independence (Dec) Annual meetings (Apr), board meetings held as needed.

Holocaust Memorial Center
Mailing Address: 28123 Orchard Lake Road • Farmington Hills, MI 48334
Contact: Lawrence Willim, Program Associate and Social Media Manager
E-Mail: info@holocaustcenter.org
Phone: (248) 553-2400
Fax: (248) 553-2433
Hours: Sun-Thu 9:30 a.m.-5 p.m. (last admission 3:30 p.m.), Fri 9:30 a.m.-3 p.m. (last admission 12:30 p.m.). Closed Jewish holidays.
Admission: $8/adult, $6/student, $6/senior, $5/children. Museum members and uniformed professional personnel are free.
Visitor Accessibility: Free on-site parking. Wheelchair accessible. Tour guide available Sun-Thu at 1 p.m., reservations requested for groups of six or more.
Website: www.holocaustcenter.org
About: The Holocaust Memorial Center Zekelman Family Campus remembers those who perished in the Holocaust and recognizes the survivors as well. By highlighting those individuals, the center seeks to contribute to maintaining a free society. Highlights at the museum include the interactive Portraits of Honor, where visitors can read and hear the stories of many of Michigan's survivors, and the Institute of the Righteous, which provides an exploration of those who took responsibility and risked their lives for Holocaust resistance.
Exhibits/Collections: Multilingual reference collection of the Holocaust, European Jewish history, and Christian-Jewish relations; videotapes, memorial books, photographs, maps, artifacts, art collection, vertical file, newspapers, and periodicals; John J. Mames Oral History Collection.
Annual Events: Annual Dinner, International Holocaust Remembrance Day, Summer Teacher Seminar, Yom HaShoah Commemoration.
Publications: Quarterly newsletter, "The World Reacts to the Holocaust," "The Rewards of Raising Righteous Children: Proceedings of the Fourth International Symposium on Altruism," "Survey of U.S. Federal, U.S. State, and Canadian Provincial Support for Holocaust Education," "Nazi Book Burning and the American Response," and "Remembering the Holocaust."

Marvin's Marvelous Mechanical Museum
Mailing Address: 31005 Orchard Lake Rd. • Farmington Hills, MI 48334
Contact: Marvin Yagoda
E-Mail: marvin@marvin3m.com
Phone: (248) 626-5020
Hours: Mon-Thu 10 a.m.-9 p.m.; Fri-Sat 10 a.m.-11 p.m.; Sun 11 a.m.-9 p.m.
Website: www.marvin3m.com
*Information may not be current.

Farwell
(Clare County)

Farwell Area Historical Museum
Mailing Address: P.O. Box 824 • Farwell, MI 48622
Contact: Alice Wilson, President
E-Mail: trishtom68@yahoo.com
Phone: (989) 588-0580
Physical Location: 221 W. Main St. • Farwell, MI 48430

✤ Historical Society of Michigan

Hours: Year-round: Mon, Wed, Fri 1:30-5:30 p.m. summer: Sat 12-4 p.m.
Admission: Free.
Visitor Accessibility: Free on-site and street parking. Wheelchair accessible. Free tour guide available.
Website: www.farwellmuseum.com

About: The Farwell Area Historical Society maintains a museum in the 1882 Ladies Library Association building. Exhibits highlight local history and include school, mill, post office, and local figures.
Annual Events: Farwell Lumberjack Days (Jul), Holiday of Lights (Nov). Meetings 3rd Wed monthly Apr-Nov, 6:30 p.m. at museum.

Tyrone Historical Society
Mailing Address: 10408 Center Rd. • Fenton, MI 48430
Contact: Barbara Burtch
Phone: (810) 629-8631
About: The business and purpose of this corporation is to preserve, advance, and disseminate knowledge of the history of Tyrone Township.
Exhibits/Collections: Many township artifacts are on display in museums in Hartland and Fenton. Original 1855 road grader on display at the township hall. Assembling photo collection.
Annual Events: Potluck dinners alternate months starting Jan.

F Fenton
(Genesee County)

Fenton Historical Society
Mailing Address: 310 South Leroy St. • Fenton, MI 48430
Contact: Donna Seger
Phone: (810) 629-8458
Site/Location: A.J. Phillips Fenton Museum
Hours: Sun 1-4 p.m.
Admission: Free.
Visitor Accessibility: Free on-site parking. Wheelchair accessible. Free tour guide available.
Website: http://fentonhistsoc.tripod.com/
About: The Fenton Historical Society makes the history of Fenton available to the public and schools. It maintains the A.J. Phillips Fenton Museum in the personal office of A.J. Phillips, who owned a factory that made wooden snow shovels, ironing boards, screen windows, and doors. Exhibits include wars that Fenton residents served in, school memorabilia, and items that once belonged to Phillips.
Exhibits/Collections: The genealogy research room houses books, photos, family history, early newspapers, and transcriptions of vital records.
Annual Events: Meetings 4th Wed Sep-May, 7:30 p.m.
Publications: "Fenton Postcards," "The Village Players."

Pioneer Memorial Association of Fenton and Mundy Townships
Mailing Address: P.O. Box 154 • Fenton, MI 48430
Contact: Phyllis Heusted
E-Mail: podunkpioneers@aol.com
Phone: (810) 655-5451
Site/Location: Podunk House
Physical Location: 2436 North Long Lake Road • Fenton, MI 48430
Hours: By appointment
Admission: Free.
Visitor Accessibility: On-site parking. Partially wheelchair accessible; Podunk House is not. To schedule a tour, call (810) 629-8747.
Website: www.addorio.com/podunk
About: The Podunk House is the last remaining structure from a trading post that included a grist mill, a post office, and homes. It was rescued from demolition and moved to its current location on the north end of Lake Fenton. The museum has expanded to include two additional buildings that house displays on local farming, barbering, steamboats that transported people from one end of the lake to the other, early schools, and the lives of early settlers.
Exhibits/Collections: 1834 pioneer home furnished with period items.
Annual Events: Pioneer Day Festival (Sat after Labor Day). Meetings 2nd Tue, 7 p.m. at museum.
Publications: Newsletter (Podunk Pioneer Papers). See website for periodic updates.

Ferndale
(Oakland County)

Ferndale Historical Society
Mailing Address: 1651 Livernois • Ferndale, MI 48220
Contact: Garry Andrews, President
E-Mail: garryandrewsmich@comcast.net
Phone: (248) 545-7606
Site/Location: Ferndale Historical Museum
Hours: Mon-Wed 10 a.m.-1 p.m., Sat 1 p.m.-4 p.m. Appointments available.
Admission: Donations accepted.
Visitor Accessibility: On-site parking. Partially wheelchair accessible. Tour guides available; 24 hours notice needed for special tours.
Website: www.ferndalehistoricalsociety.org
About: The Ferndale Historical Museum is housed in a building given to the city by Canadian Legion Post No. 71.
Exhibits/Collections: Collections dating from the 1800s-present, large military installation covering all of America's greatest wars, histories of all 8,000 structures in Ferndale. Local historical and genealogical collection.
Annual Events: Memorial Day and Veterans Day open houses. Board meetings 4th Thu monthly, 6 p.m. at museum.
Publications: Quarterly newsletter (Crow's Nest).

Fife Lake
(Grand Traverse County)

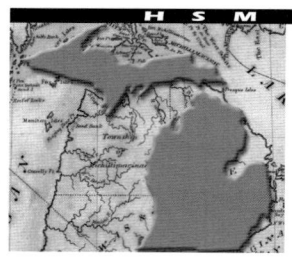

Fife Lake Historical Society
Mailing Address: P.O. Box 305 • Fife Lake, MI 49633
Contact: Fel Brunett
Phone: (231) 879-3342
Site/Location: Fife Lake Historical Museum
Physical Location: 136 E. State St. • Fife Lake, MI 49633
Hours: Call for current hours.
Admission: Free.
Visitor Accessibility: On-site parking. Wheelchair accessible. Guides available.
Website: http://www.fifelake.com/chamber/historical.htm
About: The Fife Lake Historical Society was organized in 1967 to provide displays of local history and prehistory. Nearby are the Fife Lake Historical Fire Barn, which features a 1936 fire truck, uniforms, and large wheeled fire-fighting equipment, and an 1878 one-room school.

Michigan History Directory

Exhibits/Collections: Local archaeological collection, large collection of late-19th-century and early-20th-century artifacts. Genealogical records, store inventories, fraternal group records.
Annual Events: Buffalo BBQ (Jul), High Noon (Jul).

Flat Rock
(Wayne County)

Flat Rock Historical Society
Mailing Address: P.O. Box 337 • Flat Rock, MI 48134
Contact: Cindy Fesko, President
E-Mail: feskos.fesko13@gmail.com
Phone: (734) 782-5220
Site/Location: **Memory Lane Village**
Physical Location: 25200 Gibraltar Road • Flat Rock, MI 48134
Hours: 2nd Sunday monthly 1-4 p.m. Also by appointment.
Admission: Free.
Visitor Accessibility: Free on-site parking shared with Flat Rock Library. Partially wheelchair accessible. Tour guide available during open houses and by appointment.
Website: www.flatrockhistory.org
About: Formed in 1975 to save Munger General store, the Flat Rock Historical Society now maintains the following historic buildings: C.J. Munger Store (b. 1875), Flat Rock Hotel (b. 1896), Carriage House (b. 1860), DTI Caboose (b. 1926), and the Wagar House (b. 1875). Special exhibits change monthly.
Exhibits/Collections: Local history room maintained at Flat Rock Library. Early Flat Rock and Brownstown Township records. Archives are open by appointment.
Annual Events: Flea market (May and Oct), Flat Rock Speedway. Meetings 2nd Wed (Feb, Apr, Sep, and Dec), 6 p.m. at Flat Rock Hotel.
Publications: Quarterly newsletter. "Images of America: Flat Rock."

Winifred Mae Oestrike Hamilton-Collection
Mailing Address: Local History Room-Flat Rock Public Library, 25200 Gibraltar Rd. • Flat Rock, MI 48134
Contact: Lila Fedokovitz
E-Mail: lila-flatrock@comcast.net
Phone: (734) 782-2430 • *Fax:* (734) 789-8265
Hours: Wed, Sat 12-4 p.m.
Admission: Donations accepted.
Visitor Accessibility: Parking lot located behind library. Wheelchair accessible. Tour guides sometimes available (donations accepted).
Website: http://flatrockhistory.org
About: A joint effort of Flat Rock Public Library and Flat Rock Historical Society to preserve local historical materials.
Exhibits/Collections: Covers Brownstown Township, Flat Rock, and surrounding area. Collection includes cemetery records, Vreeland and Wagar family research, N.J. Dutch records, more than 100 family records, Delbert Wagar diaries 1892-1915, photos.
Annual Events: Flea Market (May, Oct).
Publications: "Images of America - Flat Rock, MI."

Flint
(Genesee County)

Applewood Estate
Mailing Address: Ruth Mott Foundation Archives, 1400 E. Kearsley St. • Flint, MI 48503
Contact: Deborah Elliott, Estate Manager
E-Mail: delliott@ruthmott.org
Phone: (810) 233-3835
Fax: (810) 232-6937
Hours: See website.
Admission: Free. Please consider bringing food or personal care items to be donated to local shelters.
Visitor Accessibility: On-site parking. Free guided tours are available for groups of 10 or more; call ahead.
Website: www.applewood.org
About: Applewood is the estate of the Charles Stewart Mott family, built by Mr. Mott in 1916. The estate is listed on the National Register of Historic Places. Ruth Mott gave Applewood to the Ruth Mott Foundation upon her passing in 1999. It features the original home and barn, 34 acres of stately trees, and the heritage apple orchard for which it was named. Buildings include the Jacobean-Revival Residence, gatehouse, barn, and chicken coop.
Annual Events: Monthly Garden Day (May-Sep, Dec). See online calendar for special events.

Flint Genealogical Society
Mailing Address: P.O. Box 1217 • Flint, MI 48501-1217
Contact: Dale Ladd
Phone: (810) 237-3439
Website: http://www.rootsweb.ancestry.com/~mifgs/
About: Encourages, aids, and shares research education in genealogy. Helps to publish and provide historical and genealogical materials.
Exhibits/Collections: Genesee County materials including cemetery, marriage, and death records. Acquisitions and publications open to public at Flint Public Library, General Reference Section, 1026 E. Kearsley, Flint, MI 48502.
*Information may not be current.

Flint Historic District Commission
Mailing Address: Department of Planning & Development, 1101 S. Saginaw • Flint, MI 48502
Contact: Megan Hunter, Director
Phone: (810) 766-7436 • *Fax:* (810) 766-7351
Hours: Mon-Fri 9 a.m.-5 p.m.
Visitor Accessibility: Street parking. Wheelchair accessible.
Website: www.cityofflint.com
About: Established by city ordinance in 1979. Reviews plans for new construction, additions, alterations, and demolition in order to protect historical, architectural, and archeological features within historic districts.
Annual Events: Meeting 1st Thu monthly, located at Flint City Hall.

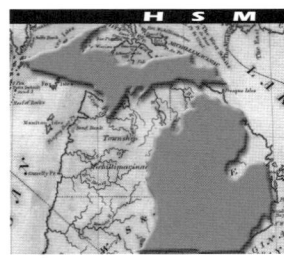

Genesee County Historical Society
Mailing Address: 316 Water St. • Flint, MI 48503
Contact: David White, President
E-Mail: dwhite@kettering.edu
Phone: (810) 410-4605
Fax: (810) 410-4908
Site/Location: **Durant-Dort Carriage Company Headquarters**
Hours: Memorial Day-Labor Day by appointment.
Admission: Free.
Visitor Accessibility: Free parking behind building. Wheelchair accessible. Tour guide available by apointment.
Website: www.geneseehistory.org
About: The society actively supports the preservation of the history of Genesee County and seeks to increase community understanding of the area's rich and varied past through its programming and publications. The society's museum is located in the restored Durant-Dort

Historical Society of Michigan

Carriage Company Headquarters, the birthplace of the General Motors Corporation. Today, the building is a National Historic Landmark that features photo exhibits, carriages, and furniture.
Exhibits/Collections: Durant-Dort Office Building. Collections located at Buick Gallery and Sloan Museum in Flint.
Annual Events: Board of Directors meet monthly. Heritage Day Dinner (May).
Publications: Newsletter, Citizen.

Genesee County Parks and Recreation Commission
Mailing Address: 5045 Stanley Road • Flint, MI 48506
Contact: Gary Pringle, Village Manager
E-Mail: parkswebteam@gcparks.org
Phone: (800) 648-7275 • *Fax:* (810) 736-7220
Site/Location: **Crossroads Village & Huckleberry Railroad**
Physical Location: 6140 Bray Road • Flint, MI 48505
Hours: May-Sep: Wed-Sun and Holidays 10 a.m.-5 p.m. See website for Oct-Dec hours.
Admission: $10/adult, $9/senior, Children $8/children. Additional charge for train, boat, and/or amusement rides. Fees vary for special events.
Visitor Accessibility: Free parking. Wheelchair accessible. Self-guided.
Website: www.geneseecountyparks.org
About: Interpreters in period costumes represent American life in the 1800s at Crossroads Village & Huckleberry Railroad. With 34 historic structures, the 51-acre village is also home to the Huckleberry Railroad, a narrow-gauge steam railroad, and the Genesee Belle, a paddle wheel riverboat.
Exhibits/Collections: Narrow-gauge steam engines, railway cars of the 1800s and early 1900s. Antique amusement rides of early 1900s. Structures of mid- to late-1800s, including blacksmith shop, print shop, and water-powered mill.
Annual Events: Weekend Themes (Memorial Day-Labor Day), Huckleberry Hustle 5K Trail Run, 5K Walk, and Little Berry Dash (Jul), Day Out with Thomas (Aug), Ladies Night Out (Nov), Halloween Ghosts & Goodies (Oct), Christmas at Crossroads (Nov-Dec).

Genesee Historical Collections Center
Mailing Address: Frances William Thompson Library, 303 W. Kearsley • Flint, MI 48502
Contact: Paul Gifford, Senior Associate Librarian
E-Mail: pgifford@umflint.edu
Phone: (810) 762-3402 • *Fax:* (810) 762-3133
Hours: Mon-Fri 1-5 p.m. and Wed 6-10 p.m.
Visitor Accessibility: On-site parking. Wheelchair accessible.
Website: www.umflint.edu/library/archives
About: Part of academic library.
Exhibits/Collections: University of Michigan-Flint records. Manuscripts and books relating to history of Flint and Genesee County.
*Information may not be current.

Kettering Archives
Mailing Address: Kettering University, 1700 University Ave. • Flint, MI 48504
Contact: David White, Archivist
E-Mail: dwhite@kettering.edu
Phone: (810) 762-9890
Fax: (810) 762-9550
Hours: Mon-Fri 9 a.m.-4 p.m., research by appointment only.
Visitor Accessibility: On-site parking. Wheelchair accessible.
Website: www.kettering.edu/archives
About: Established in 1974 as a collection of industrial history.
Exhibits/Collections: Papers of industrial organizations and individuals, including Charles F. Kettering and Billy Durant. Crooks Photo Collection, an extensive pictorial history of Flint and Genesee County. Archives of Kettering University.
Annual Events: Author and Art Fair (Oct), Book Sale (May), lectures twice a year.
Publications: "Wm C. Durant, In His Own Words," Chevrolet Photo Album.

Sloan*Longway
Mailing Address: 1221 E. Kearsley St. • Flint, MI 48503
Contact: Cathy Gentry, Marketing Manager
E-Mail: sloan@sloanlongway.org
Phone: (810) 237-3450
Site/Location: **Alfred P. Sloan Museum**
Hours: Mon-Fri 10 a.m.-5 p.m., Sat-Sun 12-5 p.m.
Admission: $9/adult, $8/senior, $6/youth (2-11), children 1 and under free.
Visitor Accessibility: Free on-site parking. Wheelchair accessible.
Website: www.sloanlongway.org/sloan-museum
About: The Sloan Museum features exhibits and displays relating to regional history, historic automobiles, and hands-on science. In the "Flint and the American Dream" exhibit, dramatic settings, video programs, and hundreds of artifacts and photographs portray the area's tumultuous 20th-century history.
Exhibits/Collections: 100,000 artifacts ranging from prehistoric stone implements to antique textiles and prototype automobiles. Photographs and papers of Flint and Genesee County history. Buick engineering papers, service manuals, and sales literature.
Annual Events: Auto Fair (Jun), Golden Memories Car Show (Sep).
Other Sites/Locations: **Buick Automotive Gallery and Research Center** • Location: 303 Walnut St., Flint, MI 48503 • Hours: Mon-Fri 10 a.m.-5 p.m., Sat 12-5 p.m. • Admission: $9/adult, $9/junior. Includes admission to Alfred P. Sloan Museum. • Visitor Accessibility: Free on-site parking. Wheelchair accessible. Self-guided. • The Buick Automotive Gallery and Research Center features more than 25 classic and concept Buicks, Chevrolets, and other locally built automobiles. Automobiles exhibited include five concept cars designed by Buick: 1951 XP-300, 1954 Wildcat II, 1956 Centurion, 1963 Silver Arrow I, and 1977 Phantom. A Hellcat Tank Destroyer built by Buick during World War II is also on display.

Sons of Union Veterans of the Civil War
Mailing Address: Department of Michigan, SUVCW, 3914 Larchmont St. • Flint, MI 48532
Contact: Donald Shaw, Commander
Phone: (810) 234-5800 • *Fax:* (810) 232-2466
Physical Location: Department of Michigan SUVCW, 535 Mayflower Dr. • Saginaw, MI 48638
Website: www.suvcwmi.org
About: A geneologically based fraternal organization dedicated to preserving the memory and objectives of the Grand Army of the Republic. Activities vary and are conducted through the organization's 23 local branches.
Annual Events: Department Encampment.
*Information may not be current.

Stockton Center at Spring Grove
Mailing Address: 720 Ann Arbor St. • Flint, MI 48503
Phone: (810) 238-9140 • *Fax:* (810) 238-9152
Hours: Tours by appointment.
Admission: $5/inidividual.
Visitor Accessibility: Free on-site parking. Wheelchair accessible. Free tour guides available.
Website: www.stocktoncenter.org
About: Dedicated to the historical preservation, education, environmental enhancement, and beautification of the Flint community. Original home to Col. Thomas Stockton and his wife Maria, daughter of Jacob Smith. It is also the location of the first St. Joseph Hospital in Flint.
Annual Events: Annual meeting (Apr), Halloween event (Oct), Christmas event (Dec).

Traveling Museum of Afrikan Ancestry & Research Center
Mailing Address: P.O. Box 660 • Flint, MI 48501
Contact: Kathryn Hunter-Williams, Curator/Founder
E-Mail: afrikanancestry@att.net
Phone: (810) 789-7324 • *Fax:* (810) 789-7327
Website: http://mbahf.netfirms.com
About: Offers outreach programs with traveling exhibits and lecture series on underground railroad.
Exhibits/Collections: Repository for collecting, documenting, and preserving contributions and achievements of people of Afrikan ancestry. 3,000 resources online, links to database, photos, and sketches on website.
Annual Events: "We're Movin' On" Afrikan American Festival (Jul), Kwanzaa Celebration (Dec).
Publications: Bimonthly newsletter (Agiza Histia Habari).
Information may not be current.

HSM MEMBER
Whaley Historic House Museum
Mailing Address: 624 E. Kearsley St. • Flint, MI 48503
Contact: Samantha Engel, Executive Director
E-Mail: 1885@whaleyhouse.com
Phone: (810) 471-4714
Hours: 1st and 3rd Sat of month 10 a.m.-1 p.m.
Admission: $5/adult, $3/student, $3/children.
Visitor Accessibility: Free on-site parking. Partially wheelchair accessible; first floor only. Tour guide available.
Website: www.whaleyhouse.com
About: The Whaley Historic House Museum was once the home of the prominent Whaley family of Flint. The home now serves as a museum that spreads Flint's history, while demonstrating life during the Gilded Age (late-19th-century America). The home, which is listed on the National Register of Historic Places, contains many items once owned by the Whaley family, as well as by other prominent Flint families. All items are, however, true to the Gilded Age.
Exhibits/Collections: Whaley family papers and photographs.
Annual Events: Christmas at the Whaley Historic House Museum (Dec). Monthly board meetings.

Flushing
(Genesee County)

HSM MEMBER
Flushing Area Historical Society
Mailing Address: 431 W. Main St. • Flushing, MI 48433
Contact: Daniel Anderson, President
E-Mail: fahs@att.net
Phone: (810) 487-0814
Site/Location: **Flushing Area Museum and Cultural Center**
Hours: May-Dec: Sun 1-4 p.m. Closed all holiday weekends.
Admission: Free.
Visitor Accessibility: Free on-site parking. Wheelchair accessible. Self-guided.
Website: www.flushinghistorical.org
About: The Flushing Area Historical Society manages the history and culture of the area in and around Flushing. The society maintains the Flushing Depot, which operates as a museum and cultural center. The restored 1888 Grand Trunk depot museum features railroading and local history, veterinary medical equipment, drugstore items, 1930s kitchen appliances, and a shaving mug display.
Exhibits/Collections: 20,000 obituaries with index from Flushing Observer, family histories, research materials on homes and businesses. A database is underway for all major articles in the Flushing Observer from 1882-1980s.
Annual Events: Candlewalk (Dec). Meetings 3rd Mon monthly (Jan-May, Sep-Nov), 7:30p.m. at museum.
Publications: Newsletter, "Flushing Sesquicentennial History, Vol. I (1835-1985), Vol. II (1835-1987), and Vol. III (1835-1998)."

Fowlerville
(Livingston County)

HSM MEMBER
Livingston Centre Historical Village
Mailing Address: P.O. Box 372 • Fowlerville, MI 48836
Contact: Jennifer Rhodes, Office Manager
E-Mail: fair@fowlervillefamilyfair.com
Phone: 517-223-8186
Fax: 517-223-0280
Physical Location: 8800 W. Grand River Ave. • Fowlerville, MI 48836
Hours: By appointment or during fairground events.
Admission: Donations accepted.
Visitor Accessibility: Free on-site parking. Partially wheelchair accessible. Tour guides available by appointment.
Website: www.fowlervillefamilyfair.com
About: The Livingston Centre Historical Village includes eight buildings: 1869 home of early settlers, 1872 Grand Marquette Depot, 1906 Methodist Church, 1880s barn with silo, 1910 barber shop, 1870 cobbler shop, and 1882 schoolhouse and blacksmith shop.
Exhibits/Collections: Several original collections from period and specific buildings within them.
Annual Events: Meetings 1st Thu monthly, Fowlervile Fairgrounds office.

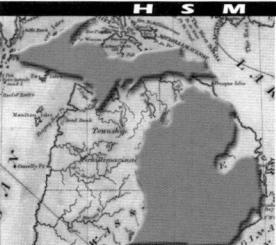

Frankenmuth
(Saginaw County)

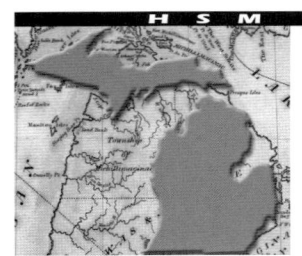

Frankenmuth Historical Association — *HSM MEMBER*

Mailing Address: 613 S. Main St. • Frankenmuth, MI 48734
Contact: Ammiee Kotch
E-Mail: fhaoffice@airadv.net
Phone: (989) 652-9701
Site/Location: **Frankenmuth Historical Museum**
Physical Location: 613 South Main Street • Frankenmuth, MI 48734
Hours: Mon-Thu 10 a.m.-5 p.m., Fri-Sat 10 a.m.-7 p.m., and Sun 12-6 p.m.
Admission: $2/adult, $1/student, $5/family. Paid admission gives visitor free admission to Lager Mill Museum.
Visitor Accessibility: Free public parking. Wheelchair accessible. Self-guided.
Website: www.frankenmuthmuseum.org
About: The Frankenmuth Historical Association preserves, communicates, and celebrates the heritage of the Franconian communities. In addition to its two museums, the association maintains the Log Cabin in Cross Park as well as Fischer Hall. The association also provides education programs for local schools, scout groups, etc. The programs can be held on site, in the classroom, historic Fischer Hall, or at the Log Cabin in Cross Park. The Frankenmuth Historical Museum focuses on the history of Frankenmuth. Exhibits change quarterly.
Exhibits/Collections: 16,000 artifacts. Extensive research material on German immigration and socialization.
Annual Events: Volunteer Luncheon (Feb and Jul), Annual Meeting (Mar), Spring Reception - members only (May), Fundraising Auction (Nov). Board meetings last Mon monthly.
Publications: "Images from America Frankenmuth," "Frankenmuth: A Valuable Work Ethic," "A Pictorial History of Frankenmuth," "Visions Realized: Frankenmuth's Geographical, Political, Boundary, Govermental Structure and Public Works History, 1919-1979." "How Firm A Foundation: The Founding of St. Lorenz Luthern Church and the Community of Frankenmuth," "Fischer Hall: Frankenmuth's Gathering Place."
Other Sites/Locations: **Lager Mill Brewing Museum** • Location: 701 Mill St., Frankenmuth, MI • Hours: Mon-Thu 11 a.m.-7 p.m.; Fri-Sat 10 a.m.-9 p.m.; Sun 12-6pm. • Admission: Adults $2, Students $1, Family $5. Paid admission gives visitor free admission to Frankenmuth Historical Museum. • Visitor Accessibility: Free on-site parking. Wheelchair accessible. Self-guided. • The Lager Mill Brewing Museum shares Frankenmuth's brewing heritage and explores the brewing process. The two-story brewing museum is housed in the historic Nickless-Hubinger flour mill along the Cass River. Displays include antique signs, glasses, and bottles.

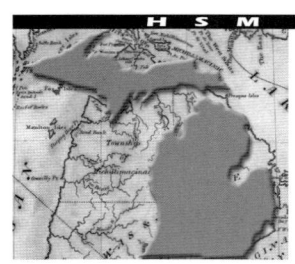

Michigan's Military & Space Heroes Museum — *HSM MEMBER*

Mailing Address: 1250 Weiss St. • Frankenmuth, MI 48734
Contact: John Ryder
E-Mail: michown@ejourney.com
Phone: (989) 652-8005
Hours: Mar-Dec: Sat-Sun 10 a.m.-5 p.m.
Admission: $5/adult, $4/senior (65+), $2/student (6-18), Children 6 and under free.
Visitor Accessibility: On-site parking. Wheelchair accessible. Tour guides available.
Website: www.michigansmilitarymuseum.com
About: Nurtures memories of those from Michigan who heeded the summons to military service from the Spanish American War to the War on Terror and of those who served in the nation's space program. Attractions include uniforms of five Michigan govenors, the largest collection of Medals of Honor in the United States, Michigan space pioneers, and the uniforms of all 13 Michigan astronauts.
Annual Events: Patriot's Day, September 11th Memorial Ceremony; the Frankenmuth Bavarian Festival Parade. Biannual board of director's meeting in Frankenmuth.
Information may not be current.

Frankfort
(Benzie County)

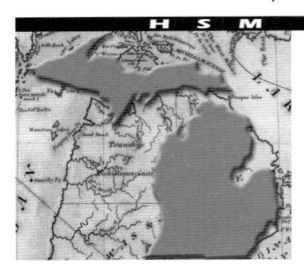

Friends of Point Betsie Lighthouse, Inc. — *HSM MEMBER*

Mailing Address: P.O. Box 601 • Frankfort, MI 49635
Contact: Charles Clarke, Treasurer
E-Mail: info@pointbetsie.org
Phone: (231) 352-7644
Hours: May-Oct: Sat 10:30 a.m-5 p.m., Sun 12:30-4:30 p.m. Jul-Aug: Thu-Fri 10:30 a.m.-4:30 p.m.
Admission: $4/adult, $2/children (0-12), children 6 and under free.
Visitor Accessibility: Free street parking. Wheelchair accessible. Tour guide available.
Website: www.pointbetsie.org
About: The Friends operate the Point Betsie Light Station, which is owned by Benzie County. Supports the restoration, preservation, and maintenance of the historic lighthouse, which remains an official navigational aid maintained by the U.S. Coast Guard. Volunteers provide interpretive information about the lighthouse and site. Extensive displays of light-keeping and lifesaving at Point Betsie. The century-old 4th Order Fresnel Lens is a featured display.

Franklin
(Oakland County)

Franklin Historic District Commission

Mailing Address: Franklin Village Hall, 32325 Franklin Rd. • Franklin, MI 48025
Contact: Gary Roberts, Chair
E-Mail: clerk@franklin.mi.us
Phone: (248) 626-9666 • *Fax:* (248) 626-0538
Hours: Mon-Fri 9 a.m.-5 p.m.
Admission: Call ahead for current prices.
Visitor Accessibility: Public parking available. Wheelchair accessible.
Website: www.franklin.mi.us
About: A governmental body operated under Michigan conformed legislation, Franklin was the first nationally registered district in Michigan. Historic district guidelines are available in the office and on the website.
Annual Events: Meetings 1st Mon monthly, 7:30 p.m. at Franklin Village Hall.

Franklin Historical Society

Mailing Address: P.O. Box 250007 • Franklin, MI 48025
Contact: Ann Lamott, President
E-Mail: info@franklin-history.org
Physical Location: 26165 13 Mile Rd. • Franklin, MI 49412
Hours: 1st Sat 1-3 p.m., also by appointment.

Admission: Free.
Visitor Accessibility: Free on-site parking.
Website: http://franklin-history.org
About: Preserves and protects objects, sites, and buildings that are of interest in the history of Franklin. Museum in 1951 ranch home donated by Derwich family.
Exhibits/Collections: Artifacts and documents of Franklin community and organizations.
Annual Events: Meetings 2nd Thu monthly, 7 p.m. at museum.
Publications: Biannual newsletter.

Village of Franklin Historic District Commission
Mailing Address: 32325 Franklin Rd. • Franklin, MI 48025
Contact: Eileen Pulker, Clerk
E-Mail: clerk@franklin.mi.us
Phone: (248) 626-9666 • *Fax:* (248) 626-0538
Visitor Accessibility: Free on-site parking. Wheelchair accessible. Self-guided.
Website: http://www.franklin.mi.us

Fraser
(Macomb County)

Fraser Historical Commission
Mailing Address: c/o Fraser Public Library, 16330 14 Mile Rd. • Fraser, MI 48026
Contact: Marilynn Wright
Phone: (586) 294-6633 • *Fax:* (586) 294-5777
Site/Location: **Baumgartner House and Hemme Barn**
Physical Location: 18577 Masonic Avenue • Fraser, MI 48026
Hours: 1st Sun monthly 1-4 p.m., 2nd Sun (Jun, Sep). Closed Jan-Feb, Jul.
Admission: Donations accepted.
Visitor Accessibility: Parking next to museum. Partially wheechair accessible; depot welcome center and Hemmer Barn only. Free tour guide available.
Website: www.micityoffraser.com
About: The Fraser Historical Commission preserves two historical buildings: The Baumgartner House and Museum and Hemme Barn. The commission also hosts tours, raises funds to support the property, and writes articles regarding Fraser's history.
Exhibits/Collections: Collection of items featuring strawberries.
Annual Events: Flea Market and Resale (spring and fall), Fall Dinner Show (Oct). Meetings 1st Mon monthly (except Jan, Jul), 7 p.m. in the depot's welcome center.
Publications: Biannual newsletter (Strawberry Preserves).

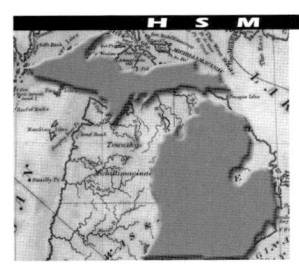

Fraser Historical Society
Mailing Address: PO Box 26155 • Fraser, MI 48026
Contact: Julie Racine, Treasurer
E-Mail: jaracine0186@yahoo.com
Phone: (586) 293-0186
Site/Location: **Baumgartner House**
Physical Location: 18577 Masonic Avenue • Fraser, MI 48026
Hours: 1st Sun monthly.
Admission: Free.
Visitor Accessibility: Free on-site parking. Not wheelchair accessible. Free tour guide available.

About: The Fraser Historical Society supports the work of Fraser Historical Commission by helping with tours of the 1865 Baumgarten House and fundraising activities.
Exhibits/Collections: Several collections stored in Baumgartner House Museum.
Annual Events: Flea Market (spring and fall).
Publications: Biannual publication (Strawberry Preserves).

Fremont
(Newaygo County)

Fremont Area District Library Local History Room
Mailing Address: 104 E. Main St. • Fremont, MI 49412
Contact: Susan Herrick, Reference Librarian
E-Mail: fadl@fremontlibrary.net
Phone: (231) 928-0253
Fax: (231) 924-2355
Hours: History Room: Mon, Tue 10 a.m.-1 p.m.; Fri 10 a.m.-1 p.m., 2 p.m.-5 p.m. Also by appointment.
Visitor Accessibility: On-site parking. Wheelchair accessible.
Website: www.fremontlibrary.net
About: Preserves Newaygo County's history as well as documents the histories of the families who helped form it. Also helps beginners learn their history by teaching and assisting patrons with their family trees.
Exhibits/Collections: Compiled local history and family histories. Extensive collection of obituary, marriage, birth, and anniversary records.

Fremont Historical Society
Mailing Address: 445 Lewis Ln. • Fremont, MI 49412
Information may not be current.

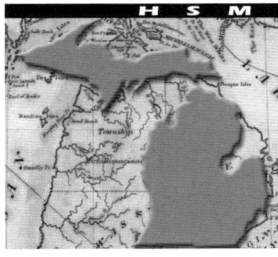

Terry Wantz Historical Research Center
Mailing Address: 10 W. Main St., P.O. Box 2 • Fremont, MI 49412
Contact: Sandy Vincent Peavey, Director
E-Mail: sandy.historycenter@gmail.com
Phone: (231) 335-2221
Fax: (231) 335-2221
Hours: Tue-Wed 10 a.m.-7 p.m., Thu-Fri 10 a.m.-5 p.m., 1st and 2nd Sat monthly 10 a.m.-2 p.m.
Admission: Free.
Visitor Accessibility: Free on-site parking. Wheelchair accessible. Tour guide available.
Website: www.wantzhistorycenter.com
About: A nonprofit historical research center that preserves and archives Newaygo County's history and that works toward preserving the past through oral histories and gathering family histories.
Exhibits/Collections: Newaygo County genealogies and histories.
Annual Events: Cemetery Walk, Gen Chat.
Publications: "World War I: Letters Home," "Newaygo County 1920-1980."

Gagetown
(Tuscola County)

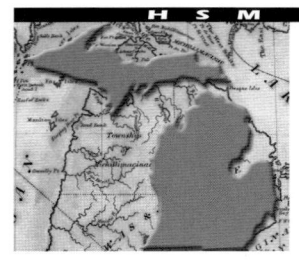

Friends of the Thumb Octagon Barn
Mailing Address: P.O. Box 145 • Gagetown, MI 48735
Contact: Rose Putnam, President
Phone: (989) 665-0081
Physical Location: 6948 Richie Rd. • Gagetown, MI 48735
Hours: May-Sep: Daily 9 a.m.-6 p.m. Oct: By appointment only.
Admission: $2/self-guided tour, $5/guided tour.
Visitor Accessibility: Free on-site parking. Wheelchair accessible. Tour guides available upon request.
Website: www.thumboctagonbarn.org
About: This volunteer group is committed to the preservation and restoration of the Thumb Octagon Barn Complex as an educational tool for preserving the area's rural and agricultural history. The 70-foot-high, 8,000-square-foot Octagon Barn was part of the "Mud Lake Estate," built by banker James Purdy in the 1920s. Site includes the Craftsman-style Purdy home, a one-room school, grain elevator, and blacksmith shop.
Exhibits/Collections: Logging equipment, milk parlor, milk wagon, fire truck, hand tools, hay equipment, sugar beet equipment, bean sorters and separators, working legs in grain elevator, Thumb-Two Cylinder display, buggies, and hand plows.
Annual Events: School tours (May), Themed tea parties (Jun-Aug), Bluegrass concert (Jul), Fall Family Days (Sep), Christmas Open House, Countywide Historical Museums Open House, Steam School (Aug).
Publications: The Story of the "Mud Lake Estate."
Information may not be current.

Gaines
(Genesee County)

Swartz Creek Area Historical Society
Mailing Address: 11353 W. Cook Rd. • Gaines, MI 48436
Contact: Tim Buda, Secretary & Treasurer
E-Mail: tbuda@shianet.org
Phone: (989) 271-9193
Physical Location: Swartz Creek City Hall, 8083 Civic Drive • Swartz Creek, MI
Hours: Mon-Fri 9 a.m.-4:30 p.m.
Admission: Free.
Visitor Accessibility: Free on-site parking. Wheelchair accessible. Free tours by appointment.
Website: www.swartzcreekhistory.com
About: Preserves, collects, and displays any material related to the history of the Swartz Creek area. Educates local students about their history. Mini museum in Swartz Creek City Hall. Revolving exhibits include a large display of the Crapo Farm, including artifacts made by American Indians who once lived on the farm.
Annual Events: Meetings 2nd Wed monthly, 7 p.m. at Swartz Creek City Hall, 8083 Civic Drive.
Publications: Bi-monthly newsletter. "Going Up the Swartz."
Information may not be current.

Galesburg
(Kalamazoo County)

Galesburg Historical Museum
Mailing Address: 190 E. Michigan Ave. • Galesburg, MI 49053
Contact: Keith Martin, Curator
Phone: (269) 665-9011
Hours: Wed 4:30-6:30 p.m., Sat 10 a.m.-2 p.m.
Admission: Donations accepted.
Visitor Accessibility: On-site parking. Wheelchair accessible. Self-guided, guided tours available with advance notice. Call (269) 665-9953 to make reservations.
Website: www.galesburgcity.org
About: The Galesburg Historical Museum serves as a repository for historical artifacts from the Galesburg and surrounding areas. The museum's exhibits include an 1860s linear four-room house (kitchen, parlor, dining room, and bedroom).
Exhibits/Collections: Photos, early business history, military memorabilia, railroad and interurban history, small appliances, and General William Rufus Shafter history, and more.
Annual Events: Greater Galesburg Days (Jun). Board meets 3rd Wed monthly.

Galien
(Berrien County)

Galien Woods Historical Society
Mailing Address: P.O. Box 162 • Galien, MI 49113
Contact: Donna Potter
Physical Location: 107 S. Grant St. • Galien, MI 49113
Hours: Year round: Tue 9 a.m.-12 p.m. Aug: Sat 1-4 p.m. Also by appointment.
Admission: Free.
Visitor Accessibility: On-site parking. Not wheelchair accessible.
About: The Galien Woods Historical Society promotes interest in, preserves, and restores history, historical buildings, and objects pertaining and contributing to the area, record books, family histories, historical sites, and markers. Attractions include an 1879 restored jail.
Exhibits/Collections: Stage curtain from township hall; veteran and school pictures; record books and ledgers; settlers site map; 1860 Tri-County map; pictures and artifacts; plus collection of trophies from Galien Township high School.
Annual Events: Christmas Party (Dec), White Elephant Sale (Dec). Monthly public programs last Thu Mar-Oct at 7 p.m. and 1st Dec at 12 p.m. Call ahead to verify times.
Publications: Cemetery books and quarterly newsletter.
Information may not be current.

Garden
(Delta County)

Fayette Historic Townsite.
Please see entry under Lansing: Michigan Historical Center.

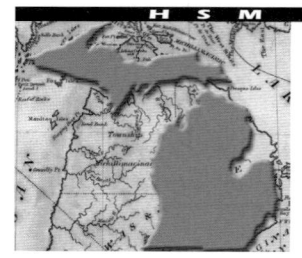

Garden Peninsula Historical Society
Mailing Address: P.O. Box 6 • Garden, MI 49835
Contact: Connie Wilson, President
Site/Location: **Garden Peninsula Historical Society Museum**

Physical Location: 6347 State St. • Garden, MI 49835
Hours: Wed-Sat 11 a.m.-3 p.m.
Admission: Free.
Visitor Accessibility: Free street parking. Wheelchair accessible. Self-guided.
About: The Garden Peninsula Historical Society Museum is located in a former schoolhouse that had an addition created to accomodate more artifacts. The museum considers local history and includes a genealogy department.
Annual Events: 4th of July Fundraiser, Honoree Dinner. Meetings 1st Mon monthly (May-Oct), 1 p.m. at museum.
Publications: Contact for list of current publications.

Garden City
(Wayne County)

Friends of the Garden City Historical Museum
Mailing Address: 6221 Merriman Rd. • Garden City, MI 48135
Contact: Mark Hammar, Board President
E-Mail: straight.farmhouse@yahoo.com
Phone: (734) 838-0650
Site/Location: **The Straight Farmhouse**
Hours: Wed and Sat 12-3 p.m.
Admission: Donations accepted.
Visitor Accessibility: Free on-site parking. Wheelchair accessible. Tour guide available.
Website: www.sfhonline.org
About: The Friends of the Garden City Historical Museum provides a museum in Garden City, which preserves the history of the community and serves as an educational center. The museum contains artifacts from the orgins of Garden City, a re-creation of a 1930s post office, Lathers General Store, Grande Parlour Banquet Room, and three floors of exhibits in the 1866 Straight Farmhouse.
Exhibits/Collections: Archives and artifacts from the early days of Garden City as well as notable business start-ups, such as the first KMart and the first Little Caesars Pizza shop in Michigan.
Annual Events: Board of directors meetings 2nd Wed monthly, 4 p.m. at Straight Farmhouse.
Publications: "Early Days of Garden City," "Chronicles of Garden City," Quarterly membership newsletter.

Garden City Historical Museum
Mailing Address: Maplewood Community Center, 31735 Maplewood • Garden City, MI 48135
Phone: (734) 421-1540 • *Fax:* (734) 422-3855
Information may not be current.

Gaylord
(Otsego County)

Gaylord Fact-Finders Genealogical Society
Mailing Address: P.O. Box 1524 • Gaylord, MI 49734
Contact: Susan Giessel, President
E-Mail: pinelake2014@gmail.com
Website: http://www.otsego.org/factfinders
About: The purpose of the Gaylord Fact-Finders is to research family histories and genealogy and to obtain documents that pertain to our heritage. All documents will be made available for public use.
Annual Events: Meetings 3rd Wed Jan-Jun and Aug-Nov, 7 p.m. at Otsego County Library.
Publications: Quarterly newsletter (Keystone).

Otsego County Historical Society
Mailing Address: P.O. Box 1223 • Gaylord, MI 49734
Contact: Jim Akans, Executive Director
E-Mail: ochsmuseum@gmail.com
Phone: (989) 732-4568
Fax: (989) 732-4568
Site/Location: **Otsego County Historical Museum**
Physical Location: 320 W. Main St • Gaylord, MI 49734
Hours: Mon-Tue, Thur-Sat 11 a.m.-5 p.m.
Admission: Free.
Visitor Accessibility: On-site parking. Wheelchair accessible. Self-guided.
Website: www.otsego.org/ochs
About: Organized in 1963, the Otsego County Historical Society Museum is located in the former cigar factory building. Exhibits highlight lumbering, farming, furniture, commerce, and the Dayton Lost Block Works of Gaylord.
Annual Events: Antique Appraisal (Sep).
Publications: Otsego Logging Calendar. "A Step Back in Time Vol 1-3," "Ghosts of the Past: Railroads of Otsego County," "Tomorrow's Saturday," "The Early History of Otsego County," "Recipes and Remembrances."
Information may not be current.

Gibraltar
(Wayne County)

Gibraltar Historical Museum
Mailing Address: 29450 Munro Ave. • Gibraltar, MI 48173
Phone: (734) 676-3900
Information may not be current.

Gladwin
(Gladwin County)

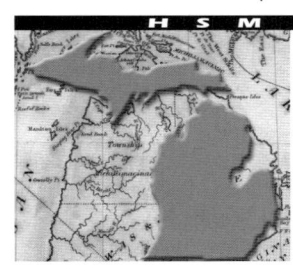

Gladwin County Historical Society
Mailing Address: 221 W. Cedar Ave. • Gladwin, MI 48624
Contact: Bruce Guy, President
E-Mail: historicalsociety@ejourney.com
Phone: (989) 426-9277
Site/Location: **Gladwin County Historical Museum**
Hours: Thu-Sat 10 a.m-4 p.m.
Admission: Free.
Visitor Accessibility: Free on-site parking. Wheelchair accessible; use rear entrance. Docent available; donations accepted.
Website: www.gladwinhistory.org
About: The Gladwin County Historical Society brings together those interested in history, especially of Gladwin County. The society collects and preserves historical photographs, written materials, and artifacts. Attractions at the Gladwin County Historical Museum include antiques belonging to the first families, WWI memorabilia, an 1850s Square Grand Piano, an antique barbershop, portable embalming table and tools, and antique hand tools.
Exhibits/Collections: Farming and logging tools, Civil War and military uniforms, and antique household utensils.
Annual Events: Log Cabin Days, Founders Day, Carriage Festival. See website for meetings schedule.

Publications: "Gladwin History: Then & Now," "Beaverton: A Century in the Making," "Gladwin Illustrated: A History in Photographs," "The First Years," "The Gladwin County First Settler Centennial 1861-1961," "My Journey From 11-11-11, A Memoir," "Settler: A Journey Into Michigans."
Other Sites/Locations: **Gladwin County Historical Village** • Location: 515 E. Cedar, Gladwin, MI 48624 • Hours: Memorial Day to Labor Day: Sat 10 a.m.-4 p.m. • Admission: Free • Visitor Accessibility: Free parking. Wheelchair accessible. • The Gladwin County Historical Village is a complex featuring a restored Michigan Central Railroad depot with seven other buildings. The collection includes a carriage house (c. 1890) with a carriage and a cutter collection at the fairgrounds.

Goodells
(St. Clair County)

St. Clair County Farm Museum
Mailing Address: 8310 County Park Dr., P.O. Box 202 • Goodells, MI 48027
Contact: Doug Porrett, History Committee Chair
E-Mail: dcporrett@hotmail.com
Phone: (810) 325-1737
Hours: Call for current hours.
Admission: Free.
Visitor Accessibility: Free on-site parking. Not wheelchair accessible. Tour guide available; reservations recommended.
Website: www.stclaircountyfarmmuseum.com
About: The St. Clair County Farm Museum acquires, preserves, demonstrates, and exhibits artifacts to provide an understanding of the agricultural heritage of St. Clair County. While farming, lumbering, and rural domestic life is addressed for all periods of the county's development, the primary focus is on the time period between 1880 and 1965, when the county farm was an active agricultural operation. Located in a restored farmhouse, the museum has a large collection of antique and vintage farming equipment.
Exhibits/Collections: Horse-drawn, steam-powered, and gas-powered farming equipment; domestic items, handmade and muscle-powered through factory-made and electrified; antiquarian books, generally related to rural and agrarian subjects; artwork, primarily prints.
Annual Events: Old Fashioned Harvest Days Steam & Horsepower Show (Aug). Meetings 3rd Tue monthly at 7 p.m.

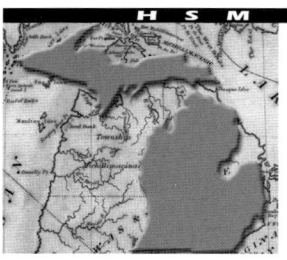

Wales Historical Society
Mailing Address: 8674 Morris Rd. • Goodells, MI 48027
Contact: Herman Weng, President
E-Mail: hermweng@gmail.com
Phone: (810) 325-1146
Site/Location: **Historic Village at Goodells County Park**
Physical Location: 8345 County Park Drive • Goodells, MI 48207
Hours: Open for schools and private tours upon request; call Herman Weng at (810) 325-1146.
Admission: Donations accepted.
Visitor Accessibility: Free on-site parking. Wheelchair accessible. Free tour guide available.
Website: www.waleshistoricalsociety.org
About: The society preserves the heritage of the Wales Township area. The society collaborates with St. Clair County at the Historic Village at Goodells County Park. Attractions include CC Peck Bank (c. 1900), Lynn School (c. 1882), Mudge Log Cabin (c. 1860), and Murphy-Ryan Farm (c. 1871). Local family archives are on display in CC Peck Bank. Extensive library of local history books located in the Lynn School. The park was once the location of the county's poor farm.
Exhibits/Collections: Archives include local township history dating from 1848-1900s, available on the society's website. Documents from Dr. Horace Modge, a Civil War doctor and director of the county's poor farm.
Annual Events: Earth Fair (Apr), School End of Year Field Days, Log Cabin Day (Jun), St. Clair County 4-H Fair (Jul-Aug), Harvest Festival (Sep). Meetings 2nd Wed monthly, either at CC Peck Bank or Wales Township Hall (depending on weather).
Publications: Annual historical calendar.
Other Sites/Locations: **Wales Township Hall** • Location: 1372 Wales Center Rd., Wales, MI 48027 • The Wales Historical Society stores its archives at the Wales Township Hall, which is listed on the State Register of Historic Sites.

Goodrich
(Genesee County)

Goodrich-Atlas Area Historical Society
Mailing Address: P.O. Box 661 • Goodrich, MI 48438
Contact: Nancy Dugas
Phone: 810-636-7194
Physical Location: 10219 Hegel Road • Goodrich, MI 48438
Hours: May-Dec: 2nd, 4th Sat 11 a.m.-1 p.m.
About: Organized in 1991. Museum opened former store in 1998. Displays memorabilia and local artifacts.
Annual Events: Good Times in Goodrich (Sep), Lunch with Santa, Christmas in Downtown Goodrich. Meetings 1st Mon (Apr-Dec).
Publications: Video of Goodrich-Atlas history.
*Information may not be current.

Gould City
(Mackinac County)

Newton Township Historical Society
Mailing Address: P.O. Box 2 • Gould City, MI 49838
Contact: Lucille Kenyon, President
E-Mail: genilady@hughes.net
Phone: (906) 586-3382
Physical Location: N6125 S. Gould City Road • Gould City, MI 49838
Hours: Not established yet.
Admission: Not established yet.
Visitor Accessibility: Street parking. Not wheelchair accessible.
Website: http://gould-city-historical-society-com.webs.com/
About: The Newton Township Historical Society's mission is to collect and preserve the history of Newton Township and make it available to others. The society aquired a museum building in October 2012 and is currently preparing the museum for the public.
Exhibits/Collections: 500-plus photos have been scanned. Local items are being collected.
Annual Events: Tea and History, Annual Meeting (Sep). Meetings 2nd Sun bimonthly at 2p.m.

Grand Blanc
(Genesee County)

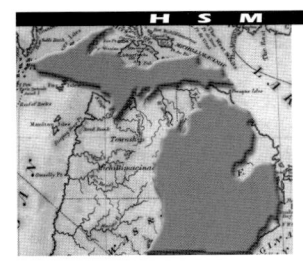

Gospel Army Black History Group
Mailing Address: 5125 Sandalwood Dr • Grand Blanc, MI 48439
E-Mail: thegospelarmy@yahoo.com
Website: thegospelarmy.com
Information may not be current.

Grand Blanc Heritage Association
Mailing Address: 203 E. Grand Blanc Rd. • Grand Blanc, MI 48439
Contact: Dan Harrett, Museum Director
E-Mail: dharrett@tir.com
Phone: 810-694-7274
Fax: (810) 694-9517
Site/Location: Grand Blanc Heritage Association Museum
Hours: Wed 10 a.m.-2 p.m.
Admission: Donations accepted.
Visitor Accessibility: Free on-site parking. Partial wheelchair accessibility. Tour guides available; trained docents can be arranged for group tours.
Website: http://www.cityofgrandblanc.com/Departments/HeritageMuseum/tabid/5996/Default.aspx/
About: The Grand Blanc Heritage Association discovers, documents, collects, preserves, researches, and exhibits any tangible materials that help establish or illustrate the history of the community and surrounding area. Located in the former 1885 Congregational Church, the museum building is listed on the Michigan Register of Historic Structures. It features four exhibit rooms, which display a restored 1922 player piano and 1875 reed organ among other artifacts.
Exhibits/Collections: Extensive collection of artifacts, historical articles, clippings, publications, quilts, and photographs. Also extensive genealogical collection (print and digital).
Annual Events: Memorial Day Open House (May), Old-Fashioned Christmas Program (Dec). Meetings 4th Mon Jan-Apr and Aug-Oct.
Publications: "Footsteps Through the 'Great White' Country: A Pioneer History of Grand Blance Township."

Grand Haven
(Ottawa County)

Grand Haven Historic Conservation District Commission
Mailing Address: Grand Haven City Hall, 519 Washington • Grand Haven, MI 49417
Contact: George Dood
E-Mail: georgedood@grandhaven.org
Phone: 616-847-3490 • **Fax:** 616-844-2051
Hours: Mon-Fri 8 a.m.-5 p.m.
Website: http://www.grandhaven.org
About: Safeguards heritage of Grand Haven by preserving landmarks and sites which reflect the city's cultural, social, economic, political, or architectural history.
Information may not be current.

Pere Marquette Historical Society
Mailing Address: P.O. Box 422 • Grand Haven, MI 49417
Contact: Bob VandeVusse, President
Website: www.pmhistsoc.org
About: Membership organization preserves history of the Pere Marquette Railway and its predecessors.
Exhibits/Collections: Archival collection is located in the Joint Archives of Holland. (See separate listing).
Publications: Newsletter (Pere Marquette Tracks).

Pere Marquette Preservation Committee
Mailing Address: Tri-Cities Historical Museum, 200 Washington Ave. • Grand Haven, MI 49417
Phone: (616) 842-0700 • **Fax:** (616) 842-3698
Hours: Mon-Sun 8 a.m.-dusk.
Admission: Free to the public, train for display only.
Website: www.tri-citiesmuseum.org/1223-locomotive.html
About: Volunteer committee of the Tri-Cities Museum works to restore and maintain Pere Marquette locomotive #1223 and other railroad equipment displayed outdoors on former terminal of the Detroit & Milwaukee Railway.
Annual Events: 1223 Ice Cream Social (Aug).

Tri-Cities Historical Museum
Mailing Address: 200 Washington Ave. • Grand Haven, MI 49417
Contact: Steven Radtke, Director
Phone: (616) 842-0700
Fax: (616) 842-3698
Hours: Summer: Tue-Fri 10 a.m.-8 p.m., Sat-Sun 12-8 p.m. Winter: Tue-Fri 10 a.m.-5 p.m., Sat-Sun 12-5 p.m.
Admission: Donations accepted.
Visitor Accessibility: Free street and on-site parking. Wheelchair accessible. Self-guided.
Website: www.tri-citiesmuseum.org
About: The Tri-Cities Historical Museum details the development and history of Northwest Ottawa County. The museum is located in the newly renovated Akeley Building, located in Grand Haven's historic downtown. Exhibits include an authentic Native-American wickiup; the 1920s Ekkens Store; a re-created Bastian and Blessing soda fountain; and displays relating to local/state geology, fur trading, lumbering, pioneers, farming, industry, banking, business, building, and general living.
Annual Events: Board of directors meet 2nd Mon monthly at museum.
Publications: Quarterly membership newsletter (The River Winds), Semiannual Journal (The Grand River Packet).
Other Sites/Locations: Grand Trunk Depot Museum of Transportation • Location: 1 N. Harbor Drive, Grand Haven, MI 49417 • Hours: Summer: Tue-Fri 10 a.m.-8 p.m., Sat-Sun 12-8 p.m. • Admission: Donations accepted • Visitor Accessibility: Free street and on-site parking. Wheelchair accessible. • The Grand Trunk Depot Museum of Transportation is located in a restored 1870 Detroit & Milwaukee Depot that showcases the history of railroading, automobiles, and maritime history on the Great Lakes.
Dewitt School House • Location: Taft Street and 180th Avenue • Hours: By appointment • Admission: Donations accepted • Visitor Accessibility: Free street parking. Not wheelchair accessible. Tour guide available. • Located in a one-room schoolhouse, the Dewitt School House offers a five-hour program highlighting the curriculum used in 1895. This program is offered the last week of April through the first week of June and is open to classes studying Michigan history. Call for reservations.

Grand Ledge
(Eaton County)

Grand Ledge Area Historical Society
Mailing Address: P.O. Box 203 • Grand Ledge, MI 48837
Contact: Marilyn Smith, Chairman
E-Mail: marnor1@comcast.net
Phone: (517) 627-5170
Fax: (517) 627-5170
Site/Location: **Grand Ledge Area Historical Society Museum**
Physical Location: 118 W. Lincoln St. • Grand Ledge, MI 48837
Hours: Tue 10 a.m.-12 p.m., Sun 2-4 p.m., Festival Days 12-4 p.m. Also by appointment.
Admission: Donations accepted.
Visitor Accessibility: Street and church parking lot behind building. Wheelchair accessible. Tour guide available; $25 by special arrangement, school groups free.
Website: www.gdledgehistsoc.org
About: The society preserves local area history, information, artifacts, and photos and shares them with the community through programs, publications, website, museum displays, and mini displays. The society works with other groups to preserve historic sites, such as the Islands and the 1880s museum, 1884 opera house, and the 1895 Ledges Playhouse (former spiritual meeting house). Housed in an 1880 Gothic Revival House, the society changes its themed exhibit each year.
Exhibits/Collections: Archives and photographs are housed at the Grand Ledge District Library; includes businesses, cultural activities, families, schools, churches, and genealogical research materials. To schedule an appointment, call (517) 627-5170.
Annual Events: Victorian Days (May), Garden Tour (Jun), Holiday Traditions Home Tour (Dec). Meetings 1st Tue of Feb-Jun, Oct and Nov, 7:30 p.m. at Grand Ledge Opera House, 121 S. Bridge St.
Publications: "Grand Ledge Remembered," "Through the Years, Vol. I & II," "GLHS Graduates," "Sincerely, Frank D. Fitzgerald," "Greetings from Grand Ledge," "Cast in Clay."

Grand Marais
(Alger County)

Grand Marais Historical Society
Mailing Address: P.O. Box 179 • Grand Marais, MI 49839
Contact: Pat Munger, President
E-Mail: gmhistoricalsociety@gmail.com
Phone: 906-494-2404
Hours: Hours vary between venues.
Admission: Donations accepted. Walking tour books $1.
Visitor Accessibility: Street parking. Partially wheelchair accessible; some venues are not. See website. Docents available at Lighthouse Keeper's House and Pickle Barrel Museum.
Website: http://historicalsociety.grandmaraismichigan.com
About: The Grand Marais Historical Society is dedicated to preserving and protecting the history of Grand Marais and Burt Township, while educating residents and visitors on the area's rich history. The society offers the Promenade Through the Past walking tour, which includes 25 historic sites and buildings throughout Grand Marais.
Exhibits/Collections: Logging, commercial fishing artifacts. Store ledgers, photos, 1900 Burt Twp. census records. Shipwreck artifacts and items relating to the Teenie Weenies and William and Mary Donahey, U.S. Life Saving Service artifacts.
Annual Events: Plant Sale (Memorial Day Weekend), Community Yard Sale (Jun), Silent Auction (Jul), Garden Tour (Jul), Historic Iris Sale (Aug). Monthly meetings Apr-Nov and as needed in the winter.
Publications: "Grand Marais," "Around Our Table."
Other Sites/Locations: **The Old Post Office Museum** • Location: N14272 Lake Ave., Grand Marais, MI 49839 • Hours: Jun-Sep: Daily • Admission: Donations accepted • Visitor Accessibility: Free street parking. Wheelchair accessible. Self-guided. • The Old Post Office Museum showcases the history of Grand Marais from its early settlement to the present day. A memorial rose garden is located behind the museum.
Lightkeeper's House Museum • Location: E22050 Coast Guard Point Road, Grand Marais, MI 49839 • Hours: Jun & Sep: Sat-Sun 1-4 p.m.; Jul-Aug: Daily 1-4 p.m. • Admission: Donations accepted • Visitor Accessibility: Free street parking. Not wheelchair accessible. Docents on site. • Built in 1906, this museum is the restored residence of the Grand Marais Lightkeeper and has been furnished in the style of the period.
Pickle Barrel House Museum • Location: N14252 Lake Ave., Grand Marais, MI 49839 • Hours: Jun & Sep: Sat-Sun 1-4 p.m., Jul-Aug Daily 1-4 p.m. • Admission: Donations accepted • Visitor Accessibility: Free street parking. Not wheelchair accessible. Docent on site. • The Pickle Barrel House is a barrel-shaped house that was built as a summer residence for author/illustrator William Donahey and his wife, author Mary Dickerson Donahey. The 16-foot-high main barrel has two stories and is attached to an 8-foot-high kitchen barrel. The museum has been furnished in the style of 1926, when it was built. A number of William Donahey's personal effects are on display, including where he created his "Teenie Weenie" cartoons.

Grand Rapids
(Kent County)

Calvin College
Mailing Address: Heritage Hall, 1855 Knollcrest Circle SE • Grand Rapids, MI 49546
Contact: Richard Harms
Phone: 616-526-6313 • *Fax:* (616) 526-7689
Site/Location: **Heritage Hall**
Hours: Mon-Fri 8 a.m.-5 p.m.
Website: www.calvin.edu/hh
About: Pioneer origins, contains extensive holdings from 1840s-present. Dutch-American settlements; immigration data and letters; and personal papers of prominent figures in the denomination Christian Reformed Church of North America, Calvin College, and Calvin Theological Seminary 1840s-present.
Publications: Origins journal, see website for list of books.
Information may not be current.

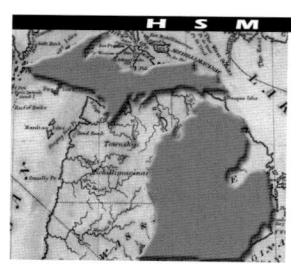

Cascade Historical Society
Mailing Address: 2865 Thornhills Ave. SE • Grand Rapids, MI 49546
Contact: Vic Gillis, President
E-Mail: vicsugoblu@comcast.net
Phone: (616) 676-9443
Fax: (616) 949-3918
Site/Location: **Cascade Historical Society Museum**
Physical Location: 2839 Thornapple River Drive • Grand Rapids, MI 49546
Hours: By appointment.
Admission: Free.
Visitor Accessibility: Free street parking. Wheelchair accessible. Tour guide available.
Website: cascadetwp.com

About: The Cascade Historical Society preserves and records the history of Cascade Township. Recently, the society initiated a program that honors historic sites in Cascade Township, is in the process of recording a complete inventory of its collection, and has begun a program that identifies the oldest structures in the township. The museum was built in the 19th century, formerly the township hall. Today, it features artifacts, photographs, and limited exhibits.
Exhibits/Collections: Artifacts and records of Cascade County. The society maintains the history room at the Cascade Township Library
Annual Events: Christmas Tree Lighting, Meetings 1st Thu monthly.

East Grand Rapids Historical Commission
Mailing Address: c/o East Grand Rapids Public Library, 750 Lakeside SE • Grand Rapids, MI 49506
Information may not be current.

Gaines Township Historical Society
Mailing Address: c/o Local History Room Gaines Township Library, 421 68th St. SE • Grand Rapids, MI 49508
Contact: Shirley Bruursema
E-Mail: libsabsarg@aol.com
Phone: (616) 698-8464
Hours: Library: Mon,Thu 12-8 p.m., Tue-Wed, Fri-Sat 9:30 a.m.-5 p.m.
Admission: Free.
Visitor Accessibility: On-site parking available. Wheelchair accessible. Tour guides available by appointment.
Website: www.gainestownship.org/residents/historicalsociety
About: Society supports the local history room to help develop awareness and encourage preservation of local history (sites, records, and memories).
Exhibits/Collections: Complete set of 1939 township books, maps, descriptions of every parcel of property. Old schoolbooks, original to 120-year-old restored school.
Annual Events: Cutlerville Days, Dutton Days.
Other Sites/Locations: **DeTray One Room Schoolhouse** • Location: 4011 100th Street, Caledonia MI 49316 • Hours: School groups by appointment only • Admission: Call for arrangements • The school is used for school groups, replicating period dress, classes, lunch pails, and outdoor games.

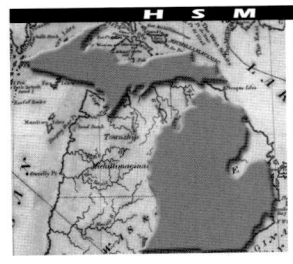

Gerald R. Ford Presidential Museum
HSM MEMBER
Mailing Address: 303 Pearl St. NW • Grand Rapids, MI 49504
Contact: Kristin Mooney, Public Affairs Specialist
E-Mail: ford.museum@nara.gov
Phone: (616) 254-0400
Fax: (616) 254-0386
Hours: Daily 9 a.m.-5 p.m.
Admission: $7/adult, $6/senior, $3/youth, children 5 and under free.
Visitor Accessibility: Free on-site parking lot. Wheelchair accessible.
Website: www.fordlibrarymuseum.gov
About: Presidential libraries and museums preserve the written record and physical history of our presidents while providing special programs and exhibits that service the community. Located in President Ford's hometown and former congressional district, this museum provides extensive exhibits on President Ford's life and career.
Exhibits/Collections: All holdings relate to the 1970s and the presidency of Gerald R. Ford, showcasing his long life and political career.
Annual Events: Mrs. Ford's Birthday (Apr), Holiday Open House (Dec). Admission to the library is free during these events.

Grand Rapids Historic Preservation Commission
Mailing Address: 1120 Monroe Ave. NW, 3rd Floor • Grand Rapids, MI 49503
E-Mail: rbaker@ci.grand-rapids.mi.us
Phone: 616-456-3451 • *Fax:* 616-456-4546
Hours: Mon-Fri 7:30 a.m.-4 p.m.
Visitor Accessibility: On-site parking. Wheelchair accessible.
Website: www.ci.grand-rapids.mi.us
About: This seven-member commission is appointed by the City Commission to review applications for work affecting the exterior of structures or resources in the Historic District or to an historic landmark.
Information may not be current.

Grand Rapids Historical Commission
Mailing Address: 33 College SE • Grand Rapids, MI 49503
E-Mail: dbarrettgr@yahoo.com
Phone: (616) 235-0914
Website: historygrandrapids.org
Information may not be current.

Grand Rapids Historical Society
HSM MEMBER
Mailing Address: c/o Grand Rapids Public Library, 111 Library NE • Grand Rapids, MI 49503
E-Mail: grhs.local@gmail.com
Phone: (616) 988-5402 x5497
Fax: (616) 988-5421
Website: www.grhistory.org
About: The Grand Rapids Historical Society collects and preserves local history materials and promotes local history through public programs and publications.
Annual Events: Annual banquet (May). Meetings, programs, lectures 2nd Thu monthly, 7p.m. at Gerald R. Ford Presidential Museum Auditorium, 303 Pearl St. NW.
Publications: Grand Rapids Times newsletter, Grand River Valley History annual magazine.

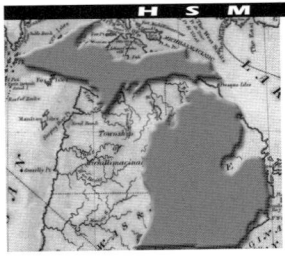

Grand Rapids Public Library
HSM MEMBER
Mailing Address: Periodical Department, 111 Library St. NE • Grand Rapids, MI 49503
Contact: Tim Gleisner, Supervisor Grand Rapids History
E-Mail: localhistory@grpl.org
Phone: (616) 988-5400
Fax: (616) 988-5421
Hours: Sep-May: Mon-Thu 9 a.m.-9 p.m., Fri-Sat 9 a.m.-6 p.m., Sun 1-5 p.m.
Visitor Accessibility: On-site and street parking for a fee on weekdays; free on weekends. Wheelchair accessible. Self-guided.
Website: http://www.grpl.org/
About: The Grand Rapids History and Special Collections Department was established in 1904, upon the completion of the Ryerson Library. When planning the "new" library, board members ensured that a "Michigan Room" was set aside in which to preserve the collections. The earliest collections came to the archives in 1905 and include the papers of John Lawrence, Rebecca Richmond, and

❦ Historical Society of Michigan

the Old Residents' Association, as well as Lewis G. Stuart's collection of maps of the Old Northwest Territory.

Exhibits/Collections: More than one million photographic images and negatives, all held in the Local History Department. A typical collection might contain letters, business documents, personal recollections, scrapbooks, photographs and other items.

Annual Events: History Detectives (Jan).

Grand Rapids Public Museum
Mailing Address: 272 Pearl St. NW • Grand Rapids, MI 49504
Contact: Kate Moore, Director of Marketing & Public Relations
E-Mail: info@grmuseum.org
Phone: (616) 929-1700
Fax: (616) 929-1780
Hours: Mon-Sat 9 a.m.-5 p.m., Sun 12 p.m.-5 p.m. Closed Easter, Thanksgiving, Christmas, and New Year's.
Admission: $8/adult, $7/senior, $3/children (3-17), Children 2 and under are free. Additional charges for special shows and exhibits.
Visitor Accessibility: Parking ramp across the street. Wheelchair accessible.
Website: www.grmuseum.org

About: Founded in 1854, the Grand Rapids Public Museum is Michigan's oldest and third-largest museum. The facility collects, preserves, and presents the natural, cultural, and social history of the region. Permanent exhibits include Streets of Old Grand Rapids, Collecting A to Z, Anishinabek: People of This Place, Habitats, Furniture City, and New Comers.

Exhibits/Collections: Nearly 1 million objects cataloged in more than 350,000 record groups. In the Community Archives & Research Center, 223 Washington SE, Grand Rapids, MI. By appointment only.

Annual Events: The Rides (Jun), Front Row for Fireworks (Jul), Ethnic Heritage Festival (winter), Night at Your Museum (winter).

Other Sites/Locations: Voigt House Victorian Museum •
Location: 115 College Ave. SE Grand Rapids, MI 49503 • Visitor Accessibility: Not wheelchair accessible. Group tours by reservation only. By appointment. • The historic 1895 Heritage Hill home of the Voigts, a prominent merchant and flour mill family. The home includes original furnishings and the family's personal possessions. A site of the Public Museum of Grand Rapids. 15,000 personal items and assorted memorabilia original to Voigt family.

Greater Grand Rapids Women's History Council
Mailing Address: PO Box 68874 • Grand Rapids, MI 49506
Contact: Falinda Geerling, President
E-Mail: info@ggrwhc.org
Phone: (616) 574-7307
Website: www.ggrwhc.org

About: Diverse group of educators, scholars, historians, business leaders, and homemakers dedicated to educating the community and celebrating the legacies of local women, preserving knowledge of their past, and inspiring visions for their future. Research & Recognition Committee researches and nominates local women for induction into Michigan Women's Hall of Fame in Lansing, Michigan.

Exhibits/Collections: Active oral history program. Bibliography and collections in local history room at Grand Rapids Public Library.

Hekman Library Calvin College
Mailing Address: Calvin College Seminary, 1855 Knollcrest Cir. SE • Grand Rapids, MI 49546-4437
Contact: Glenn Remelts, Dean of the Library
E-Mail: library@calvin.edu
Phone: (616) 526-7197 • *Fax:* (616) 526-6470
Hours: Mon-Thu 7:30 a.m.-12 a.m.; Fri 7:30 a.m.-8 p.m.; Sat 9 a.m.-8 p.m.
Admission: Free admission to library; $20/individual for guest book checkout.
Visitor Accessibility: Free on-site parking.
Website: http://library.calvin.edu/

About: The library's mission is to support the curricular needs and scholarship of the Calvin community. The library houses Heritage Hall, a collection rich in primary materials concerning the history of the Dutch in West Michigan. Heritage Hall also serves as the archives for the Christian Reformed Church in North America. Another important special collection is the Meeter Center for Calvin Studies.

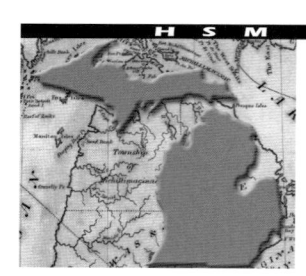

Heritage Hill Association
Mailing Address: 126 College Ave. SE • Grand Rapids, MI 49503
Contact: Jan Earl, Director
E-Mail: heritage@heritagehillweb.org
Phone: (616) 459-8950
Fax: (616) 459-2409
Site/Location: **Heritage Hill Historic District**
Hours: Mon-Thu 9 a.m.-5 p.m.
Website: www.heritagehillweb.org

About: Heritage Hill Association provides neighbors with a way of collectively building a historically preserved community. The association also offers a self-guided walking tour of the Heritage Hill Historic District, highlighting examples of American architecture from the 19th and 20th centuries.

Exhibits/Collections: Photos and histories of 1,300 houses in Heritage Hill.
Annual Events: Heritage Hill Weekend Tour of Homes (May). Board meetings 3rd Wed monthly, 7 p.m. at Saint Marys Health Center.
Publications: Bimonthly newsletter. "Almost Lost."

History Remembered, Inc./ Michigan Civil War Sesquicentennial
Mailing Address: 1691 Summerfield SE • Grand Rapids, MI 49508
Contact: Bruce B. Butgereit, Executive Director
E-Mail: civil-war@comcast.net
Phone: (616) 827-3369
Website: http://www.micw150.us/

Kent County Council for Historic Preservation
Mailing Address: 183 Bona Vista NW • Grand Rapids, MI 49504
Contact: Herb Ranta
Phone: (616) 246-4821 • *Fax:* (616) 451-9690

Site/Location: **Meyer May House**
Hours: Public hours: Tue and Thu 10 a.m.-2 p.m., Sun 1-5 p.m., call for groups of 10 or more.
Website: http://www.hsmichigan.org/grandrapids/kentco/
About: Heritage Hill home designed by Frank Lloyd Wright for Grand Rapids clothier, Meyer May. This example of Wright's Prairie style was restored to its original concept by Steelcase and opened for visitor tours in 1987. Offers a rare opportunity to view a totally designed living environment and a composition of light, planes, and space as Wright envisioned it in 1908.

*Information may not be current.

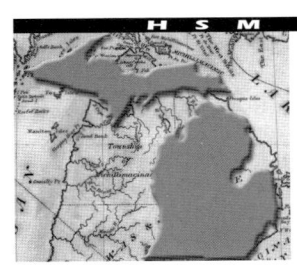

Michigan Masonic Museum & Library
Mailing Address: 233 E. Fulton St., Ste. 10 • Grand Rapids, MI 49503
Contact: Brook Tinker, Director
E-Mail: brooktinker@yahoo.com
Phone: (888) 748-4540
Hours: Mon-Fri 10 a.m.-6 p.m. Every other Sat 10 a.m.-3 p.m.
Admission: Free.
Visitor Accessibility: Free parking in the adjoining ramp. Wheelchair accessible. Tours can be scheduled during regular hours or by appointment.
Website: www.masonichistory.org
About: Housed in the lower level of the historic Grand Rapids Masonic Center, the Michigan Masonic Museum & Library is dedicated to education for the public and members of the fraternity about Free Masonry. The museum is home to a wealth of Masonic memorabilia, such as Masonic aprons dating from the 1700s, swords and other ceremonial gear, officer jewels dating from the mid-1850s, and an array of uniforms and costumes.
Exhibits/Collections: Masonic aprons dating to the 1700s, swords, ceremonial gear, masonic jewels, Masonic memorabilia. Library contains about 10,000 volumes related to Freemasonry, Michigan history, and philosophy.

Polish Heritage Society of Grand Rapids
Mailing Address: P.O. Box 1844 • Grand Rapids, MI 49501
Contact: Andy Budnick
E-Mail: phsgrandrapids@gmail.com
Phone: (616) 644-1142
Admission: Varies with event, call for details.
Website: www.polishheritagesociety.com
About: Works to foster pride in Polish and local heritage, spread knowledge about the culture, and encourage education.
Annual Events: Polish Heritage Festival (Aug), Matka Boskazielna (Aug), Wigilia DInner (Dec). General meetings spring and fall.
Publications: Polish Harvest Society Newsletter.

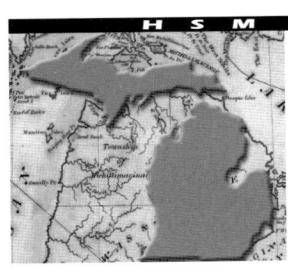

Temple Emanuel of Grand Rapids Archives
Mailing Address: 1715 E. Fulton • Grand Rapids, MI 49503
Contact: Barbara Robinson, Volunteer Archivist
Phone: (616) 459-5976
Fax: (616) 459-6510
Hours: Closed Mon. Tue-Sun 9 a.m.-5 p.m.
Admission: Free.
Visitor Accessibility: Free on-site parking. Wheelchair accessible. Tour guide or docent available (call ahead).
Website: www.templeemanuelgr.org
About: Established in 1873. Keeps and preserves important documents pertaining to the temple's activities and history. Hall of glass cases containing important documents and artifacts. Front of building has two large display cases containing other documents. Tiffany window from original building built in 1881. Present temple designed by Eric Mendelsohn and built in 1952-53.
Exhibits/Collections: Original minutes from 1873, board minutes, religious school, holidays, life events, marriages, births, bar and bat mitzvahs, confirmations, death, extensive cemetery record.

West Michigan Railroad Historical Society
Mailing Address: P.O. Box 150461 • Grand Rapids, MI 49515
Contact: Suzanne Carpenter, Treasurer
E-Mail: suzannec@iserv.net
Phone: (616) 784-7264
Site/Location: **Toledo, Saginaw, & Muskegon Depot**
Physical Location: 371 N. Union St. • Sparta, MI 49345
Hours: Jul: 3rd weekend. Also by appointment.
Admission: Free.
Visitor Accessibility: Free on-site parking. Partially wheelchair accessible; warehouse is not. Free tour guide available; appointment preferred.
About: Preserves Michigan railroad history, with emphasis on West Michigan. Includes 1880s depot, photo and lantern collections, C&O caboose, hopper car, boxcar containing running model railroad, railway velocipede, and rare roadrailer car.
Exhibits/Collections: Large collection of west Michigan depot photos and engines, both old and new, and a lantern collection. Also many early railroad timetables. Artifacts from steam railroad era.
Annual Events: Open House in conjunction with Sparta Village's "Town & Country" Days (Jul), Annual Banquet (Nov). Meetings 3rd Thu Apr-Oct, 7:30 p.m. at the Sparta Depot, Jan-Mar at member homes.
Publications: Member newsletter (The Waybill).

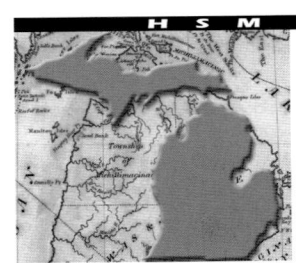

Western Michigan Genealogical Society
Mailing Address: c/o Grand Rapids Public Library, 111 Library St. NE • Grand Rapids, MI 49503
Contact: Don Bryant, President
E-Mail: wmgs@wmgs.org
Website: www.wmgs.org
About: Founded in 1954, the Western Michigan Genealogical Society preserves and makes available genealogical records, encourages and assists members in genealogical research, promotes the exchange of knowledge, and encourages the deposit of genealogical records in established libraries and archives.
Exhibits/Collections: Collection held at the Grand Rapids Public Library focuses on Kent County and the counties immediately surrounding. Member-submitted family trees and manuscripts. Online database at http://data.wmgs.org.
Annual Events: GotAncestors?! Seminar (fall). Meetings 1st Sat Sep-Jun, 1:30p.m., Ryerson Auditorium, Grand Rapids Public Library.
Publications: Quarterly magazine (Michigana), see website for complete list of publications.

Grandville
(Kent County)

Grandville Historical Commission
Mailing Address: 3195 Wilson Ave. SW • Grandville, MI 49418
Contact: Ron Wortley, President
E-Mail: grandvilleHC@hotmail.com
Phone: (616) 531-3030
Site/Location: **Grandville Museum**
Hours: 1st Wed monthly 1-4 p.m. Also 2nd Mon monthly in the evening. Also by appointment.
Admission: Free.
Visitor Accessibility: Free on-site parking. Wheelchair accessible. Tour guides available during open hours and by appointment.
Website: https://www.facebook.com/GrandvilleHistoricalCommission
About: The Grandville Historical Commission aims to discover, gather, and preserve knowledge about Grandville; to collect and classify objects, documents, and other information relating to the past of Grandville; to present and illustrate the history of Grandville and its exploration, settlement, and development; and to produce and distribute information in connection with the foregoing.
Exhibits/Collections: Pictures, obituaries, yearbooks, plat maps, and information about people and companies.
Annual Events: No.10 Schoolhouse Open Houses (Jun, Sep). Meetings 3rd Mon Jan-May and Sep-Nov, 7-9 p.m. at Grandville City Hall. Work Group Committee meets for data processing every Wed, 1-3 p.m. in basement work room.
Publications: "Images of America: Grandville," "Bend in the River," "Grandville Pictorial."
Other Sites/Locations: **No. 10 Schoolhouse** • Location: Heritage Park on Canal Avenue (Near 44th Street), Grandville, MI 49418 • Hours: By request • Admission: Free • Visitor Accessibility: Free on-site parking. Wheelchair accessible. Tour guide available during open hours and by appointment. • The No. 10 Schoolhouse has original desks, pictures of students, old books, chalkboards, clothing to try on, teacher quarters, and bell.
Information may not be current.

Grass Lake
(Jackson County)

Grass Lake Area Historical Society
Mailing Address: P.O. Box 53 • Grass Lake, MI 49240
Contact: Mike Fensler, President
Phone: (517) 522-5141
Site/Location: **Coe House Museum**
Physical Location: 371 W. Michigan Ave • Grass Lake, MI 49240
Hours: Open by appointment.
Admission: Free.
Visitor Accessibility: On-site parking. Wheelchair accessible.
Website: www.grasslakechamber.org
About: The Coe House is an 1871 brick Victorian home with period furnishings and Tuscan Vernacular architecture. Exhibits highlight local artifacts and documents.
Exhibits/Collections: Archival records, scrapbooks of local history.
Annual Events: Heritage Day (Sep), Christmas Auction (Dec). Board meets on the 3rd Wed, nine times annually.
Publications: Annual newsletter (May).
Information may not be current.

Whistlestop Park Association
Mailing Address: P.O. Box 202 • Grass Lake, MI 49240
Contact: Judy McCaslin, President
E-Mail: jojumac2@yahoo.com
Phone: (517) 522-4384
Site/Location: **Whistlestop Park & Grass Lake Depot**
Physical Location: 210 E. Michigan • Grass Lake, MI 49240
Hours: Tours by appointment.
Admission: Donations accepted.
Visitor Accessibility: Street parking. Wheelchair accessible.
Website: www.grasslakechamber.org
About: The Whistlestop Park Association restored and developed the park to enhance historical and cultural Grass Lake and to promote tourism. The Victorian stone depot includes gardens, a gazebo, and a train shed. Artwork and artifacts are displayed inside the depot.
Annual Events: Independence Day Parade, Heritage Day (Sep), Holiday Open House (Dec).
Information may not be current.

Grayling
(Crawford County)

Crawford County Historical Society & Museum Complex
Mailing Address: P.O. Box 218 • Grayling, MI 49738
Contact: Ginger Lyons, President
E-Mail: cchs49738@yahoo.com
Phone: (989) 348-4461
Physical Location: 97 E. Michigan Ave. • Grayling, MI 49738
Hours: 12-4 p.m.
Admission: Donations accepted.
Visitor Accessibility: Free street parking. Partially wheelchair accessible; the second story of the railroad depot is not accessible. Tour guides available upon request.
Website: www.grayling-area.com/museum
About: The Crawford County Historical Society maintains a museum complex that includes an 1882 historic train depot, a 1900 schoolhouse that is used to exhibit the military history of Crawford County, a log trapper's cabin, a firehouse with two restored fire engines, a farm building with a restored tractor, an early 1900 cutter(sleigh), and a retired 1920s caboose. Rooms in the depot represent a general store, schoolroom, ladies sewing room, saloon, one room cabin, and R.R. crew quarters.
Exhibits/Collections: Exhibits also include a large dollhouse, Fred Bear Memorial room, law enforcement display, history of the AuSable River, history of the AuSable Canoe Marathon since 1947, and 1930s kitchen.
Annual Events: Meetings 1st Tue monthly Mar-Nov, 5:30 p.m. at Grayling Nature Center.
Publications: Seasonal newsletter.

Hartwick Pines Logging Museum.
Please see entry under Lansing: Michigan Historical Center.

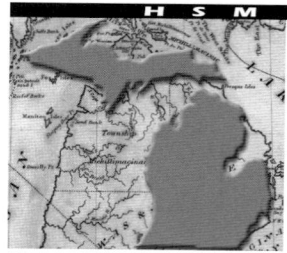

Lovells Township Historical Society
Mailing Address: PO Box 2505 • Grayling, MI 49738
Contact: Richard Perry, President
E-Mail: lovellsmuseum@yahoo.com
Phone: (989) 348-7173
Fax: (989) 348-4880
Site/Location: **Lovells Township Historical Society Museum**

Physical Location: Township Hall, 8405 Twin Bridge Road • Grayling, MI 49738
Hours: May-Sep: Wed, Fri-Sun 10 a.m.-4 p.m.
Admission: Donations accepted.
Visitor Accessibility: Tour guide available.
Website: www.lovellsmuseum.com
About: The Lovells Township Historical Society maintains two museum buildings. The 1907 Lone Pine School House shares Lovells community history and the Lovells Museum of Trout Fishing History tells the AuSable River's history.
Exhibits/Collections: Artifacts, records and archival materials on Lovells community history and trout fishing.
Annual Events: Trout Opener (Apr), Annual Members Meeting (Jun), Bear, Beaver and Banjo Fundraiser (Jul), Lovells Bridge Walk (Aug). Board of Directors meets 2nd Mon monthly.
Publications: Annual newsletter.
Information may not be current.

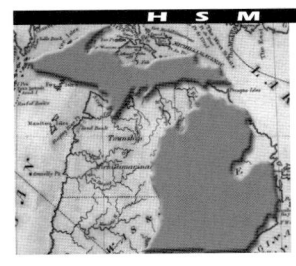

Wellington Farm Park
Mailing Address: 6771 S. Military Rd. • Grayling, MI 49738
Contact: Howard Taylor, General Manager
E-Mail: welfar32@gmail.com
Phone: (989) 529-7331
Physical Location: 6944 S. Military Rd. • Grayling, MI 49738
Hours: Jun-Oct: Daily 9 a.m.-5 p.m.
Admission: $7.50/adult, $5.50/senior, $5.50/student.
Visitor Accessibility: Free on-site parking. Wheelchair accessible. Tour guide available.
Website: www.wellingtonfarmpark.org
About: Wellington Farm is a 60-acre living history farm. The farm includes a blacksmith shop, broom shop, sawmill, grist mill, summer kitchen, carpenter shop, and livestock barn, along with the historic Stittsville Church—all fully functional and often manned and in operation by interpreters in period costume. The farm operates a shop selling handmade ice cream. Highlights include one of the first threshing machines, the largest clover huller, the first broom handle lathe, and the first belt sander ever built.
Exhibits/Collections: Vintage farm equipment and hand tools, tractors, threshing machines, and agricultural equipment.
Annual Events: Plow Day (May), Dairy Days (Jun), Music Festival (Aug), Tractor and Engine Show (Aug), Fall Folk Arts Festival (Sep), Punkin-Chunkin (Oct), Halloween Hayrides (Oct), The Farm By Lantern Light (Dec), Christmas Eve Church Service (Dec). Citizens Advisory Board of Directors meets the 3rd Tue of Jan, Apri-Jun, Sep, and Nov.

Greenbush
(Alcona County)

Greenbush Historical Society
Mailing Address: P.O. Box 222 • Greenbush, MI 48738
Contact: Jane Meyers, President
Phone: (989) 739-3911
About: Established in 1980, dedicated to perpetuating Greenbush-area history. Has preserved and maintained the 1870 one-room Greenbush School and the oldest structure in the community.
Exhibits/Collections: 1898 Elmer Car, 1929 Durant car, wooden smokehouse.

Greenville
(Moncalm County)

Fighting Falcon Military Museum
Mailing Address: 516 W. Cass St. • Greenville, MI 48838
Contact: Barbara Christensen, President
E-Mail: bachristensen@charter.net
Phone: (616) 225-1940
Hours: Apr-Nov: Sun 2-4:30 p.m. Also by appointment.
Admission: Donations accepted.
Visitor Accessibility: Free on-site and street parking. Wheelchair accessible. Private parking lot. Tour guide available during open hours and by appointment.
Website: www.thefightingfalcon.com
About: The Fighting Falcon Military Museum maintains a collection of military artifacts to educate the public as well as remember and honor the sacrifices of area men and women. The main exhibit is the restoration of an Army Air Corps CG4A, known worldwide as the "Fighting Falcon," which was purchased originally by the students of Greenville Public Schools and made locally by the Gibson Refrigerator Company. The museum is located in a restored school building, which originally opened in 1902.
Exhibits/Collections: Restored Army Air Corps CG4A "Fighting Falcon" glider, displays of supporting documents and photographs, artifacts from the Civil War, WWI, WWII, Korean War, and modern conflicts.
Annual Events: Spring into the Past Weekend Tour (May), Danish Festival in Greenville (Aug). Meetings 2nd Tue Apr-Nov, 7p.m. at museum.
Publications: Biannual newsletter (Fighting Falcon Military Museum).

Flat River Community Library
Mailing Address: 200 W. Judd St. • Greenville, MI 48838
E-Mail: gre@llcoop.org
Phone: (616) 754-6359 • *Fax:* (616) 754-1398
Hours: Mon-Thu 9 a.m.-8 p.m.; Fri-Sat 9 a.m.-5 p.m.
Admission: Free.
Visitor Accessibility: Free on-site parking. Wheelchair accessible. Self-guided.
Website: http://flatriverlibrary.org
About: Public library located within the city of Greenville, Michigan.
Exhibits/Collections: Ash and Randal Local History Room is home to a large collection of Montcalm County history, including indexes for birth, death, marriage, obituary, census, cemetery, and early pioneer records. Access to local newspaper available from 1856-present. Family histories and histories of neighboring towns/townships.
Annual Events: Open Geneology Class (1st Thu monthly at 10 a.m.).

Flat River Historical Society
Mailing Address: P.O. Box 188 • Greenville, MI 48838
Contact: Bill Garlick, President
E-Mail: frhsmuseum@att.net
Phone: (616) 754-5296
Site/Location: **Flat River Historical Museum**
Physical Location: 213 N. Franklin St. • Greenville, MI 48838
Hours: Sat-Sun 2-4:30 p.m. Also by appointment.
Admission: $2/adult, children and students free.
Visitor Accessibility: Free on-site parking. Paritally wheelchair accessible; basement and first floor only. Tour guide available by appointment.
Website: www.flatriverhistoricalsociety.org
About: The Flat River Historical Society preserves, advances, and presents the history of Montcalm County and portions of Ionia and

Kent Counties. The Flat River Historical Museum is located in the former Ridley Egg Emporium and contains several period rooms depcicting early 1900s businesses and home life. Among the displays are logging and farm equipment and early household items. The adjacent former Eureka Township Hall contains military items and artifacts from early local industries.
Exhibits/Collections: Extensive archives on local history and genealogy.
Annual Events: Spring into Past (May), Danish Festival (Aug), Holiday Open House (Dec), Annual Membership Meeting (Jul). Board meetings 3rd Tue monthly.
Publications: Quarterly newsletter, several publications on early settlement, DVD on Greenville history.

Grosse Ile
(Wayne County)

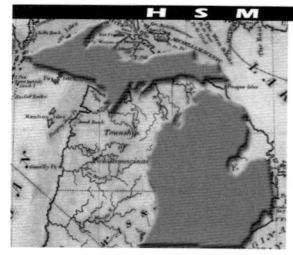

Grosse Ile Historical Society
Mailing Address: P.O. Box 131 • Grosse Ile, MI 48138
Contact: Clare Koester, Museum Committee
E-Mail: info@gihistory.org
Phone: (734) 675-1250
Site/Location: **Michigan Central Railroad Depot Museum & Customs House**
Physical Location: 25020 E. River Road • Grosse Ile, MI 48138
Hours: Sun 1-4 p.m., Thu 10 a.m.-12 p.m.
Admission: Free.
Visitor Accessibility: Free on-site parking. Not wheelchair accessible. Self-guided.
Website: www.gihistory.org
About: The Grosse Ile Historical Society collects, preserves, and interprets historical information and materials relative to Grosse Ile; teaches and promotes study and research; and generates interest in Grosse Ile history. The Michigan Central Railroad Depot Museum & Customs House features displays on railroad, community life, and significant Grosse Ile artifacts.
Exhibits/Collections: Archives stored in the Customs House.
Annual Events: Island Tour, Grosse Ile Island Fest, Lighthouse Tour (Sep). Meetings 3rd Mon Jan, Apr, and Oct.
Publications: "Grosse Ile," "Grosse Ile Then and Now," "Naval Air Station Grosse Ile."
Other Sites/Locations: **Grosse Ile Township Hall** • Location: 9601 Groh Road, Grosse Ile, MI 48138 • Hours: Mon-Fri 8 a.m.-5 p.m. • Admission: Free • Visitor Accessibility: Free on-site parking. Wheelchair accessible. Self-guided. • Exhibits at the Grosse Ile Township Hall consider naval history and Grosse Ile's legacy as a Naval Air Station through artifacts and photographs. Also on-site is a memorial garden.
Grosse Ile North Channel Light • Location: Lighthouse Point Road, Grosse Ile, MI 48138 • Hours: 2nd Sun in Sep • Admission: Varies • Visitor Accessibility: Not wheelchair accessible. Tour guide available; call (734) 675-1250 for more information. • Built in 1894, the North Channel Light is the only remaining light on Grosse Ile.

Grosse Pointe
(Wayne County)

National Society of the Colonial Dames of America
Mailing Address: 511 Lakeland St. • Grosse Pointe, MI 48230
Contact: Alice Schultes, President
Website: www.nscda.org
Information may not be current.

Wayne County Council for Arts, History, and Humanities
Mailing Address: 17728 Mack Ave. • Grosse Pointe, MI 48230
E-Mail: robert@maniscalcogallery.com
Website: www.waynearts.org
Information may not be current.

Grosse Pointe Farms
(Wayne County)

Grosse Pointe Historical Society
Mailing Address: 376 Kercheval Avenue • Grosse Pointe Farms, MI 48236
Contact: Isabelle Donnelly
E-Mail: info@gphistorical.org
Phone: (313) 884-7010
Fax: (313) 884-7699
Site/Location: **Provencal-Weir House**
Hours: Tours available Sep-Jun 2nd Sat 1-4 p.m. Also by appointment.
Admission: Free.
Visitor Accessibility: Not wheelchair accessible. Free street parking.
Website: www.gphistorical.org
About: Founded to celebrate and preserve history. Sponsors numerous interactive programs and manages facilities that preserve and protect important artifacts. Greek Revival farmhouse believed to be community's oldest surviving residence was built circa 1823. An 1840s log cabin is also located on property.
Exhibits/Collections: The resource center was established to assist visitors with scholarly or personal investigations about Grosse Pointe. The library and archives collections preserve maps, manuscripts, newspapers, magazine clippings, genealogical materials, and photos.
Annual Events: Annual Fundraiser, Talking Headstones, Christmas Party, Plaque Celebration, Valentines Party, Bicknell Lectures. Board meetings 2nd Tue Sep-Jun 7-9 p.m.
Other Sites/Locations: **Alfred B. and Ruth S. Moran Resource Center** • Location: 381 Kercheval Avenue, Suite 2, Grosse Pointe Farms, MI 48236 • Hours: Tue-Wed 10 a.m.-12:30 p.m. and 1:30-4 p.m.

Grosse Pointe Shores
(Wayne County)

Edsel & Eleanor Ford House
Mailing Address: 1100 Lake Shore Rd. • Grosse Pointe Shores, MI 48236
Contact: Cynthia Fragnoli, Office Manager
E-Mail: info@fordhouse.org
Phone: (313) 884-4222
Fax: (313) 844-5977
Site/Location: **Ford Estate**
Hours: Jan-Mar: Call for tour schedule. Apr-Dec: Tue-Sat 10 a.m.-4 p.m., Sun 12-4 p.m. Business office: Mon-Fri 8:30 a.m.-4:30 p.m.
Admission: $12/adult, $11/senior, $8/child (6-12).
Visitor Accessibility: Parking adjacent to Activities Center (free, except during large grounds events). Partially wheelchair accessible. All tours are docent-guided (no additional charge).
Website: www.fordhouse.org
About: Historic home of automotive pioneer Edsel Ford and his family. Inspires, educates, and engages visitors through exploration of its unique connections to art, design, history, and the environment while celebrating family traditions and community relationships. Permanent exhibits

include the historic garage with Ford family vehicles.
Exhibits/Collections: Paintings, graphic arts, French and English period furniture, glass, ceramics, and historic textiles.
Annual Events: Easter Brunch & Tour, Bunny Brunch, Little Goblins' Night Out, Nutcracker Teas, Winter Wonderland, Fairytale Festival. See website for additional events.

Gulliver
(Schoolcraft County)

Gulliver Historical Society
Mailing Address: 1904W County Road 431 • Gulliver, MI 49840
Contact: Marilyn S. Fischer, President
E-Mail: msfischer@hughes.net
Phone: (906) 283-3183
Site/Location: **Seul Choix Point Lighthouse**
Physical Location: 905 S Seul Choix Rd. • Gulliver, MI 49840
Hours: Jun-Sep: 10 a.m.-6 p.m.
Admission: $4/adult, $1/children (0-16).
Visitor Accessibility: Free on-site parking. Partially wheelchair accessible; lighthouse tower not accessible. Tour guide available.
Website: www.greatlakelighthouse.com
About: The Lighthouse is fully operational, built in 1895, fully restored and put back into the 1900-1920 period. The lighthouse sits in a public park along with state of Michigan public boat access. The complex has a Boat House Maritime Museum, a Fog Signal Area History Museum, a large gift shop, 30-seat theater, research/genealogy library, and the Lighthouse Museum with tower tours.
Exhibits/Collections: Lighthouse artifacts, United States Coast Guard artifacts, an 18th-century dugout canoe, two USLHE light poles, Native-American artifacts, oil houses, local fishing village artifacts, Great Lakes shipping artifacts.
Annual Events: Pot Lock Picnic (Sep), Haunted Lighthouse Tours (Oct), Christmas From the Past (Dec), Santa Arrives (Dec).
Publications: See website for list of current publications.

Gwinn
(Marquette County)

Forsyth Township Historical Society
Mailing Address: P.O. Box 851 • Gwinn, MI 49841
Contact: Rick Wills, President
E-Mail: rpwills@yahoo.com
Phone: (906) 346-5413
Site/Location: **Forsyth Township Historical Society Museum**
Physical Location: (Above Forsyth Township Hall), 106 Pine St. • Gwinn, MI 49841
Hours: Call for current hours.
Admission: Free.
Visitor Accessibility: Street parking. Not wheelchair accessible.
About: Founded in 1992, the Forsyth Township Historical Society presents programs concerning local and regional history several times a year. The museum showcases the history of the township's small mining and railroad villages from 1860s as well as the history of K.I. Sawyer Air Force Base. There's a special emphasis on the unique "model town" of Gwinn, built in 1908 by Cleveland-Cliffs Iron Company president William Gwinn Mather.
Exhibits/Collections: Numerous photos of individual villages within township. Many are of construction of Gwinn during period 1907-1915 and of K.I. Sawyer AFB during late 1950s and early 1960s.
Publications: Newsletter (Forsyth Sagas).

Hadley
(Lapeer County)

Hadley Township Historical Society
Mailing Address: P.O. Box 20 • Hadley, MI 48440
Contact: Kent Copeman
E-Mail: krc@centurytel.net
Phone: (810) 797-4026
Physical Location: 3633 Hadley Rd. • Hadley, MI 48440
Hours: By appointment.
Admission: Donations accepted.
Visitor Accessibility: Free on-site parking. Partially wheelchair accessible, lower level only. Tours provided.
Website: www.hadleytownship.org
About: The Hadley Township Historical Society collects and preserves items of historical significance to the township. It also provides a museum in the grist mill as part of the Hartwig Community Park. Features the mill's turbine, shoots, grain elevators, line shaft, and large engine.
Exhibits/Collections: Hadley Township school pictures, antique tools and equipment, period clothing, and early business displays. Lower level includes mill turbine, line shaft, and mill equipment.
Annual Events: 4th of July. Meeting 1st Thu Jun-Oct, 7p.m. at Hadley Township Office Building.
Publications: Quarterly newsletter.

Hale
(Iosco County)

Michigan Museum of Military Transportation
Mailing Address: 6831 M 65 • Hale, MI 48739
Contact: Brian Morrison
E-Mail: mmmtpresident@centurytel.net
Phone: (231) 582-2364
Website: www.mmmt.us
About: Traveling museum. Displays of vehicles, equipment, and artifacts. Transported by members and friends of museum to various events in Central Michigan. Promotes restoration of historic military vehicles. Encourages and supports military vehicle hobbyists.
Annual Events: Camp Grayling Color Tour.
Publications: Newsletter (Data Plane).
Information may not be current.

Hamburg
(Livingston County)

Hamburg Township Historical Museum
Mailing Address: P.O. Box 272 • Hamburg, MI 48139
Contact: Wayne Burkhardt, President
E-Mail: suzanne@pendragon-design.com
Phone: (810) 986-0190
Physical Location: 7225 Stone St. • Hamburg, MI 48139
Hours: Wed 4-7 p.m., Sat 11 a.m.-3 p.m.
Admission: Donations accepted.
Visitor Accessibility: Free on-site parking. Wheelchair accessible. Tour guides available.
Website: www.hamburg.mi.us

About: The Hamburg Township Historical Museum preserves and presents the history of Hamburg through local history displays, active research archives, and changing special exhibits. Permanent galleries depict life in Hamburg since 1831 and include furniture, household items, textiles, farm tools, a military gallery, archive room, and tea room.

Exhibits/Collections: Artifacts from Hamburg area. Documents, newspapers, items belonging to founder's families. General history, wedding gowns, and clothing accessories.

Annual Events: Hamburg History Days (Sep). Board of Directors meets 3rd Wed monthly, 7 p.m. at museum.

Hamtramck
(Wayne County)

Hamtramck Historical Commission
Mailing Address: 9525 Jos. Campau • Hamtramck, MI 48212
Contact: Greg Kowalski, Chairman
E-Mail: hamtramckhistory@gmail.com
Phone: (313) 893-5027
Site/Location: **Hamtramck Historical Museum**
Hours: Sat-Sun 11 a.m. to 4 p.m. and by appointment.
Admission: Free.
Website: www.hamtramckhistory.org

About: The Hamtramck Historical Museum opened in September 2013 and has 4,500 square feet of floor space for material displays and presentations. The museum highlights the rich history of Hamtramck as well as the wide diversity of the city today. The Friends of Historic Hamtramck conducts walking and bus tours of the city on request and is available for off-site slide presentations and lectures on the rich history of Hamtramck.

Exhibits/Collections: A variety of material is on display, ranging from a Prohibition Era still to automotive artifacts, that has played a role in shaping one of the most unique communities in Michigan. Housed in city hall.

Annual Events: Meetings last Wed monthly (except Dec and Jul), 6 p.m. at City Hall, 3401 Evaline.

Hancock
(Houghton County)

Finnish American Heritage Center
Mailing Address: 601 Quincy St. • Hancock, MI 49930
Contact: Joanna Chopp, Archivist
E-Mail: editor@finnishamericanreporter.com
Phone: (906) 487-7347 • *Fax:* (906) 487-7557
Physical Location: 435 Quincy St. • Hancock, MI 49930
Hours: Mon-Fri 8 a.m.-4:30 p.m.
Admission: Donations accepted.
Visitor Accessibility: Free on-site and street parking. Wheelchair accessible. Self-guided.
Website: http://www.finlandia.edu/FAHC.html

About: As part of the Finlandia University campus, the Finnish American Heritage Center preserves the rich history and heritage of Finnish Americans in the Copper Country, Michigan, and North America. In addition to the Finnish American Historical Archives, the building features several display areas in the building that highlight Finnish heritage.

Exhibits/Collections: Largest collection of Finnish/North American materials in the world, including archival materials, genealogical resources, oral histories, two 1642 Christina Bibles, artifacts, textiles, and North America's largest collection of Finnish-American artwork.

Annual Events: Finnish Independence Day (Dec), Heikinp„iv„ (Jan).

Hancock
(Houghton County)

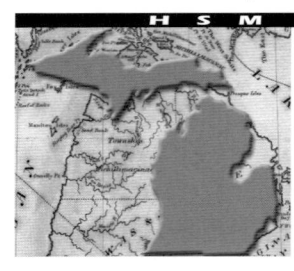

Quincy Mine Association, Inc.
Mailing Address: 49750 US Highway 41 • Hancock, MI 49930
Contact: Glenda Bierman
E-Mail: glenda@quincymine.com
Phone: (906) 482-3101
Hours: Fri-Sun 9:30 a.m.-5 p.m. May-Jun, daily mid-June to Oct.
Admission: Surface: $10/adult $10/senior, $5/youth. Full Tour: $18/adult, $17/senior, $9/youth.
Visitor Accessibility: On-site parking. Partially wheelchair accessible. Guided tours.
Website: www.quincymine.com

About: Tours include visit to museum in No. 2 hoist building, shaft house, and Nordburg Steam Hoist, the world's largest steam engine. Full tour includes cogwheel tram car to mine and wagon ride seven levels underground. Exhibit from Seaman Mineralogical Museum includes 17-ton solid copper boulder.

Hanover
(Jackson County)

Hanover-Horton Area Historical Society
Mailing Address: P.O. Box 256 • Hanover, MI 49241
Contact: Betty Jo DeForest, President
E-Mail: hhahs@frontier.com
Phone: (517) 563-8927
Fax: (517) 563-8927
Site/Location: **Conklin Reed Organ and History Museum**
Physical Location: 105 Fairview St. • Hanover, MI 49241
Hours: May-Oct: Sun 1-5 p.m. Also by appointment.
Admission: Donations accepted.
Visitor Accessibility: On-site parking. Partially wheelchair accessible. Self-guided. Group tours available by appointment; cost is $3/individual (min.10 people).
Website: http://conklinreedorganmuseum.org/

About: The Hanover-Horton Area Historical Society immerses visitors into the past by illustrating life in rural America through exhibits and events. Housed in a 1911 Quincy Box-Style Schoolhouse, the Conklin Reed Organ and History Museum displays a collection of more than 100 playable reed (pump) organs, melodeons, and harmoniums. Other attractions include a restored antique fire apparatus, 1950s-era water pump truck, restored classroom, printing press, and Model-T popcorn truck. The building is listed on the National Register of Historic Sites.

Exhibits/Collections: Photographs, postcards, and school artifacts; issues of the Hanover-Horton Local from 1891-1986; barber chair, rug loom, and a player piano.

Annual Events: Plow Day (Apr), Tractor Pull and Parade (Jul), Rust 'N' Dust (Aug), Home and Garden Luncheon (Sep), Christmas Open House (Dec), Bluegrass Bonanza.

Publications: Quarterly Newsletter (Bulletin).

Other Sites/Locations: **Hanover-Horton Heritage Park** • Location: 121 Tefft St., Hanover, MI 49241 • The Hanover-Horton Area Historical Society farms much of the land's 82-plus acres using antique equipment and holds two annual tractor pulls on a specially built track.

Harbor Beach
(Huron County)

Frank Murphy Memorial Museum
Mailing Address: 766 State St. • Harbor Beach, MI 48441
Contact: Barbara McGowan
Phone: (989) 479-9554
Physical Location: 142 S. Huron Ave • Harbor Beach, MI 48441
Hours: Jun-Aug Tue-Sun 10 a.m.-4 p.m.
Admission: $2/individual.
Visitor Accessibility: Not wheelchair accessible.
Website: http://harborbeachmi.org/frank_murphy
About: Friends group supports buildings and grounds of city-owned home of Frank Murphy, former Michigan governor who helped settle 1937 GM sit-down strike and was a justice of the United States Supreme Court. All furnishings in the house were associated with the Murphy family who occupied the site from 1890-1989. Site includes residence, Murphy law office, barn (closed to public), original Murphy home, and caretaker's house, now Harbor Beach Visitor Center.
Exhibits/Collections: Largest collection of Filipino cultural artifacts in the United States. Many documents recording events from 1890-1949, including the 1937 GM sit-down strike.
Annual Events: Carriage House Art Fair (Aug), Spring Bonnet High Tea, Gold/ Silver Friendship High Tea, Fall Fantasy High Tea, Victorian Christmas High Tea, "Dolly and Me" High Tea (Aug).

Grice House Heritage Museum
Mailing Address: 865 N. Huron Ave. • Harbor Beach, MI 48441
Contact: Barbara McGowan
Phone: 989-479-6477
Physical Location: 766 State Street Harbor Beach, MI 48441
Hours: Jun-Aug: Tue-Sun 12-4 p.m.
Admission: $2/individual.
Website: www.harborbeachchamber.com/grice.html
About: The heritage association partners with the city to operate and raise funds for the museum, home to three generations of the Grice family. Home tour includes kitchen, parlor, sewing room, and bedroom, which are furnished with articles (circa 1860-1940) donated by local residents. Also available are rooms with exhibits on local industry, Great Lakes history, and military items. Also on-site is a barn filled with farm equipment and the 1920s Adams School with furnishings typical of one-room schools.
Exhibits/Collections: Eclectic range of artifacts including farm tools, household items, clothing, quilts, furniture from Ford summer home, Fresnel Lens from Harbor Beach Lighthouse and variety of documents.
Annual Events: Grice Heritage Day (Jul).
*Information may not be current.

Harbor Beach Historical Society
Mailing Address: C/O Carol Messner, 157 N. 4th St. • Harbor Beach, MI 48441
Phone: (989) 428-3418
*Information may not be current.

White Rock School Museum
Mailing Address: 9494 White Rock Rd. • Harbor Beach, MI 48441
Contact: Kimberly Stein, Secretary
Phone: (989) 864-3817
Physical Location: 10124 White Rock Road • Harbor Beach, MI 48441
Hours: By appointment.
Admission: Free.
Visitor Accessibility: Free on-site parking. Wheelchair accessible. Tour guide available by appointment.
About: The White Rock School Museum brings together those interested in history, especially the history of the White Rock area. Set up as a 1909 schoolhouse with authentic materials, the White Rock School Museum offers educational opportunities and glimpses of the past, when one-room schools were prevalent.
Exhibits/Collections: Student, teacher, and textbook records and board minutes dating back to the 1800s.
Annual Events: Annual Picnic (Aug), Holiday Party (Dec).
Publications: "White Rock: Reflections through Time."
*Information may not be current.

Harbor Springs
(Emmet County)

Andrew J. Blackbird Museum
Mailing Address: 368 Main St. • Harbor Springs, MI 49740
Phone: (232) 526-0612
Website: http://www.visitharborspringsmichigan.com/stories/andrew_j_b
About: Andrew J. Blackbird's mark on Harbor Springs as well as the Native-American influence on Northern Michigan is preserved at the Andrew J. Blackbird Museum. Located on Main Street in Blackbird's restored house, the museum shares space with the Harbor Springs Area Chamber of Commerce. Native-American artifacts fill the museum space. This museum is across the street from the Harbor Springs History Museum.
*Information may not be current.

Harbor Springs Area Historical Society
Mailing Address: P.O. Box 812 • Harbor Springs, MI 49740
Contact: Mary Cummings, Executive Director
E-Mail: info@harborspringshistory.org
Phone: (231) 526-9771
Site/Location: Harbor Springs History Museum
Physical Location: 349 E. Main St. • Harbor Springs, MI 49740
Hours: Call or see website.
Admission: $5/adult, $3/senior and child, HSAHS members free.
Visitor Accessibility: Free on-site and street parking. Wheelchair accessible. Self-guided.
Website: www.harborspringshistory.org
About: The Harbor Springs Area Historical Society connects learning about the past with appreciating the present by preserving the area's histories and traditions. The society operates the Harbor Springs History Museum, which is housed in the former city hall building and features exhibits with hands-on activities. The permanent exhibit galleries detail the history of the Harbor Springs area, and the temporary exhibit space features new exhibits yearly that reflect a variety of topics of both local and statewide interest.
Exhibits/Collections: Historical materials, objects, and artifacts relating to Harbor Springs and surrounding area.
Annual Events: Monthly Harbor History Talks, Shay Days (Jul). Board of trustees meetings 3rd Mon monthly (except Dec) at 6:30 p.m.
Publications: Quarterly newsletter. Book: "In All The World, No Place Like This."

❀ Historical Society of Michigan

Little Traverse Bay Bands of Odawa Indians
Mailing Address: Gijigowi Library, 7500 Odawa Cir. • Harbor Springs, MI 49740
Contact: Meredith Henry, Director of the Gijiqowi Bipskaabii
Phone: (231) 242-1480 • *Fax:* (231) 242-1490
Hours: Mon-Fri 8 a.m.-5 p.m.
Visitor Accessibility: Public parking. Wheelchair accessible. Free tour guide available; call ahead.
Website: www.ltbbodawa-nsn.gov
About: Strives to preserve an authentic past and collective memory. Maintains accountability and manages organizations and resources of the Wayanakising Odawak. Maintains cultural library and provides Native North Tour.
Exhibits/Collections: Cultural library and collections, Native North Tour. Newspaper clippings, maps, church records, rolls, newsletters, reference books and materials, photographs, artifacts, genealogy resources, and oral histories.
Annual Events: LTBB Homecoming Powwow (Aug).
Information may not be current.

Harrison Township
(Macomb County)

Fashion and the Automobile
Mailing Address: 24742 Crocker Boulevard • Harrison Township, MI 48045
Contact: Victoria Mobley, Creator and Curator
E-Mail: vmobley@wowway.com
Phone: (586) 246-0312
Website: http://fashionandtheautomobile.com
About: Fashion and the Automobile is a touring exhibit that highlights the many changes wrought on popular culture by the evolution of the car. The exhibit is a virtual drive down memory lane, showcasing the relationship between fashion and automotive design by decade and how both were influenced by function, environment, lifestyle, and world events. The fashion and accessories in the exhibit are authentic. The automobiles are depicted by automotive artists' work in original fine art, photographs, and renderings.
Exhibits/Collections: Fashion and the Automobile: touring museum exhibits, vintage fashion shows, presentations, and teas.

Harrison Township Historical Commission
Mailing Address: 36175 Merilac • Harrison Township, MI 48045
Phone: (586) 463-1754
Information may not be current.

Louisa St. Clair Chapter—DAR
Mailing Address: Attn: Grace Bliss Smith, Chapter Regent, 34713 Bay Vista Dr. • Harrison Township, MI 48045
Contact: Grace Bliss Smith, Chapter Regent
E-Mail: gracemi@comcast.net
Phone: (586) 792-8571 • *Fax:* (586) 792-8893
Website: www.louisa.michdar.net
About: Local chapter for Daughters of the American Revolution.
Annual Events: Monthly meetings.
Information may not be current.

Harrisville
(Alcona County)

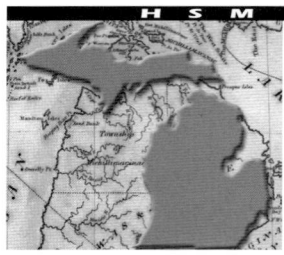

Alcona Historical Society
Mailing Address: P.O. Box 174 • Harrisville, MI 48740
Contact: Linda Klemens, President
Phone: (989) 724-6297
Site/Location: **Sturgeon Point Lighthouse and Old Bailey School**
Physical Location: 6072 E. Point Rd. • Harrisville, MI 48470
Hours: Jun-Sep: 11 a.m.-4 p.m.
Admission: Free.
Visitor Accessibility: Free on-site parking. Partially wheelchair accessible; grounds and gift shop only. Self-guided.
Website: www.alconahistoricalsociety.com
About: The Alcona Historical Society locates, preserves, protects, restores, and records the historical pieces of Alcona County and provides educational tours and programs, including exciting opportunities for residents and visitors to explore and enjoy our three museums: Sturgeon Point Lighthouse, Bailey School, and the Lincoln Depot. The Sturgeon Point Lighthouse features an authentic lens, keeper's home, and two boats used by the Coast Guard. Also on-site is an actual Alcona County one-room school house, completely restored and furnished with authentic collections.
Exhibits/Collections: Maritime artifacts.
Annual Events: Historical Day at the Lighthouse, Log Cabin Day at the Bailey School with a Strawberry Shortcake Social, Lincoln Depot Handmade Quilt Raffle, and Depot Day Celebration. Meetings 1st Tue monthly, 7 p.m. at Harrisville Library.
Publications: Quarterly newsletter.
Other Sites/Locations: **Lincoln Train Depot** • Intersection at Lake and Fisk Streets, Lincoln, MI 48742 • Hours: Call for current hours • Admission: Free • Visitor Accessibility: Free on-site parking. Wheelchair accessible. Self-guided. • The Lincoln Depot, a wooden structure that has been standing since 1886, was built by the Detroit, Bay City, and Alpena Railroad. The depot is located on Lake Street in Lincoln and served the community and the surrounding area until 1929. In December of 1998, the Lincoln Depot was officially recognized as a Michigan Historic Site. The last remaining train depot of its kind in Northeast Michigan. The display includes an actual caboose and switching engine.

Harrisville Train Depot
Mailing Address: Harrisville Depot Preservation Group, P.O. Box 546 • Harrisville, MI 48740
Contact: Cheryl Peterson
Phone: 989-724-6384
Physical Location: 114 Dock Street • Harrisville, MI 48740
Hours: Open by appointment.
About: A beautiful cut-stone train depot built on Detroit & Mackinaw Railroad in 1901. It served passengers until 1951. Under restoration.
Annual Events: Dragon Days (Sep).
Information may not be current.

Hart
(Oceana County)

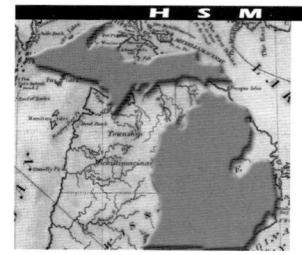

Hart Historic District Commission
Mailing Address: City of Hart, 407 State St. • Hart, MI 49420
E-Mail: ggoldberg@ci.hart.mi.us
Phone: (231) 873-2488
Fax: (231) 873-0100
Physical Location: 570 E. Lincoln • Hart, MI 49420

Hours: Jun-Sep: Tue-Sat 11 a.m.-4 p.m. Also by appointment.
Admission: $5/individual for a self-guided tour, $8/individual for a guided tour.
Visitor Accessibility: Free on-site parking. Partially wheelchair accessible. Tour guide available; refer to admission for pricing.
Website: www.ci.hart.mi.us

About: The Historic District is managed jointly by the Heritage Preservation Group and the Hart Historic Commission. Attractions include a Native-American log cabin, railroad depot, Randall School, Sackrider Church, log house, Native-American artifacts, miniature piano collection, antique animated dolls, antique pipe organ, wildlife collections, etc.
Exhibits/Collections: Local artifacts, Rider Indian artifact collection, and Mudget wildlife display.
Annual Events: Friday night concert series (Jul-Aug), Heritage Days Festival (Labor Day Weekend). Heritage Preservation Group Meeting last Thu monthly, 7 p.m.
Other Sites/Locations: Historic District buildings include: 1858 Native-American Log Cabin (Cobmoosa House), 1868 Hart Railroad Depot, 1876 Randall School, 1897 Sackrider Church, 1917 Mudget Wood Shop, 1917 Wilde Blacksmith Shop (privately owned), 1920 Schaner Feed Mill, 1947 Log House, 1993 B.R. Mudget Pavilion, 2002 Heritage Hall, 2005 Heritage Complex.
Information may not be current.

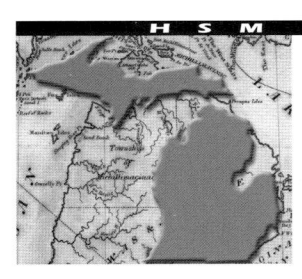

Oceana County Historical & Genealogical Society
Mailing Address: 114 Dryden St. • Hart, MI 49420
Contact: Marjorie Peterson, Publicity Chairman
E-Mail: info@oceanahistory.org
Phone: (231) 873-2600
Site/Location: **Oceana Historical Park & Museum Complex**
Physical Location: 5809 Fox Road • Mears, MI 49436
Hours: Historical & Genealogical Society: Wed 10 a.m.-4 p.m. Also by appointment. Historical Park & Museum Complex: Jun-Aug Sat-Sun 1-4 p.m.
Admission: Free.
Visitor Accessibility: Free on-site and street parking. Partially wheelchair accessible; main floor only. Tour guide available.
Website: www.oceanahistory.org

About: The Oceana County Historical & Genealogical Society collects, preserves, and disseminates knowledge of the history of Oceana County. Since its inception, the society has been gathering genealogical information about current and former residents of the county, which is available to the public at the society's headquarters in Hart.
Exhibits/Collections: Genealogical information; early county newspapers; historical and genealogical information about Native Americans in Oceana County (1897-present); cemetery records; obituaries; county post cards and photographs; histories of 114 early rural schools.
Annual Events: Postcard Show & Exchange (Jun), Special Exhibit at Old Town Hall (Jul), Annual Membership Meeting (Jul), Pleasant Afternoon (Aug).
Publications: "Oceana History, Vol. 1-3."

Hartford
(Van Buren County)

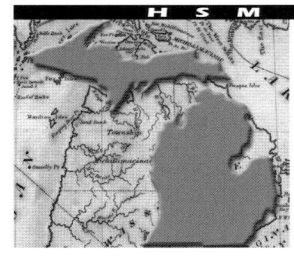

Van Buren County Historical Society
Mailing Address: P.O. Box 452 • Hartford, MI 49057
Contact: Sandra Merchant, President
Phone: (269) 621-2188
Site/Location: **Van Buren County Historical Museum**
Physical Location: 58471 Red Arrow Highway • Hartford, MI 49057
Hours: Jun-Sep: Wed, Fri-Sat 12-5 p.m.
Admission: $5/adult, $1/children (0-12).
Visitor Accessibility: On-site parking. Wheelchair accessible. Tour guide available; private tours by appointment.
About: The Van Buren County Historical Museum is housed in a former county poorhouse (b. 1884). The building features three floors of historical items and exhibits, including a one-room school, general store, music room, old-fashioned kitchen, turn-of-the-century parlor, old dentist office, and military room. There is also a replica log cabin and blacksmith works on the grounds.
Exhibits/Collections: Local archives open Wed Jun-Sep, also by appointment.
Annual Events: Soup and Spaghetti Suppers (Spr, Sum), Demonstration Day, Paranormal Tours, Murder Mystery.

Hartland
(Livingston County)

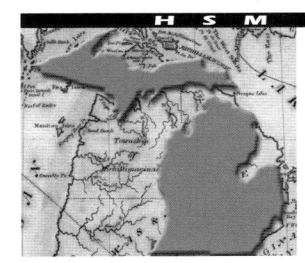

Hartland Area Historical Society
Mailing Address: P.O. Box 49 • Hartland, MI 48353
Contact: Michael Forster, Curator
Phone: (810) 229-7621
Physical Location: 3503 Avon St. • Hartland, MI 48353
Hours: Apr-Oct: Wed 2-4 p.m., Sat 10 a.m.-2 p.m. Winter: Sat 10 a.m.-2 p.m.
Admission: $1/individual donation.
Visitor Accessibility: Public parking. Not wheelchair accessible. Tour guides available; donations accepted.
Website: www.hartlandareahistory.org

About: The Hartland Area Historical Society preserves the heritage and history of Hartland Township and maintains the Florence B. Dearing Museum. The museum is housed in the former township hall and includes a farming display, a blacksmith display, looms (Hartland was noted for its weaving from 1930 to 1970), the original Hartland Post Office (est. 1837), an antique kitchen and living room, and many changing exhibits.
Annual Events: Fundraiser Dinner and Silent Auction (Feb), Annual Board Meeting (May), Potluck Dinners (May, Nov), Ice Cream Social (Jul), Heritage Day in Hartland (Sep), and Memorial Day Parade.
Publications: Quarterly membership newsletter. "Memories & Milestones," "Hartland: Weaving the Past with the Present."

Hastings
(Barry County)

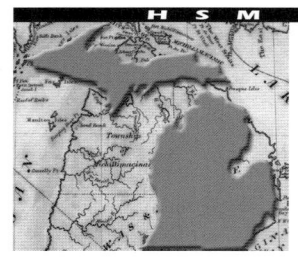

Barry County Historical Society
Mailing Address: P.O. Box 311 • Hastings, MI 49058
Contact: Mary E. Walton, President
E-Mail: bchistory64@gmail.com
Phone: (269) 838-7426
Physical Location: 532 W. Sager Rd. • Hastings, MI 49058-0311
Hours: 1st Tue monthly 7 p.m.
Admission: $10/yearly membership. Free programs.
Visitor Accessibility: Free on-site parking. Wheelchair accessible. Self-guided.
Website: https://www.facebook.com/pages/Barry-County-Historical-Society/100659980048103?fref=ts
About: Preservation and resourcing historical items and information for Barry County and the state of Michigan.
Annual Events: Meetings 3rd Thu monthly, 7:30 p.m. at the Hastings Elks Club.
Publications: Quarterly newsletter.

Historic Charlton Park
Mailing Address: 2545 S. Charlton Park Rd. • Hastings, MI 49058
Contact: Dan Patton, Executive Director
E-Mail: info@charltonpark.org
Phone: (269) 945-3775
Fax: (269) 945-0390
Hours: Office: Mon-Fri 8 a.m.-5 p.m. Park: 8 a.m.-Dusk. Village: 9 a.m.-4 p.m. Village is closed in winter.
Admission: Free, except during special events.
Visitor Accessibility: Free on-site parking except during special events. Partially wheelchair accessible. Tour guides available; $4/individual. Call (269) 945-3775.
Website: www.charltonpark.org
About: Historic Charlton Park provides educational and recreational opportunities through preservation and demonstration of early rural Michigan life, artifacts, and buildings. The park collects artifacts pertaining to Barry County and Michigan's history (from 1850 to 1930). Irving D. Charlton donated the land for the facility in 1936 and left the park approximately 100,000 artifacts. The park includes a carpenter shop, Upjohn House, blacksmith shop, barber shop, seamstress shop, township hall, hardware store, general store, museum, church, and print shop.
Exhibits/Collections: More than 30,000 artifacts represent life at the turn of the century. This includes agricultural equipment, vocational tools, furniture, textiles, housewares, fire arms, communication devices, and archival documents.
Annual Events: Tri River Musuem Tour (May), Charlton Park Day (May), Father's Day Car Show (Jun), Old Fashioned Fourth of July, Gas & Steam Engine Show (Jul), Civil War Muster (Jul), Great Lakes Longbow Invitational (Aug), August Fest (Aug), Walk in the Spirit Pow Wow (Sept), All Hallow's Eve (Oct), Of Christmas Past (Dec).
Publications: Bi-monthly village newsletter.

Hermansville
(Menominee County)

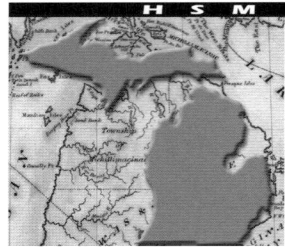

IXL Historical Museum
Mailing Address: P.O. Box 162 • Hermansville, MI 49847
Contact: Don Ducheny, Manager
E-Mail: museum@hermansville.com
Phone: (906) 498-2181
Physical Location: W5561 River St. • Hermansville, MI 49847
Hours: Memorial Day-Labor Day: 12:30-4 p.m.
Admission: $4/adult, children under 18 free.
Visitor Accessibility: Free on-site parking. Partially wheelchair accessible, outer buildings only. Tour guide available.
Website: www.hermansville.com/IXLMuseum
About: The IXL Historical Museum consists of the original 1881-1882 office building of the Wisconsin Land and Lumber Company and IXL Flooring Company of Hermansville. The main building contains four floors of lumber and hardwood flooring artifacts as well as estate furnishings. Surrounding the main office building are a complex of outer buildings: the original Hermansville Produce Warehouse, IXL Carriage House, a company house, a train depot, and caboose.
Exhibits/Collections: Lumbering artifacts and company records. Records of Blaney Park owned by Wisconsin Land & Lumber Co. Photo collection includes the town and mill, lumbering camps, and community founders.
Annual Events: Old Wheels Day and Quilt Show (Aug), Porcelain Doll Show. Meetings 2nd Wed monthly at North Central School or at museum in summer.

Thomas St. Onge Vietnam Veterans Museum
Mailing Address: N. 16462 Linden St., P.O. Box 242 • Hermansville, MI 49847
Contact: Gerald Ayotte, President
Phone: (906) 498-2309 • *Fax:* (906) 498-2409
Hours: Memorial Day-Labor Day: Sat-Sun 1-4 p.m. Also by appointment.
Admission: Donations accepted.
Visitor Accessibility: Free on-site parking. Wheelchair accessible. Free tour guide available.
Website: www.vietnam-museum-hermansville.org
About: Educates public about Vietnam War and its history through exhibits, slide shows, and presentations. Acts as a healing place for veterans and families. Attractions include tank helicopter, Anchor Coast Guard Bell, brick veterans walkway, and memorabilia from all wars.
Exhibits/Collections: Weapons, military equipment, pictures, literature, video tapes and DVDs.
Annual Events: Meetings 1st Thu monthly, 8 p.m. CST at Vietnam Vets Clubhouse.
*Information may not be current.

Hessel
(Mackinac County)

Eastern Upper Peninsula History Consortium
Mailing Address: c/o Annegret Goehring, P.O. Box 271 • Hessel, MI 49745
Contact: Annegret Goehring
About: Informal group meets twice a year to share information and activities. Occasional speakers and workshops.
Annual Events: Meetings May and Oct, 9 a.m.-2 p.m.
Publications: Publishes brochure with 20 listings of Eastern U.P. historical museums.
*Information my not be current.

Hickory Corners
(Barry County)

Gilmore Car Museum
Mailing Address: 6865 Hickory Road • Hickory Corners, MI 49060
Contact: Brittany Williams, Digital Media Coordinator
E-Mail: info@gilmorecarmuseum.org
Phone: (269) 671-5089
Fax: (269) 671-5843
Hours: Mon-Fri 9 a.m.-5 p.m. and Sat-Sun 9 a.m.-6 p.m.
Admission: $12/adult, $11/senior, $9/child (7-17), Children under 6 free. Free school tours.
Visitor Accessibility: Free on-site parking. Wheelchair accessible. Self-guided.
Website: www.gilmorecarmuseum.org
About: The 90-acre Gilmore Car Museum campus is home to nearly 400 cars, trucks, and motorcycles. Four recreated car dealerships represent each decade from 1910 to 1950. There is also a 1930s gas station and authentic 1940s diner. On display are more than 1,600 hood ornaments, 100-plus children's pedal cars, and the only full-size authentic Disney movie set outside of Disney studios or parks.
Exhibits/Collections: More than 500,000 items covering all aspects of the auto in America. Included are the Tucker Historical Collection, the Checker Cab archives, and the H. H. Franklin blueprint collection.
Annual Events: See website for schedule of car shows.
Publications: "Gilmore Car Museum: Miles from Ordinary." Quarterly newsletter (The Industry Standard).

Highland
(Oakland County)

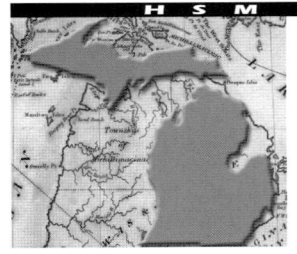

Highland Township Historical Society
Mailing Address: P.O. Box 351 • Highland, MI 48357
Contact: Diane Needham, Secretary
E-Mail: dianeneedham@comcast.net
Phone: (248) 325-5808
Site/Location: **Highland Station House**
Physical Location: 205 W Livingston Rd. • Highland, MI 48357
Visitor Accessibility: Free on-site parking available. Wheelchair accessible.
Website: www.highlandtownshiphistoricalsociety.com
About: Devoted to fostering a deeper understanding of and appreciation for the people, places, and events that make up our Highland heritage.

Hillman
(Montmorency County)

Brush Creek Mill
Mailing Address: 121 State St., P.O. Box 344 • Hillman, MI 49746
Contact: Edith Lennox, Coordinator & Director
E-Mail: brushcreekmill@myfrontiermail.com
Phone: (989) 742-2527
Physical Location: 121 S. Hillman Street • Hillman, MI 49746
Hours: Jan-Apr: Fri-Sat 12-4 p.m., May-Dec: Tue-Sat 12-4 p.m.
Admission: Free.
Visitor Accessibility: Free on-site parking. Wheelchair accessible. Tour guide available by appointment.
Website: www.brushcreekmill.com
About: The Brush Creek Mill is a history museum and area cultural center that celebrates history and promotes and provides a learning environment. It also features history about local families, as well as information pertaining to solar power, water power, wind turbines, and geothermal energy.
Exhibits/Collections: More than 2,500 pictures of the Montmorency community dating from 1889 to present, 97 DVDs featuring interviews with residents.
Annual Events: Mill River Days (Jul), Applefest and Antique Show (Oct), Festival of Lights (Dec). Meetings 2nd Mon monthly, 10 a.m.

Hillman Historical Society
Mailing Address: 121 S. Hillman Street • Hillman, MI 49746
Contact: Florence Tripp
E-Mail: brushcreekmill@myfrontiermail.com
Phone: (989) 742-4218
Admission: Free. Special event prices vary.
Visitor Accessibility: Wheelchair accessible.
About: The Hillman Historical Society collects and provides a place to have the area's local history maintained. The society also encourages an interest in the small village through recording oral histories, preserving old photographs, and assisting the Brush Creek Mill projects. The society shares the Brush Creek Mill site with their organization. Collections are displayed and change often.
Annual Events: Meetings 3rd Wed monthly, 3 p.m. at the Brush Creek Mill.

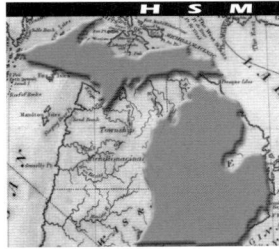

Montmorency County Historical Society
Mailing Address: P.O. Box 252 • Hillman, MI 49746
Contact: Florence Tripp, President
Phone: (989) 742-4218
Site/Location: **McKenzie One-Room School**
Physical Location: M-33 N (Montmorency County Fair Grounds) • Atlanta, MI 49709
Hours: 3rd week in Aug 10 a.m.-9 p.m.
Admission: Fair entry fee.
Visitor Accessibility: Fairground parking for a fee. Wheelchair accessible.
About: The Montmorency County Historical Society maintains the McKenzie One-Room School. It also collects and preserves artifacts and records pertaining to Montmorency County.
Exhibits/Collections: Local newspapers 1900-1991 on microfilm. Documents pertaining to the one-room schools of Montmorency County and the early timber period. Large collection of old photographs and family histories.
Annual Events: Meetings 3rd Thu Apr-Oct. Time and place vary; local radio and newspapers make announcements.
Publications: "The Lewiston Story and Montmorency County Notes," "Life in the Forest: The History of Montmorency County, Michigan," "Hillsman's 90 Years," "Blue Sky Circuit" "Life in a Lumber Camp," "Tribute to Hillsman Firefighters," "Hillman United Methodist Church," "Lewiston in the Lumbering Era I & III" "Lumbering in Early Twentieth Century Michigan: The Kneeland-Biglow Company Experience."

Information may not be current.

Hillsdale
(Hillsdale County)

Hillsdale County Genealogical Society
Mailing Address: 11 E. Bacon St. • Hillsdale, MI 49242
Contact: Janis Reister, President
Phone: (517) 523-2283
About: Working group to gather and publish records useful for genealogical research.
Exhibits/Collections: Unbound indexes (some on CD) of Hillsdale County deaths, marriages, censuses, plat maps, and newspapers.
Annual Events: Meetings 3rd Wed Mar, May, Jul, Sep, and Nov, 6:30 p.m. at Hillsdale Community Library.
Information may not be current.

Hillsdale County Historical Society
Mailing Address: PO Box 306 • Hillsdale, MI 49242
Contact: JoAnne Miller, Board Member
E-Mail: hillsdalehistoricalsociety@gmail.com
Phone: (517) 439-9547
Site/Location: Will Carleton Poorhouse
Physical Location: 180 N. Wolcott St. • Hillsdale, MI 49242
Hours: Call or see website.
Admission: Donations accepted.
Visitor Accessibility: Free on-site parking. Wheelchair accessible. Tour guide available upon request.
Website: www.hillsdalehistoricalsociety.org
About: The Hillsdale County Historical Society preserves, advances, and disseminates knowledge of the history of Hillsdale County. The society maintains the Will Carleton Poorhouse and the Fairgrounds Museum, which feature many restored artifacts and play host to several changing exhibits. The Will Carleton Poorhouse is a cobblestone house built in 1853 by Issac Vandenbergh. This building was once used as the Hillsdale County Poorhouse from 1854-1867 and was the basis for Will Carleton's poem "Over the Hill to the Poorhouse."
Exhibits/Collections: Photos, Hillsdale newspapers dating back to the 1880s, and extensive kitchen implements from the 1800s through the 1930s. County supervisor minutes relating to Poorhouse. Will Carleton books of published poetry.
Annual Events: High School History Awards (Mar), Show and Tell (Apr) Membership Picnic (Jun), William Carelton Farm Festival (Aug), Restoration/Preservation/Beautification Awards (Oct), Christmas at the Poorhouse (Dec). Board meetings 2nd Mon monthly, 7 p.m. General Membership meetings 4th Mon monthly, 7:30 p.m. in Mar, Apr, Jun, and Oct.
Publications: Quarterly newsletter, "Annual Ghost Walk Booklet."
Other Sites/Locations: Hillsdale County Fairgrounds Museum • Location: 115 S. Broad St., Hillsdale • Admission: Free • Hours: Last week of Sep: 10 a.m.-8 p.m. • Visitor Accessibility: Free steet parking. Wheelchair accessible. Tour guides are available. • The museum features a 1920s kitchen, pump organ, and player piano. The exhibits change on an annual basis.

Mitchell Research Center
Mailing Address: 22 N. Manning St. • Hillsdale, MI 49242
Contact: Bonnie McCosh, President
E-Mail: mrc@hillsdale-library.org
Phone: (517) 437-6488
Hours: Mon-Fri 10 a.m.-4 p.m., closed Thanksgiving to Mar.
Admission: Free.
Visitor Accessibility: Street parking. Wheelchair accessible.
Website: www.hillsdale-library.org/mitchell.html
About: Part of the Hillsdale Community Library housed in the historic Mitchell Building. Managed by a volunteer group supported by donations and research activities.
Exhibits/Collections: Published family genealogies, microfilmed newspapers, military, Indian, self-help, DAR, ethnic material, census, vital records, cemetery, church/military records, obituary card file, and the John Pulver Room.
Annual Events: Meetings 1st Mon Feb-Dec, 1 p.m.
Publications: Hillsdale County Cemetery Records available on CD only.

Holland
(Allegan County)

A.C. Van Raalte Institute
Mailing Address: Hope College, P.O. Box 9000 • Holland, MI 49422
Contact: Jacob Nyenhuis, Director
Phone: (616) 395-7678 • *Fax:* (616) 395-7120
Physical Location: Theil Research Center, 9 East 10th Street • Holland, MI 49423
Hours: Mon-Fri 8 a.m.-12 p.m., 1 p.m.-5 p.m.
Visitor Accessibility: On-site parking. Wheelchair accessible. Tours on occasion; call ahead for guarantee.
Website: www.hope.edu/vri
About: Department of Hope College honoring memory and vision of Rev. Albertus C. Van Raalte by studying his life, his work, and Holland, the community he founded. Dedicated to scholarly research and publication of materials relating to immigration and contributions of Dutch Americans. Sponsors lectures and presentations by members and invited guests. Works with scholars and institutions of Netherlands and other nations. Hosts foreign scholars doing research in local archives.
Exhibits/Collections: Research library, including translations of Dutch documents. Relies on holdings of the Joint Archives of Holland.
Annual Events: Sponsors two to three public lectures each year.
Publications: Published papers. See website for complete list of publications.

Association for the Advancement of Dutch-American Studies
Mailing Address: Joint Archives of Holland Hope College, P.O. Box 9000 • Holland, MI 49422
Contact: Geoffrey Reynolds, Membership Chairperson
E-Mail: archives@hope.edu
Phone: (616) 395-7798 • *Fax:* (616) 395-7197
Hours: Mon-Fri 8 a.m.-12 p.m. and 1-5 p.m.
Website: http://www.aadas.nl/
About: Membership organization encourages research and continuing interest in the history, life, and culture of the Dutch in North America. Hosts a biennial conference. Areas of interest include history, science, the arts, education, and other Dutch-American topics.
Annual Events: Biennial conference.
Publications: Biennial conference proceedings.

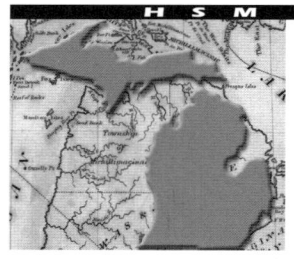

Center of African American Art and History
Mailing Address: 21 W. 16th Street • Holland, MI 49423
Contact: Ruth Coleman, President
Phone: (616) 836-8559
Fax: (616) 396-0898
Website: http://www.caaahholland.org/
Information may not be current.

Felt Estate.
Please see entry under Saugatuck: Friends of the Felt Estate.

Graafschap Heritage Center
Mailing Address: c/o Graafschap Christian Reformed Church, 5973 Church St. • Holland, MI 49423
Contact: Bill Systma
E-Mail: williamsytsma@sbcglobal.net
Phone: (616) 396-5008 • *Fax:* (616) 396-3258
Hours: Last Tue monthly 7 p.m. Also by appointment.
Admission: Donations accepted.
Visitor Accessibility: Free on-site parking. Wheelchair accessible. Free tour guide available; call ahead for reservation.
Website: www.graafschapcrc.org/heritage
About: Guided visual and hands-on tour of the local pioneer history of this 1847 settlement called "The Kolonie" as displayed in seven beautifully illustrated galleries. It has been described as the most unique center of its kind in the country including a replica of the 1848 log church.
Exhibits/Collections: Extensive genealogy records of all members who have attended the Graafschap church.
Annual Events: July 4th Patriot Community Celebration, Holland Tulip Time Festival.
Publications: See website for complete list of publications.

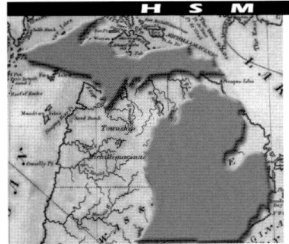

Herrick District Library
Mailing Address: 300 South River Avenue • Holland, MI 49423
Contact: Mary VanderKooy, Librarian
E-Mail: Reference@herrickdl.org
Phone: (616) 355-3100
Fax: (616) 355-3083
Site/Location: **Genealogy Department**
Hours: Mon-Tue 9 a.m.-9 p.m.; Wed-Sat 9 a.m.-6 p.m.
Admission: Free.
Visitor Accessibility: Free on-site parking. Wheelchair accessible. Self-guided.
Website: http://www.herrickdl.org
About: The Genealogy Department collects items that record the Dutch immigration to the Michigan area during the 19th century and items that report on the founding families and early settlers of the Holland area, as well as copies of vital records of Ottawa and Allegan Counties. It collects some materials that record the family migration patterns to and from the Western Michigan area. It also collects some materials that record the traditional routes of migration into the Midwest.
Exhibits/Collections: 1,400 family genealogies, various records, immigration records, Holland newspapers on microfilm, historic maps, and plat maps of Allegan and Ottawa Counties.

Historic Ottawa Beach Society
Mailing Address: P.O. Box 8462 • Holland, MI 49422-8462
Contact: Joyce Flipse Smith
E-Mail: info@historicottawabeachsociety.org
Phone: (616) 399-4648
Visitor Accessibility: Self-guided.
Website: www.historicottawabeachsociety.org
About: Fundraising continues for the Pumphouse Museum and Learning Center, located on Ottawa Beach Road adjacent to the shore of Lake Macatawa near Holland State Park. Restoration of the building begins fall 2014 following the guidelines established by the Department of Interior for restoration of historic structures. Waterfront walkway, covered pavillion, and Pumphouse Museum grounds open year-round once autumn construction is completed while fundraising continues.

Holland Area Historical Society
Mailing Address: c/o The Joint Archives of Holland, Hope College, P.O. Box 9000 • Holland, MI 49422-9000
Contact: Geoffrey Reynolds
E-Mail: archives@hope.edu
Phone: (616) 395-7798
Fax: (616) 395-7197
Website: http://hope.edu/jointarchives
About: The major goal of the society is to bring together persons with an interest in history and at the same time promote an awareness in the general public of the cultural heritage of the Holland area. The Holland Area Historical Society is not affiliated with the Holland Museum.
Annual Events: Meetings 2nd Tue 7:30 p.m. (Sep-Apr).

Holland Genealogical Society
Mailing Address: c/o Herrick District Library, 300 S. River Ave. • Holland, MI 49423
Contact: Peggy Cleair, President
E-Mail: wcleair@sbcglobal.net
Phone: (616) 399-2129
Physical Location: c/o Howard Miller Community Center, 14 S. Church St. • Zeeland, MI 49464
Admission: Free.
Visitor Accessibility: Free on-site and street parking. Wheelchair accessible. Self-guided.
Website: hollandgenealogicalsociety.wordpress.com
About: We are a diverse group with interests that go beyond Holland, Michigan. We hope to create a place to share information and ideas, grow in knowledge, and encourage everyone who comes to continue to share in our love of family history.
Exhibits/Collections: Dutch heritage, obituary file, city directories, local newspapers, genealogical resources.
Annual Events: Meetings 3rd Sat Sep-Apr, 1p.m. at Herrick library.

Holland Historic District Commission
Mailing Address: 94 W. Twelveth St. • Holland, MI 49423
Contact: Jim McKnight
E-Mail: mcjim@sbcglobal.net
Information may not be current.

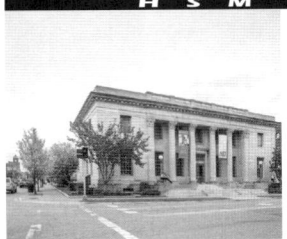

Holland Historical Trust
Mailing Address: 31 W. 10th Street • Holland, MI 49423
Contact: Paula Dunlap, Operations Manager
E-Mail: hollandmuseum@hollandmuseum.org
Phone: (616) 796-3321
Fax: 616-394-4756
Site/Location: **Holland Museum**
Hours: May-Oct: Mon, Wed-Sat 10 a.m.-5 p.m., Sun 12-5 p.m..
Admission: $7/adult, $6/senior, $4/student, children under 6 free.
Visitor Accessibility: Free street parking. Wheelchair accessible. Tour guide available.
Website: www.hollandmuseum.org

About: The Holland Historical Trust is a catalyst for the dynamic interaction of the past and present that enriches the greater Holland area. The Holland Museum features cultural attractions from the "old country," including Dutch paintings and decorative arts and exhibits from the Netherlands Pavilion of the 1939 New York World's Fair. The museum also considers local history, including Lake Michigan maritime and agricultural history.

Exhibits/Collections: Extensive paper collection of local history and Netherlands history. Separate collections include local history artifacts from start of "Holland Kolonies" to locally produced furniture, along with automotive and boat-building components.

Annual Events: Kentucky Derby (May), Ice Cream Social at Cappon House (Jun), Big Red Cruise and Lighthouse Tour (Jul), Cappon House Christmas Teas (Dec).

Publications: Quarterly newsletter (The Review).

Other Sites/Locations: **Cappon House and Settler's House** • Location: 228 West 9th St., Holland, MI 49424 • Hours: May-Dec: Fri-Sat 12-4 p.m. • Admission: $5/individual, children under 6 free • Visitor Accessibility: Free street parking. Not wheelchair accessible. Tour guide available. • The Italianate Cappon House was built by Holland's first mayor and tannery owner, Isaac Cappon, after the fire of 1871. Used by the family until 1980, the building has since been restored and furnished with Grand Rapids furniture. One of the few buildings to survive the Holland fire, Settler's House was built in 1867 by Irish Canadian shipbuilder, Thomas Morrissey. Highlights include period furnishings.

Holland Armory • Location: 16 W. 9th St., Holland, MI 49423 • Hours: Open for special events • Visitor Accessibility: Free street parking. Wheelchair accessible. Self-guided. • Housed in the historic Holland Armory are administrative offices, collection storage, and an interpretative exhibit honor Col. Geerds.

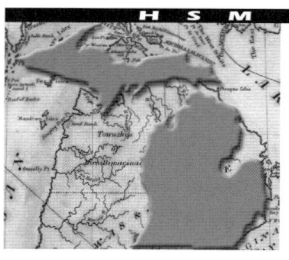

Joint Archives of Holland
Mailing Address: P.O. Box 9000, Hope College Campus • Holland, MI 49422
Contact: Geoffrey Reynolds, Director
E-Mail: archives@hope.edu
Phone: (616) 395-7798
Fax: (616) 395-7120
Physical Location: Theil Research Center, 9 E. 10th St. • Holland, MI 49423
Hours: Mon-Fri 8 a.m.-12 p.m. and 1-5 p.m.
Admission: Free.
Visitor Accessibility: Free street parking. Wheelchair accessible. Tour guide available by appointment.
Website: www.jointarchives.org

About: A department of Hope College, the Joint Archives of Holland promotes the educational mission of Hope College and its partner institutions by actively collecting, caring for, interpreting, and making available unique historical resources. Those resources include the archival collections of Hope College, Western Theological Seminary, area governmental units, and other contractual members of the Joint Archives of Holland. It serves as a history research center for students, faculty, and staff of Hope College, contractual members, and the general public.

Exhibits/Collections: Hope College and Western Theological Seminary records. Reformed Church records, including missionary activities. 19th-century Midwest Dutch immigration, Western Michigan history, maritime history, pleasure-craft industry. Pere Marquette Historical Society collection.

Publications: "Joint Archives of Holland Quarterly" newsletter.

Michigan Shipwreck Research Association
Mailing Address: 1134 Goodwood Ct. • Holland, MI 49424
Contact: Valerie van Heest, Board Member
E-Mail: valerie@michiganshipwrecks.org
Phone: (616) 566-6009
Website: http://www.michiganshipwrecks.org
Annual Events: Mysteries and Histories (May).
Publications: Email newsletter (The Explorer).

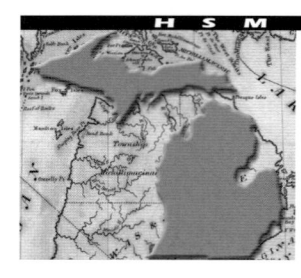

Windmill Island Gardens
Mailing Address: 1 Lincoln Ave. • Holland, MI 49423
Contact: Ad van den Akker, Manager
E-Mail: windmill@cityofholland.com
Phone: (616) 355-1030
Fax: (616) 355-1035
Hours: Apr-Oct: Daily 9:30 a.m.-5 p.m. Extended hours during Tulip Time (early May).
Admission: $8/adult, $5/children(5-15). Discounted rates for groups of 20 or more.
Visitor Accessibility: Free on-site parking. Partially wheelchair accessible. Guided tours of windmill available.
Website: www.windmillisland.org

About: The 36-acre Windmill Island Gardens commemorates Holland's Dutch heritage with DeZwaan (The Swan) windmill, built in 1761, the last to leave the Netherlands. Costumed guides provide a tour of the windmill. There is also a Story of DeZwaan movie, Amsterdam street organ, antique children's carousel, a miniature Little Netherlands, and more.

Annual Events: Tulip Time Festival (May), Historic Dutch Trade Fair (May).

Holly
(Oakland County)

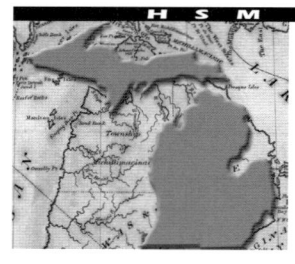

Abraham Lincoln Civil War Round Table
Mailing Address: 10035 Orchard Ridge Court • Holly, MI 48442
Contact: Worley Smith
E-Mail: alcwrt@aol.com
Physical Location: 9955 N Haggerty Road • Plymouth, MI 48170
Website: www.ALCWRT.org

Holly Historic District Commission
Mailing Address: Holly Village Hall, 920 Baird St. • Holly, MI 48442
Contact: Jerry Walker, Village Manager
Phone: (248) 634-9671 • *Fax:* (248) 634-4211
Hours: Mon-Thu 7:30 a.m.-5:30 p.m.
Visitor Accessibility: On-site parking. Wheelchair accessible.
Website: www.hollyvillage.org
About: Meets to review home/building owners' plans to do work on historic structures.
Annual Events: Meetings as needed 7 p.m. at 315 S. Broad St., Holly, MI 48442.

Holly Historical Society
Mailing Address: 306 S. Saginaw St. • Holly, MI 48442
Contact: Nancy Grimmer, President
E-Mail: hollyhistoricalsoc@comcast.net
Phone: (248) 634-9233
Site/Location: Hadley House Museum
Hours: Sun 1-4 p.m. Call for exact dates.
Admission: $2/adult.
Visitor Accessibility: Limited parking. Not wheelchair accessible. Self-guided.
Website: www.hsmichigan.org/holly
About: The Holly Historical Society organized in 1965 and acquired the 1873 Italianate Hadley House in 1986. Has original interior with period furniture. Many rooms with historical displays.
Exhibits/Collections: Genealogy room with local newspapers, photographs, and genealogical materials relating to northwest Oakland County.
Annual Events: Holly Holiday Art & Craft Show (Nov), Dickens Olde Fashioned Christmas Festival (Dec). Meetings 2nd Wed Mar-Jun and Sep-Dec, 7p.m. in museum.

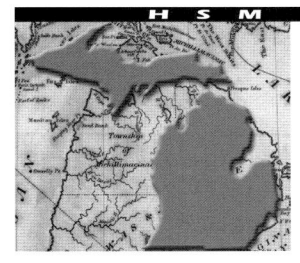

Holly Township Library
Mailing Address: 1116 N. Saginaw St. • Holly, MI 48442
Contact: Shirley Roos
E-Mail: sroos@comcast.net
Phone: (248) 634-1754 • **Fax:** (248) 634-8088
Hours: Mon-Thu 9:30 a.m.-8 p.m.; Fri 9:30 a.m.-5 p.m.; Sat 9:30 a.m.-3 p.m.
Admission: Free.
Visitor Accessibility: Free on-site parking. Wheelchair accessible. Self-guided.
Website: http://www.hollytownshiplibrary.org
Exhibits/Collections: Ben East Collection.

Holt
(Ingham County)

Holt-Delhi Historical Society
Mailing Address: 2074 Aurelius Road • Holt, MI 48842
Contact: Jacob McCormick, President
E-Mail: holtdelhihistory@gmail.com
Phone: (517) 694-2135
Hours: Call for current hours.
Visitor Accessibility: Wheelchair accessible.
About: The mission of the Holt-Delhi Historical Society is to preserve and present the history of the Holt-Delhi area and to educate residents of the interesting and important history of Holt. Established in 2014.
Annual Events: Cemetery Tours, Walking Tours.

Homer
(Calhoun County)

Homer Historical Society
Mailing Address: 505 Grandview Ave. • Homer, MI 49245
Contact: JoAnne Miller, Trustee
E-Mail: joanne.miller43@gmail.com
Phone: (517) 568-3116
Site/Location: Blair Historical Farm
Physical Location: 26445 M-60 East • Homer, MI 49245
Hours: By appointment.
Admission: Donations accepted.
Visitor Accessibility: Free on-site parking. Wheelchair accessible. Tour guides available by appointment.
Website: www.homerhistoricalsociety.org
About: The Homer Historical Society preserves Homer's history, landmarks, and stories. It also maintains Blair Historical Farm, a pioneer family farm with a barn and out buildings. Owned originally by Homer's first pioneer doctor, George Blair, the property also features the old Albion Town Hall and Grover Rural Railroad Depot—both of which were moved to the farm and renovated for use as display areas.
Exhibits/Collections: Photos, books, articles, and miscellaneous items related to Homer's history.
Annual Events: Herb Workshop (Feb), Car and Truck Show (Jul), Homer Historical Fall Festival (Sep). Meetings held last Wed monthly; call in advance to verify date/time/place.
Publications: "Ties to Homer."

Houghton
(Houghton County)

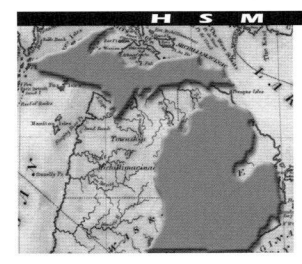

Carnegie Museum of the Keweenaw
Mailing Address: c/o City of Hougton, 616 Shelden Ave. • Houghton, MI 49931
Contact: Elsie Nelson, Director
E-Mail: history@cityofhoughton.com
Phone: (906) 482-7140
Fax: (906) 482-0282
Physical Location: 105 Huron St. • Houghton, MI 49931
Hours: Oct1-Jul 3: Tue, Thu 12-5 p.m.; Sat 12-4 p.m. Jul 5-Sep 30: Tue-Wed 12-5 p.m.; Thu 12-6 p.m.; Fri-Sat 12-4 p.m. Also by appointment.
Admission: Free.
Visitor Accessibility: Free on-site and street parking. Self-guided.
About: Opened in 2007, the Carnegie Museum of the Keweenaw is a re-use of Houghton's Carnegie Library (b. 1910). Exhibits are displayed on the main floor.
Annual Events: Night at the Museum Fundraiser (Jun), Holiday Open House (Dec). Board meetings 4th Tue monthly, 5:30 p.m. at museum.
*Information may not be current.

Isle Royale & Keweenaw Parks Association
Mailing Address: 800 E. Lake Shore Dr. • Houghton, MI 49931
Contact: Kristine Bradof, Executive Director
E-Mail: irkpa@irkpa.org
Phone: (906) 482-3627 • **Fax:** (906) 487-7170
Website: www.irkpa.org
About: Promotes understanding, appreciation, and enjoyment of Isle Royale National Park and Keweenaw National Historical Park. Educating the public about these parks will help preserve and protect them for future generations.
*Information may not be current.

Northland Historical Consortium
Mailing Address: P.O. Box 552 Houghton, MI 49931
Contact: Erik Nordberg, Secretary/Treasurer
E-Mail: northlandconsortium@gmail.com
Phone: (906) 487-2505 • **Fax:** (906) 487-2357
Website: http://northlandconsortium.wordpress.com

Historical Society of Michigan

About: Organized in 1985 with more than 40 museums, archives, and historical organizations participating from Michigan's Central and Western Upper Peninsula and Northeastern Wisconsin. Meets twice a year for training workshops, mini-conferences, tours of member institutions, and opportunities for networking. No required membership dues, though fees are charged for listings in the consortium's printed informational brochure.
Annual Events: Meetings, hosted by member institutions.
Information may not be current.

Houghton Lake
(Roscommon County)

Houghton Lake Area Historical Society
Mailing Address: 1701 W. Houghton Lake Drive • Houghton Lake, MI 48629
Contact: Agnes Feldman, President
E-Mail: chuckandag@charter.net
Phone: (989) 821-8433
Site/Location: Houghton Lake Area Historical Village
Hours: Summer: Fri-Sat 12-4 p.m. Also by appointment.
Admission: $3/individual.
Visitor Accessibility: Free onsite-parking. Wheelchair accessible. Tour guide available.
Website: www.houghtonlakehistory.com
About: The Houghton Lake Area Historical Society preserves the history of the Houghton Lake area and provideds historical education to Roscommon County and its community schools. It maintains a 13-building historic village, which replicates a 19th-century logging-era community. The site includes a one-mile nature trail, school museum, and operating general store. The adjacent historical playhouse, located at 1681 W. Houghton Lake Drive, was built in 1927 as Johnson Dance Hall.
Exhibits/Collections: Photographs and memorabilia concerning logging in the area. Douglas Houghton's surveying tools.
Annual Events: Houghton Lake Historical Days (Aug). Meetings 3rd Tue monthly Apr-Nov, 7 p.m. at Houghton Lake Playhouse.

Howell
(Livingston County)

George W. Lee Civil War Round Table of Howell
Mailing Address: 309 Victoria Park Dr. • Howell, MI 48843
Contact: Dave Finney
Phone: (517) 552-8733
Information may not be current

Howell Area Archives
Mailing Address: Howell Carnegie Library, 314 W. Grand River • Howell, MI 48843
Contact: Milton Charboneau
E-Mail: archives@howelllibrary.org
Phone: (517) 546-0720 x129 • *Fax:* (517) 546-1494
Hours: Wed, Fri, and Sat 1-5 p.m.
Website: www.howelllibrary.org
About: Collects and preserves historical materials relating to Livingston County.
Exhibits/Collections: Michigan Civil War Regiment Books Vol 1-46, Michigan Historical Collection Vol 1-40, DAR Lineage Books Vol 41-113. Materials on Livingston County including obituaries and genealogies.
Information may not be current.

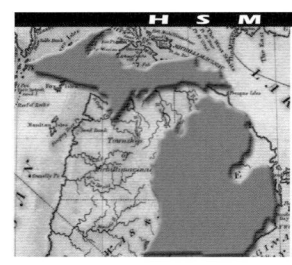

Howell Area Historical Society
Mailing Address: P.O. Box 154 • Howell, MI 48844
Contact: Bruce Powelson, Treasurer
E-Mail: howellareahistoricalsociety@gmail.com
Phone: 517-548-6876
Site/Location: Depot Museum
Physical Location: 128 Wetmore Street • Howell, MI 48844
Hours: Memorial Day-Labor Day: Sun 10 a.m.-2 p.m. Also by appointment.
Admission: Donations accepted.
Visitor Accessibility: Free on-site parking. Wheelchair accessible. Tour guide available during open hours by appointment.
Website: www.howellareahistoricalsociety.org
About: Located in the 1886 Historic Ann Arbor Depot, the society's museum houses a replica of an 1890s general store, displays, and artifacts from WWI and WWII. Railroad buffs will be particularly interested in the station master's old telegraph key, hand-operated signal levers, and collection of lanterns. The site also features an 1888 Grand Trunk wooden caboose.
Exhibits/Collections: Miscellaneous collection of artifacts from Livingston county.
Annual Events: Melon Festival (Aug), Passport to History School Tours.
Publications: Quarterly newsletter.

Howell Historic District Commission
Mailing Address: 611 E. Grand River • Howell, MI 48843
Information may not be current.

Livingston County Genealogical Society
Mailing Address: P.O. Box 1073 • Howell, MI 48843
Contact: Geunter Loepertz, President
E-Mail: milcgs@hotmail.com
Phone: (248) 529-6646
Hours: Call or visit website for current hours.
Website: www.milcgs.wordpress.com
About: The Livingston County Genealogical Society exists to encourage and assist in the study of family history, to promote the exchange of knowledge, to encourage the deposit of genealogical records, to preserve and make available the records of our ancestors for research, and to help other societies, and to publish materials of interest and use to other genealogists.
Annual Events: Meetings 1st Thu monthly, 7-9 p.m. at First United Methodist Church, Howell.
Publications: Livingston County Cemetery Records (call for detailed list), Livingston County Census.

Marine Historical Society of Detroit
Mailing Address: c/o Mark Cowles, Secretary, 514 Aberdeen Way • Howell, MI 48846
Contact: Mark Cowles
E-Mail: roger@knowyourships.com
Phone: (517) 546-5241
Hours: Call or see website.
Website: www.mhsd.org
About: Membership organization founded 1944.
Annual Events: Annual dinner, meets four to five times annually with the Lake Huron Lore Society at the Port Huron Museum.
Publications: Monthly newsletter (Detroit Marine Historian). Annual calendar of Great Lakes ships and books on Great Lakes ships and history.

Crisp Point Light Historical Society
Mailing Address: 450 W. Marr Road • Howell, MI 48855
Contact: Rick Brockway, President
E-Mail: cplhs@sbcglobal.net
Phone: (517) 230-6294
Fax: (517) 546-5283
Site/Location: **Crisp Point Lighthouse**
Physical Location: 1944 Crisp Point Road (CR-412) • Newberry, MI 49868
Hours: Jun-Oct 10 a.m.-5 p.m. Check on-line calendar for volunteer keeper status.
Admission: Free.
Visitor Accessibility: Free on-site parking. Grounds, visitors center, and restrooms are wheelchair accessible; lighthouse is not wheelchair accessible. Self-guided.
Website: www.crisppointlighthouse.org
About: The Crisp Point Light Historical Society restores and preserves the Crisp Point Lighthouse for future generations. Attractions at the lighthouse include a Fourth Order Fresnel Lens, Fresnel Buoy lens, historical photos, artifacts found on grounds, and various styles of USCG Great Lakes buoys.
Exhibits/Collections: Crisp Point Lighthouse, LHE-Era buoy lens, and related artifacts.
Annual Events: Crisp Point Light Historical Society Summer Conference (Jul).
Publications: Quarterly newsletter.

Hubbardston
(Ionia County)

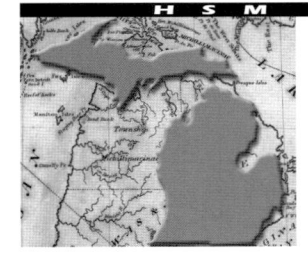

Hubbardston Area Historical Society
Mailing Address: P.O. Box 183 • Hubbardston, MI 48845
Contact: Joanne Howard, Board Member
E-Mail: hubb.northplains@gmail.com
Phone: (989) 584-3803
Site/Location: **Hubbardston Area Historical Society Museum**
Physical Location: 305 Russell Street • Hubbardston, Michigan 48845
Hours: Tue-Wed 2-4 pm. Also by appointment; call (989) 584-3803.
Admission: Donations accepted.
Visitor Accessibility: Free on-site parking. Wheelchair accessible. Tour guide available.
Website: www.hubbardston.org
About: The Hubbardston Area Historical Society seeks, promotes, and preserves the history of Ionia, Clinton, Montcalm and Gratiot Counties; completes the genealogy of the founding families; publishes findings; and secures the continuing operation and collections of the local historical museum, which is located in the Hubbardston Community Center (the former public elementary school). Attractions include Hubbardston Mill tool display, original Methodist church pump organ, and more.
Exhibits/Collections: First family genealogy completions, family histories, plat maps, Irish history collections, antique clothing display, pictures, school class photos, early editions of county history, and filed collection of obituaries by year.
Annual Events: Irish Extravaganza Fundraiser (Apr), Membership Drive (Memorial Day Weekend), Fall Social (Aug). Celebrate the Holidays (Nov). Meetings 4th Thu Mar-May and Aug-Nov, 7 p.m. at the HAHS Museum Room; refreshments are served at 6:30 p.m. Call society for information on speakers.
Publications: Quarterly newsletter. "St. John the Baptist Parish, the Beginnings," "Hubbardston Genealogy 1780-1930," "Irish Lore and Recipes," "St. Mary's and St. John the Baptist Cemetery Burial Records (seven volume)."
Other Sites/Locations: **St. John the Baptist Catholic Church Complex** • Location: 324 S. Washington St., Hubbardston, MI 48845 • Hours: By appointment • Admission: Donations accepted • Visitor Accessibility: Free on-site parking. Wheelchair accessible. To schedule a self-guided tour, call Joanne Howard at (989) 584-3803. • Built in 1868, St. John the Baptist Catholic Church was the largest building (seating 400) in Ionia County at the time of its establishment. It features 17 stained glass windows, which were installed in 1905 and registered with the Michigan Stained Glass Census Bureau in late 1990s. Other buildings on site include the rectory (b.1907), a former school (b.1919), and cemetery that was dedicated in 1884 and is still in use today.

Hudson
(Lenawee County)

Bean Creek Valley Historical Society
Mailing Address: 520 Sunrise Dr. • Hudson, MI 49247
Contact: Hazel Monahan, President
E-Mail: millsmj@cass.net
Phone: (517) 448-8858
Site/Location: **Hudson Museum**
Physical Location: 219 W. Main St. • Hudson, MI 49247
Hours: Mon, Fri 1-4 p.m., Sat 12-3 p.m. Also by appointment.
Admission: Donations accepted.
Visitor Accessibility: Free on-site parking. Partially wheelchair accessible (ground floor). Tour guide available upon request.
About: The Bean Creek Valley Historical Society is charged with finding, preserving, and passing on the history of the Hudson area, which includes the western portion of Lenawee County and the eastern portion of Hillsdale County. Visitors will see extensive, donated collections of war memorabilia, early manufacturing history, a recreated one-room schoolhouse, and pictorial highlights of the Hudson football teams national winning streak, which lasted from 1968-1975.
Exhibits/Collections: Authors Ella Flatt Keller and Will Carleton. Civil War artifacts highlighting the soldiers who enlisted in Hudson, including 4th Michigan Infantry and United States Sharpshooters. Extensive genealogical holdings for area.
Annual Events: Dinner Auction (May). Monthly meetings (except Jan-Mar) at the museum.
Publications: "Cleaning up the Muss," "History of Addision," "Reflections on the Bean."

William G. Thompson House Museum & Gardens
Mailing Address: 101 Summit St. • Hudson, MI 49247
Contact: Ray Lennard
E-Mail: rlennard@thompsonmuseum.org
Phone: (517) 448-8125
Hours: Mon, Wed, Fri 12-3:30 p.m. Also by appointment.
Admission: $7.50/adult, $5/senior, $5/student.
Visitor Accessibility: Free on-site parking. Partially wheelchair accessible. Guided tours.
Website: www.thompsonmuseum.org
About: The William G. Thompson House Museum & Gardens preserves and conveys the collections and spirit of William G. Thompson through the interpretation of the three-generational Queen Anne-style home and collections. The 1890 home features an ornate metal roof and ashler cut stone foundation. Visitors can see the

changes to the home over the years.
Exhibits/Collections: Extensive collection of oriental art, antiques, and paintings.
Annual Events: Lost Arts/Antique Appraisal Day (Aug).
Publications: "Yesterday and Today in Hudson," "Yesterday and Today in Devils Lake."

Imlay City
(Lapeer County)

Imlay City Historical Commisson
Mailing Address: 77 Main St. • Imlay City, MI 48444
Contact: Marilyn Swihart, Board Secretery
E-Mail: bswihart1904@charter.net
Phone: (810) 724-1904
Site/Location: Imlay City Historical Museum
Hours: Apr-Dec: Sat 1-4 p.m. Also by appointment.
Admission: Donations accepted.
Visitor Accessibility: Street parking. Wheelchair accessible. Self-guided.
Website: www.imlaycityhistoricalmuseum.org
About: Operates a museum and brings together those interested in history, especially in the history of Imlay City and its surrounding community. Museum opened 1978 in Historic Grand Trunk Depot. Artifacts in caboose and bunk car on-site. Displays include military display, farm tools, country doctor's operating room equipment, photos of Imlay City, and racecar driver Bob Burman.
Exhibits/Collections: Local families, microfilm record of newspapers, obituary file for genealogical research, scrapbooks.
Annual Events: Blueberry Festival (Aug), Old-Fashioned Roast Beef Supper and Auction (Oct).
Publications: Quarterly newsletter.

Indian River
(Cheboygan County)

Tuscarora Historical Society
Mailing Address: P.O. Box 807 • Indian River, MI 49747
Information may not be current.

Inkster
(Wayne County)

Inkster Historical Commission
Mailing Address: c/o Leanna Hicks Public Library, 2005 Inkster Rd. • Inkster, MI 48141
Contact: Michael Wells
Phone: (313) 563-2822 • *Fax:* (313) 274-5130
Website: http://www.inkster.lib.mi.us/board.html
About: Historical Commission works out of office in Leanna Hicks Public Library. Collects documents and records pertaining to history of Inkster while seeking space for artifact collection and displays.
Annual Events: Meetings 3rd Thu monthly, 4 p.m. at Leanna Hicks Public Library.
Information may not be current.

Interlochen
(Grand Traverse County)

Walter E. Hastings Museum
Mailing Address: Interlochen Center for the Arts, P.O. Box 199 • Interlochen, MI 49683
About: The Walter E. Hastings Nature Museum is an environmental classroom for Interlochen campers.
Exhibits/Collections: The museum houses an extensive collection of wildlife photographs; rocks and minerals; and Native-American tools, arrowheads, and other handiwork.
Information may not be current.

Ionia
(Ionia County)

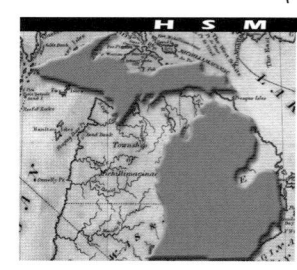

Ionia County Historical Society
Mailing Address: P.O. Box 176 • Ionia, MI 48846
Contact: Henry Knoop
E-Mail: kknoop@charter.net
Phone: (616) 527-6281
Site/Location: Blanchard House
Physical Location: 251 East Main Street • Ionia, MI 48846
Hours: Jun-Aug and Dec: Sun 1-4 p.m. Also by appointment.
Admission: $3/individual suggested donation.
Visitor Accessibility: On-site and street parking available. Not wheelchair accessible. Free tour guides available.
Website: www.ioniahistory.org
About: The Ionia County Historical Society preserves local history; shares information through museum, guided tours, presentations, and educational lectures; and operates the 1881 Blanchard Mansion, carriage house, and grounds. The basement of the Blanchard House also serves as the local museum.
Exhibits/Collections: Collections date back to 1833 and include photographs and local records.
Annual Events: Antique Appraisal (Apr), Upstairs/Downtown Tour of Ionia (May) Antique Fair (Jun), Gravesite Presentation (Oct).
Publications: Monthly newsletter (Chronicle). Available in hardcopy or online on website.

Iron Mountain
(Dickinson County)

Cornish Pumping Engine & Mining Museum
Mailing Address: P.O. Box 237 • Iron Mountain, MI 49801
Contact: Dianne Castelaz-Chiapusio
E-Mail: mrh-museum@sbcglobal.net
Phone: (906) 774-1086
Physical Location: 300 Kent St. • Iron Mountain, MI 49801
Hours: Memorial Day-Labor Day Mon-Sat 9 a.m.-5 p.m., Sun 12-4 p.m. Call for spring and fall hours.
Admission: $5/adult, $4.50/senior, $3/student, children 10 and under free.
Visitor Accessibility: Free on-site parking. Wheelchair accessible. Free tour guides available for group tours only.
Website: www.menomineemuseum.com
About: Preserves the history of the Menominee Iron Range and Dickinson County. Largest steam-driven pumping engine built in the United States. Exhibits include mining equipment and geological specimens and tell the story of iron mining on Menominee Range. Exhibit on WWII military gliders built by Ford Motor Company in Kingsford.

Dickinson County Genealogical Society
Mailing Address: c/o Dickinson County Library, 401 Iron Mountain St. • Iron Mountain, MI 49801
Contact: William Cummings, President

E-Mail: foster@chartermi.net
Phone: (906) 774-9663
Hours: Mon-Fri 9 a.m.-8 p.m., Sat 9 a.m.-5 p.m., Sun (hours vary).
Admission: Free.
Visitor Accessibility: Free street parking. Wheelchair accessible.
Website: www.dcl-lib.org/?history
About: Provides information for family history. Collection of books pertaining to the history of the Upper Peninsula.
Exhibits/Collections: Microfilm of Upper Peninsula and Northern Wisconsin census records, microfilm of local newspapers, city directories, cemetery indices.
Annual Events: Meetings 4th Thu monthly Jan-May, Sep-Oct, 1p.m. at library. 3rd Thursday in Nov, 1 p.m. at library.
Publications: Quarterly newsletter (Dickinson Diggings).

Iron Mountain Iron Mine
Mailing Address: P.O. Box 177 • Iron Mountain, MI 49801
Contact: Dennis Carollo
E-Mail: ironmine@uplogon.com
Phone: (906) 563-8077
Physical Location: US-2 • Vulcan, MI 49892
Hours: Memorial Day-Oct 15: Daily 9 a.m.-5 p.m.
Admission: $14/adult, $8/children (6-12), children 5 and under are free.
Visitor Accessibility: Free on-site parking. Wheelchair accessible. Guided tours included in admission.
Website: www.ironmountainironmine.com
About: Located nine miles east of Iron Mountain, the Iron Mountain Iron Mine keeps alive the heritage of the area's underground mining ancestors. The site provides guided underground mine tours by train of former east Vulcan mine, which produced more than 22 million tons of Iron Ore from 1870-1945.
Exhibits/Collections: Antique mining equipment, mining artifacts, and photos.

Menominee Range Historical Foundation
Mailing Address: P.O. Box 237 • Iron Mountain, MI 49801
Contact: William Cummings, Vice President/Historian
E-Mail: mrh-museum@sbcglobal.net
Phone: (906) 774-4276
Site/Location: **Menominee Range Historical Museum**
Physical Location: 300 E. Ludington Street • Iron Mountain, MI 49801
Hours: Memorial Day-Labor Day: Tue-Fri 11 a.m.-3 p.m.
Admission: $5/adult, $4.50/senior, $3/student, children under 10 free.
Visitor Accessibility: Not wheelchair accessible. Tour guides available.
Website: www.menomineerangehistoricalfoundation.org
About: The Menominee Range Historical Foundation & Museum preserves the history of Dickinson County and life on the Menominee Range. The newest addition to the site is a restored CG-4A glider, which was produced at the Ford Plant during WWII.
Exhibits/Collections: Artifacts, library materials, photographs, and other items relevant to history of Menominee Iron Range and Dickinson County.
Other Sites/Locations: **World War II Glider and Military Museum** • Location: 300 Kent St., Iron Mountain, MI • The World War II Glider and Military Museum contains a completely restored C6-4A WWII glider, WWII jeep, Ford memorabilia, and military exhibits from the Civil War through the Iraq and Afghanistan conflicts.

Iron River
(Iron County)

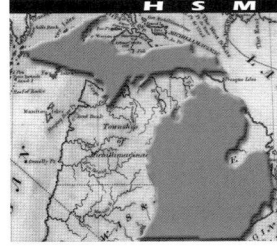

Beechwood Historical Society
Mailing Address: P.O. Box 219 • Iron River, MI 49935
Contact: Janet Melstrom, Treasurer
E-Mail: beechwoodhistoricalsociety@gmail.com
Phone: (906) 265-5652
Site/Location: **Beechwood Hall**
Physical Location: 178 Beechwood Store Road • Iron River, MI 49935
Hours: No regular hours at this time.
Admission: Free.
Visitor Accessibility: Free on-site parking. Wheelchair accessible. Self-guided.
Website: www.beechwoodhistoricalsociety.org
About: The Beechwood Historical Society preserves and shares Beechwood heritage with present and future generations. It collects, houses, and preserves artifacts, works of art, and archival materials related the history of the Beechwood community. It also provides interpretive exhibits, displays, and programs based upon the research of its members.
Exhibits/Collections: Items from the original Beechwood Post Office, logging film from local logging operation, school desks, copy of "More than a Farmer" slideshow by Marcia Bernhardt.
Annual Events: Memorial Day Services (May), Chilly Feed, Rummage Sale, Christmas Craft and Bake Sale, movie night, and history night. Meetings 3rd Mon monthly, 6 p.m. at Beechwood Hall.
Information may not be current.

Ironwood
(Gogebic County)

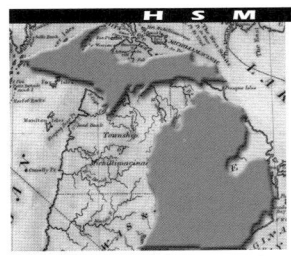

Ironwood Area Historical Society
Mailing Address: P.O. Box 553 • Ironwood, MI 49938
Contact: Gary Harrington, President
E-Mail: twolees1@chartermi.net
Phone: (906) 932-0287
Physical Location: 150 N. Lowell • Ironwood, MI 49938
Hours: Memorial Day-Labor Day: Mon-Sat 12-4 p.m.
Admission: Free.
Visitor Accessibility: Free on-site parking. Wheelchair accessible. Free guides available.
Website: https://www.facebook.com/pages/Ironwood-Area-Historical-Society-Museum/115519501803896
About: 1892 depot shared by museum and Chamber of Commerce. Focus on history of Gogebic Range and Ironwood. Exhibits include mining history and its significance to the area, as well as a representation of an early general store as stocked in early days of Ironwood. Heritage Room in Memorial Building.
Exhibits/Collections: Culturally significant artifacts and photos. Railroads, Mining, General.
Annual Events: Festival Ironwood (Jul), Meetings 2nd Tue monthly 6 p.m.
Publications: Newsletter, local historical videos.

Ironwood Carnegie Library
Mailing Address: 402 Lake Avenue • Ironwood, MI 49938
Contact: Elaine Erikson, Library Director
E-Mail: libraryboss@ironwoodcarnegie.org
Phone: (906) 032-0203 • *Fax:* (906) 932-2447
Hours: Mon, Thu, Fri 9 a.m.-5:30 p.m.; Tue 12-7 p.m.; Sat 9 a.m.-12:30 p.m.
Admission: Free.

Visitor Accessibility: Free street parking. Wheelchair accessible. Self-guided.
Website: http://www.uproc.lib.mi.us/ironwood
About: The oldest, continuously operating Carnegie Library in Michigan and the first library to have received a grant from Carnegie. The library is on the National Register for Historic Places.
Exhibits/Collections: Local history and geneaology.

Ishpeming
(Marquette County)

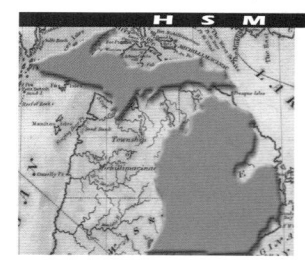

Cliffs Shaft Mining Museum
Mailing Address: 501 W. Euclid St., • Ishpeming, MI 49849
Contact: Brad Waters
E-Mail: steelworkers1@aol.com
Phone: (906) 485-1882
Fax: (906) 485-1884
Hours: Tue-Sat 10 a.m.-4 p.m.
Admission: $10/adult, $5/student (13-17), children 12 and under free.
Visitor Accessibility: Free on-site parking. Wheelchair accessible (except for service tunnel tour). Free tour guides available.
Website: http://www.gincc.org/business/index.php?q=&c=176
About: Best-preserved, most complete example of underground iron mining in Michigan. Great education outreach programs.
Exhibits/Collections: Mining artifacts, railroad artifacts, Isphemimg rock and mineral club specimens.
Annual Events: Meetings 2nd Mon monthly, 6:30 p.m.

Ishpeming
(Marquette County)

Ishpeming Historical Society
Mailing Address: 501 W. Euclid Street • Ishpeming, MI 49849
Contact: Sue Boback, President
E-Mail: ishphistoricalsociety@gmail.com
Hours: Spring-fall: Mon 10 a.m.-4 p.m. Call for additional summer hours and appointments.
Admission: Donations accepted.
Visitor Accessibility: Free street parking. Wheelchair accessible. Self-guided.
About: The Ishpeming Area Historical Society discovers, preserves, promotes, and encourages appreciation and sustained interest for the history of Ishpeming area. It focuses on Ishpeming's citizens, schools and yearbooks, famous citizens, merchants, clubs, organizations, and past times. The society is located in the former Gossard Garment Factory building, where additional spaces within the building may be viewed.
Exhibits/Collections: Movie memorabilia, Gossard Garment Factory history and artifacts, Blue Notes Drum & Bugle Corp.
Annual Events: Estate Sale (Jan), Annual Meeting with Speaker (Oct), Historic Home Tour (Jun), Seasonal Historic Home Tea. Meetings 4th Tue (Jan-Apr, Aug-Oct).
Publications: "A Visit to the Past, Vol. I and II."

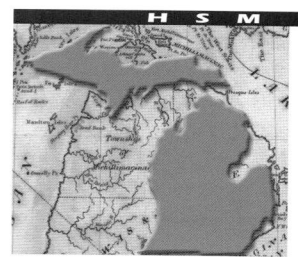

U.S. Ski and Snowboard Hall of Fame
Mailing Address: P.O. Box 191 • Ishpeming, MI 49849
Contact: Tom West, President and CEO
E-Mail: administrator@skihall.com
Phone: (906) 485-6323
Fax: (906) 486-4570
Physical Location: 610 Palms Ave. • Ishpeming, MI 49849
Hours: Mon-Sat 10 a.m.-5 p.m.
Admission: Donations accepted.
Visitor Accessibility: Free on-site parking. Wheelchair accessible. Tour guide available.
Website: www.skihall.com
About: The U.S. Ski and Snowboard Hall of Fame provides respected permanent national recognition for those who have achieved national and international success in skiing and snowboarding competition or who have contributed significantly to the development of ski sports at the national level in the United States. The museum features 15,000 square feet of exhibits, including National Honors Court, Birkebeiner diorama, Early American ski manufacturing, adaptive skiing display, Olympic collection, early snow-making equipment, and the first chair lift in America.
Exhibits/Collections: More than 75,000 artifacts, photographs, and films in its collections. Artifacts include skis from over the past two centuries, ski clothing, trophies, and a 1940s "Weasel" snow groomer.
Annual Events: Induction Ceremony (Mar/Apr), Skiing History Week (Mar/Apr), Hall of Fame Weekend and National Ski Jumpers Reunion (Sep), Ski Film Project (Nov).
Publications: Skiing History.

Ithaca
(Gratiot County)

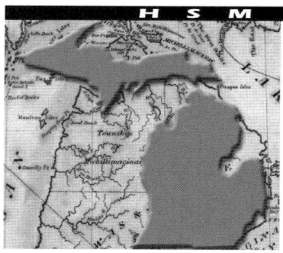

Gratiot County Historical & Genealogical Society
Mailing Address: P.O. Box 73 • Ithaca, MI 48847
Contact: Karen Emery, President
E-Mail: carol@gchgs.org
Phone: (989) 875-6232
Physical Location: Gratiot County Library, 228 W. Center St. • Ithaca, MI 48847
Admission: Free.
Visitor Accessibility: Free street parking. Wheelchair accessible. Free tour guide available.
Website: www.gchgs.org
About: Organized 1978.
Exhibits/Collections: Collection of furniture, textiles, glass and china, kitchenware, and toys. Genealogical library in Peet/Miller House. Stories and genealogies of Gratiot County families. County histories. Records of organizations, churches, and schools.
Annual Events: Meetings 3rd Mon 7:30 p.m. at genealogical library (Mar, May, Jul, Sep, Nov).
Publications: Monthly newsletter (Pages From the Past and Present), Quarterly Gratiot Genealogical Group.
Other Sites/Locations: **Gratiot County Area Historical Museum** • Location: 129 W. Center St., Ithaca, MI 48847 • Hours: Tue 12-3 p.m. • Museum in 1881 brick Victorian home.
Information may not be current.

Jackson
(Jackson County)

Ella Sharp Museum of Art & History
Mailing Address: 3225 Fourth St. • Jackson, MI 49203
Contact: Mara Wierzbicki, PR & Visitor Services Coordinator
E-Mail: info@ellasharp.org
Phone: (517) 787-2320

Fax: (517) 787-2933
Hours: Tue-Wed and Fri-Sat 10 a.m.-5 p.m., Thu 10 a.m.-7 p.m.
Admission: Combined Galleries and House: $7/adult, $5/children (5-12), $4/AAA members. Free for museum members. Prices vary for visitation to farmhouse and galley only. See website for current price listings.
Visitor Accessibility: Free on-site parking. Wheelchair accesible. Tour guide available; call ahead.
Website: www.ellasharp.org
About: The Ella Sharp Museum promotes the understanding and appreciation of art and history through exhibits, interpretation of historical buildings, and educational programs. Ella Sharp Museum includes Ella Sharp's 19th-century Hillside Farmhouse; the Dibble One-Room Schoolhouse; Eli Stilson's Log House; the Merriman-Sharp Tower Barn; and six modern galleries featuring a private Audubon sculpture and art collection, Jackson history, and a private clock collection.
Exhibits/Collections: Jackson County history, Merriman-Sharp Collection, W.H. Withington Papers, Sparks-Withington Company (Sparton), and Jackson-made automobiles.
Annual Events: Sugaring & Shearing Festival (Mar); Art, Beer & Wine Festival (Jun); Fall Harvest Festival (Oct); Christmas at Hillside (Dec).
Publications: Bimonthly newsletter (Elle News), "Merriman-Sharp Family," "My Dear Wife."
Other Sites/Locations: **Cell Block 7 Prison Museum** • Location: 3455 Cooper Street, Jackson • Admission: $15/adult, $8/children (5-12), children 5 and under free. $10/members, seniors, and military personnel. • Visitor Accessibility: Free on-site parking. Partially wheelchair accessible. Self-guided. • This exhibit brings important topics to life, including how Jackson was chosen for the site of Michigan's State Prison, major changes throughout the years, and how punishment and overcrowding were handled. Discover how and why prison life has changed. Learn about the riots, escapes, and the establishment of the Michigan Department of Corrections.

Jackson County Genealogical Society
Mailing Address: c/o Jackson District Library, 244 W. Michigan Ave. • Jackson, MI 49201
Contact: Judy Moulton
Phone: (517) 768-9266
Physical Location: United Way Building, 536-540 N Jackson • Jackson, MI 49201
Hours: Tue-Thu 1-5 p.m., Sat 10 a.m.-4 p.m.
Website: http://www.rootsweb.ancestry.com/~mijackgs/jcgs.htm
About: Dedicated to the encouragement and enhancement of genealogy, to preserve and make available records of Jackson County area and assist Jackson County-area libraries in collecting genealogical records and expanding their collections of published genealogical records. Publishes genealogical material.
Annual Events: Meetings 1st Tue monthly, 6:30 p.m. at Department of Aging, Lansing (Sep-May).
Publications: Bimonthly newsletter.
Information may not be current.

Jackson County Historical Society
Mailing Address: c/o Jackson District Library, 224 W. Michigan Ave. • Jackson, MI 49201
Contact: John Fisher, President
About: To encourage historical study and research and to preserve historical material connected with the city of Jackson. Presents programs, tapes, and DVDs on Jackson County history. Awards historical markers to appropriate structures.
Annual Events: Meetings 2nd Sat Sep-Apr, 11 a.m. at Ella Sharp Museum.
Publications: Monthly newsletter (The Broadside).
Information may not be current.

Jackson District Library
Mailing Address: 244 W. Michigan Ave. • Jackson, MI 49201
Contact: Reference Department
E-Mail: reference@myjdl.com
Phone: (517) 788-4087
Visitor Accessibility: Free on-site parking. Wheelchair accessible.
Website: www.myjdl.com
About: The Minter VanOrman Room at the Carnegie Branch houses the library's Genealogy and Jackson Local History Collections. The materials in these collections are available to the public during normal Carnegie Branch hours. All materials in the Minter VanOrman Room are restricted to library use only. Staff members and volunteers are happy to assist the public as time permits.

Jackson Historic District Commission
Mailing Address: 161 W. Michigan Ave. • Jackson, MI 49201
Contact: Barry Hicks, Project Manager
E-Mail: bhicks@cityofjackson.org
Phone: 517-768-6433 • *Fax:* (517) 780-4781
Hours: Mon-Fri 8 a.m.-5 p.m.
Visitor Accessibility: Street and on-site parking.
Annual Events: Meeting: 3rd Mon of each month, 6 p.m. at 161 W. Michigan Ave.
Information may not be current.

Jenison
(Ottawa County)

Jenison Historical Association
Mailing Address: P.O. Box 664 • Jenison, MI 49429
Contact: Liz Timmer, Chairperson
E-Mail: info@jenisonhistory.org
Phone: (616) 457-4398
Site/Location: **Jenison Museum**
Physical Location: 28 Port Sheldon Rd. • Jenison, MI 49428
Hours: 1st Tue monthly 10 a.m.-12 p.m., 3rd Sat monthly 2-4 p.m.
Admission: Donations accepted.
Visitor Accessibility: Free on-site parking. Not wheelchair accessible. Self-guided.
Website: www.jenisonhistory.org
About: The Jenison Historical Association oversees and cares for a turn-of-the-century house that is decorated with period-appropriate furnishings and features several displays regarding the history of the Jenison area. This includes "Then and Now," which compares Jenison of the past with its present, as well as a display about the interurban railroad that ran through Jenison.
Exhibits/Collections: Displays include medical instruments, a working 5-foot cash register from the L&L Store and a Morning Glory Talking Machine, period furnishings.
Annual Events: Open House (Mar-Oct), Holiday Open House (Dec). Meetings 3rd Thu monthly, 6:45 p.m. at Georgetown Township Library (1525 Balwin, Jenison).
Publications: Newsletter (Jenison Historical Association Footnotes).

Jonesville
(Hillsdale County)

Grosvenor House Museum
Mailing Address: P.O. Box 63 • Jonesville, MI 49250
Phone: 517-849-9596

Physical Location: 211 Maumee Street • Jonesville, MI 49250
Hours: Jun-Sep: Sat-Sun 2-5 p.m.
About: Home of E.O. Grosvenor, one-time Lt. Governor of Michigan. Mr. Grosvenor was head of the commission in charge of building the Michigan State Capitol Building. His home was designed by the same architect as the capitol's.
Annual Events: Christmas at Grosvenor House (Dec).
*Information may not be current.

Kalamazoo
(Kalamazoo County)

Alamo Township Historical Society & Museum
Mailing Address: Alamo Township Hall, 7901 N. 6th St. • Kalamazoo, MI 49009
Contact: Brian Smith
E-Mail: info@alamotownship.org
Phone: (269) 382-3366 • *Fax:* (269) 552-4733
Physical Location: 8119 N. 6th St.• Kalamazoo, MI 49009
Hours: May-Oct: Sat-Sun 2-4 p.m.
Admission: Free.
Visitor Accessibility: Free on-site parking. Not wheelchair accessible.
Website: www.alamotownship.org
About: Society preserves the history of Alamo and the community. Museum exhibits include period clothing, articles used in daily life, historical items from Alamo businesses, farming and railroad equipment, pioneer tools, toys, and household items.
Exhibits/Collections: Military uniforms, post office and school items, books, musical instruments, and photographs.
Annual Events: Antique tractor show (Jul).
*Information may not be current.

Clarence L. Miller Family Local History Room
Mailing Address: Kalamazoo Public Library, 315 S. Rose St. • Kalamazoo, MI 49007
Contact: Beth Timmerman
E-Mail: localhistory@kpl.gov
Phone: (269) 553-7808
Fax: (269) 553-7959
Hours: Fall-spring: Mon-Thu 9 a.m.-9 p.m.; Fri 9 a.m.-6 p.m.; Sat 9 a.m.-5 p.m.; Sun 1-5 p.m. Summer: Mon-Wed 9 a.m.-9 p.m.; Thu-Fri 9 a.m.-6 p.m.; Sat 9 a.m.-5 p.m.
Website: http://www.kpl.gov/local-history/room.aspx
About: Maintains an extensive collection of materials about all aspects of Kalamazoo County history, including businesses, institutions, buildings, and biographical and genealogical information about county residents.
Exhibits/Collections: Books relating to the history of Kalamazoo, the state of Michigan, and genealogical research; local newspapers and magazines (index available on website); file materials; maps; photographs; government documents; census; and vital records.
*Information may not be current.

Kalamazoo College Archives
Mailing Address: 1200 Academy St. • Kalamazoo, MI 49006-3295
Contact: Lisa Murphy, College Archivist
E-Mail: archives@kzoo.edu
Phone: (269) 337-7151
Fax: (269) 337-7143
Hours: See website for current hours.
Visitor Accessibility: Free street parking. Wheelchair accessible. Self-guided.
Website: https://reason.kzoo.edu/archives/
About: The Kalamazoo College Archives contains a broad range of materials on the more than 175-year history of Kalamazoo College. Located on the third floor of the recently renovated Upjohn Library Commons, the archives offer a pleasant and comfortable research room, modern storage, and an ever-advancing means of access to the materials.
Exhibits/Collections: The history of Kalamazoo College, Baptists in Michigan and the Midwest, and the settlement of Michigan. Today, the College operates independently while acknowledging its link with the American Baptist Church.

Kalamazoo County Historical Society
Mailing Address: P.O. Box 1623 • Kalamazoo, MI 49005
Contact: Tom Dietz, President
Phone: (269) 373-7900
About: Preserves the local history of Kalamazoo County through activities such as meetings, publications, markers, and tours. Supports the Regional History Day competition held in Kalamazoo.

Kalamazoo Historic Preservation Commission
Mailing Address: 415 Stockbridge • Kalamazoo, MI 49007
Contact: Sharon Ferraro
E-Mail: ferraros@kalamazoocity.org
Phone: (269) 337-8804
Fax: (269) 337-8513
Hours: Call or see website.
Website: www.kalamazoocity.org
About: Advises city commission and admininstraton on preservation issues, educates the public on history and preservation, identifies and designates historic sites, publishes books, and assists with historic tours.
Annual Events: Historic Preservation Awards of Merit. Meetings: 2nd Tue of each month, 7 p.m. at city hall, located at 241 W. South.

Kalamazoo Valley Museum
Mailing Address: 6767 W. O Ave., P.O. Box 4070 • Kalamazoo, MI 49003
Contact: Bill McElhone, Director
Phone: (269) 373-7990
Fax: 269-373-7997
Physical Location: 230 North Rose Street • Kalamazoo, MI 49007
Hours: Oct-May: Mon-Sat 9 a.m.-5 p.m.; Sun 1-5 p.m.; Fri 9 a.m.- 9 p.m. Closed major holidays.
Admission: Free.
Visitor Accessibility: Street parking for a fee. Wheelchair accessible. Self-guided.
Website: www.kalamazoomuseum.org
About: Kalamazoo Valley Museum features exhibits on science, technology, and the history of Southwest Michigan. Attractions include an interacitve Science Gallery, new History Gallery, planetarium, Challenger Learning Center, Children's Landscape preschool area,

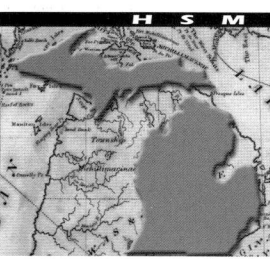

and national traveling exhibits.
Exhibits/Collections: 56,000 objects made or used in Southwest Michigan with samples of materials from other times and places. 20,000 images. Research library limited to regional history collection.
Annual Events: Fretboard Festival (Mar), Festival of Health (Mar), Safe Halloween (Oct), School Break Hands-On programs.
Publications: Magazine (MuseON).
*Information may not be current.

Old House Network
Mailing Address: 1014 Davis • Kalamazoo, MI 49008
Contact: Sharon Ferraro
Phone: (269) 349-2022 • ***Fax:*** (269) 349-2022
Website: www.oldhousenetwork.org
About: Provides educational hands-on training in the repair and rehabilitation of historic homes. Workshops cost $7-15.
Annual Events: Old House Expo. Check website for schedule and information.
Publications: Newsletter (Old House Journal).
*Information may not be current.

Southwest Michigan Black Heritage Society
Mailing Address: 471 W. South St., Suite 42A • Kalamazoo, MI 49007
E-Mail: smbhs03@gmail.com
Hours: By appointment.
Website: http://www.smbhs.org/
About: The mission of the Southwest Michigan Black Heritage Society is to nurture respect, appreciation, and study of the African-American heritage and contributions to Southwest Michigan history. Raising awareness and development of multi-cultural connections is a major concern of our organization.
Publications: "History Detectives Oral History Project," "Telling the Kalamazoo Community Race Story."

Stuart Area Restoration Association
Mailing Address: 530 Douglas Ave., • Kalamazoo, MI 49007
Contact: Lois Johnson, Executive Director
E-Mail: historicstuart@gmail.com
Phone: (269) 344-7432 • ***Fax:*** (269) 344-7346
Visitor Accessibility: Free street parking. Wheelchair accessible.
Website: http://stuartneighborhood.org
About: Stuart Area Restoration Association has been an active neighborhood association since 1973. The association's mission is to preserve its historic neighborhood and improve the quality of residential life through mutual cooperation and involvement.
Annual Events: Historic Homes Tour (Sep), Holiday Homes Tour (Dec).
Publications: Monthly newsletter (Stuart Neighborhood News).

Thirteenth Michigan Memorial Association
Mailing Address: 2315 Oakland Drive • Kalamazoo, MI 49008
Contact: Michael Culp, Director
E-Mail: 13thmi_association@att.net
Phone: (269) 342-4741
About: The Thirteenth Michigan Memorial Association is dedicated to honoring and preserving the memory of members of the Thirteenth Michigan Veteran Volunteer Infantry during the Civil War. The goal is to collect information about these men, before, during, and after the war and to act as a central distribution center for anyone wishing information on the 13th Michigan. A unit history is being created. The association is active in locating and preserving the graves of members of the 13th Michigan.
Publications: Quarterly newsletter.

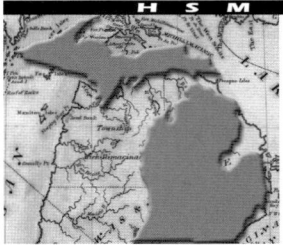

Western Michigan University Archives Regional History Collection
Mailing Address: Zhang Legacy Collections Center, 1650 Oakland Drive • Kalamazoo, MI 49008
Contact: Dr. Sharon Carlson, Director
E-Mail: arch_collect@wmich.edu
Phone: (269) 387-8490
Fax: (269) 387-8484
Hours: Sep-Apr: Tue-Fri 8 a.m.-5 p.m., Sat 9 a.m.-4 p.m.; May-Aug: Mon-Fri 9 a.m.-4 p.m.
Admission: Free.
Visitor Accessibility: On-site parking available. Wheelchair accessible. Tour guide available.
Website: http://www.wmich.edu/library/collections/archives
About: Repository for public records of 12 Southwest Michigan counties, including tax records, court records township minutes, and some naturalization records. Census records.
Exhibits/Collections: Materials documenting history of Western Michigan University and the people, places, activities of Southwestern Michigan. Yearbooks, photographs, bulletins, news magazines, scrapbooks, and Western Herald beginning with issue #1 of 1916.

Kaleva
(Manistee County)

Kaleva Historical Society
Mailing Address: P.O. Box 252 • Kaleva, MI 49645
Contact: Cynthia Asiala
E-Mail: caasiala@jackpine.com
Phone: (231) 362-2080
Site/Location: Bottle House Museum
Physical Location: 14551 Wuoksi St. • Kaleva, MI 49645
Hours: Memorial Day-Labor Day: Sat-Sun 12-4 p.m.; Sep-Oct: Sat 12-4 p.m.
Admission: $3/individual suggested donation.
Visitor Accessibility: Street parking; also church parking lot. Not wheelchair accessible. Tour guide availability/cost varies.
Website: www.kalevami.com/The_Bottle_House_Museum.html
About: The Kaleva Historical Society preserves the history of Kaleva, settled by Finnish immigrants in 1900 and stores and displays data and materials so they are available to the community. The society maintains the historic Bottle House Museum, built in 1942 by John Makinen using 60,000 soda pop bottles from his bottle factory. Rooms are dedicated to Kaleva School, business, lumbering, and agricultural tools, and more.
Exhibits/Collections: Makinen Tackle Collection, Finnish Cooperative Movement. Business room features Robert Rengo's contribution as village president, military display, artifacts of lumbering and farming.

Annual Events: Annual Members Meeting (Apr), Juhannus Solstice Celebration (Jun), Kaleva Days (Jul), Christmas Open House (Dec), WinterSoltice Lighting the Cemetery (Dec), Log Cabin Concerts. Board meets Feb, Jun, Aug, and Oct.
Other Sites/Locations: **Kaleva Depot Railroad Museum** • Location: 14420 Walta St., Kaleva, MI 49645 • Hours: Memorial Day to Labor Day: Sat 12-4 p.m. • Admission: Donations accepted • Visitor Accessibility: On-site parking. Wheelchair accessible. Tour guide availability/cost varies. • The Depot Railroad Museum features railroad memorabilia and an M&NE engine.

Kalkaska
(Kalkaska County)

Kalkaska County Historical Society
Mailing Address: P.O. Box 1178 • Kalkaska, MI 49646
Contact: Donald Bellinger
Phone: (231) 258-9719
Site/Location: **Kalkaska County Museum**
Physical Location: Located in the train depot building in downtown Kalkaska.
Hours: Jun-Aug: Wed-Sat 1-4 p.m. Aso by appointment.
Admission: Free.
Visitor Accessibility: Parking available. Wheelchair accessible. Self-guided.
Website: www.kalkaskacounty.net/kalkhistory.asp
About: Society organized 1964, museum opened 1970 in 1911 Grand Rapids & Indiana Railroad Depot. Artifacts on display are part of local history, including an 1898 Elmer, an auto built in Kalkaska by Elmer F. Johnson.
Exhibits/Collections: Information regarding people, places, businesses, early residents, churches, schools, local government, industries, export products, clubs, and organizations in Kalkaska County. Farm and lumbering artifacts, two antique cars, and military uniforms.
*Information may not be current.

Kalkaska Genealogical Society
Mailing Address: P.O. Box 353 • Kalkaska, MI 49646
Contact: Dawn Triplett
E-Mail: kalkaskadawn@hotmail.com
Phone: (231) 258-9265
Website: www.rootsweb.com/~mikgs/
Exhibits/Collections: Local history and genealogy collection held at Kalkaska County Public Library. Call for library hours (231) 258-9411.
Annual Events: Meetings 3rd Mon 7 p.m. at Kalkaska County Library (Jan-Nov).
Publications: Newsletter.
*Information may not be current.

Kent City
(Kent County)

Tyrone Township Historical Society
Mailing Address: P.O. Box 11 • Kent City, MI 49330
Contact: Ione Stark, Treasurer
E-Mail: starki@att.net
Phone: (616) 678-7220
Site/Location: **Tyrone Township Historical Museum**
Physical Location: 43 S. Main St. • Kent City, MI 49330
Hours: By appointment.
Visitor Accessibility: Street parking. Wheelchair accessible. Call ahead for tour guide availability.
Website: www.tyronetownship.org/historical_society.php

About: Supervises and maintains local historical information and artifacts.
Annual Events: Meetings Mar-Nov 2nd Tue monthly, 1 p.m.
Publications: Newsletter (Tyrone Gleanings).

Kentwood
(Kent County)

Kentwood Historic Preservation Commission
Mailing Address: 4900 Breton Ave. SE, P.O. Box 8848 • Kentwood, MI 49518
Contact: Lisa Golder
E-Mail: golderl@ci.kentwood.mi.us
Phone: (616) 554-0709 • *Fax:* (616) 656-5292
Site/Location: **Heritage Room at the Richard L. Root Branch Library**
Physical Location: 4950 Breton SE • Kentwood, MI 49518
Hours: Open during library's operating hours; refer to www.kdl.org. Call ahead for research assistance.
Visitor Accessibility: Free on-site parking. Wheelchair accessible. Self-guided.
Website: www.ci.kentwood.mi.us/committees/historical/
About: The Kentwood Historic Preservation Commission identifies, preserves, develops, and promotes the city of Kentwood's architectural, historical, and cultural heritage. The commission shares the history of Kentwood, from its beginnings as Paris Township to today, through educational programs, exhibits, displays, and other special events.
Exhibits/Collections: Collections relate to city's beginnings as a farming community through becoming a first-tier suburb and employment center in the Grand Rapids area. Collections include artifacts, photographs, documents, and oral histories.
Annual Events: Meetings 2nd Mon monthly, 6 p.m. at the Richard L. Root Branch of the Kent District Library.
Publications: "The Story of Kentwood: A History of Kentwood Michigan."
*Information may not be current.

Kimball
(St. Clair County)

Huron County Historical Society
Mailing Address: 6174 S. Branch Ln. • Kimball, MI 48074
Phone: (810) 989-0399
*Information may not be current.

Kinross
(Chippewa County)

Kinross Heritage Society
Mailing Address: P.O. Box 34 • Kinross, MI 49752
Contact: Jim Moore, President
E-Mail: ksupervisor@kinross.net
Phone: (906) 440-3840
Site/Location: **Kinross Heritage Park**
Physical Location: 6277 W. M-80 • Kinross, MI 49752
Hours: Thu-Sun 1-5:30 p.m.
Admission: Free.
Visitor Accessibility: Free parking (call ahead for busses or trailers). Museum and log cabin are wheelchair accessible. Free guide available.
Website: http://kinross.net/
About: Administered by the Kinross Heritage Society, which seeks to preserve the history of Kinross for future generations, the Heritage Park includes an 1882 log cabin; a 1902 one-room schoolhouse; a working

blacksmith shop; and early farming, household goods, and military displays. A quarter-mile nature trail completes the site.
Exhibits/Collections: Kinross Cemetery records & early birth records in Kinross Township. Military artifacts, medical items, 1900 wheelchair, and many household items.
Annual Events: Log Cabin Day (Jun), Chippewa County Fair Garage Sale (Aug-Sep). Meetings 3rd Thu monthly, at museum or Kinross Rec Center depending on weather.
Information may not be current.

Lake Ann
(Benzie County)

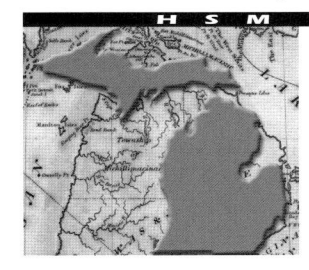

Almira Historical Society
Mailing Address: P.O. Box 91 • Lake Ann, MI 49650
Contact: Vera Carmien, President
E-Mail: info@almirahistoricalsociety.org
Phone: (231) 275-7362
Site/Location: **Almira Historical Society Museum**
Physical Location: 19440 Maple St. • Lake Ann, MI 49650
Hours: Memorial Day-Labor Day: Tue and Sat 1-4 p.m. Also by appointment.
Admission: Free.
Visitor Accessibility: Free parking. Wheelchair accessible. Tour guide available.
Website: www.almirahistoricalsociety.org
About: The Almira Historical Society was formed in 1992. The society's museum has more than 1,300 artifacts and includes the Thompson-Kuemin House. The property also includes the Almira Fire Barn Museum, which houses a 1946 international fire truck. There is also a blacksmith shop and boathouse. The Babcock House is currently being restored. Exhibits include military uniforms and American flags, vintage switchboards, wooden and brass post office boxes, early logging and farming equipment, and a fire display.
Annual Events: Lake Ann Homecoming (Jul).
Publications: "Recipes and Memories of the Almira Historical Society."

Lake City
(Missaukee County)

Missaukee County Historical Society
Mailing Address: P.O. Box 93 • Lake City, MI 49651
Contact: Susan Robinson
E-Mail: funnestnan@hotmail.com
Phone: (231) 839-4963
Site/Location: **The Old Bath House**
Physical Location: Missaukee County Park, 6201 W. Park • Lake City, MI 49651
Hours: Memorial Day-Labor Day: Fri-Sun 2-5 p.m.
Admission: $2 fee to enter park, historical society admission by donation.
Visitor Accessibility: Free parking with park admission. Wheelchair accessible. Free tour guide available.
About: The museum is located in the Old Bath House built by the CCC in the 1930s. Displays include military, agriculture, and logging.
Exhibits/Collections: Maintains local history collection in cooperation with Missaukee District Library, 210 S. Canal St. Lake City, MI 49651.
Information may not be current.

Lake Linden
(Houghton County)

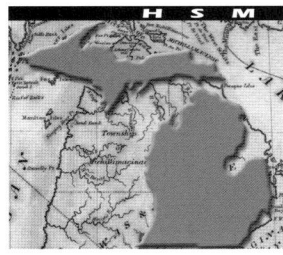

Houghton County Historical Society
Mailing Address: P.O. Box 127 • Lake Linden, MI 49945
Contact: David Pulse, President
E-Mail: info@houghtonhistory.org
Phone: (906) 296-4121
Site/Location: **Houghton County Historical Museum**
Physical Location: 53150 Highway M-26 • Lake Linden, MI 49945
Hours: Call ahead for current hours.
Admission: Museum: $5/adult, $3/senior, $3/student (6-16). Train Ride: $4/adult, $3/senior $3/student (6-16), $1/children 6 and under.
Visitor Accessibility: Free parking. Partially wheelchair accessible. Guided tours by appointment.
Website: www.houghtonhistory.org
About: The Houghton County Historical Society preserves, presents, and interprets the history and culture of the Copper Country. Exhibits include Lake Linden and Torch Lake Railroad, a steam locomotive, and a 3-foot gauge track to support tours interpreting former Calumet & Hecla Mill. Trains run weekends. The site also houses a general history museum, a 1940s log cabin, a schoolhouse, and the former 1st Congressional Church of Lake Linden with a restored pipe organ.
Exhibits/Collections: Extensive collection of local newspapers, Polk Directories, photographs, mining journals, and some family records.
Information may not be current.

Lake Odessa
(Ionia County)

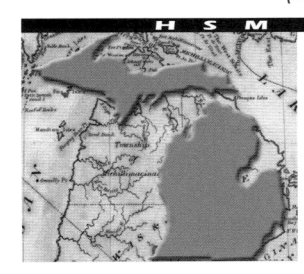

Ionia County Genealogical Society
Mailing Address: P.O. Box 516 • Lake Odessa, MI 48849-0516
Contact: Lori L. Fox, President
E-Mail: ioniacogensoc@yahoo.com
Phone: (616) 374-8455
Fax: (616) 374-8424
Website: http://ionia.migenweb.net
About: A non-profit volunteer group whose mission is to create awareness and preserve family histories within the Ionia County area. The focus of this group will be to develop genealogical resources and to assistant all those seeking local history.
Exhibits/Collections: Held in genealogy room of Freight Station Museum. Ionia County family histories, obituaries, vital records, maps, and photos.
Annual Events: Meetings 2nd Sat of each month (except Dec), 1 p.m. at the Freight Station Museum, 1117 Emerson St., Lake Odessa, MI 48849
Publications: Quarterly newsletter and Rural School newsletter

Lake Odessa Area Historical Society
Mailing Address: Page Memorial Building, 839 Fourth Ave. • Lake Odessa, MI 48849
Contact: John Waite, President
E-Mail: jrwgen@hotmail.com
Phone: (616) 374-8455
Site/Location: **Lake Odessa Museum Complex**
Physical Location: 1117 Emerson St. • Lake Odessa, MI 48849
Hours: Last Sat monthly 10 a.m.-2 p.m., last Sun monthly 2 p.m.-5 p.m.
Admission: Free.

Visitor Accessibility: On-site parking. Wheelchair accessible.
Website: www.lakeoahs.blogspot.com
About: Maintains the Lake Odessa Museum Complex, which includes the 1887 Pere Marquette Depot, a Grand Trunk Caboose, Freight Station Museum with a focus on local history, and Hosford House. Exhibits rotate on a monthly basis with permanent exhibits on local history, German Prisoner of War Camp, and Pere Marquette Railroad history.
Exhibits/Collections: Collects and preserves artifacts related to history of Lake Odessa area.
Annual Events: Military Tribute (Mem Day), High School Reunion Open House (Jun), Depot Day (Jul), Christmas Memory Tree (Nov), Christmas 'Round the Town (Nov). Meetings 2nd Thu, 7 p.m. at Lake Odessa Museum Complex.
Publications: Quarterly newsletter (Bonanza Bugle).

Lake Orion
(Oakland County)

Friends of the William E. Scripps Estate
Mailing Address: 1601 Joslyn Rd. • Lake Orion, MI 48360
Contact: Denise Bertin-Epp, President and COO
E-Mail: kcollier@guesthouse.org
Phone: (248) 391-4445
Physical Location: 1840 W. Scripps Rd. • Lake Orion, MI 48360
Visitor Accessibility: On-site parking.
Website: www.friendsofscrippsestate.org
About: Tours are currently suspended pending estate repairs.
Information may not be current.

North Oakland Genealogical Society
Mailing Address: c/o Orion Township Public Library, 825 Joslyn Rd. • Lake Orion, MI 48362
Contact: Ella Mae Schultz, Secretary
Phone: (248) 693-3000
Hours: Call or visit website for current hours.
Admission: Free.
Visitor Accessibility: Free public parking. Wheelchair accessible.
About: Meetings are centered around helping members on their search through discussion, computer, or using resources in collection.
Exhibits/Collections: Local history room contains many books on local town/village histories, also videos. Oakland County and Michigan Genealogical Collection, Canadian (Ontario & Alberta) Collection, periodicals from throughout the Northern United States.
Annual Events: Meetings 3rd Thu Mar, Apr, May and Sep, Oct, Nov, 7 p.m. at Orion Township Library.

Orion Historical Society
Mailing Address: c/o Penny Peterson, P.O. Box 817 • Lake Orion, MI 48361-0817
Contact: Penny Peterson
Website: www.orionhistoricalsociety.org
About: Society encourages active participation in preservation activities and education about Orion's history. Working with schools and other organizations to preserve historic Howarth Schoolhouse, last one-room schoolhouse in Orion Township.
Annual Events: Lake Orion boat tours for members and periodic tours of the William E. Scripps mansion.
Information may not be current.

Orion Township Public Library
Mailing Address: 825 Joslyn Rd. • Lake Orion, MI 48362
Contact: Beth Sheridan, Head of Adult Services
E-Mail: orionref@orionlibrary.org
Phone: (248) 693-3000
Fax: (248) 693-3009
Hours: Mon-Thu 9:30 a.m.-9 p.m.; Fri-Sat 9:30 a.m.-5 p.m.
Visitor Accessibility: Free on-site parking. Wheelchair accessible. Self-guided.
Website: http://www.orionlibrary.org
About: The Orion Library's mission is to serve and engage a thriving community of lifelong learners, and our vision is to be known for more than books. Our local history collection is housed in the James Ingram Room, including the Genealogy, Michigan History, and Orion History Collections. Included are books; videos; vertical files that pertain to local and Michigan history; and historical documents such as atlases, cemetery records, and other genealogical information, as well as census records and a microfiche reader.
Exhibits/Collections: Books, videos, and vertical files that pertain to local and Michigan history; historical documents, such as atlases, cemetery records, genealogical information, census records, and a microfiche reader.

Lakeside
(Berrien County)

Wilkinson Heritage Museum
Mailing Address: 15300 Red Arrow Highway • Lakeside, MI 49116
Contact: Nadra Kissman
Phone: (269) 469-2090
Hours: Apr-Dec: Tue-Sun 11 a.m.-6 p.m., Jan-Mar: Sat-Sun 12-6 p.m. Also by appointment.
About: Museum is located in former trading post of John Wesley Wilkinson, founder of Lakeside.
Exhibits/Collections: Doll collection from 1860s-1950s, Civil War letters, Lakeside-area pictures and documents. Antique clothing and household items. Articles from Wilkinson, Disbrow, Robinson and other area families.

L'Anse
(Baraga County)

Ford Center and Sawmill Museum
Mailing Address: 21235 Alberta Ave. • L'Anse, MI 49946
Contact: Kari Price, Manager
E-Mail: fordcenter@mtu.edu
Phone: (906) 524-6181
Fax: (906) 524-6180
Physical Location: US-41, 8 miles south of L'Anse
Hours: Mon-Thu 10 a.m.-5 p.m.
Admission: $5/adult, $3/senior, $2/children (5-12).
Visitor Accessibility: Free on-site parking. Partially wheelchair accessible. Tour guide available; reservations required.
Website: www.fordcenter.mtu.edu
About: The purpose of the facility is education, with a special emphasis in forestry education. The Sawmill Museum and the historic village of Alberta are open to the public. The village was created by Henry Ford in 1935 and was donated to Michigan Tech University in 1954. The university still owns and operates the village.

The exhibits in the sawmill cover its operations, Henry Ford's lumber empire, history of Alberta, sustainable forestry, logging equipment, and the importance of wood to modern life.
Exhibits/Collections: Band blade sawmill, 12 houses, pump house, two school buildings, six additional original structures, tools associated with milling/logging, photographs, documents/ledgers, some genealogical information on people who lived in Alberta, 50 video interviews.
Annual Events: Sugarbush (Spr).

Huron Island Lighthouse Preservation Association
Mailing Address: P.O. Box 381 • L'Anse, MI 49946
Information may not be current.

Lansing
(Ingham County)

Archives of Michigan
Mailing Address: Michigan Library and Historical Center, 702 W. Kalamazoo St. • Lansing, MI 48909
Contact: Mark Harvey, State Archivist
E-Mail: archives@michigan.gov
Phone: (517) 373-3559 opt. 3 • *Fax:* (517) 241-1658
Hours: Mon-Fri 1-5 p.m.
Visitor Accessibility: On-site parking for a fee. Wheelchair accessible. Staff available to assist researchers.
Website: www.michigan.gov/archivesofmi
About: Archival holdings include the official repository for records of state government and other public institutions. Accepts local government records and records from individuals and organizations relating to Michigan's history. Digitized photo collection see: www.haldigitalcollectionscdmhost.com.

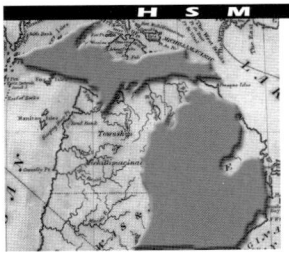

Delta Township Historical Society
Mailing Address: 4637 Clydesdale Rd. • Lansing, MI 48906
Contact: Rita LaMoreaux
E-Mail: info@deltatownshiphistory.org
Phone: (517) 323-3210
About: The Delta Township Historical Society preserves and protects the history of Delta Township.
Annual Events: Educational meetings 3rd Wed of the month, 6:30 p.m. Call or e-mail for details or meeting place.

Forest Parke Library & Archives
Mailing Address: Capital Area District Library—Local History Collection, P.O. Box 40719 • Lansing, MI 48901
Contact: Heidi Butler
Phone: (517) 334-1521
Hours: By appointment.
Website: www.cadl.org
About: Local history collection of the Capital Area District Library.
Exhibits/Collections: Lansing and Ingham County history, including 100,000-plus photographs, maps, ephemera, diaries, business and organization records, and city council minutes 1910s-1990s.

Friends of Michigan History
Mailing Address: P.O. Box 17035 • Lansing, MI 48901
Information may not be current.

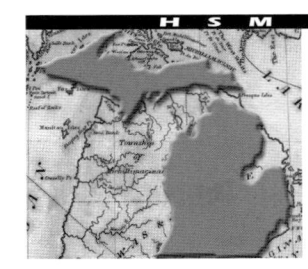

Gunnisonville Historical Community Preservation
Mailing Address: 1745 E. Clark Road • Lansing, MI 48906
Contact: Lois Baumer, Historian
E-Mail: grandmotherbee@att.net
Phone: (517) 485-8290
Website: www.gunnisonville.blogspot.com
About: The Gunnisonville Historical Community Preservation protects, preserves, and promotes the community's history and historical buildings and artifacts. The organization collects any materials/artifacts that help to define the area surrounding Clark and Wood Corners as a historical district.
Annual Events: Gunnisonville Community Day (Sep). Monthly meeting held at Gunnisonville Meadows, 1754 E. Clark Road, Lansing.
Information may not be current.

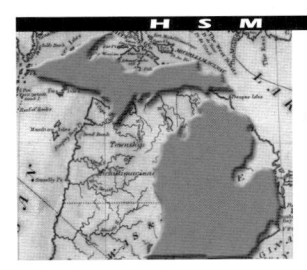

Historical Society of Greater Lansing
Mailing Address: P.O. Box 12095 • Lansing, MI 48901
Contact: Valerie Marvin, President
E-Mail: info@lansinghistory.org
Phone: (517) 282-0671
Physical Location: 124 W. Michigan Avenue • Lansing, MI 48901
Website: www.lansinghistory.org
About: The Historical Society of Greater Lansing creates and displays pop-up temporary exhibits about Lansing history at a variety of sites around Lansing, including in Lansing City Hall, located at 124 W. Michigan Ave. Visit our website to learn more about our current exhibits.

Historical Society of Michigan
Mailing Address: 5815 Executive Dr. • Lansing, MI 48911
Contact: Larry Wagenaar, Executive Director
E-Mail: hsm@hsmichigan.org
Phone: (517) 324-1828
Fax: (517) 324-4370
Hours: Mon-Fri 8 a.m.-5 p.m.
Website: www.hsmichigan.org
About: Official historical society for the state of Michigan, founded in 1828. Provides educational programs, publications, conferences, and serves local societies. Sponsors and coordinates Michigan/National History Day competition for students.
Exhibits/Collections: Michigan history books.
Annual Events: Michigan in Perspective Conference (Mar), Michigan History Day (Apr), U.P. History Conference (Jun), State History Conference (Sep).
Publications: "The Chronicle," "Michigan History Magazine," "Michigan Historical Review," "Michigan History Directory," "Historic Michigan Travel Guide."

Historical Society of Michigan

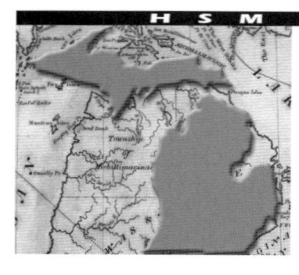

Lansing Area African-American Genealogical Society
Mailing Address: P.O. Box 22203 • Lansing, MI 48909-2203
Contact: Angela C. Moore, President
E-Mail: entpeople@yahoo.com
Physical Location: Library of Michigan, 702 W. Kalamazoo St. • Lansing, MI 48909
Hours: Aug-Jun: 2nd Sat monthly 10 a.m.
Admission: $20/individual yearly membership fee.
Visitor Accessibility: On-site parking available for a fee. Wheelchair accessible.
Website: www.laaags.org
About: Assists members in researching family genealogy and history. Conducts educational programs to assist members and general public in resources of genealogy and history research, methods unique to African-American research. Provides a forum for sharing information.

Lansing Historic District Commission
Mailing Address: Planning & Neighborhood Development Dept., 316 N. Capitol Ave. • Lansing, MI 48933
Contact: Bill Rieske
Phone: (517) 483-4091 • **Fax:** 517-483-6036
Hours: Mon-Thu 9 a.m.-5 p.m.
Visitor Accessibility: Structure parking. Wheelchair accessible.
Website: www.lansingmi.gov/pnd/hdc/index.jsp
About: Nine-member appointed commission reviews proposed additions, alterations, or demolitions to properties in designated historic districts. Commission issues a certificate of appropriateness, notice to proceed, or certificate of denial based upon the Secretary of the Interior's standards.
Exhibits/Collections: City Clerk's Office and Planning Office maintain HDC minutes. Planning office retains files on local historic districts, National Historic Registered Places, and State Registered Historic Sites in City of Lansing.
Annual Events: Meetings 1st Mon monthly, 5:30 p.m. in Suite C-3 PND Conference Room at 316 N. Capitol Ave, Lansing.
Information may not be current.

Library of Michigan
Mailing Address: Michigan Library and Historical Center, 702 W. Kalamazoo St. • Lansing, MI 48909
Contact: Edwina Murphy, Michigan Curator
E-Mail: librarian@michigan.gov
Phone: (517) 373-1580
Fax: (517) 373-5700
Hours: Mon-Fri 10 a.m.-5 p.m.; 2nd Sat monthly 10 a.m.-5 p.m.
Admission: Free.
Visitor Accessibility: On-site parking $1/hr, weekend parking free. Wheelchair accessible. Self-guided.
Website: www.michigan.gov/libraryofmichigan
About: The Michigan Legislature created the Library of Michigan to guarantee the people of this state and their government one perpetual institution to collect and preserve Michigan publications and conduct reference and research support to libraries statewide.
Exhibits/Collections: Michigan Collection, government documents, legal material, rare book room, mel.org.
Publications: Directory of Michigan Libraries.

Michigan Alliance for the Conservation of Cultural Heritage
Mailing Address: c/o Michigan Humanities Council, 119 Pere Marquette, Suite 3B • Lansing, MI 48912
Contact: Brian Jaeschke, President
E-Mail: info@macch.org
Website: http://www.macch.org/
About: A statewide organization of libraries, archives, museums, historical societies, and preservation networks founded in 1988 with support of Michigan Humanities Council to promote protection and preservation of Michigan's cultural and humanities resources for the enjoyment, education, and benefit of present and future generations. Offers help with disaster planning and educational programs.
Annual Events: Michigan Heritage Guardian Award, Angel Projects.
Publications: Conference Proceedings.

Michigan Genealogical Council
Mailing Address: P.O. Box 80953 • Lansing, MI 48908
Contact: Tom Koselka, President
E-Mail: info@mimgc.org
Phone: (517) 230-8405
Website: http://mimgc.org
About: The Michigan Genealogical Council is the umbrella organization for Genealogical Societies in Michigan.

Michigan Heritage Route Program
Mailing Address: Michigan DOT, P.O. Box 30050 • Lansing, MI 48909
Contact: Tom Doyle, Program Manager
E-Mail: doylet@michigan.gov
Phone: (517) 335-2936 • **Fax:** 517-373-9255
Physical Location: 425 W Ottawa • Lansing, MI 48909
Website: www.michigan.gov/mdot
About: Program, created in 1993, to identify, inventory, protect, enhance, and promote state trunklines and adjacent land with distinctive or unique scenic, cultural, or historic qualities.

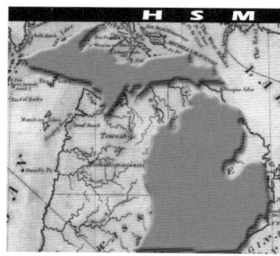

Michigan Historic Preservation Network
Mailing Address: 313 E. Grand River Ave. • Lansing, MI 48906-4348
Contact: Nancy Finegood, Executive Director
E-Mail: info@mhpn.org
Phone: (517) 371-8080
Fax: (517) 371-9090
Hours: 9 a.m.-5 p.m.
Website: www.mhpn.org
About: Statewide historic preservation organization, conducts annual conference and regional and local workshops. Advocates for preservation of Michigan's architectural heritage. Special projects include Historic Preservation Easement Program, Historic Resource Council, and Practical Preservation Program. Collaborates with State Historic Preservation Office in Michigan Historical Center.
Annual Events: Historic Preservation Conference, Fall Benefit.

HSM MEMBER

Michigan Historical Center
Mailing Address: P.O. Box 30740 • Lansing, MI 48909
Contact: Sandra Clark, Director
E-Mail: museuminfo@michigan.gov
Phone: (517) 373-3559
Fax: (517) 241-3647
Site/Location: **Michigan Historical Museum System (12 locations listed below under Other Sites/Locations)**
Physical Location: 702 W. Kalamazoo • Lansing, MI 48909
Visitor Accessibility: On-site parking; $1/hour on weekdays, free on weekends. Wheelchair accessible. Self-guided.
Website: www.michigan.gov/michiganhistory

About: The Michigan Historical Center comprises the Archives of Michigan and the Michigan Historical Museum in Lansing as well as four additional museum and historical sites in the Upper Peninsula and seven in the Lower Peninsula.

Exhibits/Collections: The Michigan Historical Center houses the Michigan Historical Museum, which contains several permanent exhibits that tell the story of Michigan from pre-European contact to present day. The museum also features a special exhibit that changes annually focusing on a theme or particular era of Michigan history. The center houses the Archives of Michigan and major genealogical collections. The center also offers several educational programs for visitors of all ages.

Annual Events: Statehood Day (Jan), Be a Tourist in Your Own Town (May), Abrams Foundation Family History Seminar (Jul).

Other Sites/Locations: **Civilian Conservation Corps Museum** • Location: 11747 N. Higgins Lake Drive, Roscommon, MI 48653 • Phone: (989) 348-2537 • E-mail: museuminfo@michigan.gov • Hours: May 27-Sep 2: Daily 10 a.m.-4 p.m. • Admission: Free, although a Michigan State Parks Recreation Passport is required for entry • Visitor Accessibility: Free on-site parking. Wheelchair accessible. • More than 100,000 young men worked in Michigan's forests during the Great Depression and lived in barracks like those on display at the Civilian Conservation Corps Museum. See how "Roosevelt's tree army" served the state, creating a legacy that we enjoy today.

Fort Wilkins Historic Complex and Copper Harbor Lighthouse • Location: 15223 U.S. 41, Copper Harbor, MI 49918 • Phone: (906) 289-4215 • E-mail: jamesb@michigan.gov • **Fort Wilkins Historic Complex** • Hours: Mid-May to mid-Oct: Daily 8:30 to dusk. Admission: Free, although a Michigan State Parks Recreation Passport is required for entry • Visitor Accessibility: Free on-site parking. Wheelchair accessible. • Built in 1844 on the rugged shoreline of Lake Superior, Fort Wilkins is a well-preserved example of mid-19th-century army life. It includes 19 buildings—12 of which are original structures dating to the 1840s. There are hands-on exhibits, interpretive signs, and a historical video titled "Beyond the Wilderness: The Fort Wilkins Story." • **Copper Harbor Lighthouse** • Hours: 10 a.m.-6 p.m. Admission: Free, although there is a charge for boat transportation to and from the lighthouse • Visitor Accessibility: Free on-site parking. Wheelchair accessible. Self-guided. • The Copper Harbor Lighthouse complex includes a restored 1848 lightkeeper's dwelling, 1844 lighthouse, and 1933 steel tower. The Copper Harbor Lighthouse marks the entrance to one of Michigan's northernmost harbors.

Hartwick Pines Logging Museum • Location: 4216 Ranger Road, Grayling, MI 49738 • Phone: (989) 348-2537 • E-mail: burgr@michigan.gov • Hours: May 1-24: Daily 9 a.m.-4 p.m. May 25-Sep 2: Daily 10 a.m.-6 p.m. Sep 3-Oct 31: Daily 9 a.m.-4 p.m. • Admission: Free, although a Michigan State Parks Recreation Passport is required for entry • Visitor Accessibility: Free on-site parking. Partially wheelchair accessible. Self-guided. • Hartwick Pines Logging Museum is situated among the towering trees of one of Michigan's largest remaining stands of old growth white pine. The exhibits return visitors to the state's 19th-century logging era, when Michigan led the nation in sawed-lumber production. The visitor center, logging camp, exhibits, and period rooms tell the stories of the loggers, river men, and entrepreneurs who powered Michigan's white pine industry.

Mann House • Location: 205 Hanover St., Concord, MI 49237 • Phone: (517) 373-3559 • E-mail: museuminfo@michigan.gov • Hours: May 27-Sep 2: Thu-Sun 10 a.m.-4 p.m. Call or check website to confirm. • Admission: Free • Visitor Accessibility: Free street parking. Not wheelchair accessible. Self-guided. • In 1883, Daniel and Ellen Mann built their two-story house in the small, picturesque farming community of Concord. Today, the Mann house features eight rooms of period furniture, including pieces from the 1840s to the early-20th century, restored flower and herb gardens, a carriage house with carriages and sleighs, and exhibits that illustrate the way Michiganians worked and played in the 19th and 20th centuries.

Michigan Historical Museum • Location: 702 W. Kalamazoo, Lansing, MI 48909 • Phone: (517) 373-3559 • E-mail: museuminfo@michigan.gov • Hours: Mon-Fri 9 a.m.-4:30 p.m., Sat 10 a.m.-4 p.m., Sun 1-5 p.m. • Admission: Adults $6, Seniors $4, Youth (5-17) $2, 5 and under free • Visitor Accessibility: On-site parking; $1/hour on weekdays, free on weekends. Wheelchair accessible. Self-guided. • The Michigan Historical Museum is the flagship of Michigan's state museum system. The museum surrounds visitors with Michigan history from the time of its earliest people to the late-20th century. The museum has five levels featuring 26 exhibits and a special exhibit.

Tawas Point Lighthouse • Location: 686 Tawas Beach Road, East Tawas, MI 48730 • Phone: (989) 362-5658 • E-mail: museuminfo@michigan.gov • Hours: See website • Admission: $2/person. Also, a Michigan State Parks Recreation Passport is required for entry. • Visitor Accessibility: Free on-site parking. Information can be provided in Braille if staff is given advance notice. Tour guide available. • In operation since 1876, the Tawas Point Lighthouse is part of Tawas Point State Park. There are other historic structures on site, including an oil house and a fog signal area.

Sanilac Petroglyphs Historic Site and State Park • Location: 8251 Germania Road, Cass City, MI 48909 • Phone: (989) 856-4411 • E-mail: museuminfo@michigan.gov • Hours: May 27-Sep2: Wed-Sun 10 a.m.-4 p.m. • Admission: Free • Visitor Accessibility: Wheelchair accessible. Free on-site parking. Self-guided. • Discovered in 1881 after a massive forest fire swept the Lower Peninsula area, the Sanilac Petroglyphs Historic Site features rock-carvings etched into the sandstone about 1,000 years ago. Native Americans created the unusual artwork that gives visitors an idea of ancient woodland life and the people who lived here before Europeans arrived.

Walker Tavern Historic Complex • Location: 13220 M-50, Brooklyn, MI 49230 • Phone: (517) 241-0731 • E-mail: museuminfo@michigan.gov • Hours: See website • Admission: Free • Visitor Accessibility: Free on-site parking. Partially wheelchair accessible. Self-guided. • In the mid-19th century, a stagecoach ride from Detroit to Chicago was a long and arduous five-day trip. Discover Michigan's agricultural and travel heritage through Sylvester Walker's stagecoach stop at a historic crossroads.

Fayette Historic Townsite • Location: 4785 II Road, Garden, MI 49835 • Phone: (906) 644-2603 • Hours: May-Oct. See website or call for hours. • Admission: Free, although a Michigan State Park Passport is required for entry • Visitor Accessibility: On-site parking; Michigan State Park Passport required for entry. Partially wheelchair accessible. Tour guide available mid-Jun through mid-Aug. • The Fayette Historic Townsite was once an industrial community that manufactured charcoal pig iron from 1867-1891. Today, it features a modern visitor center, 19 historic structures, museum exhibits, and walking tour that interpret Fayette's role as a company town. The site is administered by Michigan Department of Natural Resources.

Michigan Iron Industry Museum • Location: 73 Forge Road, Negaunee, MI 49866 • Phone: (906) 475-7857 • E-mail: jamesb@michigan.gov • Hours: May-Oct: Daily 9:30 a.m.-4:30 p.m.; Nov-Apr Mon-Fri 9:30 a.m.-4 p.m. • Admission: Donations accepted. Film costs $1/person; children 5 and under free. • Visitor Accessibility: Free on-site parking. Wheelchair accessible. Self-guided. • The Iron Industry Museum builds programs and alliances that preserve and interpret Michigan's past and help people discover, enjoy, and find inspiration in their heritage. The museum overlooks the historic site of the Carp River Forge, the first iron forge in the Lake Superior region, and interprets Michigan's rich iron mining heritage through exhibits, audio visual programs, and outdoor interpretive trails. The 23-minute documentary "Iron Spirits: Life on the Michigan Iron Range" is shown seven times daily.

Great Lakes Maritime Heritage Center • Location: 500 W. Fletcher St., Alpena, MI 49707 • Phone: (989) 356-8805 • E-mail: thunderbay@noaa.gov • Hours: Daily. See website for seasonal hours. • Admission: Free • Visitor Accessibility: Free on-site and street parking. Wheelchair accessible. Self-guided. • Located in Lake Huron, Thunder Bay is adjacent to one of the most treacherous stretches of water within the Great Lakes. Unpredictable weather, murky fog banks, sudden gales, and rocky shoals earned the area the name "Shipwreck Alley." Today, the 448-square-mile Thunder Bay National Marine Sanctuary protects one of America's best-preserved collections of more than 200 shipwrecks. The sanctuary works to protect the Great Lakes and their rich maritime heritage.

Father Marquette National Memorial Museum • Location: 720 Church St., St. Ignace, MI 49781 • Phone: (906) 643-8620 • E-mail: burnettw@michigan.gov • Hours: Daily 8 a.m.-10 p.m. • Admission: Free, although a Michigan State Parks motor-vehicle permit or Recreation Passport is required for entry to the park • Visitor Accessibility: Public parking. Wheelchair accessible. Self-guided. • Features a hiking trail with historic interpretation. Also on-site is an open-air building dedicated to the memory of missionary and explorer Father Jacques Marquette.

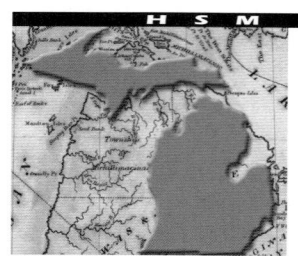

Michigan Humanities Council
Mailing Address: 119 Pere Marquette Dr., Ste. 3B • Lansing, MI 48912
Contact: Eric Nordberg
E-Mail: krhodes@mihumanities.org
Phone: (517) 372-7770
Fax: (517) 372-0027
Hours: Mon-Fri 9 a.m.-5 p.m.
Visitor Accessibility: Street parking. Wheelchair accessible: enter through rear entrance.
Website: www.michiganhumanities.org
About: Nonprofit, state affiliate of National Endowment for the Humanities. Connects people and communities by fostering and creating quality cultural programs. Offers grants for Humanities Programs; provides statewide programming.
Annual Events: Poetry Out Loud State Finals, Prime Time Programs, The Great Michigan Road. Board of directors meets triannually.
Publications: Biannual newsletter, monthly e-newsletter, annual report, Online Arts & Humanities Touring Program Directory, Online Humanities Professionals Directory, Grant Guidelines and Applications.

Michigan Museum of Surveying
Mailing Address: 220 S. Museum Dr. • Lansing, MI 48933
Contact: Lisa Jacobs
Phone: (517) 484-6605 • *Fax:* (517) 484-3711
Hours: Mon-Fri 9 a.m.-4 p.m., weekends by appointment.
Admission: Free.
Visitor Accessibility: On-site parking. Wheelchair accessible.
Website: www.surveyhistory.org
About: Presents concept of land measurement and scientific innovation through history of surveying and mapping. Collects, preserves, researches, and interprets our land-use heritage.
Exhibits/Collections: Ralph Moore Berry Library houses a publicly accessible collection of surveying and mapping related books and papers.
Information may not be current.

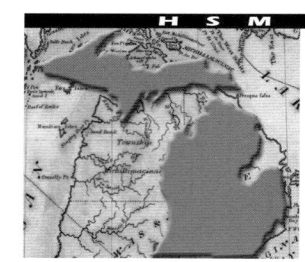

Michigan Oral History Association
Mailing Address: c/o Geneva Kebler Wiskemann, 5580 W. State Rd. • Lansing, MI 48906-9325
Contact: Geneva Kebler Wiskemann, Secretary
Phone: (517) 321-1746
Hours: By appointment.
Website: www.michiganoha.org
About: Provides for effective cooperation and communication among programs and institutions concerned with techniques, uses, and promotion of oral history in Michigan. Conducts workshops and participates in history-related events.
Annual Events: Oral History for Michiganians Conference.
Publications: Quarterly newsletter (The MOHA), "Guide for Doing Oral History." See website for list of publications.

Michigan State Historic Preservation Office (SHPO)
Mailing Address: Michigan State Housing Development Authority, P.O. Box 30740 • Lansing, MI 48909-8240
Contact: Laura Ashlee, Historian and Communications Liaison
E-Mail: preservation@michigan.gov
Phone: (517) 373-1630 • *Fax:* (517) 335-0348
Site/Location: **Michigan Library and Historical Center**
Physical Location: 702 W Kalamazoo St. • Lansing, MI 48909
Hours: Mon-Fri 8 a.m.-5 p.m. Researchers must call ahead for an appointment.
Visitor Accessibility: On-site parking.
Website: www.michigan.gov/shpo
About: The National Historic Preservation Act of 1966 required states to establish a SHPO to oversee preservation activities. Funded through the National Park Service, the SHPO works with the public, developers, nonprofits, and governmental agencies at all levels to protect archaeological sites and to identify, designate, and reinvest in historic properties. The SHPO administers incentive programs that include federal tax credits and pass-through grants and Michigan Lighthouse Assistance Program grants. The State Archaeologist is part of the SHPO.
Annual Events: Governor's Award (May). Review Board meeting 3/yr.
Publications: Lighthouses of Michigan (map), Michigan Archaeology (poster).

Michigan Supreme Court Historical Society
Mailing Address: 925 W. Ottawa St. • Lansing, MI 48915
Contact: Carrie Pickett, Executive Director
Phone: 517-373-7589 • *Fax:* 517-373-7592
Hours: Mon-Fri 9 a.m.-5 p.m.
Website: www.micourthistory.org
About: Membership organization founded 1988. Collects, preserves, and displays documents, records, and memorabilia relating to Michigan Supreme Court and other courts of Michigan. Promotes study of history of Michigan's courts. Seeks to increase public awareness of Michigan's legal heritage.
Exhibits/Collections: Portraits and busts of nearly all former Michigan Supreme Court Justices.
Annual Events: Membership luncheon (Apr).
Publications: "A Brief History of the Michigan Supreme Court," "MSC Historical Reference Guide," "Index to Special Sessions and the Verdict of History: The History of Michigan Jurisprudence Through its Significant Supreme Court Cases."

Michigan History Directory

Michigan Supreme Court Learning Center
Mailing Address: P.O. Box 30205 • Lansing, MI 48909
Contact: Rachael L. Drenovsky, Coordinator
E-Mail: drenovskyr@courts.mi.gov
Phone: (517) 373-7171 • *Fax:* (517) 373-7615
Physical Location: Michigan Hall of Justice, 925 W. Ottawa St. • Lansing, MI 48915
Hours: Mon-Fri 9 a.m.-4 p.m. Closed on state holidays.
Admission: Free. All visitors must enter through the east entrance and present a government-issued ID. A security screening is required.
Visitor Accessibility: Parking is available east of the Michigan Hall of Justice, off Allegan Street, or at the Michigan Historical Center; $1/hour. Cash payment is required. Wheelchair accessible. Tour guide available for groups of eight or more with reservation.
Website: http://courts.mi.gov/education/learning-center
About: The Michigan Supreme Court Learning Center is a gallery located within the Michigan Hall of Justice, headquarters of the state's judicial branch of government and home of the Michigan Supreme Court. The learning center educates the public about the judicial branch through tours and programs. The gallery includes interactive exhibits, including a mock trial court courtroom, with information about the history and present-day working of the judiciary. The Michigan Hall of Justice also includes a Court of Appeals courtroom and the Michigan Supreme Court Courtroom. Proceedings are open to the public.
Annual Events: Law Day (May), Constitution Day (Sep).
Publications: Justia, a seasonal e-newsletter for educators.

Michigan Women's Historical Center & Hall of Fame
Mailing Address: 213 W. Malcolm X St. • Lansing, MI 48933
Contact: Samantha Cumbow, Office Manager
E-Mail: info@michiganwomen.org
Phone: (517) 484-1880
Fax: (517) 372-0170
Hours: Wed-Sat 12-4 p.m. Also 1st Sun monthly 2-4 p.m. Closed holidays.
Admission: $3/adult, $2/student (6-18), Children 5 and under are free.
Visitor Accessibility: On-site parking. Wheelchair accessible. Tour guides available.
Website: www.michiganwomenshalloffame.org
About: Opened in 1987 by the Michigan Women's Studies Association, the Michigan Women's Historical Center & Hall of Fame was the nation's first state-level facility to focus on women's history. The organization promotes educational opportunities and honors the accomplishments of Michigan women.
Exhibits/Collections: Collection includes artifacts from inductees, traveling exhibits, and research library.
Annual Events: Women's History Month Reception (Mar), Golf Outing & Dinner (Jun), Annual Hall of Fame Induction Dinner (Oct).

Mid-Michigan Genealogical Society
Mailing Address: P.O. Box 16033 • Lansing, MI 48901
Contact: Judy Pfaff
E-Mail: pfaff@msu.edu
Phone: 517-669-3798
Website: http://mmgs.wordpress.com/
About: Encourages and assists in the study of family history and promotes the exchange of knowledge and preserving genealogical records.
Annual Events: Meetings 4th Wed Feb-Jun and Sep-Oct, 3rd Wed in Nov, 7 p.m. at Plymouth Congregational Church, Lansing.
Publications: See website.

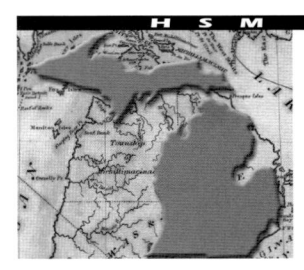

R.E. Olds Transportation Museum
Mailing Address: 240 Museum Drive • Lansing, MI 48933
Contact: William Adcock, Executive Director
E-Mail: director@reoldsmuseum.org
Phone: (517) 372-0529
Fax: (517) 372-2901
Hours: Jan-Dec: Tue-Sat 10 a.m.-5 p.m., April-Oct: Sun 12-5 p.m.
Admission: $6/adult, $4/senior, $4/student, $12/family.
Visitor Accessibility: Free on-site and street parking. Wheelchair accessible. Tour guide available; $3/individual.
Website: www.reoldsmuseum.org
About: The R.E. Olds Transportation Museum collects, preserves, studies, and interprets objects that illustrate the part Lansing played in the development of transportation. It places emphasis on the automobile and its effect on Lansing and its people. On display are 50-plus cars and trucks, Curved Dash Olds assembly line display, the first automobile built by R.E. Olds, and an EV1.
Exhibits/Collections: Vehicles, engines, R.E. Olds family artifacts, vintage clothing, aviation display, bicycle display, lawn mower display, stop sign display, Curved Dash Olds assembly display.
Annual Events: Car Capital Auto Show, Be a Tourist in Your Own Town.

Turner-Dodge House
Mailing Address: 100 E. North St. • Lansing, MI 48906
Contact: Jennifer McDaniels, Coordinator
E-Mail: DodgeTurner@gmail.com
Phone: (517) 483-4220 • *Fax:* (517) 483-6081
Hours: Tue-Fri 10 a.m.-5 p.m. Closed for holidays and special events.
Admission: $3.50/Lansing residents, $5/non-residents, $2/children.
Visitor Accessibility: On-site parking. Partially wheelchair accessible; first floor only. Several guided tour packages ($5/individual for tour, $8/individual for tour & tea, $10/individual for tour & class).
Website: http://parks.cityoflansingmi.com/tdodge
About: Classical revival home was built in 1858 by Marion and James Turner and enlarged in 1903 by daughter Abby and her husband, Frank Dodge. See website for more info.
Exhibits/Collections: Information pertaining to Turner and Dodge families.
Annual Events: Offers camps throughout the year. Special teas for adults and children. See website for current event information.
*Information may not be current.

Lapeer
(Lapeer County)

Lapeer County Genealogical Society
Mailing Address: P.O. Box 353 • Lapeer, MI 48446
Contact: Alton Hart, President
E-Mail: alhart1@charter.net
Phone: (810) 356-5406
Exhibits/Collections: Lapeer County genealogical and historical information, plus some information of surrounding counties.
Annual Events: Meetings 2nd Tue monthly Sep-Nov and Mar-May, 7 p.m. at First Presbyterian Church, Lapeer.
Publications: "Pioneer Families and History of Lapeer County," "Family Maps of Lapeer County." See website for list of available genealogical resources.

Historical Society of Michigan

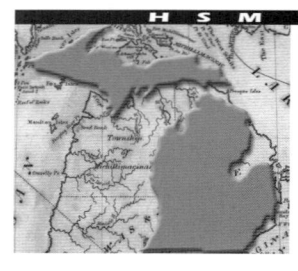

Lapeer County Historical Society
Mailing Address: P.O. Box 72 • Lapeer, MI 48446
Contact: Bill Rykhus, President
Phone: (810) 245-5808
Site/Location: **Lapeer County Historical Museum**
Physical Location: 518 W. Nepessing St. • Lapeer, MI 48446
Hours: Wed and Sat 10 a.m.-3 p.m. Also by appointment for groups.
Admission: Donations accepted. Minimal fee for groups after hours.
Website: http://www.lapeercountyhistoricalsociety.com/
About: The Lapeer County Historical Society is dedicated to the preservation of Lapeer County heritage. The Lapeer County Historical Museum includes permanent exhibits of household items and the lumber industry with rotating artifacts. Other exhibits feature important individuals or themes.
Exhibits/Collections: General artifacts from Lapeer County.
Annual Events: Farm Fest (Aug), Concert and Dessert Gala (Nov).
Other Sites/Locations: **Historic Courthouse** • Location: 235 W. Nepessing St., Lapeer, MI 48446 • Hours: May 1-Oct 31: Sat 10 a.m.-3 p.m. Also by appointment. • Admission: Free. Minimal group fee. • Visitor Accessibility: Street and public lot parking. Wheelchair accessible. Tour guide available. • Built in 1847, Lapeer's Historic Courthouse is the oldest continuously operating courthouse in Michigan. Exhibits includes restoration work and pictures/artifacts from the courthouse and early leaders in Lapeer.
Davis Brothers Farm Shop Museum • Location: 3520 Davis Lake Rd., Lapeer, MI 48446 • Hours: Aug: 4th Sat. Also by appointment. • Admission: Donations accepted; fee for groups • Visitor Accessibility: Parking on grounds. Wheelchair accessible. Tour guide available; contact Jim Davis at (810) 245-0852 or (810) 441-4803. • The Davis Brothers Farm Shop Museum features several pieces of vintage farm machinery from the early 1900s to the 1950s. Exhibits include hand tools and an operating shop. A restored sawmill operates during the Farm Fest (4th Sat of Aug).

Lathrup Village
(Ingham County)

Lathrup Village Historical Society
Mailing Address: P.O. Box 760312 • Lathrup Village, MI 48076
Contact: Robin Roberts, President
E-Mail: lvhistoricalsociety@yahoo.com
Phone: (248) 569-9390
Website: http://lvhistoricalsociety.home.comcast.net
About: Collects, restores, and preserves material of Lathrup Village and promotes preservation of historical structures of Lathrup Village. Activities include meetings, speakers, newsletter, oral history, archives, and biennial home and garden tour.

Leland
(Leelanau County)

Fishtown Preservation Society
Mailing Address: P.O. Box 721 • Leland, MI 49654
Contact: Amanda Holmes, Executive Director
E-Mail: info@fishtownmi.org
Phone: (231) 256-8878
Physical Location: 203 E. Cedar St. • Leland, MI 49654
Hours: Office Mon-Fri 9 a.m.-4 p.m. year-round. Site is open year-round. Shops are seasonal and hours vary.
Admission: Free.
Visitor Accessibility: Free, limited street parking throughout Leland and near Fishtown. Limited wheelchair accessibility. Group tours available with appointment.
Website: www.fishtownmi.org
About: Historic Fishtown's attractions include historical fishing shanties, regional foods, unique shops, and exhibits about Fishtown's past and present as a working waterfront. Some exhibits are viewable all year, others are seasonal.
Annual Events: Fun Run 5K (Jul), Heritage Celebration (Sep), Benefit Brunch at the Bluebird (Oct).
Publications: Biannual newsletter.

Leelanau Community Cultural Center
Mailing Address: P.O. Box 883 • Leland, MI 49654
Contact: Judy Livingston
E-Mail: info@oldartbuilding.com
Phone: 231-256-2131 • *Fax:* 231-256-2131
Physical Location: 111 S. Main Street • Leland, MI 49654
Hours: Mon-Thu 8:30 a.m.-2:30 p.m.
Website: http://www.oldartbuilding.com/
About: Promotes cultural enrichment programs and events. Provides gathering place for community. Ensures preservation of 85-year-old Old Art Building. Home to MSU Summer Art School.
Annual Events: Summer art programs, Leland Heritage Day Celebration (Sep).

Manitou Trail Questers
Mailing Address: P.O. Box 444 • Leland, MI 49654
Contact: Claudia Goudschaal, Secretary
Phone: (231) 386-5694
About: Contributes to the preservation of local historic buildings and as a chapter of the national organization of collectors; also supports scholarships for grad students in preservation.
Exhibits/Collections: Members maintain their own collections of glass, china, silver, textiles, boxes, jewelry, nautical, figurines, etc.
Annual Events: Meetings 1st Thu monthly. Chapters are kept small (11-20 members) so they can meet in members homes.
Information may not be current.

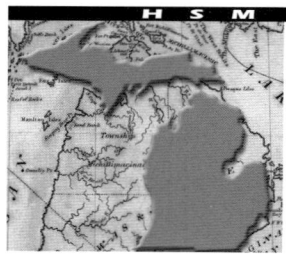

Leelanau Historical Society
Mailing Address: P.O. Box 246 • Leland, MI 49654
Contact: Francie Gits, Executive Director
E-Mail: info@leelanauhistory.org
Phone: (231) 256-7475
Site/Location: **Leelanau Historical Society Museum**
Physical Location: 203 E. Cedar Street • Leland, MI 49654
Hours: Wed-Fri 10 a.m.-4 p.m., Sat 10 a.m.-2 p.m. Call for seasonal hours or appointment.
Admission: $2/individual.
Visitor Accessibility: Free on-site parking. Wheelchair accessible. Self-guided.
Website: www.leelanauhistory.org
About: Founded in 1957, the Leelanau Historical Society seeks to inspire people to explore the past, understand the present, and envision the future of the diverse cultures in the Leelanau Peninsula and its islands. The museum preserves and displays local history and also serves as a research center. Its exhibits include Shipwrecks of the Manitou Passage, North Manitou Island, and the Native-American

Anishnabek Arts Collection.
Exhibits/Collections: Photographs, letters, manuscripts, government documents, and newspapers. Objects that represent diverse cultures of Leelanau, including collection of Anishnabek traditional arts. Researchers can browse collections on the museum's website.
Annual Events: Valentine Workshop (Feb), North Manitou Island Day Trip (Aug-Sep), Wood Boats on the Wall Live Exhibit for Heritage Day (Sep), Annual Meeting (Aug).
Publications: "Wood Boats of the Leelanau," "A Short History of the Leland Iron Works."

Lewiston
(Montmorency County)

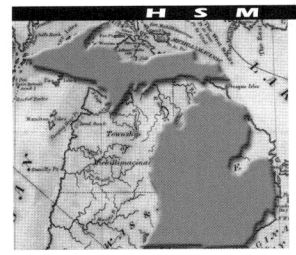

Lewiston Area Historical Society
Mailing Address: P.O. Box 461 • Lewiston, MI 49756
Contact: Lyle Cline, President
E-Mail: lewareahistsoc@gmail.com
Phone: (989) 786-2451
Site/Location: **Kneeland-Sachs Museum**
Physical Location: 4384 Michelson Ave. • Lewiston, MI 49756
Hours: Call for current hours.
Admission: Donations accepted.
Visitor Accessibility: Free on-site parking. Partially wheelchair accessible. Tour guide available during open hours or by appointment.
About: The Lewiston Area Historical Society preserves and promotes the heritage of the Lewiston area through education, preservation, family genealogies, and programs. Built in 1892, the Kneeland-Sachs Museum was the home of David Kneeland, manager of the Michelson & Hanson Lumber Company. The house was then sold to George and Martha Sachs, whose family occupied the building for the next 85 years. The museum shares their histories. The site also features a fully furnished trapper's cabin as well as a barn.
Exhibits/Collections: Photos and local family genealogies.
Annual Events: Heritage Day, Christmas at the Kneeland Home. Meetings 2nd Wed Mar-Nov.
Publications: "The Lewiston Story and Montmorency County Notes."
Other Sites/Locations: **Lunden Civilian Conservation Corps Camp** • Location: North Side of County Road 612, Lewiston, MI 49676 • Admission: Free • Visitor Accessibility: Free on-site parking. Wheelchair accessible. Self-guided. • Established in June 1933, Camp Lunden was 1 of 103 Michigan Civilian Conservation Corps Camps that planted trees; built roads, fire lines, and trout ponds; and cleared the airfield for the Atlanta airport. The camp closed in 1936 and was designated as a state historic site in 1994. Today, the site features a display of photos and documents related to the camp.

Lincoln
(Alcona County)

Lincoln Train Depot.
Please see entry under Harrisville: Alcona Historical Society.

Lincoln Park
(Wayne County)

Downriver Genealogical Society
Mailing Address: P.O. Box 476 • Lincoln Park, MI 48146
Contact: Sherry Huntington, President
E-Mail: info@downrivergenealogy.org
Phone: (734) 374-8774
Physical Location: Taylor Library, 12303 Pardee Rd. • Taylor, MI 48180
Hours: Tue-Thu 1-5 p.m.
Visitor Accessibility: Free parking. Wheelchair accessible.
Website: www.downrivergenealogy.org
About: Dedicated to the preservation of ancestral information and educating the community and its members in genealogical research.
Exhibits/Collections: Indexed files of obituaries and marriages, transcriptions of local funeral homes and cemeteries, family histories and land abstracts.
Annual Events: Beginner's Workshops, bus trip to Allen Co. Library, trip to Salt Lake City. Meetings 3rd Wed monthly Jan-Jun and Sep-Nov, 7 p.m. at St. John's Church, Wyandotte (check website or call library for changes).
Publications: More than 70 genealogical publications for sale including cemetery and funeral home records.

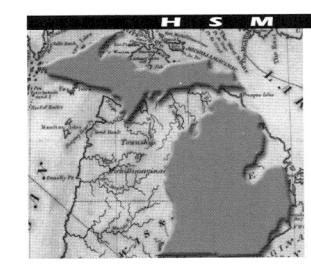

Lincoln Park Historical Society & Museum
Mailing Address: 1335 Southfield Rd. • Lincoln Park, MI 48146
Contact: Jeffrey Day, Curator
E-Mail: lpmuseum@gmail.com
Phone: (313) 386-3137
Hours: Wed, Thu, Sat 1-5 p.m.
Admission: Free.
Visitor Accessibility: Free on-site parking. Partially wheelchair accessible; ramp access to main rear entrance. Self-guided.
Website: www.lphistorical.org
About: Formed in 1954, the historical society worked for many years toward opening a museum in 1972 to collect, preserve, and exhibit materials and archival information that are important in reflecting the history and development of the Lincoln Park community since its founding in 1921 and its prior Ecorse Township history. Beginning with modest collections, the museum has grown into a permanent site in the historic Lincoln Park Post Office, its location since 1993.
Exhibits/Collections: Collections of artifacts from farmsteads, homes, schools, businesses; uniforms and period clothing; archives of local and municipal history; early maps; founding families and leading citizens; oral histories; extensive photograph collection.
Annual Events: Annual dinner (May), Commemorative Bell Ringing Ceremony (May, Nov) Holiday open house (Dec). Meetings 1st Wed monthly.
Publications: "Lincoln Park," "Growing up in Simpler Times: Memories of Lincoln Park." Quarterly newsletter.

Linden
(Genesee County)

Linden Historic District Commission
Mailing Address: Linden City Hall, P.O. Box 507 • Linden, MI 48451
Phone: (810) 735-2860
Physical Location: 210 N. Main St. • Linden, MI 48451
Website: www.lindenmi.us
About: Captures and preserves what is unique to Linden by promoting historic preservation. Aids property owners through guidance, setting standards, and seeking funding.
Annual Events: Meetings 3rd Wed monthly, 7:30 p.m. in Linden Council Chambers.
*Information may not be current.

Historical Society of Michigan

Linden Mills Historical Society
Mailing Address: P.O. Box 823 • Linden, MI 48451
Contact: Barbara Kincaid, Curator
E-Mail: lindenmills@yahoo.com
Phone: (810) 735-2860
Site/Location: **Linden Mills Historical Museum**
Physical Location: 201 N. Main • Linden, MI 48451
Hours: Jun-Oct: 2nd and 4th Sun 2-5 p.m. Also by appointment.
Admission: Donations accepted.
Visitor Accessibility: Free on-site and street parking. Free tour guides available, call ahead.
Website: www.freewebs.com/lindenmichiganhistoricalsociety
About: Dedicated to the preservation of Linden's history and the perpetuation of its museum, which is located in an 1871 Grist Mill building. Attractions include a small gift shop, surrey/buggy c. 1900 made in Linden by Beach Buggy Works, quilt exhibit, military display case, rooms of a Victorian home, general store, schoolroom, farm and dairy implements, Victorian dollhouse, large ice sled, 1860 Melodeon, weaving loom, and pump organ.
Exhibits/Collections: Historic building scale models, bridal gowns of Linden residents, Victorian clothing and accessories, vintage tools, Linden High School Band uniforms, children's toys, cameras, musical instruments/phonographs.
Annual Events: Linden Mills Days (Jun), Fairview Cemetery Tour (Sep), Holiday Happening (Dec). Meetings 2nd Tue monthly, 7:30 p.m. at Shiawassee Shores Clubhouse #1, Linden.
Publications: "Illustrated History of Linden," "Linden Area Centennial 1871-1971," "History of LMHS," "Linden Historic Buildings Driving tour," and DVD "Union Block Fire."

Livonia
(Wayne County)

Alfred Noble Library and Historical Society
Mailing Address: 11316 Merriman Road • Livonia, MI 48150-2849
E-Mail: jneussendorfer@mindspring.com
Phone: (248) 909-0824
Hours: Daily 8 a.m.-5 p.m.
Admission: Free.
Website: http://livonia.lib.mi.us/noble
About: The Alfred Noble Historical Society informs about the outstanding legacy of the world-famous civil engineer Alfred Noble, who was born in Livonia, Michigan, in 1844. He was involved in the engineering of the Panama Canal and the Weitzel Lock at Sault Ste. Marie. The society aims to preserve the civil engineering, construction, and surveying historical record in the Michigan Territory and the state of Michigan, as well as preserve emerging, present-day technologies in these sectors.
Exhibits/Collections: Tours of the Alfred Noble Branch Library.
Annual Events: Alfred Noble Birthday (Aug).

Livonia Historical Commission
Mailing Address: 20501 Newburgh Road • Livonia, MI 48152
Contact: Linda Wiacek, Program Supervisor
E-Mail: greenmead@ci.livonia.mi.us
Phone: 248-477-7375 • *Fax:* (248) 426-8568
Site/Location: **Greenmead Historical Park**
Hours: Park grounds open during daylight hours. Tours: Jun-Oct and Dec 1-4 p.m. (no holiday tours). Also by appointment.
Admission: $3/adult, $2/youth.
Visitor Accessibility: Free on-site parking. Paritally wheelchair accessible. Tour guide available during open hours and by appointment.
About: The Livonia Historical Commission is a body appointed by the mayor of Livonia to oversee Greenmead Historical Park. The commission preserves and provides the citizens of Livonia with information about the area's past through the collection and exhibition of materials relevant to the history of Livonia. The commission provides visitors with an authentic interpretation of Livonia's past. It also provides a history of Livonia through publications, programs, and activities.
Annual Events: Peter Rabbit's Adventure (May), flea market (Jun, Sep), Garden Walk (Jun), Highland Games & AMC Car Show (Aug), Halloween Walk (Oct), Christmas Walk (Dec), A Visit With Santa (Dec).
Publications: "Livonia Preserved," "Greenmead and Beyond."

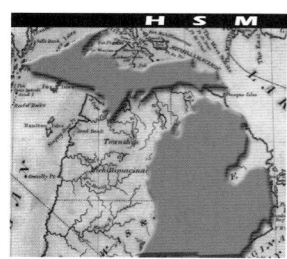

Livonia Historical Society
Mailing Address: 20501 Newburgh • Livonia, MI 48152
Contact: Bob Legel
E-Mail: greenmead@ci.livonia.mi.us
Phone: (248) 477-7375
Fax: (248) 426-8568
Website: https://www.facebook.com/Greenmead
About: Founded in 1956 to study and preserve local history. Supports Greenmead, Livonia's historical village.
Annual Events: Flea market at Greenmead (Sep), potluck (Apr), banquet (May), picnic (Aug). Speakers at Jan, Mar, Aug, and Nov meeting.
Publications: Livonia Historical Society Newsletter.

Livonia
(Wayne County)

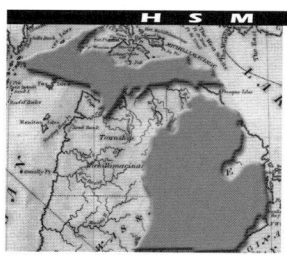

Madonna University Archives
Mailing Address: 36600 Schoolcraft Rd. • Livonia, MI 48150
Contact: Carol Vandenberg, Archivist & Reference Librarian
E-Mail: cvandenberg@madonna.edu
Phone: (734) 432-5584
Fax: (734) 432-5687
Hours: By appointment.
Admission: Free.
Visitor Accessibility: Free on-site parking. Wheelchair accessible.
Website: http://library.madonna.edu/university-archives/
About: The role of the archives is to document the history of Madonna University. This is accomplished by collecting, organizing, describing, preserving, and making available materials that portray this history through the lives and experiences of those who have influenced or changed the direction of Madonna University.

Michigan One-Room Schoolhouse Association
Mailing Address: c/o: Greenmead Historic Park, 20501 Newburgh Road • Livonia, MI 48152-1098
Contact: Lawrence Schlack, Membership Chairperson
E-Mail: greenmead@ci.livonia.mi.us
Phone: (248) 477-7375
Website: www.one-roomschool.org
About: Seeks to stimulate interest in Michigan's one-room schools and encourage preservation and interpretation of one-room schools through conferences, newsletters, awards, and consultation services. Developing an inventory of all Michigan one-room schools.
Annual Events: Michigan One-Room Schoolhouse Association Conference (May).
Publications: Biannual newsletter (The Slate).

Society of the War of 1812 in Michigan
Mailing Address: 15595 Westbrook St. • Livonia, MI 48154
Contact: Allan Treppa, President—Michigan
E-Mail: allan_treppa@sbcglobal.net
Phone: (734) 464-7702
Website: www.beaufait.com/mich1812/
About: The purpose of this society is to provide patriotic, historical, and educational material for the public.
Information may not be current.

Western Wayne County Genealogical Society
Mailing Address: P.O. Box 530063 • Livonia, MI 48153
Contact: Stephanie Smith, Vice President
E-Mail: info@wwcgs.org
Phone: (734) 513-0619
Physical Location: Livonia Civic Park Senior Center Building, 15218 Farmington Road • Livonia, MI 48154-5448
Hours: Sep-May: 3rd Mon 6:30-9 p.m. Open 4th Mon in Feb.
Admission: Membership—see website. Meetings are free and open to the public.
Visitor Accessibility: Free on-site parking. Wheelchair accessible. Self-guided.
Website: http://www.wwcgs.org
About: The society is a nonprofit organization dedicated to promoting an interest in genealogy, biography, and history. The general meetings feature a speaker or speakers whose topics educate, guide, and encourage members in compiling and preserving records related to family history.
Annual Events: Annual Genealogical Seminar. Meetings 3rd Mon monthly except Jun, Jul, and Dec.
Publications: "Livonia 1870 Census," "1876 Livonia Township map," "Maple Grove Cemetery Tombstone Inscriptions," "The Clarenceville Cemetery," "Union Church Cemetery and Livonia Cemetery," "Wyandotte Treaties with the United States 1785-1867 and with Canada 1790-1892."

Lowell
(Kent County)

Fallasburg Historical Society
Mailing Address: 13944 Covered Bridge Rd. NE • Lowell, MI 49331
Contact: Ken Tamke, President
Hours: Schoolhouse open May-Oct, Sun 2-4 p.m. Village open by appointment for tours.
Admission: Donations accepted.
Visitor Accessibility: On-site parking. Wheelchair accessible. Call for group tour pricing.
Website: www.fallasburg.org
About: Collects, preserves, advances, and disseminates knowledge of this history of the Lowell area. Fallasburg village is a nationally and state designated historic district. The 42-acre site contains a schoolhouse, two vintage barns, and three homsteads (one of which is the original John Falcas home).
Exhibits/Collections: Artifacts from mid-19th-century furniture, antique tools, and a variety of items used for rural farming/housekeeping.
Annual Events: Covered Bridge Bike Tour (Jul), Christmas in Fallasburg (Dec). Monthly meetings Mon Jan-Nov, 7 p.m. at Lowell Chamber of Commerce.
Information may not be current.

Lowell Area Historical Museum
Mailing Address: P.O. Box 81 • Lowell, MI 49331
Contact: Pat Allchin, Executive Director
E-Mail: history@lowellmuseum.org
Phone: (616) 897-7688
Fax: (616) 897-7688
Physical Location: 325 West Main St. • Lowell, MI 49331
Hours: Tue, Sat, Sun 1 p.m.-4 p.m; Thu 1 p.m.-8 p.m.
Admission: $3/adult, $1.50/child (5-17), children under 5 free.
Visitor Accessibility: Free on-site parking. Wheelchair accessible. Tour guide available.
Website: www.lowellmuseum.org
About: The Lowell Area Historical Museum preserves Lowell-area history. It is housed in the Graham Building, which was built in 1873 and used as a residential duplex. Today, the building features Victorian rooms, early Lowell history, business and industry, and the Lowell Showboat. It is listed in the National Register of Historic Places.
Exhibits/Collections: Lowell Showboat, local industry and retailing.
Publications: Quarterly newsletter. "Where the Rivers Meet," "Images of Lowell."

Vergennes Historical Society
Mailing Address: 13783 Three Mile Rd. • Lowell, MI 49331
Information may not be current.

Ludington
(Mason County)

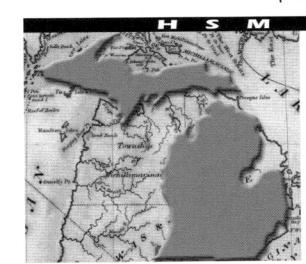

Lake Michigan Carferry Service
Mailing Address: 701 Maritime Drive • Ludington, MI 49431
Contact: Terri Brown
E-Mail: tbrown@ssbadger.com
Phone: (231) 843-1509
Fax: (231) 843-4558
Site/Location: S.S. Badger
Hours: May-Oct.
Admission: Travel fare prices listed on website.
Visitor Accessibility: Free on-site parking available. Wheelchair accessible. Self-guided.
Website: www.ssbadger.com
About: The only coal-fired steamship in operation in the United States, the S.S. Badger transports passengers and vehicles between Ludington, Michigan, and Manitowoc, Wisconsin. The ferry, which is listed on the National Register of Historic Places, has a room with displays detailing maritime history. We will be steaming into the future for many years to come, and we invite you to experience a bit of history that almost slipped away!

Mason County Genealogical Society
Mailing Address: P.O. Box 549 • Ludington, MI 49431
Information may not be current.

❋ Historical Society of Michigan

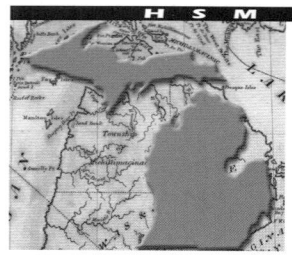

Mason County Historical Society
Mailing Address: 1687 S. Lakeshore Dr. • Ludington, MI 49431
Contact: Kate Arbogast, Executive Director
E-Mail: info@historicwhitepinevillage.org
Phone: (231) 843-4808
Fax: (231) 843-7089
Site/Location: Historic White Pine Village
Hours: May-Oct: Tue-Sat 10 a.m.-5 p.m.; Memorial Day-Labor Day Sun 1-5 p.m.; Year-round: Research library Tue, Thu 11 a.m.-4 p.m.
Admission: $9/adult, $6/children (6-17), children 5 and under free.
Visitor Accessibility: On-site parking. Wheelchair accessble. Self-guided.
Website: www.historicwhitepinevillage.org
About: Historic White Pine Village opened in 1976 and has 29 buildings, including a one-room schoolhouse, lumbering museum, blacksmith shop, fire hall, general store, trapper's cabin, sawmill, doctor's office, chapel, courthouse, print shop, maritime museum, post office, sugar house, hardware store, farmstead, cooper's shop, car museum, town hall with old-fashioned ice cream parlor, the Rose Hawley Museum, and the Mason County Sports Hall of Fame.
Exhibits/Collections: Research library includes local maps, photos, directories, information files, newspapers.
Annual Events: Music Festival and Corn Roast, Children's Days (Jul-Aug), Lumbering Days (Sep), Autumn Days (Oct).
Publications: 1890 Mason County History, 1987 Pictorial History, Centennial Farms of Mason County.

Sable Points Lighthouse Keepers Association
Mailing Address: P.O. Box 673 • Ludington, MI 49431
Contact: Peter Manting, Executive Director
E-Mail: splkadirector@gmail.com
Phone: (231) 845-7417
Physical Location: 107 S. Harrison St. • Ludington, MI 49431
Hours: 10 a.m.-5 p.m. at the lighthouses.
Admission: Admission varies between sites.
Visitor Accessibility: On-site parking available for a fee; check website for specific site fees.
Website: www.splka.org
About: The Sable Points Lighthouse Keepers Association restores and preserves area lighthouses, educates the public about those lights, and provides access to those lights.
Exhibits/Collections: Maritime artifacts, historical lighthouse photos, original handwritten keeper's journal, and interview collections.
Annual Events: West Michigan Lighthouse Festival (Jun).
Publications: Semi-annual newsletter, E-blasts.
Other Sites/Locations: **Big Sable Lighthouse** • Location: 5611 N. Lighthouse Dr., Ludington, MI 49431 • Visitor Accessibility: Not wheelchair accessible. Self-guided tours. Parking lot availble 1.8 miles away from light; Michigan parking pass required. • The Big Sable Light has a 112-foot tower for climbing. Visitors can watch a history movie. **Ludington Breakwater Lighthouse** • Location: 107 S Harrison St., Ludington, MI 49431 • Visitor Accessibility: Not wheelchair accessible. Self-guided tours. Beach parking. Info: Visitors can climb the tower. **Little Sable Point Lighthouse** • Location: 287 N Lighthouse Dr., Mears, MI 49436 • Visitor Accessibility: Wheelchair accessible. Self-guided tours. State parking lot; Michigan parking pass required. • Visitors can climb the 115-foot tower and view the original Fresnel Lens. **White River Light** • Location: 6199 Murray Rd., Whitehall, MI 49461 • Visitor Accessibility: Wheelchair accessible. Self-guided tours. Beach parking. • Visitors can tour the three-room museum as well as climb the tower.

Luzerne
(Oscoda County)

Steiner Logging and Pioneer Museum
Mailing Address: 983 W Rynd Road • Luzerne, MI 48636
Contact: Norman C. Caldwell
E-Mail: nccsurveyor@yahoo.com
Phone: (989) 889-1742
Hours: Mid-May to Oct Fri-Sun 12-4 p.m.
Admission: Donations accepted.
Visitor Accessibility: On-site parking. Wheelchair accessible. Tour guide available by appointment.
Website: www.steinermuseum.org
About: The Steiner Logging and Pioneer Museum tells the history of logging and pioneer settlements through an extensive collection of lumbering and household artifacts from the early-20th century. The museum is located in a log-sided frame building and has an extensive collection of early lumbering and farming equipment on the grounds. Also on-site is the 1885 North Fairview School.
Exhibits/Collections: Artifacts from logging and pioneering era in Oscoda County.
Annual Events: Pancake Breakfast (May).
Publications: Wilderness Chronicle.

Lyons
(Ionia County)

Lyons-Muir Historical Museum
Mailing Address: 311 E. Bridge Street • Lyons, MI 48851
Contact: Marjorie Ackerson, Secretary
Phone: (616) 527-9064
Hours: By appointment.
Admission: Donations accepted.
Visitor Accessibility: Free street parking. Wheelchair accessible. Tour guide available.
Website: https://www.facebook.com/pages/Lyons-Muir-Historical-Museum/
About: Our mission is the collection and preservation of items of local historical significance. Some of these items include household goods, clothing, tools, small machines dating from the late-19th century.
Exhibits/Collections: GAR parade flag, civil war discharge ledger, high school class photos, school yearbooks, textbooks and ledgers, early firefighting equipment, and a late-19th-century general store replica with an authentic delivery wagon.

Mackinac Island
(Mackinac County)

Stuart House Museum
Mailing Address: c/o City Clerk, P.O. Box 455 • Mackinac Island, MI 49757
Contact: Karen Lennard, City Clerk
Phone: (906) 847-8181
Physical Location: Market St. • Mackinac Island, MI 49757
Hours: May-Oct: 10 a.m.-5 p.m.
About: The former headquarters of John Jacob Astor's American Fur Company, this two-story structure was built in 1820 and also served as home for Astor's agents Robert Stuart and Ramsey Crooks.

Information may not be current.

Michigan History Directory

Mackinac Island Historical Society
Mailing Address: P.O. Box 264 • Mackinac Island, MI 49701
Information may not be current.

Mackinaw City
(Cheboygan County)

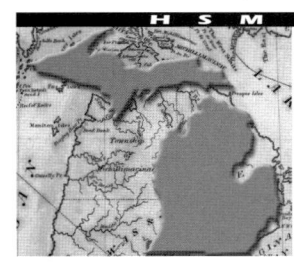

Great Lakes Lighthouse Keepers Association
Mailing Address: P.O. Box 219 • Mackinaw City, MI 49701
Contact: Terry Pepper, Executive Director
E-Mail: info@gllka.com
Phone: 231-436-5580
Fax: (231) 436-5466
Site/Location: **St. Helena Island Light Station**
Physical Location: SE Corner of St. Helena Island
Hours: Visitors with their own boats can visit anytime.
Admission: Donations requested.
Visitor Accessibility: Boat-access only. Not wheelchair accessible. Tour guides available mid-Jun to mid-Aug.
Website: www.gllka.com
About: The Great Lakes Lighthouse Keepers Association is dedicated to preserving our lighthouses and the history of the people who kept them. Offers workshops-in-residence at St. Helena Island Light Station in Northern Michigan's Straits of Mackinac. Works with other lighthouse organizations, offering direction in legislative processes and other aspects, to enable them to achieve preservation and restoration goals. Stewards of two lighthouses. St. Helena Island Light Station is a fully restored light station with live-in volunteer keeper program.
Exhibits/Collections: Hugh Murray Memorial Library available for maritime research.
Annual Events: Narration of Shepler's summer lighthouse cruises on the Straits of Mackinac, varied excursions on three of the Great Lakes.
Publications: The Beacon quarterly magazine, "Beginner's Guide to Saving a Lighthouse (available online)," "Lighting the Straits," "McGulpin Pt. Historic Site," "Instructions to Light-Keepers and Maritime Heritage Educational Resource Guide."
Other Sites/Locations: **Cheboygan River Front Range Light** • Location: 606 Water St., Cheboygan, MI 49721 • Hours: Memorial Day-Labor Day: Weekends and holidays 9 a.m.-5 p.m. • Admission: Donations requested • Visitor Accessibility: Free on-site parking. Not wheelchair accessible. Tour guides available during open hours.

Icebreaker Mackinaw Maritime Museum
Mailing Address: P.O. Box 39 • Mackinaw City, MI 49701
Contact: Lisa Pallagi, General Manager
E-Mail: contact@themackinaw.org
Phone: (231) 436-9825 • *Fax:* (888) 935-9524
Physical Location: 131 S. Huron Ave • Mackinaw City, MI 49701
Hours: May-Oct: 9 a.m.-5 p.m., Jun-Sep: 9 a.m.-7 p.m.
Admission: $11/adult, $6/childen (6-17), $35/family, children 5 and under free.
Visitor Accessibility: On-site parking. Not wheelchair accessible. Self-guided tours with docents.
Website: www.themackinaw.org
About: The Icebreaker Mackinaw Maritime Museum collects, preserves, protects, and interprets the rich maritime and marine history of the Straits of Mackinac and the Great Lakes. It features the United States Coast Guard Cutter Mackinaw WAGB-83, the world's most powerful and capable icebreaker in the world when it was commissioned in 1944. The ship was decommissioned in 2006 and now helps tell the history of its crew and the important historical and present-day contributions of the U.S. Coast Guard on the Great Lakes.
Exhibits/Collections: Entire vessel and all contents.
Annual Events: Check website for annual events.

Mackinac Associates
Mailing Address: P.O. Box 567 • Mackinaw City, MI 49701
E-Mail: mackinacparks@michigan.gov
Phone: (231) 436-4100 • *Fax:* (231) 436-4210
Website: www.mackinacassociates.com
About: Formed in 1981 as a nonprofit friends organization to support the historic and evironmental programs of Mackinac State Historic Parks.
Annual Events: Mackinac Celebration (Jun), Red, White, and Blue (Jul), Annual Meeting (Aug). Board Meeting 3-4 times per year.
Publications: Newsletter (Curiosities), see website for more publications.
Information may not be current.

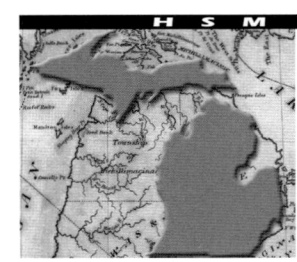

Mackinac Island State Park Commission
Mailing Address: P.O. Box 873 • Mackinaw City, MI 49701
Contact: Steve Brisson, Deputy Director
E-Mail: mackinacparks@michigan.gov
Phone: (231) 436-4100
Fax: (231) 436-4210
Site/Location: **Mackinac State Historic Parks**
Hours: Call or visit website for current hours, times vary between sites.
Admission: Call or visit website for current pricing, prices vary between sites.
Visitor Accessibility: For all sites: On-site parking adjacent to entrances. Partially wheelchair accessible (see "Guide to Access" brochure available at sites). Costumed interpretive guides daily.
Website: www.mackinacparks.com
About: Administered by the Mackinac Island State Park Commission, Mackinac State Historic Parks includes five sites located in the Mackinac Straits region of Northern Michigan: Mackinac Island State Park (established 1895), Fort Mackinac (1780-1895), Colonial Michilimackinac (1715-1780), Old Mackinac Point Lighthouse (1889-1957), and Historic Mill Creek Discovery Park (1790-1839). The commission also operates the Richard and Jane Manoogian Mackinac Art Museum and five early-19th-century historic structures (including the 1780 Biddle House and Dr. Beaumont Museum) in the Mackinac Island downtown district.
Exhibits/Collections: Live interpretive programs by costumed interpreters daily at all sites. Exhibits include period settings, themed galleries, and hands-on components. Collections include archaeological specimens, historical artifacts, and archival objects.
Publications: See website for complete list of publications.
Other Sites/Locations: **Fort Mackinac** • Location: Located on Mackinac Island • Hours: Early-May to mid-Oct: 9:30 a.m.-5 p.m. (Peak summer season hours extended to 6 p.m.) • Admission: $11/adult, $6.50/children (5-17). Fort Mackinac ticket allows entrance to downtown historic buildings during main season. • Visitor Accessibility: Tour guide available • Fort Mackinac includes 14 original buildings, including one of Michigan's oldest buildings: the Officers' Stone Quarters dating back to 1780.
Colonial Michilimackinac • Location: 102 W. Straits Ave., Mackinaw City, MI 49701 • Hours: Early-May to mid-Oct: 9:30 a.m.-5 p.m. (Peak summer season hours extended to 7 p.m.) • Admission: $11/adult, $6.50/youth (5-17) • French fur-trading village and military outpost Michilimackinac was founded in 1715. It was later occupied by the British, who abandoned it in 1780 to establish a new fort on Mackinac Island. Today, the site features a reconstructed fortified village

of 13 buildings as it appeared in the 1770s, based on evidence gathered during the nation's longest archaeological excavation.

Historic Mill Creek Discovery Park • Location: 9001 US-23, Mackinaw City, MI 49701 • Hours: Early-May to mid-Oct: 9 a.m.-4:30 p.m. (Peak summer season hours extended to 5:30 p.m.) • Admission: $8/adult, $4.75/youth (5-17) • The Straits' first industrial complex, now the site of the Historic Mill Creek Discovery Park, provided lumber for the settlement of Mackinac Island in the 1790s. Attractions include demonstrations of both hand-saw techniques and reconstructed 18th-century water-driven sawmill. There are also natural history programs, nature trails, and daily "high ropes" adventure tours.

Old Mackinac Point Lighthouse • Location: 526 N. Huron Ave., Mackinaw City, MI 49701 • Hours: Early-May to mid-Oct: 9 a.m.-4:30 p.m. (Peak summer season, hours extended to 5:30 p.m.) • Admission: $6.50/adult, $4/youth (5-17) • Erected in 1892, the Old Mackinac Point Lighthouse served more than 60 years. The castle-like structure has since been restored to its 1910 appearance and features period settings and hands-on exhibits. Interpreters lead frequent tours up the tower and in its lantern room.

Richard and Jane Manoogian Mackinac Art Museum • Location: 7070 Main St., Mackinac Island 49757 • Hours: Early-May to mid-Oct: 10 a.m.-4:30 p.m. (Peak summer season, hours extended to 6 p.m.) • Admission: $5/adult, $3.50/youth (5-17) • The Richard and Jane Manoogian Mackinac Art Museum showcases the historic artwork in Mackinac State Historic Parks' collection.

Mackinaw Area Historical Society
Mailing Address: P.O. Box 999 • Mackinaw City, MI 49701
Contact: Susie Safford, President
E-Mail: mail@mackinawhistory.org
Phone: (231) 373-9793
Site/Location: **Heritage Village**
Physical Location: 1425 West Central Avenue • Mackinaw City, MI 49701
Hours: Call or see website.
Admission: Free.
Visitor Accessibility: Free on-site parking. Partially wheelchair accessible. Tour guide available from 1-4 p.m. Sat-Mon Memorial Day-Labor Day.
Website: www.mackinawhistory.org
About: Operated by the Mackinaw Area Historical Society, Heritage Village educates visitors about the historical era of 1880-1917 as it was experienced by people living in the Mackinaw City area. The village includes Pestilence House, church, artifacts building, sawmill that cut the timbers for the Soo Locks, one-room schoolhouse, log cabin, Stimpson Homestead, machine shed, tar paper shack, and wigwams.
Annual Events: Summer Celebration (Aug). Monthly speakers 2nd Mon monthly, 7:30 p.m. at Mackinaw Library. Board meetings 2nd Mon monthly, 3 p.m. at Mackinaw Library.

Macomb
(Macomb County)

Great Lakes Lighthouse Festival Museum
Mailing Address: 15391 Haverhill • Macomb, MI 48044
Contact: Melanie Kim
E-Mail: mjk361@comcast.net
Phone: 989-595-3600
Physical Location: 7406 US 23 North • Alpena, MI 49707
Hours: May-Oct.
Website: www.lighthousefestival.org
About: The Great Lakes Lighthouse Festival Museum focuses on the history of lighthouses, underwater shipwrecks, and the U.S. Coast Guard on the Great Lakes. Artifacts pertain to the Great Lakes maritime history and include boats, buoys, lights, etc.
Annual Events: Great Lakes Lighthouse Festival (Oct).
*Information may not be current.

Mancelona
(Antrim County)

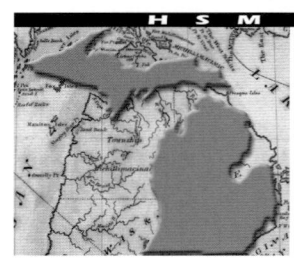

Mancelona Historical Society
Mailing Address: P.O. Box 103 • Mancelona, MI 49659
Contact: Herb Tipton
Phone: (231) 587-9687
Fax: (231) 587-0599
Physical Location: 9826 South Williams • Mancelona, MI 49659
Site/Location: **Mancelona Historical Society Museum**
Hours: Jun-Sep Sat 1-4 p.m.
Admission: Donations accepted.
Visitor Accessibility: Free on-site parking. Wheelchair accessible. Docent available Sat, June-Sep.
Website: http://www.ole.net/~maggie/antrim/mancy.htm
About: The Mancelona Historical Society opened its museum, which features an Antrim Iron Works exhibit, in 2006.
Exhibits/Collections: Historical pictures and information about early days in Antrim and Mancelona. Emil Johnson glass-plate negative collection of 60 years of photos of people of the Mancelona area.
Annual Events: Meetings 1st Tue monthly, 10 a.m. Call for location.
Publications: "Mancelona in the 20th Century."

Manchester
(Washtenaw County)

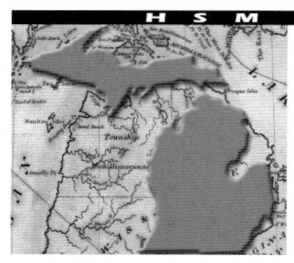

Manchester Area Historical Society
Mailing Address: P.O. Box 56 • Manchester, MI 48158
Contact: Carl Curtis, President
E-Mail: mahs-info@manchesterareahistoricalsociety.org
Phone: (517) 536-0775
Site/Location: **John Schneider Blacksmith Shop**
Physical Location: 324 E. Main St. • Manchester, MI 48158
Hours: By appointment.
Admission: Donations accepted.
Visitor Accessibility: Free street parking. Not wheelchair accessible. Tour guide available with appointment.
Website: http://manchesterareahistoricalsociety.org
About: The Manchester Area Historical Society was incorporated in 1976 and received 501(c)(3) tax status in 1977. Part of the society's mission is to maintain a museum for educational purposes and to preserve history and artifacts of the Manchester area, including the Village of Manchester and the four surrounding townships of Bridgewater, Freedom, Manchester, and Sharon, all in Washtenaw County.
Exhibits/Collections: The shop has a working forge and tools of the trade and is one of the last-remaining, intact, main street blacksmith shops. John Schneider was the last full-time blacksmith in Manchester.
Annual Events: Manchester Chicken Broil (Jul), Blacksmith Shop Open House (Jul).
Publications: Annual historical calendar, quarterly newsletter.

Michigan History Directory

Manistee
(Manistee County)

Manistee County Historical Museum
Mailing Address: 425 River St. • Manistee, MI 49660
Contact: Mark Fedder, Director
E-Mail: manisteemuseum@yahoo.com
Phone: (231) 723-5531
Hours: Jan-Mar: Thu-Sat 10 a.m.-5 p.m., Apr-May: Tue-Sat 10 a.m.-5 p.m., Jun-Sep: Mon-Sat 10 a.m.-5 p.m., Oct-Dec: Tue-Sat 10 a.m.-5 p.m.
Admission: $3/adult, $5/couple, $1/student, $7/family.
Visitor Accessibility: Street parking. Partially wheelchair accessible.
Website: www.manisteemuseum.org
About: Museum features three exhibits throughout the year. Permanent exhibits include seven different period rooms, maritime, antique dinnerware, Native-American artifacts, costumes, and dolls.
Exhibits/Collections: Newspapers, books, atlases, more than 25,000 photographs, city directories, air photos, real estate tax records, more than 100,000 file cards of Manistee ancestors, federal census forms.
Annual Events: Heritage Social (Aug).

Our Savior's Historical Society
Mailing Address: 115 Spruce St. • Manistee, MI 49660
Contact: Douglas Jensen, President
Hours: Jun-May: Sat 1-4 p.m.
Visitor Accessibility: Street parking.
About: Preserves and maintains a 19th-century Danish church building, which is the nation's oldest existing church building of the Danish Synod of the American Evangelical Lutheran Church.
Annual Events: Annual Meeting (Nov).
*Information may not be current.

S.S. City of Milwaukee
Mailing Address: P.O. Box 394 • Manistee, MI 49660
Contact: Linda Spencer
E-Mail: lspencer@carferry.com
Phone: (231) 723-3587 • *Fax:* (231) 723-3589
Site/Location: Northwest Maritime Museum
Physical Location: 99 Arthur St. (US 31) • Manistee, MI 49660
Hours: Call or visit website for current hours.
Admission: Admission for a fee.
Visitor Accessibility: On-site parking. Cardeck on City of Milwaukee for wheelchair access, tours are guided.
Website: www.carferry.com
About: To preserve railroad carferry history and Coast Guard history of the 180s. Walking tours through carferry City of Milwaukee, engine room to pilot house. Walking tour of USCG Acacia "Last of the 180s."
Exhibits/Collections: Artifacts, records, archival holdings focusing on Lake Michigan car ferries.
Annual Events: Carferry Reunion (Memorial Day weekend), Annual Meeting (Aug), Ghost Ship Weekends (Oct).
Publications: Quarterly newsletter (Box Cars and Buoys).

Manistique
(Manistique County)

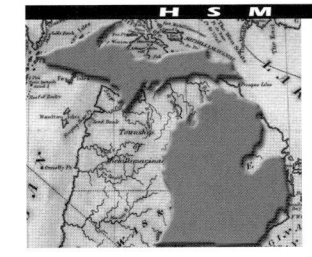

Schoolcraft County Historical Society
Mailing Address: P.O. Box 284 • Manistique, MI 49854
Contact: M. Vonciel Le Duc
E-Mail: m085@centurytel.net
Phone: (906) 341-5045
Site/Location: Pioneer Park
Physical Location: 100 Deer St. • Manistique, MI 49854
Hours: Jun-Labor Day: Wed-Sat 1-4 p.m.
Admission: $1/individual donation.
Visitor Accessibility: On-site parking. Partially wheelchair accessible. Tour guides available.
Website: http://schs.cityofmanistique.org/
About: The Schoolcraft County Historical Society preserves the history of Schoolcraft County through the collection of artifacts and photographs. The society's museum is located in a small 1910 house. The log cabin has exhibits (from 1890s). The fire engine building contains a hook and ladder truck from the 1800s as well as a 1950 La France Firetruck. The Manistique Watertower (1923) is open and contains special exhibits.
Annual Events: Pioneer Days (Jun), Appraisal Fair and Craft Show (Aug).
Publications: Historical newspaper, "Souvenir of Manistique," "Live Wire City."

Manton
(Wexford County)

Manton Area Historical Museum
Mailing Address: P.O. Box 86 • Manton, MI 49663
Contact: Paul Hallett, President
Phone: (231) 824-3208
Physical Location: 102 Griswald St. (Old US-31) • Manton, MI 49663
Hours: Memorial Day-Labor Day: Mon-Sat 1-4 p.m.
Admission: Donations accepted.
Visitor Accessibility: On-site parking. Ground floor wheelchair accessible. Tour guide available.
About: Collects and preserves the town of Manton and its ancestors' legacy. The Veterans Museum is housed in the former power plant. A diesel engine and generator that powered the city until 1959 are in place. Features old-fashioned drug store and horse-drawn hearse.
Exhibits/Collections: Artifacts and pictures of the area. Obituary and family history records.
Annual Events: Meetings 3rd Mon Apr-Oct, 7 p.m.
*Information may not be current.

Marine City
(St. Clair County)

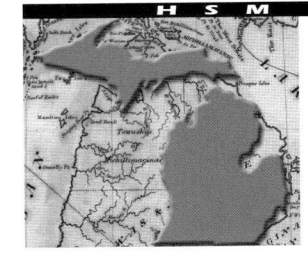

Community Pride & Heritage Museum
Mailing Address: P.O. Box 184 • Marine City, MI 48039
Contact: Gary Beals, President
E-Mail: marinecitymuseum@hotmail.com
Phone: (810) 765-5446
Physical Location: 405 South Main St. • Marine City, MI 48039
Hours: Jun-Oct: Sat-Sun 1-4 p.m.

Historical Society of Michigan

Admission: Donations accepted.
Visitor Accessibility: Free street parking. Wheelchair accessible. Tour guides available for groups of 10 or more; appointment via e-mail rewuired.
Website: www.marinecitymuseum.org
About: The Community Pride & Heritage Museum provides information on local history and shipbuilding in the area and helps teachers educate their students about the history of their community. The museum is located in a building contructed in 1847 by Eber Brock Ward to house the Newport Academy, run by his sister Emily Ward. Exhibits touch on shipbuilding, Americana, business, farming, and genealogy research.
Exhibits/Collections: Artifacts, records, and archival holdings on shipyards, military, schools, household items, farming and business. Newspapers and scrapbooks.
Annual Events: Summer Concerts. Meetings Feb-Nov 3rd Sat monthly, 10 a.m. at museum.

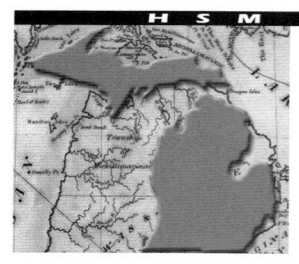

Historical Society of Marine City
Mailing Address: P.O. Box 23 • Marine City, MI 48039
Contact: Heather Bokram
E-Mail: hbokram@comcast.net
Phone: (810) 765-3567
Fax: (810) 765-5639
Physical Location: 409 N. Main St. • Marine City, MI 48039
Website: historicalsocietymarinecity.org
About: Safeguards the heritage of Marine City by preserving elements of its cultural, social, economic, political, and architectural history through promoting the restoration and beautification of the city.
Annual Events: Meetings 2nd Tue monthly, 6:30 p.m. at Heather House.
Publications: Biannual newsletter.

Marquette
(Marquette County)

Beaumier U.P. Heritage Center
Mailing Address: Northern Michigan University, 1401 Presque Isle Ave. • Marquette, MI 49855
Contact: Daniel Truckey, Director
E-Mail: heritage@nmu.edu
Phone: (906) 227-3212 • *Fax:* (906) 227-2229
Hours: 10 a.m.-4 p.m.
Admission: Free.
Visitor Accessibility: Free on-site parking. Wheelchair accessible. Self-guided.
Website: www.nmu.edu/beaumier
About: The Beaumier U.P. Heritage Center celebrates the history and culture of the people of the Upper Peninsula through programs, exhibitions, and the collection of material. The center also collects artifacts and creates displays related to the history of Northern Michigan University. The Beaumier Center features two to three temporary exhibitions each year and has a permanent installation on immigration to the Upper Peninsula. Also on-site are exhibits on the Legends of the U.P. and athletics at Northern Michigan University.
Exhibits/Collections: Artifacts of the ethnic, religious, and social diversity of the Upper Peninsula, including household, symbolic, and recreational pieces. The Northern Michigan University Collection consists of artifacts from the history of NMU.

Information may not be current.

Bishop Baraga Association
Mailing Address: 1004 Harbor Hills Dr. • Marquette, MI 49855
Contact: Len McKeen, Associate Director
Phone: (906) 227-9117
Site/Location: **The Baraga House**
Physical Location: 615 S. Fourth St. • Marquette, MI 49855
Hours: Association: Tue, Thu 8:30 a.m.-5 p.m., Fri 8:30 a.m.-12:30 p.m. Baraga House: By appointment.
Admission: Free.
Visitor Accessibility: Free on-site parking. Wheelchair accessible. Tours available by appointment.
Website: www.bishopbaraga.org
About: The Bishop Baraga Association promotes the cause for the canonization of Venerable Frederic Baraga, first Bishop of Marquette, by educating and updating members and the community at large. The association preserves the history of Bishop Baraga and the Catholic Church in the Upper Peninsula.
Exhibits/Collections: 800 letters written by Frederic Baraga, more than 1,000 letters to him from various people. Materials and artifacts relating to the life of Bishop Baraga, the Chippewa, Ottawa and American Fur Company.
Annual Events: Baraga Days Florida (Feb), Baraga Days (Sep).
Publications: Quarterly newsletter.

Marquette County Genealogical Society
Mailing Address: c/o Peter White Public Library, 217 N. Front St. • Marquette, MI 49855
Contact: Sherrye Woodworth, Corresponding Secretary
Phone: (906) 228-9510
Hours: Call for library hours.
Website: http://www.rootsweb.ancestry.com/~mimarqgs/mcgs.html
About: Society members share a common interest in genealogy, help preserve and organize sources and resources in the area, promote family research, and maintain a collection of genealogical resources.
Exhibits/Collections: Genealogy collection, local history materials, CDs and personal records held in Peter White Public Library. Call (906) 228-9510 for library hours.
Annual Events: Genealogy workshop, cemetery work bees. Meetings 3rd Wed Sep-May, 6:45 p.m. at library.
Publications: Newsletter (Lake Superior Roots).

Information may not be current.

Marquette Maritime Museum and Lighthouse
Mailing Address: P.O. Box 1096 • Marquette, MI 49855
Contact: Carrie Fries, Director
E-Mail: info@mqtmaritimemuseum.com
Phone: 906-226-2006 • *Fax:* (906) 226-2006
Physical Location: 300 N. Lakeshore Blvd. • Marquette, MI 49855
Hours: May-Oct: Daily 10 a.m.-5 p.m.
Admission: Museum or lighthouse: Adults $5, Children $3. Museum and lighthouse: Adult $9, Children $5.
Visitor Accessibility: Free on-site and street parking. Museum is wheelchair accessible; lighthouse is not. Museum docents available by request; lighthouse docents included in admission.
Website: www.mqtmaritimemuseum.com
About: The mission of the Maritime Museum is to preserve, protect, and promote local maritime history. The Marquette Maritime Museum offers two different tours. One is a self-guided tour of the Maritime Museum, which includes local shipwrecks, life-saving, lighthouse, and a WWII Silent Service Memorial. The second tour is of the Marquette Harbor Lighthouse.
Exhibits/Collections: Largest collection of Fresnel Lenses on the Great

Lakes; early life-saving and 3-D breeches buoy exhibit; local shipwrecks, including the Henry B. Smith and the Edmund Fitzgerald.
Annual Events: Maritime Month (Aug).
Publications: Quarterly newsletter (Mariner's Log).

Marquette Regional History Center
Mailing Address: 145 W. Spring St. • Marquette, MI 49855
Contact: Jennifer Naze
E-Mail: mrhc@marquettehistory.org
Phone: (906) 226-3571
Hours: Mon-Tue 10 a.m.-5 p.m., Wed 10 a.m.-8 p.m., Thu-Fri 10 a.m.-5 p.m., Sat 10 a.m.-3 p.m.
Admission: $7/adult, $6/senior, $3/student, $2/children 12 and under.
Visitor Accessibility: Free on-site parking; public parking also nearby. Wheelchair accessible. Tour guide available upon request.
Website: www.marquettehistory.org
About: The Marquette Regional History Center includes a 7,500-square-foot exhibit space with displays that depict natural history, indigenous peoples, fur trade, pioneer life, sports history, and Yooper life.
Exhibits/Collections: Collection of rare books, manuscripts, maps, genealogical files, and business records. Permanent collection includes artifacts from Paleo-Indian to contemporary life.
Publications: Quarterly history journal (Harlow's Wooden Man), Books related to Northern Michigan.

Northern Michigan University
Mailing Address: 1401 Presque Isle Ave. • Marquette, MI 49855
Contact: Marcus Robyns
E-Mail: archives@nmu.edu
Phone: (906) 227-1046 • *Fax:* (906) 227-1333
Site/Location: **University Archivist & Records Manager**
Hours: Mon-Fri 8 a.m.-12 p.m. and 1-5 p.m.
Admission: Free.
Website: www.nmu.edu/archives
About: Documents history of central Upper Peninsula of Michigan and Northern Michigan University.
Exhibits/Collections: Official records of Northern Michigan University. Depository for state and local government records of central Upper Peninsula. Records of Cleveland-Cliffs Iron Mining Company. Papers of Michigan Supreme Court Justice John Voelker.
*Information may not be current.

Marshall
(Calhoun County)

Calhoun County Genealogical Society
Mailing Address: P.O. Box 879 • Marshall, MI 49068
Contact: Marcie Telfer, Committee Chair
Admission: $15/yearly membership with electronic newsletter, $18/yearly membership with paper newsletter.
Website: www.rootsweb.com/~micalhou/ccgs.htm
About: The Calhoun County Genealogical Society is a nonprofit organization founded in 1988 for the purpose of gathering and preserving information of genealogical value; encouraging the deposit of such information in suitable dispositions; aiding genealogists in the study of family history through the exchange of knowledge; and publishing and promoting Calhoun County and other genealogical materials.
Annual Events: Meetings 4th Tue Jan-Jun and Sep-Nov at Church of Jesus Christ of the Latter-Day Saints (Marshall, MI).
Publications: Newsletter (Generations). See website for books and records in print.

Calhoun County Road Commission
Mailing Address: 13300 15 Mile Rd. • Marshall, MI 49068
Contact: Tiffany Eichorst, Environmental Services Coordinator
Phone: (269) 781-9841 • *Fax:* (269) 781-6101
Site/Location: **Historic Bridge Park**
Physical Location: 14930 Wattles Road • Battle Creek, MI 49015
Hours: 8 a.m.-8 p.m.
Admission: Free.
Visitor Accessibility: Free on-site parking. Partially wheelchair accessible.
Website: http://www.calhouncountyroads.com/parks/historic-bridge-park/
About: The Historic Bridge Park is managed by the Calhoun County Road Commission. The park, which is adjacent to the Kalamazoo River, features relocated and restored historical road bridges. The restoration techniques used on the bridges are what fabricators used 100 years ago. The park also features a small boat launch.
Annual Events: Calhoun County Parks Board meets 1st Wed monthly, 5:30 p.m. at Calhoun County Road Commission.
*Information may not be current.

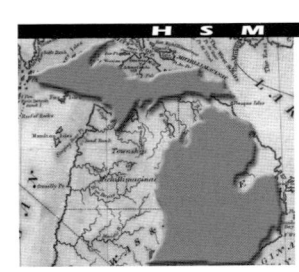

Marshall Historical Society
Mailing Address: 107 N. Kalamazoo Ave. • Marshall, MI 49068
Contact: Casey Nager, Treasurer
E-Mail: rhodes@msu.edu
Phone: (269) 781-8544
Site/Location: **Honolulu House Museum**
Physical Location: 107 N. Kalamazoo Ave. • Marshall, MI 49068
Hours: May 1-Oct 31: Daily 11 a.m.-5 p.m.
Admission: $5/individual.
Visitor Accessibility: Free on-site parking. Partially wheelchair accessible. Guided tours available; additional costs may apply for tours made by appointment during off-season hours.
Website: www.marshallhistoricalsociety.org
About: The Marshall Historical Society was organized in 1961 to preserve, protect, and promote Marshall's heritage. It has restored three historic buildings in Marshall. The Honolulu House was built in 1860 by Abner Pratt, then-consul to the Sandwich Islands. The exterior architecture is a blend of Italianate, Gothic, and Polynesian. The interior features paint-on-plaster wall and ceiling paintings restored to the splendor of the 1880s. It is listed on the National Register of Historic Places and the Historical American Building Survey.
Annual Events: Historic Home Tour (Sep), Christmas Candlelight Walk (Dec). Board of Trustees meeting 4th Mon monthly.
Publications: "Nineteenth Century Homes of Marshall" "Marshall, A Plan for Preservation."
Other Sites/Locations: **G.A.R. Hall** • Location: 402 E. Michigan Ave., Marshall, MI 49068 • Hours: May 1-Oct 31: Sat 1-4 p.m. • Admission: $3/individual • Visitor Accessibility: Free on-site parking. Wheelchair accessible. Guided tours available; additional costs may apply for tours made by appointment during off-season hours. • The G.A.R. Hall, built in 1902, currently houses Marshall memorabilia, including items from the Civil War and Spanish American War, as well as police and firefighter artifacts.
Capitol Hill School • Location: 602 Washington St., Marshall, MI

49068 • Admission: $3/inidividual • Visitor Accessibility: Free on-site parking. Wheelchair accessible. Tour guide available by appointment; additional costs may apply for groups of less than 20. • Built in 1860 adjacent to the intended Michigan state capitol, Capitol Hill School is the only survivor of three identical Gothic Revival schools. It was removed from public service in 1961 but now continues to provide a turn-of-the-century classroom experience. The Capitol Hill School is listed on the National Register of Historic Places and the Historical American Building Survey.
Information may not be current.

Marshall National Landmark Historic District
Mailing Address: 323 W. Michigan Ave. • Marshall, MI 49068
Contact: Susan Collins
E-Mail: sujocol@aol.com
Phone: (269) 781-5893
Website: www.MarshallLandmark.com
About: The tradition of historical preservation and restoration began in the 1920s. It found resonance in homes in the 1950s and culminated in 1991 when the National Park Service designated Marshall as the nation's largest National Historic Landmark District in the Small Urban category. The district has more historical markers than any other Michigan community, except Detroit.
Exhibits/Collections: Standards for rehabilitation, local records.
Information may not be current.

Walters Gasoline and Interurban Railroad Museum
Mailing Address: 220 West Michigan Ave. • Marshall, MI 49068
Contact: Richard Walters, Jr.
E-Mail: dwalters@waltersdimmick.com
Phone: (269) 789-2562
Hours: May-Oct: Sat 12-5 p.m.; Sun 1-4 p.m. Also by appointment.
Admission: Free.
Visitor Accessibility: Free on-site and street parking. Not wheelchair accessible. Tour guides available.
About: Walters Gasoline and Interurban Railroad Museum gives the public an interesting look at the early history of Marshall, Calhoun County, and the state of Michigan. The museum features photos and maps of the Marshall Interurban Railroad, which ran through downtown Marshall. There are also gasoline artifacts, Marshall and Calhoun Counties historical artifacts. Each visiting child receives a special toy. Group tours are welcome and can also enjoy shopping and dining in Marshall.
Exhibits/Collections: Gasoline artifacts, Marshall-area memorabilia, and the Historic Marshall Interurban Railway.
Annual Events: Marshall Cruise the Fountain Weekend, Marshall Home Tours, Christmas Open House.

Marysville
(St. Clair County)

Marysville Historical Museum
Mailing Address: 1111 Delaware Ave. • Marysville, MI 48040
Contact: Ann Shaw, Recreation Coordinator
E-Mail: ashaw@cityofmarysvillemi.com
Phone: (810) 364-6613, ext. 302 • *Fax:* (810) 364-3940
Physical Location: 887 Huron Rd. • Marysville, MI 48040
Hours: Memorial Day-Labor Day: Weekend Sun 1:30-4 p.m.
Admission: $1/individual donation.
Visitor Accessibility: Not wheelchair accessible.
Website: www.cityofmarysvillemi.com/museum
About: Located in the old city hall originally built for the Carpenter and Cuttle families in 1912. Hosts room-by-room displays depicting living conditions of earlier times. Other rooms devoted to particular areas of interest, including ships and automobiles. Marysville Vikings sports hallway and classroom. Historic photos and maps are displayed throughout. Operated by city recreation department.
Exhibits/Collections: Archives are located in upstairs of community center. Mayors of Marysville, pictures of police and fire departments, ships of Great Lakes and St. Clair River, Willis St. Clair Car Company.
Information may not be current.

Port Huron and Detroit Railroad Historical Society
Mailing Address: P.O. Box 217 • Marysville, MI 48040
Contact: Bud Gilbert, President
Site/Location: **Port Huron and Detroit Railroad Historical Society Museum**
Physical Location: 2100 32nd Street • Port Huron, MI 48060
Website: www.phdrailroad.com
About: The Port Huron and Detroit Railroad Historical Society was started in April 2007. The purpose was to save the office building and the roundhouse of the Port Huron & Detroit Railroad Company and to preserve the history of other railroads in Michigan.
Information may not be current.

Wills Sainte Claire Automobile Museum
Mailing Address: 2408 Wills St. • Marysville, MI 48040
Contact: Terry Ernest, Director
E-Mail: willsmuseum@sbcglobal.net
Phone: (810) 987-2854
Hours: Call ahead or see website.
Admission: $5/adult, children 12 and under are free.
Visitor Accessibility: On-site parking. Wheelchair accessible. Tour guide available for groups with advance reservation.
Website: www.willsautomuseum.org
About: The Wills Sainte Claire Automobile Museum is dedicated to preserving the history of C. Harold Wills and the Wills Sainte Clair Automobile. It features more than 12 Wills Sainte Claire Autos, which is the largest collection in the world. Exhibits feature photos, advertising, and displays relating to the factory and the city of Marysville ("The City of Contented Living").
Exhibits/Collections: Wills Sainte Clair Automobiles, photographs, advertising, original records of C.H. Wills Co. and successor Wills Sainte Claire Co., records of Marysville Land Improvement Co., personal records of C. Harold Wills.
Annual Events: Annual car show. Dates listed on website. Meetings 2nd Thu monthly, 7:30 p.m. at museum.
Publications: Gray Goose News.

Mason
(Ingham County)

Ingham County Genealogy Society
Mailing Address: P.O. Box 85 • Mason, MI 48854
Contact: Diane Bishop, President
E-Mail: icgs@icgsweb.org
Phone: (517) 676-7140
Site/Location: **Ingham County Genealogical Society Reference Room**
Physical Location: Capital Area District Library—Mason Branch, 145 W. Ash Street 2nd floor. Mason, MI 48854
Hours: Open during library hours.

Admission: Free to library members.
Visitor Accessibility: Free street parking. Partially wheelchair accessible; second-floor research room not wheelchair accessible. Self-guided. For research assistance, call ahead.
Website: www.icgsweb.org
About: Encourage and assist the study of family history. Encourage the deposit of genealogical records and assist area library in expanding and publicizing their genealogical holdings. Publish material of interest and use to genealogists.
Exhibits/Collections: Microfilmed records of Mason and townships of Ingham County. Holdings include obituary files, archived copies of county newspapers from 1876, cemetery records, township histories, and other research materials.
Annual Events: Annual Picnic (Aug), Christmas Potluck Dinner (Dec). Meetings 2nd Thu monthly (except Jan, Jun, Jul), 7 p.m. at Vevay Township Hall.
Publications: Quarterly newsletter (Inroads to Ingham). See website for list of genealogical records available.

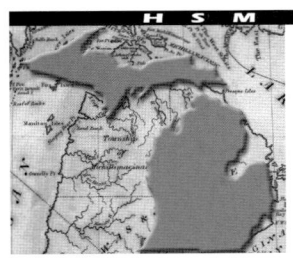

Ingham County Historical Commission
Mailing Address: P.O. Box 319 • Mason, MI 48854
Contact: Jim MacLean
E-Mail: bbennett@ingham.org
Phone: 517-676-7200
Fax: (517) 676-7264
Site/Location: Ingham County Courthouse
Physical Location: 341 S. Jefferson St. • Mason, MI 48854
Hours: By appointment. Closed Wed.
Admission: Free.
Visitor Accessibility: Free parking. Wheelchair accessible. Tour guide available.
Website: http://bc.ingham.org
About: Completed in 1904, the current Ingham County Courthouse was put on the National Register of Historic Places in 1971.
Annual Events: Meetings 1st Wed monthly, 7 p.m. at Ingham County Courthouse.

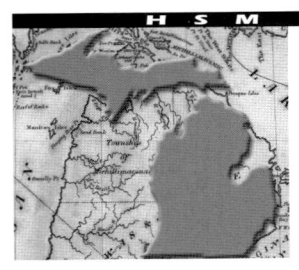

Mason Area Historical Society
Mailing Address: P.O. Box 44 • Mason, MI 48854
Contact: Jean Bement, President
E-Mail: btornholm@sbcglobal.net
Phone: (517) 697-9837
Site/Location: Mason Historical Museum
Physical Location: 200 East Oak Street • Mason, MI 48854
Hours: Tue, Thu, Sat 1-3 p.m.
Admission: Free.
Visitor Accessibility: Street parking. Wheelchair accesible. Tour guide available during open hours or by appointment.
Website: www.masonmuseum.com
About: The Mason Area Historical Society researches, preserves, and educates on the history of Mason. Exhibits include artifacts related to the history of Mason.
Exhibits/Collections: Extensive library with information pertaining to Mason area, photos, books, files, and DVDs of past programs. DVDs about area WWII veterans and history of Mason.
Annual Events: Garden Social Tour and Heritage Event (alternate years). Meetings 1st Mon monthly (or 2nd if the 1st is a holiday).
Other Sites/Locations: **The Pink School** • Location: 707 W. Ash, Mason, MI 48854 • Hours: By appointment • Admission: Free • Visitor Accessibility: Street parking. Wheelchair accessible. Tours available by appointment. • The Pink School is a one-room school that originally opened in 1854. It displays old school memorabilia, records of teachers, etc.

Mason Historic District Commission
Mailing Address: Mason City Hall, 201 W. Ash St. • Mason, MI 48854
Contact: David Haywood
Phone: 517-676-9155 • *Fax:* 517-676-1330
Hours: 8 a.m.-5 p.m.
Website: www.mason.mi.us
About: Review agency for appropriateness of development proposals in Mason Downtown Historic District.
Annual Events: Meetings 4th Mon monthly, 7 p.m. at City Hall.
*Information may not be current.

Victorian Society in America—Michigan Chapter
Mailing Address: 117 W. Sycamore St. • Mason, MI 488541640
Contact: Rex Hauser, President
E-Mail: Lameti@law.msu.edu
Phone: (517) 676-6350
Admission: $20/yearly membership fee.
About: Meets twice yearly. Provides spring and fall tours of Michigan communities that feature 19th-century architecture, culture, and historical collections. The society offers a fun traveling group to visit museums, homes, and neighborhoods (with stops for lunch and tea).
Publications: Biannual newsletter.

Maybee
(Monroe County)

Exeter Historical Society & Township Museum
Mailing Address: P.O. Box 3 • Maybee, MI 48159
Contact: Linda Badgley, President
E-Mail: lindylite13@yahoo.com
Phone: (734) 587-2100 • *Fax:* (734) 587-7220
Physical Location: 6158 Scofield Rd. • Maybee, MI 48159
Hours: Open by appointment.
Visitor Accessibility: One-room schoolhouse has entrance ramp.
About: Purpose is to preserve historic attributes of local community and promote the importance of historic preservation efforts. Maintains museum in the 1890 Exeter Township Hall. The McGodwan School was built circa 1876 and closed in 1966. The museum features displays of memorabilia, documents, and artifacts of local interest.
Exhibits/Collections: School furnishings and book collection. Township hall contains collection of early commercial and personal memorabilia from the local area. Voting booths and cannisters.
Annual Events: Open House (Oct), Trick or Treat Night (Oct). Meetings 1st Wed monthly Sep-Jun, 7 p.m. at Exeter Township Hall.
*Information may not be current.

Mayville
(Tuscola County)

Mayville Area Museum of History & Genealogy
Mailing Address: P.O. Box 242 • Mayville, MI 48744

Historical Society of Michigan

Contact: Fran Campbell
E-Mail: mayvillemuseum@hotmail.com
Phone: 989-843-7185
Physical Location: 2124 Ohmer Rd (M24) • Mayville, MI 48744
Hours: Memorial Day-Labor Day Fri-Sat 10 a.m.-4 p.m. Also by appointment.
Admission: Donations accepted.
Visitor Accessibility: Free on-site parking. Partially wheelchair accessible. Free volunteer tour guides available.
About: Founded in 1972 by area residents interested in preserving local history and culture. Museum is housed in Pere Marquette Depot, which features mastodon bones and artifacts from WWI and the Korean War. Other attractions include the West Dayton One-Room Schoolhouse, a log cabin, and an outhouse.
Exhibits/Collections: Collection of genealogy information, obituary file, and local history.
Annual Events: Flear Market, Pancake breakfast, Top Thirty Car Show (Sep), Log Cabin Days (Jun). Meetings 2nd Thu monthly, 2 p.m.; 7 p.m. in Apr, Aug, and Dec.
Publications: Annual newsletter. "Mayville Historical Video," annual calendar, "Remembering the '30s—A Collection of Stories," "A Backward Look, Reminiscences of Fostoria, Michigan."

Melvindale
(Wayne County)

City of Melvindale Historical Commission
Mailing Address: 3100 Oakwood Blvd. • Melvindale, MI 48122
Information may not be current.

Memphis
(St. Clair County)

Memphis Historical Society
Mailing Address: P.O. Box 41056 • Memphis, MI 48041
Contact: Anita Labinski, President
Phone: (810) 392-3510
Site/Location: Memphis Historical Society Museum
Physical Location: 34830 Potter St. • Memphis, MI 48041
Hours: Museum is open whenever community center is being used for public functions or MHS meetings.
Admission: Donations accepted.
Visitor Accessibility: Street parking.
About: Preserves the heritage of the city of Memphis and its surrounding community. Showcases with exhibits on Memphis history and women of Memphis area are located in community center/library building. Available to public during open hours.
Exhibits/Collections: Artifacts including clothing, postcards, photos of homes past and present, literature.
Annual Events: Meetings 4th Tue of Jan, Mar, May, Jul, Sep, 3rd Thu of Nov. Call for location.
Publications: Historic calendar (for sale at local businesses).

Menominee
(Menominee County)

Bailey Property Preservation Association
Mailing Address: W2784 County Road 338 • Menominee, MI 49858
Contact: Eileen Behrend, President
Phone: (906) 863-9716
Site/Location: West Shore Fishing Museum
Physical Location: N5156 State Highway M35 • Menominee, MI 49887
Hours: Memorial Day-Labor Day: Sat-Sun 1-4 p.m.
Admission: Donations accepted.
Visitor Accessibility: Free on-site parking. Wheelchair accessible. Tour guide available; group tours by appointment.
About: The Bailey Property Preservation Association preserves and portrays the history of the Great Lakes commercial fishing industry, in particular the history along the west shore of Green Bay. The West Shore Fishing Museum was once the site of the Charles L. Bailey Commercial Fishery. The showcase museum features a restored Victorian family home and gardens, exhibit building, twine shed, and boat shelter with a fleet of five commercial fishing boats. Walking trails extend throughout 24 acres of natural coastal property.
Exhibits/Collections: Bailey family papers and photographs; Native-American artifacts; commercial fishing artifacts; home furnishings (1895-1940).
Annual Events: Plant Sale (May), Ice Cream Social (Sep), Membership Meeting (fall). Business meetings 3rd Mon Mar-Dec.
Information may not be current.

Menominee County Historical Society
Mailing Address: P.O. Box 151 • Menominee, MI 49858
Contact: Michael Kaufman, Executive Director
E-Mail: jcallow1@new.rr.com; dmurwin@new.rr.com
Phone: (906) 863-9000
Site/Location: Heritage Museum and M.J. Anuta Research Center
Physical Location: 904 11th Ave. • Menominee, MI 49858
Hours: Memorial Day-Labor Day: Mon-Sat 10 a.m.-4 p.m.
Admission: Donations accepted.
Visitor Accessibility: Free on-site and street parking. Partially wheelchair accessible. Tour guide available; donations accepted. Large groups should make reservations.
Website: www.menomineehistoricalsociety.org
About: The Menominee County Historical Society gathers, preserves, and disseminates the history of the area. Located in a former church, the Heritage Museum focuses on the area's early history. Artifacts relate to Native Americans, early settlers, and the development of industry in the county from 1863. The Anuta Research Center is located in the rear of the museum.
Exhibits/Collections: The M.J. Anuta Research Center is open on select days each week. It holds paper artifacts, including local newspapers dating to 1871, thousands of pictures, obituaries, and books.
Annual Events: See website for events. Meetings 1st Mon monthly, 10 a.m. at Spies Public Library.
Publications: Quarterly membership newsletter, several books written by local historians, and brochures of area walking and driving tours. **Other Sites/Locations: Chappee-Webber Learning Center** • Location: Fire Number N1936 River Road, Menominee, MI 49858 • Hours: Call museum to arrange a visit • Admission: Free • Visitor Accessibility: Free on-site parking. Partially wheelchair accessible. Self-guided. • In the fall, the Chappee-Webber Learning Center brings in special speakers to teach youth about fur trading, horticulture, logging, and Native-American life. The site also features a pavillion, historical markers, and the opportunity to walk trails and along the Menominee River.
Information may not be current.

Menominee Historical Commission
Mailing Address: 1502 First St., P.O. Box 151 • Menominee, MI 49858
Information may not be current.

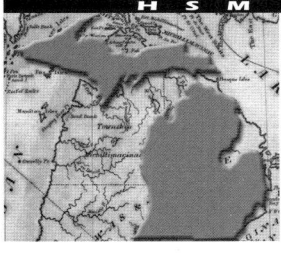

Spies Public Library
Mailing Address: 940 First St. • Menominee, MI 49858
Contact: Cheryl Hoffman, Director
E-Mail: cherylh@uproc.lib.mi.us
Phone: (906) 863-2900
Fax: (906) 863-5000
Hours: Summer hours: Mon-Fri 9 a.m.-6 p.m., Sat 9 a.m.-12 p.m. Winter Hours: Mon, Fri 9 a.m.-5 p.m., Tue-Thu 9 a.m.-8 p.m. Sat 9 a.m.-1 p.m.
Visitor Accessibility: Wheelchair accessible.
Website: www.uproc.lib.mi.us/spies

Michigamme
(Marquette County)

Michigamme Museum
Mailing Address: P.O. Box 220 • Michigamme, MI 49861
Contact: Donald Moore
E-Mail: michigammetownship@gmail.com
Phone: (906) 323-9016
Fax: (906) 323-6344
Physical Location: 110 Main St. • Michigamme, MI 49861
Hours: Memorial Day-Oct. Call for current hours.
Admission: Donations accepted.
Visitor Accessibility: Free street parking. Wheelchair accessible. Tour guide available.
About: Exhibits at the Michigamme Museum include logging, mining, "Anatomy of a Murder," a log house, and a 1900 American LaFrance Steam Fire Engine.
Exhibits/Collections: Artifacts of local interest and collection of grave site listings and obituaries.
Annual Events: Car Show and Log Cabin Days (Jun).

Middleville
(Barry County)

Thornapple Heritage Association
Mailing Address: 216 Stadium Dr. • Middleville, MI 49333
Information may not be current.

Midland
(Midland County)

Alden B. Dow Home & Studio
Mailing Address: 315 Post St. • Midland, MI 48640
Contact: Craig McDonald
E-Mail: info@abdow.org
Phone: 866/315-7678
Fax: (989) 839-2611
Hours: Tours are held Feb-Dec: Mon-Sat 2 p.m., Fri-Sat 10 a.m. Reservations required.
Admission: $15/adult, $12/senior, $7/student.
Visitor Accessibility: Free on-site parking. Not wheelchair accessible. Guided tours only.
Website: www.abdow.org
About: The Alden B. Dow Home & Studio was the home of Alden B. Dow, an organic architect. Today, his home, along with his studio, is a National Historic Landmark that is open for tours and educational programming. The Home & Studio houses original furnishings, a ceramic and glass collection from the 1930s-1960s, personal and professional libraries, historic model-scale trains, and mechanical toys.
Exhibits/Collections: 22,000 original design development and working architectural drawings with 560 corresponding job files, 1,425 publications.
Annual Events: Autumn Reflections Tours (Oct).
Publications: "Alden B. Dow Midwestern Modern."

Chippewa Nature Center
Mailing Address: 400 S. Badour Rd. • Midland, MI 48640
Contact: Kyle Bagnall, Manager of Historical Programs
E-Mail: kbagnall@chippewanaturecenter.org
Phone: (989) 631-0830
Fax: (989) 631-7070
Hours: Mon-Sat 8 a.m.-5 p.m., Sun and Holidays 12-5 p.m.
Admission: Free.
Visitor Accessibility: Free on-site parking. Wheelchair accessible. Self-guided.
Website: www.chippewanaturecenter.org
About: The Chippewa Nature Center aims to facilitate the understanding of mid-Michigan's natural and cultural resources, promote environmental awareness, and foster responsible stewardship. The Ecosystem Gallery provides hands-on exhibits, the 1870s Homestead Farm and Log Schoolhouse are open Sunday afternoons, where visitors can tour the log cabin, barn, and outbuildings; visit farm animals and an heirloom garden, and participate in historical activities.
Exhibits/Collections: Photographs, slides, audio-visuals, and a teaching collection. Natural history collection includes 2,000 specimens representing plants, animals, and geology of mid-Michigan. Archaeological collection comprises 7,000-plus cataloged artifacts.
Annual Events: Maple Syrup Day (Mar), Banff Mountain Film Festival World Tour (Apr), Native Plant Sale (May), Homestead Sundays (Jun-Aug), Fall Harvest Festival and Bio-Blitz (alternating years in Sep).
Publications: "Chippewa Nature Center: The First Twenty-Five Years," "The Cater Site: The Archaeology, History, Artifacts and Activities at this Early 19th Century Midland County Site," "Naturally: Exploring Ecosystems at Chippewa Nature Center."

Dow Gardens
Mailing Address: 1018 W. Main St. • Midland, MI 48640
Contact: Ed Haycock, Managing Director
E-Mail: haycock@dowgardens.org
Phone: (989) 631-2677 • **Fax:** (989) 631-0675
Physical Location: 1809 Eastman Ave. • Midland, MI 48640
Hours: Apr 15-Labor Day: 9 a.m.-8:30 p.m.; Labor Day-Oct: 9 a.m.-6:30 p.m.; Nov-Apr: 9 a.m.-4:15 p.m.
Admission: $5/adult, $1/students (6-17).
Visitor Accessibility: Free parking. Wheelchair accessible (wheelchairs or amigos available for rental). Group tours min. 5 people, $2/individual.
Website: www.dowgardens.org
About: Dow Gardens were started in 1899 by Herbert Dow, founder of Dow Chemical Company, on eight acres of land. Work was continued by architect Alden Dow and was expanded to 110 acres. Today the Gardens feature some of the finest seasonal horticultural displays in the Midwest. Check website for current activities, including Art in the Gardens and musical events.

Historical Society of Michigan

Grace A. Dow Memorial Library
Mailing Address: Attn. Melissa Barnard, 1710 W. St. Andrews Drive • Midland, MI 48640
Phone: (989) 837-3430
Fax: (989) 837-3468
Hours: Mon-Fri 9:30 a.m.-8:30 p.m., Sat 9 a.m.-5 p.m., Sun 1-5 p.m.
Visitor Accessibility: Free on-site parking. Wheelchair accessible. Self-guided.
Website: http://cityofmidlandmi.gov/Library

About: The Grace A. Dow Memorial Library is the public library for the city of Midland. Collections include a local history and genealogy collection and Midland newspapers on microfilm. Volunteers are available to assist researchers in the genealogy area 1-4 p.m. weekdays, generally speaking. Please call the reference desk at (989) 837-3449 to verify hours and volunteer availability.

Midland County Genealogical Society
Mailing Address: P.O. Box 2421 • Midland, MI 48641
Contact: Wilma Diesen, President
E-Mail: diesens2@centurytel.net
Phone: (989) 832-8485
Physical Location: c/o Grace A. Dow Memorial Library, 1710 W. St. Andrews Drive • Midland, MI 48640
Hours: Year-round: Mon-Fri 9:30 a.m.-8:30 p.m., Sat 10 a.m.-5 p.m.; Sep-May: Sun 1-5 p.m.
Visitor Accessibility: Free on-site parking. Wheelchair accessible.
Website: http://www.rootsweb.ancestry.com/~mimgs/

About: Serves as a focal point for genealogical activities in the Midland County area, collecting, preserving, and publishing genealogical and historical records. Purchases genealogical materials to add to the colletion at the Grace A. Dow Library. Assists with volunteer activities in the library's genealogy collection.
Exhibits/Collections: Census films from 1850-1930 of Midland and surrounding counties. Local newspapers on microfilm. Midland County obituary Index Vol. 1-3, Midland County marriage records 1855-1910, collection of some Midland County records on CD.
Annual Events: Meetings 7 p.m. monthly at the Grace A. Dow Library (Sep-Nov, Jan-May).
Publications: Newsletter (Pioneer Record). "Midland Pioneer."
*Information may not be current.

Midland County Historical Society
Mailing Address: 1801 W. Saint Andrews Rd. • Midland, MI 48640
Contact: Gary Skory, Director
E-Mail: skory@mcfta.org
Phone: (989) 631-5930 x1310
Fax: (989) 835-9120
Site/Location: **Doan History Center**
Physical Location: 3417 West Main St. • Midland, MI 48640
Hours: Wed-Sat 11 a.m.-4 p.m. Research Library Apr-Oct: Thu 1-4 p.m.
Admission: $5/adult, $3/children (4-14), children 3 and under free. Youth groups: $3/individual. MCHS members free.
Visitor Accessibility: On-site parking. Wheelchair accessible. Guided group tours available by appointment.
Website: www.mcfta.org

About: Investigates, preserves, and presents the history of Midland County. Heritage Park operates three main attractions: the Herbert D. Doan Midland County History Center, the 1874 Bradley Home Museum and Carriage House, and the Herbert H. Dow Historical Museum. The Doan History Center offers the Midland History Gallery and hands-on interactive exhibits. The Bradley Home is one of Michigan's only hands-on historic house museums. The Dow Museum chronicles the life of the Dow Chemical Company.
Exhibits/Collections: At the Dow Museum, a collection devoted to early chemistry; at the Bradley House, a collection devoted to Victorian living; at the Carriage House, a collection of horse-drawn transportation and blacksmithing.
Annual Events: Victorian Secrets (Sep), Cemetery Tour and Funeral Tea (May), Quilt Show (Apr), Bradley Home: A Family Holiday (Dec).

West Main Street Historic District
Mailing Address: City Of Midland, 333 W. Ellsworth St. • Midland, MI 48640
Contact: C Bradley Kaye, AICP, CFM, Dir of Planning & Community Development
E-Mail: bkaye@midland-mi.org
Phone: (989) 837-3374 • *Fax:* (989) 837-5733
Hours: City offices: Mon-Fri 8 a.m.-5 p.m.
Visitor Accessibility: Street parking. ADA accessible public sidewalks.
Website: www.midland-mi.org

About: Responsible for the development and administration of guidelines on which all work within the West Main Street Historic District will be reviewed and determined. There are 24 homes in the historic district, which is adjacent to four public parks and other historic sites.
Annual Events: Meetings 4th Wed of Jan, Apr, Jul, and Oct, 7 p.m.

Milan
(Washtenaw County)

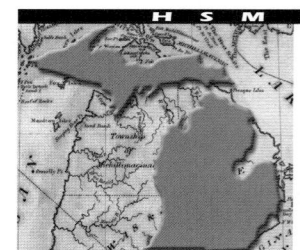

Milan Area Historical Society
Mailing Address: P.O. Box 245 • Milan, MI 48160
Contact: Anne Farmer, Corresponding Secretary
E-Mail: farmera44@att.net
Phone: (734) 439-1297
Site/Location: **Historic Hack House Museum**
Physical Location: 775 County St. • Milan, MI 48160
Hours: May-Oct: Sun 1-4 p.m.
Admission: Free.
Visitor Accessibility: Free on-site parking. Not wheelchair accessible. Tour guide available.
Website: www.historicmilan.com

About: The Milan Area Historical Society preserves the past for future generations. In addition to maintaining the Historic Hack House Museum and Old Fire Barn, the society provides public lectures and programs aimed at schoolchildren. Built in 1888 with ill-gotten funds from a sugar scandal, the Hack House remained in the Hack family until 1970. Now used as a museum, the building features artifacts of Milan and 19th- and early-20th-century America. Includes a summer kitchen, barn, a three-hole outhouse, and more.
Exhibits/Collections: Milan-area memorabilia, schools, business, homes, artifacts. Photo archives. Collection of Milan News-Leaders.
Annual Events: Spring Festival (May), Ice Cream Social (Jul), Fall Festival (Oct), Holiday Open House (Dec). Meetings 3rd Wed of Feb-May at Milan Senior Center on Nickel Court.
Other Sites/Locations: **The Old Fire Barn** • Location: 153 East Main Street, Milan, MI 48160 • Hours: Not open for tours • Visitor Accessibility: Free street parking. Partially wheelchair accessible; downstairs only. • In 1983, the Old Fire Barn was donated to the

Milan Area Historical Society, which led to the restoration of the building. Today, the building is listed on the National Register of Historic Places. The DDA and Chamber of Commerce lease office space on the first floor. It is not used as a museum.

Milford
(Oakland County)

Milford Historical Society
Mailing Address: 124 E. Commerce St. • Milford, MI 48381
Contact: Marlene Gomez, Assistant Director
E-Mail: milfordhistory@hotmail.com
Phone: (248) 685-7308
Site/Location: **Milford Historical Museum**
Hours: May-Dec: Wed, Sat 1-4 p.m.
Admission: Donations accepted.
Visitor Accessibility: Free on-site and metered street parking. Wheelchair accessible. Tour guide available during open hours and by appointment; donations accepted.
Website: www.milfordhistory.org
About: Located in an 1853 Greek revival home, the Milford Historical Museum's second floor is furnished as a home would have been in the late-Victorian Era, complete with a living room, dining room, kitchen, and bedroom. Many of the furnishings in the display are items that were manufactured in Milford. On the first floor there is a display that depicts the interior of the log cabin that Job G. Bigelow built in 1833 on the south end of Milford.
Exhibits/Collections: Genealogies of local families, history of Oak Grove Cemetery, oral histories, Milford-area photographs, tax and Census records, and every issue of the local weekly newspaper: The Milford Times.
Annual Events: Independence Day Parade (Jul), Granny's Attic Yard Sale (Jul), Homes Tour (Sep). Meetings Jan, Mar, May, Sep, Nov.
Publications: "Ten Minutes Ahead of the Rest of the World," "Moments in Time," "The Mary Jackson Teahouse Cookbook," "Jacob Tipisco—A Michigan Chippewa."
Other Sites/Locations: **Mary Jackson's Childhood Home** • Location: 642 Canal St., Milford, MI 48381 • Hours: By appointment only • Admission: Donations accepted • Visitor Accessibility: Free street parking. Not wheelchair accessible. Tour guide available by appointment. • Mary Jackson was best known as a stage, screen, and TV actress, with many movie credits and a role as one of the Baldwin sisters on the TV show Walton's Mountain.

Millersburg
(Presque Isle County)

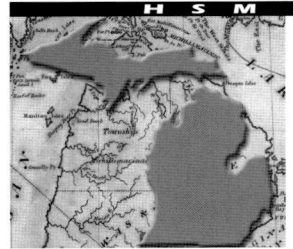

Glawe School Museum
Mailing Address: 14610 Pomranke Hwy. • Millersburg, MI 49759
Contact: Joyce Foster
Phone: (989) 733-8659
Physical Location: 40 Mile Point Lighthouse Park, US-23 North • Rogers City, MI 49779
Hours: Memorial Day-Aug: Sat-Sun 1-4 p.m.
Admission: Donations accepted.
Visitor Accessibility: Free on-site parking. Not wheelchair accessible. Docents available during open hours.
Website: https://www.facebook.com/40MilePointLighthouse
About: The Glawe School Museum is arranged as a one-room school, complete with blackboards, students and teacher desks, and piano. While the museum is located in the 40 Mile Lighthouse Society Park, it is a separate entity with its own exhibits and budget.
Exhibits/Collections: Artifacts and information about Presque Isle County one-room schools.
Information may not be current.

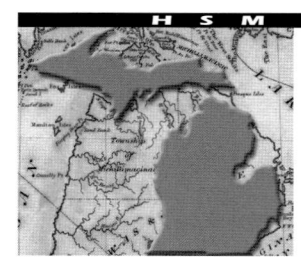

Millersburg Area Historical Society
Mailing Address: P.O. Box 30 • Millersburg, MI 49759
Contact: Virgil Freel, President
Phone: (989) 733-8210
Physical Location: 324 E. Luce St. • Millersburg, MI 49759
Hours: By appointment.
Admission: Free.
Visitor Accessibility: Free on-site parking. Wheelchair accessible. Tour guides available.
About: Preserves and celebrates the signifance of the depot as the main means of transportation and communication in the early years of the 20th century. Society showcases artifacts from the Millersburg area in the D&M Railroad Depot, the only depot remaining in Presque Isle County. Building currently under construction.
Exhibits/Collections: Photos of past residents, model of 1910 kitchen, artifacts, the Plat Book of Michigan (c.1909), and railroad memorabilia.
Annual Events: The MAHS Labor Day Homecoming, meetings 2nd Tue Apr-Oct, 7 p.m. at depot.
Publications: "Village of Millersburg 1901-2001."

Millington
(Tuscola County)

Millington-Arbela Historical Society
Mailing Address: P.O. Box 422 • Millington, MI 48746
E-Mail: millingtonarbelahistoricalsociety@hotmail.com
Phone: (989) 871-5508
Site/Location: **Millington-Arbela Historical Museum**
Physical Location: 8534 State St. (M-15 Heritage Route) • Millington, MI 48746
Hours: Apr-Dec: Fri-Sat 12-2 p.m. Also by appointment.
Admission: Free.
Visitor Accessibility: Free on-site and street parking. Partially wheelchair accessible. Tour guide available; special tours available with 24 hours notice.
About: The Millington-Arbela Historical Society mission statement is "preserving the past for the future" and is dedicated to preserving and displaying the Millington- and Arbela-area history for the public through pictures and artifacts so that citizens of tomorrow will learn of the area's yesterdays. As part of that mission, the society operates a museum and invites everyone to visit.
Exhibits/Collections: Native-American artifacts; old toys, tools, and radios; Edison record player; area veterans information; military uniforms and medals; Civil War artifacts; one-room schools; Millington yearbooks (1908-2011); obituaries; publications; agricultural tools.
Annual Events: Old-Fashioned Summer Festival, Christmas in the Village. Meetings Apr-Dec 2nd Thu monthly, 1 p.m. at the museum.
Publications: Quarterly membership newsletter. "Millington Township Cemetery," "Millington History (1854-2004) in Pictures," "Millington High School's First Hundred Years," "Annie."

Historical Society of Michigan

Mio
(Oscoda County)

Oscoda County Genealogical Society
Mailing Address: P.O. Box 15 • Mio, MI 48647
Phone: (989) 826-6741
Information may not be current.

Mohawk
(Keweenaw County)

Delaware Copper Mine Tours
Mailing Address: 7804 Delaware Mine Rd. • Mohawk, MI 49950
Contact: Lani Hendricks-Poynter, Owner/Manager
E-Mail: delminetourupmi@aol.com
Phone: (906) 289-4688 • *Fax:* (906) 289-4688
Physical Location: Off US-41, 12 miles south of Copper Harbor • Copper Harbor, MI 49918
Hours: May-Oct: Mon-Sun 10 a.m.-6 p.m.
Admission: $11/adult, $7/children (6-12).
Visitor Accessibility: Free parking. Not wheelchair accessible. Self-guided.
Website: http://delawarecopperminetours.com/
About: Dating back to 1847-1887, the Delaware Copper Mine relates the history of copper mining in the Keweenaw Peninsula. About 8 million pounds of copper were removed from the mine's five shafts, which reach a depth of 1,400 feet. The tour takes participants to the first level at 110 feet. Veins of pure copper and other geological points of interest are exposed in the walls of the mine.
Exhibits/Collections: Walking trails past mine ruins, and a small collection of mining artifacts and copper specimens.
Information may not be current.

Monroe
(Monroe County)

Genealogical Society of Monroe County
Mailing Address: P.O. Box 1428 • Monroe, MI 48161
Contact: Jim Ryland, Archivist
E-Mail: gsmcmi@gsmcmi.org
Website: www.gsmc-michigan.org
About: The society seeks to help genealogists research their ancestry in Monroe County and elsewhere. The society is currently transcribing vital records at the Monroe County courthouse, cemetery records, and local newspaper articles to make them more accessible to researchers. Archives are located on the second floor of the Monroe County Historical Museum, 126 S. Monroe Street in Monroe.
Exhibits/Collections: All Monroe County censuses on microfilm, county naturalizations, books from a variety of states and countries, and newsletters from various genealogical societies. The Betty Gay Collection. Access to Ancestry World.
Annual Events: Open House (Apr). Meetings held first Sat of each month with exceptions, 1 p.m. in Audrey M. Warrick Administration Building at Monroe County Community College.
Publications: See website for complete list of publications.

Immaculate Heart of Mary Archives
Mailing Address: 610 West Elm Ave. • Monroe, MI 48162
Contact: Donna Westley, Archivist
E-Mail: archives@ihmsisters.org
Phone: (734) 240-9695 • *Fax:* (734) 240-8328
Website: www.ihmsisters.org

Monroe County Historical Commission
Mailing Address: 126 S. Monroe St. • Monroe, MI 48161
Contact: Andrew Clark, Director
E-Mail: history@monroemi.org
Phone: 734-240-7780
Site/Location: **Monroe County Historical Museum**
Hours: Year-round: Wed-Sat 10 a.m.-5 p.m. Summer: Wed-Sat 10 a.m.-5 p.m.; Sun 12-5 p.m. Also by appointment.
Admission: Suggested donation of $4/adult, $2/children (6-17), 5 and under free.
Visitor Accessibility: Limited free on-site parking; metered street parking. Wheelchair accessible. Self-guided.
Website: http://historicmonroecounty.org/
About: The Monroe County Historical Museum focuses on the county of Monroe and its environs, along with Native Americans, early French inhabitants, life on Lake Erie and the River Raisin, Monroe County military history, George and Libbie Custer, and various aspects of Monroe County's history.
Exhibits/Collections: Manuscript collection, genealogical materials on Monroe County residents, research materials on War of 1812 and General George A. Custer. Artifacts and archives related to the development of southeast Michigan.
Annual Events: Maple Syrup Days, Fur Trade Days, Lantern Tours, Christmas Tree Festival. Commission meetings 1st Wed monthly, 7 p.m. at Monroe County Historical Museum.
Publications: Electronic newsletter (Monroe Muse). A variety of pamphlets and booklets relating to the history of Monroe County. *Other Sites/Locations:* **Navarre-Anderson Trading Post Complex** • Location: 3775 N. Custer, Monroe, MI 48162 • Hours: Seasonal and by appointment • Admission: Donations accepted • Visitor Accessibility: Free on-site parking. Partially wheelchair accessible; ramps for some but not all of the buildings. Self-guided. • An original, circa 1790s French-Canadian-built building, the Navarre-Anderson Tading Post was moved to its current site on the River Raisin as part of a French "ribbon" farm and is one of two original buildings. It has been interpreted as a French fur-trade business and home, as it had been used. Reproduction items are used in display. The Navarre-Morris cabin (circa 1810) is interpreted next to the trading post as a French summer kitchen.
Eby Log House • Location: 3775 S. Custer, Monroe, MI 48161 • Hours: Open during Monroe County Fair (end of Jul, beginning of Aug) • Admission: Free, although fair admission is required • Visitor Accessibility: Not wheelchair accessible. Self-guided. • The Eby Log House belonged to the Eby family and dates back to the late 1850s.
Martha Barker Country Store Museum • Location: 3815 N. Custer Road, Monroe, MI 48162 • Hours: Seasonal • Admission: Donations accepted • Visitor Accessibility: Free on-site parking. Wheelchair accessible. Self-guided. • Located in the former one-room Papermill School (1860s-1962), the Martha Barker Country Store Museum features a collection of circa 1910 local mercantile objects. The site is part of a complex with the Navarre-Anderson Trading Post site and supplies the parking lot for both sites.
Monroe County Vietnam Veterans Museum • Location: Visitor Center at Norman Heck Park, North Dixie Highway, Monroe, MI • Hours: May-Sep: Wed and Sat 12-4 p.m. Admission: Donations accepted • Visitor Accessibility: On-site parking. Wheelchair accessible. Group tours available by appointment; call (734) 240-7780. • Staffed by Monroe County Vietnam War veterans, this museum displays more than 1,500 original artifacts, including news releases; stories of local soldiers, sailors and airmen; magazines articles; medals/ribbons; models; dioramas; local Vietnamese artifacts; and military uniforms from the Vietnam War.
Information may not be current.

Monroe County Labor History Museum
Mailing Address: 41 W. Front St. • Monroe, MI 48161
E-Mail: lwconnerjr@mail.com
Phone: (734) 693-0446 • *Fax:* (734) 850-4217
Hours: Mon-Fri 8 a.m.-5 p.m.; Sat-Sun by appointment.
Admission: Free.
Visitor Accessibility: On-site and street parking. Wheelchair accessible. Free tour guide available.
Website: http://www.monroelabor.org/
About: Museum in one of only two CIO halls in Michigan. Dedicated by Walter Reuther in 1947. Seeks to educate about struggles and successes of organized labor movement. Visitors will experience what a working union hall looked like in the 1940s.
Exhibits/Collections: Desk from Chicago office of Industrial Workers of the World. Collection of union buttons, contracts, meeting minutes. Collection of documents of 1937 Newton Steel Strike in Monroe, library of labor related books.
Annual Events: Labor Day activities. Meetings 1st Mon of month 6 p.m. in museum.
*Information may not be current.

Monroe County Library System
Mailing Address: 840 S. Roesslur Street • Monroe, MI 48161
Contact: Nancy Bellaire, Director
Phone: (734) 241-5770 • *Fax:* (734) 241-4722
Website: www.monroe.lib.mi.us
Exhibits/Collections: Custer Collection, federal and state government documents, genealogy resources, art for loan, Michigan collection, local history collection.
Annual Events: Custer Week Celebrations.

Monroe Historic District Commission
HSM MEMBER
Mailing Address: c/o Jeffrey Green, 120 E. First St. • Monroe, MI 48161
Contact: Jeffrey Green
E-Mail: jlgreen@ci.monroe.mi.us
Phone: (734) 384-9106
*Information may not be current.

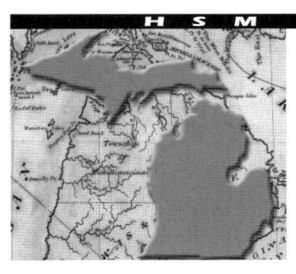

River Raisin National Battlefield Park
HSM MEMBER
Mailing Address: 1403 E. Elm Ave. • Monroe, MI 48162
Contact: Scott Bentley, Superintendent
E-Mail: scott_bentley@nps.gov
Phone: (734) 243-7136
Fax: (734) 244-5501
Hours: Visitor Center: 10 a.m.-5 p.m. Grounds: Sunrise to sunset.
Admission: Free.
Visitor Accessibility: On-site parking. Wheelchair accessible. Tour guide available by appointment.
Website: www.nps.gov/RIRA
About: The River Raisin National Battlefield Park preserves, commemorates, and interprets the January 1813 battles of the War of 1812 and their aftermath. The battlefield interprets the multi-national battle for supremacy or survival and the many different cultures involved in the land campaigns in the Old Northwest during the War of 1812.
Exhibits/Collections: Visitor center includes exhibits, artwork, orientation map, and gift shop. The battlefield has an accessible walking trail featuring interpretive signs, a picnic area, covered pavilion, and secondary loop and heritage trails.
Annual Events: Battle Commemoration (Jan), Open House (May).
Publications: Brochures and children's pamphlets on site.

Montague
(Muskegon County)

Montague Museum
Mailing Address: c/o Montague City Hall, 8778 Ferry St. • Montague, MI 49437
Contact: Sally McLouth, President
Phone: (231) 893-1155
Physical Location: 8717 Meade Street • Montague, MI 49437
Hours: Memorial Day-Labor Day: Sat-Sun 1-5 p.m. Also by appointment.
Admission: Free.
Visitor Accessibility: Free on-site parking. Not wheelchair accessible. Tour guide available.
Website: www.cityofmontague.org/museum.html
About: The Montague Museum shares state and local history through exhibits about the local industry, military, music, and Native-American history. Highlights include a local Miss America, doctor's and dentist's offices, and more. Displays include Lumber Era on White River and White Lake, local farming tools and pictures, military guns and clothing, Admiral Byrd's South Pole Explorations, Montague's 1961 Miss America, Nancy Ann Fleming, local art, photo collections, fire and police equipment, post office, and an Indian room.
Exhibits/Collections: Family records, doctor's notes, dentist books, museum organizational records, a 100-year record of local newspapers, maps, guides to historical housing and Indian sites, etc.

Montrose
(Genesee County)

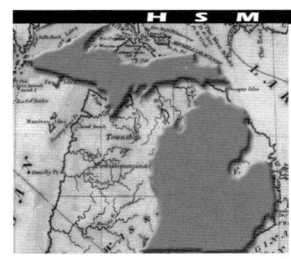

Montrose Historical & Telephone Pioneer Museum
HSM MEMBER
Mailing Address: P.O. Box 577 • Montrose, MI 48457
Contact: Joe Follett
E-Mail: staff@montrosemuseum.com
Phone: (810) 639-6644
Fax: (810) 639-6644
Physical Location: 144 East Hickory Street • Montrose, MI 48457
Hours: Sun 1-5 p.m., Mon-Tue 9:30 a.m.-3:30 p.m.
Admission: Free admission. Group tours: $2/adult, children free.
Visitor Accessibility: Free on-site and street parking. Wheelchair accessible. Guided tours available.
Website: www.montrosemuseum.com
About: Opened in 1980, the building was originally the telephone office for the Public Telephone Company and serves as both a local area and telephone museum. Hands-on working exhibits of antique telephone equipment and historical center for the area. More than 500 telephones from the 1800s to the present are on display, local history exhibits, rotating displays on loan from individual collections, and genealogy research.
Exhibits/Collections: Genealogy room with more than 12,500 entries in archives. Collection of local artifacts. Telephones and telephone equipment.
Annual Events: Blueberry Festival (3rd weekend Aug).
Publications: Newsletter (Memory Lane Gazette).

✤ Historical Society of Michigan

Mount Clemens
(Macomb County)

Macomb County Genealogy Group
Mailing Address: c/o Mount Clemens Public Library, 150 Cass Ave. • Mount Clemens, MI 48043
Contact: Ann Faulkner, Chairperson
E-Mail: macombcogg@gmail.com
Phone: 586-469-6200
Hours: Mon-Thu 9 a.m.-9 p.m., Fri 9 a.m.-5 p.m., school year Sat 9 a.m.-5 p.m., summer 9 a.m.-1 p.m.
Visitor Accessibility: Wheelchair accessible. Parking in lot.
Website: www.rootsweb.ancestry.com-mimcgg/
About: Assists members and others in researching their family history. Provides genealogical volunteers for the library, abstracts local records, and indexes local records for the library website.
Exhibits/Collections: Held at Mount Clemens Public Library.
Annual Events: Annual Genealogy Book Auction (Jun). Meetings bimonthly Fri 1 p.m., Sep-Jun 2nd Wed, 7 p.m. at Mount Clemens Public Library.
Publications: "Macomb County Genealogy Group Heritage Cookbook," "Knight, Chase and Allied Families," "Transcription of Sterling Grove Cemetery," "The Monforte Letters: Correspondence."

Macomb County Historic Commission
Mailing Address: 1 S. Main St., 7th Floor • Mount Clemens, MI 48043
Contact: Alan Naldrett, Vice-Chair
E-Mail: macombhistory@yahoo.com
Phone: (586) 469-6787
Hours: Hours: Mon-Fri 8:30 a.m.-5 p.m.
Website: www.macombcountymi.gov/historicalcommission
About: Seeks to procure, protect, preserve, and promote the historical resources and legacy of Macomb County.
Information may not be current.

Macomb County Historical Society
Mailing Address: 15 Union St. • Mount Clemens, MI 48043
Contact: Kim Parr, Director
E-Mail: crockerhousemuseum@sbcglobal.net
Phone: (586) 465-2488
Fax: (586) 465-2932
Site/Location: Crocker House Museum
Hours: Mar-Dec: Tue-Thu 10 a.m.-4 p.m., 1st Sun monthly 1-4 p.m. Closed holidays.
Admission: $4/adult, $2/child suggested donation.
Visitor Accessibility: Metered city parking lot, free street parking. Not wheelchair accessible. Guided tours only.
Website: www.crockerhousemuseum.com
About: The Macomb County Historical Society collects and preserves the area's local heritage to instill an appreciation of the community's unique history. An 1869 Italianate, the Crocker House Museum offers a late-Victorian home-life experience reminiscent of the world-renowned Mineral Bath Era of Mount Clemens in Macomb County. This home housed the first two mayors of Mount Clemens and later offered gambling and lunch room.
Exhibits/Collections: Museum collection consists of domestic artifacts and clothing ranging from the early 1800s-1911; Mount Clemens and Macomb County artifacts; local military artifacts; and Bath Era artifacts.
Annual Events: Garden Walk (Jun), Members Annual Meeting and Picnic (Jul), Cemetery Walk and Funeral Tea (Oct), Tuesday Tea Talks at Two, Mount Clemens Heritage Holiday (Dec).
Publications: "Along the Huron: The Letters of Father Pierre Degian 1825-1826," "Missionary Priest of Macomb County, Christian Clemens," "The Founder of Mount Clemens," "Crocker Chronicle: The History of Crocker House," "Depression Days in Mount Clemens," "The Pocket Diary of Robert Warner."
Other Sites/Locations: Sabin Crocker Library • Location: 36 Byron Street, Mount Clemens, MI 48043 • Hours: Available only through appointment • The Sabin Crocker Library contains local city directories, atlases, local books for historical reference, scrapbooks, films, and photographs. Genealogical files are held at the Mount Clemens Public Library.

Michigan Transit Museum
Mailing Address: P.O. Box 12 • Mount Clemens, MI 48046
Contact: Gary J. Michaels, Secretary
E-Mail: mtm1973@juno.com
Phone: 586-463-1863
Physical Location: 200 Grand Avenue • Mount Clemens, MI 48043
Hours: Sat-Sun 1-4 p.m. Train rides also offered Sun (Jun-Oct).
Admission: Donations accepted. Train rides $7/adult, $4/child.
Visitor Accessibility: Free on-site parking. Wheelchair accessible. Train rides not wheelchair accessible. Tour guide available; reservations can be made for special times and dates.
Website: www.michigantransitmuseum.org
About: One of the original Grand Trunk Railway stations, the Mount Clemens Depot originally opened for business November 21, 1859. Today, it is home to the Michigan Transit Museum, which is dedicated to the preservation of the history and legacy of railways, streetcars, and electric interurbans in Southeastern Michigan.
Exhibits/Collections: Full-size locomotives, freight cars, electric trolleys, rapid transit cars. Railroad-related archival collection.
Annual Events: Holiday Express Train Rides (Dec), Mount Clemens Heritage Holiday (Dec). Meetings 2nd Wed monthly, 8 p.m. at museum.
Publications: Monthly newsletter (The Michigan Transit Gazette).
Other Sites/Locations: Train Excursions at Joy Park • Location: Joy Boulevard, Clinton Township, MI 48036 • Train Schedule: Jun-Oct: Sun 1-4 p.m. Train departs on the hour; trip takes about 30-40 minutes. • Admission: $7/adult, $4/children • Attractions include one mile of historic railway track, first laid down in 1902, of the former Mount Clemens Sugar Company.

Mount Clemens Historic Commission
Mailing Address: 38 Washington • Mount Clemens, MI 48043
Contact: John Murphy
E-Mail: cityboymurphy@hotmail.com
Information may not be current.

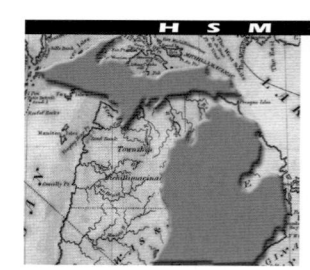

Mount Clemens Public Library
Mailing Address: 150 Cass Ave. • Mount Clemens, MI 48043
Contact: Deborah Larsen, Assistant Director
E-Mail: askmcpl@libcoop.net
Phone: (586) 469-6200
Fax: (586) 469-6668

Website: www.mtclib.org

Exhibits/Collections: The Mount Clemens Public Library houses a local history room with infomation on area and mineral bath history.

Society of Automotive Historians/ Henry M. Leland Chapter/MI

Mailing Address: P.O. Box 46024 • Mount Clemens, MI 48046
Contact: Victoria Mobley, Secretary/Treasurer
E-Mail: vmobley@wowway.com
Phone: 586/246-0312
Fax: 586/493-1953
Website: www.autohistory.org

About: The Society of Automotive Historians (SAH) actively pursues the recording, preservation, and study of cars, trucks, their technology, and the people who have contributed to that history. Founded in 1969, the national organization is devoted to all facets of automotive history, including engineering, design, economics, the lives of automotive pioneers and innovators, motorsports, the integration of motor vehicles into modern life, and culture of cars. The local Henry M. Leland Chapter in Michigan is one of the more active chapters.

Annual Events: Annual meeting/awards banquet in conjunction with the Antique Automobile Club of America's National Fall Meet in Hershey, PA, each Oct.

Publications: National SAH membership: Bimonthly SAH Journal, Automotive History Review, and Biennial Membership Directory.

Mount Pleasant
(Isabella County)

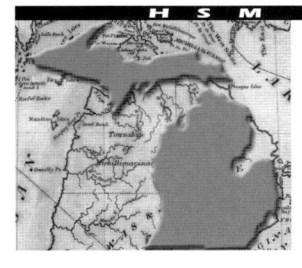

Clarke Historical Library

Mailing Address: Central Michigan University Library, Park 142 • Mount Pleasant, MI 48859
Contact: Frank Boles, Director
E-Mail: clarke@cmich.edu
Phone: (989) 774-3352
Fax: (989) 774-2160

Physical Location: First Floor, Charles V. Park Library, Central Michigan University • Mt. Pleasant, MI 48043
Hours: Mon-Fri 8 a.m.-5 p.m.
Admission: Free.
Visitor Accessibility: Metered parking. Wheelchair accessible.
Website: www.clarke.cmich.edu

About: Clarke Library is the special collections unit of Central Michigan University Libraries. The 1,200-sqaure-foot exhibit gallery features two exhibits each year. Each exhibit highlights some aspect of the library's collection.

Exhibits/Collections: Comprehensive printed collection regarding state of Michigan and Michigan history. Archives focus primarily on the geographic region north of Lansing, south of Mackinaw. Library also serves as archives for CMU.

Publications: Biannual Michigan Historical Review published in cooperation with Historical Society of Michigan. Available to HSM members.

Genealogical Society of Isabella County

Mailing Address: P.O. Box 117 • Mount Pleasant, MI 48804
Contact: Tammy L. Prout, President
E-Mail: tlcp77@hotmail.com
Phone: (989) 433-5507
Website: http://isabellagenealogy.org

About: The society seeks to preserve and organize Isabella County-area genealogical data, to encourage and assist the study of family history, and to promote continued interest in genealogical work.

Exhibits/Collections: Historical/genealogical displays in the foyer of the county building, Displays change every quarter.

Annual Events: Isabella County Youth and Family Farm Fair (Jul). Meetings 2nd Thu Mar-Dec, at 7pm.

Publications: Quarterly newsletter. See website for complete list of publications.

Michigan Barn Preservation Network

Mailing Address: P.O. Box 614 • Mount Pleasant, MI 48804
E-Mail: vera@wiltse.com
Phone: (989) 465-1216 • *Fax:* 989-465-9291
Website: www.mibarn.net

About: Active statewide organization of barn owners and enthusiasts. Committed to rehabilitation of barns for agricultural, commercial, residential, and public uses. Educational resource for barn restoration and preservation.

Publications: Triannual newsletter.

Information may not be current.

Mount Pleasant Area Historical Society

Mailing Address: P.O. Box 107 • Mount Pleasant, MI 48804
Contact: Jack Westbrook, President
E-Mail: mtpleasantmiareahistoricalsociety@charter.net
Phone: (989) 854-4409
Fax: (989) 773-5741

Physical Location: Isabella County Building, 200 N. Main St. • Mount Pleasant, MI 48858
Website: http://www.mifamilyhistory.org/isabella/MPHistoricalSociety/

About: The Mount Pleasant Area Historical Society brings together people interested in the history and heritage of the city of Mount Pleasant and Isabella County. The society aims to educate and collect any material which may help to record or illustrate the history of the region. The society maintains rotating exhibits pertaining to the county's history.

Exhibits/Collections: Scrapbooks, newspapers, photographs, vintage clothing, and microfilm of newspaper accounts of area servicemen (1940-1965).

Annual Events: Annual Isabella County Founder's Day (Feb). Meetings 1st Tue monthly, 7 p.m. at Isabella County Commission on Aging (2200 South Lincoln Road, Mt. Pleasant).

Publications: Quarterly newsletter (Looking at Mt. Pleasant), "The Elizabeth Hursh Story," "Isabella County: 150 Years in the Making."

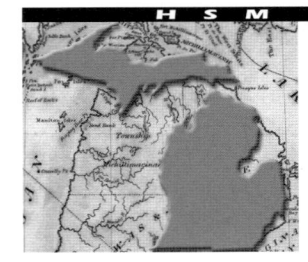

Museum of Cultural & Natural History

Mailing Address: Central Michigan University, 103 Rowe Hall • Mount Pleasant, MI 48859
Contact: Dr. Jay Martin, Director
E-Mail: cmuseum@cmich.edu
Phone: (989) 774-3829

Fax: (989) 774-2612
Hours: Mon-Fri 8 a.m.-5 p.m.; Sat-Sun 1-5 p.m.
Admission: $1/adult suggested donation, $.50/child suggested donation.
Visitor Accessibility: Street parking for a fee. Wheelchair accessible. Tours are available by reservation only.
Website: www.museum.cmich.edu

About: A unit of Central Michigan University, the Museum of Cultural & Natural History features exhibits relating to pre-historic glaciers and mastodons, Native Americans and fur traders, Civil War soldiers and lumbermen, and wildlife, including bats and walleye.
Exhibits/Collections: 13,000 artifacts focused on regional history from the middle of the 1800s on. Michigan's lumbering and pioneering periods. Full range of articles used in everyday life, including bottles, phonograph records, clothing, and woodworking tools.
Annual Events: Tour Tuesdays (Jul).
Other Sites/Locations: **1901 Bohannon Schoolhouse** • Location: Corner of West Campus Drive and Preston Street • Hours: By appointment • Admission: Free • Site Information: Parking in lot 22. Wheelchair accessible. • The restored 1901 Bohannon Schoolhouse is open by appointment for tours conducted by CMU students studying museum studies and/or public history.
*Information may not be current.

Ziibiwing Center of Anishinabe Culture & Lifeways
Mailing Address: Saginaw Chippewa Indian Tribe of Michigan, 6650 E. Broadway • Mount Pleasant, MI 48858
Contact: Shannon Martin, Director
E-Mail: ggenereaux@sagchip.org
Phone: (989) 775-4750
Fax: (989) 775-4770
Hours: Mon-Sat 10 a.m.-6 p.m.
Admission: $6.50/adult, $3.75/senior, $4.50/student, $3.75/children (5-17), children 4 and under free.
Visitor Accessibility: On-site parking. Wheelchair accessible. Docents available; group tours of 10 or more at no extra cost.
Website: http://www.sagchip.org/ziibiwing/

About: The Ziibiwing Center of Anishinabe Culture & Lifeways is an American-Indian museum that includes the permanent exhibit "Diba Jimooyung" (Telling Our Story), changing exhibit areas, collections storage area, and research center.
Exhibits/Collections: Collection of artifacts and artwork, primarily from Great Lakes Anishinabek, numbering more than 2,000 pieces. Treaty documents, Saginaw Chippewa historical material, photographs.
Annual Events: American Indian Dance (Jul), Native Fest (Jul), Pow Wow (Jul).
Publications: Electronic newsletter (E-Noodaagen), "Diba Jimooyung: Telling Our Story."

Munising
(Alger County)

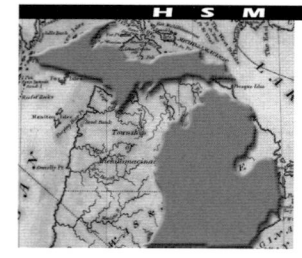

Alger County Historical Society
Mailing Address: 1496 Washington St. • Munising, MI 49862
Contact: Barbara Hermann, President
E-Mail: algerchs@jamadots.com
Phone: (906) 387-4308
Fax: (906) 387-4188
Hours: Mon-Thu 1-4:30 p.m., Fri 2:30-8 p.m., Sat 9 a.m.-5 p.m.
Admission: Donations accepted.
Visitor Accessibility: On-site parking. Wheelchair accessible.
About: In 1993, the Alger County Historical Society opened its heritage center in the former Washington Grade School. Exhibits cover history of Grand Island and the Grand Island Recreation Area, Munising Woodenware Company, barn building, homemaking, Native Americans, and sauna. There is also a fur trader's cabin and blacksmith shop on site.
Exhibits/Collections: Fay Swanberg Archive Room. Father Emil Beyer collection of pictures and scrapbooks. "Munising News" newspapers from 1900-present; historic photos of families, businesses, organizations, government; oral history tapes; several state/county/city records.
Annual Events: Breakfast By the Bay (Jul), Alger Women's Roll of Honor (Aug), ACHS Annual Dinner (May). Meetings 1st Mon monthly, 6:30 p.m. at museum.
Publications: Quarterly newsletter, "Alger County Centennial History."

Muskegon
(Muskegon County)

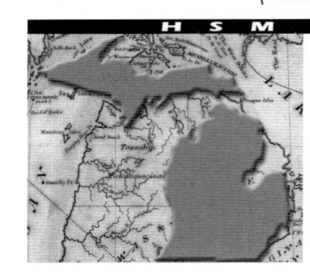

Hackley Public Library
Mailing Address: Genealogy & Local History Collection, 316 W. Webster Ave. • Muskegon, MI 49440
Contact: Mary Ferriby, Director
Phone: (231) 722-7276
Fax: (231) 726-5567
Hours: Mon-Tue 12-8 p.m. Wed-Sat 10 a.m.-5 p.m.
Admission: Free.
Visitor Accessibility: On-site and street parking. Wheelchair entrance in back. Free tour guide available by appointment.
Website: www.hackleylibrary.org

About: To inform, inspire, and delight the community by providing information, knowledge, literature, technology, and traditional innovative programs. Building contains stained glass windows, Romanesque architecture, murals, facsimile edition of The Book of Kells, and paintings.
Exhibits/Collections: Special collections: Civil War and 19th-century materials, genealogy and local history collections, Muskegon Chronicle (microfilm collection from 1869 to present), city directories (1873 to present), digital collection, Muskegon images.
Annual Events: Book sale, Hackley Lecture. See website for meetings.

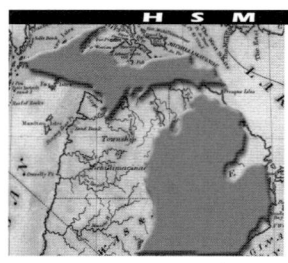

Lakeshore Museum Center
Mailing Address: 430 W. Clay Ave. • Muskegon, MI 49440
Contact: John H. McGarry III, Chief Executive Officer
E-Mail: info@lakeshoremuseum.org
Phone: (231) 722-0278
Fax: (231) 728-4119
Hours: Mon-Fri 9:30 a.m.-4:30 p.m., Sat-Sun 12-4 p.m.
Admission: Free.
Visitor Accessibility: Free on-site and street parking. Wheelchair accessible. Self-guided.
Website: www.lakeshoremuseum.org

About: The Lakeshore Museum Center preserves and interprets natural and cultural history of Muskegon County through exhibits, education, and programs. Permanent exhibits include "Michigan: from the Depths of Time," "Coming to the Lakes," "Habitat Gallery," and

"Body Works." Two hands-on galleries are available. "Michigan Through the Depths of Time" takes visitors on a 400-million-year journey beginning under the sea, through the ice age to today's Great Lakes state.

Exhibits/Collections: 10,000 photographs; newspaper articles; business, organization, and resident records; books; tax records; plat maps; and various directories pertaining to Muskegon County. Series of essays and photos are available on website.

Annual Events: Lumber Barons' Ball (Oct). Board of trustees meeting 4th Mon monthly in the center's auditorium.

Publications: Bimonthly newsletter (The Muser). "Hackley and Hume Historic Site: A Photographic History."

Other Sites/Locations: **Hackley and Hume Historic Site** • Location: 484 W. Webster Ave., Muskegon, MI 49440 • Hours: May-Oct: Wed-Sun 12-4p.m. Special holiday tours are offered between Thanksgiving and New Year's Day. • Admission: $5/adult, Children 12 and under are free. Admission is free for all guests during the month of October. • Visitor Accessibility: Free on-site and street parking. Not wheelchair accessible. Tour guide available; appointment required for groups of 10 or more. • The restored homes of Muskegon's most famous lumber barons, Charles H. Hackley and Thomas Hume, are two of the finest examples of Queen Anne-style Victorian homes in the country. Built in the late 1800s, they feature lavish woodcarvings, stenciling, stained glass windows, and period furnishings. Tours of the homes last approximately 1 1/4 hours.

The Scolnik House of the Depression Era • Location: 504 W. Clay Ave., Muskegon, MI 49440 • Hours: May-Oct: Wed-Sun 12-4 p.m. Special holiday tours are offered between Thanksgiving and New Year's. • Admission: Free • Visitor Accessibility: Free street parking. Not wheelchair accessible. Self-guided. • The Scolnik House of the Depression Era tells the story of common families living during the Great Depression. A fictional Polish Catholic family owns the two-story home and shares it with a young fictional Polish Jewish family that lives on the second floor. The house was built in the late 1880s in classic Queen Anne-inspired Folk Victorian style. The home features period furnishings, appliances, flooring, and wallpaper.

Fire Barn Museum • Location: 510 W. Clay Ave., Muskegon, MI 49440 • Hours: May-Oct: Wed-Sun 12-4 p.m. Special holiday tours are offered between Thanksgiving and New Year's. • Admission: Free • Visitor Accessibility: Free street parking. Partially wheelchair accessible; first floor only. Self-guided. • The Fire Barn Museum is a replica of the Hackley Hose Company No. 2, which was formed in 1875 after the city experienced several devastating fires. Artifacts on display include a 1923 LaFrance Class B Pumper Truck, hose carts, hooks and ladders, alarm and call box systems, uniforms, and photographs of local fires. The second floor features a uniform display and the living quarters of early firefighters.

Muskegon County Genealogical Society
Mailing Address: Torrent House, 315 W. Webster Ave. • Muskegon, MI 49440
Contact: Dawn Kelley, President
E-Mail: 1972mcgs@gmail.com
Phone: (231) 722-7276 x233
Hours: Mon-Sat: 10 a.m.- 5 p.m.
Admission: Free.
Visitor Accessibility: Free street and lot parking. Wheelchair accessible.
Website: www.genealogymuskegon.org
About: Founded 1972. Assists members and friends of society in the compilation of family histories and genealogical investigation. Carries on genealogical projects. Helps locate, preserve, produce, and deposit records of value to the genealogical community in the Hackley Public Library.
Annual Events: Family History Genealogy Workshops 2nd Sat (Jan-May, Sep-Nov) from 10:30 a.m-12:30 p.m. and 2-4 p.m. at the Torrent House. Meetings 2nd Thu monthly (except Jul, Dec), VFW Post 3195, 5209 Grand Haven Rd., Muskegon, MI 49441
Publications: Newsletter (Twig Talk).

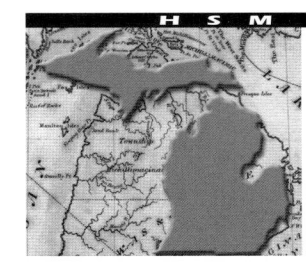

Muskegon County Historical Society
Mailing Address: 173 E. Apple Ave. • Muskegon, MI 49442
Contact: Mark Fairchild
E-Mail: fairchildma@co.muskegon.mi.us
Phone: (231) 724-6245
Information may not be current.

Muskegon Heritage Association
Mailing Address: 561 W. Western Ave. • Muskegon, MI 49440
Contact: Jim Funnell, President
E-Mail: info@muskegonheritage.org
Phone: (231) 722-1363
Site/Location: **Muskegon Heritage Museum**
Hours: Mid-May to mid-Oct: Thu-Sat 11 a.m.-4 p.m. Also by appointment.
Admission: $4/adult, $2/student, children 5 and under/MHA members free. Group rates available.
Visitor Accessibility: On-site and street parking. Wheelchair accessible. Group and special tours by appointment.
Website: www.muskegonheritage.org
About: The Muskegon Heritage Museum exhibits focus on companies that made Muskegon an industrial capital, as well as logging, foundries, and manufacturing industries. Highlights include a working Corliss Valve Steam Engine from the 1890s, operating Brunswick Bowling Alley and Automatic Pinsetter, Made in Muskegon exhibit, historical homes exhibit, and a walking tour brochure of the surrounding area near the museum.
Annual Events: Bike Time (Jul).
Publications: Muskegon's Industries.

Muskegon Historic District Commission
Mailing Address: 933 Terrace St., P.O. Box 536 • Muskegon, MI 49443
Contact: Mike Franzak, HDC Staff Liaison
Phone: (231) 724-6702 • *Fax:* (231) 724-6790
Physical Location: 933 Terrace St. • Muskegon, MI 49443
Hours: Mon-Fri 8:30 a.m.-5 p.m.
Website: www.shorelinecity.com
About: Evaluates applications for new construction, rehabilitation, additions, and demolitions of structures within historic districts.
Annual Events: Meetings 1st Tue of month, 4 p.m. in city council chambers, Muskegon City Hall, 933 Terrace, Muskegon, MI 49443.

Muskegon Railroad Historical Society
Mailing Address: 561 W. Western Ave. • Muskegon, MI 49440
Phone: (231) 726-3657
Hours: Tue 7-9 p.m., Sat 10 a.m.-2 p.m.
Website: www.mrhs-online.org
About: Organized 1982. Focus on Muskegon County and Michigan railroads. Museum collection; library; and N-, HO-, and O-gauge layouts.
Exhibits/Collections: Railroad artifacts and pictures. Library of more than 800 books, 550 videos, and railroad reference materials.
Annual Events: Fall and spring railroad shows.
Publications: Monthly newsletter (MRHS Mainline).
Information may not be current.

✤ Historical Society of Michigan

S.S. Milwaukee Clipper Preservation, Inc.
Mailing Address: P.O. Box 1370 • Muskegon, MI 49443
Contact: Ray Hilt, Museum Curator
E-Mail: milwaulkeeclipper@gmail.com
Phone: (231) 683-1590
Physical Location: 2098 Lakeshore Drive • Muskegon, MI 49441
Hours: Memorial Day-Labor Day Sat-Sun 12 p.m.-5 p.m.
Admission: $7/adult, $5/student, children under 5 are free. Groups tours by appointment.
Visitor Accessibility: Ship not wheelchair accessible. Museum wheelchair accessible.
Website: www.milwaukeeclipper.com
About: The Milwaukee Clipper is a 110-year-old National Historic Landmark and nonprofit, the last large American passenger steamship left on the Great Lakes. Visitors will see how people traveled in a steam boat in the 20th century and learn about historic Great Lakes shipping.
Exhibits/Collections: Archival collection (currently being catalogued), large collection of Great Lakes material.
Annual Events: Auction/Brunch Fundraiser (May).
Publications: Quarterly newsletter.

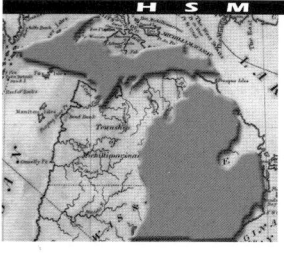

USS LST 393 Preservation Association
Mailing Address: 506 Mart St. • Muskegon, MI 49440
Contact: John Stephenson, President
E-Mail: info@lst393.org
Phone: (231) 730-1477
Fax: (231) 722-0016
Site/Location: USS LST 393 Veterans Museum
Hours: May-Oct 1: 10 a.m.-5 p.m. Open daily.
Admission: $9/adult, $6/student.
Visitor Accessibility: Free parking. Partially wheelchair accessible; main deck only. Free tour guides available.
Website: www.lst393.org
About: The USS LST 393 Preservation Association preserves USS LST 393, provides a museum on board of the ship to honor those who served in America's armed forces and educate the public about their legacy, provides educational programs for students and the general public, and honors all Americans from all branches of the service and all time eras.
Exhibits/Collections: Restored WWII USS LST 393 (350-foot landing ship tank). Artifacts from all wars and services. Books and documents relating to ships in WWII service.
Annual Events: Armed Forces Day Celebration, 4th of July Celebration. Veteran's Day Fair. Monthly meetings aboard ship.

USS Silversides Submarine Museum
Mailing Address: 1346 Bluff St. • Muskegon, MI 49441
Contact: Russel Gallas, Executive Director
E-Mail: contactus@silversidesmuseum.org
Phone: 231-755-1230
Fax: (231) 755-5883
Hours: Jun-Aug: Daily 10 a.m.-5:30 p.m.; Sep-May: Sun-Thu 10 a.m.-4 p.m., Fri-Sat 10 a.m.-4 p.m.
Admission: $15/adult, $12.50/senior, $10.50/children (5-18). WWII Veterans, Active Duty, and Children 4 and under are free.
Visitor Accessibility: Free on-site parking. Wheelchair accessible. Tour guide available during portions of the year.
Website: www.silversidesmuseum.org
About: The USS Silversides Submarine Museum honors the men and women of the military, preserves military history, and provides experiences that educate the public about past and present military history and technology. Self-guided tours of the USS Silversides Submarine Museum allow visitors to see what it was like to serve aboard the World War II submarine USS Silversides. Guests can visit the deck topside as well as the major internal compartments below deck.
Exhibits/Collections: Naval objects and archives. Maritime objects.
Annual Events: Lost Boat Ceremony (May).

Muskegon Heights
(Muskegon County)

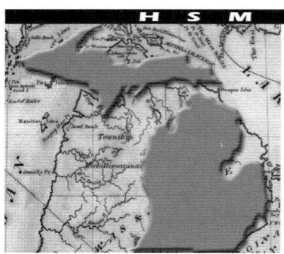

James Jackson Museum of African American History
Mailing Address: PO Box 4582 • Muskegon Heights, MI 49444
E-Mail: Ja2Jck@aol.com
Phone: (231) 739-9500
Fax: (231) 739-5574
Physical Location: 7 East Center Street • Muskegon Heights, MI 49444
Hours: Mon-Sat 3-5:30 p.m.
Admission: Free.
Visitor Accessibility: Street parking.
About: The James Jackson Museum of African American History educates the public about African-American history through exhibits, DVDs, films, literature, etc.
*Information may not be current.

Naubinway
(Mackinac County)

Top of the Lake Snowmobile Museum
Mailing Address: P.O. Box 2 • Naubinway, MI 49762
Contact: Charlie Vallier, Chairperson
E-Mail: info@snowmobilemuseum.com
Phone: (906) 477-6298
Physical Location: W11660 US-2 • Naubinway, MI 49762
Hours: Open daily 9 a.m.-5 p.m., closed Tue.
Admission: $5/adult, children 16 and under free.
Visitor Accessibility: Free on-site parking. Wheelchair accessible. Tour guide available; call ahead for group tours.
Website: www.snowmobilemuseum.com
About: The museum preserves and displays the history of snowmobiling. Ranked #1 of "13 Great Snowmobile Museums in North America." There are 83 vintage and antique snowmobiles on display. Displays include 8 machines, 12 vintage racing machines, 6 machines manufactured outside of the United States, accessories, and huge two-man chainsaw with a curious connection to snowmobiles.
Exhibits/Collections: Snowmobiles, advertising materials, equipment (suits, helmets), signs, and printed resources on history of snowmobiling.
Annual Events: Snowmobile Show & Ride (Feb), Swap Meet and Auction (Sep). Quarterly meetings held in the museum's meeting room.
Publications: Binannual newsletter.

Negaunee
(Marquette County)

Michigan Iron Industry Museum
Mailing Address: 73 Forge Road • Negaunee, MI 49866
Contact: Barry C. James, Historian
E-Mail: jamesb@michigan.gov
Phone: 906-475-7857
Fax: 906-475-9221
Physical Location: US 41 East (1 mile west of M-35)
Hours: May-Oct: Daily 9:30 a.m.-4:30 p.m.; Nov-Apr Mon-Fri 9:30 a.m.-4 p.m. Winter hours: Call or see website.
Admission: Free. Film costs $1/individual, children 5 and under free.
Visitor Accessibility: Free on-site parking. Wheelchair accessible. Self-guided.
Website: www.michigan.gov/ironindustrymuseum
About: The Iron Industry Museum builds programs and alliances that preserve and interpret Michigan's past and help people discover, enjoy, and find inspiration in their heritage. The museum overlooks the Carp River Forge, the first iron forge in the Lake Superior region, and interprets Michigan's rich iron mining heritage through exhibits, audio visual programs, and outdoor interpretive trails.
Exhibits/Collections: Emphasis on Michigan iron mining and communities.
Annual Events: Museum Open House (May); Iron, Steel, and the Automobilie: Antique Automobile Exhibit (Jun). Advisory board meets bimonthly at museum.
Publications: "No Tears in Heaven: The 1926 Barnes-Hecker Mine Disaster."

Negaunee Historical Society & Museum
Mailing Address: P.O. Box 221 • Negaunee, MI 49866
Contact: Virginia Paulson, President
Phone: (906) 475-4614
Physical Location: 303 East Main St. • Negaunee, MI 49866
Hours: June 1-Labor Day: Mon-Sat 10 a.m.-4 p.m., Sun 1-4 p.m. Also by appointment.
Admission: Donations accepted.
Visitor Accessibility: Street parking. Off-season visits welcome with appointment; call ahead for information.
Website: www.negauneehistory.org
About: Preserves the history of Negaunee and the importance of iron ore to both the local area as well to the state. Exhibits include railroad room, medical room, and women's and children's rooms.
Exhibits/Collections: Complete set of Iron Herald, the local paper. Mining artifacts, history of the city, education, sports, burial records, school yearbooks.
Annual Events: Home Tour (Jul). Meetings 1st Tue monthly (except Jan-Feb), 7 p.m. at museum; Nov, Dec, Mar, and Apr meetings are at Immanuel Lutheran Church.
Publications: Quarterly newsletter.

New Baltimore
(Macomb County)

New Baltimore Historic District Commission
Mailing Address: City of New Baltimore, 36535 Green St. • New Baltimore, MI 48047
Contact: Marcella Shinska, City Clerk
Phone: (586) 725-2151 x108 • *Fax:* (586) 725-6927
Hours: Mon-Fri 8 a.m-4:30 p.m.
Website: www.cityofnewbaltimore.org
About: Preserves and protects distinctive characteristics of buildings and places within designated historic areas. Reviews proposed work affecting the exterior appearance of any structure or site within the historic district, including construction, alteration, repair, moving of structures, demolition, and signage.
Annual Events: Meetings 1st Tue monthly 7 p.m (except Jul, Nov).

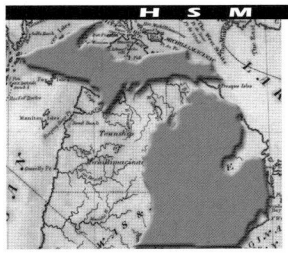

New Baltimore Historical Society
Mailing Address: 51065 Washington • New Baltimore, MI 48047
Contact: Richard Gonyeau, President
Phone: (586) 725-4755
Site/Location: **Grand Pacific House Museum**
Hours: Wed Sat 12 p.m.-2 p.m.
Admission: Donations accepted.
Visitor Accessibility: Free parking. Tour guides available.
Website: https://www.facebook.com/NewBaltimoreHistoricalSociety
About: The Grand Pacific House Museum is operated by the New Baltimore Historical Society, which strives to preserve all historical aspects of the Anchor Bay area. Originally built in 1881 for use as a hotel, then later used as a boarding house, a soda fountain shop, and a candy store, the museum building now contains exhibits about New Baltimore's history.
Annual Events: Workshops, monthly membership meetings.

New Boston
(Wayne County)

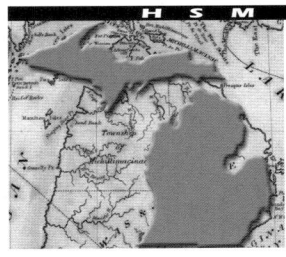

Huron Township Historical Society
Mailing Address: P.O. Box 38 • New Boston, MI 48164
Contact: Faye Bird, President
Phone: (734) 753-3109
Fax: (734) 782-2695
Site/Location: **Samuel Adams Historical Museum**
Physical Location: 37236 Huron River Drive • New Boston, MI 48164
Hours: 1st Sun monthly 1-3 p.m.
Admission: Free.
Visitor Accessibility: Free on-site parking. Wheelchair accessible. Tour guide available.
About: The Huron Township Historical Society is dedicated to the promotion of history and historical preservation at a local and global level.
Annual Events: Valentine display, Memorial Day Service, June Car Show, Volunteer Days, Historical Days Events and Activities, Monarch Butterfly Release, Annual Christmas Tree Lighting. Monthly meetings: 3rd Thu at 6 p.m.
Other Sites/Locations: **Willow School** • Location: 28399 Mineral Springs, Huron Charter Township, MI 48164 • Hours: By appointment • Admission: Free • Visitor Accessibility: Free on-site parking. Wheelchair accessible. Self-guided. • The Willow School is open for school field trips.

New Buffalo
(Berrien County)

New Buffalo Railroad Museum
Mailing Address: 106 N Whittaker St • New Buffalo, MI 49117
Contact: Katha Kissman, President
E-Mail: ask@new-buffalo-railroad-museum.org
Phone: (269) 469-8010

Historical Society of Michigan

Physical Location: 530 South Whittaker Street • New Buffalo, MI 49117
Hours: May-Sep, Thu-Mon 12-5 p.m.; Oct-Dec, Fri-Sun 12-5 p.m.
Admission: Free.
Visitor Accessibility: Parking available; wheelchair accessible.
Website: www.new-buffalo-railroad-museum.org
About: Established in 1989 to illustrate the history of the New Buffalo area and to highlight the role the railroad played in its development. Shares space in reconstructed depot with Chamber of Commerce. Operating HO model of New Buffalo and its railroad facilities. Documents and artifacts from the railroad era housed in depot and in refurbished a WWII troop car and a CSX boxcar.
Annual Events: Box Car Celebrity Buffet (spring); Museum Family Fun Day (fall).

New Haven
(Macomb County)

Save Our Depot, Inc.
Mailing Address: P.O. Box 480015 • New Haven, MI 48048
Contact: George Drake
E-Mail: kmayzie@att.net
Phone: (586) 749-6167
Physical Location: 58625 Victoria St. • New Haven, MI 48048
Hours: Sun 1-4 p.m. Also by appointment.
Admission: Donations accepted.
Visitor Accessibility: Free on-site parking. Wheelchair accessible. Tour guide available, donations accepted.
About: Formed to acquire and restore historic New Haven Railroad Depot, which is used for museum exhibits. Currently also restoring 1861 church building.
Exhibits/Collections: Photographs and local artifacts. Also collection of antique cameras.
Annual Events: Heritage Celebration Day (Aug), Victorian Christmas Tea (Dec), Cemetary Walk (Sep). Meetings 3rd Mon monthly, 7 p.m.
Information may not be current.

New Lennon
(Shaiwassee County)

Juddville Historical Society
Mailing Address: 11447 Wilkinson Rd • New Lennon, MI 48449
Contact: Irene Turk
Phone: (810) 621-4460
Hours: Open by appointment.
About: The Juddville Historical Society maintains a farm museum with various machinery and buildings. Attractions include a Raleigh gas station with cars, blacksmith's shop, one-room school of that era, and the Greek Revival home of Dr. Augustine Holcomb.
Exhibits/Collections: Old school records, tools, local artifacts.
Information may not be current.

Newaygo
(Newaygo County)

Newaygo County Museum and Heritage Center
Mailing Address: P.O. Box 361 • Newaygo, MI 49337
Contact: Roxanne Bassett, Director
E-Mail: archivist@newaygocountyhistory.org.
Phone: 866/901-7489
Fax: (231) 518-4816
Physical Location: 12 Quarterline Rd • Newago, MI 49337
Hours: May-Oct: Wed, Fri, and Sat. 12-4 p.m.; Thu 12-8 p.m.
Admission: Free.
Visitor Accessibility: Free street parking. Wheelchair accessible.
Website: www.newaygocountyhistory.org
About: The Newaygo County Museum and Heritage Center preserves Newaygo County's historical and genealogical materials for future generations through conservation, education, research, and restoration.
Exhibits/Collections: Township records and rural school ledgers. All county newspapers and census records in digital. Archives, documents, and books available at the society's office building at 1099 Wilcox Street, White Cloud.
Annual Events: Antique Appraisal Fair (spring), History Fair (Sep).
Publications: "Newaygo County's History and Biography," "Newaygo County 1850-1920," "One-Room Schoolhouses of Newaygo County, Volume I," "History of Newaygo County in the Civil War," "Lumbering in Newaygo County." See website for more publications.
Other Sites/Locations: S**aint Mary's Church** • Location: Locust and 48th, Newaygo, MI 49337 • Hours: Sep: 2nd Sun 3 p.m. • Admission: Free • Visitor Accessibility: Free street parking. Partially wheelchair accessible. Self-guided. • Built in 1853, this former Catholic church is the oldest in Newaygo County. It now serves as a meeting place for the Newaygo County Society of History & Genealogy.

Newberry
(Luce County)

Crisp Point Lighthouse.
Please see entry under Howell: Crisp Point Light Historical Society.

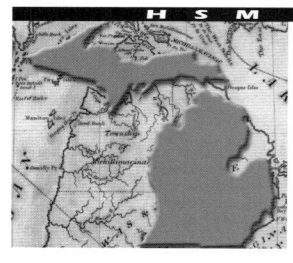

Luce County Historical Society
Mailing Address: P.O. Box 41 • Newberry, MI 49868
Contact: Sterling McGinn, Vice President
Phone: (906) 293-8417
Site/Location: **Luce County Historical Museum**
Physical Location: 411 W. Harrie St. • Newberry, MI 49868
Hours: Jun to Labor Day: Wed-Fri 1-4 p.m. Also by appointment.
Admission: Donations accepted.
Visitor Accessibility: Free parking. Wheelchair accessible. Tour guide available; call ahead for additional hour options.
Website: http://www.exploringthenorth.com/newberry/histmuseum.html
About: The society preserves and displays local artifacts and information, assists historical research, and stimulates interest in local and state history. The Luce County Historical Museum is located in the former sheriff's residence and jail (b. 1894). The brownstone, Queen Anne-style residence with attached jail features the original kitchen, dining room, parlor, and bedrooms with related artifacts. Public areas contain the men's and women's jail cells, the sheriff's office, and an 1890 judge's bench with witness stand and jury chairs.
Exhibits/Collections: Luce County History (1882-1990s), historical records, original copies of the Newbery News (1896-2004), area maps, family albums, historic picture file, oral histories, early high school yearbooks. Various artifacts.
Annual Events: Open houses (Jun and Sep).

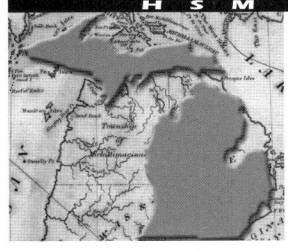

Tahquamenon Logging Museum
Mailing Address: P.O. Box 254 • Newberry, MI 49868
Contact: Peter K. Anderson, President
Phone: (906) 293-3700
Fax: (906) 293-1525
Physical Location: 9651 N M-123 • Newberry, MI 49868
Hours: Daily 10 a.m.-5 p.m.
Admission: $5/adult, $2/children (6-12), children 5 and under free. Members of the Recreation Passport Perks receive 10% off admission.
Visitor Accessibility: Free on-site parking. Wheelchair accessible. Tour guide available.
Website: www.newberrychamber.net
About: The Tahquamenon Logging Museum provides information and artifacts depicting the early logging days. Attractions include an authentic log cook shack, the original Camp Germfask CCC building, bronze CCC statue, Port Huron steam engine #6854, original Williams Family Log Home, original one-room Pratt Schoolhouse, a Goldthorpe logging truck, and nature trail.
Exhibits/Collections: Charcoal Iron Company items, blacksmith forge items, antique cash register, log books, various logging tools, Civilian Conservation Corps items, schoolhouse items, historical family items.
Annual Events: Lumberjack Breakfast (May-Aug & Oct), Music Festival & Breakfast (Jul-Aug), Original MI Fiddlers Jamboree (Sep). Meetings 2nd Thu monthly, 7 p.m. at American Legion Hall (Oct-May) and at the museum cook shack (Jun-Sep).
Publications: Brochures.

Niles
(Berrien County)

Fort St. Joseph Museum
Mailing Address: 508 E. Main St. • Niles, MI 49120
Contact: Carol Bainbridge
E-Mail: cbainbridge@nilesmi.org
Phone: (269) 683-4702 • *Fax:* (269) 684-3930
Hours: Wed-Fri 10 a.m.-4 p.m., Sat 10 a.m.-3 p.m.
Website: http://www.ci.niles.mi.us/Community/FortStJosephMuseum
About: City-owned museum located in carriage house of Victorian-period Chapin Mansion. Tells story of Niles from colonial start in 1691 to present. Featured exhibits portray history of Fort St. Joseph, built by the French in 1691, Underground Railroad in Southern Michigan, and importance of Nile's railroad and classification yards. Outstanding Lakota Indian collection, including 12 pictographs drawn by Chief Sitting Bull.
Annual Events: Christmas Holiday Open House (Dec).

Four Flags Area Genealogical Society
Mailing Address: c/o Larry Norman Sr., 2431 Eastfield • Niles, MI 49120
Phone: (269) 684-4309

Northport
(Leelanau County)

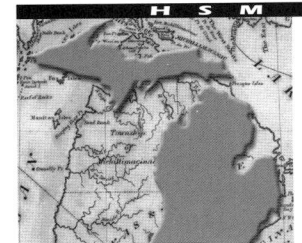

Grand Traverse Lighthouse Museum
Mailing Address: P.O. Box 43 • Northport, MI 49670
Contact: Stefanie Staley, Executive Director
E-Mail: gtlthse@triton.net
Phone: (231) 386-7195
Physical Location: 15550 N. Lighthouse Point Road • Northport, MI 49670
Hours: May: Daily 12-4 p.m.; June-Sep: Daily 10 a.m.-5 p.m.; Nov-Dec: Sat-Sun 12-4 p.m.
Admission: $4/adult, $2/student (6-18).
Visitor Accessibility: State Park Recreation Passport required. Partially wheelchair accessible.
Website: www.grandtraverselighthouse.com
About: Organized in 1985, the Grand Traverse Lighthouse Museum is located in a 162-year-old lighthouse that has been restored to resemble a keeper's home from the 1920s and 1930s. Exhibits look at area shipwrecks and local history. A restored air diaphone foghorn is demonstrated throughout year. There is also a fog signal building and oil house on-site. Visitors can climb tower.
Exhibits/Collections: All collections relate to lighthouse and maritime history. Open to researchers by appointment.
Annual Events: Autism Awareness Weekend (Jul), Lobster Fest (Aug), Haunted Lighthouse (Oct), and Christmas Open House (Dec).

Northwest Lower Michigan Historical Network
Mailing Address: c/o Grand Traverse Lighthouse Museum, P.O. Box 43 • Northport, MI 49670
E-Mail: annhoopfer@charter.net; quackenbush1@peoplepc.com
Phone: (231) 386-7195 • *Fax:* (231) 386-7195
About: Informal network of historical societies and museums in the five counties of Northwest Lower Michigan. Meets bimonthly, rotating between sites, with a program on museums or local history. Provides opportunities to share experiences, plans, and problems. Call for program information.
*Information may not be current.

Northville
(Wayne County)

City of Northville Historic District Commission
Mailing Address: 521 W. Cady St. • Northville, MI 48167
Contact: Jennifer Luikart
*Information may not be current.

Northville Genealogical Society
Mailing Address: P.O. Box 932 • Northville, MI 48167
Contact: Pat Allen
E-Mail: richpats@hotmail.com
Website: www.rootsweb.com/~mings
About: Assists members and others in pursuit of family history. Offers free assistance in local history room of Northville District Library every Mon 1-3pm.
Exhibits/Collections: At Northville District Library. Books available for reference or circulations.
Annual Events: Meetings with speaker: Sep-Jun: 2nd Sun of month 2:30 p.m. in the Carlos Meeting Room, Northville District Library. Roundtable discussion preceeds meeting at 1:15 p.m.
Publications: Members-only newsletter, Northville Cemetery books. See website for complete list of publications, including electronic genealogical research technologies.

Northville Historical Commission
Mailing Address: 215 W. Cady St. • Northville, MI 48167
Contact: Richard Starling
Phone: (248) 449-9902 • *Fax:* (248) 449-9960
Website: www.ci.northville.mi.us
*Information may not be current.

❦ Historical Society of Michigan

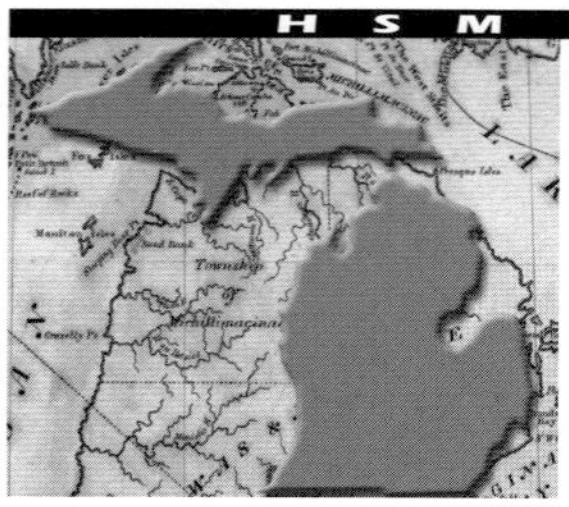

Northville Historical Society
Mailing Address: 215 Griswold Ave. • Northville, MI 48167
Contact: Abbie Holden, Office Manager
E-Mail: mrv1845@yahoo.com
Phone: (248) 348-1845
Fax: (248) 348-0056
Site/Location: Mill Race Historical Village
Hours: Mid-Jun to mid-Oct Sun 1-4 p.m.
Admission: Free.
Visitor Accessibility: Free on-site parking. Partially wheelchair accessible. Self-guided.
Website: www.millracenorthville.org

About: Founded in 1964, the Northville Historical Society discovers, collects, observes, advances, and disseminates historical knowledge of the Northville region. The society created Mill Race Village to preserve examples of architectural styles common to Northville pre-1900. The village is home to 10 relocated, reproduced, and/or reconstructed buildings: a church, school, blacksmith shop, general store, gazebo, interurban station, Georgian home, Victorian home furnished in the style of 1880, and small weaving studio.
Exhibits/Collections: Structures of Mill Race Village; Northville community history, family information, and community businesses and organizations; photos, letters, diaries, histories, maps, family trees, documents, journals, and deeds.
Annual Events: Annual Members Meeting (Jan), Independence Day Activities (Jul), Victorian Festival (Sep), Christmas in the Village (Dec), Cemetery Walk. Board of directors meeting 3rd Thu monthly.
Publications: Quarterly newsletter (Mill Race), "Welcome to Mill Race Village," "Northville, The First Hundred Years," "Images of America: Northville."

Northville Township Historical District Commission
Mailing Address: 16480 White Haren Dr. • Northville, MI 48168
Contact: John Palmer
Information may not be current.

Novi
(Oakland County)

Novi Historical Society
Mailing Address: P.O. Box 751 • Novi, MI 48375
Contact: Kathleen Mutch
E-Mail: kmmutch@yahoo.com
Phone: (248) 349-6774
Exhibits/Collections: 10,000 titles of general interest.
Information may not be current.

Oakland
(Oakland County)

Oakland Township Historical District Commission
Mailing Address: 4393 Collins Rd. • Oakland, MI 48306
Contact: Barbara Barber, Historic Preservation Planner
E-Mail: bbarber@oaklandtownship.org
Phone: (248) 608-6807
Fax: (248) 601-0106
Site/Location: Cranberry Lake Farm Historic District
Physical Location: 388 West Predmore Road • Oakland, MI 48363
Hours: Call for current hours.
Admission: Call for current admission prices.
Visitor Accessibility: Free on-site parking. Wheelchair accessible. Self-guided.
Website: www.oaklandtownship.org

About: Cranberry Lake Farm Historic District is listed in the National Register of Historic Places. The farmstead remains substantially intact and reflects the architectural and social history for the period of 1840s to 1951. The property is an example of an older farmstead in a rural setting modified into a recreational retreat of the 1930s that still exists today. The Oakland Township Historical Society provides tours and has an archives room at the site.

Oakland
(Oakland County)

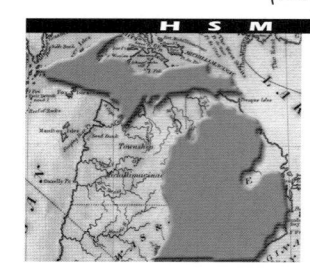

Oakland Township Historical Society
Mailing Address: 384 W. Predmore Road • Oakland, MI 48363
Contact: Colleen Barkham, Co-President
E-Mail: thsbarkham@hotmail.com
Phone: (248) 652-0712
Site/Location: Caretaker House at Cranberry Lake Farm Historic District
Hours: Call or visit website for current hours.
Admission: Free.
Visitor Accessibility: Free on-site parking. Wheelchair accessible. Tour guide available by appointment; donations accepted.
Website: www.oaklandtownshiphistoricalsociety.org

About: The society gathers, interprets, and preserves the history of Oakland Township. Traveling history exhibits that are displayed at locations include the Paint Creek Cider Mill, Rochester Hills Library, and Older Person's Commission. The society supports Cranberry Lake Farm Historic District, which has nine structures: main house, caretaker house, carriage barn, Flumerfelt Barn, silo, well house, chicken coop, pigeon house, and turkey brooder. Its museum is housed in the caretaker house, which has period furniture representing Victorian through Arts and Craft styles.
Exhibits/Collections: Barn/farm survey file, oral histories, pioneer family histories. Early 1900s photos from Clarence Kremer Collection, photos of Oakland Township (1960s-1980s) from Ed Noble Collection, and photos/documents from Walter Reuther Collection.
Annual Events: Greater Rochester Heritage Days (May), Goodison Good Tyme (Sep). Monthly programs 1st Wed monthly (Sep-Dec, Mar-Jun), 7 p.m. at Cranberry Lake Farm.
Publications: "Heritage in Oakland Township," "Goodison Walking Tour," "Barn on the Move—DVD."

Okemos
(Ingham County)

Friends of Historic Meridian
Mailing Address: P.O. Box 155 • Okemos, MI 48805
Contact: Jane Rose, Executive Director
E-Mail: meridianhistoricalvillage@gmail.com
Phone: 517-347-7300
Fax: 517-347-7300
Site/Location: Meridian Historical Village

Physical Location: 5113 Marsh Road • Okemos, MI 48805
Hours: May-Oct: Sat 10 a.m.-2 p.m.
Admission: Free.
Visitor Accessibility: Free on-site parking. Not wheelchair accessible. Tour guide available; check in at general store.
Website: www.meridianhistoricalvillage.org
About: The Friends of Historic Meridian was established in 1974 to create and sustain an active appreciation of local history by preserving and maintaining Meridian Historical Village. The village is a 19th-century living history museum with nine historic structures.
Exhibits/Collections: Small archival collection of local material (approx. 80 linear feet). Reference copies of the archival guide are available at the Okemos, Haslett, and East Lansing Public Libraries.
Annual Events: Music in the Park (Jun-Jul), Summer Day Camp (Aug), Heritage Festival (Sep), Fall Lecture Series (Sep-Oct), and Victorian Tea and Christmas in the Village (Dec). Spring Lecture series 4th Thu Mar-May.
Publications: Quarterly newsletter (The Gatekeeper).

Nokomis Learning Center
Mailing Address: 5153 Marsh Road • Okemos, MI 48864
Contact: Victoria Voges, Director
E-Mail: info@nokomis.org
Phone: (517) 349-5777 • *Fax:* (517) 349-8560
Hours: Call for current hours.
Admission: $4/individual suggested donation.
Visitor Accessibility: Free on-site parking. Wheelchair accessible. Tour guide available during open hours. School and group tours available on request; call (517) 394-5777 for information, cost, and scheduling.
Website: www.nokomis.org
About: The Nokomis Learning Center is a Native-American cultural learning center dedicated to the preservation and presentation of Anishinaabeg culture. The center offers educational programs and events focused on the history and culture of Great Lakes native America; serves as a resource for students and researchers; and engages the local native community and the community at large, in the continuation of Anishinaabeg cultural knowledge through our weekly Language and Craft Night programs, changing gallery displays, and traditional celebrations.
Exhibits/Collections: Small collection of Michigan Native-American artifacts and contemporary art. Rotating exhibits relating to Michigan Indian history, arts, and culture. Small collection of resource books.
Annual Events: Craft Night Social (every Thu 5-7 p.m.), Spring Feast (Apr), Heritage Festival (Sep), Fall Feast (Nov), Art Market: Native-American Art/Craft Work (Dec), Anishinaabemowin (Informal language class with native speakers every Thu from 7-10 p.m.).
Publications: "Tales of Nokomis," "Sisters of the Great Lakes: Art of American Indian Women," "Contemporary Great Lakes Pow Wow Regalia: 'Nda Maamawigaami (Together We Dance)."

Omena
(Leelanau County)

Omena Historical Society
Mailing Address: P. O. Box 75 • Omena, MI 49674
Contact: Doni Lystra, President
E-Mail: dlystra@sbcglobal.net
Phone: (734) 657-1897
Site/Location: **Putnam-Cloud Tower House**
Physical Location: 5045 N. West Bayshore Drive • Omena, MI 49674
Hours: Jun-Aug: Sat-Sun 1-4 p.m.; Sep-Oct Sat 1-4 p.m.
Admission: Donations accepted.
Visitor Accessibility: Free street parking. Not wheelchair accessible. Tour guide available.
Website: www.omenahistoricalsociety.com
About: The society preserves the history and culture of the Omena area. The Putnam-Cloud Tower House has been restored as a museum and community gathering place. The museum includes models of the village's buildings from 1910-1920; artifacts, including Native-American baskets; rotating special exhibits; and books by Omena authors. The society offers special educational programs and recently unveiled its first schedule of classes for children and adults—Crafts Through the Ages will be taught by local professional artists and craftspeople.
Exhibits/Collections: Tapes, letters, articles, photos, maps, books, and videos pertaining to Omena area as well as object artifacts that are from Omena area.
Annual Events: See website for information on exhibits and programs. Meetings held Jun-Sep.
Publications: Annual newsletter (Timelines), "Omena: A Place in Time."

Onaway
(Presque Isle County)

Onaway Historical Museum
Mailing Address: 20774 State St. • Onaway, MI 49765
Contact: Kelli Stockwell
Phone: (989) 733-2148
Hours: Tue-Fri 10 a.m.-2 p.m.
Admission: Donations accepted.
Website: http://www.onawayhistoricalmuseum.com/
Annual Events: Meetings 3rd Wed monthly at 5:30 p.m.
*Information may not be current.

Project Lakewell, Inc.
Mailing Address: 464 South Black River Road • Onaway, MI 49765
Contact: Lynn Johnson
E-Mail: projectlakewell@aol.com
Phone: (989) 733-2320
Admission: Call for fee options.
Website: www.projectlakewell.org
About: Project Lakewell provides first-person presentations of life during the fur trade era and classic rendezvous with a 26-foot canoe and wood batteau.

Onsted
(Lenawee County)

House of David Historeum and Preservation Society
Mailing Address: 11910 Stephenson Rd. • Onsted, MI 49265
Contact: Chris Siriano, Founder/Curator
E-Mail: houseofdavid9@aol.com
Phone: (269) 325-0039 • *Fax:* (517) 252-5061
Site/Location: **House of David Baseball Museum**
Hours: Memorial Day-Labor Day: Sat 10 a.m.-2 p.m. Mon-Fri by appointment.
Admission: $5/adult, $1/children (12-17).
Visitor Accessibility: On-site and street parking available. Weelchair accessible. Free tour guides available; call ahead.
Website: www.houseofdavidmuseum.org
About: The House of David Baseball Museum preserves, restores, displays, and teaches the history of the House of David Colony of Benton Harbor, its accomplishments, its role in baseball, the Negro Leagues, and inventions and amusement parks in 20th-century Michigan.

Exhibits/Collections: House of David memorabilia, including statues, baseball uniforms and posters, rare photographs from 1900-1950, news stories, pennants, jewelry, wall plaques, wood artwork, and souvenir pieces from the Chicago World's Fair.
Annual Events: Michigan documentary film premieres (monthly).
Publications: "The House of David: A Historical Perspective," A Compelling Curiosity (Documentary).

Ontonagon
(Ontonagon County)

Ontonagon County Genealogical Society
Mailing Address: 747 Pebble Beach Dr. • Ontonagon, MI 49953
Website: http://www.ontonagonmi.com/ocgs/
Information may not be current.

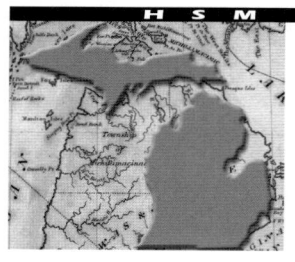

Ontonagon County Historical Society
Mailing Address: 422 River St. • Ontonagon, MI 49953
Contact: Vikki James, Business Manager
E-Mail: ochs@jamadots.com
Phone: (906) 884-6165
Site/Location: Ontonagon Historical Museum
Hours: Mon-Sat 10 a.m.-4 p.m.
Admission: $3/individual, children 12 and under free.
Visitor Accessibility: Free on-site and street parking. Wheelchair accessible. Self-guided. Historical lighthouse tours for a fee.
Website: www.ontonagonmuseum.org

About: The Ontonagon County Historical Society was founded in 1957 to collect and preserve the artifacts of the county's history and to educate the public about that history and related topics. The Ontonagon Historical Museum houses collections of mining, logging, farming, marine, and social memorabilia, displayed in room settings and cases.
Annual Events: Labor Festival(Sep).
Publications: Quarterly newsletter.
Other Sites/Locations: **Ontonagon Lighthouse** • Location: Western side of the mouth of the Ontonagon River in Ontonagon • The Ontonagon County Historical Society hosts three tours of the Ontonagon Lighthouse Tue-Sat at 11a.m., 1:30 p.m., and 3:30 p.m. The tours begin at the Ontonagon Historical Museum.

Orchard Lake
(Oakland County)

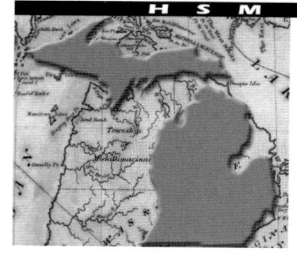

Greater West Bloomfield Historical Society
Mailing Address: 3951 Orchard Lake Road • Orchard Lake, MI 48323
Contact: Gina Gregory, Recording Secretary
E-Mail: gina@gwbhs.org
Phone: (248) 757-2451
Site/Location: Orchard Lake Museum
Physical Location: 3951 Orchard Lake Rd. • West Bloomfield, MI 48325
Hours: 2nd Sun monthly 1-4 p.m. Also by appointment.
Admission: Free.
Visitor Accessibility: Free on-site parking. Wheelchair accessible. Tour guide available on open house days; call ahead to schedule a special tour.
Website: www.gwbhs.org

About: The Greater West Bloomfield Historical Society collects, preserves, researches, and stimulates public interest in the history of West Bloomfield Township and the cities of Keego Harbor, Orchard Lake Village, and Sylvan Lake. The Orchard Lake Museum has a number of artifacts inside and outside illustrating the history of the area.
Exhibits/Collections: Items of historic value and significance pertaining to West Bloomfield Township. Includes images, oral and written histories, textiles, manuscripts, ephemera, a wooden dugout, and statue of Chief Pontiac.
Annual Events: Public tours of Apple Island (May). Board meetings 1st Wed monthly, 7 p.m. at museum.
Publications: "Song of the Heron, Reflections on the History of West Bloomfield."
Information may not be current.

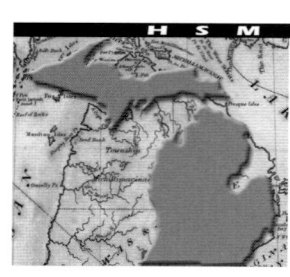

Polish Mission
Mailing Address: 3535 Indian Trail • Orchard Lake, MI 48306
Contact: Marcin Chumiecki
E-Mail: cjensen@mipolonia.net
Phone: (248) 683-0323
Site/Location: Polonica Americana Research Institute (PARI)
Hours: Mon-Tue, Fri 10 a.m.-4 p.m.
Admission: Call for current pricing.
Visitor Accessibility: Free on-site parking. Wheelchair accessible. Tour guide available.
Website: www.polishmission.com

About: Part of the Orchard Lake Schools, the Polish Mission preserves and promotes Polish and Polish-American culture, tradition, and history. The mission highlights Polish and Polish-American culture and accomplishments and serves as a repository for artifacts, archival materials, works of art, and publications. The museums, archives, and library are cornerstones of the Polish Mission's rich history and include everything from medieval royal correspondence and ancient coins to the largest Polish-related WWII collection in North America.
Exhibits/Collections: The PARI's genealogical center has experienced staff to help visitors through online databases, microfilm and microfiche, and more.
Annual Events: Constitution Day Celebration (May), Wold War II Commemoration (Sep).
Publications: Biannual journal (The Good Bews), "The History of the Polish Panorama."
Information may not be current.

Ortonville
(Oakland County)

Brandon Township Public Library
Mailing Address: 304 South St. • Ortonville, MI 48462
E-Mail: cstringer@brandonlibrary.org
Phone: (248) 627-1461
Fax: (248) 627-9880
Hours: Mon-Thu 9 a.m.-9 p.m.; Fri 9 a.m.-6 p.m.; Sat 9 a.m.-3 p.m.
Admission: Free.
Visitor Accessibility: Wheelchair accessible.
Website: www.brandonlibrary.org
Exhibits/Collections: Local history room.

Michigan History Directory

Ortonville Community Historical Society

HSM MEMBER

Mailing Address: P.O. Box 155 • Ortonville, MI 48462
Contact: Judy Miracle, President
E-Mail: jmiracle60@comcast.net
Phone: (248) 627-3893
Site/Location: **The Old Mill**
Physical Location: 366 Mill St. • Ortonville, MI 48462
Hours: Sat 10 a.m.-2 p.m. Also by appointment.
Admission: Donations accepted.
Visitor Accessibility: Free on-site and street parking. Not wheelchair accessible. Tour guide available.
Website: http://ortonvillecommunityhistoricalsoc.weebly.com
About: The Ortonville Community Historical Society represents the historical interests of Ortonville, Brandon Township, and Groveland Township. A museum is located in the Old Mill, a grist mill built in 1856 by the town's founder, Amos Orton, and still stands in its original condition with some additional improvements. The museum houses many local agricultural artifact collections, a country store replica, a display of Lakota Indian dress, an 1800s kitchen and other rooms, and a military room with uniforms and memorabilia.
Exhibits/Collections: More than 4,000 artifacts relating to pioneering of Ortonville and Brandon Township. Military collection and local photographs. Lakota Indian collection.
Annual Events: Creekfest (Jun), Septemberfest, Christmas in the Village (Dec). Meetings 1st Tue monthly, 7 p.m. at Old Mill museum.
Publications: Irregular newsletter.
Other Sites/Locations: **Mann One-Room School** • Location: 366 Mill Street, Ortonville, MI 48462 • Hours: Sat 10 a.m.-2 p.m. Also by appointment. • Admission: Donations accepted. Suggested donation of $3/student. • Visitor Accessibility: Free on-site and street parking. Not wheelchair accessible. Tour guide available. • The Mann One-Room School, which was used until the 1940s and relocated to its present location in 1985, has been refurbished in the style of the period and is used for tours and reenactments.

Oscoda
(Iosco County)

AuSable-Oscoda Historical Society & Museum

Mailing Address: P.O. Box 679 • Oscoda, MI 48750
Contact: Fred Glass, President
Phone: (989) 739-2782 • *Fax:* (989) 739-2782
Physical Location: 114 East River Road • Oscoda, MI 48750
Hours: Spring-autumn: Sat-Sun 11 a.m.-4 p.m. Summer: Thu-Sat 1-5 p.m., Sun 12-4 p.m.
Admission: Free.
Visitor Accessibility: On-site parking. Wheelchair accessible. Free group tours for five or more people.
Website: www.ausableoscodahistoricalsociety.org
About: Exhibits include Native-American artifacts, commercial fishing, shipping, shipwrecks, logging, Paul Bunyan legend, railroads, lighthouses, the AuSable River and its dams, the fire of 1911, and Wurtsmith Air Force Base.
Exhibits/Collections: Local artifacts and documents, including J.D. Hank's photo collection of logging photos in Michigan 1880s-1904 and building of "Turtle Lake Club," a private hunting club.
Annual Events: Meetings 1st Mon monthly, 7 p.m.
*Information may not be current.

Huron Shores Genealogical Society

Mailing Address: c/o Robert J. Parks Public Library, 6010 N. Skeel Ave. • Oscoda, MI 48750
Contact: Judy Sheldon, President
E-Mail: huronshoresgs@yahoo.com
Phone: (989) 739-9581
Hours: Public library hours. Also by appointment.
Visitor Accessibility: Free on-site parking. Wheelchair accessible. Self-guided.
Website: www.huronshoresgs.org
About: The Huron Shores Genealogical Society preserves and perpetuates the records of the area's ancestors, encourages the study of family history and genealogy, aids individuals in the compilation of their genealogies, and cooperates with other societies and shares information.
Exhibits/Collections: Located in the Robert Parks Public Library in Oscoda. More than 1,900 books, drawers of microfilm, cabinets of loose material, and scanned material. Plus more than 1,580 indexes.
Annual Events: Workshops (spring, fall). Business meetings 3rd Thu (Jan, Apr, Jul, and Oct) 5:30p.m.
Publications: Quarterly newsletter (The Genogram).

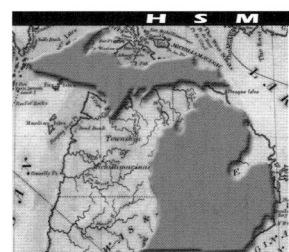

Wurtsmith Air Museum

HSM MEMBER

Mailing Address: P.O. Box 664 • Oscoda, MI 48750
Contact: Don Gauvreau, Chairman
Phone: (989) 739-7555
Physical Location: 4071 E Van Ettan • Oscoda, MI 48750
Hours: Mid-May to Labor Day: Fri-Sun 11 a.m.-3 p.m.
Admission: $5/adult, $3/children (6-12), children 5 and under are free.
Visitor Accessibility: Free parking. Wheelchair accessible. Tour guide available.
Website: www.wurtsmithairmuseum.org
About: The Wurtsmith Air Museum is located in three fighter-alert hangars on the former Wurtsmith Air Force Base. On display are aviation artifacts dating from before the Wright Brothers to the present day. There is a special emphasis on the military units that were based at Wurtsmith, beginning with its days as Camp Skeel in the 1920s. Several historic aircraft are under restoration, including a Cessna O-1A "Bird-Dog," two T-33As, a Bell UH-1H helicopter, a Waco, and a CG-4A troop glider.
Exhibits/Collections: Aircraft, artifacts, records, articles, and stories.
Annual Events: Golf Outing (Jul), Fly-in-Pancake Breakfast (Aug). Meetings 3rd Sat at 10 a.m.
Publications: Newsletter (Wurtsmith Wings).

Oshtemo
(Kalamazoo County)

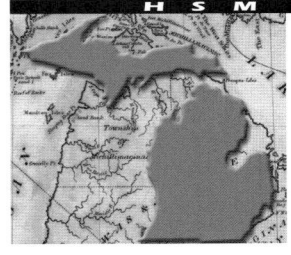

Oshtemo Historical Society

HSM MEMBER

Mailing Address: P.O. Box 297 • Oshtemo, MI 49077
Contact: Kay Oppliger
E-Mail: kdoldo61@chartermi.net
Phone: (269) 375-4753
Website: http://oshtemohistoricalsociety.org/
About: Founded in 2004 to preserve the 1882 Italianate/Greek Revival home of Benjamin and Maria Drake, who settled in the area in 1830. The society is working with the Oshtemo Township to restore the home to its former elegance and preserve the history of the rapidly developing once-rural area.
Annual Events: Meetings 3rd Thu monthly, call for time and location.
*Information may not be current.

Otisville
(Genesee County)

Otisville Area Historical Association
Mailing Address: P.O. Box 93 • Otisville, MI 48463
Contact: Dale Rock, President
E-Mail: oaha1982@yahoo.com
Phone: (810) 631-6119
Site/Location: **Otisville Museum**
Physical Location: 122 E Main St • Otisville, MI 48463
Hours: Apr-Oct: Wed 3-6 p.m.; 2nd Sunday 2-6 p.m. Also by appointment.
Admission: Donations accepted.
Visitor Accessibility: Free on-site parking. Not wheelchair accessible. Self-guided.
About: The mission of the Otisville Area Historical Association is to collect, preserve, and promote history information pertinent to the Otisville area.
Exhibits/Collections: Local history and artifacts with other changing exhibits.
Annual Events: Otisville Reunion (May). Meetings 1st Thu monthly at Forest Township Library.
*Information may not be current.

Otsego
(Allegan County)

Otsego Area Historical Society
Mailing Address: P.O. Box 424 • Otsego, MI 49078
Contact: Lyneta Nowak, Chairperson
E-Mail: oahs@otsegohistory.org
Phone: (269) 692-3775
Physical Location: 218 N. Farmer • Otsego, MI 49078
Hours: Sat 10 a.m.-2 p.m. Also by appointment.
Admission: Free.
Visitor Accessibility: Free parking. Wheelchair accessible.
Website: www.otsegohistory.org
About: The Otsego Area Historical Society illustrates the unique history of Otsego area by means of exhibits, displays, and educational programs. The society highlights the pioneer history of Michigan and the papermaking industry of Otsego, which had seven operational mills in the 20th century.
Exhibits/Collections: Various artifacts related to Otsego's history.
Annual Events: Meetings 1st Thu monthly, 6:30 p.m. at museum.
Publications: Quarterly newsletter.

Otter Lake
(Lapeer County)

Otter Lake Historical Society and Museum
Mailing Address: P.O. Box 287 • Otter Lake, MI 48464
Contact: Marcia Aikin
E-Mail: homeinol@aol.com
Phone: (810) 793-1471
Physical Location: 5844 Genesee Ave • Otter Lake, MI 48464
Hours: 1st and 3rd Sat monthly 1-3 p.m.
Visitor Accessibility: Street parking available.
About: A village small but rich in history, the Otter Lake Society and Museum's mission is to ask residents to share information and memorabilia with the community.
Exhibits/Collections: Eclectic collection including logs, logging tools, bottles from the lake, old post office boxes, historical writings, and photographs. A veteran's memorial is on-site.
Annual Events: Museum open house (Jun). Society meets quarterly.
Publications: "Otter Lake, A Bit of History."

Ovid
(Clinton County)

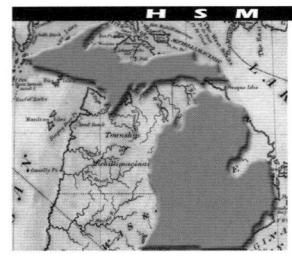

Ovid Historical Society
Mailing Address: P.O. Box 54 • Ovid, MI 48866
Contact: Roger Matthies
E-Mail: ovidhs67@yahoo.com
Phone: (989) 834-5421
Site/Location: **Mary Myers Museum**
Physical Location: 131 East Williams • Ovid, MI 48866
Hours: 2nd and 4th Sun monthly 2-4 p.m. Also by appointment.
Admission: Donations accepted.
Visitor Accessibility: Street parking.
Website: www.ovidhistoricalsociety.weebly.com
About: Organized in 1992, the Ovid Historical Society promotes history in Ovid and participates in local community events. The society maintains the Mary Myers Museum, an 1869 Italianate-style structure furnished for the period.
Annual Events: Ovid Carriage Days (Sep), meets monthly.
Publications: Quarterly newsletter.
Other Sites/Locations: **Ovid Historical Room** • Location: 206 North Main Street, Ovid, MI 48866 • Hours: Open by appointment; call (989) 834-5421 • Admission: Donations accepted • Visitor Accessibility: Street parking. • Artifacts and documents available for research. Site also features a continuous display of an 1880s carriage manufactured in Ovid.

Owosso
(Shiawassee County)

Michigan State Trust for Railway Preservation
Mailing Address: P.O. Box 665 • Owosso, MI 48867
Contact: Rich Greter, Board President
E-Mail: terry.b@mstrp.com
Phone: 989-725-9464
Site/Location: **Steam Railroading Institute**
Physical Location: 405 S. Washington St. • Owosso, MI 48867
Hours: Summer: Wed-Sun 10 a.m.-5 p.m. Winter: Fri-Sun 10 a.m.-4 p.m.
Admission: $5/individual. Excursion prices vary.
Visitor Accessibility: On-site parking. Partially wheelchair accessible to visitor's center and some back shop area. Free tour guides available on weekends.
Website: www.michigansteamtrain.com
About: The Steam Railroading Institute educates the public about steam-era railroad technology and its impact on the culture and economy of the Great Lakes region by safely operating, preserving, exhibiting, and interpreting historic railroad equipment. The Steam Railroading Institute's museum features interactive steam-era educational programs, restoration shop/engine house, and historic photo freight charters.
Exhibits/Collections: 1941 Pere Marquette #1225, a 400-ton steam locomotive; 100-foot turntable built in 1919; and 1950 C&O Pullman Sleeper. Various rail cars and artifacts. Archival holdings focused on steam railroading technology.
Annual Events: North Pole Express (Nov, Dec), fall excursions to Cadillac/Grayling. Volunteer and board meetings 3rd Sat monthly.
Publications: Quarterly member newsletter.

Owosso Historical Commission
Mailing Address: City Hall, 301 W. Main St. • Owosso, MI 48867
Contact: Mitchell Speers, Director

E-Mail: owossohistoricalcommission@gmail.com
Phone: (989) 725-0597 • *Fax:* (989) 723-8854
Site/Location: **Curwood Castle**
Physical Location: 224 Curwood Castle Dr. • Owosso, MI 48867
Hours: Mon-Fri 1-5 p.m.
Admission: $2/adult, $1/children (1-12).
Visitor Accessibility: Free on-site parking. Not wheelchair accessible. Tour guide available.
Website: http://owossohistorichometour.com
About: Maintains three city-owned historical properties.
Annual Events: Meetings 3rd Tue of each month, 7 p.m. at the Amos Gould House.

Shiawassee County Historical Society
Mailing Address: P.O. Box 526 • Owosso, MI 48867
Contact: Charles Wascher, President
E-Mail: archer@charter.net
Phone: (989) 723-2371
Site/Location: **Shiawassee County Historical Society Archives and Museum**
Physical Location: 1997 N. M-52 • Owosso, MI 48867
Hours: Apr-Sep: Sun 1-4 p.m. Also by appointment.
Admission: Donations accepted.
Visitor Accessibility: Free on-site and street parking. Wheelchair accessible. Tour guide available.
Website: www.shiawasseecountyhistsoc.org
About: The Shiawassee County Historical Society collects and displays items pertaining to Shiawassee County, especially family histories and the beginning of Shiawassee County. The Shiawassee County Historical Society Archives and Museum contains three rooms plus a long hall full of artifacts pertaining to the county.
Exhibits/Collections: Collections include household artifacts, farm equipment, period clothing, Shiawassee County memorabilia from 1800-present, Native-American tools and stones, buggies, and mammoth tusks. Open from 10 a.m.-2 p.m. on Thu for genealogical research.
Annual Events: History Meetings (Oct-Apr). Meetings 4th Sun Oct-Apr, 2 p.m. at museum.
Publications: Triannual Newsletter (Gazette). "Combined Atlases of 1875, 1895, 1915, and 1859," "Map of Shiawassee County," "One Room Schools of Shiawassee County," "Owosso A-Z."

Oxford
(Oakland County)

Northeast Oakland Historical Society
Mailing Address: Attn: Ron Brock, 1 N. Washington St. • Oxford, MI 48371
Contact: Ron Brock, President
E-Mail: info@neohs.net
Phone: (248) 628-8413
Hours: Sat 1-4 p.m., and Jun-Aug: Wed 1-4 p.m. Also by appointment.
Admission: Donations accepted.
Visitor Accessibility: Free parking; self-guided (group tours by appointment, free).
Website: http://www.neohs.net/
About: Preserves an awareness of the area's history and its artifacts. Organized and started the museum in 1972 in former Oxford Savings Bank. Changing exhibits. Gravel industry exhibit, Oxford was "Gravel Capitol of the World." Brace Beemer, the first Lone Ranger. Offers school tours, primarily local second graders.
Exhibits/Collections: Around-the-world doll collection, local furniture, tin shop display, other local artifacts. Local family genealogies and photographs, musical instruments, toys, glassware, household goods.
Annual Events: Oxford Days (Aug).
Information may not be current.

Painesdale
(Houghton County)

Painesdale Mine Shaft, Inc.
Mailing Address: P.O. Box 332 • Painesdale, MI 49955
Contact: Sherri Lewis, Trustee
E-Mail: painesdalemineshaft@yahoo.com
Phone: (906) 231-5542
Physical Location: Champion #4 Shafthouse, 42631 Shafthouse Road • Painesdale, MI 49955
Hours: By appointment.
Admission: Free.
Visitor Accessibility: Free street parking. Partially wheelchair accessible (Shafthouse and Hoist Buildings). Self-guided.
Website: www.painesdalemineshaft.com
About: Painesdale Mine Shaft, Inc., seeks to preserve and interpret copper mining Champion #4 Shafthouse, which was built in 1902 and operated until 1967. The organization offers tours of the shafthouse, hoist house, and mining captain's office.
Exhibits/Collections: Copper Range Mining Company records, family histories, mining history of Painesdale, photos, and tour maps of Painesdale.
Annual Events: Meetings 4th Tue monthly at the Captain's Office (spring-summer) and the Range VFW Lounge in South Range (fall-winter).
Publications: "Painesdale Mine & Shaft Ethnic Cookbook."

Paradise
(Chippewa County)

Great Lakes Shipwreck Museum.
Please see entry under Sault Ste. Marie: Great Lakes Shipwreck Society.

Parma
(Jackson County)

Tompkins Center Historical Society
Mailing Address: 9555 Minard Rd. • Parma, MI 49269
Contact: Patricia Tuttle
E-Mail: johnandpattuttle@yahoo.com
Phone: (517) 569-3263
Site/Location: **Tompkins Center Historical Society Sheridan Stewart Museum**
Physical Location: 10138 Tompkins Road • Rives Junction, MI 49269
Hours: 4th Sun monthly 1-4 p.m.
Admission: $2/individual.
Visitor Accessibility: Free on-site parking. Wheelchair accessible. Tour guide available; call ahead.
Website: www.tompkinshistorical.org
About: Formed in 1985, the society operates a museum and newly built replica of an 1800s one-room schoolhouse. Also available is a newly constructed frontier cabin replica, fully furnished with authentic furniture and artifacts, and several other buildings housing many artifacts of historical value.
Exhibits/Collections: Historical artifacts.
Annual Events: Freedom Festival and Steam Show (Sep).

Paw Paw
(Van Buren County)

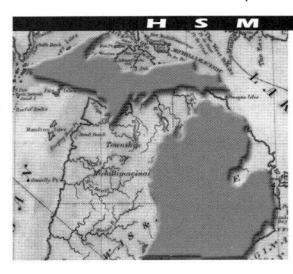

Paw Paw District Library
Mailing Address: 609 W. Michigan • Paw Paw, MI 49079
Phone: (269) 657-3800
Fax: (269) 657-2603
Hours: Mon Tue Thu 9 a.m.-8 p.m. Wed 12 p.m.-8 p.m. Fri Sat 9 a.m.-5 p.m.
Website: www.pawpaw.lib.mi.us
About: The Paw Paw District Library is dedicated to promoting education through literature and history for all age groups through the use of a local history room that contains information about the Paw Paw area, as well as photos, artifacts, obituaries, a local newspaper on microfilm, and other gathered information on local people and businesses.
Exhibits/Collections: Local newspaper (1853-current) on microfilm.

Pelkie
(Baraga County)

Hanka Homestead Museum & Restoration
Mailing Address: P.O. Box 56 • Pelkie, MI 49958
Contact: Reuben Niemisto, President
E-Mail: obheikki@up.net
Phone: (906) 334-2601
Physical Location: 13249 Hanka Rd. • Pelkie, MI 49938
Hours: Memorial Day-Labor Day: Tue, Thu, Sat, Sun 12-4 p.m.
Admission: Suggested donations only; $3/adult, $1/children.
Visitor Accessibility: Free on-site parking. Partially wheelchair accessible. Tour guides available; groups of 15 or more should call ahead.
About: To acquaint and educate visitors with Finnish homesteader's way of life and to preserve the heritage of Finnish immigrant families. Visitors will see the Hanka family homestead settled in 1896, which includes the original buildings, unchanged since the 1920s on 40 acres of the original homestead. Interpretations will include aspects common to Finnish ways of life and to the Hanka Family. The Hanka Homestead Museum Association owns the site and is a nonprofit staffed by volunteers.
Exhibits/Collections: Farm equipment, smoke sauna, period artifacts.
Annual Events: Call for details.

Laird Township Historical Society
Mailing Address: 24260 Alston Ave. • Pelkie, MI 49958
*Information may not be current.

Sturgeon Valley Historical Society
Mailing Address: P.O. Box 34 • Pelkie, MI 49958
Contact: Jack Lehto, President
Phone: (906) 353-6684
Physical Location: 15009 Pelkie Rd. • Pelkie, MI 49958
Hours: May-Sep: Sun 11 a.m.-4 p.m. Also open on holidays with same hours.
Admission: Donations accepted.
Visitor Accessibility: On-site parking (free). Not wheelchair accessible. Tour guide available upon request.
About: Historical one-room schoolhouse.
Annual Events: Meetings 3rd Thu 7 p.m. (May-Sep).
Publications: "Pelkie: Its Past and Present."
*Information may not be current.

Pellston
(Emmet County)

Pellston Historical Society & Museum
Mailing Address: P.O. Box 493 • Pellston, MI 49769
Contact: Andrew Keiser
Phone: (231) 420-0807 • *Fax:* (231) 539-8009
Physical Location: US 31 • Pellston, MI 49769
Hours: Wed 12-5 p.m.
Website: http://www.pellstonmi.com/historical.htm
About: This museum opened in 2007 in a Grand Rapids & Indiana Railroad Depot and hosts a display of local Native-American artifacts in cooperation with Little Traverse Bands.
Exhibits/Collections: Materials related to lumbering, area life, and railroad.
*Information may not be current.

Pentwater
(Oceana County)

Pentwater Historical Society
Mailing Address: P.O. Box 54 • Pentwater, MI 49449
Contact: Charles E. Bigelow, President
E-Mail: info@pentwaterhistoricalsociety.org
Phone: (231) 869-8631
Physical Location: 85 South Rutledge • Pentwater, MI 49449
Hours: May-Aug: Tue-Sat 1-4 p.m.; Sep-Oct: Thu-Sat 1-4 p.m. Also by appointment.
Admission: Donations accepted.
Visitor Accessibility: Free on-site and street parking. Wheelchair accessible. Tour guide available.
Website: www.pentwaterhistoricalsociety.org
About: The Pentwater Historical Society encourages and promotes historical awareness and knowledge of Pentwater Village and Township and Oceana County. The society offers maps for a walking tour, which takes visitors to seven different historical interpretive panels throughout the villages.
Exhibits/Collections: Artifacts relating to logging, shipping, and industry in Pentwater area.
Annual Events: Spring Membership Dinner and Program (May), Summer Membership Dinner and Program (Aug). These events are open to the public.
Publications: Quarterly newsletter (Pentwater Historical Society News).

Peshawbestown
(Leelanau County)

Grand Traverse Band of Ottawa and Chippewa Indians
Mailing Address: 2605 N. West Bayshore Dr. • Peshawbestown, MI 49682
Contact: Marjorie Jacko, Curator/Archivist
E-Mail: museum@gtbindians.com
Phone: (231) 534-7768
Fax: (231) 534-7568
Site/Location: Eyaawing Museum and Cultural Center
Physical Location: 2304 N. West Bayshore Dr. • Peshawbestown, MI 49682
Hours: Wed-Sat 10 a.m.-4 p.m.
Admission: Donations accepted.

Visitor Accessibility: Free on-site parking. Wheelchair accessible. Self-guided.
Website: http://gtbindians.org

About: The Grand Traverse Band's Museum and Cultural Center is created to establish, gather, interpret, and maintain a record of the history of the Grand Traverse Band of Anishinaabek with respect to the circle of life, honor for their families, and the telling of their true heritage. This role will promote the Tribe's belief that the culture, language, and spirit of the Grand Traverse Band shall be recognized, perpetuated, communicated, supported, and shared with the people of all nations.

Exhibits/Collections: The world's only pair of talon-locked eagles on display for all visitors to admire, which were found by a Tribal member when out for a walk with her grandmother.

Annual Events: The Expressive Culture Series, Holiday Bazaar.

Petoskey
(Emmet County)

Bay View Association
Mailing Address: P.O. Box 583, 1715 Encampment • Petoskey, MI 49770
Contact: John P. Stakoe, Executive Director
E-Mail: john@bayviewassociation.org
Phone: (231) 347-6225
Fax: (231) 347-4330
Site/Location: **Bay View Historical Museum**
Hours: Jun-Aug: Sun 11 a.m.-1 p.m., Mon and Wed 1-3 p.m.
Admission: Free.
Visitor Accessibility: Free street parking. Self-guided.
Website: www.bayviewassociation.org

About: Bay View is a Historic Chautauqua on Lake Michigan founded in 1875. Designated as a National Historic Landmark in 1987, the site has 444 cottages, two hotels, one bed and breakfast, and two auditoriums (considered to be the finest examples of Queen Anne architecture in the United States). The two oldest buildings on campus were designated as the historical museum in 1964, and the commission was established to collect, maintain, and display items that reflect Bay View's rich heritage.

Exhibits/Collections: Material dating back to the community's founding in 1875. The collections include photos, journals, letters, personal papers, all association documents.

Annual Events: Summer Festival Concerts, American Experience Week, Annual Meeting (Aug). Board of Trustees meets May-Aug.

Publications: "Beneath the Beeches," "The Story of Bay View," "Bay View An American Idea," "A Pictorial History of Bay View," "Bay View: The Summer City of Michigan," Bay View Literary Magazine (annual).

Other Sites/Locations: **Museum Cottage** • Location: Bay View Campus • Hours: Jun-Aug: Sun 11 a.m.-1 p.m. • Admission: Free • Visitor Accessibility: Free street parking. Not wheelchair accessible. Self-guided. • Open since the summer of 2012, the Museum Cottage serves as the permanent home of the Bay View Historical Museum's collection. The renovated building provides a secure, climate-controlled environment with adequate work space, proximity to the campus, and a venue for additional display areas.

Bay View Archives • Hours: Jun-Aug: Mon, Wed, Fri 1-3p.m. • Admission: Free • Visitor Accessibility: Free street parking. Wheelchair accessible. Self-guided. • Located in the lower level of the Wade Administration Building, the Bay View Archives maintains the papers of Bay View Association. This includes minutes and other documents of the association's official actions, photos of people and events, and materials related to individual cottages and their owners throughout history. Trained members of the archives commission assist members and other researchers during the archives' regular hours.

Little Traverse Historical Society
Mailing Address: P.O. Box 2418, 100 Depot Court • Petoskey, MI 49770
Contact: Michael Federspiel, Executive Director
E-Mail: info@petoskeymuseum.org
Phone: 231-347-2620
Site/Location: **Little Traverse History Museum**
Physical Location: 100 Depot Ct. • Petoskey, MI 49770
Hours: Memorial Day-Oct: Mon-Sat 10 a.m.-4 p.m.
Admission: $3/adult, children 10 and under free.
Visitor Accessibility: Free on-site and street parking. Wheelchair accessible. Self-guided.
Website: www.petoskeymuseum.org

About: The Little Traverse History Museum is housed in the 1892 Chicago and West Michigan Railroad Depot on Petoskey's waterfront. Exhibits focus on regional history and include Ernest Hemingway's personal and literary ties to the area.

Exhibits/Collections: Newspapers back to 1880s. Vertical files on local businesses, families, schools, and local topics. Photos of people, places, and events back to late-19th century. Archives available by appointment.

Annual Events: Historic Festival and Taste of the North (Jun). Monthly programs.

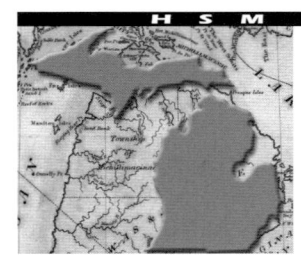

Petoskey Public Library
Mailing Address: 500 E. Mitchell St. • Petoskey, MI 49770
Contact: Drew Cherven
E-Mail: library@petoskeylibrary.org
Phone: (231) 758-3100
Hours: Mon-Thu 10 a.m.-7 p.m. (until 8 p.m. in summer), Fri-Sat 1-5 p.m.
Website: www.petoskeylibrary.org

About: Local newspapers on microfilm, local news clippings file, local history books.
Exhibits/Collections: Local artists displayed year round.
Annual Events: Book Sale (Jul).

Robert Emmet Society
Mailing Address: P.O. Box 2027 • Petoskey, MI 49720
Website: http://www.emmetsociety.org/
*Information may not be current.

Pickford
(Chippewa County)

Pickford Area Historical Society
Mailing Address: P.O. Box 572 • Pickford, MI 49774
Contact: Dianne Schmitigal, President
E-Mail: kdschmitigal@centurylink.net
Phone: (906) 647-1372
Site/Location: **Pickford Museum**
Physical Location: 175 E. Main St. • Pickford, MI 49774
Hours: Jun-Aug: Mon-Sat 9:30 a.m.-3:30 p.m. Aug-Oct: Fri-Sat 9:30 a.m.-3:30 p.m.
Admission: Donations accepted.

Visitor Accessibility: Free street parking. Self-guided. Private tours by appointment.
Website: www.pickfordmuseum.org

About: The Pickford Museum is located in a restored car dealership/hardware building that was originally built in 1912. Today, the building is listed on the National Register of Historic Places and includes a hands-on exhibit in the children's area. Exhibits regularly change and are designed to showcase life in the area from its inception in 1877 to the present. A section of the museum is devoted to ancestral portraits and a large collection of family genealogies.

Exhibits/Collections: Artifacts relating to the agricultural/dairy and lumbering/logging heritage, as well as a military exhibit and rotating collections from the educational, service clubs, churches, and merchants/business community. A 1920s-era player piano.

Annual Events: Golf Scramble (Jul), Community Days (Aug), Veterans Celebration (Nov), Quilt Show (Nov). Meetings Mar-Dec 2nd Tue monthly at museum.

Publications: Quarterly newsletter, Passages. Books include "Schools 1878-1958" and "Barns."

Pigeon
(Huron County)

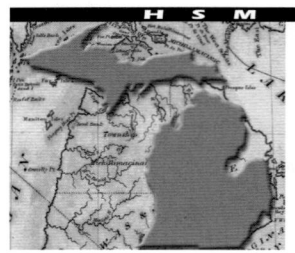

Pigeon Historical Society
Mailing Address: P.O. Box 523 • Pigeon, MI 48755
Contact: Denny Esch, President
E-Mail: eschdenny@yahoo.com
Phone: (989) 453-3242
Fax: (989) 453-2075
Site/Location: **Pigeon Depot Museum**
Physical Location: 59 S. Main St. • Pigeon, MI 48755
Hours: Museum: Thu-Fri 10 a.m.-3 p.m. Sat 10 a.m.-1 p.m.; Woelke Historical Research Center: Thu-Fri 10 a.m.-3 p.m.
Admission: Donations accepted.
Visitor Accessibility: Free public parking lot. Wheelchair accessible.
Website: www.thehchs.org/pigeonhs/index.htm

About: The Pigeon Historical Society discovers, collects, and preserves any material that may help to establish or illustrate the history of the Pigeon community and surrounding region. The Pigeon Depot Museum is located in a historical railroad depot filled with local artifacts and memorabilia. Items on display include a reed organ, pianola, hand tools, household items, turn-of-the-century clothing, railroad artifacts, 4,000 obituary cards from area, residents' books, pictures, and plat books.

Exhibits/Collections: Large collection of the history of Pigeon, its business, people, and the surrounding area.

Annual Events: Farmers Festival (Jul). See website for special events. Meetings 2nd Mon monthly; call for time and location.

Plymouth
(Wayne County)

Friends of the Plymouth Historical Museum
Mailing Address: 155 S. Main St. • Plymouth, MI 48170
Contact: Elizabeth K. Kerstens, Director
E-Mail: director@plymouthhistory.org
Phone: (734) 455-8940
Fax: (734) 455-7797
Site/Location: **Plymouth Historical Museum**
Hours: Wed and Fri-Sun 1-4 p.m. Office: Mon, Wed 9:30 a.m.-5 p.m.
Admission: $5/adult, $2/student (6-17).
Visitor Accessibility: Free street parking. Wheelchair accessible. Self-guided. Tour guide available by appointment.
Website: www.plymouthhistory.org

About: The Friends of the Plymouth Historical Museum, formally the Plymouth Historical Society, is dedicated to preserving, teaching, and presenting history through the operation and support of the Plymouth Historical Museum, which is housed in a 26,000-square-foot building donated to the society by Miss Margaret Dunning. There are three permanent exhibits, including a late-19th-century Victorian re-creation of Main Street, a series of displays of America's history as witnessed by the Plymouth community, and the Dr. Weldon Petz Abraham Lincoln Collection.

Annual Events: A Night For the Museum Fundraiser Auction (Feb), Plymouth Characters Cemetery Walk (Oct), Craft Bazaar, Bake Sale and Open House (Dec). Meeting 2nd Thu monthly (except Jun-Aug and Dec).

Publications: Bimonthly newsletter (Museum Memo).

Plymouth District Library
Mailing Address: 223 S. Main St. • Plymouth, MI 48170
Contact: Kathy Petlewski, Electronic Resoures Librarian
E-Mail: info@plymouthlibrary.org
Phone: (734) 453-0750 • *Fax:* (734) 453-0733
Hours: Mon-Thu 9:30 a.m.-9 p.m.; Fri 9:30 a.m.-6 p.m.; Sat 9:30 a.m.-5 p.m.; Sun 12-5 p.m.
Admission: Free.
Visitor Accessibility: Free on-site parking. Wheelchair accessible. Self-guided.
Website: http://plymouthlibrary.org

About: The library's mission is to help community residents meet personal, educational, and professional information needs. It keeps a collection of local history materials, including high school yearbooks, Plymouth City Directories, microfilmed copies of the Plymouth Mail/Observer Newspaper from 1887 to present, a clipping file of local topics, and several books written about the Plymouth area.

Annual Events: Summer Reading Clubs, Local Author Fair.

Publications: Quarterly newsletter (Dunning-Hough Notes).

Pointe Aux Pins
(Mackinac County)

Bois Blanc Island Historical Society
Mailing Address: P.O. Box 933 • Pointe Aux Pins, MI 49775
Contact: Betty Hutchinson, Treasurer
Physical Location: 1030 W. Huron Drive • Bois Blanc Island, MI 49775
Hours: Jul-Labor Day: Tue, Thu, Sat 10 a.m.-2 p.m.
Admission: Donations accepted.
Visitor Accessibility: On-site parking. Partially wheelchair accessible (small step at side entrance). Tour guide available.
Website: https://www.facebook.com/bbihs

About: The Bois Blanc Island Historical Society promotes interest and appreciation of the history of Bois Blanc Island. The society also collects and preserves information and artifacts of same.

Exhibits/Collections: Lumber industry tools, relics

from the soldiers on Mackinac Island who used Bois Blanc Island as a woodlot, household items, books from the island school, and cassette tapes of oral history.
Annual Events: Ice Cream Social, Book Sale, Historical Tours, and Informational Lectures.

Pontiac
(Oakland County)

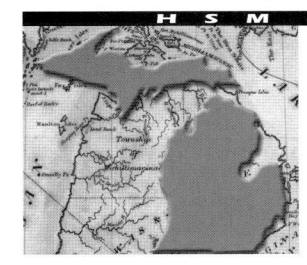

Oakland County Historical Commission
Mailing Address: 1200 N. Telegraph Rd, Dept 470, Bldg 12E • Pontiac, MI 48341
Contact: Jennifer L. Radcliff, Chair
E-Mail: jradcliffpreserv@gmail.com
Physical Location: 33 N. Main St • Clarkston, MI 48346
Website: http://www.oakgov.com/historic/Pages/default.aspx
About: The commission works to promote history throughout Oakland County and to offer a common meeting place for the many local organizations to learn and share. The historical commission advises the board of commissioners and the county executive about ways they can raise awareness of the area's history and collaborates with the Oakland County staff to enhance their on-going programs and events with information about the area's shared heritage.
Annual Events: Semi-annual workshops, tours, and seminars. Meetings 1st Tue monthly, 7-9 p.m.

Oakland County Pioneer and Historical Society
Mailing Address: 405 Cesar E. Chavez Ave. • Pontiac, MI 48342
Contact: Sara Guy, Office Manager
E-Mail: office@ocphs.org
Phone: (248) 338-6732
Fax: (248) 338-6731
Site/Location: **Pine Grove Historical Museum**
Hours: Tue-Thu 11 a.m.-4 p.m. Also by appointment.
Admission: $5/individual.
Visitor Accessibility: Free on-site parking. Partially wheelchair accessible; Wisner House is not. Tour guide available by appointment.
Website: www.ocphs.org
About: Today, Pine Grove consists of 4 1/2 acres of land, the Wisner Mansion, and several outbuildings, including a summer kitchen, outhouse, smokehouse, and root cellar. In addition to the outbuildings, there is the Drayton Plains One-Room School House and the Carriage House, which is home to the research library and archives, office, and Pioneer Museum. Please see website for info on tours, membership, hours, research, publications, news, etc.
Annual Events: Summer Social (Jul), Victorian Christmas Open House (Dec). Antique and Collectible Auctions (spring, fall)
Publications: The Oakland Gazette.

Pontiac Area Historical & Genealogical Society
Mailing Address: P.O. Box 430901 • Pontiac, MI 48343-0901
Phone: (248) 373-2629
Website: http://www.pontiac.lib.mi.us/genealog.htm
*Information may not be current.

Port Austin
(Huron County)

Huron City Museum
Mailing Address: 7995 Pioneer Dr. • Port Austin, MI 48467
Contact: Patricia Finan, Director of Programs
Phone: (989) 428-4123 • *Fax:* (989) 428-4123
Hours: Jun, Sep: Sat 10 a.m.-6 p.m. and Sun 11 a.m.-6 p.m., Jul-Aug: Thu-Mon 10 a.m.-6 p.m. and Sun 11 a.m.-6 p.m. Also by appointment.
Admission: $10/adult, $8/senior, $5/student.
Visitor Accessibility: On-site parking. Partially wheelchair accessible. Guided tours.
Website: www.huroncitymuseums.org
About: Langdon Hubbard founded this lumber town in 1854. Most of the 11 buildings on 10 acres were built after the 1881 fire that devastated Huron City. Village tour includes a log cabin, hotel, general store, Huron City Church, and U.S. Life Saving Station. Originally part of Pointe Aux Barques Lighthouse complex, the station contains artifacts from early rescue operations on the Great Lakes.
Exhibits/Collections: Original furnishings of Victorian mansion, farm equipment, life-saving station equipment, artwork, musical instruments.
Annual Events: Pioneer Day (Jun), Civil War Camp (Jul), Sawmill Day (Aug), Poetry Reading (Sep).
*Information may not be current.

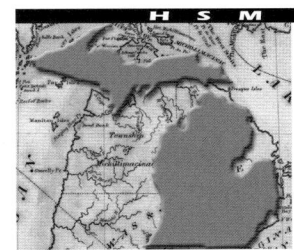

Port Austin Area Historical Society
Mailing Address: P.O. Box 450 • Port Austin, MI 48467
Contact: Martha Thuemmel, President
E-Mail: portaustinareahistoricalsociety@yahoo.com
Phone: (989) 551-5532
Site/Location: **Port Austin Area History Center**
Physical Location: 1424 Pte. Aux Barques Road • Port Austin, MI 48467
Hours: Apr-May: Sat-Sun 10 a.m.-4 p.m. Jun-Aug: Daily 10 a.m.-4 p.m. Sep-Dec: Sat-Sun 1-4 p.m.
Admission: Donations accepted.
Visitor Accessibility: Free on-site parking. Wheelchair accessible. Tour guide available; large groups should call in advance.
Website: www.portaustinhistorycenter.com
About: The Port Austin Area Historical Society's mission is to collect, preserve, and present history of the greater Port Austin area. The Port Austin Area History Center building is the renovated civic center. Exhibits include the Great Fire of 1881, Grindstone City, Port Crescent, Port Austin merchants/businesses, Port Austin manufacturing, Port Austin school items, Port Austin Air Force Station, Port Austin Reef Lighthouse, local agriculture, local homemaking, Great Lakes Storm of 1913/Howard M Hanna Jr., Union Rug Loom, 1890 cutter.
Exhibits/Collections: 50 years of local newspaper clippings, Port Austin Post 1886-1887, Huron County News 1870-1872, collection of Huron County cemeteries, John Varney Port Crescent Collection, Clevland Stone Company 1919 photos/maps.
Annual Events: Meetings 1st Thu Apr-Dec, 7 p.m. at history center.
Publications: "Life Along the Shoreline," "150 Years of Port Austin Area History," quarterly newsletter.

Port Hope
(Huron County)

Friends of Frank Murphy Museum
Mailing Address: 3038 Faye Dr. • Port Hope, MI 48468

Historical Society of Michigan

Contact: Barbara McGowan, Chairperson/Historian
Phone: (989) 428-3418
Physical Location: 142 S. Huron Ave. • Harbor Beach, MI 48441
Hours: Daily 10 a.m.-4 p.m.
Admission: $2/individual, $5/family.
Visitor Accessibility: Public parking on street and in back. Not wheelchair accessible. Tour guide present, docent by request.
About: The mission of the museum is to promote the life accomplishments of Justice Frank Murphy and to show a cross section of life in Harbor Beach from 1880 to the present. The four-building complex contains history of the Murphy family, including a law office with memorabilia and items used by the family.
Exhibits/Collections: Largest collection of Philipino cultural artificats in the United States.
Annual Events: "Dolly and Me" High Tea (Aug), Victorian Christmas High Tea (Dec), a high tea can be arranged on request. Meetings 1st Mon monthly, 12 p.m. in Visitors Center.

Port Huron
(St. Clair County)

Knowlton's Ice Museum of North America
Mailing Address: 317 Grand River Ave. • Port Huron, MI 48060
Contact: Melissa Davis, Director
E-Mail: knowltonsicemuseum@yahoo.com
Phone: (810) 987-5441
Hours: Jun-Sep: Thu-Sat 11 a.m.-5 p.m., Oct-May: Sat 11 a.m.-5 p.m.
Admission: Small admission charge.
Visitor Accessibility: Free on-site and street parking. Wheelchair accessible. Tour guide available for groups of 12 or more.
Website: www.knowltonsicemuseum.org
About: At 10,000 square feet, the Knowlton's Ice Museum houses more than 5,000 items. The ice museum depicts the natural ice-harvesting industry of long ago. It tells the history of one of the largest industries in the United States around 1880 and boasts using the water/ice resources of the Great Lakes through video, narrative, ice tools and memorabilia, and hands-on interactive displays. All items are displayed out in the open and not behind glass displays.
Exhibits/Collections: 5,000 artifacts. The ice museum also includes an antique car and truck collection, doll and buggy collection, dairy industry collection, and license plate collection.
Annual Events: Port Huron's Chilly Fest (Jan), Be a Tourist in Your Own Town (Jun).

Port Huron and Detroit Railroad Historical Society Museum.
Please see entry under Marysville: Port Huron and Detroit Railroad Historical Society.

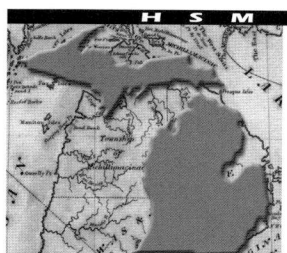

Port Huron Museum
Mailing Address: 1115 Sixth St. • Port Huron, MI 48060
Contact: Anita Varty, Director of Business Operations
E-Mail: info@phmuseum.org
Phone: (810) 982-0891
Fax: (810) 982-0053

Site/Location: Carnegie Center
Hours: Wed-Sun 10 a.m.-4 p.m.
Admission: $7/adult, $5/senior, $5/student, children 4 and under are free. Group rates available for 20-plus people; call (810) 982-0891, ext. 118 for reservations.
Visitor Accessibility: Free on-site and street parking. Wheelchair accessible. Self-guided.
Website: www.phmuseum.org
About: The Port Huron Museum celebrates the history and culture of the Blue Water Area and fosters an appreciation of other peoples and places. Through exhibitions, education, and public programs, the museum inspires knowledge of the past, participation in the present, and an imagination for the future.
Exhibits/Collections: More than 16,000 items on art, culture, and history of St. Clair County area. Great Lakes maritime history. Russell Sawyer photographic collection. Historic homes restoration information, genealogy, and general research sources.
Annual Events: 5K Tourist Trot (Jun), Blue Water SandFest (Jul), Hoptoberfest (Oct). Research group meets every Wed, 10 a.m. at Carnegie Center Museum. Family History Group meets 3rd Mon monthly, 7:30 p.m. at Carnegie Center Museum.
Publications: Quarterly newsletter.
Other Sites/Locations: Thomas Edison Depot Museum • Location: 510 Edison Parkway, Port Huron, MI 48060 • Hours: See website for hours • Admission: See museum rates • Visitor Accessibility: Free on-site parking. Wheelchair accessible. Self-guided. • The Fort Gratiot Station of the Grand Trunk Railroad, the Thomas Edison Depot, is where a teenage Thomas Edison worked during his years in Port Huron. Some of his early experiments were conducted here. A restored baggage car recreates his mobile chemistry lab. The Black Mariah Movie Theater shows films about Edison. There are also interactive displays and experiments.
Huron Lightship • Location: North side of Pine Grove Park (at the end of Prospect Place), Port Huron, MI 48060 • Hours: See website for hours • Admission: See museum rates • Visitor Accessibility: Free street parking. Not wheelchair accessible. • The Huron Lightship was a "floating lighthouse" and spent its entire career on the Great Lakes with 36 years in Port Huron. Retired in 1970, the ship has been refinished as a museum and traces the history of its service and those who served. There is a fog horn sounding on Memorial Day, Independence Day, and Labor Day.
Fort Gratiot Light Station • Location: 2802 Omar St., Port Huron, MI 48060 • Hours: See website for hours • Admission: Tours are $7/individual • Visitor Accessibility: Partially wheelchair accessible • The Fort Gratiot Light Station (b. 1829) is the oldest lighthouse in Michigan and was re-opened to the public in 2012. For information about the station's overnight program, e-mail avarty@phmuseum.org.

St. Clair County Family History Group
Mailing Address: P.O. Box 611483 • Port Huron, MI 48061
Contact: Marilyn Hebner, President
E-Mail: glgrogan@hotmail.com
Website: www.rootsweb.ancestry.com/~misccfhg
About: Encourages and assists in the study of family history. Promotes and publishes genealogical materials.
Exhibits/Collections: Collects and preserves records pertaining to St. Clair County and its people. Provides materials to Michigan Room of the St. Clair County Library.
Annual Events: Meetings held monthly at Port Huron Museum.
Publications: Quarterly newsletter (Blue Water Family Backgrounds). See website for current list of published records.

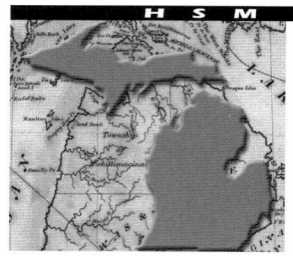

St. Clair County Library System
Mailing Address: Millage Account, 210 McMorran Blvd. • Port Huron, MI 48060
E-Mail: reference@sccl.lib.mi.us
Phone: (810) 987-7323 ext 142
Fax: (810) 987-7326
Hours: Mon-Sat 8:30 a.m.-9 p.m. Closed Sunday.

Admission: Free.
Visitor Accessibility: Free on-site parking. Partially wheelchair accessible (elevator upon request).
Website: www.stclaircountylibrary.org
About: The St. Clair County Library System relies on three principles: connections, growth, and progress. Through the use of their local genealogy records and collections, the library system provides information for the entire St. Clair County. Book, media, and online connections provide historical resources for the community.
Exhibits/Collections: Local history and genealogy, Michigan Room, including the W.L. Jenka Collection.

Port Sanilac
(Sanilac County)

Sanilac County Historical Society
Mailing Address: P.O. Box 158 • Port Sanilac, MI 48469
Contact: Thomas Fisher, President
E-Mail: sanilacmuseum@gmail.com
Phone: (810) 622-9946
Site/Location: **Sanilac County Historic Village and Museum**
Physical Location: 228 S. Ridge St. (M25) • Port Sanilac, MI 48469
Hours: Museum hours: Jun-Aug: Wed-Sun 10:30 a.m.-4:30 p.m. Office hours: Year-round: Mon, Wed, and Fri 10:30 a.m.-2:30 p.m.
Admission: Varies by event.
Visitor Accessibility: Free on-site parking. Wheelchair accessible. Tour guide available.
Website: www.sanilaccountymuseum.org
About: The Sanilac County Historic Village and Museum collects, preserves, and exhibits information, materials, objects, and buildings relating to the history of Sanilac County and the state of Michigan. Located on the 1853 estate of Dr. Joseph Loop, the museum includes 16 historic buildings: the flagship building, the doctor's 1872 Victorian mansion; theater; general store, dairy museum, carriage barn, log cabin, log barn, one-room school, hunting and fishing cabin, Native-American center, lake cottage, church, hearse shed, train depot, and barn.
Exhibits/Collections: Medical, agriculture, marine, Native American, Civil War, military, glass collections, genealogy and historical archives. Genealogy room open Wed 10:30 a.m.-2:30 p.m. or by appointment.
Annual Events: Native American, Voyageurs & Settlers Weekend (Jun), Arts & Craft Fair (Jul), Farm, Hunting & Fishing Weekend (Jul), Civil War Weekend (Aug), Antiques Yard Sale Trail (Aug), House in Mourning (Sep), Family Haunted Village (Oct), monthly concerts in museum church (Sep-Jun).
Publications: "Shingle Shavers and Berry Pickers," "The Loop-Harrison Family," "Sanilac Plat Books," "This is Walter: Letters Home from a Civil War Soldier."

Portage
(Kalamazoo County)

Air Zoo
Mailing Address: 6151 Portage Rd. • Portage, MI 49002
Contact: William Painter
E-Mail: airzoo@airzoo.org
Phone: (269) 382-6555 • *Fax:* (269) 382-1044
Hours: Mon-Sat 9 a.m.-5 p.m.; Sun 12-5 p.m. Closed Thanksgiving, Christmas Eve, and Christmas Day.
Admission: $10/adult, children 4 and under free. Individual ride tickets $2/individual.
Visitor Accessibility: Free on-site parking. Wheelchair accessible. Free tour guide available.
Website: www.airzoo.org
About: Preserves the legacy of flight for present and future generations. More than 80 aircraft in two exhibit buildings and restoration center. Numerous simulations for guests, including a balloon ride, 4D theater, 360-degree flight simulators, 3D trip to the ISS. Exhibits include Women in Aviation, Guadaleanal, and Dare to Dream.
Exhibits/Collections: Aircraft and aviation memorabilia, including an excellent collection of aircraft maintenance and reapair manuals.
Annual Events: Michigan Hall of Fame Enshrinement, Hops and Props beer tasting and casino night, Super Science Saturdays (last Sat monthly unless holiday) and Home School Discovery Days (first Tue monthly).
Information may not be current.

Portland
(Ionia County)

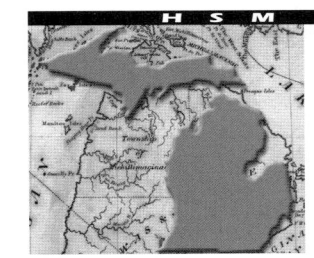

Portland Area Historical Society
Mailing Address: C/O Portland Library, 334 Kent Street • Portland, MI 48875
E-Mail: mi.pahs@gmail.com
Information may not be current.

Potterville
(Eaton County)

Potterville Benton Twp. District Library
Mailing Address: 150 Library Ln., P.O. Box 158 • Potterville, MI 48876
Contact: LuAnn Stachnik, Library Director
Phone: (517) 645-2989 • *Fax:* (517) 645-0268
Hours: Mon, Thu, Fri: 12:30-5:30 p.m. Tue: 10 a.m.-6 p.m. Wed: 12:30-7 p.m. Sat: 10 a.m.-1 p.m.
Visitor Accessibility: Free on-site parking. Wheelchair accessible.
Website: www.pottervillelibrary.org
About: The mission of the library is to provide and make readily available the library services necessary to meet the educational, informational, recreational, and cultural needs of the community.
Exhibits/Collections: Potterville News (1929-1964) newspaper on DVD.
Annual Events: Adult Winter Reading Program, All-Age Summer Reading Program.

Presque Isle
(Presque Isle County)

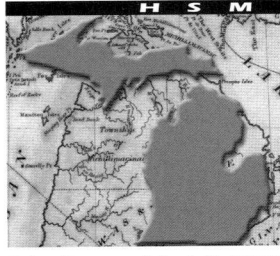

Presque Isle Township Museum Society
Mailing Address: P.O. Box 208 • Presque Isle, MI 49777
Contact: Drew Matuszak, President
E-Mail: dmatuszak@speednetllc.com
Phone: (989) 595-5419
Physical Location: 4500 E. Grand Lake Rd. • Presque Isle, MI 49777
Hours: May-Oct: Sat-Sun 11 a.m.-5 p.m.
Admission: $6/individual.
Visitor Accessibility: Free adjacent parking. Partially wheelchair accessible. Self-guided.
About: Society supports two lighthouses and a 1905 keeper's house. Towers open to climbs.
Exhibits/Collections: Artifacts dating to the 1900s.
Annual Events: 4th of July (Jul), Labor Day Picnic (Sep), Old-Fashioned Christmas. Monthly meetings held at 9:30 a.m. at Grand Lake Library.
Information may not be current.

Prudenville
(Roscommon County)

Roscommon County Genealogical Society
Mailing Address: P.O. Box 983 • Prudenville, MI 48651
Contact: Marilyn Andrick, President
E-Mail: roscogen@roscogen.org
Phone: (989) 366-1774
Site/Location: R.C.G.S. Research & Education Center
Physical Location: 2597 S Gladwin Rd • Prudenville, MI 48651
Hours: Mon 9 a.m.-1 p.m., Wed 12-4 p.m.
Admission: Free.
Visitor Accessibility: Free on-site parking. Wheelchair accessible. Self-guided.
Website: http://roscogen.org
About: The society encourages, aids, and shares knowledge of how to do genealogy research. The Research & Education Center is manned by a volunteer staff of members who educate the public on how to do their family history.
Exhibits/Collections: Family histories, county histories, cemetery records, and research books and aids. Five computers are available for Internet research; WIFI is available for laptops. Census records, newspapers, and other materials are available.
Annual Events: Meetings 2nd Thu monthly, 1 p.m. at the Old Denton Township Hall, 2597 S. Gladwin Rd., Prudenville.
Publications: Monthly newsletter (The Family Tree).

Ravenna
(Muskegon County)

Ravenna Historical Society
Mailing Address: 12278 Stafford St.• Ravenna, MI 49451
Contact: Mary De Hosler
E-Mail: hillhouse12556@aol.com
Phone: (231) 853-2400
Hours: Mar-Dec: Wed 2-4:30 p.m. Also by appointment.
About: Museum in former Odd Fellows Hall has photos, local artifacts, military collection, and school yearbooks.
Annual Events: Meetings 3rd Thu Mar-Dec, 9:30 a.m. at the museum.
*Information may not be current.

Ray Township
(Macomb County)

Wolcott Mill Metropark Historic Center
Mailing Address: 63841 Wolcott • Ray Township, MI 48096
Contact: Kathy Reidt, Interpretive Guide
E-Mail: wolcott.mill@metroparks.com
Phone: (586) 749-5997 • *Fax:* (586) 749-2835
Hours: Fri-Sun 9 a.m.-5 p.m.
Admission: $5/individual day pass.
Visitor Accessibility: Free on-site parking. Partially wheelchair accessible; path to dam is not paved. Tour guide available by appointment.
Website: www.metroparks.com
About: Built in 1845, this historic grist mill sits on the banks of the north branch of the Clinton River. The mill looks as it did in 1967 when the mill closed its doors. Also on-site is a warehouse museum, lumber barn, and long barn.
Exhibits/Collections: Roller mills, turbines, grain elevators, lumbering tools, buggies, sleigh, and broom-making equipment.
Annual Events: Civil War Skirmish, Annual Quilt and Antique Car Show, Sawdust Festival, Johnny Appleseed Festival, An Old-Fashioned Thanksgiving, Heritage Holidays.

Redford
(Wayne County)

Redford Township Historical Commission
Mailing Address: 12895 Berwyn • Redford, MI 48239
Contact: Regina Gilbert, Commissioner
E-Mail: rthc09@gmail.com
Phone: (313) 937-0310
Hours: Wed 12 p.m.-3 p.m. and by appointment.
Admission: Free.
Visitor Accessibility: Free on-site parking. Wheelchair accessible. Self-guided.
Website: www.redfordtownshiphistoricalcommission.org
About: The Redford Township Historical Commission collects and preserves historical materials relating to the history of the Northwest Territory, the state of Michigan, and the Charter Township of Redford. The commission compiles histories of the township and area and participates in other historical endeavors.
Exhibits/Collections: Fred DesAutels research, church archives, Houghton genealogy and photos, family histories and genealogies, Redford voter registration cards, census records from 1840, land patents/abstracts, Sandhill/Redford Village history and photos.
Annual Events: Meetings 1st Wed monthly, 10 a.m. Society meetings 2nd Wed, 12:30 p.m.
Publications: "Redford Township: Its Heritage and Its History," "Records of Record Cemetery," "Redford Cemetery Association."

Reed City
(Osceola County)

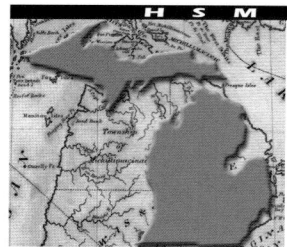

Old Rugged Cross Historical Society
Mailing Address: 4918 Park St., P.O. Box 52 • Reed City, MI 49677
Contact: Marilyn Jones, Co-President
Phone: (231) 832-5431
Site/Location: Old Rugged Cross Museum
Physical Location: 4198 Park St. • Reed City, MI 49677
Hours: May-Sep: Sat-Sun 1-4 p.m. Also by appointment. Closed on holidays.
Admission: Donations accepted.
Visitor Accessibility: On-site parking. Wheelchair accessible. Tour guides available.
About: Preserves the possessions of Rev. Geo. Bennard, author of "The Old Rugged Cross." Collects, preserves, and displays artifacts and information related to the history of the Reed City area.
Exhibits/Collections: Reed City newspapers, starting in 1874, preserved on microfilm. Archives of Osceola County Genealogical Society.
Annual Events: Crossroads Festival (Aug), Evergreen Festival (Nov). Meetings 1st Thu monthly at the museum; 1 p.m. Jan-Apr and Oct-Dec, 7 p.m. May-Sep.
Publications: Biannual newsletter (The Historian). Biannual publication (The Osceolean).
*Information may not be current.

Remus
(Mecosta County)

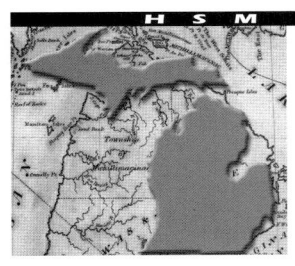

Remus Area Historical Society
Mailing Address: 324 S. Sheridan Ave., P.O. Box 71 • Remus, MI 49340
Contact: Charlene Lenon, Director
E-Mail: museum@winntel.net
Phone: (989) 967-8153
Site/Location: **Remus Area Historical Museum**
Hours: May-Oct: Wed 11 a.m.-3 p.m. Also by appointment.
Admission: Free.
Visitor Accessibility: Free on-site parking. Wheelchair accessible. Self-guided.
Website: www.remus.org
About: The Remus Area Historical Society preserves the rich heritage of the Remus area by acquiring historical artifacts and geneaology records of local families.
Exhibits/Collections: Remus Cooperative Creamery, local veterans display, local one-room schoolhouse items from the area, local churches and history.
Annual Events: Spring Tea (May), Fall Festival (Oct), Remus Heritage Days (Jul). Meetings 2nd Wed monthly, 5 p.m. at museum.
Publications: Remus Area Centennial Book 1976 Before Remus Consolidated School (2008) Remus Heritage Recipes

Republic
(Marquette County)

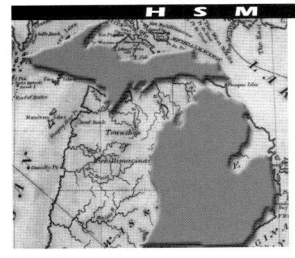

Republic Area Historical Society
Mailing Address: P.O. Box 201 • Republic, MI 49879
Contact: LaVerne Antilla, President
E-Mail: lavantl@aol.com
Phone: (906) 376-2258
Site/Location: **Pascoe House Museum**
Physical Location: 183 Cedar St. • South Republic, MI 49879
Hours: Memorial Day-Labor Day: Sat-Sun 1-3 p.m. Also by appointment.
Admission: Donations accepted.
Visitor Accessibility: Free street parking. Partially wheelchair accessible, downstairs only. Tour guide available; call ahead.
Website: www.republicmichigan.com/historical-society/
About: The Republic Area Historical Society provides programs, dispays, exhibits, and workshops for the Republic area and collects, preserves, and distributes historical knowledge of the area through resource people, oral history, research, and collection of photographs, artifacts, and documents. The Pascoe House is an 1880s house. The museum features changing exhibits.
Exhibits/Collections: Farm and logging items, church and business history, mining artifacts, household items, family genealogies, photo albums, and old publications.
Annual Events: Guest speakers, summer event, annual meeting (Nov), Christmas event (Dec). Meetings 3rd Tue monthly (except Dec), 7 p.m. at Riverview Apartments.
Publications: "Witch Lake & Environs," "Streets of Old Republic," "Life on the Farm, "Moving of Republic," "Black River." Quarterly newsletter for members.
*Information may not be current.

Richland
(Kalamazoo County)

Richland Community Library
Mailing Address: 8951 Park Street • Richland, MI 49083
Phone: (269) 629-9085
Site/Location: **Barnes and Little History Room**
Hours: Tue-Fri 1 p.m.-5 p.m. Also by appointment.
Admission: Free.
Website: www.richlandlibrary.org
About: History room honors Richland pioneers, Barnes and Little families.
Exhibits/Collections: Limited to items from the Richland/Gull Lake area. Barnes and Little Families Collection. Extensive school-related items and photographs. Village/library records. Newsclipping and newspapers from Richland 1975-1995. Family files.
*Information may not be current.

Richmond
(Macomb County)

Richmond Area Historical and Genealogical Society
Mailing Address: P.O. Box 68 • Richmond, MI 48062
Contact: Christine Rowley, President
E-Mail: richmondareahistoricalsociety@gmail.com
Phone: (586) 727-7773
Site/Location: **Richmond Historic Village**
Physical Location: 36045 Park St. • Richmond, MI 48062
Hours: By appointment only; call ahead for special event exceptions.
Admission: Donations accepted.
Visitor Accessibility: Free on-site and street parking. Wheelchair accessible. Tour guide available; donations accepted.
Website: www.richmondhistoricalsociety.org
About: The Richmond Area Historical and Genealogical Society preserves the history of the Richmond area. The Richmond Historic Village consists of a one-room schoolhouse (b. 1886), train depot (b. 1915), log cabin (b. 1850), and a museum with displays that change biannually.
Exhibits/Collections: Photographs of Richmond area families and early Richmond businesses and homes; high school yearbooks; artifacts from Richmond area; the Richmond Review (100 years) in digital format; family histories.
Annual Events: Annual Log Cabin Day (Jun), Annual Good Old Days Festival (Sep). Board meetings 1st Mon, 7 p.m. at museum.
Publications: "Images of America: The Richmond Area."

River Rouge
(Wayne County)

River Rouge Historical Museum
Mailing Address: 10600 W. Jefferson • River Rouge, MI 48218
Contact: Thomas Abair
E-Mail: rrmuseum48218@aol.com
Phone: (313) 842-4200
Physical Location: 10750 West Jefferson • River Rouge, MI 48218
Hours: Sun 12-4 p.m. except holidays.
Admission: Free.
Visitor Accessibility: Free on site parking. Wheelchair accessible. Free tour guide available.
Website: www.riverrougemuseum.com

About: Displays of city memorabilia, ship-building industry, organizations.
Exhibits/Collections: City records, tax rolls, licenses, abstracts, River Rouge Heralds 1930-1984, genealogical collection, church and census records, city directories.
Annual Events: Edmund Fitzgerald memorial service (Nov).

River Rouge Historical Society
Mailing Address: 221 Burke Street • River Rouge, MI 48218
*Information may not be current.

Rochester
(Oakland County)

Meadow Brook Hall
Mailing Address: 480 S. Adams Rd. • Rochester, MI 48309
Contact: Shannon O'Berski, Marketing & Communications Manager
E-Mail: stobersk@oakland.edu
Phone: (248) 364-6200 • *Fax:* (248) 364-6201
Hours: Schedule for tours: Summer: Mon-Sun 11:30 a.m., 12:30 p.m., 1:30 p.m., 2:30 p.m. Fall/spring: Mon-Fri 1:30 p.m., Sat-Sun 11:30 a.m., 12:30 p.m., 1:30 p.m., 2:30 p.m.; Holiday Walk Tours: Tue-Sun 11 a.m.-5 p.m., Mon 11 a.m.-9 p.m.
Admission: $15/adult, $10/senior, $10/faculty $10/alumni, Oakland University students and children 12 and under are free.
Visitor Accessibility: Free parking lot. Fully wheelchair accessible. All tours are given by a docent (included in admission cost).
Website: www.meadowbrookhall.org
About: Residence of Matilda Dodge Wilson, widow of auto pioneer John Dodge, and her second husband, lumberbroker Alfred Wilson. Constructed between 1926 and 1929, the 80,000-square-foot mansion represents one of the finest examples of Tudor-revival architecture in America.
Exhibits/Collections: Highlights include Tiffany art glass, costumes by Paul Poiret, Stickley furniture, paintings by Sir Joshua Reynolds, Sevres and Meissen porcelain, and Rookwood pottery. Extensive archives open by appointment.
Annual Events: Speakeasy, Wine, Wickets & Wheels, Wild Game Dinner, Mystery Dinner, Breakfast with Santa, Holiday High Tea, and Holiday Walk.
*Information may not be current.

Oakland University Library
Mailing Address: 2200 N Squirrel Road • Rochester, MI 48309
Contact: Dominique Daniel, Coordinator Archives/Special Collections
E-Mail: ref@oakland.edu
Phone: 248/370-2419
Hours: Mon-Fri 8:30 a.m.-4:30 p.m. (appointments preferred)
Visitor Accessibility: On-site parking at no cost. Wheelchair accessible.
Website: http://library.oakland.edu/
About: The Oakland University Archives is the official depository of materials relating to the history of Oakland University from its founding to the present. Its primary purpose is to document the history of the university and its impact in Oakland County and beyond. Oakland University Special Collections document Oakland County history, as well as Southeast Michigan history.
Exhibits/Collections: Historical records, such as tax rolls. Papers of Eugene Mack (1845-1940); journals of Abram Byron Coryell; and an Oakland County African-American Oral History Collection (1976-1982).

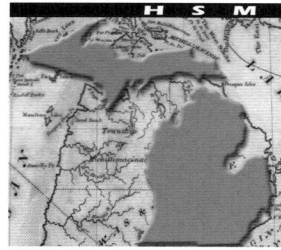

Rochester Hills Public Library
Mailing Address: 500 Olde Towne Rd. • Rochester, MI 48307
Contact: Librarians, Reference Staff
E-Mail: adult@rhpl.org
Phone: (248) 650-7130
Fax: (248) 650-7131
Hours: Mon-Thu 9 a.m.-9 p.m., Fri-Sat 9 a.m.-6 p.m., Sun 1-6 p.m. during school year.
Admission: Free.
Visitor Accessibility: Free on-site parking. Wheelchair accessible. Self-guided.
Website: http://www.rhpl.org/
About: The local history room focuses on the communities of Rochester, Rochester Hills, and Oakland Township. Holdings include, but not limited to, yearbooks, photographs, historical atlases, cemetery maps and indexes, local newspaper clippings and obits.

Rochester-Avon Historical Society
Mailing Address: P.O. Box 80783 • Rochester, MI 48308
Contact: Brian Dunphy, President
E-Mail: rahsupdates@gmail.com
Phone: (248) 266-5400
Site/Location: **World War II Honor Roll Monument**
Physical Location: World War II Honor Roll Monument, 400 Sixth St. • Rochester, MI 48307
Hours: 24 hours/7 days a week.
Admission: Free.
Visitor Accessibility: Free street parking. Wheelchair accessible. Self-guided.
Website: www.rochesteravonhistoricalsociety.org
About: The Rochester-Avon Historical Society (RAHS) was founded in 1969 to help preserve, collect, and interpret the history of the greater Rochester area for present and future generations.
Exhibits/Collections: Postcards, photographs, memorabilia of Rochester, businesses, schools. Death notices, marriages, divorces, etc; articles; oral histories of area residents, Class records and yearbooks.
Annual Events: Antique Appraisal Day (Mar), Historic Rochester Downtown Walking Tours (May-Oct), Mount Avon Cemetery Living History Walk (Sep). Monthly evening meetings 1st Thu Sep-Dec and Feb-May, 7 p.m. at Rochester Hills Public Library. Monthly daytime meetings 1st Tue Sep-Oct, Dec, and Feb-May, 12 p.m. at the Rochester Community House.
Publications: "Remembering Rochester - Vanished Rochester," "Remembering Rochester - Main Street Stories," "Home Town Rochester," "Historical Tour Guide: A Walking Tour of Rochester Michigan," "A Lively Town - 152 Years in Rochester," "Rochester Preserving History - A Pictorial Journey."

Rochester Hills
(Oakland County)

Auburn Hills Historical & Genealogical Society
Mailing Address: 1651 Bedford Square Dr., Apt. 101 • Rochester Hills, MI 48306
Contact: Ray Lucas, Treasurer
E-Mail: lucasray@ymail.com, relucasgenealogy@earthlink.net
Phone: (248) 321-5643
Hours: By appointment only.
Website: http://www.auburnhills.org/index.asp?Type=B_BASIC&SEC={3837E

About: Studying the history of Pontiac Township through Auburn Hills.
Exhibits/Collections: Newspapers, records, maps, photographs.
Annual Events: Meetings 2nd Mon, 7 p.m. at Auburn Hills Library.
Information may not be current.

Rochester Hills Historic District Commission
Mailing Address: City of Rochester Hills, 1000 Rochester Hills Dr. • Rochester Hills, MI 48309
Contact: Derek Dealcourt,
E-Mail: planning@rochesterhills.org
Phone: (248) 656-4660
Website: www.rochesterhills.org
Information may not be current.

Rochester Hills Museum at Van Hoosen Farm
Mailing Address: 1005 Van Hoosen Road, • Rochester Hills, MI 48306
Contact: Patrick J. McKay, Supervisor of Interpretive Services
E-Mail: rhmuseum@rochesterhills.org
Phone: (248) 656-4663
Fax: (248) 608-8198
Hours: Fri-Sat 1-4 p.m. Also by appointment.
Admission: $5/adult, $3/senior, $3/student.
Visitor Accessibility: Free on-site parking. Wheelchair accessible. Tour guide available.
Website: www.rochesterhills.org/museum
About: The Rochester Hills Museum at Van Hoosen Farm is a local history museum that focus on the lives of the Taylor-Van Hoosen families that settled a portion of the community in 1823. Located within Stony Creek Village (a collection of privately owned, pre-Civil War homes and listed on the National Register of Historic Places), the location was the home of five generations of the family. Prominent members of the family included Dr. Bertha Van Hoosen (1863-1952), a renowned surgeon, and Dr. Sarah Van Hoosen Jones (1892-1972), a noted breeder of Holstein cattle. The museum also serves as the repository for information about the greater Rochester community. The site includes the 1840 Van Hoosen Farmhouse, 1850 Red House, 1848 Stoney Creek Schoolhouse, 1927 Calf Barn, and exhibits inside the 1927 Dairy Barn.
Exhibits/Collections: Reference files, photographs, maps, and archival materials relating to individuals, families and history of Greater Rochester Area includes Civil War records, Van Hoosen family, historic homes, and community schools.
Annual Events: Spring on the Farm, Summer Camps, Environmental Programs, Wet and Wild Wednesdays, Stonewall Pumpkin Festival, Holiday Events.
Publications: "A History of Avon Township," "A Lively Town - 152 Years in Rochester Petticoat Surgeon," "Chronicle of Van Hoosen Centenary Farm," "If this is Hastings, Then Where is Hog's Hollow?"

Rockford
(Kent County)

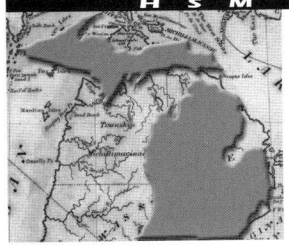

Algoma Township Historical Society
Mailing Address: 10531 Algoma Ave., • Rockford, MI 49341
Contact: Julie Sjogren, President
E-Mail: planning@algomatwp.org
Phone: (616) 866-1583
Fax: (616) 866-3832
Hours: Mon-Fri 8:30 a.m.-4:30 p.m.
Admission: Free.
Visitor Accessibility: Free on-site parking. Partially wheelchair accessible. Self-guided.
Website: www.algomatwp.org
About: The Algoma Township Historical Society preserves and protects the history of Algoma Township. The Society's display cabinets are located in the Algoma Township Hall building for the public to view. Items are exchanged in and out for a fresh display.
Exhibits/Collections: Exhibits on Algoma Township history, pictures, and artifacts located at the Township Hall. Historic Stegman Creek culvert and Historic Pine Island Bridge, both registered with the State of Michigan Historic landmarks
Annual Events: Annual Membership & Election of Officers Meeting (Aug), Memorial Day Service. Commission meetings 1st Thu monthly, 9a.m. at Chalmers School House (corner of Pine Island Drive and Fonger Street).
Publications: Quarterly membership newsletter.

Oakfield Pioneer Heritage Society
Mailing Address: 10975 12-Mile Road NE, • Rockford, MI 49341
Contact: Judith Gager, Chairman
E-Mail: jagager@aol.com
Phone: (616) 874-6271
Site/Location: **Oakfield Pioneer Heritage Museum**
Physical Location: 11009 Podunk Road NE • Greenville, MI 48838
Hours: Jun-Sep: 2nd and 4th Sun 2-4 p.m.
Admission: Donations accepted.
Visitor Accessibility: Free on-site parking. Partially wheelchair accessible; main floor only. Tour guide available.
Website: http://www.commoncorners.com/kent/kent_oakfield_ophs.htm
About: An auxiliary of the Oakfield Township Historical Commission, the Oakfield Pioneer Heritage Society identifies, gathers, and displays historical items and archives of Oakfield Township in Kent County and manages the Oakfield Pioneer Heritage Museum.
Museum displays show school, church, Gleaner, and community history, including commercial, agricultural, and residential ways of life.
Exhibits/Collections: Archives are available for genealogical research. Photos and items are displayed showing schools, churches, Gleaners, a Harvard store display, the Podunk Mill, an 1898 dishwasher, and other home and farming items.
Annual Events: Spring Into the Past (May). Meetings 3rd Thu Jun-Oct, 10 a.m. at museum.
Publications: Periodic newsletters.

Rockford Area Historical Society
Mailing Address: P.O. Box 781 • Rockford, MI 49341
Contact: Terry Konkle
E-Mail: rockfordmuseum@gmail.com
Phone: (616) 866-2235
Site/Location: **Rockford Area Historical Museum**
Physical Location: 21 S. Monroe St. • Rockford, MI 49341
Hours: Call or see website.
Admission: Free.
Visitor Accessibility: Free on-site parking. Wheelchair accessible. Tour guide available; groups can schedule an appointment by calling (616) 866-2235.
Website: www.rockfordmuseum.org

About: The Rockford Area Historical Society is dedicated to preserving the history of the Rockford area. The society has operated the Rockford Area Museum since 1975 and is now in a former county courthouse. New exhibits focus on the development of the Rockford area as a logging community and its evolution into a dynamic small city. Other exhibits tell the story of Rockford's business community, schools, connection to America's military history, agriculture, and the nearby townships that compose the Rockford area.
Exhibits/Collections: Birth and death data, family histories, cemetery indexes and obituaries, marriage records, plat maps, land patent indexes, census indexes, Civil War records, newspapers, school yearbooks, and telephone directories.
Annual Events: Make the Scarecrow Fundraiser (Oct), Annual Auction (fall). Meetings 1st Thu monthly Sep-May at community cabin.
Publications: "Rockford," "From Sawmill to City."

Rockland
(Ontonagon County)

Old Victoria Restoration
Mailing Address: P.O. Box 43 • Rockland, MI 49960
Contact: Patty Pattison, Site Manager
E-Mail: oldvictoria1899@hotmail.com
Phone: (906) 886-2617
Physical Location: 25401 Victoria Dam Road • Rockland, MI 49960
Hours: Jun 15-Oct 6: 11 a.m.-5 p.m.
Admission: Cabin tours: $5/adult, $2/children (6-12). Extended tours and group rates available; call ahead.
Website: www.facebook.com/oldvictoria
About: Four log cabins, restored at their original remote mining location, give visitors a true feeling of the life faced by copper miners and their families a century ago. Hands-on guided tours will take you back in time for an hour. The site is owned and operated by the Society for the Restoration of Old Victoria, whose members have been preserving, protecting, restoring, repairing, and interpreting the site since 1973.
Exhibits/Collections: Restored log cabins rest on a 45-acre site on which are also the remains of 16 more company log houses. Ruins of the mine are nearby.
Annual Events: Log Cabin Day (Jun), Old Victoria Craft Fair (Aug).
Publications: Newsletter.

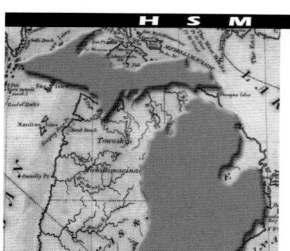

Rockland Township Historical Museum
Mailing Address: P.O. Box 296 • Rockland, MI 49960
Contact: Josie Olson
Phone: (906) 886-2821
Physical Location: 40 National Ave. • Rockland, MI 49960
Hours: Memorial Day-Sep: Daily 11:30 a.m.-4:30 p.m. Also by appointment.
Admission: Free.
Visitor Accessibility: Wheelchair accessible.
About: The Rockland Township Historical Museum is dedicated to the history of Rockland Township's people, copper mines, businesses, and first telephone system in the state of Michigan. Home settings include kitchen, dining room, parlor, and bedroom. Also mining, farming, school, and military displays.
Exhibits/Collections: Photographs, newspapers, and documents. Historical and genealogical research available.

Rockwood
(Wayne County)

Rockwood Area Historical Society
Mailing Address: P.O. Box 68 • Rockwood, MI 48173
Contact: Patricia Quick
E-Mail: jequick@sbcglobal.net
Phone: (734) 379-0674 • *Fax:* (734) 379-3007
Site/Location: Rockwood Area Historical Museum
Physical Location: 32787 Wood St. • Rockwood, MI 48173
Hours: Sun and Tue 1-3 p.m.
Admission: Donations accepted.
Visitor Accessibility: Wheelchair accessible.
About: The Rockwood Area Historical Society's museum building is a replica of the 1869 Rockwood railroad depot. The museum was dedicated in 2002. Exhibits change about three times a year. Other attractions include the restoration of a 1968 ICG caboose, which was dedicated in 2005 and is available for tours at no cost.
Exhibits/Collections: Photos, documents, stories, and artifacts relating to the Brownstown, Rockwood, and South Rockwood areas, including Detroit River Light, Pointe Mouillee, industrial and automotive industries, domestic life, and decorative arts.
Annual Events: Homemade Candy and Cookie Sale (Dec). Four annual programs with speakers, 7 p.m. at Rockwood Community Center.
*Information may not be current.

Rogers City
(Presque Isle County)

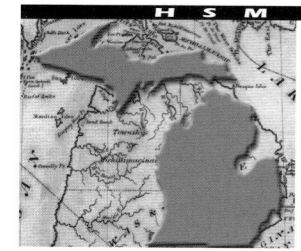

40 Mile Point Lighthouse Society
Mailing Address: P.O. Box 205, 7323 U.S. 23 N • Rogers City, MI 49779
Contact: Barb Stone
E-Mail: barbara71@hughes.net
Phone: (989) 734-4587
Fax: (989) 734-4587
Site/Location: 40 Mile Point Lighthouse
Physical Location: Presque Isle County Lighthouse Park, 7323 U.S. 23 N • Rogers City, MI 48779
Hours: Tue-Sat 10 a.m.-4 p.m.; Sun 12 p.m.-4 p.m.
Admission: Free.
Visitor Accessibility: Free on-site parking. Partially wheelchair accessible; grounds and fog signal building can be accessed via wheelchair, lighthouse has steps. Volunteer guest lighthouse keepers available for tours during open hours.
Website: www.40milepointlighthouse.org
About: The 40 Mile Point Lighthouse Society is dedicated to the restoration and preservation of 40 Mile Point Lighthouse. The society also has a guest lighthouse keeper program. Lighthouse includes a parlor, dining room, kitchen, and two bedrooms furnished in turn-of-the-century decor. The site also features nautical displays, an active 4th Order Fresnel Lens, access to the light tower, and restored 1912 Calcite Pilot House. Also on site is a fog signal building that has many nautical-themed displays.
Exhibits/Collections: Nautical artifacts, lighthouse, shipwreck, and restored 1912 Pilot house.
Annual Events: Memorial Day Weekend Open House (May), Annual Night at the Lighthouse (Oct). Board meetings monthly from Mar-Nov.

Glawe School Museum.
Please see entry under Millersburg: Glawe School Museum.

Great Lakes Lore Maritime Museum
Mailing Address: 367 N. Third St. • Rogers City, MI 49779
Contact: Dave Erickson, Director
Phone: (989) 734-0706
Hours: May 1-Dec 1: Mon-Sat 11 a.m.-4 p.m.; Sun 11 a.m.-3 p.m. Winter: Mon 10 a.m.-4 p.m. Also by appointment.
Admission: $3/adult, children 12 and under free
Visitor Accessibility: On-site parking. Wheelchair accessible.
Website: www.gllmm.com
About: The Great Lakes Lore Maritime Museum preserves the history of Great Lakes shipping and the people who worked the lakes. There is a large display of ship models, photographs, and artifacts. The memorial hall honors the crews of the Carl D. Bradley, S.S. Cedarville, Daniel J. Morrell, and Edmund Fitzgerald.
Exhibits/Collections: Ship models, drawings, photographs, and artifacts relating to Great Lakes shipping and people who served the shipping industry. Bell from Carl D. Bradley.
Annual Events: Bell Tolling Ceremony for SS Cedarville (May), Bell Tolling Cermony for the Edmund Fitzgerald (Nov), Bell Tolling Cermony for the Carl D. Bradley, and Bell Tolling Cermony for the Daniel J. Morrell (Nov).
Publications: Quarterly member newsletter.
*Information may not be current.

Presque Isle County Historical Museum
Mailing Address: P.O. Box 175 • Rogers City, MI 49779
Contact: Mark Thompson, Executive Director & Curator
E-Mail: bradleymuseum@yahoo.com
Phone: (989) 734-0123
Fax: (989) 734-0123
Site/Location: The Bradley House
Physical Location: 176 W. Michigan Ave. • Rogers City, MI 49779
Hours: May-Sep: Wed-Sun 12:30-4:30 p.m. Call ahead for Nov/Dec open hours.
Admission: Free.
Visitor Accessibility: Free street parking. The Hoffman Annex is wheelchair accessible, the Bradley House is not. Tour guide available; large groups should contact the museum in advance of arrival. Children under 12 must be accompanied by a responsible adult.
Website: www.thebradleyhouse.org
About: The Presque Isle County Historical Museum preserves local history by collecting relevant artifacts, documents, and photographs; operating a museum; interpreting the history of the county; and providing historical assistance to individuals, groups, and organizations. The Bradley House is listed on the National Register of Historic Places. The museum also operates the Hoffman Annex, which includes offices, a research room, the gift shop and bookstore, and four exhibit rooms. In addition to the permanent exhibits, two revolving exhibits are also featured.
Exhibits/Collections: Artifacts, documents, and photographs related to the history of Presque Isle County. Three major photographic collections: the Calcite Collection, the Ferris Parsons Collection, and the James and Leona Stewart Collection.
Annual Events: Northern Lake Huron Voyaguer Rendezvous (Aug), National City Festival (Aug), Christmas at the Museum (Nov-Dec). Meetings 2nd Thu Jan-Nov.
Publications: "Virgin Forests to Modern Homes," "The Baby Boomers Guide to Rogers City," "Baby Boomers II," "Before the Baby Boomers," "Harry: The Life and Times of Harry Grambau," "The Metz Fire of 1908," "Calcite and the Bradley Boats: A Pictorial History, 1912-2012," "Little Italy," "Presque Isle County," "Almost an Island: And Early History of Presque Isle County."
Other Sites/Locations: The Henry and Margaret Hoffman Annex • Location: 185 W. Michigan Ave., Rogers City, MI 49779 • Hours: May-Dec: Wed-Sun 12:30-4:30 p.m. • Admission: Free • Visitor Accessibility: Free on-site and street parking. Wheelchair accessible. Tour guide available. • The Henry and Margaret Hoffman Annex houses the museum's offices, gift shop, and numerous exhibits. Permanent exhibits include the John Bunton Collection of more than 1,000 cameras and projectors and other photographic equipment; the Calcite room with photos and other materials related to the world's largest limestone quarry; and the Bradley Boats with photos, models, and artifacts from the Bradley Transportation Fleet.

Romeo
(Macomb County)

Romeo District Library—Kezar Library
Mailing Address: 107 Church St. • Romeo, MI 48065
Contact: Stacie Guzzo, Branch Manager
E-Mail: stacie@romeodistrictlibrary.org
Phone: (586) 752-2583
Fax: (586) 336-7300
Hours: Mon-Thu 11 a.m.-7 p.m., Fri 10 a.m.-6 p.m., Sat 10 a.m.-2 p.m.
Admission: Free.
Visitor Accessibility: Free street parking. Wheelchair accessible. Self-guided.
Website: romeodistrictlibrary.org
About: The library collects historical and genealogical materials relating to Romeo, Bruce Township, and Washington Township.

Romeo Historic District Commission
Mailing Address: Village of Romeo, 121 W. St Clair • Romeo, MI 48065
Contact: Marian McLaughlin
E-Mail: villageofromeo@yahoo.com
Phone: 565/752-3565 • *Fax:* 565/752-5205
Hours: Mon-Fri 9 a.m.-5 p.m.
Admission: Free.
Visitor Accessibility: On-site parking. Wheelchair accessible (rear door entrance).
Website: www.villageofromeo.org
About: As part of the Village of Romeo's local government, the Romeo Historic District Commision reviews building permits for appropriateness of changes/additions to structures and areas in accordance to the Secretary of Interior's Standards for Historic Preservation.
Exhibits/Collections: Files on individual properties.
Annual Events: Meetings 2nd and 4th Thu as necessary.

Romeo Historical Society
Mailing Address: P.O. Box 412 • Romeo, MI 48065
Contact: Sue Kane, President
Phone: (586) 752-4111
Site/Location: Romeo Arts & Archives Center
Physical Location: 290 N. Main Street • Romeo, MI 48065

Hours: Tue 7 a.m.-9 p.m.
Admission: Free.
Visitor Accessibility: On-site and street parking. All sites wheelchair accessible. Staff available for tours.
Website: www.romeohistoricalsociety.org
About: Dedicated to the preservation, documentation, and promotion of the village of Romeo and its surrounding area.
Exhibits/Collections: Approximately 40 oil paintings, mostly by William Gibbs.
Annual Events: Christmas Candle House Tour (Dec), Barn Tour (Sep), Board meetings 3rd Thu monthly, general meetings 1st Thu monthly.
Other Sites/Locations: Bancroft/Stranahan House • Location: 132 Church St., Romeo, MI 48065 • Hours: Open Tue 7 a.m.-9 p.m. • Attractions include furniture, oil paintings, historic clothing, and more.
C. Craig Blacksmith Museum • Location: 301 N. Bailey St., Romeo, MI 48065 • Hours: Open summer, every other Sat 10 a.m.-2 p.m. A working blacksmith shop.

Romulus
(Wayne County)

Romulus Historical Society & Museum
Mailing Address: P.O. Box 74386 • Romulus, MI 48174
Contact: Pearl Varner, Museum Director
Phone: (734) 942-2340
Physical Location: 11120 Hunt St. • Romulus, MI 48174
Hours: Sun 1-4 p.m. Also by appointment.
Admission: Donations accepted.
Visitor Accessibility: On-site and street parking. Three main buildings are wheelchair accesible; caboose is not. Guided tours for groups by appointment only ($1/individual).
About: Collects and preserves the history of Romulus. Historical park includes 1839 schoolhouse (now museum), 1855 Kingsley house, 1920s windmill, 1900s railroad freight house, and 1949 caboose. Underground Railroad secret door and hiding place under Kingsley House stairs.
Exhibits/Collections: Archives stored in Kingsley House. Romulus artifacts, vintage clothing, documents, diaries, family histories, photographs, maps, high school yearbooks from 1945 to present.
Annual Events: Flea market (Jun). Meetings 3rd Wed monthly Jan-May and Aug-Nov, 7 p.m. at the museum.
Publications: Biannual newsletter.

Roscommon
(Roscommon County)

Au Sable River Center
Mailing Address: P.O. Box 363 • Roscommon, MI 48653
Contact: Albert Schultz
E-Mail: ausablerivercenter@voyager.net
Phone: (989) 275-4392
Physical Location: 211 N. Main Street • Roscommon, MI 48653
Hours: Summer: Sat-Mon afternoons. Also by appointment; call (989) 275-5826.
Admission: Free.
Visitor Accessibility: On-site parking (free). Wheelchair accessible. Call (989) 275-5826 to confirm tour guide availability.
Website: www.ausablerivercenter.org
About: Former conservation headquarters was moved and renovated by volunteers. Houses a collection of items relating to activities on the great AuSable Watershed. Model train club has replica of the town, circa 1930s, as well as David Schoppenagon's dugout canoe. Verlen Kruger's canoes, maps, and equipment from trips around and across the hemisphere.
Exhibits/Collections: Flies tied by Ann Schweigert and others.
Annual Events: Roscommon River Festival (Jul). Meetings on 3rd Thu monthly, 7:15 p.m. at the center.
Publications: Biannual water quality monitoring results. "A Train Garden."
*Information may not be current.

Civilian Conservation Corps Museum.
Please see entry under Lansing: Michigan Historical Center.

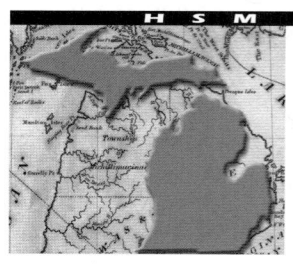

Roscommon Area Historical Society
Mailing Address: P.O. Box 916 • Roscommon, MI 48653
Contact: Ronald Swain, President
Phone: (989) 344-7386
Physical Location: 404 Lake Street • Roscommon, MI 48653
Hours: Memorial Day-Sep: Fri-Sat 12-4 p.m.
Admission: Free.
Visitor Accessibility: Free street parking. Wheelchair accessible. Tour guide available; call (989) 275-6131.
About: The Roscommon Area Historical Society preserves and protects artifacts and archives from the Roscommon and Higgins Lake areas. The society's museum is located in the 1880s-built Gallimore Boarding House that operated from 1904-1931. Rooms furnished in period style, and exhibits depict the history of the area. Richardson Schoolhouse served the community from 1914 to 1955.
Exhibits/Collections: Local artifacts spanning 1890 forward, including a parlor organ and old phonograph player. Archives concentrate on Higgins Lake and Roscommon areas. Pictures, ledger books, maps, memoirs, 49 oral history tapes.
Annual Events: Senior Birthday Party for area senior citizens, potluck dinner for the community, and Christmas in the Village. Meetings 3rd Tue Apr-Dec.

Rose City
(Ogemaw County)

Rose City Area Historical Society
Mailing Address: P.O. Box 736, 107 W. Main St. • Rose City, MI 48654
Contact: Cathy Snider, President
E-Mail: rchistsoc@hotmail.com
Phone: (989) 345-5659
Physical Location: 107 Main St. • Rose City, MI 48654
Hours: By appointment.
Admission: Free.
Visitor Accessibility: Free street parking. Wheelchair accessible. Self-guided.
Website: www.migenweb/ogemaw
About: Archives contain many papers and histories of the entire county of Ogemaw. The society has several very experienced people who will help with genealogy. The entire county of Ogemaw is covered, and the society strives to protect, save, and share all the histories they have.
Exhibits/Collections: Marriage and death records, early birth records, family histories, photos, newspapers and microfilms, maps, school records, and military files. Archive is located in the Ogemaw District Library.
Annual Events: County Expo (Apr), Ogemaw County Fair (Aug).
Publications: "Images of America: Ogemaw County," "Phebe," "Nell," "Rose City: 100 Years," "Prescott," "Civil War Letters from Sgt. Church of Williamston to his Father."

Roseville
(Macomb County)

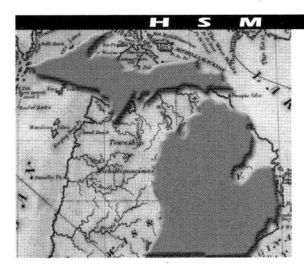

Genealogical Society of Flemish Americans
Mailing Address: 18740 E. Thirteen Mile Rd. • Roseville, MI 48066
Contact: Frances Timmerman, Chairman
E-Mail: flemishlibrary@gmail.com
Phone: (586) 777-2720
Site/Location: **Leon Buyse Memorial Library and Museum**
Hours: 2nd and 3rd Sat of each month. Also available by appointment.
Admission: Free.
Visitor Accessibility: Free on-site parking. Wheelchair accessible. Self-guided.
Website: www.flemishlibrary.org
About: Although called a Flemish American society, they help anyone wanting to learn how to research his or her past. The society wishes to teach the importance of preserving the past for future generations.
Exhibits/Collections: Collection of handmade lace samples. Large collection of death memorial cards and obituaries. The Gazette Van Detroit, in paper and microfilm. The only copy of the Gazette Van Moline on microfilm.
Annual Events: Workshops held 2nd and 4th Sat of each month (except July, 4th Sat only; and Dec, 2nd Sat only).
Publications: Flemish American Heritage Magazine.

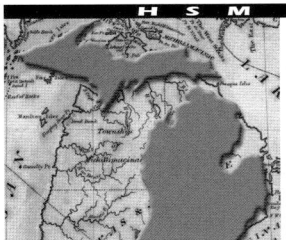

Roseville Historical & Genealogical Society
Mailing Address: c/o Roseville Public Library, 29777 Gratiot Ave., P.O. Box 290 • Roseville, MI 48066
Contact: Jackie Harvey, Library Director
E-Mail: rosevillerhgs@gmail.com
Phone: (586) 445-5407
Website: http://www.rosevillelibrary.org/rhgs.html
Exhibits/Collections: Records of Erin Township. Michigan history room in the library has books and publications on local history, Michigan history, and genealogy.
Annual Events: Meetings Tue monthly Sep-Jun, 6:30 p.m. at Erin Auditorium, Roseville Public Library, 29777 Gratiot Ave., Roseville.
Publications: Monthly newsletter. "Roseville Airport," "Wartime Memories of a Tin Can Soldier."

Roseville Public Library
Mailing Address: 29777 Gratiot Ave., P.O. Box 290 • Roseville, MI 48066
E-Mail: rsvlibrary@libcoop.net
Phone: (810) 445-5407
Hours: 9 a.m.-4:30 p.m.
Admission: Free.
About: Helping the public with research on local history and genealogy. View pictures and documents in digital form. Monthly speakers regarding historical interests. Open to the public.
Exhibits/Collections: Collections of local pictures and material, Motor City signs depicting historical businesses in front of city hall.
Publications: Newsletter (RHGS).

Royal Oak
(Oakland County)

Blue Water Chapter of the NRHSA
Mailing Address: National Railway Historical Society Archivist, P.O. Box 296 • Royal Oak, MI 48068
Contact: Michael Washenko, President
Phone: (248) 541-1000 • *Fax:* (248) 399-7963
Website: www.BluewaterNRHS.com
About: Preserves railroad history by operating rail-themed events and excursions using its fleet of historic rail cars. Open to the public.
Exhibits/Collections: Fleet of historic railroad passenger cars, including a diner, observation car, baggage car, crew sleeper, and several coaches. Library of railroad-related artifacts, books, photographs; magazines and records of Michigan railroads.
Annual Events: Meetings 2nd Thu, 7 p.m. at Royal Oak Senior Community Center.
Publications: Newsletter (Bluewater Sentinel).
Information may not be current.

French-Canadian Heritage Society of Michigan
Mailing Address: P.O. Box 1900 • Royal Oak, MI 48068
Contact: Loraine DiCerbo
E-Mail: fchsm1608@gmail.com
Admission: $25/individual yearly membership.
Website: www.habitantheritage.org
About: Promotes awareness of and appreciation for French Canadian heritage in Northern Michigan.
Exhibits/Collections: Resources located at Mount Clemens Public Library, 150 Cass in Mount Clemens. May be used during library hours, but there is no staff available to do research or respond to inquiries.
Annual Events: Meetings held at Mount Clemens Public Library. Visit website for more information.
Publications: "Michigan Habitant Heritage" Quarterly Journal.

Michigan Railroad History Conference
Mailing Address: P.O. Box 852 • Royal Oak, MI 48068
Contact: Mark Worrall, Chairperson
E-Mail: markxworrall@hotmail.com
Phone: (616) 881-1375
Website: www.michiganrailroadhistory.org
About: Presents a biennial conference covering a variety of topics relating to railroads in Michigan. See website for conference schedule and registration information.
Information may not be current.

Royal Oak Historical Society
Mailing Address: 1411 W. Webster Rd. • Royal Oak, MI 48073
Contact: Muriel Versagi, Curator
E-Mail: curator@royaloakhistoricalsociety.org
Phone: (248) 439-1501
Site/Location: **Royal Oak Historical Society Museum**
Physical Location: 1415 West Webster • Royal Oak, MI 48067

Hours: Tue, Thu, and Sat 1-4 p.m.
Admission: $2/individual donation.
Visitor Accessibility: Free on-site parking. Wheelchair accessible. Tour guide available; $2 donation/person. Tours are scheduled during hours when the museum is not open to the general public; groups should e-mail or call the society to arrange a tour.
Website: www.royaloakhistoricalsociety.org
About: The Royal Oak Historical Society preserves and displays the history of Royal Oak. It also maintains a small research library with local history written by residents, a collection of family histories, and a collection of Royal Oak High School yearbooks and newsletters. Located in the former Northwood Fire Station (built 1926), the Royal Oak Historical Society Museum displays rotating exhibits covering the history of Royal Oak from its beginnings as a township in the 1820s to today as a city.
Exhibits/Collections: Objects, maps, records, photos, books by local authors, county history. Artifacts from the founding families, farming implements, and household items. Lincoln photos and documents/letters and materials from the local schools.
Annual Events: Memorial Day Pancake Breakfast, Classic Car Show (Aug), Annual Awards Dinner (Oct). Monthly board meetings at the museum.
Publications: Quarterly newsletter.

Saginaw
(Saginaw County)

Blue & Grey Civil War Roundtable of Saginaw
Mailing Address: 3784 Nugget Creek • Saginaw, MI 48603
Contact: Dan Marino
E-Mail: danielmarino@hotmail.com
Phone: (989) 799-0044
About: Facilitates discussion and presentation of Civil War issues.
Annual Events: Meetings 1st Wed monthly.
*Information may not be current.

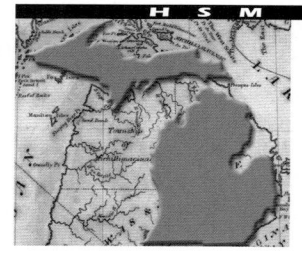

Friends of Theodore Roethke Foundation
Mailing Address: P.O. Box 20362 • Saginaw, MI 48602
Contact: Ann Ransford
E-Mail: info@roethkehouse.org
Phone: (989) 928-0430
Site/Location: **Theodore Roethke Home Museum**
Physical Location: 1805 Gratiot Avenue • Saginaw, MI 48602
Hours: Tours by appointment.
Admission: $5/individual.
Visitor Accessibility: Street parking. Not wheelchair accessible. Tours available by appointment.
Website: www.roethkehouse.org
About: The Friends of Theodore Roethke Foundation promote, preserve, and protect the literary legacy of Theodore Roethke, Michigan's Pulitzer Prize-winning poet, by restoring his family residences in Saginaw for cultural and educational opportunities. Theodore Roethke's childhood home has a Michigan historic marker, is a National Literary Landmark designation, and is on the National Register of Historic Sites.
Annual Events: Poet's Birthday Party (May), Summer Picnics (Jun-Aug), Language Arts Review for Elementary Students (Jul), and Chocolate and Beer Fundraising Party (Sep). Meetings: 3rd Wed monthly at 5:30 p.m.
*Information may not be current.

Historical Society of Saginaw County
Mailing Address: 500 Federal Ave. • Saginaw, MI 48607
Contact: Ken Santa, President/CEO
E-Mail: ksanta@castlemuseum.org
Phone: (989) 752-2861
Fax: (989) 752-1533
Site/Location: **Castle Museum of Saginaw County History**
Hours: Tue-Sat 10 a.m.-4:30 p.m., Sun 1-4:30 p.m.
Admission: $1/adult, 50¢/child. Members of the Historical Society of Saginaw County are free.
Visitor Accessibility: Free on-site and street parking. Wheelchair accessible. Guided tours by reservation; $2/individual.
Website: www.castlemuseum.org
About: The society is committed to serving the community by telling the story of the Saginaw region through exploration, preservation, and presentation of its historical and cultural heritage. Located in Castle Building, the museum offers three floors of exhibits. Programs offered include lectures, tours, and a mobile museum and classroom called History on the Move that visits local schools. The Castle Museum hosts about 40 exhibits. One of the largest working model trains in the region can also be seen here.
Exhibits/Collections: 100,000 artifacts of all types, including art, textiles, publications, photographs, and much more, all pertaining in some form or fashion to Saginaw County history.
Annual Events: Jazz on Jefferson, Community Christmas Party, Lunch and Learn Tuesdays.

Michigan Archaeology Society
Mailing Address: P.O. Box 359 • Saginaw, MI 48606
E-Mail: tk_bennett@yahoo.com
Website: www.miarch.org
About: Composed of amateur and professional archaeologists interested in preserving Michigan's archaeological history and in contributing to further archaeological research.
Exhibits/Collections: The Michigan Archaeologist.
Annual Events: Spring membership meeting (Apr), Michigan Archaeology Day (Oct).
*Information may not be current.

Public Libraries of Saginaw
Mailing Address: 505 Janes Avenue • Saginaw, MI 48607-1236
Contact: Stacy McNally, Local History & Genealogy Librarian
E-Mail: plosgene@saginawlibrary.org
Phone: (989) 755-0904
Fax: (989) 755-9829
Site/Location: **Hoyt Library History & Genealogy Collection**
Hours: Mon, Thu 12-8 p.m., Tue-Wed 10 a.m.-6 p.m., Fri-Sat 9 a.m.-5 p.m.
Admission: Free.
Visitor Accessibility: Free on-site parking. Wheelchair accessible.
Website: www.saginawlibrary.org
About: The Local History and Genealogy (LHG) Collection was created as a central repository and library of Saginaw local history in 1960 and has become one of the premier local historical and genealogical collections in the Midwest. It serves students and specialists equally well with an array of materials in the fields of genealogy,

Saginaw history, and the history of Michigan. The Collection features original source materials, such as diaries, scrapbooks, business ledgers, photographs, more than 20,000 books, microforms, and periodicals.

Saginaw Genealogical Society, Inc.
Mailing Address: P.O. Box 3767 • Saginaw, MI 48605-3767
Contact: Nancy Pavlik, President
E-Mail: saggensoc@gmail.com
Physical Location: 505 Janes Ave. • Saginaw, MI 48607
Hours: Hoyt Library: Oct-Apr: Mon-Thu 9 a.m.-9 p.m.; Fri-Sat 9 a.m.-5 p.m.; Sun 1-5 p.m.
Visitor Accessibility: On-site parking. Wheelchair accessible.
About: Helps members and friends of Hoyt Library and community learn of their ancestral beginnings through the available resources in Saginaw County (indentified in their publcations, meetings, and fieldtrips). Provides networking opportunities.
Exhibits/Collections: Third-largest genealogical collection in Michigan.
Annual Events: Meetings 2nd Tue Sep-Nov, Jan-Jun, 7 p.m. at Hoyt Library.
Publications: Quarterly publication (Timbertown Log).

Saginaw Valley Historic Preservation Society
Mailing Address: 1001 Hoyt Ave. • Saginaw, MI 48607
Contact: Thomas Mudd, President
E-Mail: muddtb88@gmail.com
Phone: (989) 754-3351
Physical Location: One Cushway Lane • Saginaw, MI 48601
Hours: By appointment only.
Admission: Donations accepted.
Visitor Accessibility: Parking area located just north of home off Cushway Lane (free). Partially wheelchair accessibly; first floor only. Tours conducted by society president.
About: Preserves and restores Saginaw's oldest remaining home as a historic attraction. Advocates and takes part in other historic preservation projects and initiatives. Attractions include dugout canoe (circa 1800), 1928 Kenmore washing machine, 1928 GE "refrigerating machine," 1928 A/C stove, and early 1800s roller-pin rope bed. Rooms in Cushway home represent different eras: kitchen (1920s/30s), dining room/parlor (1880s-1920), etc.
Exhibits/Collections: Collection of Native-American artifacts.
Annual Events: Three annual membership meetings held at Cushway Home: Cake and Cookie Bake (May), Picnic Potluck (Jul), Autumn Pie Fest (Oct). All at 6:30 p.m.

Saginaw Valley Railroad Historical Society
Mailing Address: PO Box 1714 • Saginaw, MI 48602
Contact: Joe Deneen, Curator
E-Mail: info@saginawrailwaymuseum.org
Phone: (989) 790-7994
Site/Location: **Saginaw Railway Museum**
Physical Location: 900 Maple St. • Saginaw, MI 48602
Hours: Apr-Nov: 1st and 3rd Sat 1-4 p.m. Closed holiday weekends.
Admission: Donations accepted. $20 donations receive a one-year, individual membership.
Visitor Accessibility: Free on-site parking. Partially wheelchair accessible. Self-guided.
Website: www.saginawrailwaymuseum.org
About: The Saginaw Valley Railroad Historical Society is a nonprofit organization founded in 1982 to preserve and display to the public artifacts and information that is significant to the history of American railroading. The society is in the Saginaw Railway Museum, a restored 1907 Pere Marquette Depot. It features changing displays throughout the year. Other exhibits include the Mershon switch tower, a former U.S. Navy switch engine, a C&O combine car, a static Alco locomotive, and two cabooses.
Exhibits/Collections: Donald L. Etter Collection of books and memorabilia. Also, many books, photos, and other railroad-related items.
Annual Events: Membership Meeting (Dec). Board meetings 2nd Wed monthly, 7 p.m. at the museum.
Publications: Quarterly membership newsletter (The Semaphore).
Information may not be current.

Salem
(Washtenaw County)

Salem Area Historical Society
Mailing Address: P.O. Box 75011 • Salem, MI 48175
Contact: Terry Cwik, President
E-Mail: salem_area_hs@yahoo.com
Phone: (248) 486-0669
Fax: (248) 486-0669
Physical Location: 7991 N. Territorial Road • Plymouth, MI 48170
Hours: By appointment.
Admission: Free.
Visitor Accessibility: Free on-site parking. Wheelchair accessible. Tour guide available by appointment.
Website: www.sahshistory.org
About: The Salem Area Historical Society (SAHS) was founded in 1976. Formed to archive, preserve, and inform others about the history of Salem Township and its surrounding historical associated connections. The society acquired the 1830 Dickerson Barn and the 1857 South Salem Stone School, which was used as a public school for 110 consecutive years.
Exhibits/Collections: Photographs of barns, churches, schools, and houses in Salem Township. Historical documents include genealogical materials, Civil War pension records, and township tax records.
Annual Events: Fundraising Dinner and Auction Gala (Feb), Craft and Art Fair (Aug), Barn Dance (Sep), Christmas Gathering (Dec).
Publications: "Salem Cook Book," "History of Salem Township," "Portfolio of Historical Maps of Salem Township," several monographs.

Saline
(Washtenaw County)

Saline Area Historical Society
Mailing Address: P.O. Box 302 • Saline, MI 48176
Contact: Deb Greb, President
E-Mail: salinehistory@frontier.com
Phone: (734) 944-0442
Site/Location: **Rentschler Farm Museum**
Physical Location: 1265 E. Michigan Ave. • Saline, MI 48176
Hours: May to mid-Dec: Sat 11 a.m.-3 p.m.
Admission: Free.
Visitor Accessibility: Free on-site parking. Partially wheelchair accessible; first floor only. Tour guide available; groups of 10 or more require a reservation and cost $1/individual.
Website: www.salinehistory.org
About: The Saline Area Historical Society encourages preservation and provides education and activities that best illustrate the local heritage of the Saline area. The Rentschler Farm Museum features 12 farm buildings with early 20th-century furnishings. The structure of the

farmhouse has never been changed, only paint color and wallpaper. Furnishings show the Great Depression Era of the 1930s.
Exhibits/Collections: Saline-area-related memorabilia and photographs; railroad artifacts, including a fully furnished caboose, maps, obituaries, farm tools, household furnishings 1930 and earlier; and library of books.
Annual Events: Antique Show (Jan), U.S.-12 Yard Sale (Aug), Harvest Time (Oct), Christmas on Rentschler Farm (Dec). Educational programs are offered Feb-Apr and Sep-Nov. Board meetings monthly at the depot in the winter, farm in the summer.
Publications: The Preserver newsletter, "Celebrating our Heritage," "Fire," "Voices Over the Valley," and "Rentschler Family Cookbook."
Other Sites/Locations: Saline Railroad Depot Museum • Location: 402 N. Ann Arbor St., Saline, MI 48176 • Hours: Sat 11 a.m.-3 p.m. • Admission: Free • Visitor Accessibility: Free on-site parking. Partially wheelchair accessible. Tour guide available; groups of 10 or more require a reservation and cost $1/individual. • The Saline Railroad Depot was built in 1872 and used by the railroad until approximately the 1960s. Exhibits focus on Saline history, especially during the 19th century. There is a furnished station agent's office, caboose, and livery barn.

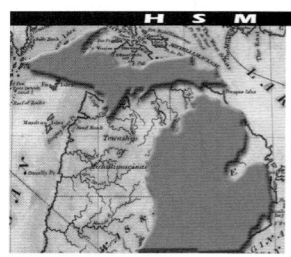

Saline District Library
Mailing Address: 555 N. Maple Road • Saline, MI 48176
Contact: Leslee Niethammer, Director
Phone: (734) 429-5450
Fax: (734) 944-0600
Hours: Mon-Thu 9 a.m.-9 p.m., Fri-Sat 10 a.m.-5 p.m., Sun 1 p.m.-5 p.m.
Admission: Free.
Visitor Accessibility: Free on-site parking. Wheelchair accessible. Self-guided.
Website: www.salinelibrary.org
About: Two exhibits at the Saline District Library celebrate Meredith Bixby, a local puppeteer who donated his collection to the city of Saline. Bixby was one of America's foremost puppeteers who traveled from 1930 to 1980. One exhibit shows the construction of a marionette and the other depicts a scene from one of his plays. The scene exhibit changes throughout the year.
Exhibits/Collections: Marionettes, stage settings, photographs, and artwork.

Saline Historical Commission
Mailing Address: 100 N. Harris • Saline, MI 48176
Phone: (734) 429-8296 • *Fax:* (734) 429-5280
Website: http://salinehistory.org/index.php
About: Seeks to safeguard the heritage of Saline, stabilize and improve property values, foster civic beauty, strengthen local economy, and promote the use of historic districts for the education, pleasure, and welfare of citizens.
*Information may not be current.

Sandusky
(Sanilac County)

Sandusky District Library
Mailing Address: 55 E. Sanilac, P.O. Box 271 • Sandusky, MI 48471
Contact: Gail Nartker, Director
E-Mail: library@sandusky.lib.mi.us
Phone: (810) 648-2644 • *Fax:* (810) 648-1904
Hours: Mon-Fri 9 a.m.-6 p.m.; Sat 9 a.m.-1 p.m.
Admission: Free.
Visitor Accessibility: Free on-site and street parking. Wheelchair accessible. Self-guided.
Website: http://sandusky.lib.mi.us
About: The Sandusky District Library is located in the heart of Michigan's Thumb. The library maintains a popular collection of printed materials, offers a variety of online services, and has public access computers and wireless connectivity for patrons and visitors alike.
Exhibits/Collections: A large collection of local history and genealogy materials specific to the surrounding area. The library provides a separate genealogy room for researchers.

Sanford
(Midland County)

Sanford Area Historical Society
Mailing Address: P.O. Box 243 • Sanford, MI 48657
Contact: Ruth Ann Nagle, President
E-Mail: logmarks@tds.net
Phone: (989) 687-9048
Site/Location: Sanford Centennial Museum
Physical Location: 2222 Smith St. • Sanford, MI 48657
Hours: Memorial Day to Labor Day: Sat 10 a.m.-5 p.m., Sun 1-5 p.m. Also by appointment.
Admission: Free.
Visitor Accessibility: Free on-site parking. Wheelchair accessible. Self-guided.
Website: www.sanfordhist.org
About: The Sanford Area Historical Society provides education and information about Sanford's local history. The museum includes eight restored and furnished historic buildings: two schools, a general store, log cabin, township hall, church, implement barn, and train depot. Inside are vintage tools, implements from the logging days, political memorabilia, a dentist's office, a barbershop, a doctor's office, a saloon, toys, and household goods. Highlights include a train engine, boxcar, two cabooses, Michigan logging wheels, covered bridge, and windmill.
Exhibits/Collections: Early Jerome Township records, first landowners, genealogies, documents, pictures, histories of business, local cemetery records. Available during public museum hours.
Annual Events: Log Cabin Day (Jun), Model Train Day (Aug), Founders Day (Sep). Meetings 3rd Wed Apr-Nov, 7p.m. at Sanford Village Office, 106 Lincoln St., Sanford.
Publications: SHS Logmarks newsletter. "Upper Tibbabawasee River Boom Towns."

Saranac
(Ionia County)

Boston-Saranac Historical Society
Mailing Address: P.O. Box 565 • Saranac, MI 48881
Contact: Marilyn Cahoon
E-Mail: marilar@att.net
Phone: (616) 693-2730
Site/Location: Saranac Depot
Physical Location: 138 N. Bridge St. • Saranac, MI 48881
Hours: Jun-Sep 2nd and 4th Sundays. Also by appointment.
Admission: Donations accepted.
Visitor Accessibility: Free on-site parking.
About: Located at the Saranac Depot. The purpose of this organization is to preserve the Boston-Saranac-area history and to inform the residents of local historical facts so future generations will take pride and interest in our culture and in their roots.
Annual Events: Meetings 3rd Mon monthly, 7 p.m. business meeting sometimes followed by special program. Saranac Bridgefest (Aug), Christmas Tea (Dec), Heritage Craft Show (Nov).
Publications: Biannual newsletter.

Saugatuck
(Allegan County)

Friends of the Felt Estate
Mailing Address: P.O. Box 675 • Saugatuck, MI 49453
Contact: Patricia Meyer, Director
E-Mail: events@feltmansion.org; patmeyer@patmeyerestoration.com
Phone: (616) 335-8982
Site/Location: **Felt Estate**
Physical Location: 6597 138th • Holland, MI 49423
Hours: See website.
Admission: $10/adult, $8/senior, $8/student.
Visitor Accessibility: Free on-site parking. Partially wheelchair accessible. Tour guide available by appointment.
Website: www.feltmansion.org
About: The Friends of the Felt Estate preserve history through the preservation of the Felt Estate. In addition to serving as the home of the Felt family, the 1920s mansion also served as housing for the St. Augustine Seminary prep school and as office space when the state used the property for a prison. Today, it features a collection of Comptometers (Dorr Felt's invention).
Annual Events: Summer tours, Harvest Festival, Holiday tours.
Publications: "The Felt Mansion: A Story of Restoration."
*Information may not be current.

Sault Ste. Marie
(Chippewa County)

Bayliss Public Library
Mailing Address: 541 Library Dr. • Sault Ste. Marie, MI 49783
Contact: Susan James, Library Manager
E-Mail: bayref@uproc.lib.mi.us
Phone: (906) 632-9331
Fax: (906) 632-3117
Hours: Tue and Thu 9 a.m.-9 p.m.; Wed and Fri 9 a.m.-5:30 p.m.; Sat. 9 a.m.-4 p.m.
Admission: Free
Visitor Accessibility: Free on-site parking. Handicap accessible.
Website: www.baylisslibrary.org
About: Bayliss Public Library is one of eight Eastern Upper Peninsula public libraries in the Superior District Library. Bayliss Library houses the Judge Joseph H. Steere Room that is open to researchers of Sault Ste. Marie and U.P.-area history. There are historical and genealogical resources available for use.
Exhibits/Collections: 17th- to 20th-century manuscripts, photograph collection.
Annual Events: Friends of Bayliss Library Valentine Sweets Sale; Friends of Bayliss Library Used Book Sales; and monthly author programs, meetings, lectures for all ages.
Publications: "From Carnegie to Bayliss: The First Hundred Years of Sault Ste. Marie's Public Library."

Chippewa County Historical Society
Mailing Address: P.O. Box 342 • Sault Ste. Marie, MI 49783
Contact: Mary June, President
E-Mail: cchs@sault.com
Phone: (906) 635-7082
Fax: (906) 635-9280
Physical Location: 115 Ashmun St. • Sault Ste. Marie, MI 49783
Hours: Office hours: 10 a.m.-4 p.m. Site hours: May-Dec: Call or see website.
Admission: Donations accepted.
Visitor Accessibility: On-site and street parking. Wheelchair access at back entrance (call ahead).
Website: www.cchsmi.com
About: The Chippewa County Historical Society promotes an appreciation of the history of the Upper Peninsula—especially Chippewa County and Sault Ste. Marie—by collecting, preserving, exhibiting, and interpreting that history for audiences of all ages and interests. The society is located in the 1889 building that originally housed the Sault Ste. Marie News, owned by Chase S. Osborn, the only governor to come from the Upper Peninsula. Attractions include American cafe, railroad, Chase Osborn, Native-American, and telephone displays.
Exhibits/Collections: Artifacts and displays created for city's Historic Water Street Homes.
Annual Events: Rendezvous in the Sault: A History Fest Event (Jul), Historic Churches of Sault Ste. Marie (Jun-Aug), Historic Water Street Homes (Sum), History Camp for 9-11 year olds (Jun), Cemetery Tours (May, Oct).
Publications: Quarterly newsletter. "Then and Now: The Changing Face of Sault Ste. Marie," "City of the Rapids: Sault Ste. Marie's Heritage," "Upbound Downbound: The Story of the Soo Locks," "Chippewa County: Memories of the 20th Century," "Fighting Fires in Sault Ste. Marie: From Horses to Horse Power."

Great Lakes Shipwreck Society
Mailing Address: 400 W. Portage • Sault Ste. Marie, MI 49783
Contact: Bruce Lynn, Executive Director
E-Mail: glshs@shipwreckmuseum.com
Phone: (906) 635-1742 • *Fax:* (906) 635-0860
Site/Location: **Great Lakes Shipwreck Museum**
Physical Location: 18335 N. Whitefish Point Rd. • Paradise, MI 49768
Hours: May-Oct: Daily 10 a.m.-6 p.m. Business office: Mon-Fri 8 a.m.-5 p.m.
Admission: $13/adult, $9/child, $38/family, children 5 and under are free.
Visitor Accessibility: Free parking. Wheelchair accessible. Self-guided. Group tours for 20 or more, call in advance.
Website: www.shipwreckmuseum.com
About: Visitors to the Great Lakes Shipwreck Museum at Whitefish Point will experience numerous shipwreck exhibits, including a permanent exhibit dedicated to the 1975 wreck of the Edmund Fitzgerald. The Fitzgerald's bell has been made a part of this exhibit. A restored lighthouse keeper's quarters, USCG Rescue Station Surfboat House, and 1920s U.S. Navy Radio Station all feature historical interpreters and a variety of thoughtful exhibits. A new hands-on exhibit and the restoration of a 1923 USCG Rescue Station Motor-Lifeboat House.
Annual Events: Edmund Fitzgerald Memorial Service (Nov), annual meeting (Apr).
Publications: Biannual member newsletter.

Sault Historic Sites
Mailing Address: 501 E. Water St. • Sault Ste. Marie, MI 49783
Contact: Lacie Wojinaroski, Administration Assistant
E-Mail: admin@saulthistoricsites.com
Phone: (906) 632-3658
Fax: (906) 632-9344
Site/Location: **Museum Ship Valley Camp**
Hours: Mid-May to mid-Oct. Call or see website for current hours.
Admission: Combination tickets and group rates available.
Visitor Accessibility: Free on-site parking. Partially wheelchair accessible.

Historical Society of Michigan

Tour guide available.
Website: www.saulthistoricsites.com

About: Sault Historic Sites was founded in 1967 to preserve, restore, and present Sault Ste. Marie history to visitors. Museum Ship Valley Camp is a 550-foot bulk carrier that was built in 1917, sailed until 1966, and was converted into a maritime museum in 1968. Visitors view all parts of the Valley Camp to see how a 29-person crew lived and worked. The cargo hold has displays of artifacts, paintings, shipwreck items, and models and exhibits about maritime history.

Other Sites/Locations: **Tower of History** • Location: 326 E.Portage St., Sault Ste. Marie, MI 49783 • Hours: Mid-May to mid-Oct: Daily 10 a.m.-5 p.m. • Admission: Combination tickets and group rates available • Visitor Accessibility: On-site and street parking. Not wheelchair accessible. • In addition to the story of the early missionaries, this 210-foot tower includes local and Native-American history and exhibits and a video presentation. The upper level features a 360-degree view of the Locks and surrounding area.

River of History Museum • Location: 531 Ashmun St., Sault Ste. Marie, MI 49783 • Hours: Mid-May to mid-Oct: Mon-Sat 11 a.m.-5 p.m. Closed major holidays. • Admission: $7/adult, $3.50/children • Visitor Accessibility: Wheelchair accessible. Free audio wands available. • The River of History Museum tells the 8,000-year history of the St. Marys River Valley, from glacial origins to Native-American occupation, French fur trade, British expansion, and U.S. independence. The river tells her story of events witnessed, people met, and changes wrought along her shores and waters.

Water Street Historic Block • Location: 405 E. Water St., Sault Ste. Marie, MI 49783 • Admission: Donations accepted • Visitor Accessibility: Street parking. Wheelchair accessible. Tour guide available. • This cooperative effort between the Chippewa County Historical Society, Sault Historic Sites, and the City of Sault Ste. Marie includes the 1793 home of early fur trader John Johnston, the Henry Rowe Schoolcraft Office (the first Indian agent in the United States), and the Kemp Industrial Museum (a museum of local industries in the former Kemp Coal Company office).

Sault Ste. Marie Historic District Commission
Mailing Address: 802 Prospect Ave. • Sault Ste. Marie, MI 49783
Contact: Jim Moody
Information may not be current.

Sault Ste. Marie Tribe of Chippewa Indians
Mailing Address: 523 Ashmun St. • Sault Ste. Marie, MI 49783
Contact: Colleen St. Onge, Cultural Repatriation Assistant
E-Mail: cstonge@saulttribe.net
Phone: (906) 635-6050
Site/Location: **Ojibwe Learning Center and Library**
Hours: Mon-Fri 8 a.m.-5 p.m.
Admission: Free.
Visitor Accessibility: Wheelchair accessible. Self-guided.
Website: http://saulttribe.com

About: The Ojibwe Learning Center and Library is located in Sault Ste. Marie and is dedicated to providing a safe zone with educational resources and authentic Anishinaabe museum items. The small library has mainly Native-American subject resources and provides Anishinaabemowin language classes in the library two days per week. The Ojibwe Learning Center and Library is committed to the preservation and protection of the Anishinaabe culture, traditions, and language.
Exhibits/Collections: All museum items are authentic Native American-made pieces.
Annual Events: Anishinaabemowin language classes.

Sugar Island Historical Preservation Society
Mailing Address: PO Box 72 • Sault Ste. Marie, MI 49783
Contact: Connie Pim, President
E-Mail: cspim@yahoo.com
Information may not be current.

Schoolcraft
(Kalamazoo County)

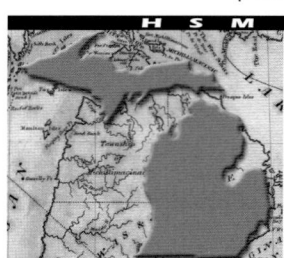

Schoolcraft Historical Society
Mailing Address: P.O. Box 451 • Schoolcraft, MI 49087
Contact: David LaLiberte
E-Mail: schoolcrafthistorical@hotmail.com
Phone: (269) 679-4304
Site/Location: **Underground Railroad House**
Physical Location: 613 E. Cass St. • Schoolcraft, MI 49087
Hours: By appointment.
Admission: $5/individual.
Visitor Accessibility: Free on-site parking. Partially wheelchair accessible; first floor only. Tour guide available by appointment.
About: Schoolcraft's first physician, Dr. Nathan Thomas, reportedly opened his home to more than 1,000 fugitive slaves as they passed through Southern Michigan on the Underground Railroad. The Underground Railroad House stands as a tribute to the courage of those who sought to escape slavery and those who gave aid.
Annual Events: 4th of July Open House. Meetings 1st Wed monthly (except Jan and Jul) at the Underground Railroad House.

Sebewaing
(Huron County)

Luckhard Museum—The Indian Mission
Mailing Address: 612 E. Bay St. • Sebewaing, MI 48759
Contact: Jim Bunke, Curator
E-Mail: cjbunke@yahoo.com
Phone: (989) 883-2539
Hours: Jun-Sep 1st Sun 2-4 p.m. Also by appointment.
Admission: Donations accepted.
Visitor Accessibility: Free on-site parking. Not wheelchair accessible. Guided tours available.
About: Highlights the work of Lutheran missionaries to Native Americans in Huron County.
Exhibits/Collections: Artifacts and relics of the early Lutheran pioneers and Native Americans of the area housed in a historic missionary building.

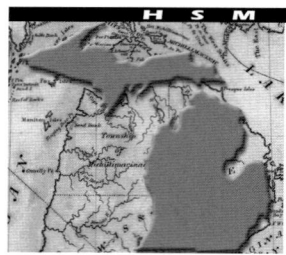

Sebewaing Area Historical Society
Mailing Address: 79 E. Bay St. • Sebewaing, MI 48759
Contact: Clarence Menzel, President
E-Mail: beegee38@sbcglobal.net
Phone: (989) 883-2391
Site/Location: **Charles W. Liken House**
Physical Location: 325 N. Center St. • Sebewaing, MI 48759
Hours: May-Nov: 1st Sat and 1st Sun monthly.
Admission: Free.
Visitor Accessibility: Free on-site and street parking. Not wheelchair accessible. Tour guide available; reservations can be made for after-hours.
Website: www.sebewaingchamber.com

Michigan History Directory

About: By using buildings and displays, the Sebewaing Area Historical Society educates the public on the history of the area's founding and the people who formed the communities, businesses, schools, churches, etc. The Charles W. Liken House was built in the early 1880s by the town's founding father. The home has since been renovated and now features replicated versions of the original furnishings.

Exhibits/Collections: Sebewaing-area artifacts, including photos, furniture, clothing, signs, tools, and records of local businesses.

Annual Events: Michigan Sugar Festival (Jun), Moonlight Madness (Oct), Christmas Open House (Nov). Meetings 2nd Thu Mar-Nov, 1 p.m. at the Charles W. Liken House.

Other Sites/Locations: **Old Sebewaing Township Hall** • Location: 92 S. Center St., Sebewaing, MI 48759 • Hours: May-Nov: 1st Sat and 1st Sun monthly • Admission: Free • Visitor Accessibility: Free on-site and street parking. Not wheelchair accessible. Tour guide available; reservations can be made for after-hours. • The Old Sebewaing Township Hall has displays pertaining to the old jail, area businesses, hunting, and doctors.

Rev. J.L. Hahn House • Location: 92 S. Center St., Sebewaing, MI 48759 • Hours: May-Nov: 1st Sat and 1st Sun monthly • Admission: Free • Visitor Accessibility: Free on-site and street parking. Not wheelchair accessible. Tour guide available; reservations can be made for after-hours. • The Rev. J.L. Hahn House is in the process of being repaired and renovated.

Selfridge ANG Base
(Clare County)

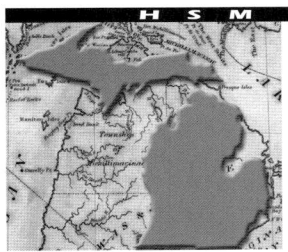

Selfridge Military Air Museum
Mailing Address: 27333 C St., Bldg. 1011 • Selfridge ANG Base, MI 48045
Contact: Louis Nigro, Lt. Col.(Retired)
E-Mail: info@selfridgeairmuseum.org
Phone: (586) 239-5035
Fax: (586) 239-6646
Hours: Apr-Oct: Sat-Sun 12-4:30 p.m. Open Memorial Day and Independence Day 12-4:30 p.m. Also available by appointment.
Admission: $4/adult, $3/children (4-12).
Visitor Accessibility: Free on-site parking. Wheelchair accessible. Self-guided tours.
Website: www.selfridgeairmuseum.org

About: Collects, preserves, and displays military artifacts and memorabilia of relevance to all past and present military units at Selfridge Air National Guard Base, in the Michigan Air National Guard, and in the Wayne/Oakland/Macomb County area. Museum buildings have displays of military photographs, uniforms, engines, and items of interest. On display in air park are more than 20 aircraft, vehicles, and missiles.

Exhibits/Collections: Research library contains books, periodicals, and special interest publications. Open to researchers by appointment.

Shelby
(Oceana County)

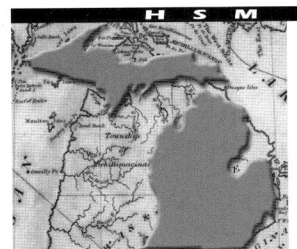

Shelby Area District Library
Mailing Address: 189 Maple St. • Shelby, MI 49455
Contact: Jeremy Gowell, Librarian
E-Mail: shelbylibrary@yahoo.com
Phone: (231) 861-4565
Fax: (231) 861-6868
Hours: Mon-Thu 9 a.m.-7 p.m., Fri 9 a.m.-5 p.m., Sat 9 a.m.-1 p.m.

Website: www.shelbylibrary.org

About: Local history committee meets monthly to discuss special topics and plan programs. Gathering historical documents, photographs, postcards, personal histories, and other local history memorabilia to be displayed in the library's local history room.

Exhibits/Collections: Genealogical materials, Hart-Montague Railtrail Collection, Shelby High School yearbooks, Oceana County plat books.

Shelby Township
(Macomb County)

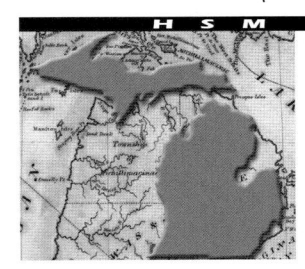

Packard Motor Car Foundation
Mailing Address: P.O. Box 182063 • Shelby Township, MI 48317
Contact: Bruce Blevins, Treasurer
Phone: (586) 739-4800
Site/Location: **Packard Proving Grounds Historic Site**
Physical Location: 49965 Van Dyke Ave. • Shelby Township, MI 48317
Hours: Call for current hours.
Admission: Donations accepted.
Visitor Accessibility: Free on-site parking. Wheelchair accessible. Tour group available by appointment; costs vary.
Website: www.packardmotorfdn.org

About: The Packard Motor Car Foundation is an educational organization dedicated to the preservation of the products, history, and properties of the Packard Motor Car Company. The Packard Proving Grounds Historic Site features seven buildings built between 1929 and 1942 (six were designed by Albert Kahn). On display are a collection of Packard automobiles and marine engines, Miss America X mahogany racing boat, and more.

Exhibits/Collections: 35,000 original Packard blueprints and other Packard memorabilia.

Annual Events: Farmer's market (May-Oct), Cars R Stars (Jun), open house (Oct). Meetings 3rd Tue monthly (except Dec).

Publications: Biannual newsletter for donors.

Shelby Township Historical Committee
Mailing Address: 52700 Van Dyke • Shelby Township, MI 48316
Contact: Clendon Mason, Chairman
E-Mail: shelbyhistory@yahoo.com
Phone: (586) 731-5102 • *Fax:* (586) 726-7227
Site/Location: **Shepherd Powerhouse Museum**
Physical Location: **Andrews Schoolhouse/Museum**
Admission: Free.
Visitor Accessibility: Free on-site parking. Free tour guides available.
Website: www.shelbyhistory.com

About: Provides assistance to citizens with their family history. Exhibits include photos, article displays, schoolhouse history, and newspaper articles.

Annual Events: Heritage Days Tour (Jun), Open House (Aug). Meetings 2nd Thu monthly, 6:30 p.m. at Andrews Schoolhouse/Museum (Sep-Jun).

Publications: "Images of America: Shelby Township."

*Information may not be current.

Shepherd
(Isabella County)

Shepherd Area Historical Society
Mailing Address: P.O. Box 505 • Shepherd, MI 48883
Contact: Janet Leiferman, Treasurer
E-Mail: neema_63@hotmail.com
Phone: (989) 828-5588
Fax: (989) 772-0718
Site/Location: **Shepherd Powerhouse Museum**
Physical Location: 314 W. Maple St. • Shepherd, MI 48883
Hours: Last Sat in Apr. Also by appointment.
Admission: Donations accepted.
Visitor Accessibility: Free street parking. Partially wheelchair accessible; ground floor only. Tour guide available by appointment.
Website: www.shepherdahs.org
About: The purpose of the society is to encourage historical study and research and to collect and preserve historical material connected with the village of Shepherd. The museum houses artifacts relevant to the Shepherd-area community, death notices for Shepherd residents, and multiple scrapbooks and published books for genealogical research on the main floor. The upper floor is composed of mini-scenes from early Shepherd houses, including a kitchen, seamstress shop, dining/living room, and a bedroom.
Exhibits/Collections: Historical artifacts of the area. Scrapbooks and genealogical materials.
Annual Events: Maple Syrup Festival Museum Open House (Apr).
Other Sites/Locations: **Little Red Schoolhouse Museum** • Location: 306 Chippewa St., Shepherd, MI 48883 • Hours: During Maple Syrup Festival. Also by appointment. • Admission: Donations accepted • Visitor Accessibility: Parking on school campus. Not wheelchair accessible. Tour guide available by appointment. • The museum houses artifacts relevant to the Shepherd school community, including many photographs of graduates and early schoolbooks. The school retains the original desks of both teacher and students, blackboard, cabinets, bell, furnace, and atmosphere of the early schoolroom.

Sidney
(Montcalm County)

North Sidney Historical Association
Mailing Address: P.O. Box 202 • Sidney, MI 48885
Contact: Wesley Thomsen, Chairman
Phone: (989) 328-2961
Site/Location: **North Sidney Church**
Physical Location: 1990 S. Grow Road • Sidney, MI 48885
Hours: Open for Memorial Day Service and special occasions.
Admission: Donations accepted.
Visitor Accessibility: Street parking. Not wheelchair accessible. Guide available upon request.
Website: www.northsidney.com
About: Church built as St. John's Church in 1903 after tornado destroyed former church of Danish emigrants. Association maintains church and cemetery.
Exhibits/Collections: Books, Bibles, photos of church and families, list of tombstones, "Heritage Wall."
Annual Events: Meetings 2nd Wed 7 p.m. at church (May, Sep), Memorial Day service.
Publications: Annual newsletter (North Sidney Messenger).
Information may not be current.

Skanee
(Baraga County)

Arvon Township Historical Society
Mailing Address: 13221 Town Rd. • Skanee, MI 49962
Contact: Mary Erickson, President
E-Mail: arvonhist@hotmail.com
Phone: (906) 524-4942
Site/Location: **Arvon Township Historical Museum**
Physical Location: Skanee/Roland Lake Roads • Skanee, MI 49962
Hours: Jun-Aug Sat 1-4 p.m., also by appointment.
Admission: Donations accepted.
Visitor Accessibility: Free on-site parking. Not wheelchair accessible. Free tour guide available.
About: To promote research related to Arvon Township and preserve historical artifacts and cultural activities. Museum is set up as a home of the early settlers. Most of the furnishings are donated items from Arvon families.
Exhibits/Collections: Artifacts of pioneering in farming, logging, and household furnishings. James Oliver Curwood books and photos of families.
Annual Events: Meetings 2nd Thu Apr-Oct, 7 p.m. at Skanee Town Hall.

Sodus
(Berrien County)

Log Cabin Society of Michigan
Mailing Address: Rock S. Edwards Farm, 3503 Rock Edwards Dr. • Sodus, MI 49126
Contact: Virginia Handy, Editor and Secretary/Treasurer
E-Mail: logcabinsociety@att.net
Phone: (269) 925-3836 • *Fax:* (269) 925-3836
Hours: By appointment.
Visitor Accessibility: On-site parking. Partially wheelchair accessible. Self-guided.
Website: www.qtm.net/logcabincrafts
About: Organized in 1988 to coordinate Log Cabin Day activities throughout the state and, in general, to collect and publicize information on log cabins in Michigan. A newsletter, Log Cabin News, has been issued since 1989. Various publications have been published, including "From the Little Log Cabin in the Lane," a history of the Palmer Park Log Cabin, and articles in books and magazines. A collection of videotapes includes television programs and films. There are about 250 members.
Exhibits/Collections: Collections of photographs, books, and articles are in the farmhouse office building.
Annual Events: Log Cabin Day (Jun). Annual meeting 3rd Sun in Oct.
Publications: Newsletter (Log Cabin News). "From the Little Log Cabin in the Lane," "Flax Craft."

South Boardman
(Kalakaska County)

South Boardman Museum
Mailing Address: P.O. Box 65 • South Boardman, MI 49680
Contact: Troy Gerning
E-Mail: sbmuseum@yahoo.com
Physical Location: 5391 Boardman Road, (Across from Post Office) • South Boardman, MI 49680
Hours: Memorial Day-Labor Day Sat 1-4 p.m., or by appointment.
Admission: Free.
Visitor Accessibility: Street parking. Wheelchair accessible. Free tour guide available.
About: Small volunteer organization seeking to preserve local artifacts

and history, including old pictures, assessment records, and some genealogy materials. Attractions include blacksmith shop, grandma's attic, parlor, Civil War letters, before and after photo display, old Post Office boxes, quilts, and clothing.
Exhibits/Collections: Documents, photographs, newspapers, furnishings.
Publications: County census, Kalkaska history, Newspaper index, Cemetery records.

South Haven
(Van Buren County)

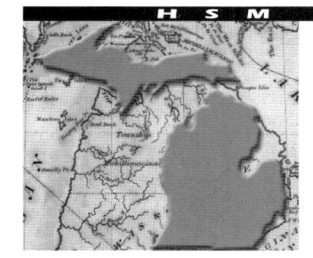

Historical Association of South Haven
Mailing Address: P.O. Box 552 • South Haven, MI 49090
Contact: Sue Hale, Administrative Coordinator
E-Mail: info@historyofsouthhaven.org
Phone: (269) 637-6424
Site/Location: Hartman School
Physical Location: 355 Hubbard St. • South Haven, MI 49090
Hours: Memorial Day-Oct: Tue-Wed 9 a.m.-4 p.m., Sun 2-4 p.m.
Admission: Free.
Visitor Accessibility: Free street parking. Wheelchair accessible. Tour guide available Sun (Memorial Day-Sep).
Website: www.historyofsouthhaven.org
About: Formed in 2002 to preserve and promote understanding of South Haven history, the Historical Association of South Haven maintains exhibits and archives in Hartman School building.
Annual Events: Spring Open House & Membership Drive Kick-Off (May), Sherman's Ice Cream Social (Jun), Songs & Stories of South Haven (Jul).
Publications: Quarterly newsletter.

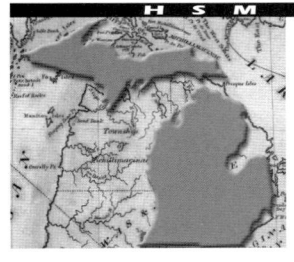

Liberty Hyde Bailey Museum
Mailing Address: P.O. Box 626, 903 Bailey Ave. • South Haven, MI 49090
Contact: John Linstrom, Director
E-Mail: lhbm@south-haven.com
Phone: (269) 637-3251
Hours: May-Sep: Wed-Sat 9 a.m.-4 p.m. Oct-Apr: By appointment.
Admission: Donations accepted. Discounts for members on special events and exhibits.
Visitor Accessibility: Off-site parking. Partially wheelchair accessible. Tour guide available; call ahead.
Website: www.libertyhydebailey.org
About: The Liberty Hyde Bailey Museum is the birthplace and childhood home of America's Father of Modern Horticulture, Liberty Hyde Bailey (1858-1954), built in the Greek Revival style in 1858. On the National Register of Historic Places, the museum is the only one in the world dedicated solely to Bailey's life and work. Also includes botanical gardens; a research center featuring the Bailey Family Library Collection; the site of blacksmith's shop and carriage barn; and an educational outreach center.
Exhibits/Collections: Rotating seasonal exhibits; a permanent exhibit detailing Liberty Hyde Bailey's life story; artifacts and documents pertaining to Bailey and his family; artifacts of the region's rural and industrial history.
Annual Events: Various seasonal programs, summer keynote speaker series, Woodshed Art Show, South Haven Garden Club Garden Walk (Jul), Blueberry Festival event (Aug).
Publications: Quarterly newsletter (The Bailey Bulletin), "The Holy Earth."

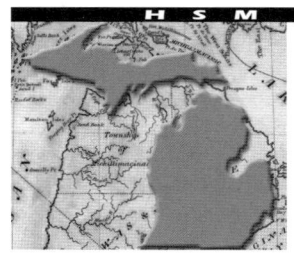

Michigan Maritime Museum
Mailing Address: 260 Dyckman Avenue • South Haven, MI 49090
Contact: Eden Morris, Director of Education and Administration
E-Mail: volunteer@michiganmaritimemuseum.org
Phone: (269) 637-8078
Hours: 10 a.m.-5 p.m.
Admission: $8/adult, $7/senior, $5/children (5-15).
Visitor Accessibility: Free on-site and street parking. Partially wheelchair accessible; main buildings only. Tour guide available for large groups; call ahead.
Website: http://michiganmaritimemuseum.org
About: The Michigan Maritime Museum is dedicated to the preservation of Michigan Great Lakes and waterways maritime history and culture. The museum collects objects related to Great Lakes maritime history with an emphasis on the state of Michigan. The museum includes permanent and changing exhibits on Michigan maritime history, a boatbuilding teaching center, and a regionally renowned research library. On-water experiences are available aboard tall ship Friends Good Will, river launch Lindy Lou, and racing yacht Bernida.
Annual Events: Blessing of the Fleet (May), Classic Boat Show (Jun), Fish Boil Fundraiser (Jul), Outboard Motor Swap Meet (Aug), Boatbuilding classes, Monthly lecture series (winter).

South Lyon
(Livingston County)

Cornish American Heritage Society
Mailing Address: 10111 Pheasant Lake Rd. • South Lyon, MI 48178
Phone: (248) 437-9736
Information may not be current.

Green Oak Charter Township Historical District Commission
Mailing Address: 12075 Nine Mile Rd. • South Lyon, MI 48178
Contact: Ruth Munzel, Vice Chair
About: The purpose of the Green Oak Township Historic District Ordinance is to safeguard the heritage of the township by preserving historical districts that reflect architectural history or elements of cultural, social, economic, or political development in the township. Districts include Green Oak Township District, Caleb-Sawyer District, Herald-Carson District, Olds-Read District, Bingham District, Johnson District, Peer-Driver District, Hammond Lintner District, and the Dean-Marentay District.

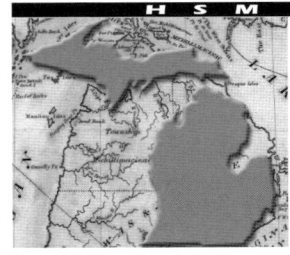

Green Oak Township Historical Society
Mailing Address: 10789 Silver Lake Road • South Lyon, MI 48178
Contact: Marilyn Harrington, President
E-Mail: stephenharrington@att.net
Phone: (248) 446-0789
Hours: By appointment.
Admission: Donations accepted.
Visitor Accessibility: On-site parking. Wheelchair accessible. Free tour guides available upon request.
Website: www.greenoaktownshiphistoricalsociety.org

About: Organized in 1974, the Green Oak Township Historical Society aims to preserve the history of Green Oak Township and the surrounding area. The organization restored the original Green Oak Township Hall, built in 1856, for public activities. The society also maintains a heritage museum, featuring artifacts from the 1800s. The museum is located adjacent to the 1856 hall.
Exhibits/Collections: Cemetery records, family histories, early tax records, histories of eight different one-room schools once located in township, and a growing library.
Annual Events: Green Oak Day (Sep). Meetings 3rd Sun Mar and May and 4th Sun Oct.
Publications: Quarterly newsletter (Green Oak Historian), "Yesteryears of Green Oak: 1830 to 1930."

Lyon Township Genealogical Society
Mailing Address: 27005 S. Milford Rd. • South Lyon, MI 48178
Contact: Cathy Cottone
E-Mail: ccottone@lyon.lib.mi.us
Phone: (248) 437-8800 x104
Hours: Mon 10 a.m.-4 p.m., Tue 2-8 p.m., Thu 10 a.m.-4 p.m., and Fri 12-5 p.m.
Visitor Accessibility: Free on-site parking. Wheelchair accessible.
Website: www.lyon.lib.mi.us
About: Helps others with genealogy.
Exhibits/Collections: Local photographs, scrapbooks, tax assessment books, funeral home records, and cemetery records. Local collection for Hudson area.
Annual Events: Meetings 3rd Tue monthly, 1 p.m. or 6:30 p.m.

South Lyon Area Historical Society
Mailing Address: P.O. Box 263 • South Lyon, MI 48178
Contact: Linda Ross, President
Phone: (248) 437-9929
Site/Location: **Witch's Hat Historic Village and Museum**
Physical Location: McHattie Park, 300 Dorothy St • South Lyon, MI 48178
Hours: Apr-Nov: Thu, Sun 1-4 p.m.
Admission: Free.
Visitor Accessibility: Free on-site parking. Partially wheelchair accessible. Guided tours available by appointment.
Website: http://www.southlyonmi.org1/223/history_of_south_lyon.asp
About: Museum operated by South Lyon Area Historical Society volunteers. Accredited by American Association of Museums. Historic village includes 1909 Queen Anne's depot and freight house, wood caboose, 1907 Washburn School, 1930s chapel, and gazebo.
Exhibits/Collections: Local history, railroad memorabilia.
Annual Events: Concerts in the Gazebo (Jun-Aug), Depot Day (Sep), Cool Yule (Dec), Meetings 3rd Tue monthly, 7:30 p.m. at Freight House.
Publications: Newsletter (Witch's Chatter).

South Range
(Houghton County)

Copper Range Historical Society
Mailing Address: P.O. Box 148 • South Range, MI 49963
Contact: Jean Pemberton, President
E-Mail: johnandjeanp@chartermi.net
Phone: (906) 482-6125
Site/Location: **Copper Range Historical Museum**
Physical Location: 44 Trimountain Ave • South Range, MI 49963
Hours: Jun: Tue-Fri 12-3 p.m. Jul-Aug: Mon-Fri 12-3 p.m. Sep: Tue-Fri 12-3 p.m. Also by appointment; call (906) 482-3097 or (906) 487-9412.
Admission: $1 donation.
Visitor Accessibility: Free street parking. Partially wheelchair accessible; flight of four stairs in entryway. Tour guide available; group tours welcome by appointment.
Website: www.pasty.com/crhm
About: The mission of the Copper Range Historical Society is to help create a sense of what the life and work experience was like during the copper mining era for the miners, loggers, farmers, businessmen, homemakers, and their families. The society's museum features copper samples, a "cooper" and his tools, photos of mining-related sites, and memorabilia. Other items on display include photos of local music hall-of-fame winners, artifacts from the Copper Range Railroad, and items from Copper Range Mining Company.
Exhibits/Collections: Mining memorabilia from mining companies that operated in Southern Houghton County, some of which are canceled payroll checks, items from a doctor's office, photos, copper ingots, and clothing.
Annual Events: Open house on first day of museum season, annual member dinner. Board meetings 1st Thu monthly.
Publications: Member newsletter (The Champion Line).

Southfield
(Oakland County)

Archives of Congregation Shaarey Zedek
Mailing Address: Attn: Judy Levin Cantor, 27375 Bell Rd. • Southfield, MI 48034
Contact: Shira Shapiro, Archivist
E-Mail: sshapiro@shaareyzedek.org
Phone: (248) 357-5544
Hours: By appointment.
Website: www.shaareyzedek.org
Publications: Bimonthly newsletter, quarterly bulletins.

Southfield Historical Society
Mailing Address: 25509 Stonycroft • Southfield, MI 48033
Contact: Gloria Kennedy, Director
E-Mail: historicsouthfield@gmail.com
Phone: (248) 356-7788
Site/Location: **Town Hall Museum**
Physical Location: 26080 Berg Road • Southfield, MI 48033
Hours: During summer concerts Jul-Aug; check www.cityofsouthfield.com for dates. Also by appointment.
Admission: Donations accepted.
Visitor Accessibility: Free on-site parking. Wheelchair accessible. Tour guide available during summer concerts or by appointment; donations accepted.
Website: http://southfieldhistoricalsociety.wordpress.com/
About: The Southfield Historical Society preserves, advances, and disseminates knowledge of the history of Southfield. At the Town Hall Museum, which is the original site of the 1872 town hall, there are many exhibits including a 1920s kitchen and displays pertaining to World War I, the Martin Luther King Task Force, and schools in Southfield.
Exhibits/Collections: Artifacts reflect early Southfield Township, its agricultural society, and daily life. Archives are housed in the history room at the Southfield Public Library, 26300 Evergreen Road, Southfield.
Annual Events: Summer concerts (Jul-Aug), Boo at the Burgh (Oct), tree lighting (Nov). Board of directors meet 2nd Wed Sep-Jun, 1:15 p.m. at the Town Hall Museum.
Other Sites/Locations: **Mary Thompson Farm House** • Location:

25630 Evergreen Road, Southfield, MI 48075 • Hours: By appointment or during special events • Admission: Donations accepted • Visitor Accessibility: Free on-site parking. Partially wheelchair accessible; first floor only. Tour guide available during special events or by appointment; donations accepted.
*Information may not be current.

Southgate
(Wayne County)

Southgate Historical Society
Mailing Address: 15043 Coventry Dr. • Southgate, MI 48195
Contact: Jim Dallos, Chairman
Phone: (734) 258-7430
Site/Location: **The Grahl House**
Physical Location: 14120 Dix-Toledo Rd. • Southgate, MI 48195
Hours: 1st weekend monthly 2-5 p.m. Also by appointment.
Admission: Free.
Visitor Accessibility: Street and lot parking behind museum. Not wheelchair accessible. Free guided tours.
About: Collects, preserves, and displays authentic documents, historical records, relics, and anything of interest/value in educational, cultural, economic, genealogical, and spiritual heritage. Promotes study and research and generates interest in the city of Southgate and the state of Michigan history. Society's museum, "The Grahl House," circa 1925, was moved to its current location in 1994.
Exhibits/Collections: Historical artifacts that were common to the local area and archived newspaper clippings, starting in 1955.
Annual Events: Site of Southgate's Easter egg hunt and visit with the Easter Bunny, Southgate Heritage Days (Aug), Visit with Santa (Dec).

Sparta
(Kent County)

Grand Rapids Civil War Roundtable
Mailing Address: c/o Daniel Dunn, 9643 Pine Island Rd. • Sparta, MI 49345
Contact: Daniel Dunn, Coordinator
E-Mail: cwhonor@comcast.net
Phone: (616) 887-9828
Physical Location: DeWitt Student Center Kuyper College, 3333 E. Beltline NE • Grand Rapids, MI 49525
Hours: 7-10 p.m. meeting days.
Admission: Free.
Visitor Accessibility: Free on-site parking. Wheelchair accessible.
Website: www.grcwrt.com
About: Dedicated to studying the Civil War and the people who fought in it. Promotes a broader understanding of the conflict and how it has shaped American history.
Exhibits/Collections: A library of Civil War-related books, videos, and magazines.
Annual Events: Monthly program on Civil War topics, 7:30 p.m. Kuyper College. Meetings 3rd Wed monthly (exceptions are Dec, Jul, Aug).
Publications: Monthly newsletter (The Valley City Reville).

Sparta Township Historical Commission
Mailing Address: 161 E. Division St. • Sparta, MI 49345
Contact: Larry Carter, President
E-Mail: history@spartahistory.org
Phone: (616) 606-0765
Site/Location: **Sparta Township Historical Commission Research Center**
Physical Location: S71 N. Union St • Sparta, MI 49345
Hours: Mon 9 a.m.-12 p.m. Also by appointment.
Admission: Free.
Visitor Accessibility: Free on-site and street parking. Wheelchair accessible. Research assistance available.
Website: www.spartahistory.org
About: The Sparta Township Historical Commission preserves and keeps alive Sparta's history for future generations. It maintains two buildings: the Meyers Schoolhouse Museum and a research center.
Exhibits/Collections: Photographs and manuscript collections pertaining to history and people of Sparta area, local maps, atlases, newspapers, obituaries, and death certificates. The Ridge Collection, military, yearbooks.
Annual Events: 5th-Grade Walking Tour, concerts in the park, Christmas Lighting Contest. Board meetings 1st Tue monthly, 7 p.m. at Commission Research Center.
Publications: "Images of America: Sparta Township," "History of Sparta Football, 1903-2010," "100 Years of Sparta Baseball."
Other Sites/Locations: **Meyers Schoolhouse Museum** • Location: 160 E. Division, Sparta, MI 49345 • Hours: By appointment • Admission: Free • Visitor Accessibility: Free on-site parking. Tour guide available. • The Meyers Schoolhouse Museum shows what life was like for students who attended one-room schoolhouses. The museum contains the history of other schools as well as the students who attended Sparta's schools.

St. Clair Shores
(Macomb County)

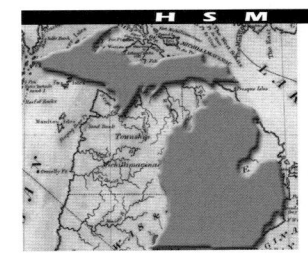

Historical Society of St. Clair Shores
Mailing Address: c/o St. Clair Shores Public Library, 22500 Eleven Mile Rd. • St. Clair Shores, MI 48081
Contact: Rose Mary Orlando, Director
E-Mail: stachowm@libcoop.net
Phone: (586) 771-9020 x271
Fax: (586) 771-8935
Website: http://www.scslibrary.org/historicalsoc.html
About: Membership organization interested in collecting, preserving, and recording the history of St. Clair Shores. Supports, helps furnish, and provides tours of Selinsky-Green Farmhouse. Helps fund special projects.
Exhibits/Collections: Household furnishings in museum, photo collection, oral histories, historical media.
Annual Events: Garden Tea Party, Santa visit. Meetings 3rd Wed monthly, 6:30 p.m. at Selinsky-Green Farmhouse Museum.
Publications: Magazine (Muskrat Tales).
*Information may not be current.

Selinsky-Green Farmhouse Museum
Mailing Address: 22500 Eleven Mile Road • St. Clair Shores, MI 48081
Contact: Mary Stachowiak, Curator
E-Mail: stachowm@libcoop.net
Phone: (586) 771-9020 • *Fax:* (586) 771-8935
Hours: Sep-May: Wed and Sat 1-4 p.m. Jun-Aug: Wed 1-4 p.m.
Admission: Donations accepted.
Visitor Accessibility: Free on-site parking. Not wheelchair accessible. Tour guide available.
Website: www.scslibrary.org/sgfm.html
About: The Selinsky-Green Farmhouse Museum represents the history of a typical family of the late-19th century. Prussian immigrants John and Mary Selinsky came to St. Clair Shores (then Erin Township) in 1868

and, by 1874, had built a log, salt-box farmhouse. The home was moved and restored by volunteers and now houses changing exhibits, period-decorated rooms, and special events.
Annual Events: Pisanki egg decorating, Santa visit, gingerbread decorating and baking, holiday open house, Woodstove Cooking Day, tea party.

St. Clair Shores Genealogical Group
Mailing Address: c/o St. Clair Shores Public Library, 22500 Eleven Mile Rd. • St. Clair Shores, MI 48081
Contact: Cynthia Bieniek, Librarian/Archivist
E-Mail: bieniekc@libcoop.net
Phone: (586) 771-9020 • *Fax:* (586) 771-8935
Hours: Arthur M. Woodford Local History Room: Tue 1-4 p.m., Thu 5-8:45 p.m. Winter: 2nd and 4th Sat 10 a.m.-12 p.m. and 1-4 p.m. Summer: 2nd and 4th Fri, same hours.
Admission: Free.
Visitor Accessibility: Free on-site parking. Wheelchair accessible. Free tours by appointment.
Website: www.scslibrary.org/genealogy.html
About: Promotes genealogy instruction and historical research through meetings, workshops, and guest speakers.
Exhibits/Collections: Digital photograph collection; Michigan/Great Lakes history; county histories; atlases; Detroit City directories; community records; high school yearbooks; genealogy books, including French-Canadian and Native American sources; databases.
Annual Events: Jan-Jun and Sep-Oct 4th Thu monthly, 7 p.m., local history center, St. Clair Shores Public Library.
Publications: Historical events published in St. Clair Shores Library newsletter. "Muskrat Tales."

St. Clair Shores Historical Commission
Mailing Address: c/o St. Clair Shores Public Library, 22500 Eleven Mile Road • St. Clair Shores, MI 48081
Contact: Gerald L. Sielagoski, Chairperson
Phone: (586) 771-9020 • *Fax:* (586) 771-8935
Hours: Summer: Wed 1-4 p.m. Winter: Wed, Sat 1-4 p.m. Also by appointment.
Admission: Free.
Visitor Accessibility: Free on-site and street parking. Not wheelchair accessible. Tour guide available during open hours and by appointment.
Website: www.scslibrary.org/historicalcomm.html
About: The St. Clair Shores Historical Commission collects and preserves historic memorabilia as well as helps operate the Selinsky-Green Farmhouse Museum. The commission establishes policies for collecting, cataloging, and preserving material related to the history of St. Clair Shores and surrounding area; residents of the area; and objects indicative of the life, customs, dress, and resources of the residents of the area.
Exhibits/Collections: Digital photograph collection, artifacts relating to farming history, artifacts of the history St. Clair Shores, Great Lakes book and journal collection, local newspapers, local history documents.
Annual Events: Annual membership meeting (spring), summer tea party.
Publications: "Muskrat Tales," "St. Clair Shores: Village on the Lake," "Jefferson Avenue Historic Tour Map," "City of St. Clair Shores, Michigan."
Information may not be current.

St. Ignace
(Mackinac County)

Father Marquette National Memorial Museum.
Please see entry under Lansing: Michigan Historical Center.

Michilimackinac Historical Society
Mailing Address: P.O. Box 735 • Saint Ignace, MI 49781
Contact: Mary Beth Powers, Business Manager
E-Mail: fortdebuademuseum@gmail.com
Phone: (906) 643-6627
Fax: (906) 643-6627
Site/Location: Fort de Buade Museum
Physical Location: 334 N. State St.• Saint Ignace, MI 49781
Hours: Tue-Thu, Sat 10 a.m.-6 p.m.; Fri 10 a.m.-9 p.m.
Admission: Donations accepted.
Visitor Accessibility: Street parking available for a fee. Partially wheelchair accessible. Tour guides available by appointment for a fee.
Website: http://michilimackinachistoricalsociety.com/
About: The Fort de Buade Museum advances the understanding of the area's shared cultural heritage through research, collection, interpretation, and exhibition of objects of historical significance. On display are the Newberry Tablets. Other exhibits include a Native-American collection, including stone tools, everyday objects, baskets, ceremonial artifacts, headdresses, and regalia; dioramas depicting a voyageur with trade goods; an 18th- to 19th-century trading post; and a representation of Chief Satigo's lodge.
Exhibits/Collections: Military and Indian weapon collection. Native-American ceremonial dress and beadwork.
Annual Events: Opening day (May), Annual Veteran Open House (Jul), Quilt Show and Raffle (Jul), St. Ignace History Week (Aug), French Frog Feast (Oct). Board meetings 2nd Thu monthly. Genealogy group meetings every Wed, 5-7 p.m.
Publications: Fort de Buade's quarterly newsletter. "Lawless Mackinac," "Michilimackinac."
Information may not be current.

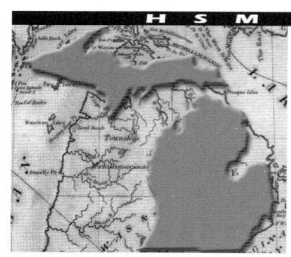

Museum of Ojibwa Culture
Mailing Address: 500 N. State St. • St. Ignace, MI 49781
E-Mail: ojibmus@lighthouse.net
Phone: (906) 643-9161
Fax: (906) 643-6076
Hours: Memorial Day-Oct: Daily. Call for current hours.
Admission: Donations accepted.
Website: www.museumofojibwaculture.net
About: Experience how Ojibwa and Huron Indians and the French lived in the Straits area 300 years ago. The museum shares the culture of the Ojibwa people. A park and exhibits show the French-Indian contact period and how the French Jesuit Missionary Jacques Marquette influenced the Indians' lives.
Information may not be current.

St. Johns
(Clinton County)

Clinton County Historical Society
Mailing Address: P.O. Box 174 • St. Johns, MI 48879
Contact: Diane Carlson, Executive Director
E-Mail: pgsmuseum@hotmail.com
Phone: (989) 224-2894
Site/Location: Paine-Gillam-Scott Museum
Physical Location: 106 Maple St. • St. Johns, MI 48879

Hours: May-Dec: Sun 1-4 p.m. and Wed 2-7 p.m.
Admission: $2/adult, $5/family.
Visitor Accessibility: Free street parking. Not wheelchair accessible. Guides available.
Website: www.pgsmuseum.com

About: The Clinton County Historical Society provides education and encourages community involvement. The Paine-Gillam-Scott Museum is located in a furnished house (b. 1860) and is reflective of Clinton County history. The carriage house has agricultural and industrial displays. There is also a doctor's office, dental office with driver's quarters, and a general store.
Exhibits/Collections: Local history and genealogical records at DeWitt Charter Township Community Center, 16101 Brook Road, Lansing.
Annual Events: St. Johns Mint Festival (Aug), Victorian Christmas (Dec).

Genealogists of the Clinton County Historical Society
Mailing Address: P.O. Box 174 • St. Johns, MI 48879
Contact: Myrna Van Epps
E-Mail: ccgensoc@yahoo.com
Phone: 517-482-5117
Physical Location: DeWitt Charter Twp Community Center, 16101 Brooks Rd. • Lansing, MI 48906
Hours: Mon-Tue 9 a.m.-4 p.m., Thu 2-6 p.m.
Website: www.dewittlibrary.com/CCHS
Exhibits/Collections: Local history and genealogical records.
Publications: Quarterly newsletter (Clinton County Trails).

St. Joseph
(Berrien County)

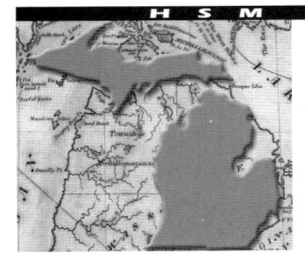

Heritage Museum & Cultural Center
Mailing Address: Priscilla U. Byrns Heritage Center, 601 Main St. • St. Joseph, MI 49085
Contact: Christina Arseneau, Museum Director
E-Mail: charseneau@theheritagemcc.org
Phone: (269) 983-1191
Fax: (269) 983-1274
Hours: Tue-Sat 10 a.m.-4 p.m.
Admission: $5/adult, $1/child (6-17), children 5 and under free.
Visitor Accessibility: Free on-site parking. Wheelchair accessible. Self-guided. Tours available.
Website: www.theheritagemcc.org

About: The Heritage Museum and Cultural Center promotes historical preservation, education, and research that relate to Benton Harbor, St. Joseph, and the surrounding region.
Exhibits/Collections: Available resources include books, reference volumes, periodicals, maps, manuscripts, business records, photographs and postcards, slides, oral history tapes, vintage films. The center's library and archive are open to researchers and the general public by appointment.
Annual Events: Public program series held monthly (Feb-Nov), evenings at the museum.
Publications: Newsletter (The Heritage Journal).

St. Louis
(Gratiot County)

St. Louis Area Historical Society
Mailing Address: 108 W. Saginaw St. • St. Louis, MI 48880
Contact: Phillip Hansen
E-Mail: stlouisdda@stlouismi.com
Phone: (989) 681-3017
Fax: (989) 681-3842
Site/Location: **St. Louis Historic Park**
Physical Location: 110 E. Crawford St. • St. Louis, MI 48880
Hours: Thu 1-4 p.m.
Visitor Accessibility: Free on-site parking. Wheelchair accessible. Guided tours can be scheduled by calling (989) 681-3017.
Website: www.stlouismi.com/1/stlouis/Historical_Society.asp

About: The St. Louis Area Historical Society preserves and displays items regarding St. Louis-area history at the St. Louis Historic Park. The park includes the society's museum, which is located in the restored Pere Marquette Train Depot that is filled with historical items and displays; the Transportation Pavilion, which includes a 1917 Republic Truck, Indian dugout canoe, and other transportation items; and a restored historic wooden tollbooth from the M-46 Plank Road.
Exhibits/Collections: Local historical artifacts include photographs, documents, a restored 1917 Republic Truck built in Alma, a hand-carved canoe from the 1880s, and a restored fire department hose reel.
Annual Events: Strawberry Shortcake Sale, 4th of July Celebration. Meetings 4th Tue monthly, 7 p.m. at the depot or city hall.
Publications: "St. Louis at 150: The Story of the Middle of the Mitten," "The Story of Colonel Elwell's Castle," "The Saratoga of the West: Story of the Magnetic Mineral Springs," "A St. Louis Album Pictorial History of St. Louis."

St. Clair
(St. Clair County)

St. Clair Historical Commission
Mailing Address: 308 S. Fourth St. • St.Clair, MI 48079
Contact: Robert Freehan, Chairperson
E-Mail: robert.freehan@gmail.com
Phone: (810) 329-6888
Site/Location: **St. Clair Historical Museum**
Hours: Open year-long Tue 9:30 a.m.-12 p.m.; May-Nov Sat-Sun 1:30-4:30 p.m.
Admission: Donations accepted.
Visitor Accessibility: Free on-site parking. Not wheelchair accessible. Docent available, prior arrangement needed for groups.
Website: www.historicstclair.com

About: The St. Clair Historical Commission preserves St. Clair history, provides historical records for history and family research, hosts historical public presentations, and maintains a public museum. The museum features a Fort Sinclair model; specialty rooms highlighting artifacts from the local area, including shipbuilding tools, shoe manufacture, period kitchen and living rooms; and a Diamond Crystal Salt Company room. The area's wooden and steel shipbuilding history is highlighted in the museum's maritime room.
Exhibits/Collections: Local artist Sam Crawford paintings; St. Clair High School pictures and yearbooks; antique tools from shipbuilding, farm, and carpentry industries; period clothing; cannon; buggy; and other artifacts.
Annual Events: Public presentations (Apr-May, Sep-Nov), Cemetery Walk (Oct).
Publications: "Fort Sinclair," "Underground Railroad."

Sterling Heights
(Macomb County)

Sterling Heights Historical Commission
Mailing Address: Sterling Heights Public Library, 40255 Dodge Park Road • Sterling Heights, MI 48313
Contact: Tammy Turgeon, Staff Librarian
E-Mail: turgeont@libcoop.net
Phone: (586) 446-2640
Fax: (586) 276-4067
Site/Location: William Upton House
Physical Location: 40433 Dodge Park • Sterling Heights, MI 48313
Hours: Open during Sterlingfest (Jul) and Sterling Christmas (Dec). Also by appointment.
Admission: Donations accepted.
Visitor Accessibility: Parking in city lot. Partially wheelchair accessible; first floor only.
Website: http://www.shpl.net/commission.htm
About: The Sterling Heights Historical Commission promotes an awareness of the community's heritage, identifies local preservation concerns, studies public policies designed to protect and preserve local history, and provides opportunities for residents to share and shape their historical legacy. The commission solicits and accepts items that depict growth and change within municipality from inception as a township in 1835 to the present. The library and commission arrange displays in the 1867 Upton House.
Exhibits/Collections: Maps, photographs, and documents relating to personal, business, educational, cultural, and recreational activities. Household accessories and personal artifacts.
Annual Events: Educational workshop (May), Sterlingfest (Jul), Sterling Christmas. Meetings 1st Thu Feb, May, Sep, and Nov at 7p.m.

Stockbridge
(Jackson County)

Stockbridge Area Genealogical & Historical Society
Mailing Address: P.O. Box 966 • Stockbridge, MI 49285
Contact: David Linderner, President
E-Mail: stockbridgeareaghs@hotmail.com
Website: www.rootsweb.com/~misaghs
Annual Events: Annual picnic (Jul), Cemetery tour (Oct). Meetings: 4th Tue of the month Mar, May, Sep, Nov.

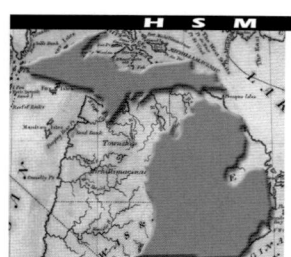

Waterloo Area Historical Society
Mailing Address: P.O. Box 37 • Stockbridge, MI 49285
Contact: Mitchell Planck, President
E-Mail: info@waterloofarmmuseum.org
Phone: (517) 596-2254
Site/Location: Waterloo Farm Museum
Physical Location: 13493 Waterloo Munith Road • Grass Lake, MI 49240
Hours: Memorial Day-Labor Day: Weekends.
Admission: $5/adult. Memberships available.
Visitor Accessibility: Free on-site parking. Partially wheelchair accessible. Tour guide available; cost included in admission.
Website: www.waterloofarmmuseum.org
About: The Waterloo Area Historical Society educates the public about pioneer Michigan farming life and history. The Waterloo Farm Museum includes several buildings, such as the farmhouse, the Really Barn, milk house, log cabin, workshop/forge, ice house, and more.
Exhibits/Collections: 1880s clothing, furnishings, farm equipment, and blacksmithing tools. Historical artifacts from Michigan farming and country living, including farm equipment, clothing, household items, and quilts.
Annual Events: Log Cabin Weekend (Jun), Antique Tractor Day (Aug), Pioneer Day (Oct), Christmas at the Farm (Dec).
Other Sites/Locations: Dewey School • Location: 11501 Territorial Road, Grass Lake, MI 48340 • Hours: By appointment • Admission: $5/adult; memberships available • Visitor Accessibility: Free on-site parking. Not wheelchair accessible. Tour guide available by appointment. • The Dewey School is a 19th-century one-room schoolhouse.
Information may not be current.

Sturgis
(St. Joseph County)

Sturgis Historical Society
Mailing Address: P.O. Box 392 • Sturgis, MI 49091
Phone: (269) 659-2512
Physical Location: 200 W. Main St. • Sturgis, MI 49091
Hours: Mon-Fri 8:30 a.m.-4:40 p.m.
Admission: Donations accepted.
Visitor Accessibility: On-site public parking available. Wheelchair accessible.
About: Preserves Sturgis history and the historic railroad depot. The museum shares former railroad depot with Chamber of Commerce.
Exhibits/Collections: 1,500 Sturgis-area items, including motorhome built from Spartan bus. Spartan buses built in Sturgis from 1947-1949. Sold in the United States and overseas, including Mexico and Saudi Arabia.
Annual Events: Meetings 4th Sun monthly, 1 p.m. in Sturges-Young Auditorium, 201 N Nottawa St., Sturgis.
Publications: Monthly newsletter.

Sunfield
(Eaton County)

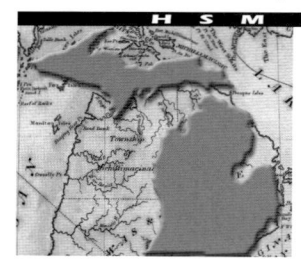

Sunfield Historical Society
Mailing Address: 161 Main St., P.O. Box 251 • Sunfield, MI 48890
Contact: Jan Sedore, President
E-Mail: sunfieldhistoricalsociety@gmail.com
Site/Location: Welch Museum
Hours: April-Dec: Mon 10 a.m.-2 p.m.; Wed 2-5 p.m.; Sat 10 a.m.-2 p.m.; Jan-Mar: Open Sat.
Admission: Free.
Visitor Accessibility: Street parking. Wheelchair accessible. Free tour guides available.
Website: www.sunfieldhistoricalsociety.com
About: A fully furnished 1860 log cabin is built within the museum. The Welch Museum also features a barn replica, a 1927 fire truck, turn-of-the-century classroom, hands-on displays, and photos of students who graduated from Sunfield High School (1914-1963). Genealogy room available for research of local area. The Sunfield Historical Society acquires, conserves, researches, and exhibits for purposes of inspiring children, connecting families, and strengthening the surrounding community.
Exhibits/Collections: The Welch Museum has exhibits and displays of artifacts from many area's surrounding Sunfield. Eaton, Barry, Ionia and Clinton Counties.
Annual Events: May Daze (May), Trunk or Treat (Oct), Christmas on Main Street (Dec).
Publications: Newsletter (Sunspot).

Michigan History Directory

Taylor
(Wayne County)

HSM MEMBER

Taylor Historical Society
Mailing Address: P.O. Box 1225 • Taylor, MI 48180
Contact: George Gouth, President
Phone: (734) 287-3835
Site/Location: **Taylor Historical Museum**
Physical Location: Taylor Heritage Park, 12405 Pardee Rd • Taylor, MI 48180
Hours: To be announced.
Admission: Free.
Visitor Accessibility: Adjacent parking available. Wheelchair accessible. Free tour guides available.
About: The Taylor Historical Society gathers local family histories and artifacts and shares them with visitors through exhibits/displays and sponsoring open houses at the museum, township hall, one-room 1882 schoolhouse, and log cabin in Taylor Heritage Park. Museum exhibits and history artifacts showcase early Taylor businesses and family life in rural Taylor Township.
Exhibits/Collections: Farm tools, historical records, published maps, site information, and handouts.
Annual Events: Summer Taylor Days, Log Cabin Day, Fall Festival, Meetings 2nd Thu monthly Sep-Jun.
Publications: Monthly membership newsletter (PRESServations).
Other Sites/Locations: **1882 One Room School** • Location: Heritage Park • Admission: $2/child plus teacher • Visitor Accessibility: Nearby parking. Wheelchair accessible. Reservations required for visitations and classrooms events; call (734) 287-3835. • Classrooms are encouraged to visit the school to experience a day back in time. The school is outfitted with hornbooks, McGuffy Readers and spellers, quillpens, inkpens, inkwells, dunce stool, hickory sticks, and real slate chalk board. Desks easily seat 25 students.

Tecumseh
(Lenawee County)

HSM MEMBER

Tecumseh Area Historical Society
Mailing Address: P.O. Box 26 • Tecumseh, MI 49286
Contact: Chris Brown, Museum Director
E-Mail: historictecumseh@gmail.com
Phone: (517) 423-2374
Site/Location: **Tecumseh Area Historical Museum**
Physical Location: 302 E. Chicago Blvd. • Tecumseh, MI 49286
Hours: Apr-Dec: Sat 10:30 a.m.-3:30 p.m.
Admission: Free.
Visitor Accessibility: Free on-site parking. Wheelchair accessible. Self-guided.
Website: https://www.facebook.com/pages/Tecumseh-Area-Historical-Museum/164792283540212?sk=timeline
About: The Tecumseh Area Historical Society collects and preserves any materials that may help establish or illustrate the history of the area. These materials are kept in the Tecumseh Area Historical Museum, which is housed in the Gothic-style St. Elizabeth Catholic Church (b. 1913).
Exhibits/Collections: Dynamic Kernel Exhibit, Meyers-Divers Airport, artifacts from the Underground Railroad, military history.
Annual Events: Vets concert, basket sale (May). Meetings 2nd Thu monthly.
Publications: Quarterly newsletter.

Temperance
(Monroe County)

HSM MEMBER

Bedford Historical Society
Mailing Address: 7318 Bentcreek Dr. • Temperance, MI 48182
Contact: Carolynn Newman, President
E-Mail: lindaski@buckeye-access.com
Phone: (734) 847-7780
Site/Location: **Banner Oak School**
Physical Location: Sterns and Crabb Roads • Temperance, MI 48182
Hours: Apr-Oct: By appointment.
Admission: Free.
Visitor Accessibility: Free on-site parking. Wheelchair accessible. Free tour guides available upon request.
About: The Bedford Historical Society collects and preserves the history of Banner Oak School a Michigan State Historic Site in Bedford Township, Monroe County. Attractions include the restored and refurnished 1871 Banner Oak One-Room School, District Number 6.
Annual Events: Colonial Craft Show (Dec). Meetings 1st Mon monthly, 7 p.m. at Bedford Library (Jackman Road, Temperance).

Thompsonville
(Benzie County)

HSM MEMBER

Michigan Legacy Art Park
Mailing Address: 12500 Crystal Mountain Drive • Thompsonville, MI 49683
Contact: Renee Hintz, Executive Director
E-Mail: director@michlegacyartpark.org
Phone: (231) 378-4963
Hours: Daily during daylight hours.
Admission: $5/adult.
Visitor Accessibility: Free on-site and street parking. Partially wheelchair accessible; call ahead to reserve a golf cart tour. Self-guided.
Website: www.michlegacyartpark.org
About: Michigan Legacy Art Park inspires awareness, appreciation, and passion for Michigan's history, culture, and environment through the arts. The 30-acre sculpture park boasts a collection of 44 major works of art and 30 poetry stones. Each sculpture helps express the Michigan experience, giving visitors a personal connection to the people, events, and natural resources that continue to shape our state. At each sculpture, interpretive signs help visitors have a deeper understanding for the art and the Michigan stories they express.
Annual Events: Summer Sounds Concert Series (Jul-Aug), daily workshops and tours (Sum), Annual Legacy Gala, Family Fun Day (Oct). Board of directors meets quarterly at Crystal Mountain.
Publications: "Michigan Legacy Art Park," "Looking to Learn."

Three Oaks
(Berrien County)

HSM MEMBER

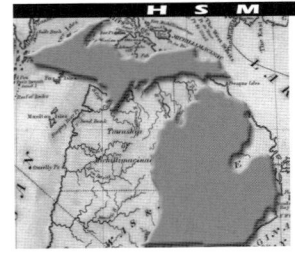

Three Oaks Township Public Library
Mailing Address: 3 N. Elm St. • Three Oaks, MI 49128-1117
E-Mail: threeoakspubliclibrary@yahoo.com
Phone: (269) 756-5621
Fax: (269) 756-3004
Hours: Tue, Thu 12-7 p.m.; Wed, Fri 10

a.m.-5 p.m.; Sat 10 a.m.-2 p.m. Closed Sun, Mon.
Admission: Free.
Visitor Accessibility: Free on-site parking. Wheelchair accessible. Self-guided.
Website: http://www.threeoaks.michlibrary.org

About: An extensive local history collection. Local newspapers (1880-1989) are digitized and searchable by keyword on-site. Large collection of items and photographs from Warren family and the Featherbone Factory.

Traverse City
(Leelanau County)

Fox Island Lighthouse Association, Inc.
Mailing Address: P.O. Box 851 • Traverse City, MI 49685
Contact: John McKinney, President
E-Mail: info@southfox.org
Phone: (231) 947-1926
Website: www.southfox.org

Grand Traverse Area Genealogical Society
Mailing Address: P.O. Box 2015 • Traverse City, MI 49685
Contact: Virginia LeClaire
E-Mail: ginintc@charter.net
Website: www.grandtraverseregion.com/gtags
About: Since 1979, Grand Traverse Area Genealogical Society has contributed more than 1,800 genealogy books, many reels of microfilm, and a number of CD-ROMS to the library. Monograph holdings now include more than 2,000 books.
Exhibits/Collections: The society's genealogy monograph collection is held at the Traverse Area District Library.

History Center of Traverse City
Mailing Address: 322 Sixth St. • Traverse City, MI 49684
Contact: Bill Kennis, Executive Director
E-Mail: museum@traversehistory.org
Phone: (231) 995-0313 • *Fax:* (231) 946-6750
Hours: Summer: Mon-Sat 10 a.m.-5 p.m., Sun 12-5 p.m.
Admission: $5/individual.
Visitor Accessibility: Free on-site parking. Wheelchair accessible. Self-guided.
Website: www.gtheritagecenter.org
About: The History Center of Traverse City preserves, promotes, and presents the history of the Grand Traverse region. The History Center of Traverse City includes a pre-written history wing, which features Native-American items; a scale Wigwam; and interactive glacier panels depicting the two glaciers that formed Michigan. Children can dig through 2,000 pounds of cherry pits to forge for a souvenir copper ingot, arrowhead, Petoskey stone, or beach stone.
Exhibits/Collections: Ice Age artifacts and Native-American crafts, logging, railroads, agriculture items, rock and minerals, Veterans exhibit, State Hospital items, blacksmithing, Victorian collection, and regional items from over 100 years.
Annual Events: Winter Sports Spectacular (Jan, Feb), Legends (Mar, Apr), Lego Exhibit (Memorial Day-Labor Day), Heritage Days and Legends (Sep), Haunted Museum (Oct), Festival of Trains (Dec). Board of directors meetings 3rd Mon monthly.

*Information may not be current.

Maritime Heritage Alliance
Mailing Address: 13268 S. West Bayshore Dr. • Traverse City, MI 49684
Contact: Sherri Freels, Office Manager
E-Mail: info@maritimeheritagealliance.org
Phone: 231-946-2647
Hours: Call or visit website for hours.
Admission: Free.
Visitor Accessibility: Call ahead for tour guide availability.
Website: www.maritimeheritagealliance.org
About: Maritime Heritage Alliance (MHA) preserves, interprets, and shares the maritime history of the Great Lakes. MHA currently owns and maintains a replica of an 1850s schooner, a cutter Champion, several other boats, and a boat restoration shop. MHA's woodshops, including the Edwin & Mary Brown Restoration Boat Shop, are housed in two large buildings. There is also a collection of vintage canoes, as well as motors and an old Singer sewing machine. All have been researched and are available for viewing.
Exhibits/Collections: Collection of old wood boats, including a Mackinaw boat and Gracie L, the first boat built by members of the MHA. Large library of nautical-themed books.
Annual Events: Spring potluck, boat auction (Jun), fall potluck (Nov). Board of directors meets 2nd Mon monthly at 5:30p.m.
Publications: Monthly newsletter.

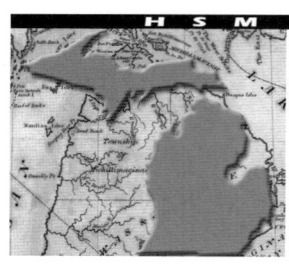

Old Mission Penninsula Historical Society
Mailing Address: 7072 Peninsula Drive • Traverse City, MI 49968
Contact: Kennard R. Weaver, President
E-Mail: dobrum@aol.com
Phone: (231) 947-0947
Fax: (231) 947-0947
Site/Location: Hessler Log Cabin
Physical Location: Lighthouse Park • Old Mission, MI 49673
Hours: Call or see website.
Admission: Free.
Visitor Accessibility: Free on-site parking. Wheelchair accessible. Self-guided.
Website: www.omphistoricalsociety.org
About: The Hessler Log Cabin features a motion-activated audio history presentation at the viewing door on the west side of the cabin, available at any time from May through October.
Exhibits/Collections: The Hessler Log Cabin and its authentic period-correct furniture contents.
Annual Events: Log Cabin Day (Jun). Meetings 1st Thu monthly, 7 p.m. at Peninsula Township Hall.
Publications: Biannual newsletter (Echoes).

Railroad Historical Society of Northwest Michigan
Mailing Address: P.O. Box 1845 • Traverse City, MI 49685
Contact: George Gregory, President
E-Mail: rrgregory@aol.com
Phone: (231) 946-6436
Physical Location: History Center of Traverse City, 322 6th St. • Traverse City, MI 49685
About: The Railroad Historical Society of Northwest Michigan encourages and advances the knowledge of railroad history. The organization promotes public interest in all areas of railroad history through the display of artifacts, a library, an NYC motor car, documents, and works of historical

significance to the railroad industry and its heritage.
Exhibits/Collections: Railroad artifacts and documents, magazine collection spanning 50 years, 200-plus railroad books, and 75-plus railroad videos.
Annual Events: Meetings 1st Tue monthly, 7 p.m. at History Center of Traverse City, 322 6th St., Traverse City.
Publications: Newsletter (Train Talk).
Information may not be current.

Traverse Area District Library
HSM MEMBER
Mailing Address: 610 Woodmere Ave. • Traverse City, MI 49686
Contact: Metta Lansdale, Director
E-Mail: info@tadl.org
Phone: (231) 932-8500
Hours: Mon-Thu 9 a.m.-9 p.m., Fri-Sat 9 a.m.-6 p.m., Sun 12-5 p.m.
Visitor Accessibility: Free on-site parking. Wheelchair accessible. Self-guided.
Website: www.tadl.org
Exhibits/Collections: Grand Traverse-area local history and genealogy.

Traverse Area Historical Society
Mailing Address: c/o Grand Traverse Heritage Center, 322 N. Sixth St. • Traverse City, MI 49684
Contact: Patricia DeAgostino
Phone: (231) 929-7663
Hours: Archive: Mon 1-4 p.m., Thu 1-7 p.m.
Website: www.traversehistory.org
About: Dedicated to preserving and presenting history of Grand Traverse region. Offices located in Grand Traverse Heritage Center where society maintains archive.
Exhibits/Collections: More than 13,000 photos, documents, and newspaper clippings related to history of Grand Traverse region.
Information may not be current.

Traverse City Historic Districts Commission
Mailing Address: 400 Boardman Ave. • Traverse City, MI 49684
Phone: (231) 922-4778
Website: www.traversecitymi.gov
About: Administrates the Historic District of Traverse City.
Information may not be current.

Women's History Project of Northwest Michigan
Mailing Address: c/o History Center of Traverse City, 322 Sixth St. • Traverse City, MI 49684
Contact: Nancy Doughty, President
Phone: (231) 995-0313
Hours: Mon-Fri 10 a.m.-5 p.m.
Admission: Varies per event/activity.
Visitor Accessibility: Free on-site and street parking. Wheelchair accessible.
Website: www.whpnm.org
About: Founded in 2000 to preserve and recognize the contributions of women to their families and communities in Northwest Lower Michigan. Book study group focusing on books by or about women (meets four times a year). Also features a display case that includes items of particular interest regarding women's history.
Exhibits/Collections: Transcribed oral histories of approximately 80 local women. Library.
Annual Events: Annual membership meeting (Oct). Souper Sunday (Super Bowl Sunday).
Information may not be current.

Trenton
(Wayne County)

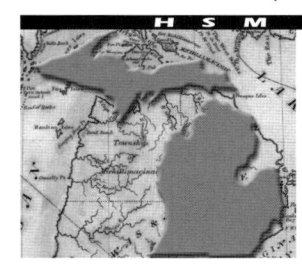

Trenton Historical Commission
HSM MEMBER
Mailing Address: 2800 Third St. • Trenton, MI 48183
Contact: Leah Inglehart
Phone: (734) 675-2130
Site/Location: Trenton Historical Museum
Physical Location: 306 St. Joseph • Trenton, MI 48183
Hours: Mar-Dec: Sat 1-4 p.m.
Admission: Donations accepted.
Visitor Accessibility: Street parking. Not wheelchair accessible. Self-guided.
Website: www.trentonhistoricalcommission.org
About: The Trenton Historical Commission collects, develops, and compiles historical data and information concerning the origin and development of the Trenton area. It oversees the maintenance and tours of Trenton Historical Museum. The Trenton Historical Museum is a Victorian-style home, built in 1881 by John and Sarah Moore. The museum is decorated in the Victorian period and contains information on history of Trenton and area artifacts.
Annual Events: Trenton Mid-Summer Festival (Jul), Victorian Christmas (Dec). Commission meets 2nd Thu monthly, 7 p.m. in city of Trenton Commission Room.

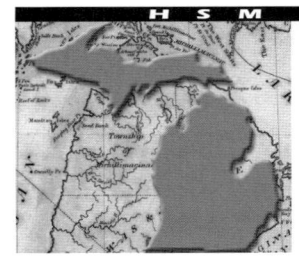

Trenton Historical Society
HSM MEMBER
Mailing Address: P.O. Box 596 • Trenton, MI 48183
Contact: Carol Ann Hendricks
Phone: (734) 676-4375
Site/Location: Trenton Historical Society Archives
Physical Location: Trenton High School, Room 1522 • Trenton, MI 48183
Hours: Wed 1-3 p.m., also by appointment.
Website: www.trentonhistoricalsociety.org
About: Established in 1987. Lucy Shirmer Collection housed in the archives contains papers used by Mrs. Shirmer in the writing of the book, "Snug Harbor," as well as various books, photos, and maps donated by the Shirmer estate. Obituary collection, Trenton High School yearbooks from 1900, Trenton Times on microfilm 1912-1973, photographs, and family biography collection.
Exhibits/Collections: See website for databases available online.
Annual Events: Hosts periodic speakers and special events.
Information may not be current.

Troy
(Oakland County)

Troy Historical Society
Mailing Address: 60 W. Wattles Road • Troy, MI 48098
Contact: Loraine Campbell, Executive Director
E-Mail: info@thvmail.org
Phone: (248) 524-3570
Fax: (248) 524-3572
Site/Location: **Troy Historic Village**
Hours: Mon-Fri 10 a.m.-3 p.m. See website for current weekend hours.
Admission: Adults $5/adult, $3/senoir, $3/children (5-12).
Visitor Accessibility: Free on-site and street parking. Wheelchair accessible. Self-guided.
Website: www.troyhistoricvillage.org
About: The Troy Historical Society stimulates discovery and promotes life-long appreciation for heritage by sharing and protecting the history of Troy and Southeast Michigan through creative, meaningful experiences that engage our stakeholders. The Troy Historic Village is a four-acre, park-like cultural and educational destination that includes 11 historic buildings.
Exhibits/Collections: 19th- and early-20th-century artifacts, archival documents, and photographs.
Annual Events: Trick or Treat in the Village (Oct), Holiday Open House (Dec). Evening talks, teas last Thu monthly, 2 p.m. Cheddar's Preschool Story Hour 1st Wed monthly, 10:30 a.m. Board meetings 3rd Tue monthly, 7 p.m. at the village.
Publications: Quarterly newsletter (Village Press), "Troy: A City from the Corners," "Fire Calls and Station Stories: The History of the Volunteer Troy Fire Department," "Troy: Our Local Community," "The Life of Solomon Caswell."

Ubly
(Huron County)

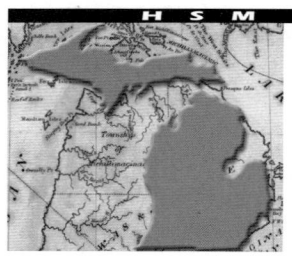

Ubly Area Historical Society
Mailing Address: P.O. Box 112 • Ubly, MI 48475
Contact: Leila Korotounova, President
E-Mail: ublyareahistoricalsociety@gmail.com
Phone: (989) 553-4892
Site/Location: **The Ten Cent Barn**
Physical Location: 1 Longuski Drive • Ubly, MI 48475
Hours: Memorial Day to Labor Day: Sun 1-4 p.m.
Admission: Donations accepted.
Visitor Accessibility: Free on-site parking. Partially wheelchair accessible; first floor only. Tour guide available; for a weekday tour, call (989) 553-4892.
Website: www.thehchs.org
About: The Ubly Area Historical Society brings together those interested in Ubly-area history to discover and collect materials. Attractions at the Ten Cent Barn include a blacksmith shop display, farm tools, household items, and historical furniture. During Homecoming Weekend in July, the museum has a "people mover" pulled by an antique tractor taking visitors to and from Memorial Park.
Exhibits/Collections: Village records, school yearbooks, cemetery information, and canning jars.
Annual Events: Village Homecoming (Jul). Meetings 4th Mon Apr-Sep, 7 p.m. at the museum or senior center.
Publications: "Celebrating 150 Years: Huron, Michigan, 1859-2009."

Union City
(Branch County)

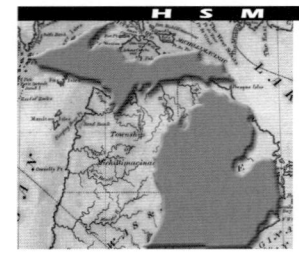

Society for Historic Preservation
Mailing Address: 210 Charlotte St. • Union City, MI 49094
Contact: Nancy Bard
E-Mail: uchistoricalsociety@yahoo.com
Phone: (517) 741-7733
Site/Location: **Hammond House Museum**
Hours: Open for special events and by appointment.
Admission: $2/adult.
About: The Hammond House Museum is located in an 1840s Greek Revival house and features an attached display area.
Exhibits/Collections: Items that pertain to the history of Union City, Burlington, and Sherwood areas. Documents, household items, memorabilia from local schools and businesses. Collection of watercolors by local artist, J.P. Palmer.
Annual Events: Home tour, teas, ice cream social, cemetery tour, road show.
Publications: Quarterly member newsletter.

University Center
(Saginaw County)

Marshall M. Fredericks Sculpture Museum
Mailing Address: Saginaw Valley State University, 7400 Bay Road • University Center, MI 48710
Contact: Marilyn Wheaton, Director
E-Mail: mfsm@svsu.edu
Phone: (989) 964-7125 • *Fax:* (989) 964-7221
Hours: Mon-Fri 11 a.m.-5 p.m., Sat 12-5 p.m.
Admission: Free.
Visitor Accessibility: Free on-site parking. Wheelchair accessible. Group tours available with advance reservation; cost is $3/individual and $2/seniors.
Website: www.marshallfredericks.org
About: The AAM accredited Marshall M. Fredericks Sculpture Museum is located on the campus of Saginaw Valley State University. The museum celebrates the artistic legacy of Marshall M. Fredericks (1908-1998) through collecting and preserving his life's work for audience enrichment. The main gallery features 200 works of bronze and plaster models that span Fredericks' 70-year career.
Exhibits/Collections: Drawings, tools, sculptures, photos and business correspondence of M. Fredericks.
Annual Events: Saints and Sinners Fundraising Gala.
Publications: Marshall Fredericks, Sculptor (Monograph), "Sketches to Sculptures," "Rendered Reality: Sixty Years with Marshall M. Fredericks."

Utica
(Macomb County)

Utica Heritage Association
Mailing Address: 7530 Auburn Rd. • Utica, MI 48317
Contact: Patrica Hallman, President
E-Mail: uticaheritage@gmail.com
Phone: (586) 781-2963
Website: www.cityofutica.org/hdc.htm
About: The Utica Heritage Association was established in 1986 to educate the public on the history of Utica and the surrounding area and collect documents and photographs to aid in that purpose. We currently

have no museum or regular program meetings. We have a book available "The History of Utica, Michigan." Our long-term project is planning for the city bicentennial in 2017.
Exhibits/Collections: There is an archival collection in a room in the basement of the Utica Public Library that can be visited by appointment. There are old maps, photos, diaries, church and organizational histories, etc.
Publications: "The History of Utica, Michigan."

Vandalia
(Cass County)

James Suggs Underground Railroad Museum
Mailing Address: 60354 N. Main, P.O. Box 162 • Vandalia, MI 49095
Contact: Martha Suggs Spencer
E-Mail: martha2521@comcast.net
Phone: (269) 476-7071 • *Fax:* (574) 232-1631
Hours: Mon-Sat 9 a.m.-5 p.m., Sun by appointment.
Admission: $6/adult, $3/student. Donations accepted.
Visitor Accessibility: Free on-site parking. Not wheelchair accessible.
About: The James Suggs Underground Railroad Museum promotes racial harmony and education on the Underground Railroad. Vandalia was one of the main stops of the Underground Railroad. Learn about the perilous journey of American slaves as they ran from the Kentucky raiders on their trail toward freedom.
Exhibits/Collections: Artifacts from the early 1800s relating to the Suggs family and the Underground Railroad. Black Suggs and white Suggs coexisting in the same household, as is detailed through the exhibits.
Annual Events: Suggs Freedom Festival. Meetings 2nd Mon monthly at 6 p.m.
Publications: "Suggs Black Back Tracks."

Underground Railroad Society of Cass County
Mailing Address: P.O. Box 124 • Vandalia, MI 49095
Contact: Cathy LaPointe, Treasurer
E-Mail: info@urscc.org
Phone: (269) 445-7358
Site/Location: **Bonine House**
Physical Location: 18970 M-60 • Vandalia, MI 49095
Hours: Call or see website.
Admission: Donations accepted.
Visitor Accessibility: Free on-site parking. Wheelchair accessible. Tour guide available; private group tours by reservation at info@urscc.org.
Website: www.urscc.org
About: The Underground Railroad Society of Cass County (URSCC) provides exploration into the origins and activities of the Underground Railroad, the unique role the people of Cass County played throughout its existence, and how it impacted history. The URSCC is restoring the house for use as a community events and UGRR education center. The carriage house will be restored as a museum.
Annual Events: Cass County UGRR "Wax Museum" (Apr/May) Underground Railroad Days (Jul), Christmas at the Bonine House (Dec). Board meets 2nd Wed monthly.
Publications: Self-guided tour booklet featuring 15 local UGRR sites in Cass County. Tour maps and pamphlets are available at the UGRR Michigan Hisotric Marker in Milo Barnes Park (M60 and Water Street in Vandalia). The tour can also be downloaded at www.urscc.org.

Vassar
(Tuscola County)

Vassar Historical Society
Mailing Address: P.O. Box 23 • Vassar, MI 48786
Contact: Corey Haubenstricker, President
Phone: (989) 823-2651
Site/Location: **Vassar Museum**
Physical Location: 450 S. Main St. • Vassar, MI 48768
Hours: Apr-Dec: Sat 10 a.m.-2 p.m.
Admission: Free.
Visitor Accessibility: Free on-site parking. Wheelchair accessible. Free tour guide available.
Website: www.vassarhistory.org
About: Promotes an interest in the history of Vassar and the surrounding townships. Exhibits pertain to Vassar High School, the founder of Vassar, Townsend North items, lumbering, and farming.
Exhibits/Collections: Historical artifacts from Vassar and its surrounding areas.
Annual Events: Spring Fling, bake sale, Riverfest Breakfast. Meetings 1st Tue monthly, 6:30 p.m.
*Information may not be current.

Vermontville
(Eaton County)

Kalamo Township Historical Society
Mailing Address: 8889 Spore Hwy. • Vermontville, MI 49096
*Information may not be current.

Vermontville Historical Society
Mailing Address: 527 S. Main • Vermontville, MI 49096
Contact: Joeann Nehmer, Society Secretary
E-Mail: joeannnehmer@yahoo.com
Phone: (517) 726-1019
Site/Location: **Vermontville Academy and Museum**
Hours: By appointment.
Admission: Free to the public.
Visitor Accessibility: Street parking for a fee. Not wheelchair accessible.
Website: www.eaton.migenweb.net/hist.vermontville.htm
About: The Vermontville museum contains two floors of the history of Vermontville, as well as items used in the early 1900s.
Annual Events: Maple Syrup Festival (Apr).

Vernon
(Shiawassee County)

Vernon Area Historical Society
Mailing Address: P.O. Box 348 • Vernon, MI 48476
*Information may not be current.

Wakefield
(Gogebic County)

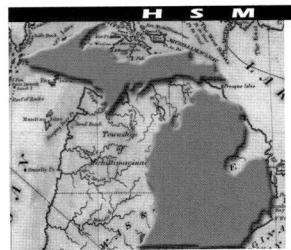

Wakefield Historical Society
Mailing Address: P.O. Box 114 • Wakefield, MI 49968
Contact: Dennis Ferson
E-Mail: djferson@att.net
Phone: (906) 224-1045
Site/Location: **Wakefield Museum**

Physical Location: 306 Sunday Lake Street • Wakefield, MI 49968
Hours: Jun-Sep: Tue-Sat 1-4 p.m.
Admission: Donations accepted.
Visitor Accessibility: Street parking. Not wheelchair accessible. Free tour guide available.
About: The Wakefield Historical Society preserves, protects, and displays artifacts of local historical interest. It also operates Wakefield Museum, which features a period classroom, doctor's office, kitchen, and general store. There is also a veterans display; mining exhibit; and "Esther's Closet," which features period fashions.
Exhibits/Collections: Artifacts of local interest dating from 1884. Mining and lumbering.
Annual Events: It's the Berries (Jun), "Fortchuly" Parade & Picnic (Jul), Christmas Faire (Dec). Meetings 2nd Tue monthly (except Jul and Dec), 2 p.m. at Sunset Manor.
Information may not be current.

Walled Lake
(Oakland County)

Commerce Township Area Historical Society
Mailing Address: P.O. Box 264• Walled Lake, MI 48390
Contact: Darlene Williams
Phone: (248) 624-2309
Information may not be current.

Warren
(Macomb County)

Warren Historical & Genealogical Society
Mailing Address: P.O. Box 1773 • Warren, MI 48092
Contact: Darlyne Slicker, President
E-Mail: warrenhistsoc@yahoo.com
Phone: (586) 258-2056 • *Fax:* (586) 258-2068
Site/Location: **Bunert One-Room Schoolhouse**
Physical Location: 27900 Bunert Road • Warren, MI 48092
Hours: 1st Sun monthly 1-4 p.m. Closed Feb.
Admission: Free.
Visitor Accessibility: Parking near entrance. Wheelchair accessible. Self-guided, contact for group tour cost. Available by appointment for group programs. Self-guided; docents provided with group programs.
Website: www.warrenhistsoc.org
About: The Warren Historical & Genealogical Society maintains the Bunert One-Room Schoolhouse and a portion of the Warren Union Cemetery. The organization works in cooperation with the Warren Historical Commission to maintain a collection of Warren history at the Warren Historical Gallery. The society brings together those interested in the history of Warren and collects and preserves materials pertaining to the historical heritage of Warren. The restored one-room Bunert School features exhibits dating back to 1875-1944.
Exhibits/Collections: Records of all historical sites past and still existing within the City of Warren.
Annual Events: Annual Honors Banquet. Society meetings: 1st Wed monthly Sep-Jun, 7 p.m. Genealogy group meetings: 2nd Thu monthly Sep-Jun, 7 p.m. in community center.
Information may not be current.

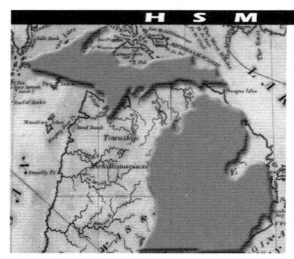

Warren Historical Commission
Mailing Address: Warren Community Center, 5460 Arden • Warren, MI 48092
Contact: Suzanne Keffer, Chair
E-Mail: histcomm@cityofwarren.org
Phone: (586) 258-2056
Fax: (586) 258-2068
Site/Location: **Warren Historical Gallery**
Hours: Mon-Fri 9 a.m.-5 p.m. Also by appointment.
Admission: Free.
Visitor Accessibility: Tour guide available upon request; donations accepted.
About: The Warren Historical Commission, in cooperation with Warren Historical & Genealogical Society, maintains a historical gallery in the Warren Community Center. The Warren Historical Gallery exhibits encompass pre-1807 "The Impassable Swamp" through the development of the city. The gallery concludes with "Warren Today 2000-Present."
Exhibits/Collections: Records pertaining to city of Warren and historic village.
Annual Events: Meetings 3rd Wed monthly, 7 p.m.

Warren Village Historic District Commission
Mailing Address: 29500 Van Dyke Ave. • Warren, MI 48092
Contact: Michelle DeDecker
Phone: (586) 795-9479
About: Mayor-appointed commission, established in the zoning ordinances, oversees the designated historic village. The city includes many historical homes, 75 years and older, that are designated historical landmarks.
Annual Events: Meetings 1st Thu monthly in village hall (except Jan).
Information may not be current.

Washington
(Macomb County)

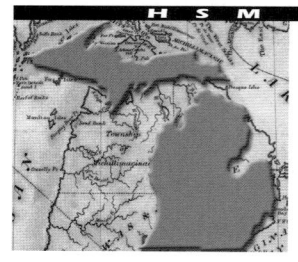

Friends of the Loren Andrus Octagon House
Mailing Address: P.O. Box 94118 • Washington, MI 48094
Contact: Susie DiPace
E-Mail: info@octagonhouse.org
Phone: (586) 781-0084
Site/Location: **Loren Andrus Octagon House**
Physical Location: 57500 Van Dyke Ave. • Washington, MI 48094
Hours: By appointment only.
Admission: $5/individual.
Visitor Accessibility: Free on-site parking. Wheelchair accessible.
Website: www.octagonhouse.org
About: The Friends of the Loren Andrus Octagon House preserve the 1860s Loren Andrus Octagon House, which was inspired by Orson Squire Fowler's publication "The Octagon House: A Home for All, Home." The society claims the house is on an old Underground Railroad route and had been used for a variety of different endeavors, ranging from an inn to the Wayne State Agricultural Program. The house has been restored and refurbished and the grounds have been restored to the Victorian era.
Annual Events: UGPR event (Feb), super weekend (Jun), quilt show (Jul), open houses (Nov), christmas events (Nov-Dec).

Michigan History Directory

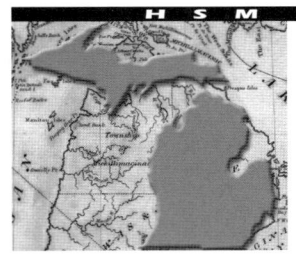

Greater Washington Area Historical Society
Mailing Address: P.O. Box 94144 • Washington, MI 48094
Contact: Ira Holcomb, President
E-Mail: holcomi@comcast.net
Phone: (248) 652-2458
Fax: (248) 652-2458
Physical Location: 58230 VanDyke • Washington, MI 48094
Hours: Jun-Nov: 2nd and 4th Sun 1-4 p.m.
Visitor Accessibility: Free on-site parking. Not wheelchair accessible. Self-guided.
Website: www.washhistsoc.org

About: The Greater Washington Area Historical Society preserves and exhibits the history of the area with documentation, pictures, and artifacts. The museum features an extensive display on George Washington. The war room has items from the Civil War, World War I, World War II, and Desert Storm. Many models of army vehicles have been placed on display. Within the museum is a Boy Scout Museum, which contains the largest collection of Boy Scout paraphernalia in Michigan.

Exhibits/Collections: Civil War, WWI and II, Native-American artifacts, freedom shrine. Pictures and historical information related to Washington area. Local genealogical records and cookbooks.

Annual Events: George Washington Birthday Celebaration (Feb), Art and Orchard Antique Show (Jun), craft show (Sep). Business meetings 2nd Thu monthly (except Dec), 10 a.m. at museum. General meetings 4th Thu monthly Mar-April and Sep-Oct, 7 p.m. at the museum

Publications: See website for complete list of publications.

Washington Township
(Macomb County)

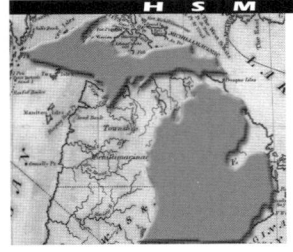

Ray Township Historical Society
Mailing Address: P.O. Box 844 • Washington Township, MI 48094
Contact: Terry Goike, President
E-Mail: info@rayhistory.org
Phone: (586) 784-9221
Website: www.rayhistory.org

About: Preserves and protects the historical significance of Ray Township's heritage. Collects, accesses, and preserves historic artifacts. Brings people with an interest in history together. Conducts oral histories. Encourages research and preservation of historic building, markers, and sites.

Exhibits/Collections: Oral history program. Photographs, surveys of historic homes, deed abstracts, early tax records, genealogical records and family histories of Ray residents.

Annual Events: See website for events. Meetings 3rd Mon Sep-May, 7 p.m. at Ray Township Senior Center.

*Information may not be current.

Sacred Spaces L.L.C.
Mailing Address: Historical Graveyard Restoration, 8277 Waschull • Washington Township, MI 48094
Contact: Laura Gheodotte
E-Mail: lghedotte@comcast.net
Phone: (586) 557-4971
Website: www.graveyardrestoration.com

Waterford
(Oakland County)

Waterford Township Historical Society
Mailing Address: Sally Strait, P.O. Box 300491 • Waterford, MI 48330
Contact: Sally Strait, President
E-Mail: sstrait649@comcast.net
Phone: (248) 683-2697
Site/Location: Waterford Historic Village
Physical Location: 4490 Hatchery Road • Waterford, MI 48330
Hours: Wed 10:30 a.m.-2 p.m.
Admission: Free.
Visitor Accessibility: On-site parking. Wheelchair accessible. Self-guided tour with audio. Tour guide available for large groups upon request.
Website: www.waterfordhistoricalsociety.org

About: This early 1900s Historic Waterford Village includes a 1919 Hatchery House, log cabin, Jacober's General Store, Drayton Plains Depot, Grand Tunk caboose and water tower, carriage house, millinery, barber shop, hardware store, print shop, doctor and dentist offices, bakery, and service station.

Exhibits/Collections: Items related to Waterford and railroads in area. Library for research and photo collection.

Annual Events: Log Cabin Days (Jun), Christmas in October.

Wayne
(Wayne County)

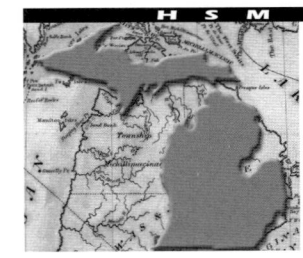

Wayne Historical Society
Mailing Address: 1 Town Square • Wayne, MI 48184
Contact: Richard Story, Museum Manager
E-Mail: rstory@ci.wayne.mi.us
Phone: (734) 722-0113
Site/Location: Wayne Historical Museum
Physical Location: North East Biddle and Main Street • Wayne, MI 48184
Hours: Thu-Fri 1-4 p.m.
Admission: Free.
Visitor Accessibility: On-site and street parking. Wheelchair accessible. Free tour guide available.
Website: www.ci.wayne.mi.us/historical_museum.shtml

About: Located in the former city offices building (c. 1878), the Wayne Historical Museum opened in 1964 and features more than 100 exhibits tracing the path from village to city.

Exhibits/Collections: Artifacts of daily life in village. Extensive early Nankin Township history and records, first landowners, genealogies, documents, histories and pictures of early businesses and industries, community leaders, local cemetery records.

Annual Events: Meetings 2nd Thu Mar-May and Sep-Nov, 7:30 p.m.

Publications: "Wayne Fire Department," "The City of Wayne."

Weidman
(Isabella County)

Barryton Area Historical Commission
Mailing Address: 6388 W. Vernon Rd. • Weidman, MI 48893
Contact: Irene Warren

E-Mail: ikgibbons@hughes.net
Phone: (989) 382-5419
Physical Location: 19730 30th Avenue • Barryton, MI 49305
Hours: Memorial Day-Labor Day: Sat-Sun 1-4 p.m.
About: The Barryton Area Historical Commission opened its museum in 1987. The commission also maintains the Titus School, Covert School, and the Ed McNeilly Memorial Building.
Exhibits/Collections: Cameras, pictures, histories, and artifacts from local residents; farming equipment; and a sleigh. Barryton Press Collection.
Annual Events: Barryton Lilac Fest (May), Christmas tree lighting (Dec).
Publications: Annual newsletter.
Information may not be current.

West Bloomfield
(Oakland County)

Chaldean Cultural Center
Mailing Address: 5600 Walnut Lake Road • West Bloomfield, MI 48323
Contact: Mary C. Romaya, Director
E-Mail: mromaya@chaldeanculturalcenter.org
Phone: (248) 681-5050
Fax: (248) 681-9191
Hours: Call for current hours.
Visitor Accessibility: Free on-site parking. Tour guide available; advance reservations required by calling (248) 681-5050.
Website: www.chaldeanculturalcenter.org
About: Set to open in fall 2014, the Chaldean Cultural Center celebrates and explores the extraordinary history, arts, traditions, and contributions of the Chaldean people from ancient times to the present, serving as a repository of the collected history and stories. It serves to promote the history and accomplishments of the Chaldean people and will cover more than 5,000 years of Chaldean history.
Publications: "The Chaldeans: A Contemporary Portrait of One of Civilization's Oldest Cultures."

Jewish Genealogical Society of Michigan
Mailing Address: P.O. Box 251693 • West Bloomfield, MI 48325
Contact: Adina Lipsitz
E-Mail: contact@jgsmi.org
Phone: (248) 968-4211 • *Fax:* (248) 855-8727
Admission: $5/non-member (events only), free to members.
Website: www.jgsmi.org
About: Founded in 1985 by Betty Provizer Starkman, the Jewish Genealogical Society of Michigan is a leader in education, research, information exchange forums, and resources for Jewish genealogy. Most of our events are hosted at the Holocaust Memorial Center in Farmington Hills, which also houses the Gayle Sweetwine Saini Memorial Library of the Jewish Genealogical Society of Michigan.
Exhibits/Collections: Collection includes more than 400 items.
Annual Events: Morris and Betty Starkman Annual Genealogy Lecture and election of officers (Jun). See website for meeting times and locations.

Jewish Historical Society of Michigan
Mailing Address: 6600 W. Maple Rd. • West Bloomfield, MI 48322
Contact: Wendy Rose Bice, Executive Director
E-Mail: info@michjewishhistory.org
Phone: (248) 432-5517
Fax: (248) 432-5540
Hours: By appointment.
Admission: Free to the public.
Visitor Accessibility: Free parking. Wheelchair accessible. Volunteer docents available for public and private tours. Volunteer speakers available for public and private events.
Website: www.michjewishhistory.org
About: For more than half a century, the Jewish Historical Society of Michigan (JHSM) has promoted and celebrated the special story of Michigan's Jewish communities, organizations, and citizens. JHSM accomplishes this through the presentation of programs, tours, events, and publications that preserve and proudly bring to life the stories of the historic Jewish community.
Exhibits/Collections: More than 900 yearbooks of Detroit-area high schools with predominately Jewish populations from 1890s to present. Leonard N. Simons Jewish Community Archives at the Reuther Library, Wayne State University.
Annual Events: "Settlers to Citizens" tours of historic Jewish Detroit; Settlers to Citizens Youth Tours of historic Jewish Detroit and JHSM Annual Meeting and Presentation of the Leonard N. Simons History Award (Spr).
Publications: Annual journal (Michigan Jewish History).

West Branch
(Ogemaw County)

Ogemaw County Agricultural Society Antique Village
Mailing Address: P.O. Box 175 • West Branch, MI 48661
Contact: Fred & Evelyn Delaney, Chairpersons
E-Mail: info@ogemawcountyfair.com
Phone: (989) 345-5393
Physical Location: 2276 Rifle River Trail • West Branch, MI 48661
Hours: 3rd week of Aug (Fair Week): 10 a.m.-9 p.m.
Admission: Fair gate fee (week of fair only). No cost by appointment.
Visitor Accessibility: Free parking. Wheelchair accessible. Tour guides available (free).
Website: www.ogemawcountyfair.com/antique_village.php
About: Quaint setting of old-time buildings at Ogemaw Fairgrounds. Log church, two log homes, school, print shop, general store, livery stable, pottery shop, tool and machine sheds, blacksmith's shop, covered bridge, stone water fountain, windmill, gas engine display, CCC bunkhouse and fire barn, heirloom garden, and a building to display memorabilia from all branches of our armed forces.
Annual Events: School programs spring and fall, Ogemaw County Fair.

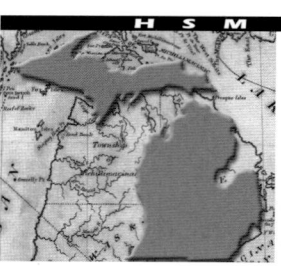

Ogemaw County Genealogical and Historical Society
Mailing Address: P.O. Box 734, 123 S. 5th St. • West Branch, MI 48661
Contact: Sally Rea, Curator
E-Mail: oghs1978@gmail.com
Phone: (989) 343-0177
Site/Location: Ogemaw County Historical Museum
Hours: Thu-Fri 10 a.m.-2 p.m. Also by appointment.
Admission: Donations accepted.
Visitor Accessibility: Street parking. Not wheelchair accessible.
Website: www.westbranch.com/ogemaw_genealogical.htm
About: The Ogemaw County Genealogical and Historical Society preserves and showcases the history of Ogemaw County through historical events, school programs, and special programs. Provides walking tours of cities and cemeteries and driving tours of historic sites in county.

Museum's exhibits change periodically.
Exhibits/Collections: Native-American items. A new collection of photos from a local photography studio, consisting of 10,000 photos.
Annual Events: Nancy Douglas Doll & Tea (Jun), Civil War Cemetery Walk (Sep).
Publications: "City of West Branch 100 Years," "First Landowners," "Footsteps through Ogemaw State Forest."

West Olive
(Ottawa/Allegan County)

Olive Township Historical Society & Museum
Mailing Address: 11903 Stanton • West Olive, MI 49460
Contact: Beverly Jaarsma, Treasurer-Secretary
E-Mail: jaarsmab@yahoo.com
Phone: (616) 875-8036
Physical Location: 11768 Polk St. • Holland, MI 49424
Hours: By appointment.
Admission: Donations accepted.
Visitor Accessibility: Parking lot. Wheelchair accesssible. Guides available by appointment, $10/individual.
Website: www.olivetownship.com/OTHS
About: Organized in 2004, the society operates a museum in the former township hall and Olive Center School. It provides educational programs and tours of historical sites. Exhibits highlight local and regional artifacts, including pioneer school, military display, and church room.
Exhibits/Collections: Artifacts and archival materials about Olive Township and nearby communities.
Annual Events: Christmas Home Tour, Memorial Day lunch and display. Meetings 4th Tue monthly, 7 p.m. at museum.
Publications: Newsletter (Olive Leaves). "Tales of Ottawa Station," "Paging the Days of Olive."
Other Sites/Locations: Ottawa School • Location: 11611 Stanton St., West Olive, MI 49460

Westland
(Wayne County)

Friends of Eloise
Mailing Address: 33748 La Crosse • Westland, MI 48186
Contact: Jo Johnson, President
Phone: (734) 522-3918
Physical Location: 623 N. Wayne Rd. • Westland, MI 48185
Hours: Sat 1-4 p.m. Closed holiday weekends.
Admission: Donations accepted.
Visitor Accessibility: Free on-site parking. Partially wheelchair accessible. Tour guides available on Saturdays or by appointment.
About: Maintains history and collects artifacts of Eloise Infirmary Group.
Exhibits/Collections: Furniture and hospital equipment. Old photographs. Patient and employee records, cemetery records, books and articles related to Eloise.
Annual Events: Meetings: 3rd Tuesday monthly at the Westland Historical Park.
*Information may not be current.

Friends of Nankin Mills
Mailing Address: 33175 Ann Arbor Trail • Westland, MI 48185
Contact: Carol Clements, Department Manager
E-Mail: friends@nankinmills.org; cclement@waynecounty.com
Phone: 724/261-1850
Fax: (734) 261-3994
Site/Location: Nankin Mills Interpretive Center
Hours: Mon-Sat 9 a.m.-4 p.m.
Admission: Donations accepted.
Visitor Accessibility: Free on-site parking. Wheelchair accessible. Tour guide available for groups with a minimum of 10 people; $2/adult and $6/child. To schedule a tour, call (734) 261-1850.
Website: www.nankinmills.org
About: The Friends of Nankin Mills works with Wayne County Parks to help tell the story of Nankin Mills, a former grist mill purchased by Henry Ford in 1918 as part of his Village Industry Project. The building is now an interpretive center, and visitors will learn about the natural and cultural history of the Nankin Mills area, including the Native American, Grist Mill, and Ford eras. They can also see various fish and reptiles as they learn about the local ecology.
Exhibits/Collections: A hydroelectric generator installed by Ford and Thomas Edison remains in the mill. Nankin Mills is part of the Motor Cities National Heritage Area, telling the story of Michigan's auto heritage.
Annual Events: Local history seminars (monthly), Hines Cruise (Aug), Native American Heritage Day (Sep), Halloween Forest Fun Hike (Oct), Holiday Fest and Mill Lighting (Dec).
Publications: "History of Westland."

Westland Historical Commission
Mailing Address: 36601 Ford Rd. • Westland, MI 48185
Contact: Jeff Koslowski
Phone: (734) 326-1110
Site/Location: Westland Historic Village Park
Physical Location: 957 N. Wayne Road • Westland, MI 48185
Hours: Sat 1-4 p.m., except holiday weekends.
Admission: Free.
Visitor Accessibility: Free on-site parking. Partially wheelchair accessible. Tour guides available on Sat or by appointment (donations accepted).
Website: www.cityofwestland.com
About: Preserves the history of Nankin Township and Westland. Maintains the museum complex, which includes the Felton Farmhouse (a typical Michigan farmhouse built in the 1850s) and the Collins House that stores the commission's historical archives. Also features an Octagon furnished with 1930s items. Includes 1918 Eloise fire engine and other Eloise items.
Exhibits/Collections: Michigan pioneering artifacts. Local cemeteries, area schools past and present, census of the 1800s, limited death records from County Poorhouse (Eloise), history of Nankin Township, and city of Westland.
Annual Events: Arm Forces Day, 1870 baseball game, craft show appraisal, Santa visit. Meetings last Tue monthly, 7 p.m. at the historic park.

Westphalia
(Clinton County)

Westphalia Historical Society
Mailing Address: P.O. Box 163 • Westphalia, MI 48894
Contact: Maggie Upson, President
E-Mail: westphalia1836@gmail.com
Phone: (989) 587-6839
Physical Location: 120 W Main St. • Westphalia, MI 48894
Website: www.westphaliahistory.weebly.com
About: The Westphalia Historical Society began in 1985. Through the years, it has published various publications and pamphlets detailing different aspects about the area's German-Catholic ancestors who settled Westphalia in 1836. It is the society's hope to preserve the past for the future.
Annual Events: Meetings 3rd Tue monthly.
Publications: "Of Pilgrimage, Prayer, and Promise," "Quiet Heroism," "Westphalia High School Reunion 1938-1950," Westphalia Historical Society Presents Historical Film Footage 1936-1981 (DVD).

White Cloud
(Newaygo County)

White Cloud Community Library
Mailing Address: 1038 Wilcox Ave., P.O. Box 995 • White Cloud, MI 49349-0995
Contact: Pamela Miller, Local History
E-Mail: localhistory@whitecloudlibrary.net
Phone: (231) 689-6631
Fax: (231) 689-6699
Hours: Tue and Fri 9:30 a.m.-5:30 p.m.; call in advance.
Website: www.whitecloudlibrary.net
About: Collection contains microfilm of Newaygo County newspapers; 1884 and 1894 state census records; county death records to 1990; cemetery indexes; numerous family manuscripts; historian Thompson's scrapbooks with handwritten history and photos; early Newaygo County marriage index; White Cloud yearbooks; Newaygo County phone books; Douglass Photo Collection; plat books and research books for Newaygo County; Robert Auw's six booklets of memories of Newaygo County; church histories; many photos; and family look-ups already on file.

White Lake
(Oakland County)

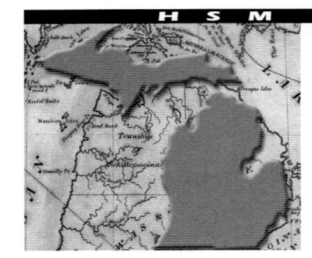

White Lake Historical Society
Mailing Address: 7525 Highland Road • White Lake, MI 48383
Contact: Barb Allison, President
E-Mail: allison@2020comm.net
Phone: (248) 684-5721
Site/Location: **Kelley-Fisk Farm**
Physical Location: 9180 Highland Road • White Lake, MI 48383
Hours: Last Tue monthly. Also by appointment.
Admission: Donations accepted.
Visitor Accessibility: Free on-site parking. Wheelchair accessible. Tour guide available; call at least one week in advance.
Website: http://www.hsmichigan.org/whitelake
About: The White Lake Historical Society brings together those interested in history, especially the history of the White Lake Township area, and shares it with all age groups. The Kelley-Fisk Farm features an 1855 farmhouse completely furnished with antiques, 1876 one-room school, turn-of-the-century barn full of farm-related antiques, and a 1930s kitchen display.
Exhibits/Collections: All buildings are equipped with historical furnishings. Schools may reserve a day at the one-room schoolhouse for a class session.
Annual Events: Easter egg hunt (Apr), storytellers event (May), farmers market (May-Oct), Annual Fisk Farm Festival (Sep), Fright Night Storytelling (Oct), White Lake Christmas Tree Lighting Festival (Dec), Visit Santa at the Farm (Dec).
Publications: "In Remembrance: A History of White Lake Township."

White Pigeon
(St. Joseph County)

U.S. Land Office Museum.
Please see entry under Centreville: St. Joseph County Historical Society.

Wahbememe Memorial Park.
Please see entry under Centreville: St. Joseph County Historical Society.

Williamston
(Ingham County)

Friends of Historic Williamstown
Mailing Address: 148 S. Putnam St. • Williamston, MI 48895
Information may not be current.

Williamston Depot Museum
Mailing Address: P.O. Box 234 • Williamston, MI 48895
Contact: Jane S. Johnson, Board President
E-Mail: tjjj@wowway.com
Phone: (517) 655-1030
Physical Location: 369 W. Grand River • Williamston, MI 48895
Hours: Mon-Fri 9 a.m.-2 p.m., 2nd Sun monthly 2-4 p.m.
Admission: Free.
Visitor Accessibility: Free on-site parking. Wheelchair accessible. Tour guide available; call ahead.
Website: http://williamstonmuseum.org
About: The mission of the Williamston Depot Museum is to collect, preserve, and display the historical record of the Williamston area. The museum provides educational opportunities through presentations, exhibits, and tours. Permanent exhibit tells the Story of Williamston from the Native Americans to the present. Content of temporary exhibits vary.
Annual Events: Native American program, Williamston History Day Tour, ice cream social (members only), annual meeting.
Publications: Biannual newsletter.

Wixom
(Oakland County)

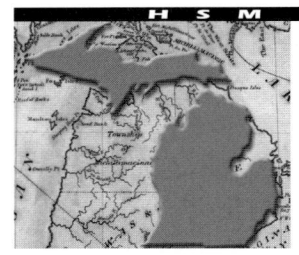

Wixom Historical Society & Museum
Mailing Address: c/o Wixom City Hall, 49045 Pontiac Trail • Wixom, MI 48393
Contact: Jackie Coulter, President
E-Mail: tgcoulter@att.net
Phone: (248) 248-0246
Site/Location: **Wixom-Wire Museum**
Physical Location: 687 North Wixom Road • Wixom, MI 48393
Hours: By appointment.
Admission: Donations accepted.
Visitor Accessibility: On-site parking. Not wheelchair accessible. Guide available by appointment.
Website: www.wixomhistoricalsociety.org
About: Museum was originally a house built for Rev. Samuel Wire (c. 1855) and used as home, church, and funeral parlor. Tiffen family lived in home 1877-1973.
Exhibits/Collections: Historical records kept at the Wixom Public Library.
Annual Events: Ice cream social (Jun), Antique Appraisal Fair (Nov), December Wassail. Meetings 3rd Monday Jan-May, Sep, and Oct.
Publications: Bimonthly newsletter.
Other Sites/Locations: **Wixom Cemetery** • Location: Across the street from the museum.

Wyandotte
(Wayne County)

Irish American Cultural Institute
Mailing Address: Metro Detroit Chapter, 17516 Birchcrest Dr. •

Wyandotte, MI 48221
Site/Location: **Metro Detroit Chapter**
Information may not be current.

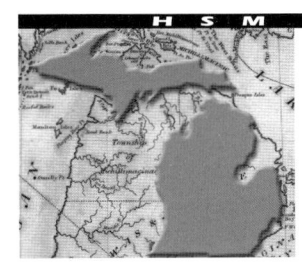

Wyandotte Museums
Mailing Address: 2610 Biddle Avenue • Wyandotte, MI 48192
Contact: Jody Egen, Director of Museums and Cultural Affairs
Phone: (734) 324-7284
Fax: (734) 324-7283
Hours: Mon-Fri 8 a.m.-5 p.m. Closed holidays.
Admission: $5/adult, $2.50/children (5-12), children 4 and under free.
Visitor Accessibility: Free on-site and street parking. Not wheelchair accessible.
Website: www.wyandottemuseums.org
About: The Wyandotte Museums are dedicated to inspiring and fostering public awareness, interest, understanding, and appreciation of the history of the city of Wyandotte and its relationship to the Downriver region. The museum preserves our mutual heritage through its historic buildings, collections, archives, publications, exhibits, programs, and special events using our shared past as a foundation for the future. The Burns Home houses the Wyandotte Museums Offices and is not open for tours.
Exhibits/Collections: 19th-century furnishings, clothing, and local history artifacts.
Annual Events: See website for events schedule.
Other Sites/Locations: **Fort-MacNichol Home** • Location: 2610 Biddle Ave., Wyandotte, MI 48192 • Hours: Apr-Dec: Thu-Sun 12-4 p.m. • Admission: $5/adult, $2.50/children (5-12), children 4 and under free • Visitor Accessibility: Free on-site and street parking. Partially wheelchair accessible; facility does not have a wheelchair-accessible restroom (although there is one in the Marx Home). Tour guide available; contact museum for group tour information and pricing.
Marx Home • Location: 2630 Biddle Ave., Wyandotte, MI 48192 • Hours: By appointment • Admission: Free • Visitor Accessibility: Free on-site and street parking. Wheelchair accessible. • The historic Marx Home, built in 1862, is a community space, where groups can meet using the first floor of the building for presentations and gatherings. It is also is used for art exhibits, receptions, live performances, and a series of monthly programs organized by the Wyandotte Historical Society.
Old Timer's Log Cabin • Location: 2815 Van Alstyne St., Wyandotte, MI 48192 • The rustic Old Timer's Log Cabin is rented to the public for parties and family gatherings.

Wyoming
(Kent County)

Wyoming Historical Commission
Mailing Address: 1155 28th SW, P.O. Box 905 • Wyoming, MI 49509
Contact: Catherine Bueche
E-Mail: wyominghistoryroom@yahoo.com
Phone: (616) 261-3508
Physical Location: Wyoming Public Library, 3350 Michael Ave. SW • Wyoming, MI 49509
Hours: Tue 10 a.m.-1 p.m., 3rd Tue monthly 10 a.m.-1 p.m., 1st and 3rd Sat 10 a.m.-1 p.m. Also by appointment.
Visitor Accessibility: Public parking. Library is wheelchair accessible. Tour guide available.
Website: www.wyomingmichiganhistory.com
About: Responsible for collecting, preserving, and making available historical and documentary material relating to the history of Wyoming. Provides periodic presentations of local interest.
Exhibits/Collections: Collections include photography, manuscripts, Wyoming City and Township records, newspapers, audiovisual material, and artifacts. Catalog of collections is available. Maps 1831-present and some plat maps available.
Annual Events: Meetings 3rd Wed Jan-Nov, 6:30 p.m.
Publications: "City of Wyoming: A History," "Wilderness to Wyoming."

Ypsilanti
(Washtenaw County)

EMU Historic Preservation Program
Mailing Address: 235 Strong Hall • Ypsilanti, MI 48197
Contact: Ted Ligibel, Director
E-Mail: tligibel@emich.edu
Phone: (734) 487-0232
Fax: (734) 487-6979
Visitor Accessibility: On-site parking. Wheelchair accessible.
Website: www.emich.edu/geo/preservation/index.php
About: A graduate program in historic preservation. Prepares students for professional service in the fields of preservation planning, historic administration, and heritage interpretation. Fosters stimulating, creative, and professional interaction among students, faculty, local and regional planning agencies, and local preservation groups in order to provide both classroom theory and practical experience.
Publications: Biannual newsletter (The Port and Lintel).

Michigan Council for History Education
Mailing Address: Eastern Michigan University, 701 Pray Harrold • Ypsilanti, MI 48197
Phone: 734-429-8030, ext. 2233 • *Fax:* 734-429-8036
Website: http://people.emich.edu/rolwell/
Information may not be current.

Michigan Firehouse Museum & Education Center
Mailing Address: 110 W. Cross St. • Ypsilanti, MI 48197
Contact: Steve Wilson, Manager
E-Mail: firemuseum@msn.com
Phone: 734-547-0663 • *Fax:* (734) 547-0669
Hours: Tue-Sat 10 a.m.-4 p.m., Sun 12-4 p.m.
Admission: $5/adult, $3/children (2-16), Children 2 and under free.
Visitor Accessibility: Parking on N. Washington and N. Huron Streets. Wheelchair accessible.
Website: www.michiganfirehousemuseum.org
About: Preserves firefighting history and promotes fire safety education. Museum consists of an original 1898 firehouse with restored bunk area and a 12,000-square-foot exhibit area on three levels.
Exhibits/Collections: More than 27 fire rigs dating from the mid-1820s to the early 1980s, bells, lights, sirens, helmets, extinguishers, alarms, and other fire-related equipment.
Annual Events: Fire Truck Muster (Aug).

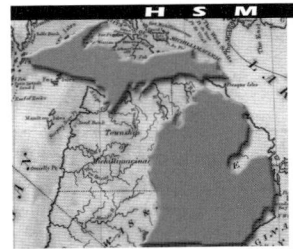

Ypsilanti Automotive Heritage Museum
Mailing Address: 100 E. Cross St. • Ypsilanti, MI 48198
Contact: Bill Nickels
E-Mail: hudsondealer@ypsiautoheritage.org
Phone: (734) 482-5200
Fax: (734) 480-2784
Hours: Tue-Sun 1-5 p.m.

❦ Historical Society of Michigan

Admission: $5/adult, Children 12 and under free.
Visitor Accessibility: Free on-site parking. Wheelchair accessible. Self-guided.
About: Located in the world's last operating Hudson auto dealership building, the Ypsilanti Automotive Heritage Museum is dedicated to Ypsilanti's auto history. The museum houses records dating back to 1927 and displays 30 vehicles and 18 cut-a-way automatic transmissions.
Annual Events: Ypsilanti Orphan Car Show (Sep).

Ypsilanti Heritage Foundation
Mailing Address: 301 N. Grove • Ypsilanti, MI 48198
Contact: Henry Prebys, President
Phone: (734) 487-0595
Website: http://yhf.org
About: Founded in 1974, seeks to increase public understanding and appreciation of Ypsilanti's wealth of historic architecture. Promotes public and private preservation efforts for conservation, rehabilitation, and utilization of historic architecture to the betterment of the whole community.
Annual Events: Historic Home Tour (Aug).
Publications: Bimonthly newsletter (Heritage News).

Ypsilanti Historic District Commission
Mailing Address: Ypsilanti City Hall, 1 S. Huron • Ypsilanti, MI 48197
Contact: HDC Assistant
Phone: (734) 483-9646 • **Fax:** (734) 483-7260
Hours: Mon-Fri 8 a.m.-5 p.m.
Admission: Free.
Visitor Accessibility: Free on-site parking. Wheelchair accessible. Self-guided.
Website: www.cityofypsilanti.com/boards/bd_historic
About: Guides all development and exterior renovations in the Ypsilanti Historic District. Any proposed work (construction/reconstruction, renovation, restoration, painting, etc.) within the district must be reviewed and approved by the HDC. Located within the planning and development department. No exhibits.
Annual Events: Meetings 2nd and 4th Tue of each month, 7 p.m. at city hall, 1 South Huron.
Publications: Semi-annual newsletter, series of fact sheets on various HDC requirements.

Ypsilanti Historical Society, Museum, and Archives
HSM MEMBER
Mailing Address: 220 N. Huron St. • Ypsilanti, MI 48197
Contact: Alvin Rudisill, President
E-Mail: yhs.archives@gmail.com
Phone: (734) 217-8236
Hours: Tue-Sun 2 p.m.-5 p.m.
Admission: Free.
Visitor Accessibility: Free on-site parking. Wheelchair accessible. Tour guide available by appointment; $1/individual for large groups.
Website: www.ypsilantihistoricalsociety.org
About: The Ypsilanti Historical Society discovers, collects, preserves, and displays materials relating to the events and history of the area. This includes printed matter, manuscripts, and museum materials illustrative of life, conditions, events, and activities of the past and present. The society's museum is located in the Asa Dow House, an 1860s brick Victorian mansion, with artifacts from the 19th and 20th centuries in a variety of displays and exhibits depicting Ypsilanti's heritage.
Exhibits/Collections: The Fletcher-White Archives maintains information with an emphasis on local history. In cooperation with the University of Michigan Digital Library, the archive is digitizing 5,000 photographs dating from the 1850s.
Annual Events: Art show (Apr), Lost Ypsilanti Exhibit, Ypsilanti Heritage Festival (Aug), quilt exhibit (Sep), Christmas at the Museum (Dec). Quarterly member meetings held at various times and locations.
Publications: Quarterly newsletter (Ypsilanti Gleanings).

Zeeland
(Ottawa County)

Pennsylvania R.R. Technical & Historical Society
Mailing Address: 4099 80th Avenue • Zeeland, MI 49464
Contact: Robert Krikke, Vice President
E-Mail: g5s472@aol.com
Phone: (616) 772-0826
Site/Location: Grand Rapids & Indiana Chapter
About: To preserve the history of the Grand Rapids & Indiana RR and its successor the Pennsylvania RR in Michigan and Indiana.
Exhibits/Collections: Quarterly meetings in member homes, with occasional programs. Also historical tours to railroad sites and attending the national organization's annual meeting.
Annual Events: Meetings quarterly, call for dates and locations.
Publications: Quarterly newsletter (The Fishing Line).

Zeeland
(Ottawa County)

Zeeland Historical Society
HSM MEMBER
Mailing Address: P.O. Box 165 • Zeeland, MI 49464
Contact: Nancy Curnick, President
Phone: (616) 772-4079
Physical Location: 37 East Main Street • Zeeland, MI 49464
Hours: Mar-Oct Thu 10 a.m.-5 p.m.; Year-round: Sat 10 a.m.-2 p.m. Business hours by appointment.
Admission: Free.
Visitor Accessibility: Partially wheelchair accessible (film shown for patrons who cannot make it to the second floor). Free parking. Self-guided, group tours available by appointment ($1 per person).
Website: www.zeelandhistory.org
About: The Zeeland Historical Museum opened in 1976 in an adjoining house and store formerly owned by Dirk Dekker. The house was restored to its original 1876 style. It features numerous local history displays as well as a resource room for local history resource. Exhibits cover topics such as Dutch immigration, the first Zeeland Bank, farming, and interurbans.
Exhibits/Collections: Local historic photographs, passenger lists of immigrants arriving by ship, family genealogies, local newspaper clippings, and information on house histories of architecturally and historically significant homes.
Annual Events: Historic Home Tour (Jun).
Publications: Newsletter (Timeline).
Other Sites/Locations: New Groningen Schoolhouse • Location: 10537 Paw Paw Dr., Zeeland, MI 49464 • Hours: By appointment • Visitor Accessibility: Wheelchair accessible • The New Groningen Schoolhouse, built at the turn of the century in 1881 and restored in recent years, is a two-room schoolhouse, complete with desks, maps, schoolbooks, and more.

*Information may not be current.

Cross Index (alphabetical by historical entity/site)

1831 Richard Gardner House	Dearborn
1845 Courthouse	Charlotte
1882 One Room School	Taylor
1883 Commandant's Quarters	Dearborn
1901 Bohannon Schoolhouse	Mount Pleasant
40 Mile Point Lighthouse	Rogers City
40 Mile Point Lighthouse Society	Rogers City
7th Michigan Cavalry Civil War Roundtable	Essexville
A.C. Van Raalte Institute	Holland
A.J. Phillips Fenton Museum	Fenton
Abraham Lincoln Civil War Round Table	Holly
Abraham Lincoln Civil War Roundtable of Michigan	Farmington Hills
Ada Historical Society	Ada
Adrian Dominican Sisters	Adrian
Adrian Historic District Commission	Adrian
Adrian Public Library	Adrian
African American Cultural & Historical Museum	Ann Arbor
Air Zoo	Portage
Alamo Township Historical Society & Museum	Kalamazoo
Alba Historical Society	Alba
Albert L. Lorenzo Cultural Center	Clinton Township
Albion College	Albion
Albion College Archives & Special Collections	Albion
Albion District Library Local History Room	Albion
Albion Historical Society	Albion
Alcona Historical Society	Harrisville
Alden B. Dow Home & Studio	Midland
Alden Depot Museum	Alden
Alfred B. and Ruth S. Moran Resource Center	Grosse Pointe Farms
Alfred B. and Ruth S. Moran Resource Center	Grosse Pointe Farms
Alfred Noble Library	Livonia
Alfred P. Sloan Museum	Flint
Alger County Historical Society	Munising
Algoma Township Historical Society	Rockford
Algonac-Clay Maritime Museum	Algonac
Algonac-Clay Township Historical Society	Algonac
Algonquin Club of Detroit & Windsor	Birmingham
Allegan County Historical Society	Allegan
Allen Area Historical Society	Allen
Allen Park Museum & Historical Commission	Allen Park
Allendale Historical Society	Allendale
Alma College Archives	Alma
Alma Public Library	Alma
Almira Historical Society	Lake Ann
Almira Historical Society Museum	Lake Ann
Almont Community Historical Society	Almont
Almont District Library	Almont
Aloha Historical Society	Cheboygan
Alpena County Library	Alpena
Alpena Historic Preservation Society	Alpena
Alpine Township Historical Commission	Comstock Park
Alpine Township Historical Museum	Comstock Park
Amasa Historical Society	Amasa
Anchor Bay Genealogy Society	Chesterfield
Andrew J. Blackbird Museum	Harbor Springs
Ann Arbor Hands-On Museum	Ann Arbor
Ann Arbor Historic District Commission	Ann Arbor
Ann Arbor Train & Trolley Watchers	Ann Arbor
Applewood Estate	Flint
Arab American National Museum	Dearborn
Arcadia Area Historical Museum	Arcadia
Arcadia Area Historical Society	Arcadia
Archdiocese of Detroit Archives	Detroit
Archives of Congregation Shaarey Zedek	Southfield
Archives of Michigan	Lansing
Arenac County Historical Society	Au Gres
Armada Area Historical Society	Armada
Arvon Township Historical Society	Skanee
Association for the Advancement of Dutch-American Studies	Holland
Athens Area Historical Society	Athens
Athens Area Museum	Athens
Au Sable River Center	Roscommon
Auburn Hills Historical & Genealogical Society	Rochester Hills
AuSable-Oscoda Historical Society & Museum	Oscoda
Automotive Hall of Fame	Dearborn
Averill Historical Museum of Ada	Ada
Bad Axe Historical Society	Bad Axe
Bad Axe Museum of Local History	Bad Axe
Bailey Property Preservation Association	Menominee
Baldwin Business Center	Baldwin
Bammert Blacksmith Shop and Phoenix Church	Eagle Harbor
Bancroft/Stranahan House	Romeo
Bangor Historical Society	Bangor
Banks Township Historical Society	East Jordan
Banner Oak School	Temperance
Baraga County Historical Museum	Baraga
Baraga County Historical Society	Baraga
Barber School	Caledonia
Barnes and Little History Room	Richland
Barry County Historical Society	Hastings
Barry Museum	Constantine
Barryton Area Historical Commission	Weidman
Bartlett/Travis House at Preservation Park	Canton
Batavia Grange	Coldwater
Battle Creek Historic District Commission	Battle Creek
Baumgartner House	Fraser
Baumgartner House and Hemme Barn	Fraser
Bay City Architectural Review Committee	Bay City
Bay County Historical Society	Bay City
Bay Mills-Brimley Historical Research Society	Brimley
Bay View Archives	Petoskey
Bay View Association	Petoskey
Bay View Historical Museum	Petoskey
Bayliss Public Library	Sault Ste. Marie
Bean Creek Valley Historical Society	Hudson
Bean Creek Valley Historical Society	Hudson
Beaumier U.P. Heritage Center	Marquette
Beaver Island Historical Society	Beaver Island
Bedford Historical Society	Temperance
Beechwood Hall	Iron River
Beechwood Historical Society	Iron River
Belding Exploration Lab Children's Museum (BEL)	Belding
Belding Museum	Belding
Belding Museum at the Historic Belrockton	Belding
Bellaire Area Historical Society	Bellaire
Bellaire Historical Museum	Bellaire
Belleville Area Museum	Belleville
Belleville Area Museum & Archives	Belleville
Bellevue Historical Museum	Bellevue
Bellevue Historical Society	Bellevue
Bentley Historical Library	Ann Arbor
Benzie Area Historical Society	Benzonia
Bergelin House Museum	Big Rapids
Bergland/Matchwood Historical Society	Bergland
Berkley Historical Committee	Berkley
Berkley Historical Museum	Berkley
Bernard Historical Society & Museum	Delton
Berrien County Genealogical Society	Benton Harbor
Berrien County Historical Association	Berrien Springs
Besser Museum for Northeast Michigan	Alpena
Big Rapids Historic Preservation Commission	Big Rapids
Big Sable Lighthouse	Ludington
Birmingham Historic District Commission	Birmingham
Birmingham Historical Museum & Park	Birmingham
Bishop Baraga Association	Marquette
Bishop Baraga Shrine	Baraga
Blair Historical Farm	Homer
Blanchard House	Ionia
Blissfield Area Historical Society	Blissfield
Bloomfield Historical Society	Bloomfield Township
Bloomfield Township Public Library	Bloomfield Hills
Bloomingdale Area Historical Association, Inc.	Bloomingdale
Blue & Grey Civil War Roundtable of Saginaw	Saginaw
Blue Water Chapter of the NRHSA	Royal Oak
Bois Blanc Island Historical Society	Pointe Aux Pins
Bonine House	Vandalia
Boston-Saranac Historical Society	Saranac
Bottle House Museum	Kaleva

Historical Society of Michigan

Organization	Location
Bowne Center School House	Alto
Bowne Center School House	Alto
Bowne Township Historical Commission	Alto
Boyne City Historical Museum	Boyne City
Branch County Genealogical Society	Coldwater
Branch County Historical Society	Coldwater
Branch District Library	Coldwater
Brandon Township Public Library	Ortonville
Breckenridge-Wheeler Area Historical Society	Breckenridge
Brethren Heritage Association	Brethren
Brighton Area Historical Society	Brighton
Brighton District Library	Brighton
Brighton Room Collection of Genealogy and Local History	Brighton
Brownstown Township Historical Commission	Brownstown
Brush Creek Mill	Hillman
Buchanan Preservation Society	Buchanan
Buckley Old Engine Club	Buckley
Buick Automotive Gallery and Research Center	Flint
Bunert School	Warren
Burton Historical Collection	Detroit
Byron Area Historical Museum	Byron Center
Byron Center Historical Society	Byron Center
C. Craig Blacksmith Museum	Romeo
Cadillac LaSalle Club Museum & Research Center	Farmington Hills
Caledonia Historical Commission	Caledonia
Caledonia Historical Museum	Caledonia
Caledonia Historical Society	Caledonia
Calhoun County Genealogical Society	Marshall
Calhoun County Historic Bridge Park	Marshall
Calumet Theatre	Calumet
Calumet Visitor Center	Calumet
Calvin College	Grand Rapids
Cannery Boat Museum	Empire
Cannon Township Historical Museum	Cannonsburg
Cannon Township Historical Society	Cannonsburg
Canton Historic District Commission	Canton
Canton Historical Society	Canton
Canton Township Historic District Commission	Canton
Capac Community Historical Museum	Capac
Capac Community Historical Society	Capac
Cappon House and Settler's House	Holland
Caretaker House at Cranberry Lake Farm Historic District	Oakland
Carnegie Center Museum	Port Huron
Carnegie Museum of the Keweenaw	Houghton
Cascade Historical Society	Grand Rapids
Cascade Historical Society Museum	Grand Rapids
Cass City Area Historical and Genealogy Society	Cass City
Cass County Historical Commission	Cassopolis
Cass County Pioneer Log Cabin Museum	Cassopolis
Castle Farms	Charlevoix
Castle Museum of Saginaw County History	Saginaw
Cedar Springs Historical Society	Cedar Springs
Ceder Springs Museum	Cedar Springs
Cell Block 7 Prison Museum	Jackson
Cell Block 7 Prison Museum	Jackson
Center of African American Art and History	Holland
Central Lake Area Historical Society	Central Lake
Central Mine Village	Eagle Harbor
Centreville Museum & History Library	Centreville
Chaldean Cultural Center	West Bloomfield
Champion-Beacon-Humboldt Historical Society	Champion
Chappee-Webber Learning Center	Menominee
Charles and Hattie Olsen Farm	Empire
Charles H. Wright Museum of African American History	Detroit
Charles W. Liken House	Sebewaing
Charles W. Liken Museum	Sebewaing
Charleviox County History Preservation Society	Boyne City
Charlevoix County Genealogical Society	Boyne City
Charlevoix Historical Society	Charlevoix
Charlevoix South Pier Lighthouse	Charlevoix
Chase Library Historical Society	Chase
Chase Township Public Library	Chase
Chassell Heritage Center	Chassell
Chassell Historical Organization	Chassell
Cheboygan Area Public Library	Cheboygan
Cheboygan County Genealogical Society	Cheboygan
Cheboygan Historic Resources Comm.	Cheboygan
Chelsea Area Historic District Commission	Chelsea
Chelsea Area Historical Society	Chelsea
Chesaning Area Historical Society	Chesaning
Chesaning Historical Museum	Chesaning
Chesterfield Historical Society	Chesterfield
Chesterfield Historical Village	Chesterfield
Chippewa County Historical Society	Sault Ste. Marie
Chippewa Nature Center	Midland
City of Brighton Arts Culture and History (COBACH) Center	Brighton
City of Melvindale Historical Commission	Melvindale
City of Northville Historic District Commission	Northville
Civilian Conservation Corps Museum	Roscommon
Clare County Historical Society	Clare
Clare County Museum Complex	Clare
Clarence L. Miller Family Local History Room	Kalamazoo
Clarke Historical Library	Mount Pleasant
Clarkston Community Historical Society	Clarkston
Clarkston Heritage Museum	Clarkston
Clarkston Historic District Commission	Clarkston
Clawson Historical Museum	Clawson
Cliffs Shaft Mining Museum	Ishpeming
Clinton and Kalamazoo Canal Society	Clinton Township
Clinton County Historical Commission	DeWitt
Clinton County Historical Society	St. Johns
Clinton Township Historical Commission	Clinton Township
Clio Area Historical Association	Clio
Clio Area Historical Depot Museum	Clio
Clyde Historical Society	Clyde
Cobblestone Farm Association	Ann Arbor
Coe House Museum	Grass Lake
Coloma Public Library	Coloma
Colonial Michilimackinac	Mackinaw City
Columbiaville Historical Society Museum	Columbiaville
Comins Restoration Association	Comins
Commerce Township Area Historical Society	Walled Lake
Community Historical Museum of Colon	Colon
Community Historical Society of Colon	Colon
Community Pride & Heritage Museum	Marine City
Conklin Reed Organ and History Museum	Hanover
Coopersville & Marne Railway	Coopersville
Coopersville & Marne Railway Railroad Station	Coopersville
Coopersville Area Historical Society	Coopersville
Coopersville Area Historical Society Museum	Coopersville
Coopersville Farm Museum & Event Center	Coopersville
Copper Harbor Lighthouse	Copper Harbor
Copper Harbor Lighthouse	Copper Harbor
Copper Range Historical Museum	South Range
Copper Range Historical Society	South Range
Coppertown USA Mining Museum	Calumet
Cornish American Heritage Society	South Lyon
Cornish Pumping Engine & Mining Museum	Iron Mountain
Courthouse Square Association	Charlotte
Courthouse Square Association Museum	Charlotte
Covert Historical Museum	Covert
Covington Township Historical Museum	Covington
Covington Township Historical Society	Covington
Cranberry Lake Farm Historic District	Oakland
Cranbrook Archives	Bloomfield Hills
Cranbrook Art Museum	Bloomfield Hills
Crawford County Historical Society & Museum Complex	Grayling
Crisp Point Light Historical Society	Howell
Crisp Point Lighthouse	Howell
Crocker House Museum	Mount Clemens
Crossroads Village	Flint
Crossroads Village & Huckleberry Railroad	Flint
Crossroads Village & Huckleberry Railroad	Flint
Crystal Falls Museum Society	Crystal Falls
Crystal Township Historical Society	Crystal
Curtis Historical Society	Curtis
Curtis Historical Society Museum	Curtis
Curwood Castle	Owosso
Davis Brothers Farm Shop Museum	Lapeer
Davison Area Historical Museum	Davison
Davison Area Historical Society	Davison
Dearborn Genealogical Society	Dearborn

Michigan History Directory

Dearborn Historical Society & Museum	Dearborn
Delaware Copper Mine Tours	Mohawk
Delta County Genealogical Society	Escanaba
Delta County Historical Society & Museum	Escanaba
Delta Township Historical Society	Lansing
Depot Museum	Howell
Depot Museum of Transportation	Grand Haven
DeTour Passage Historical Museum	DeTour Village
DeTour Reef Light	Drummond Island
DeTour Reef Light Preservation Society	Drummond Island
Detroit & Mackinaw Railway Historical Society	Bay City
Detroit Historic Designation Advisory Board	Detroit
Detroit Historic District Commission	Detroit
Detroit Historic Fort Wayne	Detroit
Detroit Historical Society	Detroit
Detroit Observatory	Ann Arbor
Detroit Public Library	Detroit
Detroit Society for Genealogical Research, Inc.	Detroit
Detroit Windsor Algonquin Club, est 1934	Birmingham
Dewey School	Grass Lake
Dewitt School House	Grand Haven
Dexter Area Historical Society	Dexter
Dexter Area Museum	Dexter
Dickinson County Genealogical Society	Iron Mountain
Dossin Great Lakes Museum	Detroit
Dossin Great Lakes Museum	Detroit
Dow Gardens	Midland
Dowagiac Area History Museum	Dowagiac
Downriver Genealogical Society	Lincoln Park
Drake Memorial House Museum	Breckenridge
Drummond Island Historical Museum	Drummond Island
Dryden Historical Depot	Dryden
Dryden Historical Society	Dryden
Durand Union Station, Inc.	Durand
Durant-Dort Carriage Company Headquarters	Flint
East Detroit Historical Society	Eastpointe
East Grand Rapids Historical Commission	Grand Rapids
East Jordan City Hall	East Jordan
East Jordan Portside Art & Historical Society	East Jordan
East Jordan Portside Art & Historical Society Museum	East Jordan
East Lansing Historic District Commission	East Lansing
East Lansing Historical Society	East Lansing
Eastern Michigan University	Ypsilanti
Eastern Upper Peninsula History Consortium	Hessel
Eaton County Genealogical Society	Charlotte
Eaton County Historical Commission	Charlotte
Eaton Rapids Area Historical Society	Eaton Rapids
Eby Log House	Monroe
Eddy Historical Collection	Saginaw
Edsel & Eleanor Ford House	Grosse Pointe Shores
Edward Lowe Foundation	Cassopolis
Edward Lowe Information and Legacy Center	Cassopolis
Edwardsburg Area Historical Museum	Edwardsburg
El Museo del Norte	Detroit
Elk Rapids Area Historical Musuem	Elk Rapids
Elk Rapids Area Historical Society	Elk Rapids
Elkton Area Historical Society	Elkton
Ella Sharp Museum of Art & History	Jackson
Ellsworth/Banks Township Historical Association	Ellsworth
Elsie Historical Society	Elsie
Empire Area Heritage Group	Empire
Empire Area Museum Complex	Empire
EMU Historic Preservation Program	Ypsilanti
Engadine Historical Museum	Engadine
Engadine Historical Society	Engadine
Engine House No. 5	Allendale
Engine House No. 5	Allendale
Evart Public Library Museum	Evart
Exeter Historical Society & Township Museum	Maybee
Exhibit Museum of Natural History	Ann Arbor
Eyaawing Museum and Cultural Center	Peshawbestown
Fallasburg Historical Society	Lowell
Farmall Acres Farm Museum	Alto
Farmington Community Library	Farmington Hills
Farmington Genealogical Society	Farmington
Farmington Hills Historic District Commission	Farmington Hills
Farmington Historical Commission	Farmington
Farmington Historical Society	Farmington
Farwell Area Historical Museum	Farwell
Fashion and the Automobile	Harrison Township
Father Marquette National Memorial Museum	St. Ignace
Father Marquette National Memorial Museum	St. Ignace
Fayette Historic State Park	Garden
Fayette Historic Townsite	Garden
Ferndale Historical Museum	Ferndale
Ferndale Historical Society	Ferndale
Fife Lake Historical Museum	Fife Lake
Fife Lake Historical Society	Fife Lake
Fighting Falcon Military Museum	Greenville
Finnish American Heritage Center	Hancock
Finnish American Historical Society	Farmington Hills
Fire Barn Museum	Muskegon
Fishtown Preservation Society	Leland
Flat River Community Library	Greenville
Flat River Historical Museum	Greenville
Flat River Historical Society	Greenville
Flat Rock Historical Society	Flat Rock
Flint Genealogical Society	Flint
Flint Historic District Commission	Flint
Flushing Area Historical Society	Flushing
Flushing Area Museum and Cultural Center	Flushing
Ford Center and Sawmill Museum	L'Anse
Ford Estate	Grosse Pointe Shores
Ford Piquette Avenue Plant	Detroit
Forest Parke Library & Archives	Lansing
Forsyth Township Historical Society	Gwinn
Forsyth Township Historical Society Museum	Gwinn
Fort de Buade Museum	Saint Ignace
Fort Gratiot Light Station	Port Huron
Fort Mackinac	Mackinac Island
Fort St. Joseph Museum	Niles
Fort Wilkins and Copper Harbor Lighthouse	Copper Harbor
Fort Wilkins Historic Complex	Copper Harbor
Fort-MacNichol Home	Wyandotte
Four Flags Area Genealogical Society	Niles
Fox Island Lighthouse Association, Inc.	Traverse City
Frank Murphy Memorial Museum	Harbor Beach
Frankenmuth Historical Association	Frankenmuth
Frankenmuth Historical Museum	Frankenmuth
Franklin Historic District Commission	Franklin
Franklin Historical Society	Franklin
Fraser Historical Commission	Fraser
Fraser Historical Society	Fraser
Fred Hart Williams Genealogical Society	Detroit
Fremont Area District Library Local History Room	Fremont
Fremont Historical Society	Fremont
French-Canadian Heritage Society of Michigan	Royal Oak
Friends of Bergland Cultural Heritage Center	Bergland
Friends of Eloise	Westland
Friends of Frank Murphy Museum	Port Hope
Friends of Historic Meridian	Okemos
Friends of Historic Williamstown	Williamston
Friends of Michigan History	Lansing
Friends of Nankin Mills	Westland
Friends of Point Betsie Lighthouse, Inc.	Frankfort
Friends of Sleeping Bear Dunes	Empire
Friends of the Felt Estate	Saugatuck
Friends of the Garden City Historical Museum	Garden City
Friends of the Loren Andrus Octagon House	Washington
Friends of the Plymouth Historical Museum	Plymouth
Friends of the Thumb Octagon Barn	Gagetown
Friends of the William E. Scripps Estate	Lake Orion
Friends of Theodore Roethke Foundation	Saginaw
G. Robert Vincent Voice Library of the MSU Libraries	East Lansing
Gaines Township Historical Society	Grand Rapids
Galesburg Historical Museum	Galesburg
Galien Woods Historical Society	Galien
GAR Memorial Hall and Museum	Eaton Rapids
Garden City Historical Museum	Garden City
Garden Peninsula Historical Society	Garden
Garden Peninsula Historical Society Museum	Garden
Gardner House Museum	Albion

Historical Society of Michigan

Gaylord Fact-Finders Genealogical Society	Gaylord
Genealogical Society of Flemish Americans	Roseville
Genealogical Society of Isabella County	Mount Pleasant
Genealogical Society of Monroe County	Monroe
Genealogical Society of Washtenaw County	Ann Arbor
Genealogists of the Clinton County Historical Society	St. Johns
Genealogy Department	Holland
Genesee County Historical Society	Flint
Genesee County Parks and Recreation Commission	Flint
Genesee Historical Collections Center	Flint
George W. Lee Civil War Round Table of Howell	Howell
Gerald R. Ford Presidential Library	Ann Arbor
Gerald R. Ford Presidential Museum	Grand Rapids
Gibraltar Historical Museum	Gibraltar
Gilmore Car Museum	Hickory Corners
Gladwin County Historical Museum	Gladwin
Gladwin County Historical Society	Gladwin
Gladwin County Historical Village	Gladwin
Glawe School Museum	Millersburg
Glen Haven General Store	Empire
Glen Haven Historic Village	Empire
Goodrich-Atlas Area Historical Society	Goodrich
Gordon Hall	Dexter
Gospel Army Black History Group	Grand Blanc
Governor John S. Barry Historical Society	Constantine
Governor Warner Mansion	Farmington
Graafschap Heritage Center	Holland
Grace A. Dow Memorial Library	Midland
Grand Blanc Heritage Association	Grand Blanc
Grand Blanc Heritage Association Museum	Grand Blanc
Grand Haven Historic Conservation District Commission	Grand Haven
Grand Ledge Area Historical Society	Grand Ledge
Grand Ledge Area Historical Society Museum	Grand Ledge
Grand Marais Historical Society	Grand Marais
Grand Pacific House Museum	New Baltimore
Grand Rapids & Indiana Chapter	Zeeland
Grand Rapids Civil War Roundtable	Sparta
Grand Rapids Historic Preservation Commission	Grand Rapids
Grand Rapids Historical Commission	Grand Rapids
Grand Rapids Historical Society	Grand Rapids
Grand Rapids Public Library	Grand Rapids
Grand Rapids Public Museum	Grand Rapids
Grand Traverse Area Genealogical Society	Traverse City
Grand Traverse Band of Ottawa and Chippewa Indians	Peshawbestown
Grand Traverse Lighthouse Museum	Northport
Grand Trunk Depot Museum of Transportation	Grand Haven
Grand Valley State University Collections & Archives	Allendale
Grandville Historical Commission	Grandville
Grandville Museum	Grandville
Grass Lake Area Historical Society	Grass Lake
Gratiot County Area Historical Museum	Ithaca
Gratiot County Historical & Genealogical Society	Ithaca
Gratiot County Historical Museum	Ithaca
Grattan Township Historical Society	Belding
Great Lakes Lighthouse Festival Museum	Macomb
Great Lakes Lighthouse Keepers Association	Mackinaw City
Great Lakes Lore Maritime Museum	Rogers City
Great Lakes Maritime Heritage Center	Alpena
Great Lakes Maritime Institute	Dearborn
Great Lakes Shipwreck Museum	Sault Sainte Marie
Greater Clinton Township Historical Society	Clinton Township
Greater Grand Rapids Women's History Council	Grand Rapids
Greater Washington Area Historical Society	Washington
Greater West Bloomfield Historical Society	Orchard Lake
Green Oak Charter Township Historical District Commission	South Lyon
Green Oak Township Historical Society	South Lyon
Greenbush Historical Society	Greenbush
Greenfield Village	Dearborn
Greenmead Historical Park	Livonia
Grice House Heritage Museum	Harbor Beach
Grosse Ile Historical Society	Grosse Ile
Grosse Ile North Channel Light	Grosse Ile
Grosse Ile Township Hall	Grosse Ile
Grosse Pointe Historical Society	Grosse Pointe Farms
Grosvenor House Museum	Jonesville
Gulliver Historical Society	Gulliver
Gunnisonville Historical Community Preservation	Lansing
Hackley and Hume Historic Site	Muskegon
Hackley Public Library	Muskegon
Hadley Township Historical Society	Hadley
Hamburg Township Historical Museum	Hamburg
Hammond House Museum	Union City
Hamtramck Historical Commission	Hamtramck
Hamtramck Historical Museum	Hamtramck
Hanka Homestead Museum & Restoration	Pelkie
Hanover-Horton Area Historical Society	Hanover
Hanover-Horton Heritage Park	Hanover
Harbor Beach Historical Society	Harbor Beach
Harbor Springs Area Historical Society	Harbor Springs
Harbor Springs History Museum	Harbor Springs
Harbour House Museum	Crystal Falls
Harrison Township Historical Commission	Harrison Township
Harrisville Train Depot	Harrisville
Harsha House Museum	Charlevoix
Hart Historic District Commission	Hart
Hartland Area Historical Society	Hartland
Hartman School	South Haven
Hartwick Pines Logging Museum	Grayling
Hartwick Pines State Park	Grayling
Heddon Museum	Dowagiac
Hekman Library Calvin College	Grand Rapids
Helena Township Historical Society	Alden
Hellenic Museum of Michigan	Detroit
Henry Ford Estate - Fair Lane	Dearborn
Henry Ford Heritage Association	Dearborn
Henry Ford Museum	Dearborn
Heritage Association of Concord	Concord
Heritage Battle Creek	Battle Creek
Heritage Hall	Grand Rapids
Heritage Hill Association	Grand Rapids
Heritage Hill Historic District	Grand Rapids
Heritage House Farm Museum	Essexville
Heritage Museum & Cultural Center	St. Joseph
Heritage Museum and M.J. Anuta Research Center	Menominee
Heritage Room at the Richard L. Root Branch Library	Kentwood
Heritage Village	Mackinaw City
Herrick District Library	Holland
Hessler Log Cabin	Traverse City
Highland Township Historical Society	Highland
Hillman Historical Society	Hillman
Hillsdale County Fairgrounds Museum	Hillsdale
Hillsdale County Genealogical Society	Hillsdale
Hillsdale County Historical Society	Hillsdale
Historic Adventist Village	Battle Creek
Historic Association of Dowagiac	Dowagiac
Historic Boston-Edison Association	Detroit
Historic Charlton Park	Hastings
Historic Courthouse	Lapeer
Historic Elmwood Cemetery	Detroit
Historic Fort Wayne Coalition	Columbiaville
Historic Hack House Museum	Milan
Historic Hack House Museum	Milan
Historic Memorials Society in Detroit	Bruce
Historic Mill Creek Discovery Park	Mackinaw City
Historic Ottawa Beach Society	Holland
Historic Village at Goodells County Park	Goodells
Historical Association of South Haven	South Haven
Historical Museum of Bay County	Bay City
Historical Preservation Society of Dundee	Dundee
Historical Society for the U.S. District Court	Detroit
Historical Society of Bancroft	Bancroft
Historical Society of Battle Creek	Battle Creek
Historical Society of Bridgeport	Bridgeport
Historical Society of Caseville	Caseville
Historical Society of Clinton	Clinton
Historical Society of Columbiaville	Columbiaville
Historical Society of Greater Lansing	Lansing
Historical Society of Marine City	Marine City
Historical Society of Michigan	Lansing
Historical Society of Saginaw County	Saginaw
Historical Society of St. Clair Shores	St. Clair Shores
History Center (The Old Schoolhouse)	Douglas

Michigan History Directory

Organization	Location
History Center at Courthouse Square	Berrien Springs
History Center of Cheboygan County	Cheboygan
History Center of Traverse City	Traverse City
History Remembered, Inc./Michigan Civil War Sesquicentennial	Grand Rapids
Holland Area Historical Society	Holland
Holland Genealogical Society	Holland
Holland Historic District Commission	Holland
Holland Historical Trust	Holland
Holland Museum	Holland
Holly Historic District Commission	Holly
Holly Historical Society	Holly
Holly Township Library	Holly
Holocaust Memorial Center	Farmington Hills
Holt-Delhi Historical Society	Holt
Homer Historical Society	Homer
Honolulu House Museum	Marshall
Horn Archaeological Museum	Berrien Springs
Horton Bay Historical Society	Boyne City
Houghton County Historical Museum	Lake Linden
Houghton County Historical Society	Lake Linden
Houghton Lake Area Historical Society	Houghton Lake
Houghton Lake Area Historical Village	Houghton Lake
Houghton-Keweenaw Genealogical Society	Calumet
House of David Baseball Museum	Onsted
House of David Historeum and Preservation Society	Onsted
Howell Area Archives	Howell
Howell Area Historical Society	Howell
Howell Historic District Commission	Howell
Hoyt Library History & Genealogy Collection	Saginaw
Hubbardston Area Historical Society	Hubbardston
Hubbardston Area Historical Society Museum	Hubbardston
Hudson Museum	Hudson
Hudson Museum	Hudson
Huron City Museum	Port Austin
Huron County Historical Society	Bad Axe
Huron County Historical Society	Kimball
Huron Island Lighthouse Preservation Association	L'Anse
Huron Lightship	Port Huron
Huron Shores Genealogical Society	Oscoda
Huron Township Historical Society	New Boston
Hyser Rivers Museum	Comstock Park
Icebreaker Mackinaw Maritime Museum	Mackinaw City
Imlay City Historical Commisson	Imlay City
Imlay City Historical Museum	Imlay City
Immaculate Heart of Mary Archives	Monroe
Indian Village Historical Collections	Detroit
Ingham County Courthouse	Mason
Ingham County Genealogical Society Reference Room	Mason
Ingham County Genealogy Society	Mason
Ingham County Historical Commission	Mason
Ingham County Historical Society	Mason
Inkster Historical Commission	Inkster
Inland Water Route Historical Society	Alanson
Ionia County Genealogical Society	Lake Odessa
Ionia County Historical Society	Ionia
Iosco County Historical Society & Museum	East Tawas
Irish American Cultural Institute	Wyandotte
Irish Genealogical Society of Michigan	Detroit
Iron County Historical Museum	Caspian
Iron County Historical Society & Museum	Caspian
Iron Mountain Iron Mine	Iron Mountain
Ironwood Area Historical Society	Ironwood
Ironwood Carnegie Library	Ironwood
Ishpeming Historical Society	Ishpeming
Isle Royale & Keweenaw Parks Association	Houghton
IXL Historical Museum	Hermansville
Jackson County Genealogical Society	Jackson
Jackson County Historical Society	Jackson
Jackson District Library	Jackson
Jackson Historic District Commission	Jackson
James Jackson Museum of African American History	Muskegon Heights
James Suggs Underground Railroad Museum	Vandalia
Jenison Historical Association	Jenison
Jenison Museum	Jenison
Jewish Genealogical Society of Michigan	West Bloomfield
Jewish Historical Society of Michigan	West Bloomfield
Jim Crow Museum of Racist Memorabilia	Big Rapids
John C. Pahl Historic Village	Allegan
John Schneider Blacksmith Shop	Manchester
Joint Archives of Holland	Holland
Jordan Valley District Library	East Jordan
Juddville Historical Society	New Lennon
Kalamazoo College Archives	Kalamazoo
Kalamazoo County Historical Society	Kalamazoo
Kalamazoo Historic Preservation Commission	Kalamazoo
Kalamazoo Valley Genealogical Society	Comstock
Kalamazoo Valley Museum	Kalamazoo
Kalamo Township Historical Society	Vermontville
Kaleva Historical Society	Kaleva
Kalkaska County Historical Society	Kalkaska
Kalkaska Genealogical Society	Kalkaska
Kelley-Fisk Farm	White Lake
Kempf House Museum	Ann Arbor
Kent County Council for Historic Preservation	Grand Rapids
Kentwood Historic Preservation Commission	Kentwood
Kettering Archives	Flint
Keweenaw County Historical Society	Eagle Harbor
Keweenaw Kernewek	Calumet
Keweenaw National Historical Park	Calumet
Kimball House Museum	Battle Creek
Kingman Museum	Battle Creek
Kinross Heritage Park	Kinross
Kinross Heritage Society	Kinross
Kitchen School	Davison
Kneeland-Sachs Museum	Lewiston
Knowlton's Ice Museum of North America	Port Huron
Lager Mill Brewing Museum	Frankenmuth
Laird Township Historical Society	Pelkie
Lake County Historical Society	Baldwin
Lake Michigan Carferry Service	Ludington
Lake Odessa Area Historical Society	Lake Odessa
Lakeshore Museum Center	Muskegon
Lansing Area African-American Genealogical Society	Lansing
Lansing Historic District Commission	Lansing
Lapeer County Genealogical Society & Museum	Lapeer
Lapeer County Historical Museum	Lapeer
Lapeer County Historical Society	Lapeer
Lapeer County Historical Society Museum	Lapeer
Lathrup Village Historical Society	Lathrup Village
Lawrence Fisher Mansion	Detroit
Leelanau Community Cultural Center	Leland
Leelanau Historical Society	Leland
Leelanau Historical Society Museum	Leland
Lenawee County Family Researchers	Adrian
Lenawee County Historical Museum	Adrian
Lenawee County Historical Society	Adrian
Lenawee County Library	Adrian
Leon Buyse Memorial Library and Museum	Roseville
Leonard N. Simons Jewish Community Archives	Bloomfield Hills
Leonard-McGlone House	Vassar
Les Cheneaux Historical Association	Cedarville
Les Cheneaux Historical Museum	Cedarville
Les Cheneaux Maritime Museum	Cedarville
Lewiston Area Historical Society	Lewiston
Liberty Hyde Bailey Museum	South Haven
Library of Michigan	Lansing
Lincoln Park Historical Society & Museum	Lincoln Park
Lincoln Train Depot	Lincoln
Linden Historic District Commission	Linden
Linden Mills Historical Museum	Linden
Linden Mills Historical Society	Linden
Little Red Schoolhouse Museum	Shepherd
Little River Railroad	Coldwater
Little Sable Point Lighthouse	Ludington
Little Traverse Bay Bands of Odawa Indians	Harbor Springs
Little Traverse Historical Museum	Petoskey
Little Traverse Historical Society	Petoskey
Livingston Centre Historical Village	Fowlerville
Livingston County Genealogical Society	Howell
Livonia Historical Commission	Livonia
Livonia Historical Society	Livonia
Log Cabin and Detroit Urban Railway Wait Station and Annex	Clay Township

Historical Society of Michigan

Organization	Location
Log Cabin Society of Michigan	Sodus
Loren Andrus Octagon House	Washington
Louisa St. Clair Chapter - DAR	Harrison Township
Lovells Township Historical Society	Grayling
Lovells Township Historical Society Museum	Grayling
Lowell Area Historical Museum	Lowell
Luce County Historical Museum	Newberry
Luce County Historical Society	Newberry
Luce-Mackinac Genealogical Society	Engadine
Luckhard Museum - The Indian Mission	Sebewaing
Ludington Breakwater Lighthouse	Ludington
Lunden Civilian Conservation Corps Camp	Lewiston
Lyon Township Genealogical Society	South Lyon
Lyons-Muir Historical Museum	Lyons
M.J. Anuta Research Center	Menominee
Maccabees Hall Museum	Caseville
Mackinac Associates	Mackinaw City
Mackinac Island Historical Society	Mackinac Island
Mackinac Island State Park Commission	Mackinaw City
Mackinac State Historic Parks	Mackinaw City
Mackinaw Area Historical Society	Mackinaw City
Macomb County Genealogy Group	Mount Clemens
Macomb County Historic Commission	Mount Clemens
Macomb County Historical Society	Mount Clemens
Madden Hall Historical Area	Adrian
Madonna University Archives	Livonia
Mancelona Historical Society	Mancelona
Manchester Area Historical Society	Manchester
Manistee County Historical Museum	Manistee
Manitou Islands Memorial Society	Empire
Manitou Trail Questers	Leland
Mann House	Concord
Mann One-Room School	Ortonville
Manton Area Historical Museum	Manton
Margaret Dow Towsley Sports Museum	Ann Arbor
Marilla Historical Society	Copemish
Marilla Museum & Pioneer Place	Copemish
Marine Historical Society of Detroit	Howell
Maritime Heritage Alliance	Traverse City
Maritime Museum	Empire
Marquette County Genealogical Society	Marquette
Marquette Maritime Museum and Lighthouse	Marquette
Marquette Regional History Center	Marquette
Marshall Historical Society	Marshall
Marshall M. Fredericks Sculpture Museum	University Center
Marshall National Landmark Historic District	Marshall
Martha Barker County Store Museum	Monroe
Martime Museum	Algonac
Marvin's Marvelous Mechanical Museum	Farmington Hills
Marx Home	Wyandotte
Mary Jackson's Childhood Home	Milford
Mary Myers Museum	Ovid
Mary's City of David	Benton Harbor
Marysville Historical Museum	Marysville
Mason Area Historical Society	Mason
Mason County Genealogical Society	Ludington
Mason County Historical Society	Ludington
Mason Historic District Commission	Mason
Mason Historical Museum	Mason
Mayhew Log Cabin & Blacksmith Barn	Elkton
Mayville Area Museum of History & Genealogy	Mayville
McFadden-Ross House	Dearborn
McKenzie School	Hillman
Meadow Brook Hall	Rochester
Mecosta County Genealogical Society	Big Rapids
Mecosta County Historical Society	Big Rapids
Memory Lane Village	Flat Rock
Memphis Historical Society	Memphis
Menominee County Historical Society	Menominee
Menominee Historical Commission	Menominee
Menominee Range Historical Foundation	Iron Mountain
Menominee Range Historical Museum	Iron Mountain
Meridian Historic Village	Okemos
Metro Detroit Chapter	Wyandotte
Meyer May House	Grand Rapids
Meyers Schoolhouse Museum	Sparta
MI Alliance for the Conservation of Cultural Heritage	Battle Creek
Michigamme Museum	Michigamme
Michigan Alliance for the Conservation of Cultural Heritage	Lansing
Michigan Archaeology Society	Saginaw
Michigan Archival Association	Detroit
Michigan Barn Preservation Network	Mount Pleasant
Michigan Central Railroad Depot Museum & Customs House	Grosse Ile
Michigan Council for History Education	Allendale
Michigan Council for History Education	Ypsilanti
Michigan Firehouse Museum & Education Center	Ypsilanti
Michigan Flywheelers Museum	Bangor
Michigan Genealogical Council	Lansing
Michigan Heritage Route Program	Lansing
Michigan Historic Preservation Network	Lansing
Michigan Historical Center	Lansing
Michigan Historical Museum	Lansing
Michigan Historical Museum System (12 Locations)	Lansing
Michigan Humanities Council	Lansing
Michigan Iron Industry Museum	Negaunee
Michigan Iron Industry Museum	Negaunee
Michigan Labor History Society	Detroit
Michigan Legacy Art Park	Thompsonville
Michigan Library and Historical Center	Lansing
Michigan Magazine Museum	Comins
Michigan Maritime Museum	South Haven
Michigan Masonic Museum & Library	Grand Rapids
Michigan Military Technical & Historical Society	Eastpointe
Michigan Museum of Military Transportation	Hale
Michigan Museum of Surveying	Lansing
Michigan Museums Association	Cheboygan
Michigan One-Room Schoolhouse Association	Livonia
Michigan Oral History Association	Lansing
Michigan Photographic Historical Society	Birmingham
Michigan Political History Society	East Lansing
Michigan Railroad Club, Inc.	Dearborn
Michigan Railroad History Conference	Royal Oak
Michigan Regimental Civil War Roundtable	Dearborn
Michigan Shipwreck Research Association	Holland
Michigan State Historic Preservation Office	Lansing
Michigan State Trust for Railway Preservation	Owosso
Michigan State University Archives & Historical Collection	East Lansing
Michigan State University Museum	East Lansing
Michigan Supreme Court Historical Society	Lansing
Michigan Supreme Court Learning Center	Lansing
Michigan Theater Foundation	Ann Arbor
Michigan Transit Museum	Mount Clemens
Michigan Women's Historical Center & Hall of Fame	Lansing
Michigan's Military & Space Heroes Museum	Frankenmuth
Michilimackinac Historical Society	Saint Ignace
Middle Island Museum on Wheels	Alpena
Midland County Genealogical Society	Midland
Midland County Historical Society	Midland
Mid-Michigan Genealogical Society	Lansing
Milan Area Historical Society	Milan
Milford Historical Museum	Milford
Milford Historical Society	Milford
Mill Race Historical Village	Northville
Millersburg Area Historical Society	Millersburg
Millington-Arbela Historical Society	Millington
Millington-Arbela Historical Society & Museum	Millington
Missaukee County Historical Society	Lake City
Mitchell Research Center	Hillsdale
Monroe County Historical Commission	Monroe
Monroe County Historical Museum	Monroe
Monroe County Labor History Museum	Monroe
Monroe County Library System	Monroe
Monroe Historic District Commission	Monroe
Montague Museum	Montague
Montmorency County Historical Society	Hillman
Montrose Historical & Telephone Pioneer Museum	Montrose
Morton House Museum	Benton Harbor
MotorCities National Heritage Area	Detroit
Motown Historical Museum	Detroit
Mount Clemens Historic Commission	Mount Clemens
Mount Clemens Public Library	Mount Clemens
Mount Pleasant Area Historical Society	Mount Pleasant

Michigan History Directory

Museum Cottage	Petoskey
Museum of Cultural & Natural History	Mount Pleasant
Museum of Ojibwa Culture	St. Ignace
Museum on Main Street	Ann Arbor
Museum Ship Valley Camp	Sault Ste Marie
Music House Museum	Acme
Muskegon County Genealogical Society	Muskegon
Muskegon County Historical Society	Muskegon
Muskegon Heritage Association	Muskegon
Muskegon Heritage Museum	Muskegon
Muskegon Historic District Commission	Muskegon
Muskegon Railroad Historical Society	Muskegon
Nankin Mills Interpretive Center	Westland
National Automotive History Collection	Detroit
National Society of the Colonial Dames of America	Grosse Pointe
Navarre-Anderson Trading Post Complex	Monroe
Negaunee Historical Society & Museum	Negaunee
New Baltimore Historic District Commission	New Baltimore
New Baltimore Historical Society	New Baltimore
New Buffalo Railroad Museum	New Buffalo
New Groningen Schoolhouse	Zeeland
Newaygo County Museum and Heritage Center	Newaygo
Newton Township Historical Society	Gould City
No. 10 Schoolhouse	Grandville
Nokomis Learning Center	Okemos
North and South Manitou Islands	Empire
North Berrien Historical Society and Museum	Coloma
North Oakland Genealogical Society	Lake Orion
North Sidney Historical Association	Sidney
Northeast Michigan Genealogical Society	Alpena
Northeast Oakland Historical Society	Oxford
Northern Michigan University	Marquette
Northland Historical Consortium	Houghton
Northville Genealogical Society	Northville
Northville Historical Commission	Northville
Northville Historical Society	Northville
Northville Township Historical District Commission	Northville
Northwest Lower Michigan Historical Network	Northport
Northwest Maritime Museum	Manistee
Northwest Michigan Engine & Thresher Club	Buckley
Norwegian Lutheran Church	Calumet
Norwegian Lutheran Church Historical Society	Calumet
Norwood Area Historical Society	Charlevoix
Novi Historical Society	Novi
Oakfield Pioneer Heritage Museum	Rockford
Oakfield Pioneer Heritage Society	Rockford
Oakland County Genealogical Society	Birmingham
Oakland County Historical Commission	Pontiac
Oakland County Pioneer and Historical Society	Pontiac
Oakland Township Historical District Commission	Oakland
Oakland Township Historical Society	Oakland
Oakland University Library	Rochester
Oceana County Historical & Genealogical Society	Hart
Oceana Historical Park & Museum Complex	Hart
Ogemaw County Agricultural Society Antique Village	West Branch
Ogemaw County Genealogical and Historical Society	West Branch
Ogemaw County Historical Museum	West Branch
Ojibwe Learning Center and Library	Sault Ste. Marie
Old Fence Rider Historical Center	Edmore
Old House Network	Kalamazoo
Old Jail	Big Rapids
Old Jail Museum	Allegan
Old Mackinac Point Lighthouse	Mackinaw City
Old Mill Museum	Dundee
Old Mission Penninsula Historical Society	Traverse City
Old Rugged Cross Historical Society	Reed City
Old Rugged Cross Museum	Reed City
Old Sebewaing Township Hall	Sebewaing
Old Timer's Log Cabin	Wyandotte
Old Victoria Restoration	Rockland
Old West Side Association	Ann Arbor
Olive Township Historical Society & Museum	West Olive
Omena Historical Society	Omena
Onaway Historical Museum	Onaway
One-Room School House	Coldwater
Ontonagon County Genealogical Society	Ontonagon
Ontonagon County Historical Society	Ontonagon
Ontonagon Historical Museum	Ontonagon
Orchard Lake Museum	Orchard Lake
Orion Historical Society	Lake Orion
Orion Township Public Library	Lake Orion
Ortonville Community Historical Society	Ortonville
Oscoda County Genealogical Society	Mio
Oshtemo Historical Society	Oshtemo
Otisville Area Historical Association	Otisville
Otisville Museum	Otisville
Otsego Area Historical Society	Otsego
Otsego County Historical Society	Gaylord
Ottawa School	West Olive
Otter Lake Historical Society & Museum	Otter Lake
Our Savior's Historical Society	Manistee
Ovid Historical Room	Ovid
Ovid Historical Society	Ovid
Owosso Historical Commission	Owosso
Packard Motor Car Foundation	Shelby Township
Packard Proving Grounds Historic Site	Shelby Township
Paine-Gillam-Scott Museum	St. Johns
Painesdale Mine Shaft, Inc.	Painesdale
Pascoe House Museum	Republic
Paw Paw District Library	Paw Paw
Pellston Historical Society & Museum	Pellston
Pennsylvania R.R. Technical & Historical Society	Zeeland
Pentwater Historical Society	Pentwater
Pere Marquette Historical Society	Grand Haven
Pere Marquette Preservation Committee	Grand Haven
Petoskey Public Library	Petoskey
Pewabic Pottery	Detroit
Pickford Area Historical Society	Pickford
Pickford Museum	Pickford
Pickl Barrel House Museum	Grand Marais
Pigeon Depot Museum	Pigeon
Pigeon Historical Society	Pigeon
Pine Grove Historical Museum	Pontiac
Pioneer Log Cabin Village	Bad Axe
Pioneer Memorial Association of Fenton & Mundy Twp	Fenton
Pioneer Park	Manistique
Pittsfield Township Historical Society	Ann Arbor
Plainfield Township Historical Commission	Comstock Park
Plank Road Museum	Breckenridge
Plymouth District Library	Plymouth
Plymouth Historical Museum	Plymouth
Point Iroquois Light Station	Brimley
Polish Genealogical Society of Michigan	Detroit
Polish Heritage Society of Grand Rapids	Grand Rapids
Polish Mission	Orchard Lake
Polonica Americana Research Institute (PARI)	Orchard Lake
Pontiac Area Historical & Genealogical Society	Pontiac
Port Austin Area Historical Society	Port Austin
Port Huron & Detroit Railroad Historical Society	Marysville
Port Huron Museum	Port Huron
Portland Area Historical Society	Portland
Potterville Benton Twp. District Library	Potterville
Prairie Historical Society	Climax
Preservation Detroit	Detroit
Preserve Historic Sleeping Bear	Empire
Presque Isle County Historical Museum	Rogers City
Presque Isle Township Museum Society	Presque Isle
Program Source International	Bloomfield Hills
Project Lakewell, Inc.	Onaway
Public Libraries of Saginaw	Saginaw
Public Libraries of Saginaw	Saginaw
Putnam-Cloud Tower House	Omena
Quincy Mine Association, Inc.	Hancock
R.C.G.S. Research & Education Center	Prudenville
R.E. Olds Transportation Museum	Lansing
Rabbi Leo M. Franklin Archives	Bloomfield Hills
Railroad Historical Society of Northwest Michigan	Traverse City
Rathbone School	Eagle Harbor
Ravenna Historical Society	Ravenna
Ray Township Historical Society	Washington Township
Red Brick Schoolhouse Museum	Cassopolis
Redford Township Historical Commission	Redford

Organization	Location
Remus Area Historical Museum	Remus
Remus Area Historical Society	Remus
Rentschler Farm Museum	Saline
Republic Area Historical Society	Republic
Richard and Jane Manoogian Mackinac Art Museum	Mackinac Island
Richland Community Library	Richland
Richmond Area Historical and Genealogical Society	Richmond
Richmond Historic Village	Richmond
River of History Museum	Sault Ste. Marie
River Raisin National Battlefield Park	Monroe
River Rapids Public Library	Chesaning
River Rouge Historical Museum	River Rouge
River Rouge Historical Society	River Rouge
Robert Emmet Society	Petoskey
Rochester Hills Historic District Commission	Rochester Hills
Rochester Hills Museum at Van Hoosen Farm	Rochester Hills
Rochester Hills Public Library	Rochester
Rochester-Avon Historical Society	Rochester
Rockford Area Historical Museum	Rockford
Rockford Area Historical Society	Rockford
Rockland Township Historical Museum	Rockland
Rockwood Area Historical Society	Rockwood
Romeo Arts & Archives	Romeo
Romeo Arts & Archives Center	Romeo
Romeo District Library-Kezar Library	Romeo
Romeo Historic District Commission	Romeo
Romeo Historical Society	Romeo
Romulus Historical Society & Museum	Romulus
Roscommon Area Historical Society	Roscommon
Roscommon County Genealogical Society	Prudenville
Rose City Area Historical Society	Rose City
Roseville Historical & Genealogical Society	Roseville
Roseville Public Library	Roseville
Royal Oak Historical Society	Royal Oak
Royal Oak Historical Society Museum	Royal Oak
S.S. Badger	Ludington
S.S. City of Milwaukee	Manistee
S.S. Milwaukee Clipper Preservation, Inc.	Muskegon
Saarinen House	Bloomfield Hills
Sabin Crocker Library	Mount Clemens
Sable Points Lighthouse Keepers Association	Ludington
Sacred Spaces L.L.C.	Washington Township
Saginaw Genealogical Society, Inc.	Saginaw
Saginaw Railway Museum	Saginaw
Saginaw River Marine Historical Society	Bay City
Saginaw Valley Historic Preservation Society	Saginaw
Saginaw Valley Railroad Historical Society	Saginaw
Saint Mary's Church	Newago
Salem Area Historical Society	Salem
Saline Area Historical Society	Saline
Saline District Library	Saline
Saline Historical Commission	Saline
Saline Railroad Depot Museum	Saline
Samuel Adams Historical Museum	New Boston
Sandusky District Library	Sandusky
Sanford Area Historical Society	Sanford
Sanford Centennial Museum	Sanford
Sanilac County Historic Village and Museum	Port Sanilac
Sanilac County Historical Society	Port Sanilac
Sanilac Petroglypphs Historic Site and State Park	Cass City
Saranac Depot	Saranac
Saugatuck-Douglas Historical Society	Douglas
Sault Historic Sites	Sault Ste Marie
Sault Ste. Marie Historic District Commission	Sault Sainte Marie
Sault Ste. Marie Tribe of Chippewa Indians	Sault Ste. Marie
Save Our Depot, Inc.	New Haven
Schoolcraft County Historical Society	Manistique
Schoolcraft Historical Society	Schoolcraft
Sebewaing Area Historical Society	Sebewaing
Selfridge Military Air Museum	Selfridge ANG Base
Selinksy-Green Farmhouse Museum	St. Clair Shores
Selinsky-Green Farmhouse Museum	St. Clair Shores
Seul Choix Point Lighthouse	Gulliver
Shelby Area District Library	Shelby
Shelby Township Historical Committee	Shelby Township
Shepherd Area Historical Society	Shepherd
Shepherd Powerhouse Museum	Shepherd
Shiawassee County Historical Society	Owosso
Shiawassee County Historical Society Archives and Museum	Owosso
Shipman Library	Adrian
Shrine of the Pines	Baldwin
Shrine of the Snowshoe Priest	Baraga
Sindecuse Museum of Dentistry	Ann Arbor
Sleeping Bear Dunes National Lakeshore	Empire
Sloan*Longway	Flint
Society for Historic Preservation	Union City
Society of Automotive Historians/Henry M. Leland Chapter/MI	Mount Clemens
Society of the War of 1812 in Michigan	Livonia
Sojourner Truth Institute	Battle Creek
Sons of Union Veterans of the Civil War	Flint
South Boardman Museum	South Boardman
South Lyon Area Historical Society	South Lyon
Southern Michigan Railroad Society	Clinton
Southfield Historical Society	Southfield
Southgate Historical Society & Museum	Southgate
Southwest Michigan Black Heritage Society	Kalamazoo
Sparta Township Historical Commission	Sparta
Sparta Township Historical Commission Research Center	Sparta
Special Collections Library	Ann Arbor
Special Collections, Grand Valley State University Libraries	Allendale
Spies Public Library	Menominee
Springfield Township Historical Society	Davisburg
St. Clair County Family History Group	Port Huron
St. Clair County Farm Museum	Goodells
St. Clair County Library System	Port Huron
St. Clair Historical Commission	St.Clair
St. Clair Historical Museum	St.Clair
St. Clair Shores Genealogical Group	St. Clair Shores
St. Clair Shores Historical Commission	St. Clair Shores
St. John the Baptist Catholic Church Complex	Hubbardston
St. Joseph County Historical Society	Centreville
St. Louis Area Historical Society	St. Louis
St. Louis Historic Park	St. Louis
Steam Railroading Institute	Owosso
Stearns Musical Collection	Ann Arbor
Steiner Logging and Pioneer Museum	Luzerne
Sterling Heights Historical Commission	Sterling Heights
Stockbridge Area Genealogical & Historical Society	Stockbridge
Stockton Center at Spring Grove	Flint
Stuart Area Restoration Association	Kalamazoo
Stuart House Museum	Mackinac Island
Sturgeon Valley Historical Society	Pelkie
Sturgis Historical Society	Sturgis
Sugar Island Historical Preservation Society	Sault Sainte Marie
Sunfield Historical Society	Sunfield
Sutherland-Wilson Farm Museum	Ann Arbor
Swartz Creek Area Historical Society	Gaines
Tahquamenon Logging Museum	Newberry
Tawas Point Lighthouse	East Tawas
Taylor Historical Museum	Taylor
Taylor Historical Society	Taylor
Taymouth Township Historical Association	Burt
Tecumseh Area Historical Museum	Tecumseh
Tecumseh Area Historical Society	Tecumseh
Temple Emanuel of Grand Rapids Archives	Grand Rapids
Terry Wantz Historical Research Center	Fremont
The Argus Museum	Ann Arbor
The Bradley House	Rogers City
The Depot	White Pigeon
The Felt Estate	Saugatuck
The Henry and Margaret Hoffman Annex	Rogers City
The Henry Ford	Dearborn
The Miller Farm	Eaton Rapids
The Old Fire Barn	Milan
The Old Mill	Ortonville
The Pink School	Mason
The Pumphouse Museum	Saugatuck
The Scolnik House of the Depression Era	Muskegon
The Straight Farmhouse	Garden City
The Ten Cent Barn	Ubly
Then & Now Genealogical Library of Allegan County	Dorr
Theodore Levin U.S. Courthouse	Detroit

Michigan History Directory

Organization	Location
Theodore Roethke Home Museum	Saginaw
Thirteenth Michigan Memorial Association	Kalamazoo
Thomas Edison Depot Museum	Port Huron
Thomas St. Onge Vietnam Veterans Museum	Hermansville
Thornapple Heritage Association	Middleville
Three Oaks Township Public Library	Three Oaks
Toledo, Saginaw, & Muskegon Depot	Grand Rapids
Tompkins Center Historical Society	Parma
Tompkins Center Historical Society Sheridan Stewart Museum	Parma
Top of the Lake Snowmobile Museum	Naubinway
Tower of History	Sault Ste. Marie
Town Hall Museum	Southfield
Train Excursions at Joy Park	Clinton Township
Traveling Museum of Afrikan Ancestry & Research Center	Flint
Traverse Area District Library	Traverse City
Traverse Area Historical Society	Traverse City
Traverse City Historic Districts Commission	Traverse City
Trenton Historical Commission	Trenton
Trenton Historical Museum	Trenton
Trenton Historical Society	Trenton
Trenton Historical Society Archives	Trenton
Tri-Cities Historical Museum	Grand Haven
Trombley/Centre House	Bay City
Troy Historic Village	Troy
Troy Historical Society	Troy
Turner-Dodge House	Lansing
Tuscarora Historical Society	Indian River
Tuskegee Airmen National Museum	Detroit
Tyrone Historical Society	Fenton
Tyrone Township Historical Society	Kent City
U.S. Land Office Museum	Decatur
U.S. Ski & Snowboard Hall of Fame	Ishpeming
Ubly Area Historical Society	Ubly
Ukrainian American Archives & Museum	Detroit
Underground Railroad House	Schoolcraft
Underground Railroad Society of Cass County	Vandalia
Union City Genealogical Society	Ceresco
University Archivist & Records Manager	Marquette
University of Detroit Mercy Library	Detroit
University of Michigan	Ann Arbor
University of Michigan	Ann Arbor
University of Michigan School of Music	Ann Arbor
Upper Peninsula Fire Fighters Memorial Museum	Calumet
USS LST 393 Preservation Association	Muskegon
USS LST 393 Veterans Museum	Muskegon
USS Silversides Submarine Museum	Muskegon
Utica Heritage Association	Utica
Van Buren County Historical Museum	Hartford
Van Buren County Historical Society	Hartford
Van Buren Regional Genealogical Society	Decatur
Vassar Historical Society	Vassar
Vergennes Historical Society	Lowell
Vermontville Academy and Museum	Vermontville
Vermontville Historical Society	Vermontville
Vernon Area Historical Society	Vernon
Vicksburg Historic Village	Vicksburg
Vicksburg Historical Society	Vicksburg
Victorian Society in America-Michigan Chapter	Mason
Village of Franklin Historic District Commission	Franklin
Wahbememe Memorial Park	White Pigeon
Wakefield Historical Society	Wakefield
Wakefield Museum	Wakefield
Wales Historical Society	Goodells
Walker Tavern Historic Complex	Brooklyn
Wallaceville School House	Dearborn Heights
Walter E. Hastings Museum	Interlochen
Walter P. Chrysler Museum	Auburn Hills
Walters Gasoline and Interurban Railroad Museum	Marshall
Warren Historical & Genealogical Society	Warren
Warren Historical Commission	Warren
Warren Historical Gallery	Warren
Warren Village Historic District Commission	Warren
Washtenaw County Historic District Commission	Ann Arbor
Washtenaw County Historical Society	Ann Arbor
Water Street Histoic Block	Sault Ste. Marie
Water Street Historic Block	Sault Ste. Marie
Waterford Township Historical Society	Waterford
Waterloo Area Historical Society	Stockbridge
Waterloo Farm Museum	Stockbridge
Watrousville Museum	Caro
Watrousville-Caro Area Historical Society	Caro
Wayne County Council for Arts, History, & Humanities	Grosse Pointe
Wayne Historical Museum	Wayne
Wayne Historical Society	Wayne
Welch Museum	Sunfield
Wellington Farm Park	Grayling
West Main Street Historic District	Midland
West Michigan Railroad Historical Society	Grand Rapids
West Shore Fishing Museum	Menominee
Western Michigan Genealogical Society	Grand Rapids
Western Michigan University Archives Regional History Collection	Kalamazoo
Western Wayne County Genealogical Society	Livonia
Westland Historic Village Park	Westland
Westland Historical Commission	Westland
Westphalia Historical Society	Westphalia
Westphalia Historical Society	Westphalia
Wexford County Historical Society	Cadillac
Wexford County Historical Society Museum	Cadillac
Wexford Genealogy Organization	Cadillac
Whaley Historic House Museum	Flint
Wheels of History Museum	Brimley
Whistlestop Park & Grass Lake Depot	Grass Lake
Whistlestop Park Association	Grass Lake
White Cloud Community Library	White Cloud
White Lake Historical Society	White Lake
White Pine Historical Society	Clare
White River Light Station Museum	Whitehall
White Rock School Museum	Harbor Beach
Wilkinson Heritage Museum	Lakeside
Wilkinson Homestead & Historical Society	Eastport
William G. Thompson House Museum & Gardens	Hudson
William L. Clements Library	Ann Arbor
William Upton House	Sterling Heights
Williamston Depot Museum	Williamston
Wills Sainte Claire Automobile Museum	Marysville
Windmill Island Gardens	Holland
Wing House Museum	Coldwater
Winifred Mae Oestrike Hamilton-Collection	Flat Rock
Witch's Hat Historic Village and Museum	South Lyon
Wixom Cemetery	Wixom
Wixom Historical Society & Museum	Wixom
Wixom-Wire Museum	Wixom
WMU Archives Regional History Collection	Kalamazoo
Wolcott Mill Metropark Historic Center	Ray Township
Women's History Project of Northwest Michigan	Traverse City
Woolley Veterinarian Building	Davison
World War II Glider and Military Museum	Iron Mountain
World War II Honor Roll Monument	Rochester
Wurtsmith Air Museum	Oscoda
Wyandotte Historical Commission	Wyandotte
Wyandotte Museums	Wyandotte
Wyoming Historical Commission	Wyoming
Yankee Air Museum	Belleville
Ypsilanti Automotive Heritage Museum	Ypsilanti
Ypsilanti Heritage Foundation	Ypsilanti
Ypsilanti Historic District Commission	Ypsilanti
Ypsilanti Historical Society, Museum, & Archives	Ypsilanti
Zeeland Historical Society	Zeeland
Ziibiwing Center of Anishinabe Culture & Lifeways	Mount Pleasant

Enjoy the Many Benefits of Membership!

For more than 180 years, the Historical Society of Michigan (HSM)— the oldest cultural organization in the state—has been committed to preserving our history.

Here's a sampling of the benefits that you will receive with an HSM membership…

Publications

Every member receives HSM's quarterly magazine, the *Chronicle*. If you upgrade to a higher level, you can get the award-winning publication *Michigan History* magazine and/or the respected academic journal *Michigan Historical Review*. You'll also earn discounts on HSM books, including the popular *Historic Michigan Travel Guide* and *Michigan History Directory*.

Conferences

As a member, you're eligible for discounted admission to HSM's annual *State History Conference* (fall) and the *Upper Peninsula History Conference* (summer), which combine tours, talks, and breakout sessions in an entertaining format. You can also join us for our annual *Michigan in Perspective: The Local History Conference* held each spring in the metro Detroit area.

Education

Are you a teacher? Enjoy discounts to our annual educator conference—*Mulling Over Michigan*—as well as lesson-plan supplements published in the *Chronicle*. HSM also coordinates the Michigan History Day (National History Day in Michigan) competition, which engages the historical and creative skills of 5,000 students each year.

Awards

Your membership fees also support HSM's annual awards program, which includes honoring individual and organizational efforts to preserve Michigan history, recognition for historic family farms, and milestone plaques for businesses and organizations.

Local Support

If you work with a local historical society, site, or museum, HSM provides you with special services that include online and print-based calendar listings, promotional assistance, web hosting, training workshops, best practices support, and much more.